THE PAPERS OF

THOMAS JEFFERSON

RETIREMENT SERIES

THE PAPERS OF
Thomas Jefferson

RETIREMENT SERIES

Volume 13
22 April 1818 to 31 January 1819

J. JEFFERSON LOONEY, EDITOR

ROBERT F. HAGGARD, SENIOR ASSOCIATE EDITOR

JULIE L. LAUTENSCHLAGER, ASSOCIATE EDITOR

ELLEN C. HICKMAN AND ANDREA R. GRAY, ASSISTANT EDITORS

LISA A. FRANCAVILLA, MANAGING EDITOR

PAULA VITERBO AND KERRY DAHM, EDITORIAL ASSISTANTS

SUSAN SPENGLER, TECHNICAL SPECIALIST

CATHERINE CLARKE COINER, SENIOR DIGITAL TECHNICIAN

PRINCETON AND OXFORD

PRINCETON UNIVERSITY PRESS

2016

Copyright © 2016 by Princeton University Press

Published by Princeton University Press, 41 William Street,

Princeton, New Jersey 08540

IN THE UNITED KINGDOM:

Princeton University Press, 6 Oxford Street,

Woodstock, Oxfordshire OX20 1TR

Library of Congress Cataloging-in-Publication Data

Jefferson, Thomas, 1743–1826

The papers of Thomas Jefferson. Retirement series / J. Jefferson Looney, editor . . .

[et al.] p. cm.

Includes bibliographical references and index.

Contents: v. 1. 4 March to 15 November 1809 — [etc.] —

v. 13. 22 April 1818 to 31 January 1819

ISBN 978-0-691-17283-5 (cloth: v. 13: alk. paper)

1. Jefferson, Thomas, 1743–1826 — Archives. 2. Jefferson, Thomas, 1743–1826 —

Correspondence. 3. Presidents — United States — Archives.

4. Presidents — United States — Correspondence. 5. United States —

Politics and government — 1809–1817 — Sources. 6. United States — Politics and

government — 1817–1825 — Sources. I. Looney, J. Jefferson.

II. Title. III. Title: Retirement series.

E302.J442 2004b

973.4'6'092 — dc22   2004048327

This book has been composed in Monticello

Princeton University Press books are printed on
acid-free paper and meet the guidelines for permanence
and durability of the Committee on Production
Guidelines for Book Longevity of the
Council on Library Resources

Printed in the United States of America

DEDICATED TO THE MEMORY OF

ADOLPH S. OCHS

PUBLISHER OF THE NEW YORK TIMES

1896–1935

WHO BY THE EXAMPLE OF A RESPONSIBLE

PRESS ENLARGED AND FORTIFIED

THE JEFFERSONIAN CONCEPT

OF A FREE PRESS

THIS EDITION was made possible by a founding grant from The New York Times Company to Princeton University.

The Retirement Series is sponsored by the Thomas Jefferson Foundation, Inc., of Charlottesville, Virginia. It was created with a six-year founding grant from The Pew Charitable Trusts to the Foundation and to Princeton University, enabling the former to take over responsibility for the volumes associated with this period. Leading gifts from Richard Gilder, Mrs. Martin S. Davis, Thomas A. Saunders III, Janemarie D. and Donald A. King, Jr., Alice Handy and Peter Stoudt, Harlan Crow, and Mr. and Mrs. E. Charles Longley, Jr., have assured the continuation of the Retirement Series. For these essential donations, and for other indispensable aid generously given by librarians, archivists, scholars, and collectors of manuscripts, the Editors record their sincere gratitude.

FOREWORD

THE 598 DOCUMENTS in this volume cover the period from 22 April 1818 to 31 January 1819, during which time Jefferson worked tirelessly to transform Central College into the University of Virginia. The Virginia General Assembly had enacted legislation in February 1818 that authorized commissioners to meet on 1 August at the tavern at Rockfish Gap to select the site of the new university. Jefferson spent months preparing for the meeting and laboring behind the scenes to ensure that his ideas about the university would be adopted. In his most important contribution, he drafted a report in advance of the gathering in which he laid out the rationale for locating the university at Central College and his vision for the organization of the university. After approval of the report at the Rockfish Gap meeting, with few significant changes to Jefferson's draft, the choice of Central College as the site of the state university still had to pass the General Assembly. Largely thanks to intense lobbying efforts in Richmond by state senator Joseph C. Cabell, the University Bill, also written by Jefferson and naming Central College as the university, became law on 25 January 1819. With Central College's transformation into the University of Virginia now assured, Jefferson focused on its future. He continued trying to bring Thomas Cooper to the faculty, and he wrote a long letter of recruitment to Nathaniel Bowditch, whose work in the fields of astronomy and mathematics Jefferson admired. Neither ultimately taught in Charlottesville. Still others had heard of Jefferson's plans and wrote to offer their services as builders and instructors.

After the conclusion of the three-day meeting at Rockfish Gap, Jefferson traveled sixty miles to Warm Springs in an effort to improve his health. Initially planning a two-week stay, he extended it, explaining to his daughter Martha Jefferson Randolph that "having no symptom to judge by at what time I may presume the seeds of my rheumatism eradicated, and desirous to prevent the necessity of ever coming here a 2ᵈ time, I believe I shall yeild to the general advice of a three weeks course." He would come to regret his visit, however, for by the time of his departure Jefferson was plagued with what was probably a staphylococcus infection on his buttocks that made travel painful and put his health in danger for some months to come. Due to this debility he was unable to make his usual autumn trip to Poplar Forest. This extended absence led Jefferson to exchange detailed letters with his manager Joel Yancey regarding work on the farms, labor assignments, provisioning, and the health of the slaves at his Bedford County properties.

Friends and visitors continued to shape and impact Jefferson's world. After working since 1816 to have the work translated and published, at long last he was able to inform Destutt de Tracy that his *Treatise on Political Economy* was in print. Historians asked Jefferson to share his memories of various members of the Revolutionary generation. At the request of Robert Walsh, he recounted anecdotes of Benjamin Franklin. Benjamin Waterhouse sought Jefferson's recollections of Samuel Adams, and William Tudor solicited information about James Otis. As usual, visitors frequented Monticello. Among them Salma Hale, a New Hampshire native, spent a day there in May 1818 and recorded his general impressions of Virginia as well as his thoughts on Jefferson and their topics of conversation, which included food, wine, and religion.

Jefferson continued to rebuild his library, ordering numerous titles from Lewis D. Belair, Mathew Carey & Son, and Fernagus De Gelone. His collection was further enriched by gifts of books, pamphlets, and essays from a wide range of correspondents. Mordecai M. Noah sent an oration he had delivered at the consecration of a synagogue in New York City, which caused Jefferson to remark that "your sect by it's sufferings has furnished a remarkable proof of the universal spirit of religious intolerance, inherent in every sect, disclaimed by all while feeble, and practised by all when in power." In thanking Charles J. Ingersoll for a pamphlet on Chinese culture and language, Jefferson wondered at the complexities of the language and speculated that the introduction of the "simpler alphabets of Europe" could enable the people of China to advance in science. Correspondents Robert Miller and Gabriel Crane attempted to interest Jefferson in their unique worldviews. Miller blended occult science and religion, while Crane sent his thoughts on the nature of light and claimed that "the Supreme" had directed him to request $5,000 from Jefferson to enable Crane to conduct further research. Multiple anonymous letters also arrived in these months, each trying to provoke Jefferson to action on some aspect of his personal religion or politics.

A notable loss occurred in Jefferson's circle with the death of Abigail Adams. His words of condolence to John Adams in November 1818 included the "comfort" that "the term is not very distant at which we are to deposit, in the same cerement, our sorrows and suffering bodies, and to ascend in essence to an ecstatic meeting with the friends we have loved & lost and whom we shall still love and never lose again."

ACKNOWLEDGMENTS

MANY INDIVIDUALS and institutions provided aid and encouragement during the preparation of this volume. Those who helped us to locate and acquire primary and secondary sources and answered our research questions include our current and former colleagues at the Thomas Jefferson Foundation, especially Anna Berkes, Jack Robertson, and Endrina Tay of the Jefferson Library, William L. Beiswanger, Diane Ehrenpreis, and Lucia C. Stanton; Phyllis S. Bendell at the American Academy of Arts and Sciences; Andrew Bourque and Vincent Golden at the American Antiquarian Society; Earle E. Spamer and Marian L. Christ at the American Philosophical Society; Gianmarco Talamona at the Archivio di Stato del Cantone Ticino, Bellinzona, Switzerland; Sean P. Casey at the Boston Public Library; Eric Pullin at Carthage College; Lish Thompson at the Charleston County Public Library; Jorie Braunold at the Chicago History Museum Research Center; Joshua A. Lascell at the Rauner Special Collections Library, Dartmouth College; Joy Siebers at the National Society Daughters of the American Revolution; Elizabeth B. Dunn at the David M. Rubenstein Rare Book & Manuscript Library, Duke University; Grant E. L. Buttars at the University of Edinburgh; Linda Thompson Robertson at the Greenwood Cemetery Association, Jackson, Mississippi; Robin Carlaw at the Harvard University Archives; Steven Smith and Sara A. Borden at the Historical Society of Pennsylvania; James N. Green at the Library Company of Philadelphia; Jeff Flannery, Joseph Jackson, Bruce Kirby, and Julie Miller at the Library of Congress; Bill Bynum, R. Thomas Crew Jr., Virginia Dunn, Dawn K. Tinnell, and Minor Weisiger at the Library of Virginia; Linda Showalter at the Marietta College Library; Anna Clutterbuck-Cook, Kittle Evenson, and Daniel Hinchen at the Massachusetts Historical Society; Jarod Kearney at the James Monroe Museum and Memorial Library; Robert Ellis at the National Archives; Paul Friday at the New Hampshire Historical Society; Bridget Sullivan at the Newport Historical Society, Newport, Rhode Island; Robert Delap at the New-York Historical Society; Brandon Westerheim at the New York Public Library; Meredith Anne Weber at Pennsylvania State University; Flavia Bucciero, Christine Pennison, and Elisabetta Piccioni at the Archivio di Stato di Pisa; Sandra Bossert and AnnaLee Pauls at the Princeton University Library; Ronald L. Becker at the Rutgers University Library; Molly Inabinett at the South Carolina Historical Society; Andreas Fankhauser at the

ACKNOWLEDGMENTS

Staatsarchiv Solothurn, Switzerland; Kelsey Duinkerken at the Scott Memorial Library, Thomas Jefferson University, Philadelphia; Gian Giacomo Migone at the University of Torino; John J. McCusker at Trinity University, San Antonio; Ken Olson at the Arthur J. Morris Law Library at the University of Virginia; Anne Causey, Petrina Jackson, Regina Rush, Ellen Welch, Penny White, and their colleagues from the Albert and Shirley Small Special Collections Library at the University of Virginia; John McClure and Candice Roland at the Virginia Historical Society; Brenda L. Wolfe at the Court of Common Pleas of Washington County, Ohio; Ray Swick of West Virginia State Parks & Forests; Susan A. Riggs at the College of William and Mary's Special Collections Research Center; and Diane Ducharme at the Beinecke Rare Book and Manuscript Library, Yale University. As always, we received advice, assistance, and encouragement from many of our fellow documentary editors, including Sara Georgini at the Adams Papers; Jennifer E. Steenshorne at the Papers of John Jay; Martha J. King and Bland Whitley at the Papers of Thomas Jefferson at Princeton University; Anne Mandeville Colony, Mary A. Hackett, Angela Kreider, and David B. Mattern at the Papers of James Madison; Cassandra Good and Daniel Preston at the Papers of James Monroe; and Neal Millikan at the Washington Papers. Genevieve Moene and Roland H. Simon transcribed and translated the French letters included in this volume; Andreas Broscheid helped with German; Coulter George assisted us with passages in Greek; Elizabeth Shanks Alexander answered a question about Hebrew; Jonathan T. Hine provided aid with Italian; and John F. Miller lent his aid with Latin quotations. The maps of Jefferson's Virginia, Jefferson's Albemarle, and the University of Virginia were created by Rick Britton. The other illustrations that appear in this volume were assembled with the assistance of Mary Davis and Christina Jackson at the Denver Art Museum; Dawn K. Tinnell, Virginia Dunn, and Meghan Townes at the Library of Virginia; Sabina Beauchard and Anna Clutterbuck-Cook at the Massachusetts Historical Society; Jayne Ptolemy and Cheney Schopieray at the William L. Clements Library, University of Michigan; Eleanor Gould at the Thomas Jefferson Foundation; and Christina Deane at the University of Virginia. We thankfully acknowledge the efforts of the able staff at Princeton University Press, including Carmina Alvarez, Leslie Flis, Dimitri Karetnikov, and our production editor, Lauren Lepow. Bob Bartleson and his associates at Integrated Publishing Solutions addressed the volume's complex typesetting needs with their usual high standards.

ACKNOWLEDGMENTS

Two names were purposely omitted from the list above so that they could be singled out for special praise as they retire. Linda Monaco's long tenure at the Papers of Thomas Jefferson at Princeton University predates the establishment of the Retirement Series, and she has been a cheerful and invaluable resource to us from the beginning. She will be greatly missed here as well as at Princeton.

Jan Lilly, senior designer at Princeton University Press, brought her decades of experience with the Jefferson Papers to the task of designing the first volume of the Retirement Series, and she did an admirable job of balancing the need to distinguish it visually from the edition's other two series while maintaining core similarities. Since then her eagle eye has saved us from innumerable errors and infelicities, and her passion for excellence and correctness has inspired us. We wish Jan and Linda only the best in the years ahead.

EDITORIAL METHOD AND APPARATUS

1. RENDERING THE TEXT

From its inception *The Papers of Thomas Jefferson* has insisted on high standards of accuracy in rendering text, but modifications in textual policy and editorial apparatus have been implemented as different approaches have become accepted in the field or as a more faithful rendering has become technically feasible. Prior discussions of textual policy appeared in Vols. 1:xxix–xxxiv, 22:vii–xi, 24:vii–viii, and 30:xiii–xiv of the First Series.

The textual method of the Retirement Series will adhere to the more literal approach adopted in Volume 30 of the parent edition. Original spelling, capitalization, and punctuation are retained as written. Such idiosyncrasies as Jefferson's failure to capitalize the beginnings of most of his sentences and abbreviations like "mr" are preserved, as are his preference for "it's" to "its" and his characteristic spellings of "knolege," "paiment," and "recieve." Modern usage is adopted in cases where intent is impossible to determine, an issue that arises most often in the context of capitalization. Some so-called slips of the pen are corrected, but the original reading is recorded in a subjoined textual note. Jefferson and others sometimes signaled a change in thought within a paragraph with extra horizontal space, and this is rendered by a three-em space. Blanks left for words and not subsequently filled by the authors are represented by a space approximating the length of the blank. Gaps, doubtful readings of illegible or damaged text, and wording supplied from other versions or by editorial conjecture are explained in the source note or in numbered textual notes. Foreign-language documents, the vast majority of which are in French during the retirement period, are transcribed in full as faithfully as possible and followed by a full translation.

Two modifications from past practice bring this series still closer to the original manuscripts. Underscored text is presented as such rather than being converted to italics. Superscripts are also preserved rather than being lowered to the baseline. In most cases of superscripting, the punctuation that is below or next to the superscripted letters is dropped, since it is virtually impossible to determine what is a period or dash as opposed to a flourish under, over, or adjacent to superscripted letters.

Limits to the more literal method are still recognized, however, and readability and consistency with past volumes are prime considerations. In keeping with the basic design implemented in the first volume of the Papers, salutations and signatures continue to display in large and small capitals rather than upper- and lowercase letters. Expansion marks over abbreviations are silently omitted. With very rare exceptions, deleted text and information on which words were added during the process of composition is not displayed within the document transcription. Based on the Editors' judgment of their significance, such emendations are either described in numbered textual notes or ignored. Datelines for letters are consistently printed at the head of the text, with a comment in the descriptive note when they have been moved. Address information, endorsements, and dockets are quoted or described in the source note rather than reproduced in the document proper.

2. TEXTUAL DEVICES

The following devices are employed throughout the work to clarify the presentation of the text.

[. . .]	Text missing and not conjecturable. The size of gaps longer than a word or two is estimated in annotation.
[ ]	Number or part of number missing or illegible.
[roman]	Conjectural reading for missing or illegible matter. A question mark follows when the reading is doubtful.
[*italic*]	Editorial comment inserted in the text.
<*italic*>	Matter deleted in the manuscript but restored in our text.

3. DESCRIPTIVE SYMBOLS

The following symbols are employed throughout the work to describe the various kinds of manuscript originals. When a series of versions is included, the first to be recorded is the version used for the printed text.

Dft	draft (usually a composition or rough draft; multiple drafts, when identifiable as such, are designated "2d Dft," etc.)
Dupl	duplicate
MS	manuscript (arbitrarily applied to most documents other than letters)
PoC	polygraph copy

PrC press copy
RC recipient's copy
SC stylograph copy

All manuscripts of the above types are assumed to be in the hand of the author of the document to which the descriptive symbol pertains. If not, that fact is stated. On the other hand, the following types of manuscripts are assumed not to be in the hand of the author, and exceptions will be noted:

FC file copy (applied to all contemporary copies retained by the author or his agents)

Tr transcript (applied to all contemporary and later copies except file copies; period of transcription, unless clear by implication, will be given when known)

4. LOCATION SYMBOLS

The locations of documents printed in this edition from originals in private hands and from printed sources are recorded in self-explanatory form in the descriptive note following each document. The locations of documents printed or referenced from originals held by public and private institutions in the United States are recorded by means of the symbols used in the *MARC Code List for Organizations* (2000) maintained by the Library of Congress. The symbols DLC and MHi by themselves stand for the collections of Jefferson Papers proper in these repositories. When texts are drawn from other collections held by these two institutions, the names of those collections are added. Location symbols for documents held by institutions outside the United States are given in a subjoined list. The lists of symbols are limited to the institutions represented by documents printed or referred to in this volume.

CSmH Huntington Library, San Marino, California
   JF   Jefferson File
   JF-BA   Jefferson File, Bixby
          Acquisition
CtY Yale University, New Haven, Connecticut
DeHi Historical Society of Delaware, Wilmington, Delaware
DeWint-M Henry Frances DuPont Winterthur Museum, Joseph Downs Manuscript and Microfilm Collection, Winterthur, Delaware
DLC Library of Congress, Washington, D.C.

NPT	Nicholas Philip Trist Papers	
TJ Papers	Thomas Jefferson Papers (this is assumed if not stated, but also given as indicated to furnish the precise location of an undated, misdated, or otherwise problematic document, thus "DLC: TJ Papers, 213:38071–2" represents volume 213, folios 38071 and 38072 as the collection was arranged at the time the first microfilm edition was made in 1944–45. Access to the microfilm edition of the collection as it was rearranged under the Library's Presidential Papers Program is provided by the *Index to the Thomas Jefferson Papers* [1976])	

DNA   National Archives, Washington, D.C., with identifications of series (preceded by record group number) as follows:

CCDCCR	United States Circuit Court of the District of Columbia, Chancery Records
CNR	Correspondence regarding the Proposed Location of the National Road
CRL	Consular Records, Leghorn
CS	Census Schedules
LAR	Letters of Application and Recommendation
LRF	Legation Records, France
MLR	Miscellaneous Letters Received
NPEDP	Naturalization Petitions to the United States Circuit and District Courts for the Eastern District of Pennsylvania
PA	Passport Applications
RWP	Revolutionary War Pension and Bounty-Land Warrant Application Files
SCACF	United States Supreme Court, Appellate Case Files
SRRWPBLW	Selected Records from Revolutionary War Pension and Bounty-Land Warrant Application Collection Files

DNAL	National Agricultural Library, Beltsville, Maryland
DNDAR	National Society Daughters of the American Revolution, Washington, D.C.
ICHi	Chicago History Museum, Chicago, Illinois
InU	Indiana University, Bloomington
KyBgW-K	Kentucky Library, Western Kentucky University, Bowling Green
KyLoF	Filson Historical Society, Louisville, Kentucky
MBCo	Countway Library of Medicine, Boston, Massachusetts
MBPLi	Boston Public Library, Boston, Massachusetts
MdAN	United States Naval Academy, Annapolis, Maryland
MdBJ	Johns Hopkins University, Baltimore, Maryland
MdHi	Maryland Historical Society, Baltimore
MH	Harvard University, Cambridge, Massachusetts
MHi	Massachusetts Historical Society, Boston
MiU-C	Clements Library, University of Michigan, Ann Arbor
MoSB	Missouri Botanical Garden, Saint Louis
MoSHi	Missouri History Museum, Saint Louis
	TJC-BC Thomas Jefferson Collection, text formerly in Bixby Collection
MoSW	Washington University, Saint Louis, Missouri
MWiW-C	Chapin Library, Williams College, Williamstown, Massachusetts
N	New York State Library, Albany
NcD	Duke University, Durham, North Carolina
NcU	University of North Carolina, Chapel Hill
	NPT Southern Historical Collection, Nicholas Philip Trist Papers
NhHi	New Hampshire Historical Society, Concord
NHi	New-York Historical Society, New York City
NIC	Cornell University, Ithaca, New York
NjHi	New Jersey Historical Society, Newark
NjMoHP	Morristown National Historical Park, Morristown, New Jersey
NjP	Princeton University, Princeton, New Jersey
NjR	Rutgers, The State University of New Jersey, New Brunswick
NN	New York Public Library, New York City
NNC	Columbia University, New York City
NNPM	Pierpont Morgan Library, New York City
NPV	Vassar College, Poughkeepsie, New York

OMC	Marietta College, Marietta, Ohio
PHC	Haverford College, Haverford, Pennsylvania
PHi	Historical Society of Pennsylvania, Philadelphia
PPAmP	American Philosophical Society, Philadelphia, Pennsylvania
PPL	Library Company of Philadelphia, Pennsylvania
PPRF	The Rosenbach of the Free Library of Philadelphia, Philadelphia, Pennsylvania
RNHi	Newport Historical Society, Newport, Rhode Island
ScCF	Charleston County Library, Charleston, South Carolina
ScHi	South Carolina Historical Society, Charleston
Vi	Library of Virginia, Richmond
ViCMRL	Thomas Jefferson Library, Thomas Jefferson Foundation, Inc., Charlottesville, Virginia
ViFreJM	James Monroe Museum and Memorial Library, Fredericksburg, Virginia
ViHi	Virginia Historical Society, Richmond
ViU	University of Virginia, Charlottesville

	JCC	Joseph C. Cabell Papers
	JHC	John Hartwell Cocke Papers
	PP	Papers from the Office of the Proctor and Papers of the Proctors of the University of Virginia
	TJP	Thomas Jefferson Papers
	TJP-CC	Thomas Jefferson Papers, text formerly in Carr-Cary Papers
	TJP-Co	Thomas Jefferson Papers, text formerly in Cocke Papers
	TJP-ER	Thomas Jefferson Papers, text formerly in Edgehill-Randolph Papers
	TJP-PC	Thomas Jefferson Papers, text formerly in Philip B. Campbell Deposit
	TJP-VMJB	Thomas Jefferson Papers, Visitors Minutes, University of Virginia and its predecessors, copy prepared after 7 October 1826 for James Breckinridge

	TJP-VMJCC	Thomas Jefferson Papers, Visitors Minutes, University of Virginia and its predecessors, copy prepared after 7 October 1826 for Joseph C. Cabell
	TJP-VMJHC	Thomas Jefferson Papers, Visitors Minutes, University of Virginia and its predecessors, copy prepared after 7 October 1826 for John H. Cocke
	TJP-VMTJ	Thomas Jefferson Papers, Visitors Minutes, University of Virginia and its predecessors, original manuscript largely in Thomas Jefferson's hand during the period of his service
ViW		College of William and Mary, Williamsburg, Virginia
	TC-JP	Jefferson Papers, Tucker-Coleman Collection
	TJP	Thomas Jefferson Papers

The following symbols represent repositories located outside of the United States:

ItPi		Archivio di Stato di Pisa, Pisa, Italy
	AFM	Archivio Filippo Mazzei
OONL		Library and Archives Canada, Ottawa, Ontario
SzBzACT		Archivio Cantonale del Ticino, Bellinzona, Switzerland

5. OTHER ABBREVIATIONS AND SYMBOLS

The following abbreviations and symbols are commonly employed in the annotation throughout the work.

Lb   Letterbook (used to indicate texts copied or assembled into bound volumes)

RG   Record Group (used in designating the location of documents in the Library of Virginia and the National Archives)

SJL   Jefferson's "Summary Journal of Letters" written and received for the period 11 Nov. 1783 to 25 June 1826 (in DLC: TJ Papers). This epistolary record, kept in Jefferson's hand, has been checked against the TJ Editorial Files. It is to be assumed that all outgoing letters are recorded in SJL unless there is a note to the contrary. When the date of receipt of an incoming letter is recorded in SJL, it is incorporated in the notes. Information and discrepancies revealed in SJL but not found in the letter itself are also noted. Missing letters recorded in SJL are accounted for in the notes to documents mentioning them, in related documents, or in an appendix

TJ   Thomas Jefferson

TJ Editorial Files   Photoduplicates and other editorial materials in the office of the Papers of Thomas Jefferson: Retirement Series, Jefferson Library, Thomas Jefferson Foundation, Inc., Charlottesville

d   Penny or denier

f   Florin or franc

£   Pound sterling or livre, depending on context (in doubtful cases, a clarifying note will be given)

s   Shilling or sou (also expressed as /)

ₜₜ   Livre Tournois

℔   Per (occasionally used for pro, pre)

„   Old-style guillemet (European quotation mark)

6. SHORT TITLES

The following list includes short titles of works cited frequently in this edition. Since it is impossible to anticipate all the works to be cited in abbreviated form, the list is revised from volume to volume.

Acts of Assembly   *Acts of the General Assembly of Virginia* (cited by session; title varies over time)

ANB   John A. Garraty and Mark C. Carnes, eds., *American National Biography*, 1999, 24 vols.

Annals   *Annals of the Congress of the United States: The Debates and Proceedings in the Congress of the United States . . . Compiled from Authentic Materials*, Washington, D.C., Gales & Seaton, 1834–56, 42 vols. (All editions are undependable and pagination varies from one printing to another. Citations given below are to the edition mounted on the American Memory website of the Library of Congress and give the date of the debate as well as page numbers.)

APS   American Philosophical Society

ASP   American State Papers: Documents, Legislative and Executive, of the Congress of the United States, 1832–61, 38 vols.

Axelson, *Virginia Postmasters*   Edith F. Axelson, *Virginia Postmasters and Post Offices, 1789–1832*, 1991

BDSCHR   Walter B. Edgar and others, eds., *Biographical Directory of the South Carolina House of Representatives*, 1974– , 5 vols.

Betts, *Farm Book*   Edwin M. Betts, ed., *Thomas Jefferson's Farm Book*, 1953 (in two separately paginated sections; unless otherwise specified, references are to the second section)

Betts, *Garden Book*   Edwin M. Betts, ed., *Thomas Jefferson's Garden Book, 1766–1824*, 1944

Biog. Dir. Cong.   *Biographical Directory of the United States Congress, 1774–Present*, online resource, Office of the Clerk, United States House of Representatives

Biographie universelle   *Biographie universelle, ancienne et moderne*, new ed., 1843–65, 45 vols.

Black's Law Dictionary   Bryan A. Garner and others, eds., *Black's Law Dictionary*, 7th ed., 1999

Brigham, *American Newspapers*   Clarence S. Brigham, *History and Bibliography of American Newspapers, 1690–1820*, 1947, 2 vols.

Bruce, *University*   Philip Alexander Bruce, *History of the University of Virginia 1819–1919: The Lengthened Shadow of One Man*, 1920–22, 5 vols.

Bush, *Life Portraits*   Alfred L. Bush, *The Life Portraits of Thomas Jefferson*, rev. ed., 1987

Butler, *Virginia Militia*   Stuart Lee Butler, *A Guide to Virginia Militia Units in the War of 1812*, 1988

Callahan, *U.S. Navy*   Edward W. Callahan, *List of Officers of the Navy of the United States and of the Marine Corps from 1775 to 1900*, 1901, repr. 1969

Chambers, *Poplar Forest*   S. Allen Chambers, *Poplar Forest & Thomas Jefferson*, 1993

Clay, *Papers*   James F. Hopkins and others, eds., *The Papers of Henry Clay*, 1959–92, 11 vols.

CVSP   William P. Palmer and others, eds., *Calendar of Virginia State Papers . . . Preserved in the Capitol at Richmond*, 1875–93, 11 vols.

DAB   Allen Johnson and Dumas Malone, eds., *Dictionary of American Biography*, 1928–36, 20 vols.

DBF   *Dictionnaire de biographie française*, 1933– , 21 vols.

Delaplaine's Repository   Joseph Delaplaine, *Delaplaine's Repository of the Lives and Portraits of Distinguished Americans*, Philadelphia, 1816–18, 2 vols.; Poor, *Jefferson's Library*, 4 (no. 139)

Destutt de Tracy, *Treatise on Political Economy*   Destutt de Tracy, *A Treatise on Political Economy; to which is prefixed a supplement to a preceding work on the understanding, or Elements of Ideology*, Georgetown, 1817 [1818]; Poor, *Jefferson's Library*, 11 (no. 700)

Dexter, *Yale Biographies*   Franklin Bowditch Dexter, *Biographical Sketches of the Graduates of Yale College*, 1885–1912, 6 vols.

DSB   Charles C. Gillispie, ed., *Dictionary of Scientific Biography*, 1970–80, 16 vols.

DVB   John T. Kneebone, Sara B. Bearss, and others, eds., *Dictionary of Virginia Biography*, 1998– , 3 vols.

EG   Dickinson W. Adams and Ruth W. Lester, eds., *Jefferson's Extracts from the Gospels*, 1983, *The Papers of Thomas Jefferson*, Second Series

Fairclough, *Horace: Satires, Epistles and Ars Poetica*   *Horace: Satires, Epistles and Ars Poetica*, trans. H. Rushton Fairclough, Loeb Classical Library, 1926, repr. 2005

Fairclough, *Virgil*   *Virgil*, trans. H. Rushton Fairclough, Loeb Classical Library, 1916–18, rev. by G. P. Goold, 1999–2000, repr. 2002–06, 2 vols.

Ford   Paul Leicester Ford, ed., *The Writings of Thomas Jefferson*, Letterpress Edition, 1892–99, 10 vols.

Harvard Catalogue   *Harvard University Quinquennial Catalogue of the Officers and Graduates, 1636–1925*, 1925

HAW   Henry A. Washington, ed., *The Writings of Thomas Jefferson*, 1853–54, 9 vols.

Heitman, *Continental Army*   Francis B. Heitman, comp., *Historical Register of Officers of the Continental Army during the War of the Revolution, April, 1775, to December, 1783*, rev. ed., 1914, repr. 1967

Heitman, *U.S. Army*   Francis B. Heitman, comp., *Historical Register and Dictionary of the United States Army*, 1903, repr. 1994, 2 vols.

Hening   William Waller Hening, ed., *The Statutes at Large; being a Collection of all the Laws of Virginia*, Richmond, 1809–23, 13 vols.; Sowerby, no. 1863; Poor, *Jefferson's Library*, 10 (no. 573)

Hoefer, *Nouv. biog. générale*   J. C. F. Hoefer, *Nouvelle biographie générale depuis les temps les plus reculés jusqu'a nos jours*, 1852–83, 46 vols.

Hortus Third   Liberty Hyde Bailey, Ethel Zoe Bailey, and the staff of the Liberty Hyde Bailey Hortorium, Cornell University, *Hortus Third: A Concise Dictionary of Plants Cultivated in the United States and Canada*, 1976

Jackson, *Papers*   Sam B. Smith, Harold D. Moser, Daniel Feller, and others, eds., *The Papers of Andrew Jackson*, 1980– , 9 vols.

Jefferson Correspondence, Bixby   Worthington C. Ford, ed., *Thomas Jefferson Correspondence Printed from the Originals in the Collections of William K. Bixby*, 1916

JEP   *Journal of the Executive Proceedings of the Senate of the United States*

JHD   *Journal of the House of Delegates of the Commonwealth of Virginia*

JHR   *Journal of the House of Representatives of the United States*

JS   *Journal of the Senate of the United States*

JSV   *Journal of the Senate of Virginia*

Kimball, *Jefferson, Architect*   Fiske Kimball, *Thomas Jefferson, Architect*, 1916

L & B   Andrew A. Lipscomb and Albert E. Bergh, eds., *The Writings of Thomas Jefferson*, Library Edition, 1903–04, 20 vols.

Latrobe, *Papers*   John C. Van Horne and others, eds., *The Correspondence and Miscellaneous Papers of Benjamin Henry Latrobe*, 1984–88, 3 vols.

LCB   Douglas L. Wilson, ed., *Jefferson's Literary Commonplace Book*, 1989, *The Papers of Thomas Jefferson*, Second Series

Leavitt, *Poplar Forest*   Messrs. Leavitt, *Catalogue of a Private Library . . . Also, The Remaining Portion of the Library of the Late Thomas Jefferson . . . offered by his grandson, Francis Eppes, of Poplar Forest, Va.*, 1873

Leonard, *General Assembly*   Cynthia Miller Leonard, comp., *The General Assembly of Virginia, July 30, 1619–January 11, 1978: A Bicentennial Register of Members*, 1978

List of Patents   *A List of Patents granted by the United States from April 10, 1790, to December 31, 1836*, 1872

Longworth's New York Directory   *Longworth's American Almanac, New-York Register, and City Directory*, New York, 1796–1842 (title varies; cited by year of publication)

MACH   *Magazine of Albemarle County History*, 1940– (title varies; issued until 1951 as *Papers of the Albemarle County Historical Society*)

Madison, *Papers*   William T. Hutchinson, Robert A. Rutland, John C. A. Stagg, and others, eds., *The Papers of James Madison*, 1962– , 38 vols.
> *Congress. Ser.*, 17 vols.
> *Pres. Ser.*, 8 vols.
> *Retirement Ser.*, 3 vols.
> *Sec. of State Ser.*, 10 vols.

Malone, *Jefferson*   Dumas Malone, *Jefferson and his Time*, 1948–81, 6 vols.

Marshall, *Papers*   Herbert A. Johnson, Charles T. Cullen, Charles F. Hobson, and others, eds., *The Papers of John Marshall*, 1974–2006, 12 vols.

MB   James A. Bear Jr. and Lucia C. Stanton, eds., *Jefferson's Memorandum Books: Accounts, with Legal Records and Miscellany, 1767–1826*, 1997, *The Papers of Thomas Jefferson*, Second Series

Notes, ed. Peden   Thomas Jefferson, *Notes on the State of Virginia*, ed. William Peden, 1955, repr. 1995

OCD   Simon Hornblower and Antony Spawforth, eds., *The Oxford Classical Dictionary*, 2003

ODNB   H. C. G. Matthew and Brian Harrison, eds., *Oxford Dictionary of National Biography*, 2004, 60 vols.

OED   James A. H. Murray, J. A. Simpson, E. S. C. Weiner, and others, eds., *The Oxford English Dictionary*, 2d ed., 1989, 20 vols.

Peale, *Papers*   Lillian B. Miller and others, eds., *The Selected Papers of Charles Willson Peale and His Family*, 1983– , 5 vols. in 6

Pierson, *Jefferson at Monticello*   Hamilton W. Pierson, *Jefferson at Monticello: The Private Life of Thomas Jefferson, From Entirely New Materials*, 1862

Poor, *Jefferson's Library*   Nathaniel P. Poor, *Catalogue. President Jefferson's Library*, 1829

Princeton Catalogue   *General Catalogue of Princeton University 1746–1906*, 1908

Princetonians   James McLachlan and others, eds., *Princetonians: A Biographical Dictionary*, 1976–90, 5 vols.

PTJ   Julian P. Boyd, Charles T. Cullen, John Catanzariti, Barbara B. Oberg, and others, eds., *The Papers of Thomas Jefferson*, 1950– , 41 vols.

PW   Wilbur S. Howell, ed., *Jefferson's Parliamentary Writings*, 1988, *The Papers of Thomas Jefferson*, Second Series

Randall, *Life*   Henry S. Randall, *The Life of Thomas Jefferson*, 1858, 3 vols.

Randolph, *Domestic Life*   Sarah N. Randolph, *The Domestic Life of Thomas Jefferson, Compiled from Family Letters and Reminiscences by His Great-Granddaughter,* 1871

Shackelford, *Descendants*   George Green Shackelford, ed., *Collected Papers . . . of the Monticello Association of the Descendants of Thomas Jefferson,* 1965–84, 2 vols.

Sibley's Harvard Graduates   John L. Sibley and others, eds., *Sibley's Harvard Graduates,* 1873– , 18 vols.

Sowerby   E. Millicent Sowerby, comp., *Catalogue of the Library of Thomas Jefferson,* 1952–59, 5 vols.

Stein, *Worlds*   Susan R. Stein, *The Worlds of Thomas Jefferson at Monticello,* 1993

Terr. Papers   Clarence E. Carter and John Porter Bloom, eds., *The Territorial Papers of the United States,* 1934–75, 28 vols.

TJR   Thomas Jefferson Randolph, ed., *Memoir, Correspondence, and Miscellanies, from the Papers of Thomas Jefferson,* 1829, 4 vols.

True, "Agricultural Society"   Rodney H. True, "Minute Book of the Agricultural Society of Albemarle," *Annual Report of the American Historical Association for the Year 1918* (1921), 1:261–349

University of Pennsylvania Catalogue   Will J. Maxwell, comp., *General Alumni Catalogue of the University of Pennsylvania,* 1917

University of Virginia Commissioners' Report   *Proceedings and Report of the Commissioners for the University of Virginia. Presented December 8, 1818,* Richmond, 1818; Poor, *Jefferson's Library,* 6 (no. 233)

U.S. Reports   *Cases Argued and Decided in the Supreme Court of the United States,* 1790– (title varies; originally issued in distinct editions of separately numbered volumes with *U.S. Reports* volume numbers retroactively assigned; original volume numbers here given parenthetically)

U.S. Statutes at Large   Richard Peters, ed., *The Public Statutes at Large of the United States . . . 1789 to March 3, 1845,* 1845–67, 8 vols.

Va. Reports   *Reports of Cases Argued and Adjudged in the Court of Appeals of Virginia,* 1798– (title varies; originally issued in distinct editions of separately numbered volumes with *Va. Reports* volume numbers retroactively assigned; original volume numbers here given parenthetically)

VMHB   *Virginia Magazine of History and Biography,* 1893–

Washington, *Papers*   W. W. Abbot and others, eds., *The Papers of George Washington*, 1983–   , 62 vols.

    Colonial Ser., 10 vols.

    Confederation Ser., 6 vols.

    Pres. Ser., 18 vols.

    Retirement Ser., 4 vols.

    Rev. War Ser., 24 vols.

William and Mary Provisional List   *A Provisional List of Alumni, Grammar School Students, Members of the Faculty, and Members of the Board of Visitors of the College of William and Mary in Virginia. From 1693 to 1888*, 1941

WMQ   *William and Mary Quarterly*, 1892–

Woods, *Albemarle*   Edgar Woods, *Albemarle County in Virginia*, 1901, repr. 1991

CONTENTS

·ᘇⱿ 1818 Ȿᘊ·

CONTENTS

CONTENTS

CONTENTS

CONTENTS

CONTENTS

CONTENTS

CONTENTS

CONTENTS

CONTENTS

CONTENTS

CONTENTS

CONTENTS

CONTENTS

·◁❧ **1819** ☙▷·

CONTENTS

[xli]

CONTENTS

MAPS

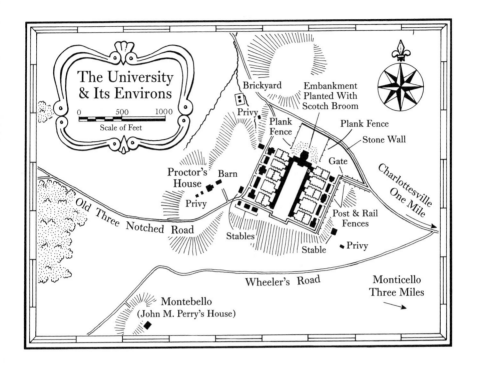

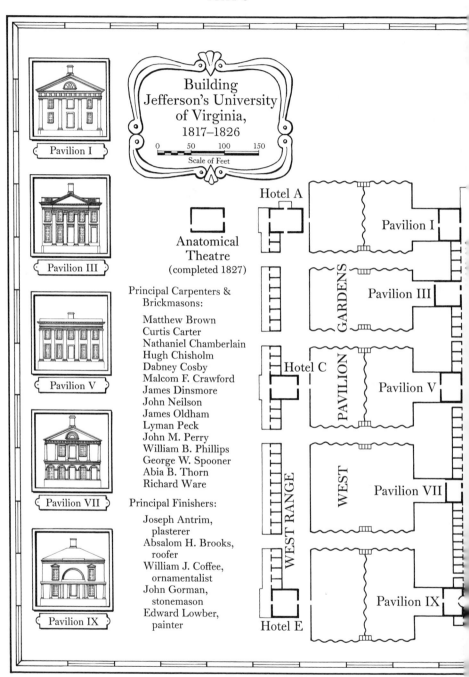

Building
Jefferson's University
of Virginia,
1817–1826

0   50   100   150

Scale of Feet

Pavilion I

Pavilion III

Pavilion V

Pavilion VII

Pavilion IX

Anatomical
Theatre
(completed 1827)

Principal Carpenters &
Brickmasons:

Matthew Brown
Curtis Carter
Nathaniel Chamberlain
Hugh Chisholm
Dabney Cosby
Malcom F. Crawford
James Dinsmore
John Neilson
James Oldham
Lyman Peck
John M. Perry
William B. Phillips
George W. Spooner
Abia B. Thorn
Richard Ware

Principal Finishers:

Joseph Antrim,
  plasterer
Absalom H. Brooks,
  roofer
William J. Coffee,
  ornamentalist
John Gorman,
  stonemason
Edward Lowber,
  painter

Hotel A

Hotel C

Hotel E

GARDENS

PAVILION

WEST

WEST RANGE

Pavilion I

Pavilion III

Pavilion V

Pavilion VII

Pavilion IX

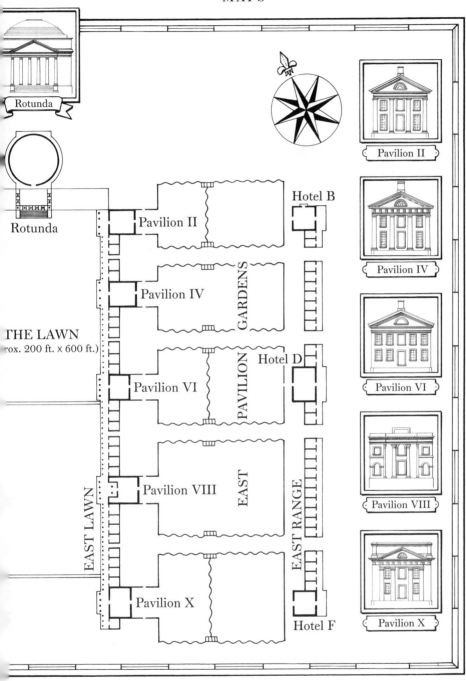

Rotunda

Rotunda

Pavilion II

Pavilion IV

THE LAWN
(approx. 200 ft. × 600 ft.)

Pavilion VI

Pavilion VIII

Pavilion X

EAST LAWN

PAVILION GARDENS

EAST PAVILION

EAST RANGE

Hotel B

Hotel D

Hotel F

Pavilion II

Pavilion IV

Pavilion VI

Pavilion VIII

Pavilion X

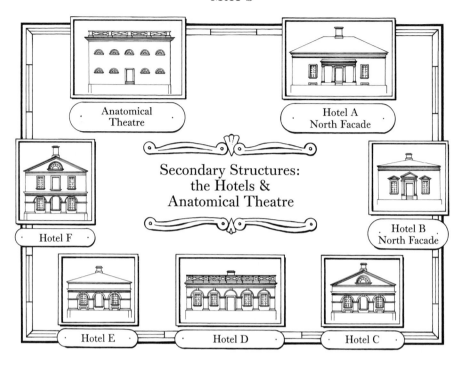

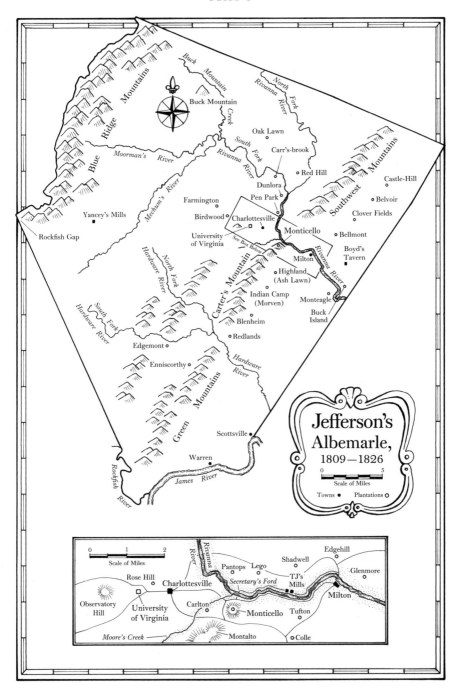

Jefferson's
Albemarle,
1809—1826

0   5
Scale of Miles

Towns •   Plantations ○

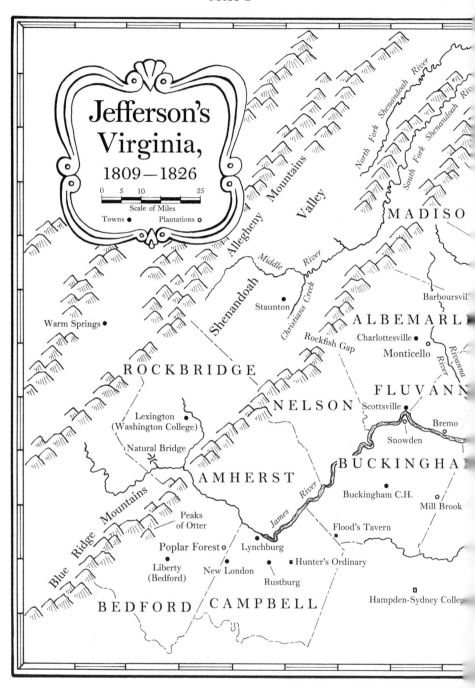

Jefferson's Virginia, 1809–1826

Scale of Miles
0 5 10   25

Towns ●   Plantations ○

North Fork Shenandoah River

South Fork Shenandoah River

Allegheny Mountains

Valley

MADISO

Middle River

Christians Creek

Staunton ●

Barboursvil

Warm Springs ●

ALBEMARL

Charlottesville ●

Rockfish Gap

Monticello

Rivanna River

ROCKBRIDGE

FLUVANN

Shenandoah River

NELSON

Scottsville ●

Lexington
(Washington College) ●

Bremo ○

Natural Bridge

Snowden ○

BUCKINGHA

AMHERST

James River

Buckingham C.H. ●

Peaks
of Otter

Mill Brook ○

Blue Ridge Mountains

Flood's Tavern ■

Poplar Forest ○   Lynchburg ●

Liberty
(Bedford) ●   New London ●   ■ Hunter's Ordinary

Rustburg ●

Hampden-Sydney Colleg ◻

BEDFORD   CAMPBELL

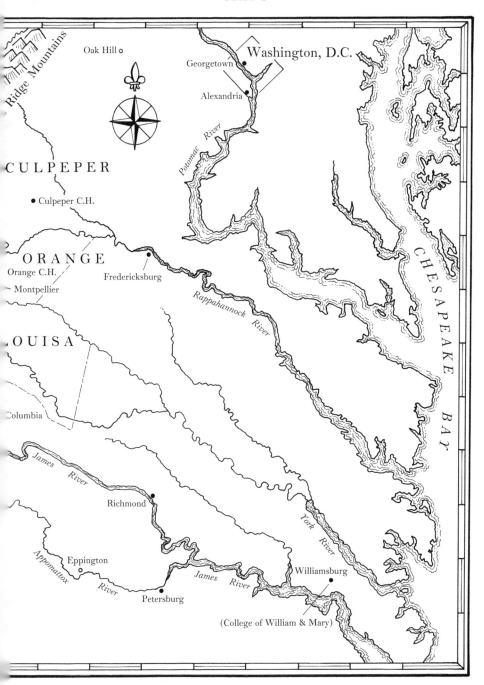

ILLUSTRATIONS

Following page 400

ROCKFISH GAP AND WARM SPRINGS BY EDWARD BEYER

In August 1818 Jefferson and his fellow University of Virginia Commissioners met for four days at the Mountain House tavern of Allen Bernard at Rockfish Gap to choose the site for the proposed University of Virginia. Following the meeting he spent three weeks at Warm Springs. The German artist Edward Beyer (1820–65) came to the United States in about 1848, spending time in Newark, New Jersey, and Philadelphia before beginning a Virginia tour of more than two years in 1854. During that time he painted many notable locations in the western part of the state, including both natural landscapes and man-made structures. In return for free board and a payment of $50, Beyer gave the owners of resort inns pictures of their establishments. These likenesses sometimes included projected improvements to the spas that were never actually constructed. The images reproduced here were part a portfolio of lithographs entitled the *Album of Virginia* that Beyer published in 1858 (*DVB*; George A. Mclean Jr., "The Life and Art of Edward Beyer," in *Edward Beyer's Travels Through America: An Artist's View; including Edward Beyer's Cyclorama*, trans. Holle Schneider [2011], ix–xx; *MB*, 2:1346).

Courtesy of the Albert and Shirley Small Special Collections Library, University of Virginia.

DRAFT OF ROCKFISH GAP REPORT

On 21 Feb. 1818 the General Assembly of Virginia passed "An Act appropriating part of the revenue of the Literary Fund, and for other purposes" which mandated the meeting of the Commissioners of the University of Virginia at Rockfish Gap on 1 Aug. 1818 and tasked them with reporting on where the university should be located, what branches of learning should be taught there, and which professorships should be established to teach these subjects. This is a page from Jefferson's earliest-known draft of the Rockfish Gap Report that the commissioners approved on 4 Aug. 1818. It shows his preliminary thoughts on organizing the professorships and curriculum. Jefferson's jump in numbering from IV at the bottom of the left-hand column to VIII at the top of the right suggests a copying error from an earlier and otherwise unknown version. Jefferson corrected this error by pasting a small scrap of replacement text on the upper right-hand portion of his tabular statement of university subjects before rewriting from sections VIII on. The row of four red stains in the middle of the page shows where Jefferson used sealing wax to affix an additional revised version of this material rather than continuing to rework it. Both sections of replacement text have been unsealed from the draft and are archivally bound with it. This draft was composed before 28 June 1818, when Jefferson enclosed a subsequent and more polished version to James Madison. Jefferson had hoped to convince Madison to compose the report himself, but the latter refused, possibly announcing his decision in person when the two men met during the 11 May 1818 meeting of the Visitors of Central College in Charlottesville (*Acts of Assembly* [1817–18 sess.], 14; TJ to Madison, 11 Apr., 28 June 1818; Minutes of Central College Board of Visitors, 11 May 1818; TJ to Spencer Roane, 28 June 1818).

Courtesy of the Albert and Shirley Small Special Collections Library, University of Virginia.

SIGNATURE PAGE OF ROCKFISH GAP REPORT

The Virginia statute that authorized the meeting of the University of Virginia Commissioners at Rockfish Gap instructed the governor to appoint a commissioner from each state senatorial district. Governor James P. Preston duly appointed twenty-four men in March 1818. Twenty-one commissioners ultimately attended the meeting at Rockfish Gap and signed the final report on 4 Aug. 1818. The absentees included commissioners from the Surry and Washington districts, who missed the meeting due to illness. Although Jefferson thought that his acquaintance Littleton W. Tazewell would be representing the Norfolk district, the *Richmond Enquirer* reported that that jurisdiction sent no commissioner "because the persons successively appointed declined the acceptance." The text of the report pictured here was the one Jefferson sent to Linn Banks, the Speaker of the House of Delegates (*Acts of Assembly* [1817–18 sess.], 14 [21 Feb. 1818]; *Richmond Enquirer*, 20 Mar., 11 Aug. 1818; TJ to Tazewell, 28 June 1818; TJ to Preston, 13 July 1818; TJ to Linn Banks and Edward Watts, 20 Nov. 1818).

Courtesy of the Library of Virginia.

WILLIAM WIRT BY CHARLES WILLSON PEALE

Jefferson's old friend Charles Willson Peale painted this likeness of William Wirt (1772–1834) during an extended stay in Washington, D.C., and Baltimore from early in November 1818 to the end of January 1819. Peale's attempt during this trip to interest the federal government in providing a permanent home for his Philadelphia museum failed. However, he took advantage of his proximity to the nation's capital to paint portraits of leading figures, which he then placed on temporary display in Washington before removing them to his museum. Peale noted that he had been urged to paint Wirt, whom he described as the "author of the life of Patrick Henry which give him a high standing in the literary line." On perusing the work himself, Peale observed that "some of his flourishes was in my mind a little extravigant, but he seems enamored with the character of Henry, therefore more execusible." In a letter to his son Rembrandt early in January, Peale noted that "my picture is a striking likeness of Mr. Wirt, altho' I shall give a few finishing touches anon." Wirt had served as one of Jefferson's counsel when he was sued in 1810 by Edward Livingston in the controversy concerning the Batture Sainte Marie. In 1818 Jefferson consulted Wirt in his capacity as United States attorney general for advice on where to prove the will of Tadeusz Kosciuszko (Peale, *Papers*, 3:635, 649, 683).

Courtesy of the Edward and Tullah Hanley Memorial Gift to the People of Denver, Denver Art Museum Collection.

ILLUSTRATIONS

HANNAH TO THOMAS JEFFERSON, 15 NOVEMBER 1818

This is a rare surviving example of a letter to Jefferson from one of his slaves, and the only one known from an enslaved woman. When Jefferson's ill health prevented him from making his usual trip to his Poplar Forest estate late in 1818, Hannah, who worked there as his cook, laundress, and housekeeper, wrote to inform him that all was well and to express her concern for his health. No evidence of a response to this letter has been found.

Courtesy of the Massachusetts Historical Society.

BENJAMIN O. TYLER'S ENGRAVED DECLARATION OF INDEPENDENCE AND SUBSCRIPTION BOOK

Benjamin O. Tyler (b. 1789), an engraver and teacher of penmanship in Washington, D.C., published his edition of the Declaration of Independence in the spring of 1818 at a cost of five dollars a copy. He managed to produce his version, notable for the attempt to reproduce the signatures accurately, earlier than his rival, the Philadelphia newspaper publisher John Binns, who had been taking subscriptions for his print of the Declaration since June 1816 but failed to release it until 1819. Although Tyler sent Jefferson a complimentary copy of the engraving, the ex-president's signature, followed by that of James Madison, appears on the first page of Tyler's subscription book. Other subscribers whose names followed on the list of more than one thousand names include many congressmen and officials, such as Secretary of State John Quincy Adams and Virginia governor James P. Preston. The book routinely indicates whether subscribers wanted their copy to be on paper or, for two dollars more, on parchment, and whether they had paid in advance. Tyler later went back and keyed his own additional notes in the margin to a section of "Remarks," where he set down biographical information on selected individuals (Enoch Reynolds to TJ, 27 June 1816; Tyler to TJ, 6 May 1818; Stein, *Worlds*, 193).

Courtesy of the Albert H. Small Declaration of Independence Collection, Albert and Shirley Small Special Collections Library, University of Virginia.

THE DECLARATION OF INDEPENDENCE BY JOHN TRUMBULL

John Trumbull's oil-on-canvas painting for the United States Capitol stands twelve feet tall and eighteen feet wide. It is an enlarged and enhanced version of an earlier painting of approximately twenty-one by thirty-one inches which Trumbull had begun in 1787 while visiting Jefferson in Paris. Trumbull evidently made his final revisions to this earlier painting as late as 1820, and an 1823 Asher B. Durand engraving owned by Jefferson, a specimen of which is displayed in Monticello's entrance hall, was based on the smaller painting. Trumbull's painting destined for Washington, D.C., was first exhibited in Boston, New York, Philadelphia, and Baltimore before it arrived at the Capitol in 1819. It was installed at its final location in the Rotunda in 1826 (Stein, *Worlds*, 124; Irma B. Jaffe, "Trumbull's 'The Declaration of Independence': Keys and Dates," *American Art Journal*, vol. 3, no. 2 [1971]: 41–9; Trumbull to TJ, 28 June 1823).

Courtesy of the Architect of the Capitol, United States Capitol, Washington, D.C.

ILLUSTRATIONS

PLAN OF THE TOWN OF CHARLOTTESVILLE

Charlottesville, named for Queen Charlotte Sophia (1744–1818), the German-born wife of the British monarch George III, was established in 1762, incorporated as a town in 1801, and attained the legal status of a city in 1888. Initially consisting of fifty acres of land, it was laid off into streets, lots, and a public square where the Albemarle County courthouse has stood ever since. This map is based on a survey done by William Woods at the request of the town trustees on 17 Dec. 1818. Several street names depicted, including Jefferson, have remained in use (*Acts of Assembly* [1762 sess.], 39 [Nov. 1762]; [1800–01 sess.], 25 [19 Jan. 1801]; [1887–88 sess.], 412 [2 Mar. 1888]; Albemarle Co. Surveyor's Book, 2:147–8).

Courtesy of the Albert and Shirley Small Special Collections Library, University of Virginia.

Volume 13

22 April 1818 to 31 January 1819

JEFFERSON CHRONOLOGY

1743 • 1826

1743	Born at Shadwell, 13 April (New Style).
1760–1762	Studies at the College of William and Mary.
1762–1767	Self-education and preparation for law.
1769–1774	Albemarle delegate to House of Burgesses.
1772	Marries Martha Wayles Skelton, 1 January.
1775–1776	In Continental Congress.
1776	Drafts Declaration of Independence.
1776–1779	In Virginia House of Delegates.
1779	Submits Bill for Establishing Religious Freedom.
1779–1781	Governor of Virginia.
1782	Martha Wayles Skelton Jefferson dies, 6 September.
1783–1784	In Continental Congress.
1784–1789	In France on commission to negotiate commercial treaties and then as minister plenipotentiary at Versailles.
1790–1793	Secretary of State of the United States.
1797–1801	Vice President of the United States.
1801–1809	President of the United States.

RETIREMENT

1809	Attends James Madison's inauguration, 4 March.
	Arrives at Monticello, 15 March.
1810	Completes legal brief on New Orleans batture case, 31 July.
1811	Batture case dismissed, 5 December.
1812	Correspondence with John Adams resumed, 1 January.
	Batture pamphlet preface completed, 25 February; printed by 21 March.
1814	Named a trustee of Albemarle Academy, 25 March.
	Resigns presidency of American Philosophical Society, 23 November.
1815	Sells personal library to Congress.
1816	Writes introduction and revises translation of Destutt de Tracy, *A Treatise on Political Economy* [1818].
	Named a visitor of Central College, 18 October.
1817	Cornerstone laid for first structure at Central College (later Pavilion VII, University of Virginia), 6 October.
1818	Attends Rockfish Gap conference to choose location of proposed University of Virginia, 1–4 August.
	Visits Warm Springs, 7–27 August.
1819	University of Virginia chartered, 25 January; named to Board of Visitors, 13 February; elected rector, 29 March.
	Debts greatly increased by bankruptcy of Wilson Cary Nicholas.
1820	Likens debate over slavery and Missouri statehood to "a fire bell in the night," 22 April.
1821	Writes memoirs, 6 January–29 July.
1823	Visits Poplar Forest for last time, 16–25 May.
1824	Lafayette visits Monticello, 4–15 November.
1825	University of Virginia opens, 7 March.
1826	Writes will, 16–17 March.
	Last recorded letter, 25 June.
	Dies at Monticello, 4 July.

THE PAPERS OF
THOMAS JEFFERSON

·《━━━━━━━》·

From Henry Dearborn

DEAR SIR,   Boston April 22ᵈ 1818

Being persuaded that you have more letters to notice than can be
perfectly convenient or agreable, I have refrained for some time from
adding to the list, we may not always be sure of what the governing
motive for our actions may be, but as far as I am capable of deciding
in the present case, my motive for writing is principally, that of saying, that neither time or space, has in any degree abated the respect
& esteem for your charactor & person which I have long entertained,
and which can never diminish while my reason continues. I frequently
reflect on the disproportion between men, in public life, who have been
& are, governed by saccred principles of strict integrity: and those of
a different charactor, and when I have found one of the former charactor, I consider him as entitled to my highest esteem. —although Mʳ
Monroe came into the Presidency under very favourable circumstancies, he has not been permitted to recline at all times on a bed of
roses, but I am confident that his good Judgement & virtuous intentions will carry him safely through. I am very sorry that Duane has
taken such hostile ground, and what is still more unaccountable is his
partiality for D. Clinton, who I have long concidered as on par, in
point of ambition and want of honest integrity, with A. Bur.— Mʳ
Clay appears disposed to play the part of John Randolph, and will
probably attach himself to the present Clintonian party.—I have frequently had the pleasure of hearing of you, by different persons, and
all agree that time has had no perceptible effect on your body or mind.
I enjoy good health, and am easey & happy in my domestic concerns,
but I can neither forgit or forgive the unjust treatment I received in
the course of the late war, I was drawn into the army against my own
inclinations, I was suspended from command in the most humiliating
and unprecedented manner, and denied any enquiry into the circumstancies on which my removal originated. and at the close of the war

[3]

I was discharged with as little regard to my feelings as any private soldier, being merely notified by a gen^l order from a Brigad^er Genl that my functions as an officer would cease on a certain day. I should not have concented to remain in the Army in time of peace, but I thought that when all circumstancies were concidered, it was not unreasonable to expect some notice from the Executive, that my services were no longer required. I have mentioned my case to you, perhaps improperly, but merely to put you in possession of the facts, as an act of Justice to myself, but with no wish or desire that they should ever go any further.—

Mr^s Dearborn Joins me in the most respectfull compliments, and best wishes for your health and happiness, with a request that you will please to present our kind & sincere regards to Mr^s & Mr Randolph & their amiable children— H. DEARBORN

RC (DLC); at foot of text: "Hon^bl Thomas Jefferson"; endorsed by TJ as received 9 May 1818 and so recorded in SJL.

Secretary of War John Armstrong was instrumental in the REMOVAL of Dear- born from active command in 1813, ostensibly to allow him time to recover from illness. Dearborn later oversaw the defense of New York until his honorable discharge on 15 June 1815 (Madison, *Papers, Pres. Ser.*, 6:461–2, 503–4, 534–5; Heitman, *U.S. Army*, 1:19, 363).

From Gamaliel H. Ward

RESPECTED SIR, Salem April 22^d 1818.—

I wrote You on the 20th January from Wilmington N^o C. by the advice of my friends there, and as the subject and my plan seem'd to excite a deal of interest & anxiety, perhaps the letter might have been intercepted, I therefore take the liberty to enclose a copy and to crave your reference thereto. But as I desired an answer to care of Robert Cochran Esqre Collector of that place and left it myself soon after I cannot yet ascertain whether or not you condescended to answer it.— Reading the Copy since I was not a little astonish'd and sensibly struck at the familiar style with which I addressd a man so much older and respectable than myself, and I now Sir humbly ask your pardon for it.—being highly elated with the prospect and the handsome Sums which were offer'd perhaps I did not duly realize who I was writing to. This therefore must be my apology and I hope will prove satisfactory to You Sir who are so well acquainted with mankind Old and Young.—I beg leave to make a further reference for my character, if necessary, which is to the Hon Secretary of the Navy B. W. Crowninshield & Nathl Silsbee Esqre, both native townsmen of mine.—

[4]

Having served the first of my time in an E.I. merchants office 5 years. at the age of 22–23 I became an E:I: Captain in E. H. Derby Esq^res employ, and having since that time followed the Sea with a variety of fortune (privateering included) perhaps my habits & manners have become a little more rough than may appear consistent & proper to those not versed in the sea faring life; therefore the Letter for which I apologize has given me some pain—fearing that an unpleasant impression might be made on the mind of a man whom I have "delighted to honour"—never but once saw—and fondly anticipate seeing on my passage to Carolina with my little family which is my present purpose.—

I beg therefore, Sir, that You will excuse me, and in your envious retirement find time to address me a few lines to Care of Genl H. A. S. Dearborn, Boston or Col° Wm R. Lee, Salem, (open for their perusal) both of which Gentlemen have been my friends in time of need.— With the hope that I shall be gratified and my future prospects be verified, I shall remain ever as before Your Mo. Ob. and respectful (young) humble Servt   GAM^L H. WARD.

P:S: A Mr Hall advertized last summer in Virginia that he could make 500 bush^s Salt a day by a new plan which has never yet been made public but seem'd to be approved of by the Editors of the Intelligencer. I Know not his principles but the advertisement led me to conjecture and to form my plan of evaporating the water by the force of Winslow Lewis' Patent (convex) Glasses the power of which may be encreased to almost any extent—say to fire a house in a very quick time: or by Concave Mirrors (if to be obtaind) the force or power of the latter I learnt in the year 1805 at Hamburgh in the worthy professor Ebelings Library; having some Cases of Books from my old friend the Rev. Mr Bentley for the Professor he invited me to visit the Library and in his private room where stood the Statue of the immortal Klopstock was also a Concave Mirror of (as near as I recollect) 18 to 24 inches diameter, which he told me was an ancient Roman Glass, the power of which he said would set on fire a Ship in a Short time; I turn'd its face to the sun and soon felt the effect in my eyes; the professor hastily threw it back observing that 'twas a dangerous thing to trifle with where materials were not fire proof.—I little thought then or since 'til now that 'twould be of service to me, but it is so, and since my two plans of encreasing the power of the Sun by the effect of Glasses—John Hogg Esqr Jus: Pac: of Wilmington, whose study and pleasure seems to be old & new inventions, in conversation explained to me a very speedy method of evaporation by steam on Count Rumford's plan of boiling water in a large vessel by means of Steam from a smaller; it struck me very forcibly and I am confident will answer an important object altho' I have not yet proved it—I mean in making fine Salt, as coarse cannot be made except by slow evaporation.—Therefore should Mr Hall's plan interfere with mine or more properly mine with his, as his is first I shall endeavour to obtain a Patent for one of my three methods, to wit, Convex Glasses. Concave Mirrors or boiling by steam and have no doubt that I shall succeed for my interest, altho' 'twas foreign to my ideas of ever supporting or enriching myself by making Salt instead of doing it as a Shipmaster & Super Cargo.—

I sometimes Sir, wonder for what I was made,—Saltmakers must at any rate owe me gratitude and the public must pay me for it so long as Salt is used and this will ever be; I therefore am confident in saying that I am not a useless member of Society.—And with respect and esteem again subscribe Your very hble & Ob. Servt

GAM^{L} H. WARD

PS. Judge Story who has read these Letters tells me the reason of my not receiving an answer to the first, must be Sir, from Your extensive correspondence and your advanced age.—
Ap^l 23^d—   G H. W

RC (DLC); endorsed by TJ as received 9 May 1818 and so recorded in SJL. RC (MHi); address cover only; with PoC of TJ to John Steele, 27 July 1818, on verso; addressed: "Honble Thomas Jefferson Monticello, Virginia"; franked; postmarked (faint) Salem [   ] Apr. Enclosure: Ward to TJ, 20 Jan. 1818.

E.I.: East India. In the Bible, a Persian king DELIGHTED TO HONOUR Mordecai

(Esther 6.6–11). The Washington *Daily National* INTELLIGENCER of 29 Sept. 1817 reprinted an article that appeared five days previously in the Norfolk *American Beacon and Commercial Diary* detailing Everard Hall's recent innovation in the manufacture of salt and indicating that he would seek to patent his discovery (see Hall to TJ, 19 Jan. 1818, and TJ to Hall, 19 Feb. 1818). Justitia pace (JUS: PAC:) is Latin for "justice of the peace."

From John Wood

DEAR SIR   Richmond 22^d April 1818.

Understanding that there will be soon a meeting of the Trustees of the Central College, I beg leave to acquaint you; that in the event of the Trustees not having procured a mathematical Professor, that I should be happy to have the professorship. I regret extremely that I was not more explicit in my answer to your letter last summer on the subject of the classical Professorship. My impressions were, that no mathematical Professorship was to be established, and my state of health then, was such, as to dread the superintendance of a number of boys in the Rudiments of Language, which was never a favourite employment with me whereas giving instruction in Mathematics always afforded me pleasure. To have my time exclusively devoted to mathematical science I have always desired; but have never been so fortunate as to obtain a situation of this description. I shall have the survey of the rivers completed during my vacation in August next; and will have no other business to interrupt in future the education of youth.—

Since receiving your letter, upon enquiry I have found, that Gilbert Wakefield is dead, but that his manuscript of a Greek Lexicon was completed and is at present in the hands of a London Bookseller. I have been informed by Mr Rice a clergyman of this city, that the English & Greek Lexicon a notice of which I observed in some review; was by a Mr Jones also the author of an English and Greek Grammar.

I have the honour to be with great esteem & respect your obliged servant   JOHN WOOD

RC (DLC); endorsed by TJ as received 6 May 1818 and so recorded in SJL. RC (DLC); address cover only; with PoC of TJ to James Madison, 28 June 1818, on recto and verso; addressed: "Thomas Jefferson Esqr Monticello by Milton"; franked; postmarked Richmond, 23 Apr.

From John Rhea

Washington 23d April 1818

John Rhea, presents the assurance of his respect and Esteem, with the enclosed copy of a Circular letter to Thomas Jefferson Esqr late President of the United States—

RC (MHi); endorsed by TJ as received 6 May 1818 and so recorded in SJL. Enclosure: Rhea to his constituents, Washington, 3 Apr. 1818, highlighting the uniqueness of the American republic, the symbiotic relationship between the state and national governments, and the status of the federal constitution as the "great charter"; summarizing United States Treasury receipts and expenditures and the rise of public debt between 1812 and 1818; inferring from a survey of domestic manufactures and imports and exports that the "quantity of domestic produce and manufacture exported from the United States, has (except in the time of the late war) been annually increasing"; commenting that the passage of an act authorizing the building of additional naval ships and steam batteries will lead to a "strong marine defence in case of future war"; noting that recent Indian removal treaties will result in "Connected settlements . . . from Mobile to Lake Erie, and from Lake Erie north of the river Ohio to Missouri"; reporting passage of an act that helps clear title to former Indian land in Tennessee; observing that the population of the country has increased fivefold since American independence; asserting that the military continues to strengthen and expand; providing a positive view of agriculture, manufacture, commerce, and civil liberties within the nation; and concluding that, as a result of the "protecting providence of the Almighty ruler of the universe," the United States has "become a great nation," which he prays will continue (printed circular in MHi: Adams Papers; filed with covering letter noted below).

Rhea sent the same CIRCULAR to James Madison on this day. Five days later he enclosed one to Secretary of State John Quincy Adams (Madison, *Papers, Retirement Ser.*, 1:247; Rhea to Adams, 28 Apr. 1818 [MHi: Adams Papers]).

From Stephen Cathalan

DEAR SIR & MY
TOO KIND PROTECTOR!   Marseilles the 25th april 1818—

your most honored Favor of the 18th January, Inclosing a Copy of the Letter your So Long Continued Friendship for me dictated to the H[ble] B. W. Crowninshield Sec[ry] of the navy, with one of his answer to you (which you was So Good, as to take the Trouble to transmit me, with & by your Good Friendly Hand) Reached me on the 21st Ins[t] by an american Vessel arived on that Day, from new york;—

my Heart has been Since it's Reciept, So Deeply oppressed by what I feel! that it is quite Impossible for me to find in any Idiom to my knowledge proper adapted words to Express to you my Everlasting Gratitude, not only for the warm Interest you took in my Behalf in 1815—at the close of the Last U.s. war, near the President, but even Since & more over, when =on Receipt of my Letter of the 8th July last, you communicated to him (then at his Seat adjacent yours) the Contents of my Said Letter and of the Papers it contained,[1] Renewing at the Same time your Intercessions in my behalf, on which he was So Good as to declare to you, he Saw nothing in the case to alarm me[2] & to add, that nothing Should, be, in any Event, done to my own Prejudice, without your previous Information on this= &[a] &[a] &[a]

I must now acknowledge to you, my Dear sir, that my Letter of Resignation, had been Influenced by the late transaction, but also by a number of Disagreable occurences, I had Experienced here, by the Competition of a Few Restless americans unjustly Jealous of me, or my So long holding this office,[3] without any plausible motives[4] on their own Part

it was not then Surprising that with So many contending Interests I was under Some apprehensions of being Dismissed,! as it had been Reported here, Even in Paris, and as I have been Informed by private Letters to me;

on the other hand, I, alone, as I have wrote it, not Long Since, in answer, I was Relying with the greatest Confidence in the Justice of the President and of the Gov[nt] of the U.s. but also (& this I did not mention it) on your Friendly Protection, in Stating & Supporting my case to the President! —

but Since you are So Good[5] as to Inform me, that you have thought it due to =the Caracter of the united states for Justice of its officers, to withold my Letter of Resignation, which is Considered as non avenue that I am allowed to continue my Services, on the assurance that they will be acceptable to the Govern[t] and under the Protection of it's Justice; Since you, the President & the hon[ble] B. W. Crowninshield Secr[y] of the Navy are So[6] Good as to have agreed that the choice is Left to me, either to Continue in office or to Retire from it, on which you are waiting for my Deliberate & Prompt answer;=

after Due Refflexion, I am Convinced that I cannot Give a more Sanguine Proof of the Sense of my Gratitude & obedience towards the U.s. Govern[t] and their members and to you Particularly, than to Declare to you that I owe to it's Justice & benevolence towards me and to my honor, which is dearer to me than my own Existance, that I wish to be Continued Still Longer in this office, and to Postpone to an other time my Second Request thro' you for obtaining Permission to Resign this Consulate,

I owe it also to you, my Dear Sir, who made your Self Responsible for me So Long as I will hold it, & I beg Leave to be assured, that this newly Repeated Proof of Confidence from you in me will Stimulate more & more my zeal to hold it Correctly & Subjoined, quam Diû me bene Gesseris & it will be at the mutual Satisfaction of the Govern[t] and of the Citizens of the united states, I hope!

as to my Friend Mr Dodge, to whom I have communicated, on Receipt your Letter of January 18 & the Copies it Inclosed & whom I offered to you as my future Successor, Should my Resignation be Granted; he is very Gratefull for all your kind Expressions & wishes, as well as those you transmitted me from the President & the Secretary of the Navy & he is aware, he being now Supported by Such Emminents Protectors, that =the Longer he will continue by his[7] Correct Conduct to merit the Succession, the more Certain he will be, to Receive it at full maturity;=[8]—he Continues to assist me in this Consulate, and as I have mentioned to you, in my Last of the 30th March, to our Mutual Satisfaction;—

I have Sent to M[r] sasserno, a Copy of the Paragraph of your Letter Concerning his appoint[mt] as consul of the U.s. at Nice, & I will not fail to Forward you his Gratefull answer for your Goodness towards him, as Soon as it will Reach me;—

I am Sorry to observe that the wines of Rivesaltes & of nice, by the Brig agent of alex[ia] W. W. Lewis Master Bound for new-york, had not yet Reached you on the 18th January, nor my Letter of the 15th Sep[ber] Inclosing my Invoice for the Same;—as to the wine of Lédenon[9] shipped in 9bre on the Brig Benefactor of alex[ia] Bound for alexandria, I hope you will have Soon after the Date of your Said Letter have Received or have heard of it's arival, & the whole at your Satisfaction;

I am Shipping on the Ship Fair Trader of alex[ia] as p[r] your order, 8 Boxes of 24 Bottles Each Red wine of the year 1814 of Bergasse, this Ship is Ready to Sail for Bouque[10] in this Gulph of Lyons, to Compleat her Cargo with Salt, Bound for alexandria; I apprehend that there will not be any other vessels for the cheasapeak in this Port before the end of august next;—[11][and in order that you may Get your Stock for Your consumption of 1819 before the next winter Sets in.]

I Intend to order & Prepare your Supply in qualities & quantities thereabout the Same, as p[r] your order by yours of 6th June 1817— without waiting for your new order & Remitance at your own Convenience;[12] I don't know whether I may at Same time Provide for your Grand Son[13] Th[s] Jef[on] Randolph Esq[r] as I did in Conformity of your Said Letter; but I think I may do it also & if when Ready there is no vessel for the cheasapeak I will Ship it for Philad[ia], new-york or Boston.

I have the honor to be with great Respect
Dear sir your most obed[t] & Gratefull Serv[t]

STEPHEN CATHALAN.

Dupl (DLC); at head of text: "2[ta]"; at foot of first page: "Thos Jefferson Esqr Monticello"; endorsed by TJ as received 30 July 1818 and so recorded in SJL. RC (DLC); endorsed by TJ as received 1 Sept. 1818 and so recorded in SJL. Enclosed in Cathalan to TJ, 2 May 1818.

A set of extracts from correspondence between Cathalan and Catherine Éléonore Ménoire Fenwick in TJ's papers may have been enclosed by Cathalan in the above letter as examples of PRIVATE LETTERS encouraging his resignation. Fenwick's husband, Joseph Fenwick, was formerly the United States consul at Bordeaux. The extracts begin with a letter from Fenwick dated Paris, 19 Jan. 1818, advising Cathalan that he should resign immediately, perhaps via a letter to the United States minister plenipotentiary in Paris (Albert Gallatin), and indicating

that she had heard complaints about him from sources that she could not disclose. Cathalan's 27 Jan. 1818 reply insisted at considerable length that the accusations against him were groundless and invited Fenwick to communicate to the source of the rumors Cathalan's refusal to consider resigning unless he heard directly from the minister plenipotentiary regarding the purported complaints. Fenwick's response dated Paris, 21 Mar. 1818, confirmed that she had transmitted the information to her acquaintance and expressed her hope for a positive outcome for Cathalan (Trs in MHi; in French; entirely in Cathalan's hand).

NON AVENUE: not having happened, annulled (OED). QUAM DIŨ ME BENE GESSERIS is a variation of "quamdiu bene se gesserint": "as long as they shall conduct themselves properly" (Black's Law Dictionary).

[1] RC: "Inclosed."
[2] Dupl: "me me."
[3] In RC preceding seven words are keyed to their proper point in text with an underscored caret.
[4] Dupl: "Motives plausible motives." RC: "plausible motives."
[5] RC: "kind."
[6] Dupl: "to." RC: "So."
[7] RC here adds "own."
[8] Closing guillemet editorially moved from left margin based on position in RC.
[9] RC here adds "I."
[10] RC: "the Port of Bouc."
[11] Remainder of paragraph, not in Dupl, supplied from RC.
[12] Preceding four words not in RC.
[13] Preceding three words not in RC.

From Thomas Appleton

SIR   Leghorn 29[h] April 1818—
The unexpected departure of the Brig. Free Ocean Capt: Bartholomew, this day for Phil[a] together with many avocations for the Squadron of Com[o] Stewart now here, allows me only the time to say, that I have shipp'd on board the above mention'd vessel, two Cases cont'g 84 bottles of montepulciano wine, which exactly balances, what you term the "atom," after paying mad[me] mazzei.—It is directed to the Care of J. Steele esq, Collector of Phil[a].—

accept Sir, the renewal of my high respect   TH: APPLETON

RC (DLC); endorsed by TJ as received 26 July 1818 and so recorded in SJL. RC (MHi); address cover only; with PoC of TJ to Lewis D. Belair, 16 Nov. 1818, on verso; addressed: "Thomas Jefferson esq monticelli Virginia"; stamped

"SHIP"; franked; postmarked Philadelphia, 18 July.

For TJ's reference to the ATOM remaining in Appleton's hands, see TJ to Appleton, 1 Aug. 1817. MAD[ME] MAZZEI: Elisabetta Mazzei Pini.

Matthew Pate's Survey of Eighteen-Acre Tract Adjacent to Poplar Forest

Ap[l] 30th 1818

Surveyed for Thomas Jefferson 18 acres of Land (by Virtue of a Land Office Treasury Warrant granted to him the 27th day of June 1812 for 100 acres & N° 4915) Situate in the County of Bedford & Bounded as follows viz Begining at pointers Corner to his own popler forest tract thence along his own lines S 40$\frac{1}{2}$ E 68 poles to pointers S 62 W 38 poles to Cobbs Corner Red oak thence along his line N 43$\frac{1}{2}$ W 81 poles to a stake in a line of the Said popler forest tract thence along said line N 75 E 47 poles to the first Station—

MATTHEW PATE S.B.C

NB there being a ballance of 82 acres of the above warrant Still unappropriated[1] it is therefore retaind in my Office for further use.—

MATTHEW PATE S.B.C

MS (Vi: RG 4, Land Office Plats and Certificates); in Pate's hand; docketed in a clerk's hand: "Thomas Jefferson's 18 acres Bedford Rec^d 2nd July 1818. G^t issued 1st June 1819 $2.53 Recorded and Book H page 16"; filed with covering sheet docketed in a clerk's hand: "Platt & Certificate of T. Jeffersons land."

An undated bill from Pate lists the charges for this survey: "Thos Jefferson to the Sur^{er} of Dr Bedford

To making two Locations &C.— $1.02
To making one Survey 18 acres— 5.25
$6.27"
(MS in ViU: TJP; in Pate's hand, with his signature and docket: "Acc^t T. Jefferson with M P. SBC"; endorsed by TJ: "Surveyor of Bedford").

TJ received a land grant for this property dated 1 June 1819, which reads "Peter V. Daniel Esqr Lieut: Governor of the commonwealth of Virginia To all to whom these presents shall come Greeting Know Ye that in conformity with a survey made on the thirtieth day of April 1818; by virtue of a Land Office Treasury warrant Number 4915 issued the 27th June 1812; there is granted by the said Commonwealth, unto Thomas Jefferson A certain tract or parcel of Land, containing Eighteen acres situate in the County of Bedford and bounded as followeth to wit: Beginning at pointers corner to his own poplar forest tract thence along his own lines South forty and a half degrees East sixty eight poles to pointers, South sixty two degrees West thirty eight poles to Cobbs corner red oak thence along his line, North forty three and a half degrees West eighty one poles to a stake in a line of the said poplar forest tract, thence along said line North seventy five degrees East forty seven poles to the Beginning, To have and hold the said tract or parcel of Land with its Appurtenances, to the said Thomas Jefferson and his heirs forever. In witness whereof, the said Peter V. Daniel Esqr Lieut: Governor of the commonwealth of Virginia hath hereunto set his hand and caused the lesser seal of the said commonwealth to be affixed at Richmond on the first day of June in the year of our Lord One thousand eight hundred and Nineteen and of the Commonwealth the forty third" (FC in Vi: RG 4, Land Office Grant Book, 68:139–40; at head of text: "Thomas Jefferson 18 acres Bedford Ex^d"; with notation in left margin: "October 4th 1821. del^d to Mr Bernard Peyton." Peyton enclosed a copy of the patent to TJ in a letter of 11 Oct. 1821.

[1] Manuscript: "unapropiated."

Thomas Eston Randolph's Memorandum on Wheat Delivered to Thomas Jefferson

[April 1818?]

Memo: for Thos Jefferson Esqre

	bush^{s} ℔s
Whole Amount of Wheat deliver'd	1894.12

Bar^{s} ℔	
355.31	Flour equal thereto
710 bush^{s}	Bran
177	S. stuff

					bar^{s} ℔s
Flour deliver'd on account of wheat crops					349.63 vizt
1817		Family bar:	shipp'd bar:	Carrier	
Sept^{r}	27th	1.			
Oct^{r}	1	.100			
	23	7.			
Nov^{r}	3		50.	Wm Johnson	
	18	36	96.	ditto	
Dec^{r}	3		30.	ditto	
	22	98			
	25	25			
1818					
Jan^{y}	19		50.	ditto	
Feb^{y}	5		107.	ditto	
		16.63	333		
			16.63		
			349.63		bar^{s} ℔s
			5.164	due to you	349.63

Rent Flour

1817			
Oct^{r}	18	43	by T. E. Randolph's boat
	24	7	Saml Howell
1818			
Jan^{y}	29	50	T. E. Randolph
		100	
		100	due, 50 thereof 31 Ult^{o}, other 50—the 30th June next
		200	

MS (MHi); entirely in Randolph's hand; undated, with date conjectured from reference to fifty barrels being due "31 Ult°," presumably 31 Mar. 1818. Possibly enclosed in Randolph to TJ, 1 July 1818.

s. STUFF: "shipstuff."

To Wilson Cary Nicholas

[DE]AR[1] SIR   Poplar Forest May 1. 18.

I recieved at this place, and yesterday only your favor of the 19th. if it has not loitered on the road, it mus[t] have been at Lynchburg with which I have but uncertain communications. were a hesitation possible at the request it contains, it would proceed only from the wish to leave at the close of life as clear a state of things as possible for those who are to come after me; to be able, as they say, to turn key and go, cheerly. but this consideration yields to the desire of rendering you service. I willingly therefore return you the papers you inclosed, with my endorsements, as I shall those which may hereafter, be necessary for their continuance, reposing my self with entire confidence in your care & assurances for you well know that a Virginia farmer has no resource for meeting sudden and large calls for money.   the unskilful management of my farms has subjected me to some temporary uneasiness, which better management & better seasons will, I trust, require not more time to relieve than I ma[y] yet expect, and spare me the only pain of unreadiness whic[h] I could feel at the hour of departure. ever & affectionately

 Your's   TH: JEFFERSON

PoC (DLC); on verso of Charles Johnston to TJ, [5 Dec. 1817]; edge trimmed; endorsed by TJ. Enclosures not found.

[1] First two letters of word missing due to polygraph malfunction.

From Stephen Cathalan

DEAR SIR   Marseilles 2[d] of May 1818

Confirming you my here inclosed letter of the 25th April ult°; this is to remit you herewith the invoice of 8 Boxes containing together 192 Bottl[s] old red wine of Bergasse & one Basket Macaroni, I have Shipped on the Ship Fair Trader,[1] G[ge] Fletcher master, for Alexd[a] to be forwarded to you by the collector of that district, amounting to F 257, 70[c] which please to pass on my credit; you will make me remitance when convenient to you.

You will observe by that Invoice, that I have Shipped also one boxe marked on the top $\frac{TJ}{SC}$ 9 of 24 Bottles red wine 1814 of Bergasse, which I beg you to divide with your Grand Son, reffering you to what I have mentioned about it in the Said invoice; I will thank you to give me your opinion on that wine after having tasted it.[2] M[r] Bergasse has offered me Since it is bottled, 50 bottles of the Said wine[3] for 30 Bottles[4] I would give him in exchange. it is a proof how this wine has improved in quality, after having passed[5] the tropick.

The boxes for wine being made to contain[6] only 12 or 24 Bottles I could not Send you the exact number of 200 you requested.[7] When I ordered that invoice to M[r] Bergasse, in order to Save you the high duty on wine in bottles imported in the U.S. great deal higher than when imported in cask, I ask'd him one cask of 60 Gallons[8] or 29 to 30 veltes of that wine of 1814 instead of about 200 bottles for you, but he refused it Saying that having but a very Small quantity of that years' wine remaining unsold in his celar, he could not Sell it[9] in casks, (but only in boxes & bottled) as he did last year to me; even Should I pay it to him at the rate of f 1 ℈ bottle deducting the cost of bottles, Corks &[c].[10] you must observe that I paid him that cask (which produced to me 290 B[lles]) in May last only F 150. it is true wine has risen much Since & I offered him for Such one[11] f 180 with F 10 more for the doble cask; he added that he was also apprehensive it would not be properly bottled on the Spot of Consumption &[ca] which would of course hurt the reputation of this[12] wine.[13] as you must have a[14] quantity of empty bottles,[15] I intend in my first invoice to Send you one cask of his wine 1817. which[16] is the best year we have Since 10 years for the good quality of wine & you will See after bottled in your celar how it will improve[17] one or two years after, not accounting how much money you will Save in receiving it in Cask.—after having experienced a dryness Since june 1816, in this corner of Europe which threatened to distroy[18] not only the crops of corn, wine, olive[19] &[ca] but also[20] the vineyard, olive & fig trees, since the 20th Ult[o] we have at last abundant & nourishing[21] Showers of rain which have Saved our pending crops with appearance of plantifull one, as well as our vineyard & fruit trees. our Springs exausted begin to run again & the country around Marseilles is beautyfull indeed now

I have the honor to be very respectfully dear Sir
Your obedient & very humble Servant[22]

STEPHEN CATHALAN.

Dupl (MHi); in a clerk's hand, with corrections and signature by Cathalan; at head of text: "Duplicata"; at foot of first page: "Th[s] Jefferson Esq[r] &[c] &[c]"; with

Dupl of second enclosure conjoined; endorsed by TJ as received 30 July 1818 and
so recorded in SJL. RC (MHi); with MS
of second enclosure conjoined; endorsed
by TJ as receieved 1 Sept. 1818 and so recorded in SJL. Enclosure: Cathalan to
TJ, 25 Apr. 1818. Other enclosure printed
below.

The customs COLLECTOR at Alexandria
was Charles Simms. YOUR GRAND SON:
Thomas Jefferson Randolph.

[1] Dupl: "Treader." RC: "Trader."
[2] RC begins new paragraph here.
[3] RC here adds "1814—of the 8 Boxes I
have Shipped for you."
[4] Dupl: "Bottes." RC: "Bottles."
[5] RC here adds "thro or under."
[6] Dupl: "countain." RC: "contain."
[7] RC here adds "from me."
[8] Dupl: "Galloons." RC: "Gallons."

[9] RC here adds "put up."
[10] Instead of preceding word, RC reads
"Boxes & packing."
[11] RC here adds "for you."
[12] Instead of preceding word, RC reads
"his Choiced."
[13] RC begins new paragraph here.
[14] RC here adds "large."
[15] RC here adds "at your Seat."
[16] Dupl: "wich." RC: "which."
[17] Instead of preceding word, RC reads
"Turn Good."
[18] Instead of preceding two words, RC
reads "of loosing."
[19] RC here adds "figs."
[20] Instead of preceding word, RC reads
"of distroying."
[21] Dupl: "last aboundant & nurishing."
RC: "Least, abundant & nourishing."
[22] Instead of preceding six words, RC
reads "your most obed[t] & devoted Serv[t]."

Invoice of Items Shipped

Invoice of Sundries Shipped by order for the account & risk of Thom[s]
Jefferson Esq[r] at Monticello Virg[a] on board the american Ship Fair Trader[1]
of Alexend[a] Geor[g] Fletcher master Bound for Alexd[a] Virg[a] & to be consigned
to the Collector of the district at Alexandria   Viz—

T.J. S.C.	Eight boxes of 24 bottles each red wine 1814 Bergasse Bordeaux claret Fashon containing together:		
	192 Bottles a f 1 ₱ Bottle		F 192
"	one basket Macaroni of Naples Weighing Mars[lle] old weight ₶ 102 net à f 53.50[c] ₱ 100₶		54 57
TJ SC n° 9	one box of 24 bottles red wine Bergasse provening from one cask, I Sent in d[ble] Cask to Senegal in may last as a trial, in order to be returned to me, as it is reported that when the claret has passed twice[2] the tropick is great deal improved this cask on return here has proved So. the 24 bottles to be divided between Th[s] Jefferson & his grand Son Randolph Jefferson Esq[r]		
	Charges		246 57
	Export duty on the wine	4 65	
	D[tto] on the Macaroni	76	
	Portage & Craftage of the Whole	3 12	
	Canvas & packing of Macaroni	2 60	11 13
		Errors Excepted	F 257 70

Marseilles the 28th of April 1818

STEPHEN CATHALAN.

Dupl (MHi); in a clerk's hand, signed by Cathalan; adjacent to signature in Cathalan's hand: "⅌ 2ᵗᵃ"; conjoined with Dupl of covering letter. MS (MHi); in Cathalan's hand; conjoined with RC of covering letter.

¹ Dupl: "Treader." MS: "Trader."
² MS here adds "thro'."

To John Wayles Eppes

DEAR SIR   Poplar forest May 3. 18.

I set out from this place for Monticello tomorrow morning and shall leave this letter at Flood's. I have engaged Francis's board with mr Dashiell himself, who takes only three others. Francis will be much pleased with the family, which is a very genteel one, and they live well as I saw by going in upon them at their dinner unexpectedly. he is an excellent teacher as I judged, at his examination, by the progress and correctness of three boys particularly who had begun with him at Christmas. he desired me to give him what directions I pleased as to Francis and he would exactly observe them; but not knowing what progress he had made this last winter in Greek particularly, I could only desire him provisionally that if Francis had done with the Greek testament, to put him into the Cyropedia of Xenophon rather than Lucian. if he has not one, mr Yancey will get it for him at Cottom's bookstore in Lynchburg as I leave directions for his being furnished there with any books he will have occasion for. he should bring his Bezout with him, as mr Dashiell is a good mathematician, and will teach him every branch of Arithmetic, Algebra, & Geometry as far as he chuses. an Euclid also if he has one. Dashiell is a strict, but rational disciplinarian. at his examination I observed a medal given as a premium to a youth who had excelled <u>in the observation of order, decorous conduct, & respect to his teacher</u>. this premium I am in hopes to see Francis obtain at the next examination. he is to find his own bed & bedding. as I have nothing of that kind here but the strict necessary, he will have to bring a mattras & bed clothes. I direct mr Yancey to have a trussel bedstead made, as that would be heavy to bring, and to let it be only 3. feet wide that he may not have to take in a bedfellow which is so apt to render the propagation of the itch so general at schools. I hear nothing of it here, but at Dʳ Carr's school it is the pest of the neighborhood, and we are kept in eternal dread of it at Monticello. his whole school lodges in one room.

I have not yet recieved the subscription paper I sent you yet it is very essential we should know what our funds are. but I inclose you another paper equally essential, which is an authority, to be signed by every subscriber to the College, enabling the visitors and Proctor to transfer the whole property of the College to the President and directors of the literary fund, on the condition that the University is fixed at the Central college. this in fact is only authorising them to recieve from the public a subscription of 15,000 D. a year to the same institution to which they have subscribed. I must request your active attention, dear Sir, to this paper as it's early return to me is very important; & to send me also the subscription paper. the general inattention to the return of these has already thrown us back a year for a 3ᵈ professorship, as we could not engage for building until we were sure of the funds. there is a possibility of opening our grammar school in July, but perhaps not till winter. the uncertainty as to the incorporation of the University with our college checks our operations much. I forgot to mention that mr Dashiell's school is now in vacation till the 1ˢᵗ of June, by which day Francis should be here. he had better go on his arrival to mr Yancey's who will do whatever is necessary for him. I shall be here myself within 3. weeks from that time. if Francis is not better employed at home during this month, we should be happy to see him at Monticello, where learning his progress I could better advise mr Dashiell as to his course. ever & affectˡʸ yours.

Tʜ: Jᴇꜰꜰᴇʀꜱᴏɴ

RC (Mrs. Francis Eppes Shine, Los Angeles, 1946; photocopy in ViU: TJP); at foot of first page: "Mʳ Eppes." PoC (CSmH: JF); on reused address cover of Bernard Peyton to TJ, 27 Nov. 1817 (see note to Francis Brooke to TJ, 27 Nov. 1817); edge trimmed; endorsed by TJ.

ᴛʀᴜꜱꜱᴇʟ: a variant of "trestle" (*OED*). The enclosed copy of the ᴘᴀᴘᴇʀ ᴇǫᴜᴀʟʟʏ ᴇꜱꜱᴇɴᴛɪᴀʟ has not been found, but it is quoted in full in the 27 July 1818 Deed to the President and Directors of the Literary Fund. The ᴘʀᴏᴄᴛᴏʀ was Nelson Barksdale.

A missing letter of 15 May 1818 from Eppes to TJ is recorded in SJL as received 4 June 1818 from Mill Brook.

From Patrick Gibson

Sɪʀ   Richmond 4ᵗʰ May 1818

Not having received the order from Mʳ Thoˢ J Randolph as I expected by last mail, I obtained <u>permission</u> of the Cashier to draw the money, engaging to furnish him with the order in a few days—and have been endeavouring in vain to procure a check, or dft to remit to Mʳ Vaughan, I have therefore written to that Gentleman on the subject, requesting him to draw upon me for $1000. on your account, and have forwarded him your letter—Mʳ Thomas E Randolph has paid me $313.50, on your accoᵗ in lieu of 38 bls: S:f: flour at 8¼$—

With much respect I am
Your obᵗ Servᵗ   Pᴀᴛʀɪᴄᴋ Gɪʙꜱᴏɴ

RC (MHi); endorsed by TJ as received 9 May 1818 and so recorded in SJL. RC (DLC); address cover only; with PoC of TJ to Charles J. Ingersoll, 20 July 1818, on verso; addressed in John G. Robert's hand: "Thomas Jefferson Esqr Monti-cello"; franked; postmarked Richmond, 4 May.

S:F: "superfine."

From Beverly Waugh

Baltimore City

ILLUSTRIOUS FELLOW CITIZEN,   Light Street May 5th 1818

I take the liberty to inclose a short treatise on the "evidence and authority of the Christian Revelation," by the Revd Thos Chalmers. In doing so, I trust my mind is influenced by pure motives.

I need not remark to you Sir, that truth is an important object, worthy of our most vigorous, and continued pursuit. Of this, you must be deeply sensible. Can you, then have the smallest objection, to hear every thing that can be said in regard to truth? Will you ever abandon the paths of sober investigation, and dilligent inquiry? I hope not. Therefore, notwithstanding you have read much, and thought much, yet may it not be expected, that you will give the inclosed Book, a fair & honest reading. His style cannot but please you, and I think you will find his logick, equal to his rhetorick.

Will you have the goodness Sir, when you shall have read the work to express to me, your opinion on its' merits.

Praying for Eternal interests I remain Dear Sir Your Obedient Servant   BEVERLY WAUGH

Minister of the Gospel in the Methodist Episcopal Church

RC (MdHi: Vertical Files); between dateline and salutation: "Thomas Jefferson Esqr"; endorsed by TJ as received 13 May 1818 and so recorded in SJL. Enclosure: Thomas Chalmers, *The Evidence and Authority of the Christian Revelation* (Edinburgh, 1814, or a later ed.; Poor, *Jefferson's Library*, 9 [no. 520]).

Beverly Waugh (1789–1858), Methodist clergyman, was a native of Fairfax County. He developed his business skills as a young man managing a store in Middleburg. At the age of fifteen Waugh joined the Methodist Episcopal Church, and by twenty he had been admitted as a preacher in the Baltimore Conference. He was ordained a deacon in 1811 and an elder two years later, and he was secretary of the Baltimore Conference, 1813–28. The General Conference elected Waugh in 1828 to assist Methodist Episcopal book agent John Emory. In 1831 they jointly published an edition of *The Works of the Reverend John Wesley, A.M.* When Emory entered the episcopacy in 1832, Waugh succeeded him as the denomination's primary book agent. In that capacity he managed the publishing house in New York City and provided leadership following a devastating fire there in 1836. In May of that year he was elected bishop at a meeting of the General Conference in Cincinnati. As bishop, Waugh contended with rising abolitionist influence. Himself a member of the American Colonization Society, he was determined to keep the church from adopting either a proslavery or an abolitionist stance. When it formally split over the issue in 1845, Waugh remained in Baltimore but sided with the northern faction. He was the church's senior bishop from 1852 until his death (*ANB*; *DAB*; Theodore L. Flood and John W. Hamilton, eds., *Lives of Methodist Bishops* [1882], 225–62; Matthew Simpson, ed., *Cyclopædia of Methodism* [1878], 903–5; Baltimore *Sun*, 10 Feb. 1858).

From Benjamin O. Tyler

City of Washington
VENERABLE AND RESPECTED SIR May 6th 1818

I received your very interesting letter of the 26th of March 4 days after date, for which I return you my most grateful thanks. At the request of several of your particular friends in this place I have taken the liberty to publish it, for whatever emanates on a National subject, from the pen of Columbia's Illustrious Statesman and Patriot will ever excite the attention of his fellow citizens. I hope therefore I have not taken an unwarrantable liberty. I have completed the publication of the Declaration of Independence and it is the first and only copy of facsimilies of the signatures ever copied from the original or[1] published. At the Destruction of the public buildings by the British, the Magna Charta of American Freedom was very nigh being destroyed, it being about the last thing Mr King (the Gentleman who had charge of the American Archives[2] in the Department of State) saved as he was leaving the office. At that time I believe there never had been a [cor]rect copy printed, the first correct copy printed is in the late [edi]tion of the laws of the United States, taken from the original manuscript by J. B. Colvin Esqr. Had it have been destroyed at that time the signatures of those American Statesmen and patriots would have been forever lost. It will ever be a source of the highest gratification to me, that I have been able to execute and multiply such a number of authentic copies, in a cheap and elegant style, that it may be in the power of almost every American to possess the charter of their freedom and thereby preserve it entire for the benefit of millions yet unborn—I have enclosed you a copy on parchment on a roller, which I request of you to accept as a testimony of my just respect and esteem for one of the most distinguished and undeviating supporters of the liberty and Independence of my native country.

That your life may be as long and happy, as it has been glorious and useful to your country, is the[3] sincere prayer of your much obliged
and obedient Servant BENJAMIN O. TYLER

RC (MHi); torn at seal; with Tyler's facsimile of TJ's signature, followed by "Esquire," at foot of text serving as internal address; endorsed by TJ as received 14 May 1818, but recorded in SJL as received the previous day. Enclosure: Tyler's print of the Declaration of Independence, reproduced elsewhere in this volume.

Tyler had issued a proposal dated Washington, 12 Feb. 1818, "FOR PUBLISHING BY SUBSCRIPTION, A SPLENDID EDITION OF THE DECLARATION OF AMERICAN INDEPENDENCE," which reads: "COPIED from the original in the Secretary of State's Office, with the FAC SIMILIES of the signatures of all those patriotic defenders of *liberty* who signed it, 'at a time that tried men's souls,' and mutually pledged to each other their LIVES, their FORTUNES, and their sacred HONOR to support it.

It is a fact, which very few are aware of, that there has never been a *correct* copy of this important document published. In the original it is headed thus:

'*In Congress July 4th*, 1776. *The Unanimous Declaration of the Thirteen United States of America.*' But in the Journals of the old Congress (as well as several other inaccuracies, omissions &c. from which our printed copies are taken) the preamble is thus printed: '*A Declaration by the Representatives of the United States of America in Congress assembled.*'

It must be obvious to every one, that an authentic copy should be published, as it is [an important state paper, from which more public good has emanated than any other ever composed by man. The object of] the present publication is to present to the American people a correct and elegant copy of that instrument, which secured to their fathers a deathless name, and to *them* extends *liberty* and *happiness.* Is it a concern unworthy the descendants of those sages who declared us FREE, and of those HEROES who achieved our *Independence*, to make the charter of their *freedom* a decoration for the parlour or an ornament for the drawing-room? As such the publisher designs it, that every American who duly appreciates the value of *liberty* and *independence* can point his children to it, and say, 'there hangs the pledge which secured your *liberty* and rescued you from the jaws of tyranny.' The publisher, in order to give it its proper construction and emphasis, has been particular to copy every capital as in the original; observing the same punctuation, and executed the emphatical words in a great variety of ornamental hands, and is not only a correct copy, but an elegant specimen of penmanship, and engraving designed and executed by the publisher, (a native American,) in the most beautiful manner after the style of his Eulogy to the memory of the illustrious WASHINGTON, and engraved by Peter Maverick, Esq. of New York, a celebrated engraver, (also a native American) in whose hands it has been several months; the whole being truly American, and worthy the patronage of every friend of liberty and the 'Rights of Man.'

The following certificate of the Hon. Richard Rush, at that time acting Secretary of State, (written by him,) with the seal of the Secretary of State's Office attached to it, will be engraved on the plate in a fac similie of Mr. Rush's hand writing, as a testimony of its authenticity.

Department of State, September 10, 1817.

THE foregoing copy of the Declaration of Independence has been colated with the original instrument and found correct. I have myself examined the signatures to each. Those executed by Mr. Tyler, are curiously exact imitations, so much so, that it would be difficult, if not impossible, for the closest scrutiny to distinguish them were it not for the hand of time, from the originals.

RICHARD RUSH."

Tyler concluded that the publication was "now engraving on a plate 24 by 30 inches, the same size as the original, and will be ready for delivery to subscribers in April next, at five dollars per copy, payable on delivery.

A few copies will be printed on parchment at seven dollars, those who prefer them will please add the word *parchment* to their names" (broadside pasted into subscription book in ViU: Albert H. Small Declaration of Independence Collection, torn and chipped at crease, with missing text supplied from Georgetown

National Messenger, 1 Apr. 1818; reprinted in *National Messenger* [and later in other newspapers] with additional note: "It is hoped that printers generally through the U.S. who feel disposed to encourage this great National work, will give the above one or two insertions in their respective papers").

Tyler's subscription book at ViU contains more than one hundred pages of subscriber signatures, with TJ's at the head of the list, followed by James Madison's. Tyler visited Monticello sometime near the end of July 1818. He may have arrived just prior to the 31 July 1818 departure of TJ and Madison for Rockfish Gap and obtained both signatures at that time (Martha Jefferson Randolph to Jane H. Nicholas Randolph, [ca. 31 July 1818] [NcU: NPT]). Immediately following Madison's signature are those of three sitting cabinet members, John Quincy Adams, William H. Crawford, and John C. Calhoun. Included in the book is an additional MS prospectus and subscription list for a proposed volume entitled "A Naval Monument," which was to include portraits of American naval heroes, the United States Navy's coat of arms, and images of great American sea battles; and a nine-page section, keyed to selected names on both lists, providing "Remarks" on subscribers, including, when available, their birth and death dates and the significant political offices they held. Both TJ's and Madison's entries include their service as United States president and their death dates.

[1] Preceding five words interlined.
[2] Manuscript: "Archiives."
[3] Manuscript: "is the is the."

Salma Hale's Visit to Monticello

I. SALMA HALE TO DAVID HALE, 5 MAY 1818

II. SALMA HALE TO WILLIAM PLUMER, 8 MAY 1818

III. SALMA HALE TO ARTHUR LIVERMORE, 16 MAY 1818

IV. SALMA HALE'S NOTES ON HIS VISIT TO MONTICELLO, [AFTER 1818]

EDITORIAL NOTE

New Hampshire congressman Salma Hale arrived at Monticello on 7 May 1818 and departed the following day. He and TJ exchanged letters once later in the year, after which they had no further interaction (Hale to TJ, 13 July 1818; TJ to Hale, 26 July 1818). The details of the visit can be gathered from the documents printed below, most of which have been found only in later printed versions.

I. Salma Hale to David Hale

DEAR SIR,— CHARLOTTESVILLE, May 5, 1818.

I am now in the heart of Virginia about 2 miles from the residence of Mr. Jefferson. I have travelled thro a poor country, and over bad roads, and feel a little the worse for the toil.

To-morrow I shall visit Mr. Jefferson to whom I have a letter of introduction. I shall then look around me a little and return home as quick as possible.

The principal part of Virginia thro which I have travelled is a level sandy pine plain, there are many log huts, and a very few good houses, not near so many as in the county of Cheshire, excepting in Richmond. The chimneys are at each end, and outside.

The land yields ten or fifteen bushels of corn to the acre, and about as much wheat. Every step I take makes me love New Hampshire better.

Yours   S. HALE.

May. 7. I have just returned from visiting Mr. Jefferson, with whom I have spent a very agreeable day. He appears to be very rich, has a large brick house on the top of a mountain, and lives happy and contented.

Printed in Massachusetts Historical Society, *Proceedings* 46 (1913): 403; with note that the letter had been franked and addressed to "Mr. DAVID HALE. Alstead New Hampshire."

Salma Hale (1787–1866), public official, attorney, and author, was born in Alstead, Cheshire County, New Hampshire. Trained as a printer, he was editor of the Walpole *Political Observatory*, 1805–08. Hale studied law and in 1812 became clerk of the court of common pleas for Cheshire County and later of New Hampshire's supreme court. When a Republican state legislature attempted to transform Dartmouth College into a public institution in 1816, Hale became a trustee of the resulting Dartmouth University. He was acting with William Wirt as the university's counsel in 1819 when the United States Supreme Court ruled against the state and restored control to the original college trustees. Hale completed one term in the United States House of Representatives, 1817–19. Between 1823 and 1846 he served intermittently in both houses of the state legislature. Hale published a textbook *History of the United States* (New York, 1825), which went through multiple editions, and *Annals of the Town of Keene* (1826; rev. ed., 1851), Keene being his place of residence from 1813. In 1834 he gave up his clerkships and was admitted to the bar. Hale died in Somerville, Massachusetts (*Biog. Dir. Cong.*; *New England Historical and Genealogical Register* 21 [1867]: 292; Charles H. Bell,

The Bench and Bar of New Hampshire [1894], 418–9; Brigham, *American Newspapers*, 1:490; Andrew J. King and Alfred S. Konefsky, eds., *The Papers of Daniel Webster: Legal Papers* [1982–89], 3:95, 100, 157, 161–2, 168, 173–5; John King Lord, *A History of Dartmouth College, 1815–1909* [1913], 111, 290; Amherst, N.H., *Farmers' Cabinet*, 6 Dec. 1866).

This letter was probably addressed to Hale's father, David Hale (ca. 1758–1822), rather than his brother David Hale (1783–1822), an attorney in Newport, New Hampshire (Albert Welles, *History of the Buell Family in England . . . and in America* [1881], 365; Bell, *Bench and Bar of New Hampshire*, 413; Keene *New-Hampshire Sentinel*, 28 Sept., 9 Nov. 1822).

Only the address cover of Hale's LETTER OF INTRODUCTION from William Pope, 5 May 1818, has been found (RC in DLC; with PoC of TJ to Robert Walsh, 20 July 1818, on verso; addressed: "Thomas Jefferson Esquire and Col° Thomas M Randolph Monticello" by "Salma Hale Esquire"; recorded in SJL as received 7 May 1818 from "Montpelier" [Pope's Powhatan County estate], with the additional notation "by mr Hale"). Pope (1762–1852) was an attorney and state legislator whose only other correspondence with TJ occurred in 1808 while he was representing Powhatan in the Virginia House of Delegates (Pope to TJ, 30 May 1808 [ViW: TC-JP]; Leonard, *General Assembly*, 249, 253, 267, 271; "Pope Ancestry," *WMQ*, 1st ser., 24 [1916]: 196–7).

II. Salma Hale to William Plumer

Dear Sir,   Charlottesville. Virginia May 8th 1818

I spent yesterday with Mr Jefferson. In conversation he was quite unrestrained, bestowing praise or censure wherever he thought either deserved.

He laments much that no good history has ever yet been published of our revolution. That by Botta, an Italian, he thinks best. Speaking of yours he regreted that you had not begun at the close of the revolutionary war, as he might then hope to see a history of a period concerning which the public know even less than of the preceding one. You might afterwards go back as Hume did. He observed that Barlow once promised to write such a history, & that he furnished him with three cases of documents, but he never wrote a word nor opened the cases, which were afterwards returned & are now in the Congressional Library. He thinks the letters of men in active life are the best documents.

If I can be of service to you at Washington next winter in searching the library, remember to command me

Monticello is a delightful retreat—The country around is tolerably fertile—the roads execrable. Mr J's house is enclosed by a forest

With great respect
Your Obdt Servant   S. Hale

RC (DLC: Plumer Papers); addressed: "His Excellency William Plumer Epping N.H"; franked; postmarked Charlottesville, 9 May.

In the latter part of his presidency TJ offered to supply Plumer with materials for a history of the United States. He regretted (REGRETED) Plumer's ambitious decision to start the work with the discovery of America, and in fact the author did not complete or publish it (Plumer to TJ, 27 Apr. 1810, and note). David Hume began his influential history of England with a volume on the reigns of James I and Charles I and AFTERWARDS extended it backwards and forwards from the invasion of Julius Caesar to the Glorious Revolution of 1688 (*ODNB*).

III. Salma Hale to Arthur Livermore

Dear Sir,—   Richmond, Vir., May 16, [18]18.

A few days ago I returned from an excursion into the interior of Virginia, having been absent a fortnight. Five or six days I spent with a Mr. Pope, a lawyer and planter, of Powhatan, one day at Monticello, and two at Barboursville, and during the whole time was as happy, as cordial and elegant hospitality could make a stranger. Mr. Pope is a brother of the Mr. P. mentioned by Mr. Wirt in his preface, and spent several days at Washington during the Session. He is not remarkable for talents, but is all life and laughter, and is well known throughout Virginia for his convivial humour. Mr. Jefferson I found on the top of his mountain surrounded with curiosities, and himself not the least. The base of Monticello is five or six miles in circumference, and entirely covered with a thick forest. On the summit is a plain of four or five acres, in the center of which stands the house, which is of brick, and exposed to every wind that blows. On three sides is a prospect extending fifty, seventy, and one hundred miles mostly over a level and cultivated country. Mr. J. does not appear to have suffered much from age. He is cheerful, social, and unreserved— talked of politics some but of literature and religion more. Of Gov. Langdon, he spoke with great respect, but regretted that in his old age he had become gloomy and unhappy. His house is filled with paintings and Indian relics, and a view of his rooms affords as much gratification as of a museum.

Barboursville is a most elegant retreat in the midst of the mountains. The Gov. has a large plantation—say 5000 acres,—and more than one hundred negroes. Last year he sowed 750 bushels of wheat, and had not the fly committed devastation, would have reaped 8000. Of tobacco and corn he raised good crops. I do not think that he has much disposable wealth, as his object appears to be to improve and embellish his plantation which is new. In this employment he appears to live cheerful, contented and happy. Here I heard yankee doodle played delightfully on a piano, and it brought to my recollection the celebrated Swiss song of Ranz des Vaches.

I have had a good opportunity to become acquainted with the Virginia character. Take the people *en masse*, and they are not so estimable as the yankees. The best are perhaps better. The soil is far from fertile, and it would be impossible for a family to live on one hundred acres as they do in N. H.

In a day or two I shall commit myself to the winds and waves,— which a wise ancient observed was one of the three follies he had been guilty of. I *reckon* he had been sea sick. I hope I shall arrive at home in season to be at Concord. Whom shall we make Senator? Will not Plumer want it? I presume he cannot get it but I hope we shall have some one who will do honor to the State.

The Season is uncommonly late here. Winter yet lingers, and the farmers, and all others look sad. Perhaps I have seen Virginia at an inauspicious moment, but its aspect now does not make me regret that my lot was cast in New Hampshire. With great regard

Your Obdt Servt. S. HALE.

Printed in Massachusetts Historical Society, *Proceedings* 46 (1913): 404–5; brackets in original; with note that the letter had been franked and addressed to "Hon. ARTHUR LIVERMORE Holderness New Hampshire."

Arthur Livermore (1766–1853), attorney and public official, was born in Londonderry (later Derry), New Hampshire, and admitted to the bar in 1791. Appointed a justice of the superior court of New Hampshire in 1798, he was elevated to chief justice in 1809 and named an associate justice of the reorganized supreme court in 1813, serving until 1816. Livermore represented his home state in the United States House of Representatives, 1817–21 and 1823–25, during which he opposed the Missouri Compromise and the extension of slavery. He served as chief justice of the state court of common pleas from 1825 until the court was abolished in 1832, after which he held no public office (*DAB*; Charles H. Bell, *The Bench and Bar of New Hampshire* [1894], 55–8; Boston *Daily Atlas*, 6 July 1853).

THE GOV.: James Barbour. A type of Alpine melody, the RANZ DES VACHES, supposedly made Swiss troops in foreign service homesick, and the expression was more widely used in describing tunes with similar effects on other nationalities (*OED*). The WISE ANCIENT was Cato the Elder, of whom Plutarch observed: "And as for repentance, he said he had indulged in it himself but thrice in his whole life: once when he entrusted a secret to his wife; once when he paid ship's fare to a place instead of walking thither; and once when he remained intestate a whole day" (Plutarch, *Cato*, book 9, in *Plutarch's Lives*, trans. Bernadotte Perrin, Loeb Classical Library [1914–26; repr. 2006], 2:328–9).

IV. Salma Hale's Notes on his Visit to Monticello

[after 1818]

In the year 1818, I paid a visit to Mr. Jefferson, in his retirement at Monticello. During the visit, the credibility of history became a topic of conversation, and we naturally adverted to that of our own country. He spoke with great freedom of the Patriots and heroes of our revolution, and of its gloomy and brilliant periods. I will give the substance of a part of his remarks. "No correct history of that arduous struggle has yet been, or ever will be, written. The actors in important and busy scenes are too much absorbed in their immediate duty, to record events, or the motives and causes which produced them. Many secret springs, concealed even from those upon whom they operate, give an impulse to measures which are supposed to be the result of chance; and a fortuitous concurrence of causes is often attributed to the concerted plan of leaders who are themselves as much astonished as others at the events they witness. They who took an active part in those important transactions can hardly recognize them as they are related in the histories of our revolution. That of Botta, an Italian, is the best. In all of them, events are misrepresented, wrong motives are assigned—justice is seldom done to individuals, some having too much, and some too little praise. The private correspondence of three or four persons in different official stations at that time, would form the best history. I have heard that Mr. Adams is writing something on the subject. No one is better qualified than he to give the reader a correct impression of the earlier part of the contest. No history has done him justice, for no historian was present to witness his conduct in the Continental Congress. In his zeal for independence he was ardent; in contriving expedients and originating measures he was always busy; in disastrous times, when gloom sat on the countenances of most of us, his courage and fortitide continued unabated, and his animated exhortations restored confidence to those who had wavered. He seemed to forget every thing but his country and the cause which he had espoused. I must, however, say that I always thought him less fond of the principles of enlarged liberty, than of independence; but the experience of the last thirty years has perhaps convinced him that, to accomplish any good purpose, the government we have established is strong enough." H.[1]

1818. (Richmond and Monticello between Sessions.)

Once when at W[ashington][2] in 1818 having learnt that Mr. Charter, my former partner in the printing business at Walpole [New Hampshire], resided at Richmond, and never having seen the ocean except once or twice from its shore, I determined to visit that city, and return home to Boston by water. On my way thither, I called on a gentleman Mr. Pope, whom I had before seen; and from him I learned that the residence of Mr. Jefferson was not far distant. I expressed a desire to see him and he very civilly offered me a letter of introduction. The next day I rode to Charlottesville, and, on the following forenoon, I ascended to his residence on Monticello, by a steep road, which nearly encircled it. His dwelling house stood on the north border of a plateau containing several acres of level land, the middle of the house being an oblong, and each end a half circle. On enquiring at the door, I was told that Mr. Jefferson was taking his usual walk in his grounds, and was invited to enter and await his return. In a short time, I saw him thro the window among the trees, a tall, spare man, walking towards the house, throwing his legs about unmindful of his steps, like a man in a reverie. On entering he gave me a civil welcome, and, after reading the letter of introduction, took his seat, and began to converse on common topics, saying, however, nothing of politics. He spoke with interest of Lewis and Clark's tour over the Rocky Mountains, a history of which lay on the table, and with animation and pathos of the feelings and sufferings of the revolutionary period.

He observed, in substance, that he had read no history that gave such a glowing account of them as they deserved. Botta's was the best. Marshall's was an unimpassioned narrative of events, and failed to give a just idea of the intense feelings, lofty purposes, and constant sufferings of the people, during that period. The world did not know, and does not now know, how sad and dismayed, at various times, was the Continental Congress, to whom the posture of affairs was better known than to the people. It was at these times, when the rest of us were dispirited and silent, that the loud voice of John Adams, the Ajax of the body, resounded through the hall, revived our spirits and restored our confidence. To him, more than to any other man, is the country indebted for independence.

After staying an hour or two, I desired him to order a servant to lead my horse to the door. "Oh, no," said he, "you must not leave me so soon; you must dine with me and sleep with me. But this is just the time when I invariably take a ride; and it is moreover my duty to visit, to day, the workmen on the University grounds and see what they are doing. Here are books, at your service, and you will find walks about the grounds. that may amuse you, till my return."

I passed the time as he suggested very agreeably, and also in examining curiosities in the spacious hall, such as the skeleton, not wholly perfect, of a mammoth, and skeletons or bones, and stuffed skins, of other animals, which once inhabited Virginia, and of which some had been extinct. I saw there also a shirt, woven of steel wire, which he said was found in the southern part of the State.

On his return after an absence of a few hours, we were summoned to dinner. He offered me several kinds of wine, but said that he drank none but *lachryma Christi*, which was made from grapes that grew on the sides of Mount Vesuvius. I tasted of a dish, which was new to me, concocted of corn meal and grated cheese. He remarked that he was very fond of corn meal, in all the modes in which it could be presented as food for man; that when minister to France, he saw none, and longed for it; that when he visited Rome, observing "American Corn Meal," on a shop door, he ordered a small quantity to be sent to his lodgings, and gave directions how to prepare it. "On tasting it, I found that the bread or cake had been made of your hard, dry northern corn—I'd as lief eat sawdust." He offered me tomatoes, with the remark, that he introduced that plant, into this country, from Europe.

After dinner, the Christian religion became a topic of conversation. In the course of it I remarked that I had lately seen quoted, in a pamphlet, a letter from him, expressing a doubt whether Jesus Christ was the Son of God, and classing him with the great men of antiquity—Zoroaster, Socrates, Confucius, &c. He remembered no such letter; but after reflecting a while, he observed that something like that might have been said in his correspondence with Dr. Rush. This pamphlet, I observed, was the first of a series, seven or eight in all, on the subject of Unitarianism, and was published alternately by opponents and professors of that doctrine. The information interested him, and he was gratified when told that, on my return home, copies of all of them should be sent to him.

Printed in Massachusetts Historical Society, *Proceedings* 46 (1913): 405–8; undated; at head of text: "MEMORANDA BY SALMA HALE," followed by Roman numeral "I." and an editorially omitted opening paragraph describing a conversation in which an unidentified fellow traveler from "the middle states," a former Loyalist, credited Massachusetts rather than Virginia as being the cradle of the American Revolution and supplied an anecdote on the contributions of John Adams.

The PAMPHLET was Thomas Belsham, *American Unitarianism; or a Brief History of "The Progress and Present State of the Unitarian Churches in America"* . . . *Extracted from his "Memoirs of the Life of the Reverend Theophilus Lindsey," printed in London, 1812* (Boston, 1815). Printed on pp. 46–7 is an extract from TJ's letter to Joseph Priestley of 9 Apr. 1803 in which he included an outline of his syllabus of Jesus's doctrines (*PTJ*, 40:157–9). TJ had written SOMETHING LIKE THAT in a 21 Apr. 1803 letter to Benjamin Rush, where he enclosed his completed syllabus (*PTJ*, 40:251–5). The SERIES was probably the set republished as *Tracts on the Unitarian Controversy* (Boston, 1816), which included the Belsham pamphlet along with eight other works. On 13 July 1818 Hale sent TJ an unspecified collection of individual imprints of these tracts.

Long afterwards, in conversation with the New York state journalist and author William Henry Bogart, Hale described his visit as "among the most fortunate incidents of his life," recalling that "Mr. Jefferson welcomed him, scarcely noticing his letters of introduction, and at once made his arrangements for the day, telling him that he claimed an hour and a half for his exercise on horseback, and at all other times proposed to be interesting to his guest. He conversed fully, freely, but always as if pronouncing judgment on men and affairs, formed after mature deliberation, and not admitting of contradiction; an air and way of becoming authority, in him entirely appropriate. His powers of conversation were especially fascinating to young men." Bogart added of TJ that "Ex-President Tyler declared him to be the most charming talker he ever knew,—that he never disputed, except with philosophers, but yet always gave his opinion as fixed and settled" ([Bogart], *Who Goes There? or, Men and Events* [1866], 39–40).

[1] After this initialed signature is an editorial notation that the text to this point had been endorsed by Hale: "Conversation with Jefferson." A Roman numeral "II." comes after that, indicating that the text that follows was a separate memorandum by Hale.

[2] This and succeeding set of brackets in original.

From Mordecai M. Noah

Dear sir,   New York May 7ʰ 1818

You will pardon the liberty I take, in transmitting to you a Discourse, delivered at the consecration of a Jewish Synagogue in this City, which I trust may have sufficient novelty, if not interest to induce you to peruse.

Nothing I am persuaded can be more gratifying to you, than to See the Jews in this Country in the full enjoyment of civil and religious rights, to know that they possess equal privileges, and above all to feel, that to your efforts in the establishment of our Independance and formation of our Government, they in great part, owe these inestimable privileges.

There are few in the Civilized, or if you please in the Christian World, that can boast of having reached forth the hand of assistance towards these unfortunate and persecuted people. The example which our Country has Set, now operates favourably in Europe, and the Jews are attaining consequence and distinction abroad,—Nothing, I have every reason to believe, would afford you more gratification, than to See the primitive people restored to their ancient rights, and taking their rank once more among the Governments of the earth, and however problematical this event may appear, I am well Satisfied, that preparations are now making towards effecting the emancipation of the Jews in Asia & Africa. The result I trust may be favourable, & I hope to See them draw from this country, that talent & political experience, which is only to be found in Governments equally tolerant.

accept Dear sir, my Sincere wishes for your health & long life, and the assurance that I am with veneration & respect,

Your obedient, Humble servant,   M M Noah.

RC (MHi); at foot of text: "Thᵒˢ Jefferson"; endorsed by TJ as received 17 May 1818 and so recorded in SJL. Enclosure: Noah, *Discourse, delivered at the Consecration of the Synagogue of* ק״ק שארית ישראל *in the City of New-York, on Friday, the 10th of Nisan, 5578, corresponding with the 17th of April 1818* (New York, 1818; Poor, *Jefferson's Library*, 10 [no. 548]).

Mordecai Manuel Noah (1785–1851), journalist, author, public official, and Jewish community leader, was a native of Philadelphia who began publishing political articles in newspapers in that city and Charleston, South Carolina, during his early years. In 1811 President James Madison appointed him to serve as the first American consul at Riga, but he never assumed the post. Instead, he accepted the same position at Tunis. During his consular service there, Noah was tasked with freeing American seamen who were being held in Algiers. His failure to secure freedom for most of these captives culminated in his recall in 1815. In order to maintain secrecy for the mission and pursue conspiracy charges against one of his agents, the United States government claimed that the Algerian government had objected to Noah's religious affiliation. This led him to publish two works in defense of his actions: *Correspondence and Documents Relative to the Attempt to Negotiate for the Release of the American Captives at Algiers; including Remarks on our Relations with that Regency* (Washington, 1816), and *Travels in England, France, Spain, and the Barbary States, in the years 1813–14 and 15* (New York, 1819; Poor, *Jefferson's Library*, 7 [no. 331]). On his return to the United States, Noah settled in New York City, where he edited a succession of newspapers beginning with the *National Advocate.* In 1820 he approached the New York state legislature with a proposal to establish a Jewish colony on Grand Island in the Niagara River. By 1825 Noah had acquired land there and laid the cornerstone for his planned Jewish refuge in a widely publicized ceremony, but the settlement never progressed further. He was also notable as a playwright, authoring multiple dramas staged during his lifetime. Noah died in New York City (*ANB*; *DAB*; Jonathan D. Sarna, *Jacksonian Jew: The Two Worlds of Mordecai Noah* [1981]; DNA: RG 59, LAR, 1809–25; *JEP*, 2:188, 193, 347, 348 [13, 27 Nov. 1811, 31 May, 1 June 1813]; Brigham, *American Newspapers*, 1:672; Madison, *Papers, Pres. Ser.*, 2:506–7, and *Retirement Ser.*, 1:252–3, 286–7, 352–3; *New-York Daily Tribune*, 25 Mar. 1851).

Noah also sent copies of the enclosed DISCOURSE to James Madison and John Adams (Madison, *Papers, Retirement Ser.*, 1:252–3; Noah to Adams, 24 July 1818 [MHi: Adams Papers]).

From John Vaughan

DEAR SIR.   Philad. May 7[th1] 1818

Your favor of 8 April desiring me to remit to Europe 1000$ which M[r] Patrick Gibson of Richmond was to remit to me on your ⅜—& also his of 4 May Informing he could not procure a Dft & desiring me to Draw—are both this moment received—I shall negociate the Dft as speedily as may be—& procure the Dfts on Paris to lodge there for the payment of

120$ Value to Mess. DeBure freres Booksellers Paris
420   Catalan Marseilles
460.   Tho[s] Appleton Leghorn

I shall apply tomorrow to M[r] Girard & if he will supply a Bill shall procure it from him, otherwise from Mess LeRoy Bayard & C[o] of New York from whom I am in the habit of procuring them—

You shall be advised of my proceedings
I remain with great respect Yours sincerly   JN VAUGHAN

RC (MHi); endorsed by TJ as received 13 May 1818 and so recorded in SJL. RC (MHi); address cover only; with PoC of TJ to Patrick Gibson, 30 July 1818, on verso; addressed: "Thomas Jefferson Monticello V[a]"; franked; postmarked Philadelphia, 7 May.

[1] Reworked from "6th."

From William F. Gray

SIR,   Fred,burg May 8th 1818

SIR,   Fred,burg May 8th 1818

By the next stage that leaves this place for Charlotesville, I will forward to you a Box which has been addressed to my care,—I presume by Mr Milligan.

It gives me much pleasure to be thus able to serve you.

Respectfully   WM F. GRAY

RC (DLC); endorsed by TJ as received 11 May 1818 and so recorded in SJL. RC (MHi); address cover only; with PoC of TJ to Charles Simms, 30 July 1818, on verso; addressed: "Thomas Jefferson, Esq. Montecello"; franked; postmarked Fredericksburg, 10 May.

To Lewis D. Belair

SIR   Monticello May 10. 18.

I lately recieved from mr Fernagus de Gelone the inclosed list of books which he desired me to forward to you after perusal. I see nothing on it which I would desire at this time, except Quenon Dictionn. Grec Francois 8vo which if among the books he sends to you I should be glad to recieve, or if you can get him to send it to you. he says he is about forwarding to you a large parcel of foreign books. if you should make a catalogue of them I should be glad of an early receipt of one. I salute you with respect   TH: JEFFERSON

PoC (DLC); on verso of portion of reused address cover of Daniel Brent to TJ, 19 Feb. 1818; at foot of text: "Mr Lewis D. Belair. bookseller No 96. Broadway N.Y."; endorsed by TJ. Enclosure not found.

Lewis Descoins Belair (ca. 1792–1875), bookseller, was born to French émigrés shortly after they fled Saint Domingue. He settled in Philadelphia by 1816 and operated bookshops specializing in foreign works there and in New York City by 1818. Belair was among the French immigrants who invested in the Vine and Olive Colony, which received a congressional land grant in 1817 in present-day Alabama. While returning from a visit to his 480-acre tract in 1822, Belair stopped at Monticello during one of TJ's absences. He never settled in Alabama and eventually sold the land. Belair later served as a justice of the peace in Philadelphia County.

At his death he left his family bequests totaling $128,000, with an additional $24,000 plus the "residue of the estate" going to eight charitable organizations in Philadelphia, including the Apprentices' Library and the French Benevolent Society (James Robinson, *The Philadelphia Directory for 1816* [Philadelphia, 1816]; *New-York Gazette & General Advertiser*, 14 July 1818; Belair to TJ, 6 Nov. 1818, 24 Aug. 1822; Kent Gardien, "The Domingan Kettle: Philadelphian-Émigré Planters in Alabama," *National Genealogical Society Quarterly* 76 [1998]: 173–87, esp. 184; Rafe Blaufarb, *Bonapartists in the Borderlands: French Exiles and Refugees on the Gulf Coast, 1815–1835* [2005], 25, 166, 190; *ASP, Public Lands*, 5:16, 26; *Proceedings and Debates of the Convention of the Commonwealth of Pennsylvania* [1837], 3:566; *Philadelphia Inquirer*, 16, 18, 29 Oct. 1875).

To Mathew Carey

DEAR SIR   Monticello May 10. 18.

On my return after an absence of 3. or 4. weeks I find here your favors of Apr. 11. and 18. the miniature bible and the books which came thro Capt Peyton. I will pray you now to send me the 3. books below mentioned, and also to bear in mind a former request of Chipman's book, the select addresses & Bridgman.

the books below mentioned might come by mail, if sent one by one & at a week's distance from one another so as not to overburthen any one of our Charlottesville mails. the route by water is tedious. send the Virgil first. I salute you with friendship & respect

                                                    TH: JEFFERSON

Virgil. the Delphin edition with English notes
De viris illustribus Romae. Hardie's edn of N. York with a dictionary at the end
McMahon's gardening.

RC (PHi: George M. Conarroe Autograph Collection); at foot of text: "Mr Carey"; endorsed by Carey as received 15 May 1818 and answered the following day. PoC (DLC); endorsed by TJ.

To Richard Claiborne

[DEAR] SIR   Monticello May 10. 18.

Were I twenty years younger your fav[or] [. . .] [n]ot recieved till Oct. 16. should not h[ave] [. . .] long unacknoleged. but the torpor of age is on me, [. . .] writing is particularly slow and irksome. this oblig[es me] to brevity. I remember well your duck foot paddle and am pleased to learn that you expect to make it a means of defence; altho I hope there will be no occasion for it in your time or mine. one war is enough for one man's life; but you & I have seen two: surely there is not a third in reserve for us: but if there is I hope[1] that your combination of steam with the foot of the Duck and thorns of the porcupine will be an useful annoyance. with assurances of my continued friendship I pray you to accept those also of my great respect.

                                                    TH: JEFFERSON

PoC (DLC); on verso of reused address cover to TJ; upper corners torn; at foot of text: "Col^o Richard Claiborne"; endorsed by TJ.

TJ RECIEVED Claiborne's letter of 4 July 1817 on 16 Oct. of that year.

[1] Preceding two words interlined.

To Ferdinando Fairfax

Monticello May 10. 18.

Th: Jefferson presents his compliments & his thanks to mr Fairfax for the pamphlet he has been so kind as to send him, and has the pleasure to concur with him in all it's pacific sentiments. peace & prosperity are twin-brothers; so are war & demoralisation. one war in one man's life is enough. Th:J. has seen two, and both pro aris et focis. he desires mr Fairfax to be assured of his continued esteem & salutes him with great respect.

PoC (DLC); on verso of reused address cover to TJ; dateline at foot of text; endorsed by TJ.

PRO ARIS ET FOCIS: "on behalf of our altars and hearths," quoting Cicero, *De*

Natura Deorum, 3.40 (*Cicero. De Natura Deorum, Academica*, trans. Harris Rackham, Loeb Classical Library [1933; rev. ed., 1951; repr. 1994], 380–1).

Notes on Mutual Assurance Society Policy

[ca. 10 May 1818]

	D		D
A. Scale house. insured	320.	valued	400
B. Transfer	200.		250
C. Warehouse	288		360
	808		1010
D. Warehouse	160		200
E. Warehouse	240.		300
	400		
	1208		1510

the houses D. & E. being blown down the valuation was reduced to 1010.D. and the insurance of the 1510. having been 9.11 D that of the 1010.D. is thus found

As 1510 : 9.11 :: 1010 : 6.09

my new warehouse was built in 1811.

the Warehouse C. was taken down in 1814[1]

1809. Aug. 27. p^d by G. & J.[2] to W. Dawson fee on valuan of my mill 11.40.

Sep. 5. p^d Benj. Brown for the fire insur^{ce} co. 63.55 being a requisition on the former insurance of Mont^o house.

1811. Apr. 3. pd by E. Bacon to B. Brown 28.24

1813. Aug. 7. gave ord. on G. & J. for 43.27 for the houses at Monticello for the years 1811.12.13 inclusive.

1818. May 10. inclosed to Ja^s Rawlings order on P. Gibson for
71.90 arrearages for the insurance of Mont° house
for 1814.15.16.17.18. with interest.

MS (MHi); written in TJ's hand on both sides of portion of reused address cover; undated.

[1] Recto ends here.
[2] Abbreviation for "Gibson & Jefferson," here and below.

To James Rawlings

SIR   Monticello May 10. 18.

Yours of Mar. 21. came to hand in the moment of my departure on a journey from which I am but just now returned, or the answer should not have been so long delayed. these arrearages have occurred from inattention partly, but chiefly from the circumstance that no agent has applied for them. I now inclose an order on mr Gibson for 71.90 insurance & interest from 1814. to 1818. inclusive on my house at this place, and if I could be reminded, or recollect it myself annually, it should be punctually paid in Richmond in the same way.

I tender you the assurance of my respect   TH: JEFFERSON

RC (Heritage Auctions, auction 6084, Beverly Hills, Calif., 4 Oct. 2012, lot 34076); at foot of text: "Mr James Rawlings." PoC (MHi); on verso of portion of reused address cover of Joel Yancey to TJ, 5 Mar. 1818 (see note to TJ to Yancey, 14 Mar. 1818); endorsed by TJ. Enclosure not found.

To Gamaliel H. Ward

SIR   Monticello May 10. 18.

The original of yours of Jan. 20. never came to hand. the copy with that of Apr. 22. is just now recieved. I am always glad to hear of the establishment of an useful manufacture, and none is more so than that of salt; but being quite a stranger to it's various processes, I am unable to give any opinion on the subject. I can therefore only wish your undertaking may be succesful and, with my thanks for the personal civility of your letters I tender you my respectful salutations.

TH: JEFFERSON

PoC (DLC); on verso of reused address cover of Alden Partridge to TJ, 20 Feb. 1818; at foot of text: "Mr Gamaliel H. Ward"; endorsed by TJ.

[35]

Minutes of Central College Board of Visitors

Charlottesville. 11 May. 1818.

At a regular meeting of the Visitors of the Central College on 11th May 1818, at which[1] Thomas Jefferson, James Madison, John H. Cocke, & Joseph C. Cabell, were present, it was agreed, that it being uncertain whether Thomas Cooper would accept the Professorship of Chemistry, in the event of his not doing so, it would be expedient to procure a Professor of Mathematicks.[2] It was also agreed to allow the Proctor of the College the sum of two hundred dollars for the present year.

May 11. 1818.[3]

JAMES MADISON
TH: JEFFERSON
J. H. COCKE
JOSEPH C. CABELL.

MS (ViU: TJP-VMTJ); in Cabell's hand, signed by Madison, TJ, Cocke, and Cabell. Tr (ViU: TJP-VMJCC). Tr (ViU: TJP-VMJHC). Tr (ViU: TJP-VMJB). Tr (ViU: TJP); extract entirely in TJ's hand; subjoined to Trs of Minutes of Central College Board of Visitors, 7 and 8 Oct. 1817; addressed: "For Mr Cabell"; enclosed in TJ to Cabell, 1 Mar. 1819.

[1] Instead of this word, VMJB Tr reads "Charlottesville."
[2] Cabell here canceled "and that Mr Jefferson should be authorized to." Tr in TJ's hand ends here.
[3] Preceding three words in TJ's hand.

From Joseph Milligan

DEAR SIR   Georgetown May 11th 1818

I have sent a box of Books for you to the care of W^m F Gray of Fredericksburg it contains Tacitus 8 vols and two other Octavo volumes also a folio volume which is either yours or Miss Randolph^s it was left with me by Mrs Madison—at the time it was left I had nothing of that kind to bind and when I was binding for you last year it was forgotten I have put into the box four Books for Mr Carr which I will esteem as a great favour if you will inform him you have got them they are Bowditchs Navigator Blunts Coast pilot and Malham^s Naval Gazetteer in two Volumes—

On the 8th of April I sent you a proof of the Political Economy I have not yet received it Corrected: with the proof that you sent me on the 9th April you sent a small note saying you would set out for Bedford the next day and return again about the 1st May If you are now at

[36]

monticello I will put another printer to work and get the political economy printed with[1] as much dispatch as possible

    yours With Esteem and respect   JOSEPH MILLIGAN

I have reced yours of the 7th   J:M

RC (DLC); lacking postscript; endorsed by TJ as received 23 May 1818 and so recorded in SJL. RC (DLC); cover with address and adjacent postscript; with PoC of TJ to William F. Gray, 7 Oct. 1818, on verso; addressed: "Thomas Jefferson Esqr Monticello Milton (virginia)"; stamp canceled; franked; postmarked Georgetown, 13 May.

Neither TJ's SMALL NOTE to Milligan of 9 Apr. 1818 nor that of 7 May 1818 (YOURS OF THE 7TH) are recorded in SJL, and neither has been found.

[1] Manuscript: "whith."

From William Short

DEAR SIR   Philad^a May 11. 1818

Knowing your present aversion to writing, & knowing also how much you are <u>accablé</u> by inevitable correspondence, I have abstained for some time from adding to this load. If I break in upon you at this moment it is because I am in search of information that I know not where to look for otherwise, & indeed which I can have no certainty of finding from you—If you recollect, among the articles which you were so good as to attend to for me before my return to America, was a parcel of land near Norfolk. This was a purchase made of Co^l Harvie in the way of exchange for my lands on Roanoak. It was done at the moment of my departure for Europe, & I have no further recollection of particulars; so that I do not now know where to look for the title. I take for granted a title as usual was made & executed but I remember nothing about it.

A friend of mine at Richmond has lately at my request, had a search made in the records of the Genl Court, but no vestige is to be found there. There is a mere possibility that the instrument may have been recorded in the county Court of Norfolk, but I do not see how that could well be, as the contract was made at Richmond & neither Harvie or myself were afterwards at Norfolk. I shall however have a search made in those records; but merely for the sake of leaving nothing undone, for I have not the least expectation of finding it there.

Now as you were so good as to have the taxes on this land paid for some years by the late Co^{lo} Newton, I have thought it barely possible you might be able to give me some light on the subject. Co^{lo} Newton, as he paid the taxes, must have ascertained at least the quantity of the land, & thus may perhaps have had access to some title, that would guide me, if I could know where or of what nature it was. If perchance you have any recollection of the manner in which you placed this business in the hands of Co^{lo} Newton, or from whence you derived your information as to it, I shall take it as a particular favor if you will let me know it; or if you can suggest to me any circumstance that may guide me in my searches after the means of establishing the existence of this title in me.

The friend mentioned as being now at Richmond, formerly resided at Norfolk, & there paid for me the taxes on these lands, after the line traced by his predecessor Co^{lo} Newton. He says these lands stand charged to me as proprietor on the books of the commissioner of the land tax, & the quantity stated there at 1000. acres. This entry must have been made of course from the deed or title I should suppose, & might guide me if I could ascertain how or by whom the entry was made.

My Richmond friend who is a lawyer at that bar, gives this opinion in his late letter to me—"If the deed cannot be found, there is sufficient evidence of your right to demand, & have one, to enable you to obtain it from the representatives of Harvie by a suit in Equity, should they refuse to make it voluntarily." But I sh^d really think this a slender reliance—for it seems to me that a deed is the sine quo non to prove a title, but that it can be proved only by itself in propria persona. However I am no lawyer & hope I am wrong in this; for as the deed is not recorded in the Genl Court I have little hope of finding it elsewhere.

I feel a great disposition to commune with you a little (by availing myself of this letter) on all that I hear said here by sensible & moderate men, truly attached to their country, of public men & public measures—but I fear you will think this letter already too long, & I therefore condemn myself to forego the pleasure, which is so grateful to every one, of opening his heart & his mind to a friend in whose judgment & in whose liberality he has ever had unbounded & unshaken confidence.

I will therefore stop here & add only assurances of all those sentiments with which I have ever been, dear sir,

faithfully your friend & serv^t   W: SHORT

RC (MHi); endorsed by TJ as received 23 May 1818 and so recorded in SJL; with notation by TJ on verso related to his 29 May 1818 response: "send him my lre of Oct. 17. 99. to Newton & Newton's Oct. 23. to me. copy of entry of Mm book 99. Nov. 21. deed probably recorded in Norf c^{ty} where the lands lie if not to be found, the Harvies will execute one, or compellable in a c^t of equity."

ACCABLÉ: "overburdened." For the 10 Dec. 1784 land patent for one thousand acres of Green Sea lands in Norfolk County (the PARCEL OF LAND NEAR NORFOLK) assigned by John Harvie (1742–1807) to Short, see Benjamin Harrison (ca. 1751–99) to TJ, 18 July 1798, and first enclosure (*PTJ*, 30:459–60). The FRIEND OF MINE AT RICHMOND was Merit M. Robinson (Robinson to Short, 1 May 1818 [DLC: Short Papers]).

From Francis Adrian Van der Kemp

DEAR AND RESPECTED SIR! Oldenbarneveld 11 May 1818.

I take again the liberty of Sending you a few lines—and this without any further apologÿ, as I take it for granted that you do me the justice, that I can not wish, to intrude on your more Serious occupations, or importune you, for making a Sacrifice of your precious time, in answering these:—what value I may place on one of your lines—I do not desire these at that rate—and on this footing I do not hesitate, to continue writing

I do not recollect if I asked in a former—if you was acquainted with the contents and the author of a Book—published in Italy about the latter part of the 15th Century—called by Sacchetti libretto aureo—with the title „Ammaestramento degli Antichi„,[1]—if So—I Should be gratified—if in a moment of leisure you did gratify me with this information.

I mentioned, I believe, that I had accepted to translate[2] in English—the old Dutch Records of this State—It was done with So much courtesy, it was urged by my high respected friends that I could not decline—at least to try, here I could Succeed—

I expected to meet an immense mass of dross—but after decyphering these heiroglyphics—at the risk of loosing my Sight, I discover a precious treasure—for the Statesman—the historian—& merchant. Although their Political principles were highly Aristocratical even despotic—betraying themselves often in a language rather congenial to an absolute master than to Republicans and their Religious tenets were those of Bigots—yet their commercial views were luminous—and to this all other considerations must give way—They appointed as early as 1652[3] a Minister, to preach in English, to gratify their Subjects—they reprimanded their clergy—to gain the Lutherans, to whom they would not allow a free exercise of Religion—They were the principal carriers of Virginia and N. England, and provided Both these colonies with European and West-Indian goods—while they preserved the monopoly of the fur-trade and Salt—but carefully prevented the establishment of a printing press—every placard being printed in Holland while they had established a Latin school—and a

Botanical garden—on a Small Scale[4] As early as 1659 they permitted the N. Netherland merchants, to trade on France Spain—Italy—the caribean Islands and any where else—to try the experiment, if the company would be benefitted by Such an extensive privilege—and under this pretext, a considerable quantity of good from the South and the North was Shipped in N. amsterdam for Europe.

I could enlarge upon these topics, was I Sure, that it would be acceptable—and if I may meet with any peculiarity worthy your notice—I Shall deem it a duty—to make a memorandum of Such a point. your courtesy will now permit me Some farther enquiries—leaving the time and manner of answering to you unconditionallÿ—but earnestly Soliciting the continuance of your Honoured remembrance, as I owe it to your kindness in 1788, you will permit me to recall this to your memory, that I received So many marks of regard from Several of the wise and good—now alas! chiefly departed. The portrait of Dr. Wistar—Sent me lately by mrs Busti, as knowing how highly I respected that man, calls to my mind—the engraving of yours—in De La Plaine's Repository—for which I am endebted to our Gov. Clinton— Is this correct—Characteristic? or if there is a better—may I expect it, Sooner or later from you? I See not how this boon can be deny'd, after what has been granted.

From that Biography I learn—that „a Summary view of the rights of British America„ has been written by you and was published in 1774. So too a reply to the propositions of Lord North in 1775. neither of these productions I have ever Seen.

The first Book I purchased in Philadelphia—on my visit to Mount Vernon—in 1788—were your Notes on Virginia—the edition of that year—I never Did See any other—from the Biography it appears— that Several have been published—one of 1797. with an app—to defend the authenticity of Logans Speech. This I had read in Europe in the voyageur Americain—or rather in the app. of it Precis Sur l'amerique Septentrionale Pag. 229 Published Amst. by C. Shuring 1783—which I presume was borrowed from Raynal's Hist. Phil: T. ix. Pag. 47 ed. de Geneve 1783—because a whole § was literally borrowed from it. pag—48—Did Raynal obtain it from you—or might he have received it from that distinguished foreigner—whom you notice in your advertisement of Febr. 27. 1787—the Raynal too ought to have given his Source—but Such dutifulness—or generosity was not congenial to a man, who when he did good, wanted its trumpetting through the Streets—

Did you receive more Substantial and correct information about the Mammoth in the N.W— parts on the Missouri, as that which was communicated through the N. Papers? Such an enquiry deserved encouragement by offered rewards from our Philosophical Societies.

Permit me to assure you, that I remain with the highest respect— Dear and respected Sir! Your most obed— and obliged Serv[t]

Fr. Adr. van der Kemp

RC (DLC); dateline at foot of text; endorsed by TJ as received 23 May 1818 and so recorded in SJL. RC (DLC); address cover only; with PoC of TJ to Caesar A. Rodney, 7 Oct. 1818, on verso; addressed: "Thomas Jefferson LLD at his Seat Monticello Virginia"; franked; postmarked Trenton, N.Y., 12 May.

Bartolomeo da San Concordio was the AUTHOR of *Ammaestramenti degli Antichi* (Florence, 1661). In an edition of novellas by Franco SACCHETTI, editor Gaetano Poggiali referred to San Concordio's work as the "aureo libretto" ("golden booklet") (Poggiali, ed., *Delle Novelle di Franco Sac-*

chetti Citadino Fiorentino [Florence, 1724], 1:lxx). Van der Kemp posed the same query regarding this work to John Adams in a letter of 8 May 1818 (MHi: Adams Papers).

APP: "appendix." T.: "tome" ("volume"). The DISTINGUISHED FOREIGNER noticed in the ADVERTISEMENT prefaced to TJ's *Notes on the State of Virginia* was Barbé Marbois.

[1] Omitted closing guillemet editorially supplied.
[2] Manuscript: "transate."
[3] Manuscript: "i652."
[4] Preceding fifteen words interlined.

To Daniel Brent

[ca. 12 May 1818]

Th: Jefferson asks the favor of mr Brent to give a passage to the inclosed letters to mr Gallatin & mr Beasley, by the first <u>safe</u> conveyance with the dispatches of the department of state. he returns him many thanks for past favors, and will often have to apologize for future troubles. he salutes him with assurances [of great] [respect?]

PoC (DLC: TJ Papers, 213:37968); on verso of reused address cover of Thomas P. Mitchell to TJ, 24 Feb. 1818; undated, with placement at 12 May 1818 based on Brent's acknowledgment in his 15 May reply and TJ's SJL notation concerning the enclosed letters; endorsed by TJ and recorded in SJL, however, as a letter of 10 May 1818; closing faint. Enclosures: (1) TJ to Albert Gallatin, 9 Apr. 1818. (2) TJ to Reuben G. Beasley, 8 Apr. 1818. (3) TJ to Thomas Appleton, 4 Apr. 1818, and enclosure. (4) TJ to Stephen Cathalan, 5 Apr. 1818. (5) TJ to de Bure Frères, 5 Apr. 1818, and enclosure. (6) TJ to Victor Adolphus Sasserno, 5 Apr. 1818.

From John Gardiner

SIR   General Land Office 12th May 1818

I pray you accept the enclosed Map, as a mark of the respect of Sir your obed[t] serv[t]   JOHN GARDINER

RC (MHi); at foot of text: "Thomas Jefferson Esqr Virginia"; endorsed by TJ as received 18 May 1818 and so recorded in SJL. Enclosure: Gardiner, *Map of the late Surveys in the Southern District of the Alabama Territory* (Philadelphia, [ca. 1817]).

From David Bailie Warden

Dear Sir,   Paris, 12 may, 1818—

I have the pleasure of sending you by Captain Corran bound to newyork, a small parcel containing some pamphlets, catalogues of Books, and a file of a french newspaper—the <u>annales</u> <u>des</u> <u>Politiques</u>— If you will send me a list of the Books which you wish to have, I think that I could procure them for you a great deal cheaper than if furnished by any Bookseller, especially if you can allow some months for their collection. Owing to the late political changes the sales of private Libraries are frequent, and sometimes Books can be purchased at a low rate.—I have sold the <u>ms</u> of my account of the united states, in England and in France on very advantageous terms, and I feel less anxious concerning an american edition. Some of my friends at newyork and Philadelphia have written to me to dissuade me from this project, and have pointed out difficulties and circumstances of an unpleasant kind connected with every plan of subscription, of which I was not aware. Yesterday Professor Pictet called on me on his way to England, and informed me that mr. Terill is well, and that he is very much pleased with his progress.—with respect to mr. and mrs Randolph, I am, dear Sir, very devotedly

your obliged Servt   D. B. Warden

RC (DLC); at foot of text: "Thomas Jefferson Esquire, monticello"; endorsed by TJ as received 2 Sept. 1818 and so recorded in SJL. FC (MdHi: Warden Letterbook).

To Patrick Gibson

Dear Sir   Monticello May 13. 18.

on my return to this place I found here your letter of May 4. but on enquiry from my grandson, to whom I had written from Bedford to request his immediate transmission of an order in your favor on the bank of the US. he told me he had forwarded one on the 4th inst. the day of the date of your letter. presuming therefore that it has been recieved, I must now pray you to make the remittance which was the chief object of obtaining the discount, that is to say to Messrs Leroy

& Bayard of New York, my 2^d of the three instalments to them of 2083.D. 20 cents each with interest from Jan. 1. 1816. till paid. this being now due, [I] inform them by the present mail that they may soon expect the remittance thro' you. I salute you with friendship & respect   TH: JEFFERSON

PoC (MHi); on verso of reused ad- MY GRANDSON: Thomas Jefferson
dress cover of Jedidiah Morse to TJ, 24 Randolph.
Feb. 1818; one word faint; at foot of text:
"Mr Gibson"; endorsed by TJ.

From Thomas Jordan

SIR   Washington 13th May 1818

I took the liberty of applying to you for the above am^t by Letter dated some weeks back, requesting you would have the kindness to remit me the am^t to the care of Doctor May of this City, but as I have not had the pleasure of hearing from you, I presume it must have escaped your recollection, therefore beg leave to remind you, which hope you'll pardon

Having received all the Subscriptions here, I purpose leaving this city tomorrow for Baltimore, where I shall remain for some days, and shall feel honoured by your reply with the above amount, to care of Doctor Stewart Army & Navy Surg^n &^{c} Baltimore

Remain Sir most Respectfully y^{rs} &c   THO^s JORDAN

[at head of text:]
Honble Thos Jefferson To Kimber & Richardson   ⎫
                                     Philadelphia D^r⎰
1814—To 3 Volumes of the Emporium of Arts & Sciences ⎫ $10.50
            new Series   ⎰

RC (DLC); endorsed by TJ as received 20 May 1818 and so recorded in SJL; additional notation by TJ: "Newspapers."

To LeRoy, Bayard & Company

MESS^{RS} LEROY & BAYARD   Monticello May 13. 1818.

I, by mail of this day, desire mr Gibson of Richmond to remit to you 2083. D 20 c with interest from Jan. 1. 16. till paid, in discharge of my 2^d bond to mess^{rs} V. Staphorsts and Hubard, which will be done without any other delay than that of finding a bill or other medium of remittance, and will I hope get safely to hand. I salute you with assurances of great esteem & respect.   TH: JEFFERSON

PoC (DLC); on verso of a reused address cover from James Pleasants to TJ; endorsed by TJ.

From James Rawlings

Office of the Mutual Ass^e Society
SIR,   Richmond 14th May 1818.

Your favour of the 10 Ins^t with a Draft on Patrick Gibson of this place came to hand by yesterday's mail—The draft has been paid, and I now enclose you a Receipt for the quotas of the years 1814, 1815, 1816 1817 & 1818 being all of the demands of the M A. Sy for Insurance of y^r buildings at Monticello up to the end of this year—.

Very Respty Y^r Most Ob   JAMES RAWLINGS
                                               P Ag^t M A Sy

RC (MHi); endorsed by TJ as a letter about "Fire insurance" received 23 May 1818 and so recorded in SJL; additional notation by TJ: "paym^ts Mont^o house 1814.15.16.17.18." RC (MHi); address cover only; with PoC of TJ to Anthony Finley, 7 Oct. 1818, on verso; addressed:

"Thomas Jefferson Esqr Monticello. Albemarle"; stamp canceled; franked; postmarked Richmond, 15 May.

P AG^T M A SY: "Principal Agent Mutual Assurance Society."

ENCLOSURE

Receipt from the Mutual Assurance Society

Thomas Jefferson
To the Mutual Assurance Society against Fire on Buildings of the State of Virginia, Dr.
To Quotas of the years **1814 1815 1816 1817 & 1818** on
    Buildings in **Albemarle** insured by Declaration No. **389.**
    12\frac{84}{100}$ **each year** $64.20.
        Interest   7 70.
                Office of the M. A Society Richmond 14 May
                1818. $71.90.
                Received payment p^r a draft on Patrick
                Gibson

                                               JAMES RAWLINGS
                                               P Agent M A Sy

MS (MHi); printed form, with blanks filled by Rawlings rendered in boldface above.

From John Vaughan

D SIR   Philad. May 14. 1818

Not being able to negociate the Dft I prevailed upon one of the Banks here to take it on Deposit & purchased of Mr Stephen Girard the following Dfts on James Laffite & Co Paris to my order dated 12 May at 60 Days S^t the fourths of which I now enclose to you having Sent on the firsts to new York to be forwarded & the seconds will go by next opportunity viz

N° 382 for 2415 F^s a 5^{25} 460 $ Endorsd to Thom^s Appleton
    381 for 2205 "   "   420 End^d to Stephen Cathalan
    380. for   630 "   "   120 En^d to DeBure freres
                      $ 1000

I shall advise the opportunities as soon as ascertaind

I remain with respect Your friend &c   JN VAUGHAN

M Correa is here <u>just arrived</u> & much recovered from his late indisposition,

M Cooper highly appreciates the kind interest you have taken in his favor, but from the exertions made for him by his friends he concieves himself bound to await the start of the trial here

Dr Dorsey is chosen to the Anatomical Chair—The Nominations to the Vacancy created of the Materia Medica are to be made the first Tuesday in June The Election to be by special meeting a few days after—There is full expectation that D Coxe will fill that Chair

On first Tuesday in June the Nominations will take place for the Chemical Chair & the Election a few days after. This is understood to be the tontine—The Moment the decision is made, if M^r C & his friends are disappointed—he Devotes himself to your Institution & that Devotion will I concieve carry great weight his knowledge is so various & so great on the points he may be wanted to teach, he inspires his pupils with so warm an attachment to the science they pursue, & put them in the way so completely of pursuing it by themselves—That he will be eminently Useful in founding of a New Establishment—

He regrets that he was not able to be with You on 11 May but he had been obliged to give a Course of Mineralogy (twice a Day) & could not with honor desert it—he has been indisposed for two or three weeks but is now better

RC (MHi); on a sheet folded to form four pages, with letter on p. 1, address on p. 2, and postscript on pp. 3–4; addressed: "Thomas Jefferson Monticello Virginia"; stamp canceled; franked; postmarked Philadelphia, 14 May; endorsed by TJ as received 23 May 1818 and so recorded in SJL. Enclosures not found.

Mᴿ c: Thomas Cooper.

From Daniel Brent

Dᴇᴀʀ Sɪʀ,   washington, Depᵗ of State, May 15. 1818.

I have just had the Honor to receive your note of the 12th, enclosing an open Letter for mʳ Gallatin at Paris, which I immediately sealed, and one for mʳ Beasley at Havre, and requesting that I would give these Letters a Conveyance, with the public Despatches.

I have the satisfaction to inform you that they will forthwith be sent to the Collector of the Customs at Baltimore, with a request to him from this Department, that he will forward them by the earliest opportunity he may have to their respective destinations.

I have the Honour to remain, with sentiments of the greatest respect & Esteem,

Dear Sir, your obedᵗ & very humble servᵗ   Dᴀɴɪᴇʟ Bʀᴇɴᴛ.

RC (DLC); endorsed by TJ as received 23 May 1818 and so recorded in SJL. RC (DLC); address cover only; with PoC of TJ to William Alston, 6 Oct. 1818, on verso; addressed: "Mʳ Jefferson, Monticello"; franked; postmarked.

The ᴄᴏʟʟᴇᴄᴛᴏʀ ᴏꜰ ᴛʜᴇ ᴄᴜsᴛᴏᴍs ᴀᴛ ʙᴀʟᴛɪᴍᴏʀᴇ was James H. McCulloch.

From Bennett H. Henderson

Sɪʀ   Glasgow Barren County Ky May 15ᵗʰ 1818

Some years ago I made a deed to James L Henderson for my interest in Some land lying around the town of Milton I took a bond for the Conveyance of a tract of land in this Country to which he never had a title when this deed was made I was an infant but that Circumstance I Should never have taken an advantage of had I not been deceiv,d my brother is dead leaving no indemnity for[1] the Consideration of the said land therefore I am to loose my right or resort to the laws which protect infants my situation in life is such that I cannot dispence with this protection. for owing to the Cunning of mankind I have been overreachᵈ & left poor indeed

I understand you have bought this property or is in possession of it if this be a fact my situation may be releiv,d as no man liveth Knows better how to appreciate my case. to be at law with you would be among the most painful Situations my utmost endeavor therefore will be to avoid it if any reasonable Sacrafice on my part can affect it.

I wish you to examine the Subject & act with that Spirit of Justice becoming your elevated character Say in your wisdom what I ought to have. make me a proposition within the pale of reason & I shall be glad to accede to it. rather than go to law I had a thought of taking half its Value and thereby put an end to a Contest which otherwise Nessessity & Justice to my own feelings will Compel me to embark in. it would only be Nessasary to prove my infancy which can be done by Several respectable witnesses I hope to hear from you & hope you will Consider me as Seeking hardly Justice & beleive me when I say to you that the above Statement is true. if you have any desire to Come to an amicable settlement I will refer you to Mr William D Meriwether who has full power to do business for me I am Sir yours &c.

BENNETT H HENDERSON

RC (ViU: TJP); addressed: "His Excellency Thomas Jefferson Esqr Monticello Albemarle County Virginia"; franked; postmarked Hartford, Ky., 18 May; endorsed by TJ as received 15 June 1818 and so recorded in SJL.

For the 18 Sept. 1802 DEED TO JAMES L HENDERSON, see *PTJ*, 38:579–80. For more on TJ's purchase of the lands in question, see Robert F. Haggard, "Thomas Jefferson v. The Heirs of Bennett Henderson, 1795–1818: A Case Study in Caveat Emptor," *MACH* 63 (2005): 1–29.

[1] Manuscript: "for for."

From Mathew Carey & Son

SIR   Philad^a May 16. 1818

By this day's mail we forward Virgil, & in a few days we will forward V. Romæ & McMahon—

We rec^d yesterday a few Law Books from London, among which were nine of Bridgman, one of which we have this day forwarded to care of Capt. Peyton, in a box to W. H. Fitzwhylsonn of Richmond—

We shall advise Capt. P. by this day's mail of it—   Your obed serv^t √ M. CAREY & SON

Chipman & Addresses cannot be procured here. Should we meet with them, they shall be forwarded.—

[*at head of text, with above dateline adjacent to first line:*]
Hon. Thos Jefferson

Bo^t of M. Carey & Son

1 Virgil with English Notes	4—
1 McMahon's Gardening	3.50
1 Bridgman's Index	30—
1 Viri Romæ	1—
	√ $38.50

RC (MHi); in the hand of a representative of Mathew Carey & Son; endorsed by TJ as a letter from Mathew Carey received 23 May 1818 and so recorded in SJL.

To John Adams

DEAR SIR   Monticello May 17. 18.

I was so unfortunate as not to recieve from mr Holly's own hand your favor of Jan. 28. being then at my other home. he dined only with my family, & left them with an impression which has filled me with regret that I did not partake of the pleasure his visit gave them. I am glad he is gone to Kentucky. rational Christianity will thrive more rapidly there than here. they are freer from prejudices than we are, and bolder in grasping at truth. the time is not distant, tho' neither you nor I shall see it, when we shall be but a secondary people to them. our greediness for wealth, & fantastical expense has degraded and will degrade the minds of our maritime citizens. these are the peculiar vices of commerce.

I had been long without hearing <u>from</u> you, but I had heard <u>of</u> you thro' a letter from Dr Waterhouse. he wrote to reclaim against an expression of mr Wirt's, as to the commencement of motion in the revolutionary ball. the lawyers say that words are always to be expounded secundum subjectam materiam,[1] which in mr Wirt's case was Virginia. it would moreover be as difficult to say at what moment the revolution began, & what incident set it in motion, as to fix the moment that the embryo becomes an animal, or the act which gives him a beginning.   But the most agreeable part of his letter was that which informed me of your health, your activity, & strength of memory; & the most wonderful that which assured me that you retained your industry & promptness in epistolary correspondence. here you have entire advantage over me. my repugnance to the writing table becomes daily & hourly more deadly & insurmountable. in place of this has come on a canine appetite for reading. and I indulge it: because I see in it a relief against the taedium senectutis; a lamp to lighten my path thro' the dreary wilderness of time before me, whose bourne I see not. losing daily all interest in the things around us, something else is necessary to fill the void. with me it is reading, which occupies the mind without the labor of producing ideas from my own stock.

I enter into all your doubts as to the event of the revolution of S. America. they will succeed against Spain. but the dangerous enemy is within their own breasts. ignorance and superstition will chain their minds & bodies under religious & military despotism. I do believe it would be better for them to obtain freedom by degrees only; because that would by degrees bring on light & information, & qualify them to take charge of themselves understandingly; with more certainty if in the mean time under so much controul only as may keep them at peace with one another. surely it is our duty to wish them independance and self-government, because they wish it themselves, and they have the right, and we none, to chuse for themselves; and I wish moreover that our ideas may be erroneous, & theirs prove wellfounded.   But these are speculations, my friend, which we may as well deliver over to those who are to see their developement. we shall only be lookers on, from the clouds above, as now we look down on the labors, the hurry, & bustle of the ants & the bees. perhaps in that super-mundane region we may be amused with seeing the fallacy of our own guesses, & even the nothingness of those labors which have filled and agitated our own time here. en attendant, with sincere affections to mrs Adams & yourself, I salute you both cordially.

TH: JEFFERSON

P.S. there is now here a mr Coffee, a sculptor & Englishman, who has just taken my bust, and is going on to take those of Madison & Monroe. he resides at New York and promises me he will ask permission to take yours & send me one. I hope you will permit him. he is a fine artist. he takes them about half the size of life in plaister.

RC (MHi: Adams Papers); addressed: "John Adams esquire late President of the US. Quincy. Mass."; franked; postmarked Charlottesville, 19 May; endorsed by Adams; docketed by Charles Francis Adams. PoC (DLC); endorsed by TJ.

MY OTHER HOME: Poplar Forest. RE-CLAIM AGAINST: "dispute, challenge, contest" (*OED*). SECUNDUM SUBJECTAM MATERIAM: "according to the subject matter" (*Black's Law Dictionary*). TAE-

DIUM SENECTUTIS: "weariness of old age." EN ATTENDANT: "in the meantime."

William J. COFFEE wrote to Adams on 16 Oct. 1818 asking permission to take the former president's bust and stating his terms. Adams declined the offer on 18 Nov. because he was grieving the loss earlier that month of his wife, Abigail Adams (Andrew Oliver, *Portraits of John and Abigail Adams* [1967], 235).

[1] Manuscript: "materiem."

To Henry Dearborn

DEAR SIR   Monticello May 17. 18.

I duly recieved,[1] on my late return to this place your acceptable favor[2] of Apr. 22.   in looking back on past life the greatest pleasure I feel, is in recollections of the friends who have been my fellow-laborers, & my greatest happiness in the harmony and affection in which I lived & parted with them. of the manner in which your command in the army was made to cease, no one felt stronger disapprobation than myself. but it did not injure you. it was seen to proceed from the dominion of passion over a mind of much strength generally, but of more weakness in that particular. the sense of your services is deeply engraven on the public mind, & before that tribunal, you were not the suffering party.   of the latter circumstance, mentioned in your letter, I never before heard; nor can I account for it. it may have been inattention in a croud of business; I am sure it was not a want of friendship; for I have heard from the then President expressions of the deepest regret & indignation at the manner of the[3] former transaction.

That federal fortress which we had to storm, & to enter first the breach effected is now compleatly mastered, and all, within & without, is quiet. what is next? what are to be our future parties? for parties must be wherever men are free, and wherever their minds & faces are unlike. I confess I am puzzled with this question. there seems to be a strange jumble at present. Duane is making common cause with the federalists. Randolph is federal by nature & by his passions. Clay is on the start somewhere. I do not know where the Clintons are; of such medley complexion are the parties of that state. I suspect the new division will be between those who wish to strengthen the legislative branch, and the partisans of Executive power: or, in other words, they will step into the shoes of the original whigs & tories of England. the last will derive vast aid from the 150. lawyers in Congress. such a multitude, whose trade is talking, renders Congress incapable of getting on with the business of the nation, and forces it to transfer it's functions to the Executive. this singular circumstance, unforeseen by the framers of the constitution, threatens to make that, in experience, an impracticable government, which the soundest theory had pronounced the wisest work of man.[4] the never-ending debates of Congress make me almost willing to try Bonaparte's dumb legislature. however it will last my time as it is, and perhaps yours, altho' you have a long course to run before you reach my term. and I sincerely wish it may be as long as you please, & as happy as you please. we all retain an affectionate remembrance of mrs Dearborne, and great pleasure at having been favored with the opportunity of making her acquaintance. on this subject mrs Randolph dwells with undiminished pleasure, and, in imagination, places herself often in Boston, while her 11. children (for she has now reached that number) chain her physically at home. but wherever we are, there is but one prayer among us, that mrs Dearborne and yourself may have the full measure of the poet's wish for

'Long life, long health, long pleasures and a friend.'

Th: Jefferson

RC (CtY); fragment, lacking dateline, salutation, much of first page, and signature, with missing text supplied from PoC. PoC (DLC); on reused address cover to TJ; torn and damaged at seal; at foot of first page: "Gen¹ Dearborne"; endorsed by TJ.

John Armstrong possessed a MIND OF MUCH STRENGTH GENERALLY. The THEN PRESIDENT was James Madison. Members of Napoleon's DUMB LEGISLATURE lacked the right to speak but could vote by throwing a black or white ball into an urn (William Barré, *History of the*

French Consulate, under Napoleon Buonaparte [London, 1804], 366). Different versions of a 1723 poem by Alexander Pope, "To Mrs. M. B. on her Birth-day," give variations of the phrase LONG LIFE, LONG HEALTH, LONG PLEASURES AND A FRIEND (Pope, *Minor Poems*, ed. Norman Ault and John Butt [1954], 244–7).

¹ RC trimmed following first two letters of word.
² RC resumes here.
³ RC ends here.
⁴ RC resumes here.

From William H. Fitzhugh

Sir   Ravensworth (near Alexandria)¹ May 18ᵗʰ 1818

At the request of some of my neighbors, I have undertaken to ask your opinion and such information, as your own experience will enable you to give, as to the most direct line of communication between the City of Washington, and that section of the country in which you reside. From the former place a turnpike road, designed to intersect the <u>Little River turnpike</u> between the six & seven milestones, has already been commenced, and will be completed (most probably) in the course of the ensuing summer. We now have it in contemplation, to continue the same road across to Yates' ford on Bull Run, & thence to Norman's ford on the Rappahannoc, unless some more eligible points can be discovered—Should we succeed in getting it so far, we think it fair to calculate on seeing it extended, in the course of a few years, to our brethern beyond the mountain—Indeed unless we are very much mistaken in our estimate of the importance of such a road, it must be embraced in any general plan of internal improvement, that may be adopted either by the State or the national government—

We have been induced to apply to you, Sir, for information on this subject, from knowing that, at one time, you frequently travelled the route over which we propose to pass; & from having understo[od]

[51]

that you had formerly suggested a similar undertaking to the one, in which we are now about to engage—

Hoping, Sir, that you will pardon the liberty, a stranger has taken with you,

I have the honor to subscribe myself very respectfuly Yrs &—&c—

W. H. FITZHUGH

RC (MHi); edge trimmed; endorsed by TJ as received 29 May 1818 and so recorded in SJL; with TJ's Notes on Itch Lotion, [ca. 29 May 1818], subjoined. RC (DLC); address cover only; with PoC of TJ to Mathew Carey, 6 Oct. 1818, on verso; addressed: "The Hon[bl] Thomas Jefferson Monticello Albemarle County Virginia"; franked; postmarked.

William Henry Fitzhugh (1792–1830), public official, was the son of TJ's friend William Fitzhugh, proprietor of Ravensworth in Fairfax County. In 1808 he graduated first in his class from the College of New Jersey (later Princeton University), and he inherited Ravensworth on his father's death the following year. Fitzhugh also owned property in Stafford and represented that county in the Virginia House of Delegates, 1811–16. From 1819–23 he was a state senator for a district that included Fairfax County, and in the 1828–29 session he was again in the House of Delegates representing Fairfax. Fitzhugh was one of the Fairfax County delegates to the state constitutional convention of 1829–30. As a vocal supporter of democratic reforms, he voted against the final document. An early member of the American Colonization Society, by 1820 Fitzhugh was one its vice presidents, a position he held until his death. Writing as "Opimius," he engaged in a newspaper debate with colonization critic John W. Nash. At the time of his death near Cambridge, Maryland, Fitzhugh owned at least two hundred slaves. He included a provision in his will freeing his slaves after 1850 and offering to pay their expenses and a fifty-dollar bounty to any of them willing to immigrate to Africa (*MB*, 2:1071; *Trenton Federalist*, 10 Oct. 1808; Leonard, *General Assembly*; *Proceedings and Debates of the Virginia State Convention, of 1829–30* [1830], esp. 882; American Society for Colonizing the Free People of Colour of the United States [later the American Colonization Society], *Annual Report* 2 [1819]; 13 [1830]; *Controversy between Caius Gracchus and Opimius in Reference to the American Society for Colonizing the Free People of Colour of the United States. First Published in the Richmond Enquirer* [1827]; Fairfax Co. Will Book, Q:57–9, 68–75; Washington *Daily National Intelligencer*, 24 May 1830; Washington *Daily National Journal*, 26 May 1830; gravestone inscription in Pohick Episcopal Church Cemetery, Lorton).

[1] Parenthetical phrase interlined.

To Reuben Haines

Monticello May 18. 18.

I am truly thankful, Sir, for the honor done me by the Academy of Natural sciences of Philadelphia in electing me a corresponding member of their society. at an earlier period of life I might have endeavored to deserve it in fact, but now can only do it by good wishes for it's success, & by assurances that I should be gratified by any occasion of being useful to it.

I am particularly gratified by the perusal of the journal you have been so kind as to send me; in which I find many distinguished papers on subjects of much interest. be so good, Sir, as to present my sincere acknolegements to the Academy, and to accept yourself the assurance of my high respect.   TH: JEFFERSON

RC (PHC: Robert B. Haines III Collection); addressed: "Mr Reuben Haines Corresponding Secretary of the Academy of Natural sciences Philadelphia"; franked; postmarked Charlottesville, 21 May; endorsed by Haines as received 24 May 1818 and read by the Academy two days later. PoC (DLC); on verso of reused address cover of Thomas Cooper to TJ, 20 Feb. 1818; endorsed by TJ.

To Joseph Milligan

DEAR SIR   Monticello May 18. 18.
    I have recieved safely the Tacitus and other books sent you to be bound, except 'a Treatise on internal navigation'[1] in small 8vo which I am in hopes you have. it may be sent me by mail. should it by any accident have got mislaid or lost, as it was printed in N. York, I would pray you to get it from there & send it by mail, well bound. it is important to me as I am just about building some locks on our river, and relied on that book for instruction.   I recieved with my own books some on navigation, which not being for me, I expect are for m[r Car]r, who I suppose will call for them. there is one of them h[owever?] I would wish you to procure & send me. this is Bow[ditch's] Practical navigator, the Stereotype edition of New York. 1817. b[e so] good as to cut it in two between the 264th & 265th pages, and bind it handsomely in 2. vols.
    You informed me when here that you could furnish me with Bacon's abridgment as cheap as I could import it. pray let me know the minimum price at which you could furnish that & the other law books stated below. on the moderateness of price will depend whether I take them. I salute you with friendship   TH: JEFFERSON

Bacon's abridgment. most improved edition
Comyn's Digest.
Coke's Institutes. 8vo edn
Fonblanque's Equity
Abridgment of cases in Equity. 8vo edn

PoC (MHi); on verso of reused address cover of Thomas Appleton to TJ, 20 Dec. 1817; torn at seal and ink stained; postscript adjacent to signature; at foot of text: "Mr Millegan"; endorsed by TJ.

[1] Omitted closing quotation mark editorially supplied.

From Peter Poinsot

MONSIEUR.   Cette 18 Mai 1818

À la recommandation de mon digne & vertueux ami le Genéral Kosciuzko Je me permis de vous écrire le 25 Juin dernier, & vous envoyai une de ses lettres par la voye de Mr Barnett mon ami, votre Consul Genéral a Paris, & le duplicata le 15 Juillet Suivant par Bordeaux, N'ayant pas été favorisé de vos nouvelles. Je viens Solliciter de vôtre bienveillance, pour vous prier de vous interesser pour moi, pour les terres que je reclame, qui Sont Situées dans le Comté de Monongalia de 1200 Acres, & dont la révolution de france m'a empeché de reclamer, Je vous demande cette grace, oui je vous la demande, en mémoire du meilleur[1] de mes amis que j'ai perdu,[2] (& dont je n'avais cessé d'être en relation d'amitié depuis 1783 à Philadelphie où[3] je lui fus recommandé par Mr Thomas de Bukaty Envoye Extraord^re de la Cour de Pologne a Londres Son ami & le mien) Je joignis dans le tems, en duplicata, copie litérale, & le plan de mes terres. Il vous plaira permettre que je me réfère à leur contenu. Dans l'esperance que vous aurez la bonté de[4] faire faire les recherches convenables pour m'assurer de leur Situation & les moyens pour m'en rendre possesseurs.[5] Dans cette douce attente Je prie Vôtre Excellence d'agreer l'assurance des Sentimens d'Estime et de la plus haute Considération avec lesquels je suis

De Vôtre Excellence Le trés humble[6] obeissant serviteur

POINSOT DES ESSART

& si il y avait des impositions foncières[7] a payer, Veuïllez m'en instruire afin que je puisse faire passer les fonds necessaires pour les acquitter de suitte   PE

EDITORS' TRANSLATION

SIR.   Cette 18 May 1818

At the recommendation of my worthy and virtuous friend General Kosciuszko, I took the liberty of writing you last June 25 and sending you one of his letters through my friend Mr. Barnet, your consul general at Paris, and the duplicate through Bordeaux on 15 July. Not having been favored with any news from you, I solicit your kindness and ask you to take an interest on my behalf in the land I am claiming in Monongalia County, consisting of 1200 acres, and which I have been prevented from claiming by the French Revolution. I ask this favor of you, indeed I do so in memory of my best friend, whom I have lost (and with whom I had remained friends since meeting him in 1783 in Philadelphia, where I was recommended to him by his friend and mine, Mr. Thomas de Bukaty, envoy extraordinary in London of the Polish court). In my previous letters I enclosed, in duplicate, a literal copy of the deed and a map of my land. Please allow me to refer you to their contents, in the hope that you will kindly have the appropriate research done in order to confirm the location of that land and the means at my disposal to take possession of it. In this pleasant expectation, I ask Your Excellency please to accept the assurance of my respect and of the highest consideration with which I am,

Your Excellency, your very humble obedient servant

POINSOT DES ESSART

And if there are property taxes to be paid, please be so kind as to inform me, so that I can transfer the necessary funds to pay them immediately

PE

RC (DLC); endorsed by TJ as received 30 July 1818 and so recorded in SJL. RC (MHi); address cover only; with PoC of TJ to Lewis D. Belair, 23 Nov. 1818, on verso; addressed: "To The Honourable Thomas Jefferson, Esq Late President of the Unitated States Montecello"; stamped "SHIP"; franked; postmarked New York, 22 July. Dupl (DLC); torn at top margin; endorsed by TJ as received 11 Sept. 1818 and so recorded in SJL. Dupl (MHi); address cover only; with PoC of TJ to John Barnes, 21 Dec. 1818, on verso; addressed: "To The Honourable Thomas Jefferson Esqʳ late Président of the United States Montecello"; stamped "SHIP"; franked; postmarked Charleston, 21 Aug. Translation by Dr. Genevieve Moene.

LE DUPLICATA was dated 10 July 1817, not 15. Franciszek BUKATY was the Polish envoy in London.

[1] RC: "meiller." Dupl: "meilleur."
[2] Instead of preceding three words, Dupl reads "la mort m'a enlevé" ("death removed from me").
[3] Unmatched opening parenthesis preceding this word editorially omitted.
[4] Manuscript: "de de."
[5] Postscript, keyed to this point with a caret in RC, is integrated into text of Dupl.
[6] Dupl here adds "& trés" ("and very").
[7] RC: "foncière." Dupl: "foncieres."

To Quinette de Rochemont

DEAR SIR   Monticello May 18. 18.

On my return to this place after an absence of some weeks I found the letter of Feb. 11. with which you favored me by mr Holly. his visit (about the latter end of April) happened unluckily to be during that absence. I am infinitely indebted to you for the two pamphlets of Constant & Scheffer, which, with those you formerly sent me, have given me a more satisfactory view of the state and prospects of Europe than every thing I had read or heard before. I am now satisfied that the mass of mind in France & the countries North of that has taken a solid direction, which may be momentarily checked, but will ultimately attain it's determined object, that of a government in which the people shall, by their representatives, ha[ve an] effectual controul. the horrors of Robespierre, and devastating frenzies of Bonaparte have indeed produced an ebb in the current of reformation; but the tide will return, and will overwhelm in it's course all obstacles opposing it. the liberty of the press, the entering wedge of reformation, is justly viewed as the instrument first to be secured. and it doubtless is an instrument of difficult management. it's abuses are most afflicting; but those it prevents are more so. punishment for the publication of <u>injurious falsehoods,</u> is the only, altho' insufficient remedy. but our experience has proved that even these may be neglected, and that the good sense of readers soon recoils the calumnies on the authors of them.

I hope that on your return you will find your foreign oppressors withdrawn, or withdrawing, that you will have a safe entrance into your own country, and a welcome reception by it's friends. I know enough of France, as well as of my own country to be sensible that the habits and society of that country must be reluctantly exchanged for those of ours: and that the chief merit of this, in the eye of the stranger must be the inviolable asylum it offers to persecuted worth. be assured, dear Sir, that my wishes are all alive for the accomplishment of a government to your country, as free as order will permit, for a safe and happy return to it for yourself and your worthy son, and that you carry with you the sentiments of my highest esteem and consideration.

TH: JEFFERSON

PoC (ViW: TC-JP); on reused address cover of Patrick Gibson to TJ, 23 Feb. 1818; two words faint; at foot of first page: "M. le baron Quesnai de Rochemont"; endorsed by TJ.

To John Wood

DEAR SIR   Monticello May 18. 18.

I deferred answering your favor of Apr. 22. until I could mention it's contents to the Visitors of the Central college, whose semiannual meeting was to take place on the 10th inst. this however was a tribute of respect to your application, rather than from any expectation of effect from it; because circumstances had already put it beyond our power. our funds enable us, as yet, to establish but two professorships. Dr Cooper's qualifications in the Physiological sciences, and in that of law also had already induced our engagement with him; and measures for procuring a classical teacher from Europe had brought us to the end of our tether. this, I know can be of no consequence with you in a country calling every where [for] the employment of such talents as yours, and where the choice of places will rest with

yourself.—this letter shall be followed by an immediate return of your
M^claurin's fluxions, which I would not have kept so long but in the
belief that your absence on other business suspended your want of it.
the grounds of the fluxionary calculus were what I wished to recover.
these the early part of the 1st vol. has given me, and a general rein-
vestigation would require more time than the age of 75. will have to
spare. I salute you with assurances of great esteem & respect.

Th: Jefferson

PoC (DLC); on verso of reused address cover to TJ; torn at seal; at foot of text: "M^r
John Wood"; endorsed by TJ.

To Benjamin Henry Latrobe

Dear Sir   Monticello May 19. 18
    Your favor of Apr. 14. is just now at hand. that of Mar. 7. had been
recieved in due time, with the book of prices, for which I ought not
to have been contented with internally thanking you, as I certainly
and cordially did. but you have no conception of the drudgery of letter writing to which I am subjected, and which really renders life a
burthen. writing too is become a slow & painful operation from a
stiffening wrist, the consequence of an antient dislocation. these things
place me often in default with my friends. you had a right to hear
from me on another subject, the progress of our College, in which you
were so good as to take an interest, and to contribute to it from the
store of your time and talents.   the pavilion we had begun before
the reciept of your draughts is not yet [fin]ished, but will be so in the
course of the month of July. we shall within [. . .] d[ays?] commence
your Palladian Corinthian, being the left hand figur[e] of [t]he upper
row on your paper, in which we permit no alteration but the [s]ubsti-
tution of a flat, for the pyramidal roof, which, seen over the pediment,
has not, we think, a pleasing effect. were we left to our own funds,
they would not extend beyond a 3^d or 4th pavilion, which would probably be your 3^d & 5th or perhaps 2^d in the same line. but the legislature has appropriated 15,000.D. a year to an University; & we think
it nearly certain they will engraft it on our stock, which we offer them
if they will adopt our site. this will call, in the first instance for about
16. pavilions, with an appendix of 20. dormitories each: and we expect each pavilion with it's dormitories to cost about 10,000.D. our
funds may be called 60,000.D. and the legislature will have to add
about 100,000. more to compleat these buildings, exclusive of your
central one, which would be reserved for the Center of the ground.

we propose 10. professors, each of whom will have his pavilion & dormitories, and for each two professorships we must erect an hotel of the same good architecture. these we shall assign to French families, who will undertake to board the students on their own account, and thus furnish the means of their learning to speak French, by interdicting the utterance of an English word within their doors. we mean to accept of no professor who is not of real eminence in his profession, and consequently we must go to Europe for many of them. this is our plan, resting at present on no other uncertainty but that of the adoption of the Central college for the scite of the University. several of your fronts, altho' beautiful, cannot be brought within our limit of 34. or 36. feet.

I learned with great grief your abandonment of the Capitol. I had hoped that, under your direction, that noble building would have been restored and become a monument of rational taste & spirit. I fear much for it now. to [my]self personally it can be of little moment; because in the public bui[ld]ings which will be daily growing up in this growing countr[y] [you?] can have no competitor for employ. I sincerely wish you as much as you can wish yourself, & salute you with undiminished friendship & respect   TH: JEFFERSON

PoC (DLC); on reused address cover of Bernard Peyton to TJ, 12 Mar. 1818; torn at seal; at foot of first page: "B. H. Latrobe esq."; endorsed by TJ.

From James P. Preston

SIR   Richmond May 20th 1818

From the determination of Mr Baldwin the late Engineer to withdraw from the service of the State, The President and Directors of the Board of Public works, are under the necessity of appointing a suitable person to supply[1] the vacancy thus produced. Mr F. R. Hassler now of New Ark, New Jersey, is among others an applicant for the appointment. In his letter to the Secy of the Board in reference to the means of obtaining information respecting his qualifications, as an Engineer he says, "I take the liberty to name in this view the following; Brigadier General Joseph G, Swift, Mr Jefferson, and Mr Madison, former presidents of the United States who may remember me from my transactions relative to the Survey of the Coast." This gentleman was formerly the Attorney General, and also the director of Roads, Bridges, and Canals for the Canton of Berne in Switzerland; I mention this fact respecting him in order to aid your recollection.

Being convinced that you are frequently interrupted and harrassed by applications of this kind, I would not voluntarily have added to your trouble; but as you are perfectly acquainted with the important duties that the Engineer to the Board of Public works, will have to perform, in relation to the great object of internal improvements contemplated by the State & also of the consequent injuries that error or incapacity in the Engineer[2] might produce to the Commonwealth, I trust my appology for the trouble thus imposed, by endeavouring to obtain the best information to aid the Board in making a proper selection, will be found in the responsibility which I owe to the Board and the Public, and in the justice due to the Applicants

With every consideration of respect I have the honor to be your Ob^t Servt   JAMES P. PRESTON

RC (DLC); endorsed by TJ as received 27 May 1818 and so recorded in SJL. RC (MHi); address cover only; with PoC of TJ to William J. Coffee, 6 Oct. 1818, on verso; addressed: "Thomas Jefferson esquire Monticello Albemarle County"; franked; postmarked Richmond, 23 May. FC (Vi: RG 57, Board of Public Works, Applications for Position of Principal Engineer); in Preston's hand and endorsed by him.

Thomas Moore succeeded Loammi BALDWIN as the principal engineer of Virginia's Board of Public Works in July 1818 (Baltimore *Niles' Weekly Register*, suppl. to vol. 15 [1818/19]: 40; *JHD* [1818–19 sess.], 6 [7 Dec. 1818]).

On this day Preston sent a letter of similar purport to James Madison (Madison, *Papers, Retirement Ser.*, 1:288–9).

[1] RC: "suply." FC: "supply."
[2] Word interlined in FC in place of "appointment."

To John Cook

Monticello May 21. 18.

Th: Jefferson presents his compliments and his thanks to Mr Cook for the N° of mr Frend's Astronomical amusements of 1818. which he has been so kind as to send him. he has looked over it with pleasure, and considers it as an instructive publication for many who have not time to devote to a more serious study of the subject. he salutes mr Cook with respect.

PoC (MHi); on verso of an unrelated cover sheet, in an unidentified hand, which reads "Thomas Jefferson Acct with William Watson Bal $111.29"; dateline at foot of text; endorsed by TJ.

To Thomas Jordan

SIR   Monticello May 21. 18.

On my return home after an absence of 3. weeks, I found here your letter of Apr. 20. and it was not till yesterday that I could procure an US. 10.D. bill; and just in that moment recieved your 2ᵈ favor of May 13. I now therefore inclose 10.50 D to the care of Dʳ Stewart as you desired. the perplexity of keeping the numerous little accounts for periodical publications had occasioned it to escape me that I was debtor for the Emporium, or it should have been paid in due time. Accept the assurance of my respect.   TH: JEFFERSON

PoC (DLC); on verso of reused address cover of Joseph C. Cabell to TJ, 11 Mar. 1818; at foot of text: "Mʳ Thoˢ Jordan"; endorsed by TJ, with his additional notations: "Newspapers. Emporium" and "10.50 D inclosed."

From John McKinney

                                   Green Creek Bourbon County Kentucky
DEAR SIR   May 21ˢᵗ 1818—

After my best Respects to you, I would just inform you, I Never have had it in my power to procure to you, the Panther skin, you Requested Me to have with it's head & Teeth, feet & Nails (or Claws) all to it, & to be as near in form, as possible like as if it was alive—But I still Look out to have it: as soon as possible & if I Do, I will forward it to you, with all speed—

Also, I now have in my care Six Elks, Three Bucks & three Does—Belonging to my Son, who lives in Missouri Territory, he brought[1] them up about two or three[2] years Ago—(however he brought up three Bucks & one Doe, & the[3] Doe, has had Two fawns, both Does,[4] Since) I have lately Recᵈ a letter from my Son, Requesting me to Sell them; & Remit the money to him, as quick as possible, as he Stands in Need of it—& not to fail Selling them; the first chance I could have—Now Sir—I have had Several applications for them But a Gentleman, who inform'd me a few Days ago, that, he hear'd you Wishe,d, to purchas some of that Specious—& Requested me to let you know, so that if you want them, you could get them—A Gentleman in this state had Some, he Sold a Buck[5] & Doe for $600—& a short time before he sold a Single Buck; for five hundred.—Now Sir—if you wish to purchas them, & will Write me a Line, & what you are willing to give; if The price will justify my Taking them to you, I will either Take, or have them Taken to you, as soon as the

Nature of Cases; will permit—That is to Say I will Deliver Two of the Bucks; & three Does—(as a gentleman has the Lent of one, of the Bucks, to his Two Does[6]—& perhaps, will wish to keep him another Season—or altogether—) The Description of them are as follows (Towit) The Two Bucks now at home—here, is (I believe) about four years old—this Summer—the oldest Doe, is about five years old, She is with fawn, & I Expect the next Doe, which is now in next month, Two years old—may be with fawn too, But not certain—The Third Doe, is one year old, in next month—all very thriving ones— Now Sir—If they Suit you—& you wish me to forward them to you, you will be So good, as to Drop me a line by male—to Paris, where I can get it & if you do write I will thank you to do it Immediately, as I Shall Sell Immediately, if appertunity Serves—After giving you Time to write—I am with[7] every Centiment of Esteem; your Sincere frend in affinity &[c]   JOHN MKINNEY

RC (MoSHi: TJC-BC); at foot of text: "The Hon[le] Tho[s] Gefferson Esq[r] Albemarl C[ty] Virg[a] state"; endorsed by TJ as received 11 June 1818 and so recorded in SJL.

John McKinney (d. 1825), teacher, public official, and land investor, was a native of Augusta County. Severely wounded during Lord Dunmore's War at the 1774 Battle of Point Pleasant, by 1785 he had moved to Kentucky. Except for a stay of several years in Missouri, McKinney remained in Kentucky thereafter. While it was still a part of Virginia, he represented Bourbon County in the House of Delegates in 1790. When Kentucky became a state in 1792, McKinney represented his county in the resulting constitutional convention and supported an unsuccessful effort to remove guarantees of slaveholding from the new charter of government. In 1783, while serving as a schoolteacher, he reportedly killed a mountain lion that had attacked him in his classroom, thereby acquiring the nickname of "Wildcat" (Otto A. Rothert, "John D. Shane's Interview with Mrs. John McKinney," *Filson Club History Quarterly* 13 [1939]: 157–66; Sylvia Pettit Welch, "Pioneer John McKinney," *Filson Club History Quarterly* 14 [1940]: 103–16; Henry R. McIlwaine and John Pendleton Kennedy, eds., *Journals of the House of Burgesses of Virginia, 1619–1776* [1905–15], 1773–76 vol., pp. 182, 204, 229; DNA: RG 15, RWP; Leonard, *General Assembly,* 179; *Journal of the First Constitutional Convention of Kentucky, Held in Danville, Kentucky, April 2 to 19, 1792* [1942], v, 10; KyBgW-K: McKinney Papers).

[1] Manuscript: "brought brought."
[2] Preceding two words interlined.
[3] Manuscript: "the the."
[4] Superfluous closing parenthesis editorially omitted.
[5] Manuscript: "Book."
[6] Manuscript: "Dows."
[7] Manuscript: "with with."

From Thomas Ritchie

DEAR SIR   [ca. 21 May 1818]

After all my exertions, it is impossible for me to execute your commission.

I cannot find in this City one map of V^a which is not pasted on linen and mounted on Rollers.—The Agent of the map resides here; but he has no[1] Copy of the description you desire.—A new Edition of it is in hand, and he has therefore pushed off the old ones as fast as he could.

If you will instruct me to purchase a linen mounted one for you, at $10, I will try to put it up in any way you may direct.—I need not say how much pleasure it will give me.

Truly Your Friend,   THOMAS RITCHIE

RC (MHi); undated; endorsed by TJ as received 29 May 1818 from Richmond and so recorded in SJL; notation by TJ beneath endorsement: "May 31. wrote note declining a map on linen & rollers" (note not found and not recorded in SJL). RC (DLC); address cover only; with PoC of TJ to James Breckinridge, 6 Oct. 1818, on verso; addressed: "Thomas Jefferson Esqr Charlottesville"; franked; postmarked Richmond, 21 May.

TJ requested the COMMISSION of Ritchie in a letter written in April 1818 after TJ's arrival at Poplar Forest on the 14th of that month, not found and not recorded in SJL but described in TJ to James Leitch, 28 May 1818.

[1] Word interlined in place of "one."

From John McKinney

                                      Green Creek, Bourbon County Kentucky
HON^D SIR   May 23rd 1818—

With esteeme, I imbrace this appertunity, of writing to you—Alho, I wrote you the other Day by male—as the Bearer Mr Thatchers, is to pass through your County, & whereas our males, have lately, been very Uncertain—I have thought it most adviseable to write by him, too[1] as I am now Anxous for[2] an Answer Imme[diately]—

Sir—I was formerly Acquainted wi[. . .] have been Several times at your Dwelling—you once spoke to me, whilst I lived in agusta C^{ty} Virg^a to Secure you if I could, a Panther skin, Case,d, with the head Teeth, & feet & Claws all on—& to be nearly in the Same Shape as if alive—I have not yet had it in my power to procure it—But if I ever do have it, I will most certainly forward it to you Immediatily—

But Sir—I have now in my care Six Elks, Three Bucks & one Doe, brought, up, from Missouri, by my Son who lives there—The Doe,

Since, has had Two Doe fawns—the oldest Buck & Doe is (I belive about five years old) the other Two Bucks, is about four years old, this Summer—the Second Doe, is in next month Two years old, the third Doe—is one year old next month—the old Doe is with young, & I expect the Two years old is, (but I am not certain) the other or third one; is one year old, next month—

Also Sir—I have been Requested by a Gentleman, lately from your County; To write to you, as he informe,d me; you wished to purchase some of these Specious—My Son has wrote me a few Days ago—to Sell them the first appertunity, or as quick as I could—& Remit the money to him, as he Was in Want of Some now.—& Sir—if you wish to purchase, I will thank you for a few lines, & state to me what you can afford to give—I Can till you what a Gentleman Sold three Elks he had out here; I believe last fall was a year—he sold one Buck & Doe for Six hundred Dollars, & a Short time before, he sold one Buck, for five hundred Dollars & Lately, I have been Told that Such Things in that Countery and with you would command, one thousand Dollars per pair—But Sir—I can Easily be Settisfied, for my Trouble taking them there (or Sending them) & will Submit the mater to you & will just Request the favour of you; for a line on the Subject, as quick as possible which I will certainly Answer—& if you Request them there, I will have Two Bucks & Three Does to you; as quick as Circomstances will admit, The Third Buck, I have Le[...] [...] to a Gentleman, who has Two Does—for Last year—& perhaps [...] wish to keep him, another Season, or perhaps purchas him altog[ethe]r—But if he Returns him, I will take him along with the Rest, & then there will be just the Three pair—I just wish you the Refusel, as I intend Selling as Soon as I can—agreeable to my Sons Directions—I hope Sir—you will Excuse haste &c Whilst I Remain, with every centiment of esteeme yours in affinity &c

JOHN MKINNEY

RC (MoSHi: TJC-BC); mutilated at seal; at foot of text: "The Hon^le Thos Gefferson—Esqr Albermarl-Cty. Virg^a state"; endorsed by TJ as received 7 Aug. 1818 and so recorded in SJL, which indicates that it was received at Warm Springs.

TJ's reply to this letter, not found, is recorded in SJL as written 8 Aug. 1818 from Warm Springs, with TJ's summary: "declining offer of elks." See also TJ to McKinney, 15 June 1818.

[1] Word interlined.
[2] Manuscript: "to for."

From John M. Perry

DEAR SIR   Central College 26 May 1818

I have unexpectedly to go to Lynchburg again—My son Tho[s] has got So much worse since I left there that my Brother has sent a Messenger for me a second time—M[r] Dinsmore who will hand you this has promised to begin to work on the pavillion I have undertaken to do for the College—I hope by this arrangement that we shall be yet able to have it done in time or So near that it will not make So much difference—M[r] Dinsmore will make everry arrangement[1] with you respecting the manner in which the work will be done I shall press M[r] Brown to Come on the moment I get to Lynchburg to Commence laying the bricks will ready by the middle of next week—

respectfully y[r] Ob; S[t]   JOHN M PERRY

RC (CSmH: JF); endorsed by TJ as received 27 May 1818 and so recorded in SJL.

[1] Manuscript: "arangemant."

To John Gardiner

Monticello May 28. 18.

Th: Jefferson presents his compliments to mr Gardiner and his thanks for the handsome Map of the Alabama territory, which he has been so kind as to send him. the rapid advance of that portion of our country into notice and estimation renders it now entirely interesting. he salutes mr Gardiner with esteem and respect.

PoC (MHi); on verso of reused address cover of Charles Willson Peale to TJ, 2 Mar. 1818; dateline at foot of text; endorsed by TJ.

To James Leitch

DEAR SIR   Monticello May 28. 18.

at the meeting of the Commissioners at Rockfish gap it will be very important to have a copy of Madison's map of Virginia with lines traced on it through the different places proposed for the University, so as to shew the quantum of population on each side of those lines. it should be one of those with the boundaries of the counties colored, but not their whole surface. I wrote to mr Ritchie from Poplar Forest in April to request him to forward me such an one, but not having heard from him I suppose my letter to have miscarried or some other good cause to have prevented it. will you be so good as to procure it for me, and bring or send it up. it will be safe to make enquiry of mr Ritchie in order to prevent a double execution of the request. I salute [y]ou with friendship and respect[1]   TH: JEFFERSON

PoC (DLC); on verso of a reused address cover from James Leitch to TJ; one word faint; at foot of text: "Mr James Leitch"; endorsed by TJ.

For this year's new edition of Bishop James MADISON'S MAP OF VIRGINIA, see TJ to Madison, 29 Dec. 1811, and note, and Stein, *Worlds*, 386–7.

[1] Manuscript: "request."

To Mordecai M. Noah

SIR   Monticello May 28. 18.
    I thank you for the Discourse on the consecration of the Synagogue in your city, with which you have been pleased to favor me. I have read it with pleasure and instruction, having learnt from it some valuable facts in Jewish history which I did not know before. your[1] sect by it's sufferings[2] has furnished a remarkable proof of the universal spirit of religious[3] intolerance, inherent in every sect, disclaimed by all while feeble, and practised by all when in power. our laws have applied the only antidote to this vice, protecting our religious, as they do our civil rights by putting all on an equal footing. but more remains to be done. for altho' we are free by the law, we are not so in practice. public opinion erects itself into an Inquisition, and exercises it's office with as much fanaticism as fans the flames of an Auto da fé. the prejudice still scowling on your section[4] of our religion, altho' the elder one, cannot be unfelt by yourselves. it is to be hoped that individual dispositions will at length mould themselves to the model of the law, and consider the moral basis on which all our religions rest, as the rallying point which unites them in a common interest; while the peculiar dogmas branching from it are the exclusive concern of the respective sects embracing them, and no rightful subject of notice to any other. public opinion needs reformation on this point, which would have the further happy[5] effect of doing away the hypocritical maxim of 'intus ut lubet, foris ut moris.' nothing I think would be so likely to effect this as to your sect particularly as the more careful attention to education, which you recommend, and which placing it's members on the equal and commanding benches of science, will exhibit them as equal objects of respect and favor.[6] — I should not do full justice to the merits of your discourse, were I not, in addition to

that of it's matter, to express my consideration of it as a fine specimen of style & composition. I salute you with great respect and esteem.

TH: JEFFERSON

RC (facsimile in catalogue for Sotheby's auction, New York City, 29 Oct. 1986, lot 76 [cover illustration]). PoC (DLC); at foot of text: "Mʳ Mordecai M. Noah." Tr (DLC: TJ Papers, ser. 9); endorsed: "For the Rev. Dʳ Pearson Harvard." Extract printed in New York *National Advocate*, 28 Jan. 1819, and elsewhere.

[1] *National Advocate* text begins with this word.
[2] Preceding three words interlined.
[3] Word interlined.
[4] *National Advocate*: "sect."
[5] Word not in *National Advocate*.
[6] *National Advocate*: "power," with the extract ending here. RC contains a non-authorial closing bracket at this point.

INTUS UT LUBET, FORIS UT MORIS: "in private do as you like, in public behave as is the custom."

To James P. Preston

SIR   Monticello May 28. 18.

The letter of the 20ᵗʰ with which you have honored me did not come to hand until yesterday. with mr Hassler I have not the pleasure of a personal acquaintance; but I have information entirely satisfactory of his scientific character. as an Astronomer and Mathematician he is certainly highly qualified; and the former commission you mention him to have held of Director of roads, bridges and canals in Switzerland, would raise a presumption of his possessing practical knolege also. whether his residence and employment in this country have enabled him to become familiar with it's natural resources, which often furnish us with unexpensive means of[1] doing what in Europe can be effected but at great cost, I am quite uninformed. if mr Hasler's practical talents should stand on as good evidence as those of his competitors, I have no doubt he must be far before them in Mathematical qualifications. I have the honor to salute your Excellency with great esteem and consideration.   TH: JEFFERSON

RC (Vi: RG 57, Board of Public Works, Applications for Position of Principal Engineer); addressed: "His Excellency Governor Preston Richmond"; franked; postmarked Charlottesville, 30 May; endorsed by Preston as a letter "respecting Mʳ Hasslers qualifications for Principal Engineers" received 1 June 1818. PoC (MHi); on verso of reused address cover of Wilson Cary Nicholas to TJ, 9 Mar. 1818; endorsed by TJ.

[1] Manuscript: "of of."

To Hugh Steel

Sir   Monticello May 28. 18.

Your favor of Apr. 12. came to hand on the 23^d instant. withdrawn by the effect of age, from the labors of correspondence to which that has rendered me unequal, I am able only to forward your letter and communication to a member of the American Philosophical society at Philadelphia. it is long since I resigned the office of their President, and Dr Wistar, who succeeded me is lately dead, and no successor yet appointed. I pray you to accept the assurance of my respect.

                                                       Th: Jefferson

PoC (MoSHi: TJC-BC); on verso of reused address cover of Alden Partridge to TJ, 24 Mar. 1817; at foot of text: "Doct^r Hugh Steel. Bellville"; endorsed by TJ.

On 1 Jan. 1819 the American Philosophical Society elected Robert Patterson to be Caspar Wistar's SUCCESSOR as president (APS, Minutes [MS in PPAmP]).

To Archibald Stuart

Dear Sir   Monticello May 28. 18.

Our fathers taught us an excellent maxim 'never to put off to to-morrow what you can do to day.' by some of their degenerate sons this has been reversed by never doing to-day what we can put off to tomorrow. for example I have been more than a year intending to send you a Merino ram, <u>next week,</u> and week after week it has been put off still to <u>next week,</u> which, like tomorrow, was never present. I now however send you one of full blood, born of my imported[1] ewe of the race called Aguerres, by the imported ram, of the Paular race which belonged to the Prince of peace, was sold by order of the Junta of Estremadura, was purchased and sent to me in 1810. by mr Jarvis our Consul at Lisbon. the Paular's are deemed the finest race in Spain for size & wool taken together, the Aguerres superior to all in wool, but small.—supposing the season with you has not yet given you peas, the opportunity has enticed me to send you a mess.

I have not yet communicated your hospitable message to mr Madison but shall soon have an opportunity of doing it. to my engagement I must annex a condition that in case of an adjournment to Charlottesville you make Monticello your head quarters. but in my opinion we should not adjourn at all, and to any other place rather than either of those in competition. I think the opinion of the legislature strongly implied in their avoiding both these places, and calling us to one between both. my own opinion will be against any adjournment, as long as we can get bread & water & a floor to lie on at the gap[2] & particularly against one Westwardly, because there we shall want <u>water</u>. but my information is that we shall be tolerably off at the Gap. that they have 40. lodging rooms and are now making ample preparations. a waggon load of beds has past thro' Charlottesville, which at that season however we shall not need. I will certainly however pay you a visit, probably on the day after our meeting (Sunday) as we shall not yet have entered on business. be so good as to present my respects to mrs Stewart and to be assured of my constant friendship

TH: JEFFERSON

RC (ViHi: Stuart Papers); addressed: "The honble Judge Stuart Staunton." PoC (MoSHi: TJC-BC); on verso of reused address cover of Giovanni Battista Fancelli to TJ, 11 Nov. 1817; endorsed by TJ.

For TJ's prior invocation of the EXCELLENT MAXIM, see his letters to Joel Barlow, 16 Apr. 1811, James Maury, 25 Apr. 1812, and Paul A. Clay, [ca. 12 July 1817]. The Spanish statesman Manuel de Godoy was known as the PRINCE OF PEACE.

[1] Preceding two words interlined in place of "an."
[2] Preceding four words interlined.

To John Vaughan

TH: JEFFERSON TO MR VAUGHAN.   Monticello May 28. 18.

The 4th of exchange for M[r] Appleton recieved in yours of May 14. happened to be overlooked by you, on endorsing, & is now returned for your signature, with a request to seal & forward under the cover by any opportunity. it is in fact only to make security more secure. mr Steel's papers are for communication to the society.

I thank you for the information respecting the competitions for the professorships, and will be still more thankful for the result of the moment which decides mr Cooper's destination. I salute you with great friendship & respect.

RC (PPAmP: Vaughan Papers); dateline at foot of text; addressed: "John Vaughan esquire Philadelphia"; franked. Enclosures: Hugh Steel to TJ, 12 Apr. 1818, and enclosure.

On this date TJ recorded in SJL that, under cover of this letter, he sent Thomas Appleton a 4TH OF EXCHANGE, not found, for $460.

From John Adams

Quincy May 29. 1818

As Holly is a Diamond of a Superiour Water, it would be crushed to pouder[1] by mountainous oppression in any other Country. Even in this, he is a light Shining in a dark place. His System is founded in the hopes of Mankind: but they delight more in their Fears. When will Men have juster Notions of the Universal eternal Cause? Then will rational Christianity prevail. I regrett Hollys Misfortune in not finding you, on his Account to whom an Interview with you would have been a lasting Gratification.

Waterhouses Pen "Labitur et labetur,." He has let it run on with too much fluency. I have not a tenth part of the Vivacity, Activity, Memory, or Promptitude and punctuality[2] in Correspondence[3] that he ascribes to me. I can answer but few of the Letters I receive, and those only with Short Scratches of the Pen.

I agree[4] with you that "it is difficult to say at what moment the Revolution began." In my Opinion it began as early as the first Plantation of the Country. Independence of Church and Parliament was a fixed Principle of our Predecessors in 1620 as it was of Sam. Adams and Chris. Gadsden in 1776. And Independence of Church and Parliament were always kept in View in this Part of the Country and I believe in most others. The Hierarchy and Parliamentary Authority[5] were dreaded and detested even by a Majority of professed Episcopalians.

I congratulate you on your "Canine Appetite for reading."[6] I have been equally voracious for Several Years and it has kept me alive.
It is policy in me to despize and abhor the "Writing Table" for it is a Bunch of Grapes out of reach; Had I your Eyes and Fingers I Should Scribble forever, such poor Stuff as you know I have been writting by fits and Starts for fifty or Sixty years without ever correcting or revising any thing.[7]

Helluo as I am, I hunger and thirst after what I Shall never See, Napolions Publication of the Report of his Institute of Cairo. Denons Volumes have excited an inextinguishable Curiosity for an unattainable Object.

Mr Coffee has been mentiond to me by my Son.[8] He will be welcome. But though Robin is alive he is not alive like to be. Mr Coffee must be very quik[9] or Robbin may die in his hand.

Mr Binon a French Artist from Lyons who has Studied eight years in Italy has lately taken my Bust. He appears to be an Artist and a Man of Letters, I let them do what they please[10] with my old head.

When We come to be cool in the future World, I think We cannot choose but Smile at the gambols of Ambition Avarice Pleasure Sport and Caprice here below. Perhaps We may laugh like the Angels in the French Fable. At a convivial repast of a Clubb of Choice Spirits of whom Gabriel and Michael were the most illustrious, after Nectar and ambrosia had Sett their hearts at Ease, they began to converse upon the Mechanique Cœleste. After discussing the Zodiack and the Constellations and the Solar System they condescended to this Speck of dirt the Earth, and remarked Some of its Inhabitants, The Lyon the Elephant the Eagle and even the Fidelity Gratitude and adroitness of the Dog. At last one of them recollected Man. What a fine Countenance! What an elegant figure! What Subtilty, Inginuity, Versatillity Agility! And above all, a rational Creature! At this the whole board broke out into a broad Ha! Ha! Ha![11] that resounded through the Vault of Heaven: exclaiming "Man a rational Creature"! How could any rational Being[12] even dream that Man was a rational Creature?

After all, I hope to meet my Wife and Friends, Ancestors and Posterity, Sages ancient and modern. I believe I could get over all my Objections to meeting Alec Hamilton and Tim Pick, if I could perceive[13] a Symptom of Sincere[14] Penitence in either.

My fatigued Eyes and Fingers command me very reluctantly to subscribe abruptly   JOHN ADAMS.

RC (DLC); addressed by Susanna Boylston Adams Clark (Treadway): "Thomas Jefferson Esqre Monticello. Virginia"; franked; postmarked Boston, 29 May; endorsed by TJ as received 9 June 1818 and so recorded in SJL. FC (Lb in MHi: Adams Papers).

LABITUR ET LABETUR: "glides, and will glide" (Horace, *Epistles*, 1.2.43, in Fairclough, *Horace: Satires, Epistles and Ars Poetica*, 264–5). HELLUO: "glutton" (*OED*). DENONS VOLUMES: Vivant Denon, *Voyage dans la Basse et la Haute Égypte, pendant les campagnes du Général Bonaparte*, 2 vols. (Paris, 1802; Sowerby, no. 3947). In the game of robin's alive (ROBIN IS ALIVE) a burning object is passed quickly from person to person (William Wells Newell, *Games and Songs of American Children* [1883], 135–6).

In accord with an 1818 resolution of the Massachusetts General Assembly, a public subscription financed the creation of a bust of Adams for display in Faneuil Hall in Boston. The French artist Jean Baptiste BINON duly executed the sculpture in marble. Benjamin A. Gould sent TJ a plaster copy in 1825 (Andrew Oliver, *Portraits of John and Abigail Adams* [1967], 179–87; Stein, *Worlds*, 228, 229; Gould to TJ, 14 July 1825; TJ to Gould, 5 Aug. 1825). MECHANIQUE CŒLESTE ("celestial mechanics"): "the branch of astronomy that deals with the mathematical theory of the motions of celestial bodies" (*OED*). TIM PICK: Timothy Pickering.

[1] FC: "powder."
[2] RC: "puntuality." FC: "punctuality."
[3] RC: "Correspondenc." FC: "correspondence."
[4] FC: "think."
[5] FC here adds "over."
[6] Omitted period at right margin editorially supplied.
[7] RC: "any. thing."
[8] Omitted period at right margin editorially supplied.
[9] FC: "quick."

[10] FC: "like."
[11] Preceding two words present in RC and added to FC by Adams.

[12] Preceding two words present in RC and added to FC by Adams.
[13] FC: "see."
[14] Word not in FC.

To James Le Ray de Chaumont

SIR   Monticello May 29. 18.

I recieved lately a copy of your Address to the Agricultural society of Jefferson county in New York, which presuming to have come from yourself, I beg leave here to return you my thanks for the pleasure derived from it's perusal. I see with great satisfaction these societies rising up, in different parts of the several states, and I expect from them much advantage to the agriculture of our country, by spreading generally a knolege of it's best processes. we have lately established one in the district in which I live, under the title of the 'Albemarle society of agriculture' of which mr Madison is President, and many of it's members are distinguished for correct and skilful practices in their farms. time will perhaps affiliate these district societies to a Central one in each state, and these again to a Central society for the United States, which will compleat their organisation. such selections of matter may then be made as may bring within moderate compass the most precious parts of the knolege of the whole. with my fervent wishes for the prosperity of your society accept the assurance of my great esteem and respect.

TH: JEFFERSON

RC (NjP: Andre deCoppet Collection); addressed: "J. Le Ray de Chaumont esquire Watertown Jefferson county. N.Y."; franked; postmarked Charlottesville, 30 May; endorsed by Le Ray de Chaumont. PoC (DLC); on verso of reused address cover of Francis W. Gilmer to TJ, 18 Mar. 1818; endorsed by TJ.

James Le Ray de Chaumont (1760–1840), farmer and land investor, was the son of Jacques Donatien Leray de Chaumont, a host and friend of Benjamin Franklin during the latter's service as United States minister plenipotentiary to France and a provider of essential military supplies and aid to the American cause during the Revolution. TJ was acquainted with both father and son during his stay in Paris, and the son acted as a

courier for letters and diplomatic correspondence when he came to the United States in 1785 to petition Congress for reimbursement for his father's services. While on that mission Le Ray de Chaumont was naturalized as a United States citizen, married an American, and joined a group of exiled French nobility who were speculating in land. The extensive landholdings he acquired in New York included two Jefferson County towns named for him, Leraysville (later Leray) and Chaumont. Le Ray de Chaumont divided his time thereafter between the United States and France, with his longest stay at his Leraysville mansion occurring between 1816 and 1832. James Monroe visited him there in 1817. Le Ray de Chaumont's friends and associates included Madame de Staël Holstein,

Gouverneur Morris, DeWitt Clinton, and Alexander Hamilton. A strong supporter of canals and turnpikes, from 1817–29 Le Ray de Chaumont also served as the first president of the Jefferson County Agricultural Society, and he was elected president of the New York State Agricultural Society before his departure for France in 1832. He died in France (J. L. Tierney, "James Donatien LeRay de Chaumont," United States Catholic Historical Society, *Historical Records and Studies* 15 [1921]: 55–69; NIC: James Le Ray de Chaumont Papers; Thomas J. Schaeper, *France and America in the Revolutionary Era: The Life of Jacques-Donatien Leray de Chaumont, 1725–1803* [1995], 335–7; Roger G. Kennedy, *Orders From France: The Americans and the French in a Revolutionary World, 1780–1820* [1989], 37, 39–40; *PTJ*, 8:54–5, 88–90, 90–1, 13:286–7; Leonard W. Labaree and others, eds., *The Papers of Benjamin Franklin* [1959–], esp. 28:239; Harold C. Syrett and others, eds., *The Papers of Alexander Hamilton* [1961–87], 26:40–3, 46–52, 53–4, 60–6; New York *Commercial Advertiser*, 28 Sept. 1816; Daniel Preston and others, eds., *The Papers of James Monroe* [2003–], 1:513–4).

The ADDRESS was Le Ray de Chaumont, *An Address, delivered at the meeting at the Agricultural Society of Jefferson County, December 29, 1817* (New York, 1818; Poor, *Jefferson's Library*, 6 [no. 270]), which opens by summarizing the proceedings of that day's meeting, including the election of DeWitt Clinton as an honorary member and a resolution to promote the use of domestic fabric by fining members who wear clothing made of foreign material five dollars per year; continues with Le Ray de Chaumont's presidential address outlining the purpose of the society, highlighting the benefits of the local climate and soil, calling on members "to take all proper measures for the advancement of agriculture" as the surest way to promote American freedom, happiness, morality, and wealth, and urging the "fair countrywomen of Jefferson County" to advance domestic manufactures; and concludes with the society's articles of association and by-laws, a table of agricultural premiums to be offered for 1818, a sketch of the proceedings of the meeting of 2 Mar. 1818, and letters from Clinton, John Adams, and others.

On 4 Feb. 1818 Le Ray de Chaumont sent Adams an earlier edition of his *Address* (Watertown, 1818) that lacks the appended material from March 1818 (MHi: Adams Papers). In his response dated Quincy, 12 Feb. 1818, Adams commented that "Thirty nine years ago, I little thought, I should live to see the heir apparent to the princely Palaces and gardens of Passy, my fellow citizen in the Republican wilderness of America, laying the foundation of more ample domains, and perhaps more splendid Palaces. I observed the motto of the Hotel de Valentinois, which I had then the honour to inhabit, 'Se sta bene non se move.'—'If you stand well, stand still.' but you have proved the maxim not to be infallible, and I rejoice in it" (FC in Lb in MHi: Adams Papers; printed in 2d ed. of Le Ray de Chaumont's *Address*, 17).

From Thomas Jordan

SIR   Baltimore 29th May 1818

On my arrival in town this morning I had the honour of receiving your very polite favour of 21st Instant, Covering ten Dollars, and Fifty Cents, being the amount of your subscription for the Emporium of Arts & Sciences due Kimber & Richardson of Philadelphia, in whose name I beg leave to return you my sincere, and gratefull thanks &

Remain Sir with every Respect Your most Obedient and humble Servant   THOS JORDAN

RC (DLC); at head of text: "Honourable Thomas Jefferson"; endorsed by TJ as received 9 June 1818 and so recorded in SJL; additional notation by TJ: "Newspapers."

Notes on Itch Lotion

[after 29 May 1818]

$$60^{grs} = 1. \text{ drachm}$$
$$\underline{8} \text{ drachms} = 1. \text{ oz}$$
$$480. \text{ grs} = 1. \text{ oz}$$
$$\underline{16} \text{ oz.} = 1. \text{ pint}$$
$$2880$$
$$\underline{480}$$
$$7680 = 1 \text{ pint}$$
$$\underline{3840}$$
$$11520 = 1\frac{1}{2} \text{ pint or } 24 \text{ oz.}$$
$$\tfrac{1}{12} \quad 960 = 2 \text{ oz.}$$

Cor. sub. 5 grs
Sal. Am. 10 grs
water   2. oz.

MS (MHi); entirely in TJ's hand; at foot of, and oriented upside-down to, RC of William H. Fitzhugh to TJ, 18 May 1818.

COR. SUB.: "corrosive sublimate" (mercuric chloride). SAL. AM.: "sal ammoniac" (ammonium chloride).

TJ composed this document no earlier than 29 May 1818, when he received the unrelated letter at the bottom of which he jotted these notes. He may have written them in connection with a painful infection on his buttocks contracted that summer at Warm Springs (*MB*, 2:1346).

TJ's calculations could derive from a recipe for "Itch Lotion" found on p. 312 of James Ewell, *The Planter's and Mariner's Medical Companion* (Philadelphia, 1807; Sowerby, no. 893): "Take of Corrosive sublimate, one drachm; Crude Sal Amoniac, two drachms; Water, one pint and a half. Mix." A recipe differing only in specifying one quart of water appears on p. 607 of the 5th ed. of Ewell's work, entitled *The Medical Companion* (Philadelphia, 1819; Poor, *Jefferson's Library*, 5 [no. 183]), a copy of which TJ received from the author late in 1819 (Ewell to TJ, 12 Oct. 1819; TJ to Ewell, 7 Nov. 1819).

To William Short

DEAR SIR   Monticello May 29. 18.

On the reciept of your favor of the 11th (which did not come to hand till the 23^d) I proceeded to examine my papers as to the information they might give you on the subject of your Green sea lands. the result I now send you, to wit, my original letter to Col° Newton, his answer, and an entry in my pocket Memorandum book which I found under the date of Nov. 21. 99. I am not able to say where I got the information of my letter to Col° Newton; but I have not a doubt of it's correctness, and think it highly probable I still possess what gave me the information itself, but not recollecting from whom it came, I do not know under what name to look for it in the immense mass of my papers. the letters inclosed however are fully sufficient to enable you to get to the source of your title. if mr Harvie executed a conveyance it must have been recorded either in the <u>county</u> court of Norfolk where the lands lay, or in the General court. if he did not execute a deed, his heirs are bound to do it, & certainly will not hesitate. if he executed a deed & that is lost, it is equally incumbent on them to execute a[1] deed of confirmation, which, on refusal, they would be decreed to do by a court of Chancery one of whose important functions is the reestablishment of lost title papers. but mr Harvie's sons are honorable men & will not put you to a suit in Chancery the delays and expences of which are interminable. your legal friend in Richmond cannot fail, from the letters now inclosed to trace & ascertain your title.   Our central College is likely to be adopted by the legislature as their University. our plan will call for 10. Professors, whom we are determined to procure of the first order of science in their respective lines which are procurable on either side of the Atlantic. I am named one of 24. Commissioners (one from each Senatorial district) who are to meet at Rockfish gap on the 1st of Aug. and to select and report to the legislature the most suitable place, on which the legislature are ultimately to decide. the expectation is that $\frac{2}{3}$ of the votes will be for the Central college, a mile above Charlottesville. after this meeting I shall pass the months of Aug. and Sep. in Bedford. I am still able to take that journey in an easy carriage; and indeed shall now go there within about 3. weeks. I ride also on horse back 5. or 6. miles every day, but I cannot walk further than my garden, and weaken very fast: and notwithstanding this increasing debility I enjoy perfect health. my wrist, the dislocation of which you remember in Paris, by it's stiffening renders writing slow and painful, and obliges me to place here the assurance of my constant & affectionate friendship & respect.

Th: Jefferson

RC (ViW: TJP). PoC (MHi); on reused address cover of David Gelston to TJ, 14 Mar. 1818; at foot of text: "Wm Short"; endorsed by TJ.

TJ here enclosed copies of his letter to Thomas Newton of 17 Oct. 1799, Newton's response of [23 Oct.] 1799, and TJ's

Memorandum Book entry of NOV. 21. 99 reading "Debit W. Short 33/9 5.D. pd. by G. Jefferson to the Auditor for taxes of his Green sea lands for 93.94.95.97" (*PTJ*, 31:216–7, 218; *MB* 2:1008).

[1] TJ here canceled "new."

From James Sloan

Baltimore, May, 29 1818.

Permit me, sir, to present you a copy of, "Rambles in Italy," as a[1] sincere though slight acknowledgement of the pleasure, and instruction I have derived from your Notes on Virginia, and as a testimony of my admiration, of your talent and accomplishment

I have the honour to remain with much respect yours

JA[s] SLOAN JUNR

RC (DLC); dateline at foot of text; endorsed by TJ as received 4 June 1818 and so recorded in SJL. RC (DLC); address cover only; with PoC of TJ to Joseph Dougherty, 6 Oct. 1818, on verso; addressed: "To His Excellency, Thomas Jefferson, Monticello, Virginia." Enclosure: [Sloan], *Rambles in Italy; in the Years 1816....17. By an American* (Baltimore, 1818; Poor, *Jefferson's Library*, 7 [no. 320]).

James Sloan (ca. 1786–1819), author and attorney, graduated from the College of New Jersey (later Princeton University) in 1805. Henry M. Brackenridge met him during a visit to Baltimore and described him as "the most accomplished young man" he encountered there. Sloan died in Baltimore (*Princeton Catalogue*, 117; Brackenridge, *Recollection of Persons and Places in the West* [2d ed.; 1868], 135–6; *Baltimore: Its History and its People* [1912], 2:113; Sloan to TJ, 4 July 1818; Philadelphia *Franklin Gazette*, 8 Apr. 1819).

[1] Manuscript: "a a."

From Horatio G. Spafford

Spa[fford's] Settlement, Venango Co.,
W. Pa., 5 Mo. 29, 1818.

RESPECTED FRIEND—

I take the liberty to enquire for thy health, & am anxious to learn if any of the seeds, with which I am stocking my Farms, would be acceptable on thine? I have lately obtained some very superior <u>oats</u>, from Russia, & some <u>summer wheat</u> & <u>Summer rye</u>; four or 5. varieties of <u>wheat</u>, from Europe & Africa, & some seed of the <u>Lupinella</u>, from Italy. I presume it is probable the most or all of these seeds may be in thy possession already, & many others, as valuable & rare: but if not, I should be glad to send small specimens, from any or all such as I have. I should also esteem it a favor to receive from thee any seeds that thou may have to spare, of kinds adapted to this climate. I hear much of the ruta baga, or Swedish turnip, as it is called in England, but am unable to procure any of the seeds. I am now wholly employed on my farms, & in opening roads, erecting mills, &c., forming a new Settlement in these vast forests. The land is handsome, well wooded & watered, & the soil good—the climate, delightful. Our situation is so wild, that we have to bring all our provisions 15 miles, & our task is [Severe] accordingly. I came here in December last, & have nearly got cleared for a crop, 12 acres, all the opening then is in sight.

With anxious wishes for the prolongation of thy valuable life, with health & happiness, I remain, very respectfully, thy friend,

HORATIO GATES SPAFFORD.

RC (MHi); dateline torn; one word illegible; endorsed by TJ as received 26 June 1818 and so recorded in SJL. RC (DLC); address cover only; with PoC of third page of TJ to William H. Crawford, 10 Nov. 1818, on verso; addressed: "Thomas Jefferson, LL.D. late President of the United States, Monticello, Va."; franked; postmarked Franklin, Pa., 6 June.

To James W. Wallace

DEAR SIR   Monticello May 29. 19. [1818]

On the Suddenness of the request in the moment of your departure for a keep-sake in the style of Gen¹ Washington's & General Braddock's razors, I could not at once recollect any thing exactly suitable. it has since occurred that the travelling razor case which I have been in the habit of using, might be a deposit for those razors, and make a compact thing of the whole, and as it is light I send it by mail for your acceptance with the assurance of my great esteem and respect.

TH: JEFFERSON

PoC (DLC: TJ Papers, 215:38423); misdated; on verso of a reused address cover from John Barnes to TJ; at foot of text: "Doctʳ Wallace"; endorsed by TJ as a letter of 29 May 1818 and so recorded in SJL.

From Thomas A. Digges

Dᴿ SIR.   Washington 30ᵗʰ¹ May 1818 Tennisons Hotel

A variety of untoward incidents, to which we are all doomd, has for the last three summers rebutted my attempts to visit You and our good friends at Montpellier, and I was peculiarly vexd in Octoʳ last that I could not by a proferrd seat in Mʳ Bagots Barouche to Mʳ Madisons & to have partaken of the pleasurable scenes they enjoyd there and of which they yet speak in rapturous delight:—The Minister haveing concievd a quite different character of The <u>President</u> to what He had found in the lively converse & abilities of The <u>Man</u>.   I have enjoyd his Mʳ Bˢ descriptions of our friend very much, and altho he repeats His regret for his non visit to Montecello, I have yet had no clue <u>as to why</u> it was not so contriv'd as to His seeing You.

My mother <u>Atwoods</u> family migrating from the close vicinity of Lord
Bagots seat in Staffordshire and my frequent summers visits in it to
Sir F^s Burdetts, Lord Littletons &c^a &c^a gave me an oppertunity of
knowing more of that Shire & the central parts of England with y^e
Elder Inhabitants of it, has causd much laughter & fun between us—
He has uniformly been much liked <u>here</u>, and M^rs B (of the Welling-
ton Irish Stock) is all affability & attention—very different from the
Dame Merry, who it seems yearns & is very anxious to get back to
Her former elevation.

Your neighbour Mr Nelson (who was all the last session a fellow-
liver in this hotel <u>where I keep a room</u>) got hither last night from a
detour round by winchester, and lost by a few hours only, the seeing
The President & party gone on the survey of the lower Chesapeake,
or, I guess the Judge would have made one of the party Voyagers
from Annapolis.—On my consulting him I have concluded to send
You to the care of Mr Faris the Coach & mail contractor at Fredricks-
burgh, a peck or somewhat more of English-growth Spring Sown²
seed Wheat.   I can get to Faris's without trouble or expence p^r
the dayly going steamboat, (the only vehicle I can at present travel
in from a fistula compla^t) and it will find safer conveyance either by
coach or waggon by boxing it in preferance to a bag too apt to rub or
get cut in ye common conveyances.

I got some of this spring-growth seed wheat rather too late for trial
this year although I have put a quart of it on trial in a gardenbed, &
reserve the bulk for next spring. I have seen at times a great portion
of spring sown wheat at the Mark-lane London Market sold at equivalent price's with their other common wheats and have also observd its
utility & commendations in Gloucestershire, Kent, mr Cokes of Hol-
kum in Norfolk, the Isle of Thanet &c^a and have every belief it would
answer well with us which I hear it does do in the state of N York.

I am determind to give it a fair trial from my remembrance in early
life, (tho I am now only <u>77</u>) that it was a very rare experiment in this
quarter to sow wheat in the fall! May it not in some measure remove
the Evil of the <u>Fly</u>? for although my home farm at F Warburton (all
but ruind by a lawless soldiery & the Fort workmen) being on a high
peninsula between two Side creeks & the River in front towards M^t
Vernon and never afflicted wth the fly, yet the neighbouring wheat
feilds are very often destroyd by it.—   The Seed which I send is
of a medium sizd excellent grain, rather dark in colour & weighs 63^lb
p^r struck bush^l.

The kind of wheat <u>now</u> generally used hereabouts (for we have lost
that of the <u>early white</u> small graind of better weight) is of the Red or

golden stemmd colour & is very apt to loose its seed in handling if not cut a little unripe.

I hope You continue to enjoy good health—accept my kindest & most grateful remembrances & good wishes & with compliments to all your amiable Family I remain   Yr ob^t &^ca &^ca

THO^s A DIGGES

Since writing the above, I am pressd to do an act of service to a very deserving and respected Clerk in The Treasury office—Mr Columbus Fenwick the only Son & representative of Mr Joseph Fenwick whom You may have known as the <u>French</u> partner of Genl Jno Mason, many years our Consul at Bordeaux and whose numerous family, highly respectable, are of the stock of our first setlers in St Marys Co^y Maryland.—It is Sir (if You know Mr Geo washington Campbell our lately appointed minister to Russia) to give my friend Mr Columbus Fenwick a recommendatory to Mr Campbell as a Secretary of Legation.

When Mr Campbell, (with^3 whom I am very intimate) left this, to return hither in a few weeks, leaving his family in Mrs Wilsons, to proceed to His Embarkation at Boston in the Guerriere^4 frigate; He had proferrd to the subject of this solicitation^5 the takeing Him into His family as a private Secretary, He Mr Campbell <u>then</u> nor anyone here supposing but that the Resident <u>Secretary of Legation</u> was Still to be continued at Petersburgh: But it seems He has resignd, and that Mr Pinkney just now announcd to be arrivd at Annapolis and there waiting to meet The President & party (who this morning left the City for embarking from thence to view the lower waters of the Chesapeak) Has left his Son, a very promising Young man tho yet in his teens, as temporary <u>Sec^y of Legation</u> at Petersburgh.

Mr Columbus Fenwick, although more Independant than Clerks generally are, from the acquirements of His Father who maintains a most honorable & fair name as well as the attainment of an independant fortune, could not prudently yeild up His present Salary for the uncertainty of what m^r Campbell could afford to give Him.

I have always noticd and regarded M^r C Fenwick on account of His acquirements and Gentlemanly intercourses within the first circles here and particularly with all the foreign ministers from a full knowlege of the French & Spanish languages; and nothing but such would induce my presumeing thus upon your time.

Any item from You to Mr Campbell might probably produce a mutual benefit to both, and gratify the Father, whom I have ever respected as an honorable minded and well directed man & good Citizen of these States meaning very shortly to fix and remain therein—

RC (DLC); at foot of text: "Tho[s] Jefferson Esq[r] Montecello"; endorsed by TJ as received 4 June 1818 and so recorded in SJL; notation by TJ on verso: "his indisposn Bagot. wheat Fenwick."

Francis Columbus Fenwick (1793–1858) was appointed United States consul at Nantes in 1821 and served there until 1838. He died in Bordeaux (Richard K. MacMaster, ed., "The Tobacco Trade with France: Letters of Joseph Fenwick, Consul at Bordeaux, 1787–1795," *Maryland Historical Magazine* 60 [1965]: 54; *JEP*, 3:257, 260, 5:186 [21 Dec. 1821, 2 Jan. 1822, 28 Jan. 1839]; *New York Herald*, 14 Mar. 1858).

Charles Bagot, the British minister plenipotentiary to the United States, and his wife, Mary Charlotte Anne Wellesley-Pole Bagot, visited James and Dolley Madison at MONTPELLIER between 12 and 20 Oct. 1817 (Madison, *Papers, Retirement Ser.*, 1:123). M[r] FARIS: Hazelwood Farish. Digges would not turn 77 until July 1819. Fort Warburton (F WARBURTON), later Fort Washington, was on land adjacent to Warburton Manor, Digges's family estate in Maryland.

Later in 1818 William Pinkney's son Charles Pinkney became secretary of the United States legation at Saint Petersburg in place of William R. King, the RESIDENT SECRETARY OF LEGATION (*JEP*, 3:45, 46, 143, 150 [20, 23 Apr. 1816, 27, 30 Nov. 1818]).

[1] Reworked from "29th."
[2] Preceding two words interlined.
[3] Omitted opening parenthesis editorially supplied.
[4] Manuscript: "Gurriere."
[5] Manuscript: "solicition."

From Patrick Gibson

SIR   Richmond 30th May 1818—

Our banks being still unwilling to draw upon the North on the receipt of your favor of the 13th Ins[t]—I wrote to Mess[rs] LeRoy & Bayard to draw upon me for the amount due by you which they have done say $2387.69 which is placed to your debit.[1] I have not received from M[r] Robertson the money you mentiond in your letter of the 21st ult[o]— M[r] Thomas E Randolph has sent down by his own boat, Twenty seven barrels flour on your account, which have been ducked by the breaking of the boat, I have not yet been able to dispose of them, but shall do so, as soon as possible—I inclose you two notes for your signature—The Virg[a] bank is curtailing 25 p[r] C[t] on perm[t] paper—I shall however put in yours for the full amount, and reduce my own for the present—

With much respect I am Your ob[t] Serv[t]   PATRICK GIBSON

1st June. I have sold your 27 bls: damag'd flour to S J. Crump at 6½$—I got the Inspector to examine the quality, who said that if sound he could not have passed them for more than x mid[gs] & fine—

RC (MHi); between dateline and salutation: "Thomas Jefferson Esq[re]"; endorsed by TJ as received 9 June 1818 and so recorded in SJL. Enclosures not found.

X MID[GS]: "cross middlings."

[1] Omitted period at right margin editorially supplied.

From Archibald Stuart

DEAR SIR   Staunton 30th May—18

I have to acknowledge with many thanks The rec^t of a fine look-ing Merino Ram by your servant and I am really ashamed of myself for not having saved you the Trouble of sending him—He will be a Valuable acquisition to me & my neighbours—

The peas you were so good as to send us are a great rarity, we shall have none of our own for a fortnight to come—

The Legislature I presume in directing The Com^{rs} to Meet at Rockfish Gap were desirous of avoiding any expression of their Opin-ion as to the Scite of the University but after the Com^{rs} have met there can be as little objection to their adjourning even to one of the places in Competition (should their convenience require it) as finally to select it for the Scite of the U—   I hope the proprietor of the house at the gap will not put himself to much expense on our Account as I feel confident That all he can do will not answer the purpose & that we shall be compelled to adjourn elsewhere—

Gen^t Opposed to Staunton as the Scite of ye U. ought not to object to an adjournment to that place particularly as the want of <u>pure water</u> there may add great weight to the Considerations in favor of its rival places—I am therefore for adjourning to Staunton on the evening of our meeting; & I believe it is the Genl expectation that you & Mr Madison will be prepared to submit such a report to our body as we ought to adopt—

I send you a Specimen of ye Cheese we made last summer—

adieu I am yours most sincerely   ARCH^D STUART

RC (MHi); endorsed by TJ as received 31 May 1818 and so recorded in SJL. RC (DLC); address cover only; with PoC of TJ to Honoré Julien, 6 Oct. 1818, on verso; addressed: "The hon^{ble} Thomas Jefferson Esqr Monticello."

To William H. Fitzhugh

SIR   Monticello May 31. 18.

In answer to the enquiries of your letter of the 18th as to the com-munications between Georgetown ferry & this quarter, I must observe there are three general routes practised, the lower one by Freder-icksburg, the upper one by Fauquier C.H. and a middle one by Ste-phensbg. this last is many miles shortest, much the levellest, and being the particular one enquired after in your letter, I shall confine myself to it. according to Triplett's survey

from Georgetown ferry by the way of Centerville to Gaines's[1] tavern are	$31\frac{3}{4}$ miles;
but by Lane's, Ravensworth, Yates's ford & Songster's are but	$19\frac{4}{10}$ miles
as measured by myself by an accurate machine to my carriage; making a difference	$12\frac{1}{3}$ miles.
from Gaines's[2] tavern to Stephensburg, by Triplett's survey	$38\frac{1}{3}$ miles
from Stephensburg to Orange C.H. as measured by myself	$21\frac{44}{100}$
from Orange C.H. to Charlottesville, nearly all measured by myself	$\underline{30.}$
	$89\frac{3}{4}$

the mail stage road from Washington thro' the great trading towns is necessary for commerce, but another thro' the middle of the state below & parallel with the mountains is wanting for the body of the country, and the route I have noted is precisely that wanted, which continued on to N. Orleans would place that within 1000. miles of Washington, thro' a level country, and always clear of the mountains. but these are objects for the rising generation, and not for that going off the stage. Accept the assurances of my great respect.

TH: JEFFERSON

PoC (MHi); on verso of reused address cover to TJ; at foot of text: "W. H. Fitzhugh. esq."; endorsed by TJ. Tr (DNA: RG 77, CNR); filed with Alexander Macomb to Board of Engineers, 24 Dec. 1824.

For TRIPLETT'S SURVEY (MS in DLC: TJ Papers, 233:41695), see TJ to Richard Fitzhugh, 26 Mar. 1805 (MHi). The ACCURATE MACHINE with which TJ measured mileage using his CARRIAGE was his odometer (Stein, *Worlds*, 362–3).

[1] Tr: "Baines's."
[2] Tr: "Baines's."

From Caleb Atwater

SIR,   Circleville, Ohio June 2nd 1818.

Attatched to the Philosopher whom I address from my earliest years, permit me to lay before you, a letter addressed to President Monroe concerning the antiquities in the West. Perhaps I am committing an error, by intruding on that dignified repose, which by your distinguished services in the cause of literature, your country and of the freedom and happiness of mankind you so richly merit. To add any thing to the honors which have been so justly awarded to you by your country and the enlightened, the virtuous and good of all civilized countries, is beyond my humble powers.

The letter which accompanies this note, has not been answered by him to whom it was originally addressed, perhaps never will be, but it was written for the eye of the enlightened part of the community and as one of them, I ask your opinion of it and the opinions advanced in it, whenever you find the leisure to do so.

I have lately written an essay on the prairies and barrens of the west, which is now in the hands of the printer for publication in Prof. Silliman's Journal. I have also written an essay on the prevailing currents of air in this country, which will also appear in that Journal, in which I have maintained doctrines taught by you many years since, on that subject. Some ignorant pretenders to science, had controverted them but I have supported your theory as to our climate, by bringing forward new facts and additional considerations, all which you will see in due time.

I am now writing Notes on Ohio in the manner of yours on Virginia. I do not thus entitle my work because I deem myself capable of writing any thing which shall equal your immortal work, but because under that humble and unassuming title I can write what I please. Any hints from you, if your time leisure and circumstances permit, concerning my intended publication, will be thankfully received and gratefully acknowledged.

My letter on our antiquities is translated into the German language and will be sent across the Atlantic and published on the continent of Europe. I am shortly about to write a memoir on the Geological formation of this part of the American continent which will probably be published in Silliman's Scientific Journal to which it is already pledged. I have no favorite theories on any of these subjects to establish, but intend to confine myself to a statement of facts, deducing therefrom only such conclusions as necessarily follow.

Without books and separated as I am from the society of learned individuals, I need assistance on many interesting subjects concerning which, did not your years and other and higher avocations probably forbid it, I should ask you for information. As it is I forbear and beg that you would pardon this intrusion on your repose and that you would accept my highest reverence for your talents, as well as highest esteem for your many virtues.   Your very obed^t hum^b serv^t

CALEB ATWATER.

P.S. A stone which I take to be the Yu stone of Tartary and China is now in my possession. It is in all respects similar to the one found in the mound at Chillicothe and described by me in my communication to Pres^t Monroe, except the one I have is manufactured from a species of marble like the Italian. I have several stone axes which were found in our tumuli, a tooth of the mammoth called mastodon, which was dug out of a salt well, a great distance below a stratum of rock very hard but of the secondary kind, imbedded in which were found many organic remains. Our highest rocks are all of them oceanic, those in our lower grounds are fluviatic. The former contain the fossil remains of marine shells and anima[ls] [. . .] the latter contain the fossil remains of she[lls] & animals, such as our ponds, lakes rivers contain at this time. Your's truly   C.A.

RC (DLC); damaged at seal; addressed: "His Excellency Tho: Jefferson Esq. late President of the United States Monticello Virginia"; franked; endorsed by TJ as received 17 June 1818 and so recorded in SJL. Enclosure: Atwater to James Monroe, Circleville, 1 Jan. 1818, describing the ancient fortifications and earthen mounds of Ohio and speculating on the reasons these earthworks were constructed and the origins of their builders (*American Monthly Magazine and Critical Review* 2 [1818]: 333–6).

Caleb Atwater (1778–1867), attorney, public official, and author, was a native of North Adams, Massachusetts, who graduated from Williams College in 1804. After working as a teacher in New York City and training as a Presbyterian minister, Atwater was admitted in 1809 to the New York bar. A business failure caused him to move in 1815 to Circleville, Ohio, where he practiced law and pursued his interest in local antiquities and earthworks. Atwater served one term in the Ohio House of Representatives, 1821–22. In that office and thereafter he promoted education and internal improvements. Following an unsuccessful run by Atwater for the United States House of Representatives and a short-lived newspaper editorship, in 1829 President Andrew Jackson appointed him as a commissioner to conduct negotiations with the Winnebago Indians. A treaty was successfully concluded, and Atwater drew on his experiences in his *Remarks Made on a Tour to Prairie du Chien* (1831). His numerous publications also include a volume of collected *Writings of Caleb Atwater* (1833) and *A History of the State of Ohio, Natural*

and Civil (1838). Atwater died in Circleville (*ANB*; *DAB*; Clement L. Martzolff, "Caleb Atwater," in Ohio Archaeological and Historical Society, *Publications* 14 [1905]: 247–71; Calvin Durfee, *Williams Biographical Annals* [1871], 250–1; Madison, *Papers, Pres. Ser.*, 2:138–9; Jackson, *Papers*, esp. 5:421–2, 7:43–7).

Atwater's essays on THE PRAIRIES AND BARRENS OF THE WEST and THE PREVAILING CURRENTS OF AIR were dated by him 28 May and 23 July 1818 and appeared in the *American Journal of Science* 1 (1818–19): 116–25 and 266–86, respectively. TJ had discussed the prevailing winds MANY YEARS SINCE in his *Notes on the State of Virginia* (*Notes*, ed. Peden, 76–7). Atwater's LETTER ON OUR ANTIQUITIES was published as a "Description of the Antiquities discovered in the State of Ohio and other Western States" in American Antiquarian Society, *Transactions and Collections* 1 (1820): 105–267, and large portions were excerpted or summarized in translation, with inadequate authorial attribution, in Friedrich Wilhelm Assall and Franz Joseph Mone, eds., *Nachrichten über die früheren Einwohner von Nordamerika und ihre Denkmäler* (1827), 1–81.

In his 1 Jan. 1818 letter to James Monroe, Atwater described the stone FOUND IN THE MOUND AT CHILLICOTHE as a three-inch-long pendant of black marble, "exactly such a one as the Emperor of China and the highest grades of his officers now wear around their necks" (*American Monthly Magazine* 2 [1818]: 334–5).

[1] Omitted period at right margin editorially supplied.

From John Barnes

Dear Sir— George Town Co^a 4^h June 1818

lest you should not have noticed the inclosed, curious dispute at Soleure—respecting the late, venerable dec^d Genl Kosciusko, of which probably you have—or may soon expect to learn, from his Relative or Confidential friends I judge it proper to inclose it, for your Goverment

most Respectfully & sincerely
I am Sir Your most Obed^t serv^t JOHN BARNES,

RC (MHi); at foot of text: "Thomas Jefferson Esqr Monticello"; endorsed by TJ as received 9 June 1818 and so recorded in SJL.

Barnes presumably enclosed a clipping from the Washington *Daily National Intelligencer* of 4 June 1818 that described a CURIOUS DISPUTE "respecting the possession of the remains of the venerated patriot General Kosciusko. The Prince Tablonowsky arrived at Soleure on the 16th ult. in order to claim the body, for the purpose of its receiving funeral honors in Poland, when the General's executor unexpectedly protested against the removal, alleging that Koskiusko had expressly desired to be buried with simplicity, and had chosen Switzerland for the interment of his remains. Thus the affair appears to rest for the present." The Washington paper claimed to take its report from the London *Courier*, but it actually appeared in at least two other London newspapers, the *Morning Chronicle* and *Morning Post*, both 17 Apr. 1818 and both misspelling the name of Prince Jablonowski. Within a few days the British press reported that any such dispute had been resolved and that Tadeusz Kosciuszko's remains were on their way to Kraków (London *Courier*, 23 Apr. 1818).

From William King (of South Carolina)

Sir, South Carolina, Greenville District. June 4th 1818.

some time past, I ventured to write to you on a subject that may perhaps be of great utility to the commercial world; but have receiv'd no answer. It is almost with a trembling hand, that I write a second time: the dread of not being noticed by one of the first Men in the united States, intimidates my mind. But the nature of the case induces the measure. If not mistaken, I have discovered a method for finding the Longitude at Sea, which differs from all others that have been in Use. A method plain & easy, in which, both the Longitude & Lattitude may be found by the same observation: and has nothing to do with the equation of time in the calculation.

Mr Samuel Farrow (formerly a Member of Congress) advised me, to write to President Jefferson; & send a Copy of s^d Plan, for his persual.

I who am a native of Virginia, (&¹ in sentiment a real American) most earnestly request & desire that you would notice this communication;

& that you will pleas to write, & give me leave to send your excelency a Copy in manuscript; for your persual. & you will greatly oblidge, Sir, one that sincerly wishes your happiness & prosperity through life.

WILLIAM KING

N.B. The above mentioned discovery has been made after intense study for years.

RC (DLC); endorsed by TJ as received 28 June 1818 and so recorded in SJL. RC (MHi); address cover only; with PoC of TJ to Patrick Gibson, 3 Nov. 1818, on recto and verso; addressed: "Thomas Jefferson Esq′ State of Virginia, Monteselo"; stamped; postmarked Spartanburg Court House, 9 June.

[1] Omitted opening parenthesis editorially supplied.

From André Thoüin

MONSIEUR ET CHER CORRESPONDANT   Paris le 5 Juin 1818

J'ai eu l'honneur de vous faire passer en février d[erl] au moyen de Mr Beasly, consul des Etats unis d'amerique au havre de grace, mon envoi annuel de Semences. Il était composé de 73 Espèces differentes qui m'ont parues manquer à votre collection et devoir vous être agréables. J'y ai Joint comme de coutume une liste de nos desiderata et quelques brochures que J'ai cru devoir vous intéresser. Je desire que cet envoi vous Soit parvenu en bon état qu'il vous ait fait plaisir et que vous m'en accusiez la reception en même tems que celle de ce paquet.

Il renferme une instruction rédigée par les professeurs du museum d'histoire naturelle de france pour Ses correspondants dabord et essentiellement, ensuite pour les voyageurs et enfin pour les Employés du Gouvernement dans Ses colonies et les autres parties du monde; cette brochure vous donnera une idée de nos collections tant en productions de la nature vivante que morte qui, Sont réunies dans nos Jardins, dans les Serres, dans notre ménagerie et dans nos galeries d'histoire naturelle. Si vous trouvéz quelques objets n'importe dans quel regne qui manquent à nos dépots et que vous puissiez nous envoyer ils Seront reçus avec plaisir; votre nom Sera placé Sur les étiquettes fixées à ces objets qui seront déposés dans nos Galeries d'instruction publique, afin d'associer les nombreux naturalistes de toutes les parties du monde qui les fréquentent, à notre Juste reconnaissance. de plus nous vous offrons, Monsieur, de vous procurer en Echange des productions dont vous pourréz nous enrichir, celles de notre pays ou de tout autre que nous avons doubles et qui manquent à votre Collection Soit particulière, Soit publique. c'est ainsi qu'on peut sans s'appauvrir, et même en S'enrichissant mutuellement propager les

Elémens des connaissances exactes qui doivent tourner au profit et au bonheur de l'humanité.

Je vous recommande, Monsieur, de prendre en considération ces Echanges dont L'objet étant d'unir les Savants par de nouveaux rapports peut concourir au grand œuvre de lier plus intimement les hommes entre Eux et de contribuer par ce moyen à la découverte des principes de la meilleure organisation Sociale, but vers le quel tendent tous les peuples Européens.

Agréez Je vous prie, Monsieur et Venerable correspondant mes Salutations tres respectueuses   A. Thoüin

EDITORS' TRANSLATION

SIR AND DEAR CORRESPONDENT   Paris 5 June 1818

Last February I had the honor of sending you my annual shipment of seeds through Mr. Beasley, consul of the United States at Le Havre. It contained 73 different species that I thought might be both lacking from your collection and pleasing to you. As usual I included a list of our desiderata and a few brochures that I believed would interest you. I hope that this shipment has reached you in good shape, that it pleased you, and that you will acknowledge both its receipt and that of the present parcel.

It contains the instructions of the professors of the Muséum d'Histoire Naturelle de France, written first and principally for their correspondents, next for travelers, and finally for government employees in the colonies and other parts of the world. This brochure will give you an idea of our collections, which consist of animate and inanimate natural productions assembled in our gardens, greenhouses, menagerie, and natural history galleries. If you find that you could send us any object, from any kingdom of nature, that our collection is lacking, it will be received with pleasure. Your name will be placed on the tags affixed to these objects, which will be deposited in our galleries of public instruction in order to allow the numerous naturalists visiting from all around the world to join in our justifiable gratitude to you. Furthermore, Sir, in exchange for the products with which you might enrich us, we offer to obtain for you those of our country, or any other, of which we have duplicates and which your collections, either private or public, might lack. In this way one can, without impoverishing oneself, and even while enriching one another, propagate the elements of accurate knowledge that may benefit and increase the happiness of humanity.

Sir, I recommend that you take into consideration these exchanges, the purpose of which is to unite scholars through new relationships that may, in turn, contribute to the great work of connecting men more closely to one another and thus aid in the discovery of the best principles of social organization, a goal toward which all Europeans aim.

Please accept, Sir and venerable correspondent, my very respectful salutations   A. Thoüin

RC (DLC); on printed letterhead of the "Administration du Muséum d'Histoire Naturelle, au Jardin du Roi"; at foot of first page: "M. Th. Jefferson Correspondant de l'Institut, de la Societé centrale d'agriculture, du Museum d'histoire Naturelle de france &c. a Monti cello en virginie, Etats unis d'amerique"; endorsed by TJ as received 11 Sept. 1818 and so recorded in SJL. Translation by Dr. Genevieve Moene. Enclosure: *Instruction pour les Voyageurs et pour les Employés dans les Colonies, sur la manière de recueillir, de conserver et d'envoyer les Objets d'Histoire Naturelle. Rédigée sur l'invitation de Son*

Excellence le Ministre de la Marine et des Colonies, par l'Administration du Muséum Royal d'Histoire Naturelle (Paris, 1818; Poor, *Jefferson's Library*, 7 [no. 303]; TJ's copy in MBPLi). Enclosed in David Bailie Warden to TJ, 13 July 1818.

[1] Preceding three words interlined.

From William Plumer

DEAR SIR,   Epping (NH) June 7. 1818

Permit me to enclose to you a copy of my message to the legislature at their present session—& to assure you that I am with much respect & esteem

Sir,
your friend & servant   WILLIAM PLUMER

RC (MHi); at foot of text: "Hon Thomas Jefferson Monticello V^a"; endorsed by TJ as received 20 June 1818 and so recorded in SJL. Enclosure: Plumer, *Message from His Excellency The Governor of New-Hampshire, To The Legislature, June 4, 1818* ([Concord?, 1818]; probably Poor, *Jefferson's Library*, 11 [no. 689]), summarizing his recommendations for the new legislative session; calling for reforms in the judicial system, such as allowing the superior court "exclusive jurisdiction of all *real actions*" and "original concurrent jurisdiction of all *personal actions*, where the sum demanded in damages shall be fifty dollars or more" (pp. 4–5); encouraging repeal of the law allowing the superior court to review civil cases and adoption of laws to limit "small vexatious suits" (p. 5); suggesting reform of the laws on debtor imprisonment in order to curtail the costs associated with such actions; highlighting the need for an annual court session in "some central and convenient part of the State" (p. 9); proposing the prohibition of lotteries not authorized by the legislature; requesting more stringent laws to insure accurate militia rolls and asking for a requirement that the cloth used in manufacturing uniforms be of "*American manufacture*" (p. 10); championing prison reform and noting that he will submit to the legislature several pamphlets on the subject sent him by Jeremy Bentham; and reporting that an advance of six thousand dollars from the United States Treasury for "services performed during the late war" has been paid into the state treasury (p. 12).

On 28 July 1818 Plumer sent a copy of the enclosed address to James Madison, noting that it was his "*last* public message" to the New Hampshire legislature, as he planned to retire from office the following June (Madison, *Papers, Retirement Ser.*, 1:318–9).

From LeRoy, Bayard & Company

SIR   Newyork June 8 1818.

We have been honor'd with your valued favor of the 13^h ult^o and on the 23^d ult^o we valued upon M. Patrick Gibson, as directed by him, \$2387.69.—@ 1 d. S^t being for

The principal of your bond to Mess N & J & R Van Staphorst

     \$1000.—with Interest to the 1 day of January 1816   2083.20

    Interest from 1 Jan^r 1816 to 7^h June 1818   <u>304.49.</u>

There then only remains the 3^d bond for \$2083.20 with Interest from January 18<u>16</u>.

Enclosed you will please to find the Second Bond receipted.

We have the honor to remain with utmost respect & consideration Sir Your obed^t Sts   LEROY BAYARD & Co

RC (DLC); in the hand of a representative of LeRoy, Bayard & Company; at foot of text: "The Honorable Thomas Jefferson Monticello"; endorsed by TJ as received 15 June 1818 and so recorded in SJL. Enclosure: bond of TJ to the firm of van Staphorst & Hubbard, 26 Mar. 1797, one of two TJ enclosed to van Staphorst & Hubbard in a letter of 27 Mar. 1797, and printed there (*PTJ*, 29:330–1; additional PrC in DLC: TJ Papers, 101:17338–9, entirely in TJ's hand, lacking signatures of witness, justice, and county clerk, with unfilled blanks for names and date in attestation, lacking docket).

From Peter S. Du Ponceau

DEAR SIR   Philadelphia 9th June 1818

I have the honor of enclosing to you the Prospectus of the first Volume of our Historical Transactions now in the press. You will see by it that your <u>Alumni</u> are not idle, & you will, no doubt, rejoice in the good effects of the encouragement which you have constantly given to our Society, & particularly to this Committee, who Still solicit the continuation of your patronage.

I have the honor to be With the greatest respect Dear Sir Your most obed^t hum^l serv^t PETER S. DU PONCEAU

RC (DLC); at head of text: "Thomas Jefferson, Esqr"; endorsed by TJ as received 20 June 1818 and so recorded in SJL.

Prospectus for Transactions of the Historical and Literary Committee of the American Philosophical Society

[ca. 9 June 1818]

IN THE PRESS,

AND WILL BE PUBLISHED IN THE COURSE OF THE PRESENT YEAR,

BY ABRAHAM SMALL, NO. 112 CHESNUT STREET, PHILADELPHIA,

TRANSACTIONS

OF THE

Historical and Literary Committee of the American Philosophical Society,
Held at Philadelphia for promoting Useful Knowledge.

VOL. I.

ABOUT three years ago a permanent Committee of the American Philosophical Society was established, for the special purpose of promoting Historical Knowledge and General Literature. From the first moment of their institution, this Committee have been assiduously engaged in preparing and collecting memoirs, original letters, state papers, and other[1] documents, to serve as materials for the HISTORY OF THE UNITED STATES and of the STATE OF PENNSYLVANIA, and they have already on hand as much as will make up several interesting volumes, which they mean to publish successively, together with the results of their future labours and researches, for the information of their fellow-citizens, and the dissemination of Useful Knowledge.

Although this Publication, from its nature, will be essentially miscellaneous, the Publisher understands that the Committee have determined to dedicate each of their volumes, as much as possible, to a particular branch of the General Subject. For this reason, the volume now about to be published, will be composed entirely of matter relating to the Indian Nations of this part of North America. These Aborigines of our Country are fast decreasing in numbers, and will in time either be amalgamated with us by civilisation, or otherwise disappear by the operation of causes which cannot be controlled; we should, therefore, avail ourselves of all the opportunities which we now have, of becoming more intimately acquainted with the manners, customs, languages, and with every thing that relates to a People, who, for so many centuries before us, possessed the whole of the country which we inhabit.

The volume we are now about to present to the Public, will consist of:

No. I.—An Historical Account of the Indian Nations who once inhabited Pennsylvania and the neighbouring States; by the Reverend JOHN HECKEWELDER, of Bethlehem, a Member of the Historical Committee, and for many years a Missionary of the Society of the United Brethren among the *Lenni Lenape*, or *Delaware Indians*.

This Historical Account will form the greatest part of the present volume, which will consist of 450 to 500 pages octavo. The Author, by a residence of between 30 and 40 years among the Indians, has had the opportunity of acquiring a perfect knowledge of their manners, customs, habits, and language; and the Publisher thinks he may safely assert that his work will be found highly curious and interesting. It is divided into chapters, and contains not only an account of the traditions of these People respecting their own history before and since the arrival of the Europeans on this Continent, but the fullest details that have ever been given on the subject of their Religion, Education, Manners, Character, Usages, Opinions, and Habits;—the whole illustrated by a great number of Characteristic Anecdotes.

Much as has already been written on the subject of the Indian Nations of America, it will be found, from the perusal of *Mr. Heckewelder's* work, that much yet remains to be known respecting them. The Indians are here exhibited in a new and interesting point of view—such as they were before they became contaminated by European vices.

No. II.—A Correspondence between the *Rev. Mr. Heckewelder* and the Secretary of the Historical Committee, on the Subject of Indian Languages, chiefly in respect of their grammatical forms and constructions, which are now known to differ essentially from those of the Languages of the Old World, and form a new and interesting Subject of Metaphysical Disquisition.

No. III.—A Grammar of the Language of the *Lenni Lenape*, or *Delaware Indians*. Translated from the German MS. of the late REV. DAVID ZEISBERGER. The Historical Committee, in their late Report to the Philosophical Society, printed in the first volume of the Philosophical Transactions, New Series, give it as their opinion, "That it is the most complete Grammar that they have ever seen of any of those languages which are called *barbarous*." It is indispensably necessary to elucidate the Correspondence which precedes it.

The Publisher having undertaken to print this volume at his own risk, on its success will greatly depend the future exertions of the Historical Committee for the benefit of their fellow-citizens. They do not wish to derive any profit from their labours, but they have not the means of publishing at their own expense. The Printer, who has[2] relied on the taste and discernment of an enlightened Public, not less than on their patriotism, ventures to hope that he will be supported in this undertaking by all the friends of learning and the well-wishers to the literary reputation of their country.

☞ *The Price will be* $3 50 *in Boards.*

MS (DLC: TJ Papers, 213:38003–4); printed text of four numbered pages, with two handwritten corrections; undated.

Peter S. Du Ponceau was corresponding SECRETARY of the American Philosophical Society's Historical and Literary Committee.

[1] Reworked in an unidentified hand from "others."

[2] An unidentified hand here canceled "solely."

From François André Michaux

P^is ce 10 juin, 1818.

hommage de l'Auteur,   F A. MICHAUX

E D I T O R S '   T R A N S L A T I O N

Paris 10 June, 1818.

a tribute from the author,   F A. MICHAUX

RC (MoSHi: TJC-BC); dateline at foot of text; at head of text: "a Monsieur Th. Jefferson ex-president des Etat Unis"; endorsed by TJ as received 11 Sept. 1818 and so recorded in SJL. Translation by Dr. Genevieve Moene. Enclosure not found.

To Patrick Gibson

DEAR SIR   Monticello June 11. 18.

Your favor of May 30. came to hand yesterday and I now return the two notes signed, & with them a 3^d of which my grandson is endorser, which I will pray you to date & put in at it's proper time.

In my letter of Apr. 21. I mentioned the sale of tob° to mr Robertson amounting to 887.34 out of which I should have to pay him about 500.D. and that the balance should be remitted you. when I came however to adjust this matter with mr Yancey, I learnt from him that he had borrowed on my account about 300.D. from mr Robertson for some plantation expences, which were to be repaid him. of this I had not been aware, & it so nearly stopped the whole sum in mr Robertson's hands that I gave no order as to the small balance. this taking place in the moment of my departure from Bedford, I put off writing to you until I should get home, where an accumulation of letters recieved in my absence & calling for answers, put it quite out of my recollection until the reciept of your favor of May. 30. or it should have been sooner explained. there was still to be sold some remainder of the last year's tobacco, which I directed mr Yancey to effect and remit to you. I have not yet heard of the sale, but shall go there in about a fortnight and see that it be made, & the proceeds remitted you. Accept the assurance of my great esteem and respect

TH: JEFFERSON

PoC (MHi); on verso of reused address cover of Joseph Delaplaine to TJ, 11 Mar. 1818; at foot of text: "Mr Gibson"; endorsed by TJ. Enclosures not found.

MY GRANDSON: Thomas Jefferson Randolph.

To Bernard Peyton

DEAR SIR   Monticello June 12. 18.

You know we are engaged in the establishment of a Central college near Charlottesville, and we are sure you will have your children educated at it. on that ground we claim a right to give you occasional trouble with it's concerns. we wish to cover our buildings with slate, and we believe all our lands on Henderson's & B. island creeks to be full of what is excellent, we wish therefore to get a workman a slater[1] to come & examine it, and if found good, to undertake our work. there is a mr Jones, a Welshman who did some excellent work in Charlottesville, and who is supposed to be now in Richmond. if you can prevail on him to come, we would prefer him because we know him. if not to be had, then we request you to search out some other good slater and send him on to us, to examine our quarries, and say whether the slate is good. we will pay the expenses of his coming & returning and wages for the time he is making the examination, and if he chuses, we may set him to work immediately. but he must come without delay, because I go to Bedford within a fortnight to be absent 3 weeks, and his coming during my absence wou[l]d answer no purpose. I inclose you a specimen of our slate from which he may form some judgment of the probability of finding what will answer. be so good as to do us this good turn without delay & to be assu[re]d of my constant esteem & respect.   TH: JEFFERSON

PoC (ViU: TJP); on verso of reused address cover to TJ; two words faint; at foot of text: "Capᵗ Peyton"; endorsed by TJ.

B. ISLAND: Buck Island.

[1] Preceding two words interlined.

To James Leitch

June 13. 18.

a hand vice
some German steel to be chosen by the bearer.   TH:J.

RC (ViHi: Preston Family Papers); dateline beneath signature; written on a small scrap; at foot of text: "Mʳ James Leitch." Not recorded in SJL.

From Bernard Peyton

D^R SIR   Rich^d 13 June 1818

I send you by Mr Johnsons Boat a small Bundle of Books shipped to my care by Mr Carey of Philadelphia.—They reached me only a day or two since & this is the first conveyance which has presented itself—   I am always glad of an opportunity to render you service—

Very respectfully sir Your assured friend & Mo: Obd: Servt:

                      B. PEYTON

RC (MHi); addressed: "Thomas Jefferson Esq Monticello"; endorsed by TJ as received 20 June 1818 and so recorded in SJL.

From Frank Carr

                 Bentivar June 15th 1818

Frank Carr avails himself of Mr Jefferson's kindly proffered attention to letters from Mr Terrell's friends, and asks the favor of him to put the enclosed in a way to reach him. F. Carr tenders sentiments of high consideration.

RC (ViU: TJP-CC); addressed: "Mr Jefferson Monticello"; endorsed by TJ as received 16 June 1818 and so recorded in SJL. Enclosures not found.

To Thomas A. Digges

DEAR SIR   Monticello June 15. 18.

a letter from the shadows of 41. to 43. (for these I suppose are the years of our births) is like one of those written from the banks of the Styx, it is so long since we have exchanged salutations, that I had almost been afraid to hazard mine to you without inclosing in it an Obolus as postage for Charon. I wish too that your letter had given a better account of your health and situation. to be driven from one's home by lawless dilapidations on it is a great aggravation of the afflictions of age. I vary mine voluntarily 3. or 4. times a year by visits to a possession in Bedford county about 80 or 90. miles South from this, where I am comfortably fixed, and make considerable stays. I believe I was absent on one of these trips when mr & mrs Bagot paid their visit to mr Madison. I should certainly have been very happy to have recieved them here and the more so had you been of their party. altho' withdrawn from all medling with public affairs, I have not withdrawn from all anxieties for the future; and convinced as I am that no two countries on earth [. . .] hurt one another so much as his and ours, I should h[ave] freely invoked his cultivation of what ought to be between them, & co[. . .] of what ought never to have been. I am sensible of the difficulties produced by the incendiary newspapers on both sides, by their insolent taunts and provocations, in constant counteraction of the interests of their country and the sounder dispositions of their governments: but men in the high stations of administration on both sides must be supposed to have minds far above these senseless passions.

I thank you for thinking of me as to the spring wheat. my family will try it with pleasure, medling little myself with the affairs of the farm. for altho' I enjoy uninterrupted health, yet I daily become more feeble in body. I perform my journies to Bedford in an easy carriage, and ride 6. or 8 miles on horseback every day without fatigue; but I do not walk further than my garden. I observe your request on the subject of mr Fenwick; but in the first place I have no rights on the attentions of mr Campbell, and have moreover been long since obliged to renounce all solicitations of the government. for a while after I left it I endeavored to serve my friends in this way: but disgusted at length with the suppliant attitude in which it kept me constantly before them I was forced to relieve them and myself by an inflexible resolution to cease from that teazing corvée.[1] could I break thro' this rule for any body it should be at your request. but I am sure you will be sensible that it's undeviating observance is essential to the state of rest and tranquility which is the summum bonum at our age. —I shall not relinquish the hope of seeing you here again altho' once disappointed, nor cease from sincere prayers for a long continuance of your health & happiness   TH: JEFFERSON

PoC (DLC); on reused address cover of Bernard Peyton to TJ, 23 Mar. 1818; torn at seal, with some missing text rewritten by TJ; at foot of first page: "Thomas Digges esq."; endorsed by TJ.

TJ was at Monticello during the October 1817 visit of Charles BAGOT and his wife to Montpellier; he departed 16 Nov. 1817 for Poplar Forest (TJ to Madison, 15 Nov. 1817; *MB*, 2:1340).

[1] Omitted period at right margin editorially supplied.

From Patrick Gibson

Sir   Richmond 15th June 1818 —

Your favor of the 11th Inst is received inclosing the two notes I had
forwarded for your signature as also one in favor of Thos J Randolph,
which shall be attended to, but as I before informed you, it is <u>neces-
sary</u> that I should have his check to enable me to draw the nt prds and
apply it towards the payment of the old note — It would be the better
plan and subject to no possible abuse, to lodge with me a power of
Atty to act for him in that special case —

With much respect and esteem I am

Sir Your ob Servt   Patrick Gibson

RC (MHi); between dateline and salutation: "Thomas Jefferson Esqre"; endorsed by TJ as received 20 June 1818
and so recorded in SJL.

Nt prds: "net proceeds."

To John McKinney

Sir   Monticello June 15. 18

Your letter of May 21. is just now recieved; and I have to thank you
for the elks you have been so good as to offer me: but the advance of
years has taught me to wind up old cares rather than engage in new
ones, and I have lost all interest in things of this kind. for the same
reason I will pray you to take no further trouble about the Panther's
skin as mentioned in your letter, as the object of that also is among
those I have laid aside.

with my thanks for your attention accept the assurance of my
respects.   Th: Jefferson

PoC (MoSHi: TJC-BC); on verso of reused address cover of Jerman Baker to TJ,
24 Mar. 1818; at foot of text (faint): "[M]r John McKinney"; endorsed by TJ.

From James Oldham

Deare Sir   Richmond June 15th 1818.

In 6 or 8. days I sett oute for Saint Louis in the Missouri Territory
houses are in Grate demand there and money more plenty than in
Richmond, for 6 months past I have been makeing arangements for
the Trip and shall be able to commence worke as soon as I arive there,
my asortement of Ironmongery Suffitient for 10 or 12 plain houses

arived at new Orleans 10 of Aprail and will be at Saint Louis before me, I think[1] it will not be in my power to do much this yeare than to prepare for the next, the Timber being very large and unwealdy there cannot be much done in cutting it by hand and I cannot devise any cheper plan than the Steem Ingine which will come very high, building is intirely checked heare for the present and I feare will be for some considerable time to come, I wished very much to of solde my property heare but it is impossable to sell to any advantage, & have Leased it for 3 years in the corse of that time I hope Richmond will asume a very different appearance from the present, adue and may heaven bless you.

    With Grate Respect I have the Honor to be Sir Your Ob[t] Sev[t]

J; OLDHAM

RC (MHi); endorsed by TJ as received 20 June 1818 and so recorded in SJL. RC (MHi); address cover only; with PoCs of TJ to Joseph Milligan, 25 and [ca. 25] Oct. 1818, on recto and verso, respectively; addressed: "Tho[s] Jefferson Esq[r] Monticello"; franked; postmarked Richmond, 15 June.

[1] Manuscript: "thing."

To James Sloan

Monticello June 15. 18.

    I have deferred, Sir, my thanks for the compliment of your volume on Italy, until I could read it, and return them avec connoissance de cause. I have now read it with great pleasure, and not without edification: for altho, as the preface observes, that country has been the theme of so many pens that novelty on it's subject is difficult, yet these wrote on Italy as it was before the Corsican Volcano directed the destroying course of it's lava over her fair fields. we were yet to learn her present state, and the dispositions with which she had passed from one tyranny to another. this you have supplied. and altho' much has been said of her edifices, her statues and paintings, yet it has not been better said than in this volume, which is truly a model of classical style in these beautiful arts, as Whateley's book is on that of landscape gardening. the Reviewers may attack your neologisms, but I thank you for them. I know no other way by which a language can be improved, or kept up with the advance of the age, but by coining new words for new ideas, and better words for old ones: and if they are contented to become stationary, let us go on without them. I have experienced but one disappointment in reading your book, that of not finding the Pantheon among your enchanting descriptions. this building, I consider as the perfection of Spherical, as the Maison carrée is of Cubic architecture. the former I know only from models and drawings; but, to feast on the latter, I went twice to Nismes, staid 10. days each time, & each day stood an hour, morning, noon & night, fixed as a statue to a single spot, and entransed in the beauties of it's form and symmetries.   I believe I should have felt, as you have described, the immortal beauties of Rome, had the leisure been my lot of visiting those monuments of the sublimest works of man. you are young, and have still your race to run. that you may reach it's last mete with the splendor promised by that with which you leave it's first is the prayer with which I close my acknolegements for your attentions, and tender my salutations of esteem & respect.

TH: JEFFERSON

PoC (DLC); on verso of reused address cover to TJ; at foot of text: "James Sloan jun[r] esq."

AVEC CONNOISSANCE DE CAUSE: "with full knowledge of the case." The CORSICAN VOLCANO was Napoleon. WHATELEY'S BOOK: Thomas Whately, *Observations on Modern Gardening* (2d ed., London, 1770;

Sowerby, no. 4227; Poor, *Jefferson's Library*, 12 [no. 727]).

TJ visited Nîmes (NISMES) in March and May 1787. Even before seeing the Maison Carrée in person there, TJ had settled on it in 1785 as his model for the Virginia state capitol in Richmond (*PTJ*, 8:534–5, 11:424, 443, 13:274).

From John M. Perry

SIR   Central College. 18th Jun. 1818
the Brick layers got here yesterday and will begin to lay Some time this evening—I Should be glad you Could make it Convenient to Come to the building to day—the dormetorries will be laid off[1] to day—the Circle next the Road is Staked off So that you Can See how to fix on the level
    your obt. Servant   JOHN M PERRY

RC (ViU: TJP); addressed: "Thomas Jefferson Esquire Monticello"; endorsed by TJ as received 18 June 1818.

[1] Manuscript: "of," here and below.

From Bernard Peyton

DEAR SIR,   Rich[d] 18 June "18
    I was favord by the last mail with your esteem[d] letter of the 12th: current enclosing a piece of Slate which I lost no time in submitting to the judgment[1] of the best skilled Quarrier in this City; (M[r] Baker Beaven,) he has no doubt but it will work well provided there be

enough of it to make it an object—I have engaged him to go immediately to Monticello and receive[2] your instructions;—his conditions are, that his travelling expences shall be defrayed & allowed usual wages whilst making the experiment, should it succeed, and you desire to employ him to cover the buildings now erecting for the Central College, he will do so, & from the very high recommendations I have received from the most respectable[3] Mechanicks & Builders here as to his ability, industry, sobriety & general good conduct, I can venture to recommend him to you as well qualified to perform the service you desire, more especially that part of it relating to the examination of the slate, he tells me he has been regularly raised to the Quarrying of slate as well using it afterwards on buildi[ngs—?]He has been employed by the Government lately to cover the Capitol with slate which has been executed entirely to their satisfaction & he is now engaged in Covering a very large & elegant Court House erecting by the Corporation of Richmond—I state these facts merely to shew you the estimation in which he is held here in these respects: he promises to set out to-day or tomorrow & loose no time on the way; I sincerely hope he may turn out to your satisfaction—

The M[r] Jones you speak of I have made dilligent enquiry for, but without success.

You have the best assurance of my support & good will towards the rearing & future prosperity of the Central College by my subscription, compared with my situation in life—I hope therefore you will feel no hesitation in calling on me at all times for any services it is in my power to afford towards the advancements of this all important undertaking. Should I be blessed with a family of Children, I shall feel proud to have them educated at an institution founded (in a great degree) by you & conducted (as I am sure it will be) under your own eye & superintendence & on the best possible principles—I have a Nephew now in waiting for its completion—

I forwarded you a few days since by M[r] Johnson a Bundle of Books which I hope has been safely rec[d].—With great[4] respect sir

Your obd: Servt: B. Peyton

RC (MHi); bottom edge chipped; endorsed by TJ as received 20 June 1818 and so recorded in SJL.

[1] Manuscript: "judgmeent."
[2] Manuscript: "receve."
[3] Manuscript: "respecable."
[4] Manuscript: "greast."

From Bernard Peyton

DEAR SIR   Rich^d 18 June 1818

The bearer of this Mr Baker Beaven is the Gentleman who I have employed to examine your Quarry of Slate & who I am persuaded you will find entirely qualified to discharge that duty—I have written you more fully by this day's mail on this subject to which I now refer you

In haste

Very respectfully sir Your obd Servt B. PEYTON

RC (MHi); endorsed by TJ as received 21 June 1818 and so recorded in SJL.

To Joseph Darmsdatt

DEAR SIR   Monticello June 19. 18.

I am now to ask from you my annual supply of fish. that is to say 6. barrels of herrings to be forwarded by the Lynchburg boats to the care of Archibald Robertson merchant of that place and 6. barrels of herrings and 1. of shad to be forwarded to Milton by the boats of that place, and to be so good as to send me a note of the cost that I may provide payment.

Accept the assurance of my antient and continued friendship and respect.   TH: JEFFERSON

PoC (MHi); on verso of reused address cover of George Washington Jeffreys to TJ, 30 Mar. 1818; at foot of text: "Mr Darmsdat"; endorsed by TJ. Enclosed in TJ to Daniel Call, 13 May 1820, and Call to TJ, 18 May 1820.

Darmsdatt's missing response of 4 July 1818 is recorded in SJL as received 18 July 1818 from Richmond. It was also enclosed in TJ to Call, 13 May 1820, and Call to TJ, 18 May 1820.

To Thomas Ritchie

DEAR SIR   Monticello June 19. 18.

I find it impossible to get a copy of Madison's map without linen or rollers, and as it is indispensable to have one at the meeting of the Commissioners for the University I must pray you to get me one of those which you say can be had with linen & rollers. I should prefer [one] with the borders of the counties coloured, but not the body.   the agent who has them, will roll one very securely in a plenty of strong paper, and deliver it to Capt Peyton, who knows the boats which come to Milton. he will for[ward it sa]fely to me by one

[99]

of them a[nd] the agent at the same time pres[en]ting this letter to mr Gibson, [and] reciev[ing] payment from him [so?] [that the] only trouble I mean to give you in the business is to put this letter into the hands of the agent and request an immediate execution of it. accept my salutations and assurances of great esteem & respect.

Th: Jefferson

PoC (DLC); on verso of reused address cover of Dupl of Patrick Gibson to TJ, 13 Apr. 1818; faint; at foot of text: "Mr Ritchie"; endorsed by TJ.

To Caleb Atwater

Monticello June 21. 18.

I thank you, Sir, for the paper you have been so kind as to send me, and I have read with pleasure the disquisition on the origin of our Indians. this long contested question seems no nearer it's solution now than when first proposed. I am glad to see the ingenuity of others employed in such investigations, but have lost all interest in them myself. the advance of years tells me they are not for my day, and a stiffening wrist, from an antient injury to it, makes writing so slow and painful an operation as to force me to decline all occasions calling for it, & not of indispensable necessity. I have particularly to thank you for your kind expressions towards myself, and recieve, in the goodwill of my fellow citizens, a full reward for any service I could ever render them. I pray you to accept for yourself the assurances of my great respect and esteem. Th: Jefferson

PoC (DLC); at foot of text: "Mr Atwater"; endorsed by TJ.

To Mathew Carey

DEAR SIR Monticello June 21. 18.

The miniature Bible came safely, and Bridgman and McMahon are arrived at Richmond and are now on their way here. the Viri Romae came also safely but was lost by an accident soon after it's arrival, wherefore I must ask another copy of the same edition with a dictionary at the end. I inclose you 50. Dollars which, covers my balance if I keep our account right. but there is the article of the 2. vols of the American register which I know not the cost of. I must request you to send me Pike's journal of his expedition to the Arkansaw, the Red river E^tc a large 8vo   the Viri Romae may come by mail because it is small, and Pike also because wanting in haste. I salute you with friendship & respect.   TH: JEFFERSON

RC (William Reese Company, New Haven, Conn., 2004); at foot of text: "Mr Cary"; addressed: "Messrs Matthew Carey & son Philadelphia"; franked; postmarked Charlottesville, 23 June; endorsed by Carey as received 26 June 1818 and answered the following day. PoC (DLC); on verso of reused address cover of Thomas Perkins to TJ, 23 Mar. 1818; endorsed by TJ.

To Patrick Gibson

DEAR SIR   Monticello June 21. 18.

I recieved last night your favor of [. . .] 15th. am sorry my awkwardness in business gives you so much trouble. I had supposed that the promisee of a note endorsing the note, authorised the holder to write over his signature an authority to recieve the money. I now correct the error by inclosing you a power of attorney from my grandson giving as fully as I know how to express it a power for the present and all subsequent renewalls and salute you with affectionate esteem and respect.   TH: JEFFERSON

PoC (MHi); on verso of reused address cover of Francis Adrian Van der Kemp to TJ, 5 Apr. 1818; torn at seal; at foot of text: "Mr Gibson"; endorsed by TJ. Enclosure not found.

MY GRANDSON: Thomas Jefferson Randolph.

To William Plumer

                                                   Monticello June 21. 18.

Th: Jefferson presents his compliments to Governor Plumer, and his thanks for the copy of his message, recieved yesterday. it is replete as usual with principles of wisdom. nothing needs correction with all our legislatures so much as the unsound principles of legislation on which they act generally. the only remedy seems to be in an improved system of education. he is happy in every occasion of saluting Govr Plumer with friendship and respect.

PoC (ViW: TC-JP); on verso of an address cover from TJ to William Tilghman; dateline at foot of text; endorsement by TJ torn.

From Thomas Cooper

D^R SIR   June 24. 1818

Dr Coxe's election comes on the first Tuesday of next month. They talk of deferring the election for chemical professor to the first Tuesday in September. I am not sufficiently instructed to know the causes of this inconvenient determination.

I send you, ad interim, a Syllabus of lectures of which I have delivered two courses. They have produced very complimentary letters of approbation from both my classes, and so far they have been very satisfactory to [me].   accept my best wishes; always.

THOMAS COOPER.

RC (ViU: TJP); mutilated at seal; addressed: "Thomas Jefferson Esq Montecello Virginia"; franked; inconsistently postmarked Philadelphia, 23 June; endorsement by TJ torn. Recorded in SJL as received 28 June 1818.

ENCLOSURE

Thomas Cooper's Geology Syllabus

[ca. 24 June 1818]

SYLLABUS

Of the Lectures of Thomas Cooper, Esq. M. D. as Professor of Geology and Mineralogy in the University of Pennsylvania.

Of the characters of mineral substances, as distinguished by the sight, the touch, the taste, the smell, the hearing.

Of the means of distinguishing mineral substances artificially; by the file, the knife, the blow-pipe, the mineral acids: by their crystallization and the goniometer; their phosphorescence, their refraction, their magnetism and polarity, their electricity, specific gravity, &c.

Of the specific gravity of the globe of the earth, according to Sir Issac Newton, Mr. Michell,[1] Mr. Cavendish, Drs. Maskelyne and Hutton.

Of the crust of the globe so far as we have yet pierced into it.

Of mineral classification: 1. By families, founded on external characters. *Werner* in Germany, and his followers, *Jameson* in Scotland, and *Thomson* in England. 2. By chemical characters, *Kirwan, Babington, Kidd, Clarke,* in England. 3. By the primitive crystal, and the crystallographic variations, according to certain laws of decrement and increment; *Romé de Lisle, Haüy,* and his followers of the French school. 4. The system of the present lecturer; viz. mineralogy founded upon geological situation and connexion, with the reasons for proposing the plan[2] now first adopted.

Of the foundation of geological science, viz. regularity of position of the formations and strata that compose the crust of the earth. Definition of formation, viz. a series of alternating and intermixing strata,[3] apparently formed within one and the same limited period.

[102]

Causes of anomaly and exception: viz. volcanic action; action of water; atmospheric decomposition; avalanches.[4] Wherein, of strata deficient in the usual series; of partial irregularities in the position of strata; boulder stones, and other rolled and misplaced masses of rocks, heterogeneous to the district where they are found.

Of the division of the formations, into primitive, transition, secondary, alluvial and volcanic. Cautions against the implicit adoption of the theories whereon these names are founded.

Of the PRIMITIVE formations, viz. granitic, magnesian, calcareous, and argillitic.

Of the *granitic* formation, viz. the old granite, gneiss, imbedded[5] large grained granite, mica slate. Of the hornblende and syenite[6] (sometimes called the primitive trap rocks) alternating and intermixed with the granitic formation.

Of the substances composing the granitic formation, viz. quartz, feldspar, mica, hornblende.

Of the substances non-metallic, occasionally found in the granitic formation; viz. schorl and tourmalin, sibarite, garnet, beryl, cymophane, topaz, pyrophysalite, scapolite, spodumene, andalusite, jade, phosphate of lime, fluate of lime, idocrase, allalite, prehnite, &c. &c.

Of the *magnesian* formation, consisting of chlorite, steatite, talc, amianth, serpentine. Of the alternating and intermixing primitive or *magnesian limestone*.[7]

Of the substances non-metallic found in the magnesian and limestone formations: asbestos, bitter spar, staurotide, automalite, diallage, kyanite, tremolite, actynolite, epidote, dolomite, &c. Of the connexion between hornblende,[8] epidote and actynolite.

Of partial and intermixing beds, nodules, and strata; of quartz, syenite, and porphyry. Of the as yet indistinct line of division between the primitive and transition formations: of the psammites of the French geologists: reasons for retaining the transition class: of the distinctive characters of the transition class, viz. 1. Absence of crystallization in the mass. 2. Aggregate of worn fragments and particles imbedded in a paste. 3. Commencement of organic remains. 4. Werner's character of the argillaceous nature of transition hornblende. 5. Characters now first proposed for investigation by the present lecturer, viz. the carbonaceous and destructible colouring matter prevalent in transition slates and limestones; and the presence of non-bituminous anthracite.

Of the TRANSITION rocks:[9] of clay-slate passing into transition clay-slate: grauwackes, grauwackeshists, limestones, and transition traps, viz. hornblende, sienitic or hornblende rocks, and greenstones.

Of the substances found in the transition class: jaspar, flint-slate, lydian stone, whetslate, gypsum, anthracite,[10] graphite, asbestos accompanying anthracite; organic remains of transition, viz. *small* crustaceæ, and impressions of the smaller and first class of vegetables.[11]

Of the various kinds of zeolyte in primitive and transition rocks; the produce of infiltration.

Of the old red sandstone: its doubtful character: and of the substances found connected with the old red sandstone; viz. rock salt, gypsum, jet, &c.

Of the SECONDARY, floetz, or horizontal formations: of the mountain, or metalliferous limestone, and the sandstone strata and lavas accompanying it:

of the bituminous coal formation; the sandstone usually subtending it; the strata composing and intersecting it, neptunian and volcanic: of the magnesian limestone; of the strata intervening between the magnesian and lias limestone: wherein of the oolite of England; quere if this be not a tufous deposit from thermal waters? Of the strata above the lias limestone ascending to the chalk: of the strata in Europe above the chalk: of the absence (according to the present state of observations) of the chalk and other more recent floetz deposits within the bounds of the United States.

Of the substances found in the secondary strata: crystallized and amorphous quartz, millstones, fullers' earth, lithograhic stones; of the surturbrand, amber, &c. near or in the alluvial.

Of the organic remains of the secondary strata. Quere, are strata really characterized by organic remains? and if so, to what extent?

Of the ALLUVIAL SOIL and the organic remains found in it: of the relative ages of organic remains, and the animals to which they belonged: of madrepore and coralline islands.

Of VOLCANIC formations; viz. of modern and active volcanoes, and the substances found therein; ashes and cinders; cellular, compact, and porphyritic lavas: of idocrase, and ejected portions of primitive rocks: of the mineral termed nepheline, meionite, and sommite; of obsidian, pumice, tufa, puzzolane or terras, zeolyte, augite or volcanic hornblende, olivine or peridot, sulphur, salts, &c. &c. Of mud-lavas.

Of ancient and extinct volcanoes: wherein of columnar basalt, amorphous basalt, porphyry, greenstone, whinstone, toadstone[12] or mud-lava. Of the volcanic interpositions called dykes.

Of the geodes, zeolytes, prehnites, jaspars, agates, quartz, olivine, &c. found in the air-cells of ancient volcanoes, and formed by infiltration.

Of the[13] volcanic origin of Werner's newest floetz trap formation.

Of BASINS: 1. Of coal basins, Richmond, Virginia; Rive de Gier[14] in France, &c. 2. Of chalk basins; of the Paris basin, the London basin, the Isle of Wight basin. 3. Of the great basin of the Mississippi.

Of MINERAL WATERS: 1. Saline. 2. Hepatic and carbonic. 3. Chalybeat. 4. Thermal.

Of METALLIC SUBSTANCES in veins, beds, or strata: of the metallic substances generally found in the primitive: as pyrites, magnetic and octahedral iron; titanite, rutilite, menachanite; molybdena; tin; &c. &c.

Of other metallic substances common to the formations.

Of METEOROLITES and falling stars.

Of theories and COSMOGENIES, and the insufficiency of any yet proposed taken singly, to account for known appearances.

When the substances are exhibited *in* the rocks, as they are actually found in nature, with their accompanyments, they convey, as I think, far more precise information than any[15] hand specimen or cabinet collection can possibly afford. For the motto of mineralogy, is that of man in the civilized world; *noscitur à socio:* "shew me your companions and I will tell you who you are." I insert the preceding syllabus of my lectures, as containing a *new* arrangement at least; and as suggesting views of the subject not to be found in the usual systems of mineralogy.—T. C.[16]

Broadside (PPAmP); undated; with one handwritten correction. Printed in *Port Folio* 6 (Aug. 1818): 117–20; at head of text: "FOR THE PORT FOLIO."

[1] Broadside and *Port Folio*: "Mitchell."

[2] *Port Folio* here adds "of mineralogical classification."

[3] Instead of preceding four words, *Port Folio* reads "strata occasionally alternating and intermixing."

[4] *Port Folio* adds "rock-" preceding this word.

[5] Broadside: "inbedded." *Port Folio*: "imbedded."

[6] Omission of first two letters of this word corrected in an unidentified hand in broadside.

[7] Broadside: "limestome." *Port Folio*: "limestone."

[8] Broadside: "horneblende." *Port Folio*: "hornblende."

[9] After the colon *Port Folio* here adds "of porphyry," followed by another colon.

[10] *Port Folio* here adds "black chalk."

[11] *Port Folio* here adds "fishes, &c."

[12] *Port Folio* here adds "amygdaloid."

[13] *Port Folio* here adds "probable."

[14] Broadside and *Port Folio*: "Guir."

[15] *Port Folio* here adds "insulated."

[16] *Port Folio* here adds "Two courses have been delivered, one in the fall of the year 1817, the other in the spring of 1818."

To James Wilkinson

DEAR GENERAL   Monticello June 25. 18.

A life so much employed in public as yours has been, must subject you often to be appealed to for facts by those whom they concern. an occasion occurs to myself of asking this kind of aid from your memory & documents. the posthumous volume of Wilson's Ornithology, altho' published some time since, never happened to be seen by me until a few days ago. in the account of his life, prefixed to that volume his biographer indulges himself in a bitter invective against me, as having refused to employ Wilson on Pike's expedition to the Arkansa, on which particularly he wished to have been employed. on turning to my papers I have not a scrip of a pen on the subject of that expedition; which convinces me that it was not one of those which emanated from myself: and if a decaying memory does not decieve me I think that it was ordered by yourself from St Louis, while Governor and military commander there; that it was an expedition for reconnoitring the Indian and Spanish positions which might be within striking distance; that so far from being an expedition admitting a leisurely and scientific examination of the natural history of the country, it's movements were to be on the alert, & too rapid to be accomodated to the pursuits of scientific men; that if previously communicated to the Executive, it was not in time for them, from so great a distance, to have joined scientific men to it; nor is it probable it could be known at all to mr Wilson and to have excited his wishes and expectations to join it. if you will have the goodness to consult your memory and papers on this subject, & to write me the result you will greatly oblige me.

My retirement placed me at once in a state of such pleasing freedom and tranquility, that I determined never more to take any concern in public affairs: but to consider myself merely as a passenger in the public vessel, placed under the pilotage of others, in whom too my confidence was entire. I therefore discontinued all corrrespondence on public subjects, and was satisfied to hear only so much,[1] true or false, as a newspaper or two could give me. in these I sometimes saw matters of much concern, and particularly that of your retirement. a witness myself of the merit of your services while I was in a situation to know and to feel their benefit, I made no enquiry into the circumstances which terminated them, whether moving from yourself or others. with the assurance however that my estimate of their value remains unaltered, I pray you to accept that of my great and continued esteem and respect.   TH: JEFFERSON

RC (ICHi: Wilkinson Papers); mutilated at folds, with missing text supplied from PoC; at foot of text: "Maj^r Genl Wilki[nson]." PoC (DLC); edge trimmed; endorsed by TJ.

PREFIXED to the concluding ninth volume of Alexander Wilson, *American Ornithology; or, The Natural History of the Birds of the United States* (Philadelphia, 1808–14; Sowerby, no. 1022), is editor George Ord's biography of Wilson, which describes his desire to participate in an exploratory mission to Louisiana, mentions a letter of 6 Feb. 1806 from William Bartram to TJ recommending Wilson (DLC), and prints Wilson's letter to TJ of the same date (pp. xxxi–xxxii). Ord complained that in failing to reply to the letter, TJ disregarded Wilson's "pretensions of Genius, and the interests of Science" (p. xxxiii).

[1] TJ here canceled "as," but he did not delete it in PoC.

From Mathew Carey & Son

D^R SIR   Philad^a June 27. 1818

Your favour of 21st inst. came to hand yesterday with fifty dollars for w^h please to accept our thanks—

Agreeably to your directions we have forwarded the above books per mail, w^h we hope will come safely to hand.—

The price of Walsh's American Register 2 Vols. is $6—

We shall forward next week, per mail, an extensive Supplement to our Catalogue, w^h is now in the press—

Yours respectfully

M. CAREY & SON

√

[*between dateline and salutation:*]
Hon: Thos Jefferson

	Bo^t of M Carey & Son	
1 Viris Romae		$1.00
1 Pikes Journal of his		
Expedition to the Arkansaw &^c	}	3.00
	√	$4.00

RC (MHi); in the hands of two different representatives of Mathew Carey & Son, with dateline and account in one hand and body of letter in the other; endorsed by TJ as a letter from Mathew Carey received 18 July 1818 and so recorded in SJL. RC (MoSHi: TJC-BC); address cover only; with PoC of TJ to George Wyche, 10 Nov. 1818, on verso; addressed: "Hon: Thos Jefferson Monticello Virg^a"; franked; postmarked Philadelphia, 27 June.

At some point after receiving this letter, TJ prepared a memorandum of his account with Mathew Carey & Son in which he listed the titles and total cost of works the firm sent him on 8, 23 Jan., 11 Apr., 16 May, and 27 June 1818, along with his payments to Mathew Carey of 15 Jan., 1 Mar., and 21 June 1818 (MS in DLC: TJ Papers, 213:38011; entirely in TJ's hand; undated; corner torn).

To John Barnes

DEAR SIR   Monticello June 28. 18.

I know not from whom or what quarter the inclosed letter to Wanscher comes, nor whether he is still living. I suppose it is from Germany, and invoke your charity to dispose of it according to circumstances. I do it with the more pleasure as it gives me new occasion to repeat to you the assurances of my constant friendship and respect.

TH: JEFFERSON

PoC (MHi); on verso of reused address cover of William Peck to TJ, 10 Apr. 1818; at foot of text: "Mr Barnes"; endorsed by TJ. Enclosure not found.

To Mathew Carey

DEAR SIR   Monticello June 28. 18.

Soon after the date of my letter of the 21st I recieved Bridgman's Index safely, and had taken for granted McMahon was coming with it. but as it did not come, I presume it has either been forgotten or is lodged by the way. in either case I ask your information & attention to it; and further that you will be so kind as to inform me whether a copy of Baron Grimm's memoirs (16. vols 8vo) can be had, and at what price? I salute you with friendship and respect

TH: JEFFERSON

RC (PHi: Lea & Febiger Records); addressed: "Mʳ Matthew Carey Philadelphia"; franked; postmarked Milton, 30 June; endorsed by Carey as received 2 July and answered 5 July 1818. PoC (DLC); on verso of reused address cover to TJ; endorsed by TJ.

To James Madison

DEAR SIR   Monticello June 28. 18.

Being to set out in a few days for Bedford from whence I shall not return till about a week before our Rockfish meeting, I have been preparing such a report as I can, to be offered there to our colleagues. it is not such an one as I should propose to them to make to an assembly of philosophers, who would require nothing but the table of professorships, but I have endeavored to adapt it to our H. of representatives. I learn, that in that body the party decidedly for education, and that decidedly opposed to it, are minorities of the whole, of which the former is strongest. that there is a floating body of doubtful & wavering men who not having judgment enough for decisive opinion, can make the majority as they please. I have therefore thrown in some leading ideas on the benefits of education, wherever the subject would admit it, in the hope that some of these might catch on some crotchet in their mind, and bring them over to us. nor could I, in the report, lose sight of the establishment of the general system of primary, & secondary schools preliminary to the University. these two objects will explain to you matters in the report, which do not necessarily belong to it. I now inclose it, and ask your free revisal of it both as to style and matter, and that you will make it such as yourself can concur in with self-approbation. I would be glad to find it at home on my return, because if the corrections should make a fair copy necessary I should have little time enough to copy it. observe that what I propose to be offered to the board is only from page 3. to 17 which sheets are stitched together. the detached leaves contain the white population of every county taken from the last census, estimates of the comparative numbers on each side of the divisional lines which may come into view, and such a report as these grounds may[1] seem to[2] authorise in the opinion of those who consider the Central college as the preferable site. I shall this day write to judge Roane and invite him to come here a day or two beforehand as I hope you will, that we may have a consultation on it. I know of no other member who will probably pass this way whom it would be particularly desirable to consult, without endangering jealousy. the 1ˢᵗ day of August happens of a Saturday. the roughness of the roads will induce me to go on horseback, as easier than a carriage; but as it is 30. miles from here to the Rockfish gap, which is more than I could advisably try in one day, I would propose that we ask a dinner and bed from mr Divers on the Thursday evening, which will give[3] us 23. miles for the next day. this of course would require Wednesday for our consultation, and Tuesday[4] at furthest for the arrival of yourself & Judge Roane here. my liaisons with Tazewell oblige me to ask him to make this a stage, and to propose to him to be here on the Wednesday, to take the road hence together. I am in hopes mrs Madison will think it more agreeable to come and while away your absence with mrs Randolph. judge Stewart is zealous that as soon as we meet at the gap, we should adjourn to Staunton, and he invites you and myself to make his house our quarters while there; this I mention to you because he desired it but entirely against any adjournment myself, that we may avoid not only the reality but the suspicion of intrigue; and be urged to short work by less comfortable entertainment. as we shall probably do nothing on Saturday, I shall have no objection to go home with him that evening, and return into place on Monday morning. in the hope of seeing you here in good time for consultation and the journey I salute you with affectionate friendship   TH: JEFFERSON

RC (DLC: Madison Papers). PoC (DLC); on reused address cover of John Wood to TJ, 22 Apr. 1818; torn at seal; endorsed by TJ. Enclosures: (1) TJ's Draft of the Rockfish Gap Report, [ca. 28 June 1818], printed below at 4 Aug. 1818. (2) TJ's Notes on the Geographic Center of Virginia's Population, [before 28 June 1818], printed below at 4 Aug. 1818.

OUR H. OF REPRESENTATIVES: the Virginia House of Delegates.

[1] Word interlined.
[2] TJ here canceled "render."
[3] Manuscript: "gives."
[4] TJ here canceled "evening."

To Bernard Peyton

DEAR SIR   Monticello June 28. 18.

I must ask the favor of you to return the inclosed Certificate for me to the land office and to pay the usual fees (I believe 1. or 2. Dollars) which mr Gibson will reimburse according to custom. will you have the goodness whenever cotton can be had in Richmond to buy 2. of the smallest bales to be had for me and send one by the Milton boats and the other by the Lynchburg boats to the care of mr Archibald Robertson of that place. bales of from 1. to 200 ℔ would suit me. I

am tired of apologising to you, but not of troubling you. affectionately
yours   TH: JEFFERSON

PoC (MHi); on verso of reused address cover of John Armstrong to TJ, 10 Apr. 1818 (see note to TJ to Armstrong, 20 Mar. 1818); at foot of text: "Capt Peyton"; endorsed by TJ. Enclosure not found.

To Spencer Roane

DEAR SIR   Monticello June 28. 18.
    I was much rejoiced to see your name on the roll of Commis[n] to
meet at Rockfish gap and to report to the legislature on the subject of
an University. the day of our meeting will be important in the history
of our country because it will decide whether we are to leave this fair
inheritance to barbarians or civilised men. the subject of our consul-
tations is vast, because it spreads over all science, and will I hope
engage several of our Colleagues to prepare such sketches at least of
a report as will require more consideration than can be given to it
there. I pressed mr Madison very much to undertake this task, but he
perseveringly threw back the undertaking on myself. I shall accordingly prepare the best sketch I can, and the object of this letter is to
pray you to make a stage of this place, and to meet mr Madison here
a day or two beforehand that we may advise on what will be proposed.
I mention this to nobody but yourself and him, to avoid jealousy, and
that even this little conciliabulum may be unknown & unsuspected.
we shall leave this together the Thursday preceding the 1st of Aug.
would ask you therefore to give us the Wednesday at this place and
of course that you should arrive here on Tuesday at farthest as he
will. I set out within 3. or 4. days for Bedford, but shall be returned
in time to recieve you here. and in the hope you will do me this favor
I salute you with high respect and friendship.
                                                      TH: JEFFERSON

PoC (DLC); on verso of reused ad-   CONCILIABULUM: "assembly."
dress cover to TJ; one word faint; at foot
of text: "Judge Roane"; endorsed by TJ.

To Horatio G. Spafford

DEAR SIR,   Monticello June 28. 18.

Your favor of May 29. came to hand 2. days ago. age and a stiffening wrist render[1] writing slow and painful, and oblige me to adopt almost a lapidary stile: this is the effect of an antient dislocation of the wrist. I have given up my farms to be managed by my family, and take no concern in them myself. I tried the Ruta baga when first brought from England and found it the best table-turnep I ever saw. but the seed I now get is so degenerated as to yield nothing but sallad. I inclose you some seed of the sprout kale which I recieved from France some years ago. sow it, and treat it exactly as cabbage, only leave it in it's place all winter. about the 1st of Dec. it will give you delicious sprouts, and, with us, 3. crops in the course of the winter. it is a valuable garden vegetable, and unknown in this country. with you it may be necessary in the winter to cover the head with loose straw which may not hinder the growth of the sprout. I must here conclude with my best wishes for success & happiness in your new establishment and assurances of my esteem & respect.   TH: JEFFERSON

RC (NNPM); with alterations in punctuation, capitalization, and emphasis, presumably by Spafford, editorially omitted; addressed: "Mr Horatio G. Spafford Venango. Pa"; franked; postmarked Charlottesville, 30 June; endorsed by Spafford as received 15 July 1818. PoC (MHi); on verso of reused address cover of John Hollins to TJ, 10 Apr. 1818; edge trimmed and mutilated at seal; endorsed by TJ.

[1] PoC: "renders."

To Littleton W. Tazewell

DEAR SIR   Monticello June 28. 18.

I was much pleased to see your name on the roll of Commissioners who are to meet at Rockfish gap on the 1st of Aug. to report to the legislature on the subject of an University: because a dozen winters ago I had recieved testimony of your zeal on this subject in a letter you then wrote to me, in my answer to which I expressed opinions which have been little changed. this zeal gives me confidence that you will not on this occasion decline giving us your aid. as you will pass within sight of Monticello, the object of this letter is to pray you to make a stage of it. the roads are so rough that I shall go on horseback as the easiest conveyance, but not thinking it advisable to encounter the whole (about 27. or 28 miles) in one day I shall ask a dinner & bed of my neighbor mr Divers, on the Thursday which will shorten the next day's ride 7. miles. mr Madison will be here, and if you will take the road hence with us, and are not acquainted with mr Divers, we will make you so, and engage a hearty welcome. I am just setting out for Bedford from whence I shall return in time for this meeting and shall hope the pleasure of recieving you here on the Wednesday preceding the 1ˢᵗ of Aug. at furthest. I salute you with great friendship & respect.   Tʜ: Jᴇꜰꜰᴇʀsᴏɴ

RC (NjMoHP: Lloyd W. Smith Collection); addressed: "Littleton W. Tazewell esq. Norfolk"; franked; postmarked Milton, 30 June. PoC (MHi); on verso of reused address cover of Benjamin Henry Latrobe to TJ, 14 Apr. 1818; endorsed by TJ.

Tazewell supplied ᴛᴇsᴛɪᴍᴏɴʏ of his support for a state university in a letter to TJ of 24 Dec. 1804 (DLC). TJ expressed his ᴏᴘɪɴɪᴏɴs in his response of 5 Jan. 1805 (NjMoHP: Smith Collection).

Account with Reuben Perry

1817   Mʳ Thomas Jefferson In A/c with R. Perry.
          To one pair Stock Brick moulds @ $13.00
1818   "   one Bed Trussel @   6.00
                                                                   $19.00
   Recᵈ of Joel Yancy Six Dollar of the above
             29ᵗʰ June 1818   R Pᴇʀʀʏ

MS (ViW: TC-JP); written in Perry's hand on a small scrap; endorsed by TJ: "<Chisolm Hugh.> Perry Reuben."

From James H. McCulloch

Sɪʀ   Custom House Baltᵒ June 30 1818
   Two letters recᵈ from you directed severally to Monsʳ Cathalan Marseilles & Debures freres Paris, were committed to the master of the Ship Ea which cleared hence yesterday for Bordeaux, with directions to deliver them to Mʳ Strobel American consul there & recommend them to his particular attention.
   The uncertainity of better conveyances offering in any short time, induced me to make use of this; it would have encreased the pleasure of the service to have had more direct opportunities at command. Whatever it may please you to require here, will be attended to with the utmost satisfaction.
   I remain Sir very respectfully Your obliged frᵈ & Servᵗ
                                                   Jᴀˢ H Mᶜᴄᴜʟʟᴏᴄʜ

RC (DLC); endorsed by TJ as received 18 July 1818 and so recorded in SJL. RC (DLC); address cover only; with PoC of first two pages of TJ to William H. Crawford, 10 Nov. 1818, on recto and verso; addressed: "Thomas Jefferson Esq. Monticello near Charlottesville Albemarle County Virginia"; stamped; postmarked (faint) Baltimore, [3]0 June.

TJ's TWO LETTERS of 28 May 1818 to Stephen Cathalan and de Bures Frères, recorded in SJL but not found, were sent under cover to McCulloch in a letter of the same date, also not found but recorded in SJL with the additional notation "covering the 2. preceding." Immediately above that in SJL, at the entry for the letter to Cathalan, TJ added the notation "4th of exchange 420. D," and at that to de Bures Frères he noted "do 120."

From John Armstrong

DEAR SIR,   Red-hook 1 July 1818

About the 1st week in May last I received a request from an old and useful friend, to whom I could not well refuse a kindness, solliciting from me a letter of introduction to yourself and another to Mr W. C. Nicholas. and adding, that he would set out for some of the watering places in your state about the 10th of that month. I accordingly gave him a few lines for each of you and committed to his care the enclosed letter in relation to Gen. K. To my great surprise in a visit I had from the gentleman yesterday, he replaced in my hands & as he received them, the two letters & the notice. With the Capriciousness of a Dyspeptic, he had altered the direction of his march and had entirely forgotten, that if anything arose to disturb his first intentions, he had engaged to forward by mail the letter marked 2. I much regret this circumstance, as it may have tended to disappoint Mr Julian's expectations, which after all, are perhaps not less likely to suffer by the very scanty materials I am able to furnish. I have a number of the General's letters, but they are written in bad English and have besides very little connexion with political events or public men.

accept dear Sir, the assurance of my very cordial regard & esteem.

JOHN ARMSTRONG

RC (DLC); endorsed by TJ as received 19 July 1818 and so recorded in SJL. RC (DLC); address cover only; with PoC of TJ to William Wirt, 10 Nov. 1818, on verso; addressed: "Thomas Jefferson Esq. late President of The U. S. Monticello Virginia"; franked; postmarked New York, 9 July.

GEN. K.: Tadeusz Kosciuszko. For JULIAN'S EXPECTATIONS, see Marc Antoine Jullien to TJ, 30 Nov. 1817, and TJ to Armstrong, 20 Mar. 1818.

John Armstrong's Notes on Tadeusz Kosciuszko

[before 10 May 1818]

Circumstances relating to gen. Kosciusko previously to his joining the American Army.

K. was born in the grand Dutchy of Lithuania in the year 1752. His family was noble & his patrimony considerable. circumstances which he justly appreciated, for as belonging to himself they were never matter of boasting and rarely subjects of notice and as the property of others only regarded as advantages when accompanied by good Sense & good morals. The workings of his mind on the subject of civil liberty, were early and vigorous. before he was twenty the vassalage of his serfs filled him with abhorrence and the first act of his manhood was to break their fetters.

In the domestic quarrel between the King and the dissidents in 1764 he was too young to take a part, but the partition of Poland in 1772 (of which this quarrel was one of the pretences) engaged him in th[e defence] of his country and Soon made him Sensible of the value of military education which he afterwards sought in the Schools of Paris. It was there & while prosecuting that object that he first became Acquainted with the name of America and the nature of the war in which the British [colonies were then engaged] with the mother Country. In the summer of 1776 he embarked for this country and in October of that year was appointed by Congress a Colo. of Engineers.

[2^d] Services of the Gen. during the W[ar].

In the Spring of 1777 he joined the Northern Army and in July following the writer of this notice left him on Lake Champlain engaged in strengthening our works at Ticonderoga and Mount Independence. The unfortunate character of the early part of this Campaign is [sufficiently] known. In the retreat of the American army Kosciusko was distinguished for activity and courage and upon him devolved the choice of camps & posts and everything connected with fortification. The last position taken by the Army while commanded by Gen. Schuyler was on an island in the Hudson near the mouth of the Mohawk river and within a few miles of Albany. Here Gates, who had superseded Schuyler, found the Army on the   day of August. Public feeling & opinion were strikingly affected by the arrival of this Officer, who gave it a full and lasting impression, by ordering the Army to advance upon the enemy. The state of things at that moment are well and faithfully expressed by that distinguished officer Col. Udney Hay, in a letter to a friend. "Fortune„ says he "as if tired of persecuting us, had began to change & Burgoyne had suffered materially on both his flanks—but these things were not of our doing; the main Army, as it was called, was hunted from post to pillar and dared not to measure its strength with the enemy; much was wanting to reinspire it with confidence in itself—with that Self respect without which an Army is but a flock of Sheep—a proof of which is found in the fact, that we have thanked in General Orders a detachment double the force of that of the enemy, for having dared to return their fire. From this miserable State of despondency & terror, Gates's arrival raised us as if by magic. We began to hope and then to act—our first step was to Stillwater and we are now on the heights, called Bhemus's looking the enemy boldly in the face. Kosciusko has Selected the ground and has covered its weak point (its' right) with redoubts from the hill to the river,,.

In front of this camp thus fortified two battles were fought [which] eventuated in the retreat of the enemy and his surrender at Saratoga.

The value of Col. Kosciusko's services during this campaign and that of 1778 will be found in the following extract from a letter of General Gates written in the Spring of 1780. "My dear friend, after parting with you at York Town, I got safely to my own fireside and without inconvenience of any kind excepting sometimes cold toes & cold fingers. of this sort of punishment however I am it seems to have no more, as I am destined by the Congress to command in the South. In entering on this new and (as Lee says) most difficult Theatre of the war, my first thoughts have been turned to the Selection of an Engineer, an Adj^t General and a Qu[artermaster] General. Kosciusko, Hay & yourself, if [I can prevail upon] you all are to fill these offices and will fill them well. [The excellent] qualities of the Pole, which no one knows better [than] yourself are now acknowleged at H.Q. and may induce others to prevent his joining us—but his promise once given, we are sure of him,,.

The invitation of Gates, for which the preceeding extract had prepared us, was given and accepted, and tho' no time was lost by K., his arrival was not early enough to [enable] him to give his assistance to his old friend & General—but to Green (his successor) he rendered the most important Services to the last moment of the War, and which were Such as drew from that officer the most lively, ardent & repeated Ac[know]legments—which induced Congress, in October 1783, to bestow upon him the brevet of Brig. General and to pass a vote declaratory "Of their high sense of his[1] faithful and meritorious[2] conduct,,.

The war having ended he now contemplated returning to Poland and was determined in this measure by a letter from Prince Joseph Poniatowsky, nephew of the King & Generalissimo of the army. It was however ten years after this Period (1783) before Kosciusko drew the Sword on the frontier of Cracovia.

———

3^d Conduct of K in France.

[When] Bonaparte created the Dutchy of Warsaw & bestowed it on the king of Saxony great pains were taken to induce K. to lend himself to the promotion & support of that polity. [Having withstood] both the smiles & the frowns of the minister of [police, a last attempt] was made thro' the General's countrywoman and friend, the Princess Sapieha. the argument she used was founded on the condition of Poland, which, she said, no change could make worse—and that of the Gen. which even a small change might make better—"but[3] on this head I have a Carte blanche, Princess,, answered the Gen. (taking her hand & leading her to her carriage) "it is the first time in my life I have wished to shorten your visit—but you shall not make me think less respectfully of you than I now do,,.

When these attempts had failed, a manifesto in the name of Kosciusko, dated at Warsaw & addressed to the Poles, was fabricated & published at Paris. When he complained of this abuse of his name, &c the Min. of Police advised him to go to Fontainbleau.

MS (DLC: TJ Papers, 236:42391–4); entirely in Armstrong's hand; undated; damaged by ink corrosion and edge trimmed, with losses supplied from *HAW*; addressed: "Thomas Jefferson Esq. late President of the U.S. Monticello near Charlottesville Alb: Virginia"; beneath address: "(2)." Printed in *HAW*, 8:494–7.

Kosciuszko was BORN in 1746, not 1752. The Battle of Bemis (BHEMUS'S) Heights, 7 Oct. 1777, helped ensure British defeat in the Saratoga campaign. For Kosciuszko's commissioning as a BREVET brigadier general at the close of the Revolutionary War, see Worthington C. Ford and others, eds., *Journals of the Continental Congress, 1774–1789* (1904–37), 25:646n, 673 (4, 13 Oct. 1783).

[1] Armstrong here canceled "long."
[2] Armstrong here canceled "Services."
[3] Omitted opening quotation mark supplied from *HAW*, here and below.

From Thomas Eston Randolph

DEAR SIR   Ashton 1st July 1818

Inclos'd you will receive your Mill account, which I believe you will find correct—The balance due to you I will make immediate preparation to discharge—as well as the loss sustain'd on the last 27 barrels of flour damaged in my Boat—

Should you want more flour for your family use, we can procure it from the Back country waggons, and Mr Colclaser will be particular in the choice of it—The money balance we can give you a draft on Richmond for—in the course of twenty days or perhaps can furnish the money[1] here in that time—The delay I hope will not put you to inconvenience—

I must ask the favor of you to leave such directions with your workmen about the Mill repairs as will ensure its being ready in due time—that being a matter <u>all</u> important—Mr Rogers has made arrangements by engaging Teams, to commence delivering wheat in few days after finishing his harvest—I would have waited on you—but Mrs Randolph is from home, and all my people are out harvesting—I am very sincerely Yours   THOS ESTON RANDOLPH

RC (MHi); dateline at foot of text; addressed: "Thomas Jefferson Esqe Monticello"; endorsed by TJ as received 1 July 1818 and so recorded in SJL; additional notation by TJ on verso: "flour balce money loss. repairs."

The MILL ACCOUNT enclosed here may have been Randolph's Memorandum on Wheat Delivered to TJ, [Apr. 1818?].

[1] Manuscript: "mony."

To Baker Beaven

SIR   Monticello July 2. 18.

We have employed 4. hands 3. days in searching for slate, and came to what is of a proper thickness and fine color, but not in sheets of any size. I have no doubt we could obtain these, if we had now time to pursue it. but as other things press, and it seems very uncertain at what depth we can obtain such as ought to be used, we postpone it to the winter. I will send you a sample of what we found if I can meet with a conveyance and when we resume the business again, we shall probably trouble you again on the subject. accept the assurance of my esteem & respect.   TH: JEFFERSON

PoC (MHi); at foot of text: "Mʳ Baker Beaven"; on verso of reused sheet with canceled notation in TJ's hand: "Catalogue of books at Monticello"; mistakenly endorsed by TJ as a letter of 2 July 1819 but correctly recorded in SJL.

Baker Beaven (Beavin; Bivans) (1785–ca. 1821), slater and plasterer, began his training in Baltimore in 1803 when he was indentured by his father to Cornelius Walker, with whom he was due to remain until his twenty-first birthday in 1806. He died in Richmond (Harford Co., Md., Orphans' Court Proceedings, Book AJ1, 21 July 1803; Richmond City Hustings Court Will Book, 3:131).

To George Divers

DEAR SIR   Monticello July 2. 18.

I have been intending in some of my college visits to go on and ask a dinner of you, but latterly my daily rides have been in the opposite direction to explore a slate quarry a mile or two below Milton. why our family has not been to see yours cannot be said but for the lazy reason of never doing to-day what can be put off to tomorrow. I set out for Bedford tomorrow, and shall return just in time for the meeting of Aug. 1. at Rockfish gap. the roughness of the road will induce me to prefer a horse, and as it is too far for me to ride in one day I propose on the Thursday preceding to ask a dinner & bed of you, which will enable me to get to the gap on Friday evening, our meeting being for Saturday. mr Madison will be with me, and probably judge Roane & mr Tazewell, [so t]hat we shall lumber you up pretty well for an evening. affectionately your's.   TH: JEFFERSON

PoC (MHi); on verso of reused address cover of Bernard Peyton to TJ, 16 Mar. 1818; mutilated at seal; at foot of text: "Mʳ Divers"; endorsed by TJ.

From Levett Harris

I received a few days Since from Professor Fischer of Moscow, two Copies of his <u>Essai Sur la Turquoise et Sur la Calaite</u>, with a request that I would Seek to make one of them acceptable to Mr Jefferson.

In hastening to meet the request of Mr Fischer I beg leave to profit of the occasion to bring myself anew to your kind remembrance.

Among the lively recollections I Shall long retain of my visit to Monticello, that of the friendly wishes you were pleased to express on the Subject of my further diplomatic Service, is not the least impressive, and I confess I was not without Sanguine expectations that the design of the President was in unison with those wishes—I may also add, and without vanity, that Such was the calculations of the leading characters in this City and in a neighboring State—Such too was the impression of many Senators & representatives, testified to me at Washington.—   My Claims to Consideration were alike recognized in almost every official letter I received during my diplomatic Service, and afforded a pledge as to the dispositions of the Government on my return.

I repaired last Winter to the Seat of Government, and was received with kindness by the Chief-Magistrate.—I Soon perceived however, that what I was So anxious for, and which I flattered myself the President would pronounce favorably upon, was not to be obtained.

A Gentleman from Tennessee has been appointed to Russia.—I Shall not presume to go much further into detail at the moment, but I need not add that I expected a different treatment.

You know Sir, that the first relations with Russia were opened by me—that I paved the road to the Diplomatic Establishment, and I may add[1] that my reports in the Department of State also Shew, that what has been done advantageous to my Country is Some what the result of my labors.

The Emperor Alexander besides, & his Ministers, had testified a wish for my return—This wish was often pronounced to me as to a Continuance at the seat of Empire—it was emphatically uttered at the day of my taking leave by both the Empresses, and I believe has been officially announced to this Government.

If we value the dispositions of Russia—dispositions which at this moment above all others are, I think, to be cherished, it is manifest that they could not be cultivated with more effect than by deputing a person to that Court, who had had the good fortune to make himself agreeable to its Sovereign.

I Shall Say nothing of the last events that took place at St Petersburg, on which the President has been pleased to heap Eulogy on my Conduct—tho I might indulge in some important reflections which would bring me very near an interesting opinion I remember having exchanged with You Sir, the morning I took my leave of Monticello, and which, without disguise, I may Say relates to the Gentleman now in the Occupation of the principal place in the Cabinet. But it is proper perhaps that I defer to a more apposite period addressing you further[2] on this Subject.

I pray You to allow my very respectful Compliments to be made acceptable to Mr & Mrs Randolph and Miss Randolph, and to accept the renewed Sentiments of the most profound respect & veneration with which

I am, Dear Sir, Your most obedient and devoted Servant

LEVETT HARRIS.

RC (DLC); at foot of first page: "Thomas Jefferson late President of the United States"; endorsed by TJ as received 18 July 1818 and so recorded in SJL. Enclosure: Gotthelf Fischer, *Essai sur la Turquoise et sur la Calaite* (Moscow, 1816; Poor, *Jefferson's Library*, 5 [no. 173]; TJ's copy in MiU-C).

George W. Campbell (the GENTLEMAN FROM TENNESSEE) had been appointed the United States envoy extraordinary and minister plenipotentiary to Russia. BOTH THE EMPRESSES: the mother and wife of Alexander I of Russia, Maria Feodorovna and Elizabeth Alexeievna. The LAST EVENTS THAT TOOK PLACE AT ST PETERSBURG probably refers to the Kosloff affair (see James Monroe to TJ, 22 Oct. 1816, and note). As secretary of state, John Quincy Adams occupied the PRINCIPAL PLACE IN THE CABINET.

[1] Manuscript: "aad."
[2] Word interlined.

To William King (of South Carolina)

SIR   Monticello July 2. 18.

Your letter of June 4. is received as the former one had been in due time. it was not answered because the effects of age oblige me to withdraw from all correspondence which is not of absolute necessity, and especially on subjects of the difficulty of that your letter presents. I am afraid, you are not aware of all it's difficulties. there are 3. persons, known to myself, capable of deciding on the merit of your discovery; these are Doct[r] Patterson of Philadelphia, mr Hasslaer in the service of the US. and mr Bowditch of Salem in Mass. I name these because they are known to me. doubtless there are many others unknown to me. but if, thro' any friend, you can get the opinion of either of these, you may be assured of it's correctness in a much higher degree than from any opinion of mine. for the good of mankind as well as of yourself, I wish you entire success in your invention.

Th: Jefferson

PoC (DLC); on verso of a reused address cover from Francis Adrian Van der Kemp to TJ; at foot of text: "Mʳ William King"; endorsed by TJ.

To Thomas Eston Randolph

Dear Sir   Monticello July 2. 18.

Your's of yesterday was recieved last night. you need take no trouble about the flour balance, till you have it of your own; and as to the damaged 27. barrels I mean to bear my own part of that misfortune, so that you have nothing to make up on that account. I set out tomorrow for Bedford & shall be back by the 20ᵗʰ. mr Bacon will be starting about that time for Missouri, and will want some money from me; so that it is possible that the money balance may be a convenience then, unless mr Bacon should think it safer to take with him a note payable in bank, rather than the cash itself.   I went to the mill this morning with a view to advise with Powers[1] & mr Colclaser what is to be done in the inside [of?] the mill. but mr Colclaser was absent. I have therefore desired mr Bacon to go with mr Colclaser & Powers thro the mill, and decide what is necessary to be done, & whatever can be done by Powers & Davy they are to go on with: but what requires a greater force can be done only after harvest; but it may begin the day after the people are discharged from the harvest field. by that time however I shall be back.   I salute you with affection & respect   Th: Jeffer[son]

PoC (MHi); on verso of reused address cover of Thomas Cooper to TJ, 19 Apr. 1818; torn at seal; signature faint; at foot of text: "T. E. Randolph esq."; endorsed by TJ.

[1]Manuscript: "Power," here and below.

From John Barnes

Dear Sir—   George Town Coᵃ 3ᵈ July 1818.

Your very particular favʳ 28ʰ Ultᵒ Covering—"I know not from whom the inclosed letter to Wanscher comes—nor whether he is still living, I suppose, it is from Germany. and invoke your Charity to dispose of it according to Circumstances.—I do it, with the more pleasure—as it gives me New Occasion to Repeat to you—the Assurance of my Constant friendship and Respect."—

So unexpected address (respecting myself) and withal, coming thro your hands without—a further Clew whereby to unravel this mysterious Appearance—I cannot allow my self the liberty—of breaking—no less—then three confidential Seals—if any, the least you have—I shall be happy to receive them, and thereby—not only satisfy my curiosity—but justify—(if need be) any Agency that may possibly Occur in its Contents—respecting—

Sir—

your very Obed^t servant   JOHN BARNES,

PS. let me ask the fav^r of you—to open said letter. its contents may indicate some other person—it is however to be presumed my Name Accompanied—the letter to you,—

RC (MHi); endorsed by TJ as received 18 July 1818 and so recorded in SJL. RC (MHi); address cover only; with PoC of TJ to Charles Simms, 27 Oct. 1818, on verso; addressed: "Thomas Jefferson Esqr Monticello—Virg^a"; franked; postmarked Georgetown, 4 July. Enclosure not found.

From Anthony Charles Cazenove

SIR   Alexandria July 3^d 1818

I was favor'd in its time with your obliging note of 25th Decr for which I return my grateful acknowledgements.

Having for some years been in the habit of importing the different qualities of Murdoch's fine Madeira Wine, some of which I generally keep on hand for sale, but generally upon the orders I receive from many gentlemen in various sections of the United States, I take the liberty to ask you if you feel disposed to order some, when I should be happy to be favor'd with your commands, or those of any of your friends who may be so disposed, to whom I will be much obliged to mention my name.

A vessel Sailing from hence in a few days for Madeira would be a very good opportunity to forward any orders you might be pleased to favor me with, & which if annual would save you the trouble of ordering hereafter. I have now on hand some of Messrs Murdoch's fine high colour'd L.P. approaching to their Burgandy, in pipes, & half pipes; which I imported nearly 2 year's ago, & I sell at importation cost, being intended to supply those Gentlemen who prefer not to wait till imported for them; but have no Burgandy Madeira.

It is well to observe that the price of the L.P. has fell from £75– stg to which it had risen to £60– stg in the Island, with an additional charge of 20/– p pipe when shipped in halfpipes or quarter casks.

It is shipped under insurance when no counter directions are given, & may be shipped direct to almost any of the principal ports of the Union, frequent opportunities offering from Madeira.—When intended for any other port than this, the correspondent of the gentleman ordering, would of course require to be named.

Permit me to request you freely to command my services here, in any other respect, whenever they can be agreable, & believe me with highest regard, very respectfully   Sir

Your most Obed[t] Serv[t]   ANT CH[s] CAZENOVE

RC (MHi); dateline at foot of text; endorsed by TJ as received 18 July 1818 and so recorded in SJL. RC (MHi); address cover only; with PoC of TJ to John Steele, 27 Oct. 1818, on verso; addressed:

"The Hon[ble] Tho[s] Jefferson Monticello Virg[a]"; franked; postmarked.

L.P.: "London Particular."

From William S. Jacobs

SIR   S[t] Croix July 3rd 1818

Had death not berefted me of my much esteemed friend & Patron, Doctor Wistar, the Contents of my present respects would 'ere this have been comunicated to you, but being thus unfortunately deprived I hope from the well Known Kindness of your disposition that you'll excuse the liberty I thus take

It is now twenty three years past since I resided in the family of that good and great man, where I had frequently the Advantage of being in your Company—I was then engaged in making Anatomical Preparations for the Doctor, which you did me the honor of admiring so much, particularly, the preparations of the Ear, on a large Scale, made of Wax & Stone.—Since the Year 1804 I have resided in the Danish Westindia Islands, extensively engaged in the practice of Physic; my future stay will be on the Island of S[t] Thomas where under present Circumstances the practice is preferable to S[t] Croix, particularly would it be to me so could I be so fortunate as to obtain through your Kind influence the Appointment of American Consul, for which I humbly soliscit your Kindness—This Appointment has been since M[r] Harrison was recalled vacant, & by late accounts rec[d] from Philad[a] was yet

S[t] Thomas is the Rendez-vous of the Westindies, sailors from every nation crowd the Streets from morning til night, frequent broils &

Quarrells take place, which would allways come under my notice in case of Americans being in the Question so well from my Capacity as a magistrate as well as a Physician & in case of appointed Consul to all certainty the only one for the American, great many Advantages might in my Opinion thereby fall in favor to the American Sailors

Having thus laid my humble Soliscitation for your Interest in my behalf before you, I pray the forgiveness of the liberty thereby taken— which will be ever gratefully acknowledged by

sir Your humble & most Obe^t Servant.

W^M S. JACOBS. MD—

RC (MoSHi: TJC-BC); at foot of first page: "Thomas Jefferson Esqre Virginia"; endorsed by TJ as received 26 July 1818 and so recorded in SJL.

William Stephen Jacobs (1772–1843), physician, was born in Brabant. He served in the armies of Austria and France, eventually attaining the rank of assistant surgeon before deserting through the British lines. By 1795 Jacobs settled in Philadelphia. He was quickly integrated into its scientific community and worked as a dissector at the University of Pennsylvania under the direction of Caspar Wistar. Jacobs executed chalk drawings of megalonyx claw fossils that became the basis for engravings that appeared, along with articles on the animal by TJ and Wistar, in volume 4 of the American Philosophical Society's *Transactions*. In 1801 Jacobs received a medical degree from the University of Pennsylvania. The following year he was admitted to membership in the American Philosophical Society, and he served as librarian of Philadelphia's Chemical Society, 1801–02. Jacobs published *The Student's Chemical Pocket Companion* (Philadelphia, 1802). He moved to Saint Croix in aid of his

health in 1803, continued to practice medicine, and died there (William E. Horner, "Obituary Notice of D^r W S. Jacobs of St Croix," MS in PPAmP: APS Archives, Memoirs of Deceased Members, 1783–1855; Wyndham Miles, "William Stephen Jacobs," *Journal of Chemical Education* 24 [1947]: 249–50; *PTJ*, 29:xxxix, 300, 39:32–3; *Catalogue of the Medical Graduates of the University of Pennsylvania* [2d ed., 1839], 41; APS, Minutes, 16 July 1802 [MS in PPAmP]; H. Carrington Bolton, "Early American Chemical Societies," American Chemical Society, *Journal* 19 [1897]: 718; DNA: RG 59, LAR, 1817–25).

Robert Monroe HARRISON was appointed United States consul at Saint Thomas in 1816. A disagreement with the Danish governor general over the treatment of American seamen led to Harrison's recall in 1818. Nathan Levi was next appointed to the consulship there in 1826 (*JEP*, 3:29, 31, 504, 513 [14, 26 Feb. 1816, 17 Feb., 9 Mar. 1826]; Worthington C. Ford, ed., *Writings of John Quincy Adams* [1913–17], 6:361–3; *Baltimore Patriot & Mercantile Advertiser*, 5 June 1818; New York *Commercial Advertiser*, 10 Sept. 1818).

From Wilson Cary Nicholas

MY DEAR SIR   [received 3 July 1818]

Under cover to Mr Dandridge I enclose two notes which you will be so good as to endorse, and after sealing my letter, you will be pleased to give it the earliest conveyance by the mail to Richmond. In renewing this kindness to me, be pleased again to accept the strongest assurances, that whether I live or die, you nor yours, shall never receive the slightest inconvenience from your goodness to me.

I am with the greatest respect your much obliged

W. C. NICHOLAS

RC (DLC: TJ Papers, 215:38476); undated; addressed: "Thomas Jefferson Esq"; endorsed by TJ as received 3 July. Recorded in SJL as an undated letter received 3 July 1818 at Poplar Forest. Enclosures not found.

From Charles J. Ingersoll

SIR   Philadelphia 4. July 1818

Mr Wilcocks, the American Consul at Canton in China, has sent me, by a late arrival from that country, a Chronological View, and Dialogues, with English translations, as specimens of Chinese Literature, or rather, of English advancement in it, which he desires me to present to you in his name—

I avail myself of this occasion to renew the assurances of respectful consideration with which I remain, Sir,

Your most obedient servant   C. J. INGERSOLL

RC (NNPM); at foot of text: "Mr Jefferson"; endorsed by TJ as received 19 July 1818 and so recorded in SJL. Enclosures: (1) Robert Morrison, *A View of China, for Philological Purposes; containing A Sketch of Chinese Chronology, Geography, Government, Religion & Customs. designed for the use of persons who study the Chinese Language* (Macao, 1817; Poor, *Jefferson's Library*, 14 [no. 910]). (2) [Morrison], *Dialogues and Detached Sentences in the Chinese Language; with a free and verbal Translation in English. collected from various sources. Designed as an Initiatory Work for the Use of Students of Chinese* (Macao, 1816; Poor, *Jefferson's Library*, 14 [no. 911]).

Benjamin Chew Wilcocks (1776–1845), merchant and public official, made a number of trading voyages between Philadelphia and Canton, China, starting in the 1790s. He served as United States consul at Canton, 1813–22, and remained based there for another five years before returning permanently to Philadelphia. During his years abroad Wilcocks was heavily involved in the illegal opium trade and spent at least one year in India (Charles P. Keith, *The Provincial Councillors of Pennsylvania* [1883], 332; James Robinson, *The Philadelphia Directory, City and County Register, for 1802* [Philadelphia, 1802], 260; Wilcocks file in DNA: RG 59, LAR, 1809–17; *JEP*, 2:313, 316, 3:314 [31 Dec. 1812, 15 Jan. 1813, 23 Dec. 1822]; Jean Gordon Lee and Philip Chadwick Foster Smith, *Philadelphians and the China Trade, 1784–1844* [1984], 44–6; Jacques M. Downs,"American Merchants and the China Opium Trade, 1800–1840," *Business History Review* 42 [1968]: 418–42; gravestone inscription in Saint Peter's Episcopal Churchyard, Philadelphia).

From James Sloan

Baltimore July 4 1818

your kind letter was not more flattering to my vanity as an author, than grateful to those feelings, which yeild enjoyments far more precious, than any which flow from the mere praise of men. It is delightful to find exemplified in you, the unfading charms of literature, and the juvenile lustre they cast upon the dignity of declining years. <u>Your</u> praise will ever be to me the highest encouragement, as it gives me reason to beleive, that the hours I have devoted to solitude, and study were not wholly mispent.

From the sentiments of your letter, which have nothing of the cold formality of compliment; but appear to me to be the warm expression of the heart I may, I trust without appearing vain and presumptuous, inform you that some of my friends are at this moment endeavouring to procure for me the place of Secretary to Mr Campbell, minister to Russia. The pleasure I take, in the study of foreign languages, and the time I have devoted to french literature, render this situation peculiarly desirable to me. The practice of the law in which I am at present engaged, affords no field for the display of acquisitions of this kind. They might be useful in the situation of which I speak. The President the Secretary of state, the Attorney general, and Mr Campbell, have, by some of my friends, been already favorably impressed with respect to my character for which I could obtain a still greater number of vouchers: but the decision of the Executive in my favour would be sooner and more effectually secured by that sanction which <u>your</u> name carries with it, and that influence which it has long possessed and ever must possess over the hearts of the people of this country.

I have the honour to remain yours with much esteem & respect

Ja^s Sloan jun^r

RC (DLC); addressed: "To His Excellency Thomas Jefferson. Monticello"; franked; postmarked (faint) [Baltimore], 4 July; endorsed by TJ as received 18 July 1818 and so recorded in SJL.

Later this year the United States Senate confirmed President James Monroe's appointment of Charles Pinkney as secretary to the American legation in Russia (*JEP*, 3:143, 150 [27, 30 Nov. 1818]).

From Mathew Carey & Son

SIR   Philad. July 5. 1818—

Your favour of 28th inst. is rec[d]

We had supposed that M[c]Mahon's Gardening was forwarded per mail, when ordered by you, but upon examination, we find that the package had not been forwarded. It is now sent per mail, & we hope will arrive safe.—

Baron Grimm's Memoirs cannot be obtained here either in French or English.—We can readily obtain it for you from London or Paris.—The price we do not know, but if you wish it in French, it will be very low.—

Your obd serv[ts]   M CAREY & SON

√

RC (MHi); in the hand of a representative of Mathew Carey & Son; endorsed by TJ as a letter from Mathew Carey "sen[r]" received 19 July 1818 and so recorded in SJL. RC (DLC); address cover only; with PoC of TJ to Honoré Julien, 8 Nov. 1818, on verso; addressed (in a different hand): "Hon: Thos Jefferson Monticeleo V[a]"; franked; postmarked Philadelphia, 6 July.

To Wilson Cary Nicholas

DEAR SIR   Poplar Forest July 6. 18.

The letter to mr Dandridge which you intrusted to me, I delivered the next morning to mr Hunter to be put into the post office at Concord, a mile from his house[.] he promised to do it the same day himself, and said the stage would take it on this day, and deliver it in Richmond on the 8th which I trust will be done. certain that I shall not suffer in your hands, I administer to this accomodation with pleasure and add the assurances of my great friendship and respect.

TH: JEFFERSON

PoC (MHi); edge trimmed; at foot of text: "Col[o] Nicholas"; endorsed by TJ.

To Richard N. Thweatt

DEAR SIR   July 6. 18.

I have for some months been expecting a cask of Scupernon wine which mr Burton of N. Carolina was so kind as to procure for me. I have not heard from mr Burton himself thro' what channel he forwarded it, but Francis Eppes tells me he thinks it was either addressed to your care or to that of mr Johnson a merchant of Petersburg. I take the liberty of troubling you with this enquiry, and with the further request, if it be in Petersburg to have it forwarded to mr Patrick Gibson of Richmond who will pay all expences of transportation E⁺c. & to drop me a line of information. with my apologies for this trouble accept the assurance of my great esteem & respect.

Tн: Jefferson

PoC (MHi); on verso of Bernard Peyton to TJ, 27 Nov. 1817 (see note to Francis Brooke to TJ, 27 Nov. 1817); at foot of text: "Rich⁺ Thweatt esq."; endorsed by TJ. Recorded in SJL as written from Poplar Forest.

TJ probably meant John Wayles Eppes, not FRANCIS EPPES.

From Robert Walsh

Dear Sir   Philadelphia July 6ᵗʰ 1818
Not being able to resist my itch for scribbling, I have undertaken, in concert with Judge Cooper and a gentleman of New York, to contribute to a magazine of which I take the liberty of sending you two Numbers. The first article of each is of my doing, and the "Reflections on the Institutions of the Cherokees" are from the pen of Mʳ F. Gilmer so well known, and so piously attached, to you. The notices of new European books, & of the latest improvements may Serve to amuse a moment of your leisure.

In addition to what I have written in the magazine concerning Franklin, I have promised Mʳ Delaplaine to furnish him with a biographical sketch for his Repository, of the same illustrious philosopher. There is not, however, here, much of that kind of tradition concerning him, which would enable me to give an air of novelty or particular discrimination, to the performance.

I must not further obtrude upon you, unless it be to tender my respectful compᵗˢ to Coˡ & Mʳˢ Randolph, and to renew the assurance of the profound consideration with which I am,

Dear Sir, Your very obᵗ Servant   Robert Walsh Jᴿ

RC (DLC); endorsed by TJ as received 19 July 1818 and so recorded in SJL. RC (DLC); address cover only; with PoC of TJ to John Farrar, 10 Nov. 1818, on verso; addressed: "Thomas Jefferson Esqʳᵉ Monticello Virginia"; stamp canceled; franked; postmarked Philadelphia, 7 July. Enclosure: *Analectic Magazine*, vol. 11, no. 6 (June 1818), and vol. 12, no. 1 (July 1818); Poor, *Jefferson's Library*, 14 (no. 925).

Walsh's FIRST ARTICLE OF EACH of the enclosed magazine issues was a book review, the first a discussion of William Temple Franklin's edition of Benjamin Franklin's memoirs (pp. 449–84) and the second an essay on three accounts of Italian travel (pp. 1–36).

From Brett Randolph

RESPECTED SIR,   Culpeper 7. July <u>1818.</u>

In the year <u>1801</u>, I improvidently abandoned a lease of 14 years upon a farm in this County in the expectation of being appointed to an office in Frederick'sburg where I unavoidably remained untill I had nearly exhausted my small pecuniary resources—and unfortunately, soon after I had resumed the occupation of a farmer, the times became unfavorable and I have been for several years struggling with adversity in a state of poverty little short of absolute want. A recurrence, to this circumstance is not intended, as a murmur at what is some times aptly termed private griefs, but merely, as introductory to a most respectful request, in the sequel. It has been suggested to me very recently, that the post office at Richmond will probably be vacated. I would, with the aid of two of my Son's, in all the details, discharge the duties of that station;—and in the event, of the Office becoming vacant, permit me good Sir, to <u>solicit</u> you to interest yourself so far in my behalf, as to name me to the proper authority, as one whose chief care it would be, faithfully, to perform his duty—and that you will be pleased to excuse this obtrusion on your time,—and accept, the respectful consideration of Sir, your most Ob^t Sev^t

BRETT RANDOLPH JR

RC (MHi); endorsed by TJ as received 18 July 1818 and so recorded in SJL. RC (DLC); address cover only; with PoC of TJ to William F. Gray, 8 Nov. 1818, on verso; addressed: "Thomas Jefferson Esqr Monticello Albemarle County Virginia" by "mail"; franked; postmarked Stevensburg, 8 July.

Brett Randolph (1766–1828), farmer, was a native of Henrico County who made several unsuccessful attempts to obtain an appointment to public office. In 1795 TJ and Francis Eppes (ca. 1747–1808), acting as executors of the John Wayles estate, began a chancery lawsuit against Randolph and his brothers, including David Meade Randolph (ca. 1759–1830). The complicated effort to make the Richard Randolph estate responsible for payment of a debt failed four years later when an appeals court ruled in favor of the Randolph heirs. Randolph died at Goshen, Lowndes County, Mississippi (*VMHB* 34 [1926]: 163; *PTJ*, 28:285–91; Albert Gallatin to TJ, 18 Apr. 1805 [DLC]; TJ to Gallatin, 20 Apr. 1805 [NHi: Gallatin Papers]; DNA: RG 59, LAR, 1809–17; correspondence in ViW: Beverly Papers; *Richmond Enquirer*, 26 Feb. 1828).

From John Wharton (1771–1845)

8th July 1818

Mr Jefferson, will Oblige a Friend, in giving his Opinion upon the Subject of Oliver Evans^s Pattent Rights, Particularly his Hopperboy; Whether under the act of Congress he can Claim unlimited

Damages—or Whether he is the Inventer of the Hopperboy—or Whether there was a Renewal of the patent right of the Hopperboy.[1] Your answer to those Enquireries together with any other information upon the subject will be thankfuly Received by Sir Your Most Obedient
Serv[t]   JOHN WHARTON

RC (MoSHi: TJC-BC); dateline at foot of text; endorsed by TJ as received 9 July 1818 and so recorded in SJL.

John Wharton (1771–1845), miller, served in the Virginia militia from late in 1802 until 1806. He was commissioner of the revenue for Bedford County, 1808–15, and by 1820 he operated a mill. In 1830 Wharton owned twenty-six slaves (Mary Denham Ackerly and Lula Eastman Jeter Parker, *"Our Kin": The Genealogies of Some of the Early Families who*

Made History in the Founding and Development of Bedford County Virginia [1930], 221–3; Vi: Wharton Papers; Bedford Co. Order Book, 15:21, 138, 281; 16:104, 215, 331; 17:51; 18:6; DNA: RG 29, CS, Bedford Co., 1830; Bedford Co. Will Book, 12:1–2, 15:112–5, 328–9).

For the ACT OF CONGRESS, see Isaac McPherson to TJ, 3 Aug. 1813, and note.

[1] Omitted period at right margin editorially supplied.

From Thomas Lehré

DEAR SIR,   Charleston S° C[a] July 9th 1818—
    I have taken the liberty of Sending you the enclosed paper, by which you will see, that your Republican friends here, at the celebration of our National Independence, have not failed, to give you, as one of our standing Toasts.—
    With my best wishes for your Welfare and happiness through life I remain Dr Sir Yours Sincerely   THO: LEHRÉ

RC (DLC); endorsed by TJ as received 19 July 1818 and so recorded in SJL.

For the ENCLOSED PAPER, see note to Lehré to TJ, 10 July 1818.

From John H. Cocke

SIR,   Bremo July 10. 1818
    Correct opinions in the liberal arts being the result of more cultivation than has fallen to my lot, and having the highest confidence in your taste in Architecture, I have taken the liberty to desire Mr Neilson to call on you with the plan of my Building for the purpose of consulting you upon some points which he will explain:—not doubting, that such a trespass upon your valuable time will be readily excused,

& any information freely given that may aid in redeeming this branch of the arts from its hitherto neglected State in Virginia—

Yours with high respect & Esteem   J. H. COCKE

RC (CSmH: JF); endorsed by TJ as received 28 July 1818 and so recorded in SJL. RC (DLC); address cover only; with PoC of TJ to Destutt de Tracy, 24 Nov. 1818, on verso; addressed: "M^r — Jefferson Monticello In care of Mr Neilson."

From Thomas Lehré

DEAR SIR   Charleston S^o C^a July 10th 1818—

By yesterday, and this days mail, I have Sent you three of the daily papers of this City by which you will see how grateful even our rising generation are towards you. It is with the greatest pleasure I inform you, that I have of late received letters from a number of your old friends in various parts of this State, in which they express a great desire to know whether I can inform them of the State of your health, at the Same time offering up their prayers to the Throne of Grace that you may enjoy[1] a long Life, and every blessing this World affords, as a just reward for your great and meritorious Services to our Dear and beloved Country.—

Our friends in this part of the Union, feel a lively Interest in the Emancipation of our Fellow Men in South America, and are anxious to know how our affairs with Spain, are likely to terminate. Whenever you can find time to drop me a line on the above Subjects, be assured it will be received with great pleasure. I remain with every sentiment of esteem—Dear Sir Yours most Sincerely

THO: LEHRÉ

RC (DLC); at foot of text: "Thomas Jefferson Former P. of the U.S."; endorsed by TJ as received 22 July 1818 and so recorded in SJL.

The DAILY PAPERS OF THIS CITY that Lehré sent in this letter and that of 9 July 1818 probably included the Charleston *City Gazette and Commercial Daily Advertiser* of 7, 9, and 10 July. The issue of 7 July reported the toasts of the Saint Andrew's Parish Independence Day celebration, the ninth of which was to "THOMAS JEFFERSON and JAMES MADISON.—The two brilliant constellations who have guided the American people to glory and happiness—May the light they have shed, never be obscured." Two days later the newspaper published the toasts of the '76 Association, with the fourth honoring "*Thomas Jefferson*, the *polar star* of *Republicanism*—Let us steer by this brilliant light, and we will pursue the strait course." Finally, on 10 July the paper printed an account of the Charleston Republican Artillery's celebration, with its fourth toast saluting "*Thomas Jefferson.—* Next to Mount Vernon, we turn a grateful eye to Monticello's height."

[1] Preceding four words interlined.

To John Wharton (1771–1845)

SIR   Poplar Forest July 10. 18.

I had formerly occasion to consider with attention Oliver Evans's right to a patent for his elevators, conveyers, and hopper boys, and satisfied my self that the elevator and conveyor had been in use some thousand years. of the hopper boy I found no evidence but I was afterwards assured that it had been invented in Maryland and Pensylvania and in use some years before the date of Evans's patent. he has however in 3 or 4. instances recovered damages in the inferior courts of the US. against persons using them without his licence. the question has never been carried before the Supreme court. the ground of the last decision I am told was that whether he had a right or not under his original patent, Congress had given it to him absolutely by their act in his favor. what damages however are recoverable, I am not able to say, not having the act of Congress here. his corn-crusher stands only on his patent right, and is a gross plagiarism. a smith of the name of Davies in George town made them commonly several years before Evans's patent, and I have one now in a mill which was in use long before his patent. the only difference is that Daviess' screw was placed horizontally, & Evans's vertically. but as to his claims under the special law of Congress, I believe it is safest, however unjust, to acquiesce in them. Accept the assurance of my great respect.

TH: JEFFERSON

RC (Vi: Wharton Papers); addressed: "Capt John Wharton Bedford." PoC (MoSHi: TJC-BC); on same sheet as RC of R. Pollard to TJ, 6 Dec. 1817; endorsed by TJ.

For earlier discussions of Oliver Evans's RIGHT TO A PATENT and his CORN-CRUSHER, see TJ to Isaac McPherson, 13 Aug. 1813, and note; TJ to Charles Willson Peale, 13 June 1815, and note. DAVIES: Thomas Davis.

From Patrick Gibson

SIR   Richmond 11th July 1818.

I hand you inclosed sales of your 67 bls: flour Nt Prds $484.90 at your credit, also copy of your accot Curt to this day balanced by $375.25 to your debit and lest something may occur to cause me to neglect it at the proper time I inclose you two notes, for renewal of those due next month—I have received a small box of seeds from Alexandria, will you be pleased to direct the disposal of it

With much respect I am
Sir Your ob: Servt   PATRICK GIBSON

Messrs Baker & Fulsom have called for paym^t of some fish sent you I have deferred it until I sh^d hear from you

RC (MHi); between dateline and salutation: "Thomas Jefferson Esqre"; endorsed by TJ as received 19 July 1818 and so recorded in SJL. Enclosures not found.

N^T PRDS: "net proceeds."

From Samuel J. Harrison

Sunday July 12. 1818.

S J Harrison presents his respects to m^r Jefferson, & regrets that he is deprived of the pleasure of Dining with him today, by the Sudden Indisposition of one of his Children.

RC (ViU: TJP); with PoC of TJ to John Wharton (d. 1829), 29 July 1819, on verso; dateline at foot of text; addressed: "Thomas Jefferson Esqr Poplar Forest."

From Salma Hale

SIR,   Keene, NH. July 13. 1818

I have collected and send you the pamphlets containing the Unitarian controversy which you expressed a desire to see when I visited you lately at Monticello. The whole impression being sold, I have been obliged to borrow two or three from a friend, and if you feel indifferent about retaining you would oblige me by returning them

This controversy has been eagerly read in New England—and the consequence, I think, will be the dissemination of liberal principles, and a victory not distant over bigotry & fanaticism.

With great respect Your Obdt Servt   SALMA HALE

RC (DLC); at foot of text: "Th. Jefferson Esquire"; endorsed by TJ as a letter from Salma "Hales" received 22 July 1818 and so recorded in SJL. For the enclosures see Hale's Notes on his Visit to Monticello, [after 1818], document 4 in a group of documents on Salma Hale's Visit to Monticello, 7–8 May 1818, and note.

To James P. Preston

SIR   Poplar Forest July 13. 18.

I recieved in due time your Excellency's letter of Mar. 18. covering the appointment with which you were pleased to honor me as one of the Comm^rs under the act concerning the University. meaning to accept the trust, it did not occur in the moment that I ought to say so, and to prevent any suspence which my silence might occasion in your mind on the subject. the reciept of your second favor of May 20. which after a long absence from home, found me here, first brought to my attention the culpable failure in duty which occasioned you the trouble of a second notification. entirely sensible of this inadvertence, I sollicit your Excellency's pardon, with the assurance that it proceeded from absence of reflection solely. my high respect for yourself personally, as well as the sense of a duty omitted, call for this apology, with an addition of the tardy assurance that I accept the appointment with which you have honored me, and will render under it every service in my power. with my regrets at this incident be pleased to accept the sincere expressions of my high consideration and esteem.

TH: JEFFERSON

RC (Vi: RG 3, Preston Executive Papers); addressed: "His Excellency Governor Preston Richmond"; franked; postmarked Lynchburg, 16 July; endorsed by Preston as TJ's letter "accepting the app^t of Comm^r to fix the Site for the University," received 20 July 1818. PoC (NPV: Autograph Files Collection); with notation at foot of text that TJ's great-grandson Wilson Cary Nicholas Randolph presented the text to Vassar College on 3 Nov. 1905.

Preston's LETTER OF MAR. 18, not found, is recorded in SJL as received 28 Mar. 1818 from "Counc. chamb." Its enclosure was evidently TJ's formal appointment as one of the University of Virginia commissioners. While TJ's copy has not been found, it presumably differed from the version sent to James Madison only in the specific information filled in by hand. Madison's copy, dated Richmond, 18 Mar. 1818, cited the 21 Feb.

1818 statute requiring appointment by the governor of "twenty-four discreet and intelligent persons" to form a "Board of Commissioners to aid the Legislature in ascertaining a permanent scite for a University and for other purposes" and appointed Madison, "by and with the advice of the Council of State," as the commissioner for his senatorial district (printed form with blanks filled in by a clerk, signed by Preston, in DLC: Madison Papers; printed in Madison, *Papers, Retirement Ser.*, 1:239).

Preston's SECOND FAVOR OF MAY 20, described above as a SECOND NOTIFICATION of TJ's appointment as a University of Virginia commissioner belatedly received at Poplar Forest, is not recorded in SJL and evidently distinct from the letter of that date printed above, which is on a different subject and was received at Monticello.

From Edmund Bacon

DEAR SIR.   July 14 1818.

I have to trouble you againe respecting my preparation of going to the western country. I am desireous to go to view it before I carry my family if I can do so without too much inconvenience to us both as much depends on my mooving this comeing fall on a letter which I expect to recieve in a few weeks from one of my brothers. when my

brothers was here in Jan:y I made arraingments with them to procure me land. if I should recieve information that they have done so
positively before I arrive there to see it I expect I had as well moove.
but the last letter that I receved states that they hoped to Keep the
oppertunities to perchase open untill my arrival I have written to them
that propersition was most sootable to me and if I can ride out to
make my own choice would certainly be most desireable to me for it
is very often the case that what one likes another disappoves of I have
considerd the business in this way that I should have untill the middle of July to say whither I will ride out or moove I think should I
ride out that I could be much better spaired August and september
than October and November. for in the too last months comes on the
sooing the graine fattening my pork feeding and attending to the
stock and in the two other months none of this interfears. and another
advantage to me is the sooner I can get out the better for fear some
arraingment might be made disagreable to me I expect I should be
oblijed to get from you 5 or 600 dollars that if I might find an oppertunity to perchase I might by ading that sum to other money be
able to do so. after I secure land should I like well enough to perchase
at this time imagin I may pospone mooving for some time or I may
detirmen to moove in the fall of 1819. should I dislike the part of the
country so as not to perchase my wish would be that you would recieve back the money on my return upon interest the business of my
going I well Know is very inconvenient to you but I think that if you
should be away while I may be gone that if you would leave with my
son written instructions that things would be done very well and in
all cassis of deficulty I would get Mr Randolph to direct in your absence and of course should expect my wagers to cease during my
absence from home in this affair I wish you to be as little subjic to
deficulties as possoble and in an important matter like that of a man
fixing his home for life wish to do what will be most to my interest
and satisfaction upon this matter you will be pleased to consider and
inform me what is sootable to you
in October and November we will be obliged to recieve our corn and
many other business that would not be on us sooner. and I have some
prospect of a neighbours company if I can go in July or August. but
that is no very graite object I wish to soot your convenienc[e] as well
as I can

    I am Yours sincerly   E: Bacon

RC (ViU: TJP-ER); dateline at foot of text; edge trimmed; adjacent to signature: "Mr. Jefferson"; endorsed by TJ.

From Edmund Bacon

S<small>IR</small>.   [ca. 14–29 July 1818]

I have been very closely considering upon the business of mooving. since our last conversation I find that my family is desireous of going so that it seems that perhaps I had better try to do so for I must confess that a home of good land is very desireous. but in this attempt I consider it my duty to proceed as much to your interest as in my power. I am truly sorry that the unforchinate chainge of the deminished prices of produce has taken place at a time when I have commenced arraingments to call upon you for money. and was it not for true necessaty I would scorn the Idea of doing so. I have recieved a letter from my brother saying that the public lands in St Louis county whare I expect to purchase has not yet commence'd but it is supposed the sales will take place in that county this fall or winter and it is important that I should be prepared to secure land when ever that sales take place consequently it is important that I should go thare to examin and pick out my land before the sales.

I have found a man that says that he thinks it will be convenient to give me money for a draught on Richmond payable on the first of November. he said that he thaught it probable that he could do so but could not say possitively that he would he said that if it should be in his power that he would require two pr cent discount pr month. this is as low as we may expect. but the important point is to be certain of the money. for it would be a considerable injury to me to get ready and then to meet with a disappointment my impresion is that if you could say something to him that he would do any way to Oblige you both as to certainty of the money and terms the man is Irie Garrett the sherief. I am affraid that I shall meet with deficulties in geting a sum I have in a Gentlemans hands. I shall try what I can do immediately. but hope I shall succeede to my wish as I am very much advise'd by my brothers to come to that part of the world at any rate and I am interested so that I must go some way or loose money if I can be accomodateed without two grait a loss to you. if I cannot moove I shall be under the necessaity to ride out. but as the Journey is graite I wish to make but one trip if I can avoid it. however I have always found you two good towards me not to be willing to be governed by your convenience that is I have a wish to do what is best for myself and to be as accomodateing to you as I possoblely can and wish to consider your interest with my own

I am Yours sincerly   E: B<small>ACON</small>

RC (MHi); undated, but evidently composed between Bacon's letters to TJ of 14 and 29 July 1818; with different opening on verso reading only "Sir. with respect of"; addressed: "Mr Jefferson."

From John Hancock Hall

SIR   Washington 15. July 1818.

Several years since, I formed the resolution of collecting information, from time to time, as opportunities occured, & of acquiring by all proper means a thorough knowledge of every thing relative to the American Militia—with a view to its being instrumental to the public welfare at some future period—At the time of forming this resolution it appeared to me <u>probable</u> that a good system for the American Militia would be established by the Govt. long before my stock of information upon the subject would have become sufficiently complete to be of much publick importance—but as it also appeared to me <u>possible</u> that that event might not thus take place I determined to improve, with prudence, every opportunity for the acquisition of such knowledge which might occur, & have continued[1] to do it to this moment— Years have now passed away & so little has yet been effected by the National Govt. in regard to our Militia, that a good system for them is still as much a desideratum as ever—Believing it in my power to contribute somewhat toward effecting this important object—I feel desirous of taking the proper steps in regard to it, & none but those which are proper

& with a view of profiting by your experience, take the liberty of respectfully soliciting your attention to the subject, & your advice in regard to the course best calculated to ensure success,

Being a Stranger to you, it would perhaps not be improper for me to state, that as the perfection of their fire[2] arms, especially small arms, constitutes a most important point in regard to our Militia—I have in attending to <u>that</u> subject, succeeded in combining, in one piece, all the advantages of the best rifles & of the best muskets, with other <u>important</u> advantages possessd by neither of those arms, & all this has been effected with great simplicity—

I shall, tomorrow sett off for Harpers' ferry, Virginia—by the direction of Govt. & shall remain there six weeks or more—& should wish, if agreeable to you to enter into farther communications upon the subject of the American Militia—

Most respectfully I am Sir Your obt. servt,   JOHN H. HALL

RC (DLC); endorsed by TJ as received 19 July 1818 and so recorded in SJL. RC (MHi); address cover only; with PoC of TJ to John Barnes, 11 Nov. 1818, on verso; addressed: "Thomas Jefferson Esq. late President—U.S—Milton Va."; franked; postmarked Georgetown, 16 July.

John Hancock Hall (1781–1841), inventor, was a native of Maine. By 1803 he was serving in the Portland Light Infantry, and by 1811 he had invented a mechanism for loading rifles at the breech. When he made his patent application later that year, William Thornton, the Patent Office superintendent, claimed to have developed the same technology. Ultimately they agreed to patent the firearm improvement in both their names. Hall spent the next several years trying to secure a position manufacturing his breech-loading rifles for the United States government. In 1819 he was awarded a contract and began working to produce the firearms at the federal armory in Harper's Ferry, where he remained for the next two decades. Hall was an early champion of the efficiency and utility of interchangeable parts, and at Harper's Ferry he installed machinery and implemented techniques that helped to transform the manufacture of firearms from craft to industry. In 1840 ill health caused him to move to Missouri, where he died (Roy T. Huntington, *Hall's Breechloaders: John H. Hall's Invention and Development of a Breechloading Rifle with Precision-made Interchangeable Parts, and Its Introduction into the United States Service* [1972]; Madison, *Papers, Pres. Ser.*, 3:181; *List of Patents*, 98; Merritt Roe Smith, *Harpers Ferry Armory and the New Technology: The Challenge of Change* [1977]; *Pittsfield* [Mass.] *Sun*, 8 Apr. 1841).

[1] Manuscript: "contined."
[2] Word interlined.

From David Bailie Warden

DEAR SIR,   Paris, 15 July 1818—

I have the pleasure of sending you the inclosed copy of a circular letter "Instruction pour Les Voyageurs &ᶜ &ᶜ"[1] which the Professors of the Royal museum request you to communicate to some of the naturalists of the United States.   I am, dear Sir, with great respect,

your very obliged Servant   D. B. WARDEN—

RC (DLC); endorsed by TJ as received 11 Sept. 1818 and so recorded in SJL. RC (DLC: TJ Papers, 205:36548); address cover only; with PoC of TJ to Stephen Cathalan, 21 Dec. 1818, on verso; addressed: "Thomas Jefferson Esquire monticello"; notation in Reuben G. Beasley's hand: "Havre, July 24ᵗʰ 1818. forwarded by yr. ob. Servant R G Beasley"; stamped "SHIP" and "FREE"; postmarked New York, 31 Aug. Enclosure: André Thoüin to TJ, 5 June 1818, and enclosure.

[1] Omitted closing quotation mark editorially supplied.

From James Madison

[16 July 1818]

I have postponed the return of the two papers, to the present time, in consequence of your intimation, that you would not return from Bedford till about a week before the day of assembling at Rockfish, and I shall note that this letter is not to be forwarded from Monticello.

affectionate respects   JAMES MADISON

RC (ViU: TJP); undated and possibly fragmentary; at foot of text: "Mᵣ Jefferson." Recorded in SJL as a letter of 16 July 1818 received six days later from Montpellier. Enclosure: enclosures to TJ to Madison, 28 June 1818.

From John Adams

DEAR SIR   Quincy July 18. 1818

Will you accept a curious Piece of New England Antiquities. It was a tolerable Catechism[1] for The Education of[2] a Boy of 14 Years of age, who was destined in the future Course of his Life to dabble in so many Revolutions in America, in Holland and in France.

This Doctor Mayhew had two Sisters established in Families in this Village which he often visited and where I often Saw him, He was intimate with my Parson Bryant and often exchanged with him, which gave me an Opportunity often to hear him in the Pulpit. This discourse was printed, a Year before I entered Harvard Colledge and I read it, till the Substance of it, was incorporated into my Nature and indelibly engraved on my Memory.

It made a greater Sensation in New England than Mᵣ Henrys Philippick against the Parsons did in Virginia. It made a Noise in Great Britain where it was reprinted and procured the Author a Diploma of Doctor in Divinity.

That your Health and voracious Appetite for reading may long continue is the Wish of your Old Friend and

humble Servant   JOHN ADAMS

RC (DLC); at foot of text: "President Jefferson"; endorsed by TJ as received 30 July 1818 and so recorded in SJL. FC (Lb in MHi: Adams Papers). Enclosure: Jonathan Mayhew, *A Discourse concerning Unlimited Submission and Non-Resistance to the Higher Powers: With some Reflections on the Resistance made to King Charles I. And on the Anniversary of his Death: In which the mysterious Doctrine of that Prince's Saintship and Mar-* *tyrdom is unriddled* (Boston, 1750; Poor, *Jefferson's Library*, 9 [no. 532]).

Patrick Henry's 1 Dec. 1763 PHILIP-PICK during the Parsons' Cause controversy is discussed in Richard R. Beeman, *Patrick Henry: A Biography* (1974), 13–22; see also William Wirt to TJ, 27 July 1814, and note. The enclosed work by the Boston clergyman Jonathan Mayhew defending popular resistance to unjust political authority was REPRINTED in Richard Barron, ed., *Pillars of Priestcraft and Orthodoxy Shaken* (London, 1752), 2:259–335. Mayhew received A DIPLOMA OF DOCTOR IN DIVINITY from King's College (later part of the University of Aberdeen) in 1749 (Peter John Anderson, ed.,

Officers and Graduates of University & King's College Aberdeen, MVD–MDCCCLX [1893], 100).

[1] RC: "Chatechism." FC: "Catechism."
[2] Preceding three words interlined.

From Frank Carr

[received 18 July 1818]

M[r] Jefferson will oblige F. Carr by giving the enclosed letter to M[r] Terrell its[1] proper direction & placing it in the channell by which it may most speedily reach its destination. F Carr asks M[r] J. to accept assurances of highest respect.

RC (ViU: TJP-CC); undated; endorsed by TJ as received 18 July 1818 and so recorded in SJL. Enclosure not found.

[1] Manuscript: "is."

From Mr. Couscher

[received 18 July 1818]

En Cas que mr Jeferson veuille profiter du Retour en france du voyageur qui lui a apporté des lettres; pour faire reponse ou le charger de quelques Comissions

m[r] Jeferson pourra lui faire parvenir à New york où ce voyageur doit S'embarquer;

Son adresse est, à Mr Couscher, chez m[r] Regniard Marchand, William Street N° 32—

EDITORS' TRANSLATION

[received 18 July 1818]

Should Mr. Jefferson wish to benefit from the return to France of the traveler who brought him some letters, by sending replies or entrusting him with any commissions

Mr. Jefferson can reach him in New York, where this traveler is to embark;

His address is, to Mr. Couscher, chez Mr. Regnard, merchant, William Street N° 32—

RC (MHi); written on an undated scrap; endorsed by TJ as a "note left at Mont[o] July. — 1818," received 18 July. Recorded in SJL as an undated "note of address left at Mont[o]" received 18 July 1818. Translation by Dr. Genevieve Moene.

[139]

From John G. Robert (for Patrick Gibson)

SIR   Richmond 18 July 1818

I send you by Mr Ja^s Johnson Two boxes wine rec^d from Alex^r & one box Seeds—toll of which thro' the Columbia Canal will be p^d M^r J by you—

  Y^{rs} respectfully   PATRICK GIBSON
               ⚘ JOHN G. ROBERT

RC (MHi); in the hand of a representative of Gibson & Jefferson; dateline at foot of text; addressed: "Thos Jefferson Esqr Monticello" by "Mr Johnson"; endorsed by TJ as a letter from Gibson of 18 Aug. received 1 Sept. 1818 and so recorded (with TJ's bracketed notation that it concerned "wines by Johnson") in SJL.

From George Rogers (for Bernard Peyton)

SIR.   Richmond 18 July 1818.

By Mr James Johnson you will receive One Box Merchandize, which was Shipped to me from Norfolk by Messrs Moses Myers, & Son. You will please pay Mr Johnson freight as customary—&C.

  Yores respc'y   B. PEYTON
               ⚘ GEO: ROGERS

RC (MHi); addressed: "Thomas Jefferson Esqr Monticello Virginia"; with initialed note by Peyton on address cover: "Pay toll at columbia on the within goods"; endorsed by TJ as a letter from Peyton received 1 Sept. 1818 and so recorded in SJL.

To John C. Calhoun

SIR   Monticello July 20. 18.

During the last session of Congress, I took the liberty of addressing to you an application for military services during the revolutionary war, from M. Poirey, Secretary and Aid de camp to Genl. La Fayette. I saw, in the proceedings of Congress published in the public-papers, that you had been so kind as to put it under way, and that it was before a Commee of Congress. seeing nothing done on it afterwards, I presume it was laid over with the mass of unfinished business to another session. being to write to M. de la Fayette shortly I should be very happy to be able to state to him the present situation & prospect of the claim of his friend. his gratification alone could induce me to trespass on your time with a request of a line of information of what I may say to him. the same motive I hope will be my apology for this trouble, to which I add the assurance of my[1] sincere respect and high consideration.   TH: JEFFERSON

PoC (DLC); on verso of reused address cover of John Cook to TJ, 20 Apr. 1818; at foot of text: "John C. Calhoun esq. Sec^y at War"; endorsed by TJ.

According to the PROCEEDINGS OF CONGRESS published in the 3 Apr. 1818 *Richmond Enquirer*, on 28 Mar. 1818 John Rhea of the House Committee on Pensions and Revolutionary Claims "reported a bill making provision for the claim of M. Poiroy, as secretary and aid-de-camp to Major General La Fayette; which was twice read and committed."

[1] Word interlined.

To Patrick Gibson

DEAR SIR   Monticello July 20. 18.
    On my return here from Bedford I find your favor of July 11. covering my account to that date, balance in your favor 375.25 and I observe that a draught of mine of June 24. in favor of James Leitch for 120.D. is not entered which would add so much to the balance. to meet this I have 21. Bar. flour now in the mill to be forwarded by mr T. E. Randolph as soon as the state of the river will admit, and the last of the month after next he will forward 50. Barrels more. but I have an earlier resource in a sum of money I expect to recieve, which of itself will cover my balance, and any other draughts which I may be under a necessity of making, which will be moderate, and made but in case of necessity. the bill of mr Baker for fish I will thank you to pay
    The crop of wheat we have just got in cannot be got to market but [in] the course of the winter. from this place it will be 550. Barrels of flour, certain, as I now recieve it in fixed rents. from Bedford the crop of wheat will be considerably below mediocrity, I suppose not more than 200. Barrels of flour. our tob° planted there should bring about 20,000 ℔. these articles, if prices are favorable, will enable me to meet my last Dutch instalment in the spring and to commence the reduction of my notes in bank, which will be my next and most important concern. in the meantime I think I may say with certainty that such moderate draughts as I may be constrained to make on you shall be covered with little delay. I return you the notes signed. I suspect the box of seeds is an annual one which I recieve from the public garden of France, and which I give to some of the botanical gardens of the US. if the direction is French this is certainly so, and I would then direct a proper disposal of it. if not French it may be forwarded her[e.] Accept the assurance of my friendly esteem & respect
                                                    TH: JEFFERSON

PoC (MHi); on verso of reused address cover of John Adams to TJ, 28 Jan. 1818; torn at seal; edge trimmed; at foot of text: "Mr Gibson"; endorsed by TJ. Enclosures not found.

The order in favor of JAMES LEITCH settled four debts: $10 he paid for TJ "in charity" on 11 May 1818, a $30 payment to Larkin Powers on 23 May, and loans from Leitch to TJ of $30 on 20 May and $50 on 20 June 1818 (*MB*, 2:1345).

To Charles J. Ingersoll

SIR   Monticello July 20. 18.

On my return, the day before yesterday, after a long absence from this place, I found here your favor of July 4. with the two Chinese works from mr Wilcox which accompanied it. I pray you to accept my thanks for the trouble you have taken in forwarding them, and, if you are in correspondence with mr Wilcox, & should have other occasion to write to him, I must request you to express to him my sense of his kind attention in sending me these works. they are real curiosities, and give us a better idea of the state of science in China than the relations of travellers have effected. it is surely impossible that they can make much progress with characters so complicated, so voluminous, and inadequate as theirs are. it must take a life to learn the characters only, & then their expression of ideas must be very imperfect. I imagine that some fortuitous circumstance will some day call their attention to the simpler alphabets of Europe, which with proper improvements may be made to express the sounds of their language as well as of others, and that then they may enter on the field of science. I think missionaries to instruct them in our alphabet would be more likely to take good effect, and lead them to the object of our religious missionaries, than an abrupt introduction of new doctrines for which their minds are in no wise prepared.   with my thanks be pleased to accept the assurance of my great esteem & respect.

TH: JEFFERSON

PoC (DLC); on verso of reused address cover of Patrick Gibson to TJ, 4 May 1818; at foot of text: "Mr C. J. Ingersoll"; endorsed by TJ.

To Thomas Lehré

DEAR SIR   Monticello July 20. 18

I am thankful to you for your favor of the 9th inst. and particularly so to my friends who think me worth their recollections. entirely withdrawn from all attention to public affairs and seeking the rest, which age now renders indispensable, I still see with pleasure the republican principles of our constitution so generally prevalent, as to give me confidence in their permanency and that most of those who had other partialities have come over to the majority. I pray you to be assured of my continued esteem and respect.   TH: JEFFERSON

PoC (DLC); on verso of reused address cover of Thomas Jordan to TJ, 20 Apr. 1818; at foot of text: "Thoˢ Lehré esq."; endorsed by TJ.

From Bernard Peyton

DEAR SIR   Richᵈ 20 July 1818
I recᵈ on friday a large Box from Norfolk containing articles for you, shipped from New Orleans by way of Boston, all the expences on which from the latter place (Boston) I have paid & forwarded it the same day by Mʳ Johnson's Boat to you & hope it will reach you safely—   Mʳ Ritchie left a Map with me some time since for you, which I forwarded by Coˡ Randolph's Cart.[1] I suppose it has reached you before this.

I understand that the commissioners for fixing upon the scite for the University of Virginia, who reside below this City, will unite with those from the other side of the mountain in endeavouring to fix it on that side, with the hope of keeping up old Williamsburg: To fix it at Charlottesville they think would be fatal to their hopes; how far this may be the fact, I am not prepared to say, & merely mention it, that you may not be taken by surprise—

Very respectfully sir Your Mo: Obd: Servt:

                                         BERNARD PEYTON

RC (MHi); addressed: "Thomas Jefferson Monticello," with "Miltone" added in an unidentified hand; franked; postmarked (faint) [Richmond], 20 July; endorsed by TJ as received 22 July 1818 and so recorded in SJL.

[1] Omitted period at right margin editorially supplied.

To Robert Walsh

DEAR SIR   Monticello July 20. 18.
On my return from Poplar Forest the day before yesterday I found here your favor of the 6ᵗʰ with the two Nᵒˢ of the Analectic magazine, for which I thank you. on learning that yourself and judge Cooper were to contribute to that work, I had determined to become a subscriber,

and knowing of no one in this state who is authorised to recieve subscriptions to it, I will avail myself of this occasion of praying you to have my name set down as a subscriber. I have not yet had time to look over the N^{os} you were so kind as to send me, but know beforehand that I shall recieve pleasure & information from whatever comes from either yourself or Judge Cooper. still the plan of this work will not fill the void which is made by the discontinuance of the American register. I looked to that work to keep us up with the new advances of science in Europe.   The buildings for our Central college are going on with some spirit, and during the next week is the meeting of the Commissioners who are to report to the legislature whether it ought not to be adopted for the University; and of such a report I have little doubt.[1] in that case I think we shall make it a place of note.   I am still to apologize for not returning your Grimm; and am constantly pressing it's readers here to get thro' it. in the hope I might save the risk of it's return by stage I had written to M. Carey to know if a copy could be had there which could be delivered you at short hand; but he informs me no one can be had. your own therefore shall be returned with little further delay.   Accept the assurance of my friendly esteem & respect.   TH: JEFFERSON

RC (facsimile in James D. Julia Inc., Fairfield, Me., online auction catalogue, 22–24 Aug. 2006, lot 819); at foot of text: "Mr Walsh." PoC (DLC); on verso of reused address cover of otherwise unlocated letter from William Pope to TJ and Thomas Mann Randolph (1768–1828), 5 May 1818 (see note to Salma Hale to David Hale, 5 May 1818, document 1 in a group of documents on Salma Hale's Visit to Monticello, 7–8 May 1818); endorsed by TJ.

[1] Omitted period at right margin editorially supplied.

To John Barnes

DEAR SIR   Monticello July 21. 18.

Believing you knew Martin Wanscher, to whom the inclosed letter is addressed, my letter to you was so short as to be unintelligible. he was a plaisterer living in Alexandria, and was the one I employed to come on and plaister my house, which he did about 10. years ago, and returned to Alexandria. he was a German, and I suppose from his acquaintance with me, instructed his friends in Germ[a]ny to inclose their letters to me. this one came inclosed to me, and having some idea that I had heard he was dead, but not certain of it, I took the liberty of requesting you to send it to him if living, or to his family if dead, for he had a family. I return it now therefore with the same request. the letter being in German, it would be useless to open it either for your or my information. if he is neither living nor left any representative, if you will be so good as to return it to me, I will give it a place among my papers, in case any body should appear to call for it. I hope you enjoy good health, and assure you of my constant esteem & respect. TH: JEFFERSON

PoC (MHi); on verso of a reused address cover from José Corrêa da Serra to TJ; one word faint; at foot of text: "Mr Barnes"; endorsed by TJ. Enclosure not found.

To Levett Harris

DEAR SIR   Monticello July 21. 18.

On my return from a visit to a distant and occasional residence of mine, I found here your letter of the 2^d inst. with the Essay of Professor Fischer for whose attention in sending it to me I am very thankful, and, should you have other occasion to write to him, I will pray you to express my thanks to him. I assure you that I am disappointed in your failure to be nominated to Petersbg. soon after I had the pleasure of your visit here, I had a full conversation with the President on your subject & of the mission to St Petersbg, and the favorable terms in which he spoke of you, & of your fitness for it, led me to expect your appointment. I consider the friendship of the emperor, and his present station as Arbiter of Europe, as of the utmost importance to the US. while there is a combination of sovereigns whose league seems to have for object the maintenance of kingly government generally. my belief is that you would have been acceptable to him, and that your knolege [of] the ground would have given you advantages which a stranger will be long acquiring. no doubt that reasons unknown to either you or myself have dictated the present appointment. with my regrets on public, as well as personal account, be pleased to accept the assurance of my great esteem and respect.

TH: JEFFERSON

PoC (DLC); on verso of reused address cover to TJ; one word faint; at foot of text: "Levett Harris esq."; endorsed by TJ.

To Brett Randolph

DEAR SIR   Monticello July 21. 18.
Your favor of the 7th inst. is the first intimation I have recieved of any expected vacancy in the post office of Richmond: nor does any thing known to me induce me to suppose it probable. I sincerely sympathise with you in the circumstances which render that appointment desirable to you, and will willingly take some occasion to make you known to the President who is daily expected at his seat adjoining me. the number of applications with which I was overwhelmed, on my retirement from the government, to ask appointments to office for others, obliged me to lay it down as a law of conduct never to take part in any of those sollicitations. this however will not prevent my favorable mention of your case by way of conversation with the President. with my wishes for your success accept the assurance of my great respect and esteem.   TH: JEFFERSON

PoC (ViW: TC-JP); at foot of text: "Brett Randolph esq."; endorsed by TJ.

To James Sloan

DEAR SIR   Monticello July 21.
Your favor of July 4. arrived here during a visit to a distant and occasional residence of mine. the request it contained would have been literally and cordially complied with had it been permitted by the law I have been obliged to lay down for my own government in such cases. on my retirement from the government the intimate friendship between my successor & myself naturally induced a general supposition that applications for office thro' myself would be favorably recieved. this drew on me such a mass of applications for recommendation, as employed fully half my time, and kept me eternally in the attitude of a supplicant at the feet of the government: and obliged me to come to a determination to withdraw from those offices with rigor, and with rigor I have observed the resolution, because a departure from it in a single instance would disarm me of it's pro[tection?] in every one. the President is daily & hourly expected at his seat adjoining me, being known to be on the road. I shall certainly see him the day after his arrival. this will give me opportunities of conversation when I will with great pleasure draw it incidentally in some way towards yourself and express to him the sentiments which I think myself justified in entertaining with respect to yourself. and if these can

have the effect of favoring your wishes present or future[1] it will be a circumstance of gratification to me　　　in the mean time be assured of my great esteem & respect　　　　　　　Th: Jefferson

PoC (DLC: TJ Papers, 213:38041); on verso of reused address cover to TJ; partially dated; ink stained; at foot of text: "James Sloane esq."; endorsed by TJ as a

letter of 21 July 1818 and so recorded in SJL.

[1] Preceding three words interlined.

From Gerard Troost

Sir—　　　　　　　　　　　　　Capesable July 21[t] 1818—

I have the honor to transmit you two books one of Mr Faujas de St Fond and the other of Dr Kesteloot with a letter of Mr Thoúin. having been Captured at Sea—and having been Subjected to other disasters of war, are the reasons why I was not able to forward them Sooner as I only receive them this Spring.

It is only by accident that I can Send you this works put under my care; it was not my original intention to remain in this Country; I was Sent by Louis King of Holland to the Island of Java; but finding at that time no opportunity to leave this country and the Island being take afterwards by the Brittish, I abandoned that project and have established myself in Philadelphia where I have erected a chemical laboratory which has andswered very well my expectations—have also erected the first and at present the only factury of Alum in the United States at the Magothy river near Annapolis Maryland—and am resolved to Spend the rest of my life in this happy Country—

I anticipated the pleasure of presenting these books to you personally but owing to the nature of my occupation which reqúires my unremitted attention at this time, the Alum establishment having been burnd Down lately, I am deprived of that Satisfaction and have to resort to the usual mode of conveyance by letter—

One of my friends Dr Julius Ducatel is ere long going to Europe he will Spend Some time in Paris, and will See Mr Faujas, Thoúin and other Scientific men, he will with pleasure convey any commands You will charge him with—He will leave this Country the middel of August next—In case You please to favour him with any. Letters directed to Dr Juliús Ducatel Baltimore will come at hand—

I have the honor to be respectfully—
Sir Your most obedient Servant　　　　　　G. Troost

RC (MHi); at head of text: "The honorable Thomas Jefferson"; endorsed by TJ as received 1 Sept. 1818 and so recorded in SJL. Enclosures: (1) Jacob L.

Kesteloot to TJ, 6 Nov. 1809, and enclosure. (2) Barthélemy Faujas de Saint-Fond to TJ, [ca. Nov. 1809], and enclosure. (3) André Thoüin to TJ, 20 Mar. 1810. Enclosed in Julius T. Ducatel to TJ, 3 Aug. 1818.

Gerard Troost (1776–1850), scientist, was a native of Holland who obtained medical and pharmaceutical training through apprenticeships at Leiden and Amsterdam. His wide-ranging interests included geology, and in 1807 Louis Bonaparte, king of Holland, appointed him to assemble a royal mineral collection. In preparation for that mission Troost studied crystallography with René Just Haüy and geology with Abraham Gottlob Werner, and he originally planned to join a scientific expedition to Java but instead settled in Philadelphia in 1810. He became the first president of the Academy of Natural Sciences of Philadelphia in 1812, and he was elected to the American Philosophical Society in 1816. Troost was also involved in an unsuccessful effort to establish an alum manufactory in Maryland. By 1821 he was teaching mineralogy at the Philadelphia Museum and chemistry at the Philadelphia College of Apothecaries (later the Philadelphia College of Pharmacy). In 1825 Troost joined Robert Owen, William Maclure, Thomas Say, and Charles Alexandre Lesueur in an attempt to establish a utopian society at New Harmony,

Indiana. Two years later the society was struggling and Troost moved his family to Nashville, where until his death he served as a professor at the University of Nashville. He was also appointed the first state geologist for Tennessee, held the post for many years, and was responsible for the first geological map of the state. Although Troost published extensively during his lifetime, his final work on the fossil crinoids of Tennessee, which he had submitted to the Smithsonian Institution for publication just before his death, lingered for decades in the hands of the reviewer James Hall, who plagiarized some of his work. The research was not released under Troost's name until 1909 (*ANB*; *DAB*; *DSB*; Leonidas C. Glenn, "Gerard Troost," *American Geologist* 35 [1905]: 72–94; Joseph W. England, ed., *The First Century of the Philadelphia College of Pharmacy, 1821–1921* [1922], 63–8, 397; APS, Minutes, 19 Jan. 1816 [MS in PPAmP]; *Philadelphia Journal of the Medical and Physical Sciences* 2 [1821]: 207; *Public Acts passed at the stated session of the Nineteenth General Assembly of the State of Tennessee* [1832], 43–4; *Richmond Enquirer*, 27 Aug. 1850; Elvira Wood, "A Critical Summary of Troost's Unpublished Manuscript on the Crinoids of Tennessee," Smithsonian Institution, United States National Museum, *Bulletin* 64 [1909]: v–150).

From James Cutbush

Office of the US. Medical Depar't Philad^a

SIR,   July 22^d 1818

I herewith enclose you two addresses which were delivered on the ever memorable 4th of July: the one of Dr Jacksons is justly considerd a valuable exposition of the rise, progress, and downfall of kingdoms & republics, and the causes which produced them. The principles drawn from the history of government serve, as they do, to recall us to preserve, protect & perpetuate[1] our happy system of government. You no doubt were acquainted with the Doctor's father, the apothecary & physician, and the friend of Dr Hutchinson & other staunch republicans. I shall say nothing of the other address, which contains some typographical errors; the intention of it, however, was to <u>unite</u>

the democratic party in this district, and to shew the absurdity of inventing new names, as old school & new school &c It is remarkable, that, at our dinner, <u>nearly</u> every man voted for Hiester or the old school candidate, and <u>every</u> man for Mr Monroe, Mr Madison & yourself. The toast for Mr Monroe was printed, so that none but Duane and a few others of the <u>old school</u> in this state will, or may be expected to oppose the reelection of Mr M.   It is this:

"The president of the U. States—The confidence of the democratic party in his principles and integrity, placed him at the helm of state; his administration has strengthened that confidence."

Although this was drank with repeated applause, yet the present governor of our state was not drank; so that, take it all in all, the democratic division in this state is local, and confined in the last election, to two democratic candidates.

You will excuse the liberty I have thus taken, in communicating these ideas. I feel pleased that we are likely to bring about an union of the contending <u>interests</u>.

The plan of cultivating Indian corn, for which Mr Hall obtained a patent and on which subject I wrote you when at Norfolk V^a has been tried with us, but with no success; it has also been tried in New Hampshire, and failed.

very respectfully Your devoted friend, & Obed^t Servt

JA^s CUTBUSH.

RC (DLC); at foot of text: "His Excellency Thos Jefferson. Monticello"; endorsed by TJ as received 30 July 1818 and so recorded in SJL. Enclosures: (1) Samuel Jackson, *An Oration, Delivered, at the County Court-House, Philadelphia, on the Forty-Second Anniversary of American Independence* (Philadelphia, 1818; Poor, *Jefferson's Library* 13 [no. 826]; TJ's copy in ViU), describing the Fourth of July as the "sabbath of our liberties" and contrasting the commemoration of the Declaration of Independence with the way that "Other nations celebrate with heartless pomp, and idle pageantry, the birth day of a despot, whom they dare not approach" (pp. 2–3); predicting that, thanks to the expansion of population and promotion of internal improvements, "Republic will rise on republic; empire stretch beyond empire, till either ocean constitute the boundaries of free and confederated America" (p. 4); declaring that the "discovery of this country, and the adoption of a free and enlightened system of government, have been designed by Providence to effectuate the perfection of the human character and the advancement of society" (p. 4); surveying the history of civilization, including the fall of Rome and development and demise of the feudal system; positing a direct connection between European settlement in the Americas "and the declaration of our freedom, as parts of the divine scheme for the gradual improvement of man; and progressive perfection of society" (p. 11); and concluding that, since "Faction and disunion, alone, threaten our safety," the preservation of the "Union of the states" is paramount (p. 12). (2) Cutbush, "An Address, Delivered at the SHEPHERDESS, on the Fourth of July 1818, to a company of citizens, by request" (Philadelphia *Franklin Gazette*, 13 July 1818), connecting the principles of liberty, equality, and the natural rights of man as expressed in the Declaration of Independence with the same ideas articulated in the United States Constitution; declaring that the nation emerged as a direct result of the "hand of Providence"; emphasizing the importance of educating children to "*know* their rights, their liberties, their inheritance"; praising TJ as author of the Declaration of Independence and quoting from his letter to Benjamin O. Tyler of 26 Mar. 1818; inferring that the blood spilled in the American Revolution sealed "a covenant between God and man, and of rational liberty and just equality"; lauding the contributions of Benjamin Franklin, John Adams, TJ, John Hancock, Robert Morris, Tadeusz Kosciuszko, and Lafayette, as well as American military victories; recalling TJ's declaration in his first inaugural address that all citizens are both federalists and republicans but denying that most members of the Federalist party support a "federalism which springs from pure principles, and is identified with republicanism"; analyzing Jean Jacques Rousseau's theory of the social contract and demonstrating its application to a republican form of government; and concluding that everyone shares responsibility for protecting the Union by preserving republican principles, supporting arts,

manufactures, and internal improvements, diffusing science, and implanting in the "rising generation correct views of political jurisprudence."

In 1801 TJ corresponded briefly with the DOCTOR'S FATHER, David Jackson (*PTJ*, 32:415–6). The Republican party in Pennsylvania had divided into OLD SCHOOL & NEW SCHOOL factions. Joseph Hiester, the OLD SCHOOL CANDIDATE for governor of Pennsylvania in 1817, lost to William Findlay but defeated him three years later at the next gubernatorial election (Philip S. Klein and Ari Hoogenboom, *A History of Pennsylvania* [2d ed., 1980], 128–34). The TOAST FOR Mᴿ MONROE was given at an Independence Day celebration addressed by Cutbush, which was organized by a "private company of citizens." Their fourth toast honored TJ as "The author of the Declaration of Independence. A brilliant star in the constellation of '76" (*Franklin Gazette*, 10 July 1818).

[1] Manuscript: "pepetuate."

From James Monroe

DEAR SIR   washington July 22. 1818

I expected long before this to have had the pleasure of seeing you in Albemarle, but the necessity of being here, on the receit of Genˡ Jackson's report, of his operations in Florida, & in the expectation of the return of our commissʳˢ from Buenos Ayres, whom I wishd to meet, detaind me in Loudoun till lately, when on the occurrence of both events I returnd to the city.

The occurrence at Pensacola, has been full of difficulty, but without incurring the charge of committing a breach of the Constitution, or of giving to Spain just cause of war, we have endeavour'd to turn it to the best account of our country, & credit of the commanding General. We shall tell the Spanish minister, that the posts will be deliverd up, but that their attack, was owing to the misconduct of the Spanish officers, whose punishment woᵈ be demanded of his govᵗ, and that his govᵗ must keep a strong force in Florida, to enable it to comply with the stipulation of the treaty of 1795, which would be rigorously enacted. The proof of misconduct in the Spanish officers, in stimulating the Indians to make war, furnishing them with munitions of war to carry it on &ca, is very strong. It has appear'd to be altogether improper, to hold the posts, as that would amount to a decided act of hostility, and might be considerd an usurpation of the power of Congress. To go to the other extreme has appeard to be equally improper,[1] that is, to bring Genl Jackson to trial, for disobedience of orders, as he acted on facts which were unknown to the gov^t when his orders were given, many of which indeed occurr'd afterwards; & as his trial, unless he should ask it himself, would be the tryumph of Spain, & confirm her in the disposition not to cede Florida.

I lately transmitted to Mr Madison a copy of a paper, written at Moscow, by order of the Emperor, as the basis of his instructions to his ministers at the allied courts, relative to the differences between Spain & her Colonies, & likewise a copy of a letter which I have written to Gener^l Jackson, on the subject [men]tiond above, for your joint information. Those papers, will give you full information, on both subjects. I shall leave this to day or tomorrow for Loudoun, whence I shall proceed without delay with my family for Albemarle, where I hope to find you in good health.

with great respect & esteem your friend & servant

JAMES MONROE

RC (DLC); edge chipped; endorsed by TJ as received 30 July 1818 and so recorded in SJL.

The SPANISH MINISTER was Luis de Onís.

The COPY OF A PAPER, WRITTEN AT MOSCOW, BY ORDER OF THE EMPEROR, was a 17 Nov. 1817 "Russian Memorial on the Negotiation relative to the Question of Rio de la Plata, and, in general, on the Pacification of the Colonies; for communication to the interested Courts and to the Cabinets of the Mediating Powers." It laid out the plan of Emperor Alexander I for negotiations between the monarchs in Madrid and Rio de Janeiro that could return the Rio de la Plata to Spanish control and restore the allegiance of other Latin American colonies to their European rulers (Tr in MHi: Adams Papers, in French, filed with George W. Erving to John Quincy Adams, 26 Feb. 1818; English translation in William R. Manning, ed., Diplomatic Correspondence of the United States Concerning the Independence of the Latin-American Nations [1925], 3:1853–9). Monroe enclosed the document to James Madison on 18 May 1818, and Madison responded three days later (Madison, Papers, Retirement Ser., 1:287–8, 289–90).

The LETTER WHICH I HAVE WRITTEN TO GENER^L JACKSON, dated Washington, 19 July 1818, gave Monroe's reaction to Andrew Jackson's explanation of his military activities in Pensacola, presented the government's official position, and explained its future course of action (Jackson, Papers, 4:224–8).

On this date Monroe advised Madison that "I send you a copy of my letter to Genl Jackson, which will unfold to you, our views on the whole subject. I wish you to shew this paper, & the Russian document to Mr Jefferson, in confidence, when you see him" (RC in DLC: Madison Papers; printed in Madison, Papers, Retirement Ser., 1:309).

[1] Remainder written in a different ink.

From Margaret Page

Dear and most respected Sir! Williamsburg, July 22nd 1818

DEAR AND MOST RESPECTED SIR! Williamsburg, July 22nd 1818

Presuming on the pure and generous friendship! with which you so many years distinguish'd my lamented Husband! I take the liberty to introduce to you <u>our</u> only surviving Son (John Page) whose delicate State of health requires that he should take a Journey to the Springs; and having to pass thro' your Neighbourhood—Reverence, Gratitude, and Affection! excite his anxious Wishes to behold You!

With deep Interest, and peculiar pleasure, I learn, the present State of your Health, inspires the Hope of many years continuance of your invaluable Life! Oh! long may it be protracted for the happiness of All who know and Love You!

The unfading rememberance of the kindness and attention I received from my dear Mrs Randolph, during my Visits at Monticello, still warms my Heart, and I beg leave to offer her, and her amiable Family, its best affections and most grateful attachment! and to assure you, revered Sir, that among its last Sentiments will be what I owe to your Friendship and Beneficence.

With the highest consideration

I am, dear Sir. most respectfully yours MARGARET PAGE.

RC (MHi); endorsed by TJ as received 21 Aug. 1818 and so recorded in SJL.

Margaret Lowther Page (ca. 1760–1835), poet, moved from New York City to Williamsburg in 1790 when she married TJ's friend John Page, then a congressman and later (1802–05) governor of Virginia. Both Page and her husband wrote poetry and exchanged their work with other authors, including fellow Williamsburg resident St. George Tucker. In 1790 the three collaborated on a volume of privately printed poems (copy in ViW, lacking title page, but with Margaret Page's handwritten annotations). Page shared her poems with friends and published several in literary magazines, including the *Port Folio* and Mathew Carey's *American Museum*. She died in Williamsburg (Joseph M. Flora and Lucinda H. Mackethan, eds., *The Companion to Southern Literature* [2002], 947, 971; Richard Channing Moore Page, *Genealogy of the*

Page Family in Virginia [2d ed., 1893], 80; *ANB*, 16:902–3; *PTJ*, 38:283–4; Daphne Hamm O'Brien, "From plantation to Parnassus: Poets and poetry in Williamsburg, Virginia, 1750–1800" [Ph.D. diss., University of North Carolina, Chapel Hill, 1993], 43–4, 160, 169; Washington *Daily National Intelligencer*, 30 Oct. 1835).

John Page (ca. 1799–1838), attorney, attended the College of William and Mary, represented Williamsburg in the Virginia House of Delegates, 1825–26, and sat in the Senate of Virginia, 1832–36. In 1827 he was named to his alma mater's board of visitors, which he chaired as rector by 1835. Page died in Richmond (*William and Mary Provisional List*, 31, 54; Leonard, *General Assembly*; Page, *Genealogy of the Page Family*, 80; Nathan Reingold, Marc Rothenberg, and others, eds., *Papers of Joseph Henry* [1972–2008], 2:457–60; Marshall, *Papers*, 12:61–2, 552; *Richmond Enquirer*, 23, 30 Oct. 1838).

To Marc Antoine Jullien

Sir   Monticello. July 23. 18.

Your favor of Mar. 30. 17. came to my hands on the 1ˢᵗ of March 1818. while the statement it contained of the many instances of your attention in sending to me your different writings was truly flattering, it was equally mortifying to percieve that two only, of the eight it enumerates, had ever come to my hands; and that both of my acknolegements of these had miscarried also. your first favor of Nov. 5. 09. was recieved by me on the 6ᵗʰ of May 10. and was answered on the 15ᵗʰ of July of the same year, with an acknolegement of the reciept of your Essai general d'education physique, morale, et intellectuelle, and of the high sense I entertained of it's utility. I do not recollect thro' what channel I sent this answer; but have little doubt that it was thro' the office of our Secretary of State, and our minister then at the court of France.

In a letter from Mʳ E. I. Dupont of Aug. 11. 17. I recieved the favor of your 'Esquisse d'un ouvrage sur l'education comparée' which he said had been recieved by his father a few days before his death; and on the 9ᵗʰ of Sep. 17. I answered his letter, in which was the following paragraph. 'I duly recieved the pamphlet of M. Jullien on education, to whom I had been indebted some years before for a valuable work on the same subject. of this I expressed to him my high estimation in a letter of thanks, which I trust he recieved. the present pamphlet is an additional proof of his useful assiduities on this interesting subject, which, if the condition of man is to be progressively ameliorated, as we fondly hope & believe, is to be the chief instrument in effecting it.' I hoped that mr E. I. Dupont in acknoleging to you the reciept of your letter to his father, would be the channel of conveying to you my thanks, as he was to me of the work for which they were rendered. be assured, Sir, that not another scrip, either written or printed, ever came to me from you; and that I was incapable of omitting the acknolegements they called for, and of the neglect which you have had so much reason to impute to me. I know well the uncertainty of transmissions across the Atlantic, but never before experienced such a train of them as has taken place in your favors and my acknolegements of them. you will percieve that the letter I am now answering was eleven months on it's passage to me.

The distance between the scenes of action of Genˡ Kosciuzko & myself, during our revolutionary war, his in the military, mine in the civil department, was such, that I could give no particulars of the part he acted in that war. but immediately on the reciept of your letter, I wrote to Genl Armstrong, who had been his companion in arms, & an Aid to Genl Gates, with whom Genl Kosciusko mostly served, and requested him to give me all the details within his knolege; informing him for whom, and for what purpose they were asked. I recieved, two days ago only, the paper of which the inclosed is a copy, and copied by myself, because the original is in such a handwriting as, I am confident no foreigner could ever decypher. however heavily pressed by the hand of age, and unequal to the duties of punctual correspondence, of which my friends generally would have a right to complain, if the cause depended on myself, I am happy to fin[d] that in that with yourself there has been no ground of reproach. least of all things could I have omitted any researches within my power which might do justice to the memory of Genl Kosciuzko, the brave auxiliary of my country in it's struggle for liberty, and, from the year 1797. when our particular acquaintance began, my most intimate and much beloved friend. on his last departure from the US. in 1798. he left in my hands an instrument appropriating, after his death, all the property he had in our public funds, the price of his military services here, to the education and emancipation of as many of the children of bondage in this country as it should be adequate to. I am now too old to undertake a business de si longue haleine; but I am taking measures to place it in such hands as will ensure a faithful discharge of the philanthropic intentions of the donor. I learn with pleasure your continued efforts for the instruction of the future generations of men, and, believing it the only means of effectuating their rights, I wish them all possible success, & to yourself the eternal gratitude of those who will feel their benefits, & beg leave to add the assurance of my high esteem & respect.　　　　　　　　　　　　　　　　Th: Jefferson

PoC (DLC); one word faint; at foot of first page: "M. Jullien." Enclosure: Tr in TJ's hand (not found) of John Armstrong's Biographical Sketch of Tadeusz Kosciuszko, printed above at 1 July 1818.

Jullien's letters of MAR. 30. 17 and NOV. 5. 09 were actually dated 30 Nov. 1817 and 15 Nov. 1809, respectively. DE SI LONGUE HALEINE: "requiring so much time and labor."

From William Kean

Sir.　　　　　　　　　　　　　　　　　　　　Norfolk 23^d July 1818.

Having conceived an Idea that a safe and cheap substitute might be contrived for Steam Navigation, I have ventured to make an essay for that purpose, on the principles of the known properties of water & Atmospheric Air; and being desirous of obtaining the opinion of the first Scientific Character in the United States, I take the liberty of Sending you herewith a Copy of the Drawing & Specifications of my invention, which have been recently deposited in the Patent Office. But owing to an opinion given by the Superintendant of that Office, to the Secretary of State, I have been refused a Patent on the Supposition that it is intended for a Perpetual motion, and Coming within a rule of the Office that requires a model for inventions of that description. It never was my intention that it should be named or likened to a Perpetual motion, well knowing the folly of attempting any thing of that kind, to be constructed of materials Subject to friction and decay.

Having as yet made no experimental efforts to test the principle, and being of opinion that a model made of diminished Size, so as to be floated in a Tub of Water in the Patent Office, it would be barely possible to give the invention a fair trial. In Consequence of which I have postponed further progress, but shall await the Honour of recieving your judgment on the practicability of bringing it to perfection, and Should be happy to adopt any alterations or improvements you might be pleased to Suggest.

I have little to add to the explanations already given, you will be pleased to notice that the well aperture, during the time the machinery will be in operation, will be covered with a large body of water, so that no air can possibly escape from the well or Chest in that direction.

You will be so good to pardon this trouble from a Stranger, who is, with the Greatest respect, Your Obedient & Humble Servant.

W^M KEAN.

RC (MoSHi: TJC-BC); endorsed by TJ as received 30 July 1818 and so recorded in SJL. RC (DLC); address cover only; with PoC of TJ to Peter Poinsot, 25 Nov. 1818, on verso; addressed: "Thomas Jefferson Esqre Monticello." Enclosures not found.

The patent office SUPERINTENDANT was William Thornton. The SECRETARY OF STATE was John Quincy Adams.

To Franz X. Zeltner

SIR   Monticello in Virginia July 23. 18.

I recieved but lately your favor of Oct. 29. announcing to us the death of Genl Kosciusko. to no country could that event be more afflicting, nor to any individual more than to myself. I had enjoyed his intimate friendship and confidence for the last 20. years, & during the portion of that time which he past in this country, I had daily opportunities of observing personally the purity of his virtue, the benevolence of his heart, and his sincere devotion to the cause of liberty. his anterior services during our revolutionary war had been well known & acknoleged by all. when he left the US. in 1798. he left in my hands an instrument, giving, after his death, all his property in our funds, the price of his military labors here, to the charitable purpose of educating and emancipating as many of the children of bondage in this country as it should be adequate to. at that time I had strength & vigor of mind sufficient to undertake the execution of his philanthropic views: but the 20. years elapsed since that time, now weigh on me so heavily, and have brought me so near the term of all human concerns that it would be imprudent for me to undertake a business of so long execution. I am therefore taking measures to have it placed in such hands as will ensure a faithful discharge of his philanthropic views. I fear some difficulty in obtaining the aid of our courts of justice from the want of an official certificate of his death. except the public papers, which could not be recieved in evidence, your letter is the only document I possess of that fact, and being unauthenticated by any public magistrate, our courts will find difficulty in acknoleging it's authority. if I could, thro your means or that of any other person, recieve a certificate of his death, authenticated by the civil authorities of the place, it would facilitate and ensure the execution of his benevolent purpose.

Your emigrant countrymen who reach these shores are certain of finding employment which will ensure to them abundant subsistence and comfort. one only of them has come into my neighborhood, Louis Leschot of Neufchatel. he is settled in a neighboring village as a watchmaker, is an excellent, sober, and industrious citizen, and is making money faster than he knows what to do with it. but there seems to be a combination of the oppressors of human rights employing the atrocious means of engaging the masters of the vessels in which they take their passage, to carry them to other countries, and to wear them out by delays, by sickness, want, scanty food, and long passages, to discorage and defeat their endeavors at seeking an asylum, in these states, from the oppressions of Europe. the sufferings some of them have been made to undergo, by these flagitious instruments of despotism and crime are horrible to relate.

I pray you to accept the assurance of my high respect and esteem.

TH: JEFFERSON

RC (SzBzACT); addressed: "Monsr F. X. Zeltner cidevant Prefet National du Canton de Soleure à Soleure en Suisse"; stamped; postmarked. PoC (CSmH: JF-BA); on reused address cover to TJ; endorsed by TJ.

To William Huntington

July 2[4?] 18

Th: Jeffe[r]son asks the favor of mr H[u]ntington to dine with hi[m] on Sunday ensuing.

RC (DNDAR); dateline at foot of text; damaged at crease. Not recorded in SJL.

William Huntington (b. ca. 1794), merchant, educator, and Episcopal lay preacher, was a native of Connecticut who moved to Albemarle County by December 1817 and operated a dry-goods store in Charlottesville until at least 1824. Although financial difficulties obliged him to sell some property in 1820, he managed to save his business, and TJ began purchasing books and other goods from him in 1821. By 1825 Huntington had moved to Charlotte Court House, where he continued his mercantile pursuits, worked as a schoolteacher, and served as an Episcopal lay minister especially active among the enslaved population of Char-

lotte County. In 1860 his combined personal and real estate in that county was valued at $4,600 (*MB*; ViHi: Huntington Papers; Vi: RG 48, Personal Property Tax Returns, Albemarle Co., 1818; Albemarle Co. Deed Book, 22:115–6, 183–4, 224, 267, 23:218–9, 254–5; Elizabeth Trist to Nicholas P. Trist, 15 June 1820 [DLC: NPT]; Charlottesville *Central Gazette*, 24 Nov. 1820, 31 May 1822; *Journals of the Conventions of the Protestant Episcopal Church in the Diocess of Virginia. from 1785 to 1835, inclusive* [1835], 151; DNA: RG 29, CS, Charlotte Co., 1850, 1860).

An undated invitation reads "Th: Jefferson asks the favor of mr Huntington to dine at Monticello tomorrow" (RC in NN: Lee Kohns Memorial Collection).

From the Seventy-Six Association

DR Sir,   Charleston 24th July 1818 —

Be pleased to accept of the '76, Association a Copy of an oration delivered on the 4th Inst: by one of their members, as a mark of the high Esteem, which, as a body, they entertain for your Sentiments and Character.

The style and political principles of this production, it is believed, will meet your Cordial approbation.

With Sentiments of high Respect we are Yours &c

> Jno: B. Legare
> A. H: Ohara
> Jno: Sommers
> Edw^D P. Simons[1]
> Rich^D Osborne
> Standing Committee of the '76 Ass: —

RC (MHi); written entirely in an unidentified hand; adjacent to first signatory: "Thos Jefferson Esqr"; endorsed by TJ as received 1 Sept. 1818 and so recorded in SJL. Enclosure: Henry Laurens

Pinckney, *An Oration, delivered in St. Michael's Church, before an assemblage of the inhabitants of Charleston, South-Carolina; On the Fourth of July, 1818. In Commemoration of American Independence;*

by appointment of The '76 Association, And published at the Request of that Society (Charleston, 1818; Poor, *Jefferson's Library*, 13 [no. 826]; TJ's copy in ViU, inscribed "Dear Sir By order of 76 asso I trasmit this—R R Reid Sec '76"), surveying the recent past and declaring that the nation had accomplished the goals of the founders and that "the descendants of patriots are not unworthy of their origin, and that the halo of fame, which encircled our ancestors, has been brightened and enlarged by the brilliant acheivements of their children" (p. 6); calling for a renewal of appreciation for the outcome of the American Revolution; noting that "The spirit of gratitude, however, is awaking from its trance," as evidenced by the commissioning of the historical paintings of John Trumbull for the United States Capitol (p. 11); summarizing Napoleon's rise and fall in France and recalling the victorious battles of the War of 1812; celebrating American forms of government as founded on "equal rights, and its principal ornament, the universal happiness, of all classes of citizens" (p. 20); and concluding with the hope that freedom will spread to South America, for, "if heaven has in store a scene, which shall strike confusion to the heart of tyranny, and stimulate man to struggle for his rights, it will be, when the new world is released from the thraldom of the old, when the chorus of freedom shall re-echo from the Mississippi to La Plata, from the heights of Bunker to the vallies of Peru, and when millions upon millions, and hosts upon hosts, shall exclaim, with one enthusiastic burst of thankfulness and rapture, ALL AMERICA IS FREE!!!" (p. 29).

John Berwick Legare (1794–1850), attorney, was a native of Charleston who graduated in 1815 from Yale College (later Yale University). He was admitted to the Charleston bar in 1818, and four years later he gave the Seventy-Six Association's annual Independence Day speech. In 1832 Legare attended the South Carolina Union Convention, at which he signed a protest against the Ordinance of Nullification. He died in Charleston (Dexter, *Yale Biographies*, 6:773; *A Catalogue of*

the Linonian Society, of Yale College, *Founded September Twelfth, 1753* [1841], 41; *A Catalogue of the Connecticut Alpha of the ΦBK* [1826], 23; Legare, *An Oration, delivered in St. Michael's Church, Charleston, South-Carolina, on the Fourth of July, 1822; before the '76 Association* [Charleston, 1822]; Baltimore *Niles' Weekly Register*, 29 Dec. 1832).

Arthur Harper O'Hara (1794–1826), attorney, was a native of Charleston. He graduated from South Carolina College (later the University of South Carolina) in 1812, was a student at the Litchfield Law School in Connecticut in 1814, and in 1820 ran unsuccessfully for the South Carolina House of Representatives on the Republican ticket. O'Hara died in Charleston (*Roll of Students of South Carolina College, 1805–1905* [(1905)], 5; *The Litchfield Law School, 1784–1833* [1900], 16; Charleston *City Gazette and Commercial Daily Advertiser*, 7 Oct. 1820, 26 Sept. 1826; Saint Philip's Episcopal Church Burial Register, Charleston [ScCF microfilm]).

John Withingham Sommers (d. 1848) was a factor and accountant in Charleston who inherited property in Saint Paul's Parish in 1828 and owned eighty-four slaves in 1840 (Abraham Motte, *Charleston Directory, and Strangers' Guide, for the year 1816* [Charleston, 1816], 79; James R. Schenck, *The Directory and Stranger's Guide, for the city of Charleston . . . for the Year 1822* [Charleston, 1822], 79; DNA: RG 29, CS, S.C., Colleton Co., 1840; James A. Strobhart, *Reports of Cases in Equity, argued and determined in the Court of Appeals of South Carolina* [1848–51], 4:37–58).

Edward Peter Simons (ca. 1794–1823), attorney, studied at the College of Charleston before graduating from Yale College (later Yale University) in 1814. He was admitted to the Charleston bar in 1818. Simons served in the state militia, was a city warden, and was elected twice to the lower house of the state legislature, in 1820–21 and 1822–23. Before completing his second term he was killed in a duel in Charleston (Dexter, *Yale Biographies*, 6:702–3; *BDSCHR*, 5:242–3; *A Catalogue of the Connecticut Alpha of the ΦBK* [1826], 22; Charleston *City Gazette* and Commercial Daily Advertiser, 8 Oct. 1823; Boston Columbian Centinel, 22 Oct. 1823; Samuel Gilman, Funeral Address, Delivered at The Second Independent Church, Charleston, [South-Carolina] at the interment of Edward Peter Simons [Charleston, 1823]; gravestone inscription in Unitarian Church Cemetery, Charleston).

Richard Osborne (Osborn) was a factor in Charleston from at least 1806–24. Margaret Obsborn was listed as a widow at his former address in 1831 (Negrin's Directory, and Almanac, for the year 1806 [Charleston, 1806], 61; Directory and Stranger's Guide, for the City of Charleston [Charleston, 1824], 71; Morris Goldsmith, Directory and Strangers' Guide, for the City of Charleston . . . from the fifth census of the United States [1831], 100).

On this date the Standing Committee sent the same oration to James Madison (Madison, Papers, Retirement Ser., 1:316).

[1] Manuscript: "Simmons."

From Julius B. Dandridge

SIR,   RICHMOND, JULY 25th, 1818.

I am instructed by a resolution of the Board of Directors of this Office, to notify you, that a curtailment of at least 12 1-2 per cent. to take effect from the first Wednesday in August next, and to continue for at least eighteen weeks, has been determined on. You will therefore please be prepared to pay up at least 12 1-2 per cent. on your notes as they become due for the period above mentioned.

Your's respectfully   J: B DANDRIDGE Cash[r]

RC (MHi); printed text, with closing and signature by Dandridge; with RC of Patrick Gibson to TJ, 27 July 1818, subjoined; printed at head of text: "**OFFICE BANK UNITED STATES**"; based on TJ's endorsement of subjoined letter, he also received this letter on 30 July 1818, and it is so recorded (as a letter from "Bank US Richmond") in SJL.

Julius Burbridge Dandridge (ca. 1770–1828), banker, was a nephew of Martha Washington. He became the discount clerk of the Bank of Virginia in Richmond at its founding in 1804. Shortly after it was organized early in 1817, Dandridge was chosen as the cashier of the Richmond branch of the Second Bank of the United States. In 1820 the bank accused him of misfeasance and nonfeasance throughout his tenure, forced him to resign, and sued him and six of his sureties in the federal courts for the $50,000 bond with which he had guaranteed his good performance. The case was eventually appealed to the United States Supreme Court before being remanded to the Circuit Court for Virginia and settled in 1833 with a payment by at least one of the sureties. Meanwhile, Dandridge had died in Richmond after falling from "a narrow path leading along the precipice" of a ravine (WMQ, 1st ser., 5 [1896]: 36; Washington, Papers, Retirement Ser., 3:436; Marshall, Papers, 9:324–6, 10:374–95; Richmond Enquirer, 1 Sept. 1804, 29 Apr. 1828, 7 June 1833).

To Salma Hale

SIR   Monticello July 26. 18.

I thank you for the pamphlets you have been so kind as to send me, which I now return. they give a lively view of the state of religious dissension now prevailing in the North, and making it's way to the South. most controversies begin with a discussion of principles; but soon degenerate into episodical, verbal, or personal cavils. too much of this is seen in these pamphlets, and, as usual, those whose dogmas are the most unintelligible are the most angry. the truth is that Calvinism has introduced into the Christian religion more new[1] absurdities than it's leader had purged it of old ones. our saviour did not come into the world to save metaphysicians only. his doctrines are levelled to the simplest understanding: and it is only by banishing Hierophantic mysteries and Scholastic subtleties, which they have nick-named Christianity, and getting back to the plain and unsophisticated precepts of Christ, that we become <u>real</u> Christians. the half reformation of Luther and Calvin did something towards a restoration of his genuine doctrines; the present contest will, I hope, compleat what they begun, and place us where the evangelists left us. I salute you with esteem and respect.   TH: JEFFERSON

RC (NhHi); at foot of text: "Mr Salma Hales." PoC (DLC).

For THE PAMPHLETS here enclosed, see Hale's Notes on his Visit to Monti-

cello, [after 1818], document 4 in a group of documents on Hale's Visit to Monticello, 7–8 May 1818, and note.

[1] Word interlined.

Central College Donors and Founders to the University of Virginia Commissioners

[before 27 July 1818]

Whereas by an Act of the General Assembly for appropriating a part of the revenue of the literary fund to the endowment of an University and for the appointment of Commissioners to enquire & report to the legislature a proper site for the same, the said Commissioners are authorized "to receive any voluntary contributions whether conditional or absolute, whether in land, money, or other property, which may be offered thro them to the Treasurer[1] and directors of the literary fund, for the benefit of the University" Be it therefore known that we the subscribers, contributors & founders[2] of the establishment of the Central College near Charlottesville do hereby authorise

& empower[3] the visitors of the said College, or a majority of them or the Proctor[4] thereof, to offer thro the said commissioners to the President & directors of the literary fund, the said Central College, with all the lands, moneys, credits & other property thereto belonging, and of the same to make an absolute conveyance. On Condition that the lands of the said College be ultimately adopted by the legislature as the site of the said university. In Witness whereof, we have hereto subscribed our names.[5]

W^M MITCHELL	JAMES MADISON
JOEL YANCEY	J. H. COCKE
CHA^S JOHNSTON.	JOSEPH C. CABELL
H. HARRISON.	ZACHARIAH NEVIL
RICH^D POLLARD	HENRY DAWSON
ROB. MORRISS	RO: RIVES
THO^S WELLS	W. C RIVES.
W^M GARTH	JOHN P. COBBS.
MOSES PEREGOY.	LANDON CABELL
JOHN FRETWELL	THOMAS J MCLELLAND
HUGH CHISHOLM	DIXON DEDMAN
SAM^L CARR.	CLIF: HARRIS.
N H LEWIS.	CHARLES BROWN
DAVID ISAACS	REUBEN MAURY
LEWIS TEEL	MANN PAGE
PETER PORTER	J. H. MARKS
N. BRAMHAM	FRANCIS M^CGEHEE
SAM^L L HART	I. A. COLES
JOHN WINN	JNO COLES
IRA GARRETT.	JAMES LINDSAY
JOHN JONES	MARTIN THACKER
FRA^S B. DYER	CHRISTOPHER HUDSON
JOHN WATSON L.M.	JOHN HARRIS.
JOHN SLAUGHTER	RICHARD WOODS
JO: BISHOP	JOHN DUNKUM
J. GOSS	DANIEL M. RAILEY
JA^S MINOR	THO: WOOD
BEN: HARDIN.	JOHN F: CARR
WILLIAM DUNKUM	HENRY CHILES
JA^S O. CARR.	ACHILLES BROADHEAD
DRURY WOOD.	MICAJAH WOODS
WILL CABELL	TUCKER COLES
GEO: CALLOWAY.	JAMES LEITCH
JOHN H CRAVEN	J. W. GARTH

Frank Carr.
Jno: Minor
Wᴹ Brown
Jas: Clark
James H Terrell
Ira Harris
Nelson Barksdale
Garland Garth.
Thoˢ J. Randolph
Wᴹ Woods
John M. Perry.
Geo: M. Woods
Danᴸ F. Carr
Alex: Garrett
William Leitch
Jaˢ Dinsmore.
samᴸ Dyer senᴿ
Tho: Eston Randolph
Joseph Coffman
John Hudson

V. W. southall
Geo: W Kinsolving
Wᴹ Watson
John C. Ragland
samᴸ Leitch.
O. Norris.
P. Minor.
Th: Jefferson
Jeremiah A. Goodman
Arthur Whitehurst
John Walker.
Jesse Garth.
J: Pollock
John Fagg
C. Wertenbaker
Wᴹ H. Meriwether
Allen Dawson
Elijah Brown
James Wood
Th: W. Maury
Zachariah shackleford.

I do hereby certify that the foregoing is a true copy of the original deed signed by the subscribers whose names are thereto annexed, which was laid before the board of Commissioners for the University of Virginia on the first day of August 1818.

Th: W. Maury secʸ to the Board

Tr (Vi: RG 79, House of Delegates, Speaker, Executive Communications); entirely in Maury's hand and signed by him. Dft (photocopy in ViU: TJP); entirely in TJ's hand; lacking signatures and Maury's certification; on verso of Dft of announcement by Nelson Barksdale described below. Printed in *University of Virginia Commissioners' Report*, 29–31, with signatories in different sequence.

On verso of Dft is an announcement from Nelson Barksdale to Central College Subscribers, [ca. 1 Apr. 1818]: "The subscriber being appointed Proctor to the Central college near Charlottesville, with authority to recieve all contributions thereto gives notice to the Contributors that their 1ˢᵗ instalment is now due, and requests that it may either be deposited in

the Richmᵈ bank of Virgᵃ, or remitted to the sbscrbr at Charlˡᵉ whichever is most to their convenience. those who have so far favᵈ that instn as to recieve subscription papers are <*desired*> requested without delay to inclose the same to mr J. the visitor residing nearest to the place" (photocopy of Dft in ViU: TJP; entirely in TJ's hand; undated; at head of text: "Central College"). Subjoined to this text is an undated tally in TJ's hand of Central College resources:

"Glebes		3195.86
Albemarle		29360.
Cumberland	1660	
	150	2090
	280	
Fluvanna		1490
Lynchburg		900
Nelson		1052.

Messrs Tucker & Coalter	300	
Wm Brent. Acquia.	100	
	38487.86	
Winchester	900.	
papers ret^d	39387.86	
known Messrs Carter &		
Harris	1000."	

The ACT OF THE GENERAL ASSEMBLY was "An Act appropriating part of the revenue of the Literary Fund, and for other purposes" (*Acts of Assembly* [1817–

18 sess.], 11–5 [21 Feb. 1818], quote on p. 14). L.M.: "Little Mountain."

[1] *University of Virginia Commissioners' Report*: "President."
[2] Preceding two words interlined in Dft.
[3] Preceding two words interlined in Dft.
[4] Preceding eight words interlined in Dft, with following word omitted there.
[5] Dft ends here.

Conveyance of Central College Properties to the President and Directors of the Literary Fund

To all persons to whom these presents shall come, Nelson Barksdale of the county of Albemarle, Proctor of the Central College within the same county, Greeting.

By[1] virtue of the powers granted to me by certain homologous instruments of writing, signed[2] and executed by the sundry subscribers,[3] contributors & founders of the said College, which several[4] instruments are all of the same tenor, and expressed in these words following,[5] to wit, 'Whereas[6] by an act of the General assembly for appropriating a part of the revenue of the literary fund to the endowment of an University, & for the appointment of Commissioners to enquire and report to the legislature a proper site for the same, the sd Commissioners are authorised "to recieve any voluntary contributions, whether conditional or absolute, whether in land, money or other property which may be offered thro' them to the President and Directors of the literary fund, for the benefit of the University" Be it therefore known that we the subscribers, contributors and founders of the establishment of the Central college near Charlottesville, do hereby authorise and empower the Visitors of the said College, or a majority of them, or the Proctor thereof to offer thro' the sd Commissioners to the President & Directors of the literary fund the sd Central College with all the lands, monies, credits and other property thereunto belonging, and of the same to make an absolute conveyance: On Condition that the lands of the sd College be ultimately adopted by the legislature as the site of the sd University; in witness whereof we have hereunto subscribed our names.' as by the sd several instruments with the names duly subscribed in the proper handwriting of each subscriber will more certainly appear:[7] Know Ye that I the sd

Nelson Barksdale, Proctor of the sd College,[8] by this my deed, indented, sealed & delivered[9] in consideration of the sum of one dollar to me in hand paid for the use of the[10] sd College, & of the condition precedent herein after stated, do give, grant, bargain & sell, offer and convey[11] to the sd President & Directors of the literary fund for the benefit of the sd University of Virginia now proposed to be established, all the lands, monies,[12] credits & other property, of whatever form, nature or value, to[13] the sd Central College belonging,[14] wheresoever the same may be, or in whatsoever hands, to have & to hold the same to the sd President & Directors of the sd literary fund & their successors, to & for the sole use & benefit[15] of the sd University of Virginia: On the Condition precedent that the lands of the sd Central[16] College in the said county of Albemarle be ultimately adopted by the legislature of this Commonwealth, or by those whom they shall authorise thereto, as the site of the sd University of Virginia;[17] which condition being previously fulfilled this deed is to be in full force, but otherwise to[18] become void & of no effect. In testimony whereof I have hereto set my hand & seal this 27th[19] day of July 1818.[20]

Signed, sealed ⎫ FRANK CARR
& delivered in ⎬ JAS LEITCH   NELSON BARKSDALE
presence of ⎭ JAMES BROWN   proctor to the C College

In the Office of the County Court of Albemarle the 27th day of July 1818

This Indenture was produced to me in my office the date above and Acknowledged by Nelson Barksdale Proctor to the Central College party thereto to be his hand and seal Act and deed and admitted to record According to Law

Teste

ALEX: GARRETT C:A:CC

MS (ViU: TJP); on indented paper; in TJ's hand, signed by Carr, Leitch, Brown, and Barksdale, with signed postscript in Garrett's hand; signed docket by Garrett: "Barksdale. Proctor C. College to President & Directors of the L. Fund } Deed 27th July 1818 acknowledged by Nelson Barksdale before me in my office the date above according to Law & thereupon admitted to record"; further notations in Garrett's hand: "Examined" and "Recorded Page 238." Dft (ViU: TJP); entirely in TJ's hand; partially dated July 1818; endorsed by TJ: "N. Barksdale to Pres. & Dir. lity fund } Deed." Tr (Albemarle Co. Deed Book, 21:238–9; dated 27 July 1818). Tr (Vi: RG 79, House of Delegates, Speaker, Executive Communications); entirely in Garrett's hand, with "A Copy" and his additional attestation at foot of text; docketed by Garrett: "Barksdale Proctor to C College to President & Directors of the L Fund } Deed," with his further notations of "Copy" and "Examined." Enclosed in TJ to Linn Banks and Edward Watts, 20 Nov. 1818. Printed in *University of Virginia Commissioners' Report*.

[1] Preceding this word in Dft, TJ canceled "Know ye, that."

[2] Word interlined in Dft in place of "subscribed by."

[3] In Dft TJ here canceled "& found."

[4] Word interlined in Dft.

[5] Dft: "in the following words."

[6] Instead of text from this point through "hereunto subscribed our names," Dft reads "E[t]c."

[7] Sentence interlined in Dft.

[8] In Dft TJ here canceled "do."

[9] In Dft TJ here canceled "offer, give, grant, bargain."

[10] Preceding three words interlined in Dft.

[11] Preceding three words interlined in Dft, with "absolutely" canceled before "convey."

[12] Dft: "money."

[13] Dft: "of whatever form or nature to," interlined in place of "of."

[14] Word interlined in Dft.

[15] Preceding two words interlined in Dft.

[16] Word not in Vi Tr.

[17] Preceding two words interlined in Dft.

[18] In Dft TJ here canceled "remain."

[19] Word added by Barksdale in MS to space left blank in MS and Dft.

[20] Dft ends here.

From Patrick Gibson

Sir   Richmond 27th July 1818

I received this morning your favor of the 20th Ins[t] returning the two notes signed, but on the one payable to Tho[s] J. Randolph you have failed to obtain his signature, and as his power of Att[y] to me does not authorize my indorsing a note in his name, I send it you inclosed.[1] On the 18th I gave in charge to James Johnson (boatman) 2 cases of Wine and the small box of seeds, which I am sorry to find should not have been sent up—I have paid Baker & Folsom $19.50 on your acco[t] and to Fitzwhylsonn & Potter $31.75—as also your dft to Leitch—   With much respect I am

Your ob[t] Serv[t]   Patrick Gibson

RC (MHi); between dateline and salutation: "Thomas Jefferson Esq[re]"; endorsed by TJ as received 30 July 1818 and so recorded in SJL. Enclosure not found.

TJ reused the address covers from this and Gibson's later letter of this date, both franked and postmarked Richmond, 27

July, for the PoCs of his letters of 20 Nov. 1818 to Joseph C. Cabell and 24 Nov. 1818 to David Bailie Warden. Which address cover went with each PoC has not been determined.

[1] Omitted period at right margin editorially supplied.

From Patrick Gibson

Sir   27th July

Since writing you of this date I have received the above notice, You will therefore be pleased to fill up the note for $2625.—   I fear this unexpected resolution will occasion much distress, as it will without doubt oblige the State banks to curtail, so as to meet the demand, which this ma[y] produce upon them (to the am^t of $700.000) and which they are not in a situation to do without it   Respectfully Yours   PATRICK GIBSON

the note had better be sent blank as the Bank <u>may</u> curtail more than $12\frac{1}{2}$ pc^t

RC (MHi); partially dated; edge trimmed; subjoined to RC of Julius B. Dandridge to TJ, 25 July 1818; endorsed by TJ as received 30 July 1818 and so recorded in SJL.

To John Steele

DEAR SIR   Monticello July 27. 18.
    I have just recieved a letter of Apr. 29. from mr Appleton of Leghorn informing me he had shipped by the brig Free Ocean Capt Bartholomew, sailing that day for Philadelphia 2. cases of Florence wine of Montepulciano, containing 84. bottles for me addressed to your care. as I presume the letter came by the same vessel, & that she is arrived, I take the liberty of requesting you to forward the cases by any trust-worthy vessel to the care of mr Patrick Gibson in Richmond. and if you will be so good as to drop me a line of the amount of duties, freight E^{t}c it shall be remitted with no other delay than what will result from an absence of 3. or 4. weeks on a journey, on which I shall set out two days hence: as your letter will lie here unopened until my [re]turn. with my apology for this trouble accept the assurance [of my] great esteem and respect.   TH: JEFFERSON

PoC (MHi); on verso of reused address cover of Gamaliel H. Ward to TJ, 22 Apr. 1818; damaged at seal; at foot of text: "John Steele esq."; endorsed by TJ.

To James Leitch

DEAR SIR   Monticello July 28. 18.
    I shall set out the day after tomorrow for the Gap, and after our business done I shall visit Staunton, and, being so far on the way shall visit the Warm springs to which I have been going and ought to have gone 2. or 3. years ago. but I must borrow of you the money for my journey which I suppose will take 100.D. I am the more reluctant on this because I cannot reimburse it by an immediate draught on Richmond[1] finding I have overdrawn my funds there between 3. & 400.D. soon after my return, or in all September at furthest, I shall

be in funds again to meet every thing. moderate sized bills will do best for the road if you can spare them. Your's with friendship & respect. TH: JEFFERSON

PoC (DLC); on verso of reused address cover to TJ; at foot of text: "Mr James Leitch"; endorsed by TJ.

THE GAP: Rockfish Gap.

[1] Preceding two words interlined.

From Edmund Bacon

DEAR SIR. July 29 1818.

upon a close look at my ploughs I find the wood work of one requires to be made intirely new and I shall want it next week I want to set my ploughs agoing at any rate before I leave home I want to so a field of rye in August.

I informed Mr Randolph that I had a demand on him for money considering it best to give him time if his money was not ready his answer strongly insinueates that it will be some little time before it will be convenient to pay me and of course will prolong the time of my seting out: Mr Dawson has given me the money for the note by deducting 6 pr cent which gives me a little less money but it will make no differance taking 6 pr cent from 327

$$\begin{array}{r} 6 \\ \hline \end{array}$$

19,62   600

19.62

$ 580 38

I am yours &C E: BACON

RC (ViU: TJP-ER); dateline at foot of text; addressed: "Mr Jefferson"; endorsed by TJ as received 29 July 1818.

On 28 July 1818 TJ recorded giving Bacon an order on Thomas Eston Randolph "for 272.82 the cash balce. due to me on our late settlement. Gave him also my note for 327.18 payable in 60 days" (MB, 2:1345). Bacon's own description of this transaction indicated that he had assigned the latter note to Martin Dawson for $307.38 and that TJ was to pay Bacon the difference of $19.80 "or to charge him with 580. instead of 600$" (ViU: Bacon Memorandum Book, 1802–22).

To Patrick Gibson

Dear Sir Monticello July 29. 18.

I shall set out tomorrow for the meeting of the Commissioners on the subject of our University, at the Rockfish gap, and when our business there is finished I shall proceed to the Warm springs and probably not return hither till the last week in August. altho' I have already overdrawn my funds in your hands, yet, as mentioned in mine of the 20th some neighborhood transactions oblige me to trespass on your indulgence. before my departure I must make one draught on you for 174. D 70 c and perhaps another for 63.60 D which will place me at ease until my resources begin to come in. this will be in September when I will take care to replace my over-draughts on you.

For fear of unexpected protraction of my absence I inclose you a renewal of my note in the bank of the US. which was not renewed on the l[ast?] occasion with the other two. I salute you with friendship & [respec]t. Th: Jefferson

P.S. 2. boxes of wine are just arrived for me at Philadelphia, & will be forwarded to you. I will pray you to send them by Johnson's boat.

PoC (MHi); on verso of a reused address cover to TJ in the hand of a representative of Gibson & Jefferson; damaged at seal; adjacent to signature: "Mr Patrick Gibson"; endorsed by TJ. Enclosure not found.

To Joel Yancey

Dear Sir Monticello July 29. 18.

According to promise I now inclose you mr Morris's and Majr Pollard's reciepts for their 1st instalments to the Central College. I shall set out tomorrow for the meeting at Rockfish gap, and when our business is done there I shall go on to the Warm springs. I shall probably be back the last week of August, and be with you a fortnight after. I salute you with friendship and respect.

Th: Jefferson

PoC (MHi); on verso of portion of reused address cover to TJ; at foot of text: "Mr Yancey"; endorsed by TJ. Enclosures not found.

Yancey's previous letter to TJ of 1 June 1818, not found, is recorded in SJL as received 7 June 1818 from Poplar Forest.

To Edmund Bacon

TH:J. TO Mʀ BACON.   July 30. 18.

I inclose you two draughts on mr Gibson, the one in favor of mr Woods for 174.70 and the other in favor of yourself for 63.85 this last is to enable you to pay 48.85 to mr Maupin and 15.D. to mr Stout. the two former sums include interest from last court. I am afraid it may not be convenient to mr Lietch to advance money for these draughts, and that it is merely an accomodation to me that he has done it; but he would probably inclose the draughts and have the money brought up by mail at my risk and expence, and pay it when recieved. this would occasion to the parties only a week's delay after court. I inclose a note to mr Powers to mend your ploughs, but in truth this should be done by one of the plantation men. if James does not know how, he ought to learn as is done in the other plantations. I start to-day for the Gap & springs. to be back the 25ᵗʰ of Aug. if you go before that I wish you a good & prosperous journey.

PoC (MHi); on verso of portion of re-used address cover to TJ; endorsed by TJ. Not recorded in SJL. Enclosures not found.

On this date TJ recorded payments to John woods for "57.9 Bar. corn @ 3.D.,"

to Charles W. maupin for "16⅕ Bar. corn @ 3.D.," and to Isaiah stout for "2000. ℔ fodder wth. interest." Larkin powers had recently replaced Rolin Goodman as TJ's head carpenter (*MB*, 2:1345n, 1346). THE GAP & SPRINGS: Rockfish Gap and Warm Springs.

To Allen Bernard

SIR   Monticello July 30.

The Commissioners for the University of Virginia being to meet at your tavern the day after tomorrow (Saturday) I propose to be with you tomorrow evening (Friday) the bearer, with my baggage will be with you some hours before. as I supposed you might find it difficult to provide beds for so many, and it was convenient to me to send a mattrass & trussels for myself, I have done so, preferring that kind of lodging in summer to a bed. I am told your house is very large, and has a great number of lodging rooms. if I could have ever so small a lodging room to myself, it would be a great indulgence to me, and the only one I would ask of you. but if you cannot spare it I shall be contented. I trust you will give to the Commissioners a preference of accomodations over meer strangers, and thus prevent all idea of adjournment to another place, which some of them think of, but which I hope will not be listened to. I am Sir

Your humble servᵗ   TH: JEFFERSON

PoC (DLC: TJ Papers, 213:38050); on verso of reused address cover of James Madison to TJ, 20 Apr. 1818; partially dated; at foot of text: "Mʳ Barnet"; endorsed by TJ as a letter to "Barnet" of 30 July 1818 and so recorded (with additional notation: "Rockfish gap") in SJL.

Allen Bernard (ca. 1763–1834), innkeeper and public official, was a longtime justice of the peace in Fluvanna County, which he represented during eight sessions of the Virginia House of Delegates, 1796, 1801–02, 1805–06, 1809–12, and 1813–15. Immediately after leaving the legislature he ran a hotel in Richmond.

On 8 July 1818 Bernard bought approximately eight hundred acres in Augusta and Nelson counties at Rockfish Gap, including the tavern at which the University of Virginia Commissioners met the following month. At some point the establishment became known as the Mountain House, and a later depiction of it is reproduced elsewhere in this volume. Bernard died at his home in Nelson County (Leonard, *General Assembly*; William Couper, *History of the Shenandoah Valley*, 2:728–9; Augusta Co. Deed Book, 42:406–7, 45:159–60; *Richmond Enquirer*, 25 July 1834).

From Joseph C. Cabell

DEAR SIR,   Warminster 30ᵗʰ July. 1818.

I send you by my brother William, the signatures of the majority of the subscribers to the funds of the Central College in Nelson County to the deed of conveyance of the property of the College to the Commonwealth on the condition of the location of the University at the Scite of the College. I have met with the ready assent of every subscriber to whom I have yet presented the paper; & I am confident there will not be a single dissenting voice. Indeed it is solely to be ascribed to my own forgetfulness that the paper has not yet been presented to all the subscribers. It did not occur to my recollection till to-day, that the assent of the subscribers should be ready for the meeting of the[1] Commissioners; my notion had been that it must be procured by the meeting of the[2] Assembly. I will thank you to send the paper back by my brother and I will not fail to procure the signature of every subscriber.

I remain, dear Sir, most respectfully & truly yours

JOSEPH C. CABELL

RC (ViU: TJP-PC); at foot of text: "Mʳ Jefferson"; endorsed by TJ as received 1 Aug. 1818 and so recorded in SJL, where TJ indicated that it had been received at "Rockfish gap."

The DEED OF CONVEYANCE is printed above at 27 July 1818. The enclosed text with signatures from Nelson County has not been found.

[1] Cabell here canceled "Visitors."
[2] Cabell here canceled "subscribers."

To Patrick Gibson

DEAR SIR   Monticello July 30. 18.

   my letter of yesterday had gone off, and the draughts therein mentioned had been delivered out of my hands, and I was in the moment
of setting out for Rockfish gap, when your letter of the 27th with the
notification from the bank of the US. came to hand. that notification
is really like a clap of thunder to me, for god knows I have no means
in this world of raising money on so sudden a call; my whole & sole
dependance being only on the annual income of my farms. it is the
more distressing as I am obliged to set out instantly for the meeting
of the Commissioners and it does not give me time for consideration.
I subscribe a note however for a blank sum and send it to my grandson to sign and forward to you and throw myself on your friendship
to get me thro' the scrape as well as can be done. more time & consideration than I now have will [. . .] to enable me to see my way out
of this difficulty which comes upon me entirely unaware. in the mean
time I renew the assurances of my gratitude to you, and of my great
esteem & respect.   TH: JEFFERSON

PoC (MHi); on verso of reused address   MY GRANDSON: Thomas Jefferson
cover of John Vaughan to TJ, 7 May   Randolph.
1818; mutilated at seal; at foot of text:
"Mr Gibson"; endorsed by TJ.

To Charles Simms

SIR   Monticello July 30. 18.

   I this moment recieve from Mr Cathalan of Marseilles information
that he has shipped for me on board the ship Fair trader G. Fletcher
master 8. boxes of claret & a basket of Maccaroni, & that the ship is
bound to Alexandria. being in the moment of departure on a journey
to be absent a month, I take the liberty of requesting that these things
may in the mean time be forwarded to mr Gibson of Richmond: and
if you will be so good as to send me a note of the duties and charges
they shall be remitted immediately on my return. I pray you to accept
the assurance of my great esteem & respect.   TH: JEFFERSON

PoC (MHi); on verso of reused address cover of William F. Gray to TJ, 8 May 1818;
at foot of text: "Colo Charles Simms"; endorsed by TJ.

From James Le Ray de Chaumont

SIR   Le Raysville 31 July 1818

An Absence from home has prevented me from having the honor to answer sooner the letter you favored me with. I am extremely grateful to Mrs Morris to have procured me such a great gratification as has been bestowed on me by your most kind and benevolent letter. Indeed I did not feel bold enough to send you my feeble pro-duction and trespass in such a manner upon your precious moments. I was very glad to find that in your district you have established a society of Agriculture. I have no doubt that the public good will be benefitted by it and the more so as many of its members are distinguished for correct and skillful practice in their farms

I hope that the time is very near when they will carry into effect your ideas about central societies in each State affiliated to one great central Society for the United States. As a private individual I did every thing I could last winter to promote the desired aim. I wrote to the head quarters at Washington and went to sollicit the legislature of our State for that purpose. We were indeed very near to carry the point for our state. There is no doubt among the well informed people that the institution will be adopted by the next Legislature

Knowing your friendly interest for the Family of the Grands, I must inform you of the loss they have met with by the death of the youngest brother Grand d'Hauteville. He had left long ago the banking business and had retired with a large fortune in a handsome estate near Vevay where he was distinguished by his agricultural pursuits and his generous encouragement for the advances of the art upon which he constantly corresponded with me. The two surviving brothers have a very independant fortune and enjoy it honorably & with prudence. The eldest in Switzerland and the youngest at Paris

With great regard, I remain
Your most obd^t Ser^vt   LE RAY DE CHAUMONT

RC (DLC); addressed: "To the Honble Th^s Jefferson Monticello Virginia"; stamp canceled; franked; postmarked Leraysville, 7 Aug.; endorsed by TJ as received 1 Sept. 1818 and so recorded in SJL.

A missing letter from Ann C. MORRIS to TJ of 16 Mar. 1818 is recorded in SJL as received 24 Mar. 1818 from Morrisania, her estate near New York City. Presumably it concerned the conveyance to TJ of Le Ray de Chaumont's address to the Agricultural Society of Jefferson County (see TJ to Le Ray de Chaumont, 29 May 1818).

From Richard N. Thweatt

Dear Sir,   Petersburg July 31st[1] 1818

Yours of the 6th inst. I have just received. The wine you speak of, Col Burton procured and sent to Mr Johnson, a merchant of this town. Mr Johnson informs me that in a few days after he received it, he met with Mr Eppes, and after telling him that he had a cask of wine for you, requested to know what he should do with it,— Mr E. told him he had better send it to Mr P. Gibson, in Richmond; this, Mr Johnson says, he did—He appeared much surprised that you had not received the wine, as several months have elapsed since he sent it to Richmond—I have requested Mr Johnson to find out, as he does not at present recollect, the captain or master of the vessel by whom he sent it—As you have not heard any thing of it, it is more than probable that the wine[2] never reached Mr Gibson, or you would have received it long before this—

I assure you, Sir, it gives me great pleasure in attending to any request of yours, and I hope you will not hesitate in calling upon me whenever you have occasion to do so—I consider it no "trouble"— and therefore requiring no apology on your part—With Sentiments of the highest respect

I am yours &c   Richard N. Thweatt

RC (MHi); endorsed by TJ as received 1 Sept. 1818 and so recorded in SJL. RC (MHi); address cover only; with PoC of TJ to Joseph Milligan, 29 Nov. 1818, on verso; addressed: "Thomas Jefferson Esqr Charlottsvell Albemarle"; stamped; postmarked Petersburg, 4 Aug.

[1] Manuscript: "31ts."
[2] Word interlined in place of "cask."

To Patrick Gibson

Dear Sir   Rockfish gap Aug. 1. 18.

I recieved[1] your letter of July 27. just as I was setting out for this place and my company waiting for me. I wrote therefore the hasty thoughts of the 1st moment. but after consideration on the road I wrote back to my grandson to begin the grinding my wheat instantly and sending it down as soon as ground. he can get down before the first curtailment as much as will supply that and will go on to provide immediately against the successive ones: and you may rest assured that you shall be exposed to no inconvenience by the paper you have been so kind as to endorse for me. under this assurance I hope your mind will be at rest, and I salute you with great friendship and respect.

Th: Jefferson

SC (MHi); at foot of text: "Mʳ Gibson"; endorsed by TJ.

A missing letter from TJ to his GRANDSON Thomas Jefferson Randolph of 30

July 1818 is recorded in SJL, as are undated letters, not found, from Randolph to TJ received 31 July and 20 Sept. 1818.

¹ Manuscript: "recived."

From Robert Walsh

DEAR SIR   Philadelphia August 1ˢᵗ 1818

I send you another N° of the Analectic magazine;—not, however, as to a subscriber. It was by no means my intention to subject you to a double tax. That of even looking thro' such light matter is enough, and, perhaps, the more onerous of the two in your estimation. I have no pecuniary interest in the circulation of this journal.

There is no branch of "internal improvement" in which I feel so deep a concern as in that of liberal instruction; and I do not expect to See a proper Institute formed in this Country but under Such auspices as your's, & those of the few men whom you may train to the right mode of thinking on the subject. It gives me, therefore, infinite pleasure to hear of your fair prospects at Charᵗᵉ'ˢ-Ville. In a short notice of Mʳ Breck's pamphlet in the n° of the A. magazine now sent, I have thrown out a few loose ideas Concerning a Faculty of Moral science in the University of Pennsyᵃ.

I pray you not to think of returning Grimm, until the members of your excellent family have fully satisfied their Curiosity. I sincerely wish I could contribute further to their gratification in the same or any other way.

most respectfully & faithˡʸ Your obᵗ servᵗ

ROBERT WALSH Jᴿ

RC (DLC); endorsed by TJ as received 1 Sept. 1818 and so recorded in SJL. RC (DLC); address cover only; with PoC of TJ to Mathew Carey, 28 Nov. 1818, on verso; addressed: "Thomas Jefferson Esqʳᵉ Monticello Virginia"; franked; postmarked Philadelphia, 3 Aug.

On pp. 148–55 of the enclosed issue of the ANALECTIC MAGAZINE, vol. 12, no. 2 (Aug. 1818), Walsh reviewed Samuel BRECK'S Sketch of the Internal Improvements already made by Pennsylvania (Philadelphia, 1818). Walsh acknowledged the strengths of the University of Pennsylvania while elaborating on what he perceived to be its failings. He called for reduced focus on medical science, with its emphasis on the highest-paid careers, and increased attention to the moral sciences, "which lead to the most perfect civilization" and a "closer connexion with our sublimest and dearest interests, the religious and political" (pp. 151–2).

From Francis Eppes

Dear Grandpapa   New London Academy August 2^d 1818

I found on my arrival here the day that we parted that the Trustees were assembling for the trial of Watts, after Spending most of the day in warm debate he was Suspended untill he should beg Mr Dashiels pardon; and promise good behaviour in future, and this in the presence of the whole school, to my great surprise he agreed to these humiliating conditions and was admitted, all goes on now as before and a sullen calm has succeeded to the storm that was once threatning in its aspect, Mr Dashiel is not as much respected I think by the students as formerly

By this time you have decided on the place for the university and I hope that the Central College is adopted, as the situation is an healthy one and the most eligible indeed in the state, and because it would afford me the greatest pleasure imaginable to finish my education there it being under your direction. I have commenced Xenophon, and Horace also, though I am afraid that I cannot get through the Arithmetic this session—I have heard nothing from the Forest since I saw you—Give my love to Aunt Randolph and the family. believe me to remain your

Affectionate Grandson   Francis Eppes

RC (MHi); endorsed by TJ as received 1 Sept. 1818 and so recorded in SJL. RC (MHi); address cover only; with PoC of TJ to Cérès de Montcarel, 29 Nov. 1818, on verso; addressed: "Thomas Jefferson Esqr monticello N^r Milton Albermarle Co."; stamped; postmarked New London, 3 Aug.

THE FOREST: Poplar Forest.

From Julius T. Ducatel

Sir   Baltimore Augt 3^d 1818—

My friend Dr G. Troost has recommended to my care a small box addressed to you, containing I believe a work of Mr Faujas. Not knowing exactly how to have it forwarded, I thought that confiding it to the politeness of Cap^n Fergusson of the Norfolk packet who in his turn is to recommend it to the care of one of his friends in Norfolk, would be the most probable mean of having it arrive at its destination.[1] I have this day Sent it to him & hope it will safely come to hand—

By Post I enclose you several letters from Paris & one from Dr G. Troost, & take this opportunity of offering my Services to you as I am about visiting Europe towards the end of the present month. If you be willing, Sir; to honour me with your confidence & to accept of my offers you may depend upon my exactitude in delivering into proper hands any thing you may confide to my care—

I have the honour of Subscribing myself gratefully obliged to you for your devotion to the interests of these States of which I have the advantage of being a Citizen   Your Ob^t Sev^t

JULIUS T. DUCATEL

RC (MHi); at head of text: "Thomas Jefferson Esqre"; endorsed by TJ as received 1 Sept. 1818 and so recorded in SJL. Enclosures: Gerard Troost to TJ, 21 July 1818, and enclosures.

Julius Timoleon Ducatel (1796–1849), scientist and educator, was born in Baltimore and studied at Saint Mary's College (later Saint Mary's Seminary and University) in that city before continuing his education in Paris, 1818–22. On his return to the United States he taught successively at the Mechanics' Institute of Baltimore, the University of Maryland, and Saint John's College in Annapolis. He provided instruction in chemistry, pharmacy, and geology. In 1832 the Maryland legislature appointed Ducatel to complete geological surveys for a new map of the state. He continued this work until funding ceased in 1841. Ducatel undertook a geological expedition to the upper Mississippi in 1843 and another to the Lake Superior region three years later. Elected to the American Philosophical Society in 1832, his most notable published work was a *Manual of Practical Toxicology* (1833). Ducatel died in Baltimore (Eugene Fauntleroy Cordell, *The Medical Annals of Maryland, 1799–1899* [1903], 383; *Memorial Volume of the Centenary of St. Mary's Seminary of St. Sulpice* [1891], 81, 84; APS, Minutes, 20 Jan. 1832 [MS in PPAmP]; *American Journal of Science and Arts*, 2d ser., 8 [1849]: 146–9).

[1] Omitted period at right margin editorially supplied.

From Anthony Finley

SIR,   Philad^a August 3^d 1818

Your "Notes on Virginia," having become scarce, and being frequently enquired for, I take the liberty of writing to you relative to them, and asking your permission to print an edition, if you have not made an arrangement for that purpose elsewhere.

If I should reprint it, I would be glad to have a <u>corrected</u> copy for my printer to use, that he might avoid the errors which crept into some of the former editions. My object would be to make a handsome octavo volume.

When you have leisure you will oblige me by a few lines—and I would also thank you to say whether you could make any additions which you think would enhance the value of the work

You will, I trust, sir, excuse the liberty I have taken, to which I am prompted by a desire of seeing a well executed edition of your valuable "Notes" in circulation.

I am, very respectfully, Your ob^t s^t   ANTH^Y FINLEY

P. S. I send accompanying a sheet of my edition of D^r smiths Moral Sentiments, as a specimen of the type, & manner in which I think the "Notes" should be printed.

RC (MHi); endorsed by TJ as received 1 Sept. 1818 and so recorded in SJL. RC (DLC); address cover only; with PoC of TJ to Albert Gallatin, 24 Nov. 1818, on recto and verso; addressed: "Hon. Thomas Jefferson Monticello Virginia"; franked; postmarked Philadelphia, 3 Aug.

Finley enclosed a printed SHEET, not found, from his edition of Adam Smith, *The Theory of Moral Sentiments* (Philadelphia, 1817).

From William F. Gray

RESPECTED SIR,   Charlottsville Aug. 3. 1818

I had intended to pay my respects to you at Monticello, but on my arrival here I found you had set off for the Mountain Top, and I could not, with any propriety, break in upon your important avocations there with a business so much of a personal and private nature.

My object in taking the liberty to address you in this way, is, in the first place, to ask your attention to the accompanying Catalogue of Books, which contains most of the articles, in my store; and, to solicit your orders, either for any thing contained therein, or for any thing from the Northern[1] Towns of the U. S. or from Great Brittain, in the procuring of which my agency can be serviceable. As I declare in my advertisement, my correspondence abroad, enables me to get, with tolerable ease and certainty, any Books in the American or English markets; or, any Philosophical Aparatus that are commonly used in Schools or Colleges. And if no other arrangement has been made, I tender my services for the supply of the Central College, or, of the University, if it should be established here, with the above named articles; and I take the liberty, Sir, of soliciting your consideration of the subject, and, if you shall think proper, you[r] influence in procuring me the agency. My terms shall be satisfactory.

Another subject, to which I beg your attention—Several of my friends in this neighbourhood, have suggested to me the expediency of establishing a branch of my business at Charlottsville. As my business has not led me to an acquaintance with the character of this section of the state, I am, of course, totally unable to judge what would be the chance of success in such an enterprize. Will you, Sir, have the goodness to give me your opinion on the subject. If it shall suit your inclination and convenience, please to say what you think would be the chance of support from the adjacent country, and what from the

College: for, without the patronage of the College I apprehend the undertaking would be futile.

If I do effect an establishment here I shall endeavour so to conduct it as to <u>merit</u> success at least.

I shall be much gratified, Sir, at hearing from you at your convenience; and if you shall think proper to give me a part of your orders, I am sure I shall execute them to your satisfaction. I will guarantee the safe delivery in Charlottsville, of any thing you may order; and will cheerfully attend, as heretofore, to any thing directed to my care.

Very Respectfully,

Sir, Your Obt. Svt.   W^M F. GRAY

RC (DLC); edge trimmed; addressed: "Thomas Jefferson, Esq. Monticello"; endorsed by TJ as received 1 Sept. 1818 and so recorded in SJL.

THE MOUNTAIN TOP: the Mountain House Inn at Rockfish Gap. The enclosed CATALOGUE OF BOOKS may have been *A Catalogue of Books and Stationary, for sale by Gray & Cady, Booksellers and Stationers, Fredericksburg–Va. September, 1817* (Fredericksburg, 1817).

Filed and probably enclosed with this letter is an undated prospectus headed "THE EDINBURGH AND QUARTERLY REVIEWS, *PUBLISHED BY KIRK AND MERCEIN, NEW-YORK*," extolling the virtues of European literary journals, particularly the abovementioned British publications; highlighting their widespread circulation, translation into foreign languages, extensive range of articles, and quality of composition; encouraging Americans to become acquainted "with the best models of classic taste and purity in our

language" so as to "compel us to equal, if not to surpass them"; noting that Kirk & Mercein are the "sole proprietors of the American edition" and able to deliver it to "every part of the United States, with regularity, and at a very small expense to the subscriber"; stating that each journal is published quarterly "at the moderate price of *five dollars* a year, which is less than half the price of a daily newspaper"; and concluding with a paragraph in a different typeface probably added at Gray's behest, reading "The publishers of the above Works, have appointed Wm. F. Gray their Agent for Fredericksburg, and the adjacent counties, who will receive subscriptions, and deliver the Books to the subscribers in the vicinity of Fredericksburg free of charges, or will forward them to any part of the country in any way most convenient to the subscribers" (broadside in DLC: TJ Papers, 213:38056).

[1] Manuscript: "Norther."

To William Kean

SIR   Rockfish[1] gap. Aug. 4. 1818.

Your favor of the 13th was handed me in the moment of my setting out from home to attend a meeting of Comm^{rs} on the subject of our University at this place from whence I am proceeding to the Springs. the impracticability of considering duly such a subject as that of your letter on a journey would be a sufficient apology for returning the papers without an opinion on them, but the truth is that the torpor of age presses heavily on me and does not permit me to apply[2] the intensity of mind which difficult subjects require, and I have long since lost[3] all familiarity with them. your justice will, I am sure, excuse the return of your papers unconsidered and yield the indulgence to age which that obliges me to ask. with the assurance of my great respect

Th:J.

Dft (MoSHi: TJC-BC); written on a half sheet; at foot of text: "M[r] W[m] Kean"; endorsed by TJ. Enclosures not found.

Kean's letter OF THE 13TH was actually dated 23 July 1818. THE SPRINGS: Warm Springs.

[1] Reworked from "Sta."
[2] Reworked from "and disables me from applying," with last word inadvertently left unchanged.
[3] Reworked from "and has occasioned me to lose."

The Founding of the University of Virginia: Rockfish Gap Meeting of the University of Virginia Commissioners

I. PROCEEDINGS OF ROCKFISH GAP MEETING OF THE UNIVERSITY OF VIRGINIA COMMISSIONERS, 1–4 AUG. 1818

II. THOMAS JEFFERSON'S NOTES ON THE GEOGRAPHIC CENTER OF VIRGINIA'S POPULATION, [BEFORE 28 JUNE 1818]

III. THOMAS JEFFERSON'S DRAFT OF THE ROCKFISH GAP REPORT OF THE UNIVERSITY OF VIRGINIA COMMISSIONERS, [CA. 28 JUNE 1818]

IV. THOMAS JEFFERSON'S NOTES ON CURRICULAR DEFINITIONS, [AFTER 28 JUNE 1818]

V. ROCKFISH GAP REPORT OF THE UNIVERSITY OF VIRGINIA COMMISSIONERS, 4 AUG. 1818

VI. THOMAS JEFFERSON'S STATEMENT OF THANKS TO THE UNIVERSITY OF VIRGINIA COMMISSIONERS, [CA. 4 AUG. 1818]

EDITORIAL NOTE

On 21 Feb. 1818 the Virginia General Assembly approved "An Act appropriating part of the revenue of the Literary Fund, and for other purposes," which authorized the creation of the University of Virginia. Under the provisions of the statute the governor was to appoint a commissioner from each of the state's twenty-four senatorial districts to attend a meeting at the tavern in the Rockfish Gap of the Blue Ridge Mountains on 1 Aug. 1818 to discuss the proposed university. They were charged with reporting to the legislature on a site for the university, its buildings, the curriculum, the number and specializations of the professorships, and any general provisions necessary for its governance and organization. Governor James P. Preston began appointing commissioners in March 1818. Shortly thereafter Jefferson began his own efforts to ensure that Central College near Charlottesville would be chosen over Lexington or Staunton as the site of the University of Virginia, and to lay out a plan of education that he hoped would be adopted for it.

Months before the meeting was due to take place, Jefferson started composing a report for consideration at Rockfish Gap. He initially attempted to convince his fellow commissioner James Madison to draft it. Jefferson wrote to him in April 1818 that he hoped they could "confer on our campaign of Rockfish gap" at the scheduled 11 May 1818 meeting of the Central College Board of Visitors. Madison apparently refused to undertake writing the report when the two men met then.

Between the May meeting and 28 June Jefferson prepared at least two full drafts of the report, the second and cleaner of which he then enclosed to Madison along with his notes calculating the geographic center of Virginia's population. Jefferson had begun by discussing the healthiness of possible locales as a factor in choosing a site, but in its final form the report primarily emphasized proximity to the center of population. In order to argue convincingly that Central College was the best location based on this criterion, he drew on data from the 1810 United States federal census. Throughout the spring and summer of 1818 Jefferson also attempted to acquire a recently updated version of Bishop James Madison's map of Virginia with which to illustrate his argument at the meeting.

Even as he worked to ensure that Central College would be selected as the university's site, Jefferson sought to maintain the appearance of disinterested objectivity. The draft report that he sent to Madison late in June included language declaring Central College to be the commissioners' preferred location, but he informed him that he would not show the commissioners these introductory pages. Jefferson also suggested that he, Madison, and Spencer Roane gather in secret at Monticello before the meeting to "advise on what will be proposed."

To strengthen Central College's appeal to the commissioners, late in July Jefferson prepared documents authorizing transfer to the state of the college's subscription funds and properties should it be chosen as the university. Unaware of what resources the supporters of Lexington or Staunton would offer, he left blanks in his drafts to be filled in with this information at the meeting. Jefferson did, however, emphasize in the introduction to all versions of his report that the choice of location ought not to be based solely on which place offered the highest bid. He was also adamant that in order to avoid outside influences, the members of the commission were not to adjourn to any of the proposed locations but instead remain at Rockfish Gap for the duration of their deliberations. For his part Jefferson maintained an air of neutrality and the customarily reserved stance of a presiding officer by saying little in open meeting. Commissioner John G. Jackson later confirmed that Jefferson had only given his opinion by voting when his name was called.

While Jefferson was preparing for the meeting at Rockfish Gap on behalf of Central College, Lexington's supporters were also marshaling their resources. Late in July 1818 citizens of that town formed a committee to draft a memorial presenting Lexington's offer to the commissioners. It was instructed to join forces with similar representatives of the interests of Washington College (later Washington and Lee University). James McDowell presented the resulting memorial and reported that their offer made a good impression on the commissioners, who were particularly impressed by a sizable pledge of land and slaves by local resident John Robinson. Lexington's backers also conducted their own investigation into the population center of Virginia based on the 1810 census.

The University of Virginia Commissioners opened their meeting on Saturday, 1 Aug. 1818, and immediately and unanimously chose Jefferson to preside. After some debate on the three proposed sites, the commissioners postponed a decision on that vexed issue and instead named a select committee headed by Jefferson to prepare a report on all other subjects under consideration. This committee met in secret, ostensibly to help prevent circulation of the report before it could be communicated to the General Assembly. When the commissioners reconvened on Monday morning, 3 Aug., they recommended Central College as the location of the University of Virginia by a vote of sixteen for that location, three for Lexington, and two for Staunton. Jefferson and the rest of the select committee quickly revised their report to reflect this decision and presented it to the whole meeting, where it passed unanimously. The following day the twenty-one members in attendance signed fair copies of the report. As adopted at Rockfish Gap, it adhered closely to the document that Jefferson had been drafting for months. These signed copies were forwarded to the speakers of the House of Delegates and Senate of Virginia on 20 Nov. 1818 along with copies of the commissioners' proceedings and the conveyance of Central College's assets. With the commissioners' official report in hand, the General Assembly began the process of considering and ultimately passing Jefferson's Bill to Establish a University (printed below at 19 Nov. 1818), which enacted their recommendations. Although the vote at Rockfish Gap on the location of the University of Virginia was divided, surviving records suggest that the deliberations as a whole were quick and relatively uncontentious, with the serious efforts by the proponents of Lexington and Staunton apparently reserved for debate over the university bill in the legislature (*Acts of Assembly* [1817–18 sess.], 11–5; Madison, *Papers, Retirement Ser.*, 1:239; TJ to Madison, 11 Apr., 28 June 1818; Thomas Ritchie to TJ, [ca. 21 May 1818]; TJ to Ritchie, 19 June 1818; TJ to James Leitch, 28 May 1818; TJ to Archibald Stuart, 28 May 1818; Stuart to TJ, 30 May 1818; TJ to Roane, 28 June 1818; TJ to Littleton W. Tazewell, 28 June 1818; TJ to George Divers, 2 July 1818; Stuart to McDowell, 4 July 1818 [ViU]; TJ to Preston, 13 July 1818; John Ruff to McDowell, 22 July 1818 [ViU]; Andrew Alexander to McDowell, 22 July 1818 [ViU: McDowell Papers]; Central College Donors and Founders to the University of Virginia Commissioners, [before 27 July 1818]; Conveyance of Central College Properties to the President and Directors of the Literary Fund, 27 July 1818; McDowell to Unknown, 3 Aug. 1818 [typescript in ViU]; *MB*, 2:1346; TJ to Martha Jefferson Randolph, 4 Aug. 1818; Jackson to Cabell, 13 Dec. 1818 [ViU: JCC]; George Wythe Randolph to James L. Cabell, 27 Feb. 1856 [ViU: JCC]).

I. Proceedings of Rockfish Gap Meeting of the University of Virginia Commissioners

The Commissioners for the "University of Virginia" having been required by law to meet at the tavern in Rockfish gap on the blue ridge, on this first day of August 1818—the following members attended (to wit) Creed Taylor, Peter Randolph, William Brockenbrough, Archibald Rutherford, Archibald Stuart, James Breckenridge Henry E. Watkins, James Madison, Armistead T. Mason, Hugh Holmes, Philip C Pendleton, Spencer Roane, John Mc Taylor,[1] John G. Jackson, Thomas Wilson, Philip Slaughter, William H Cabell, Nathaniel H. Claiborne, Thomas Jefferson, William A. G. Dade & William Jones, and their appointments being duly proven, they formed a board and proceeded to the discharge of the duties prescribed to them by the act of the Legislature entitled "An Act appropriating a part of the revenue of the literary fund, and for other purposes."[2]

Thomas Jefferson Esqr was unanimously elected President of the board, & Thomas W. Maury appointed secretary, who appeared and took his seat as such.

The board proceeded to the first duty enjoined on them (to wit) to enquire & report a proper scite for the University; whereupon the towns of Lexington & Staunton, and the central College, were severally proposed; and after some time spent in debate thereon, on motion of Mr Rutherford it was

Resolved that the consideration be postponed for the present

On motion by Mr Dade (who stated it to be his object to ascertain the sense of the board on the question, whether the board would visit the several places proposed for the scite of the University at the same moment that he himself was opposed to the adoption of such resolution) that when this board adjourns, it shall be to Lexington in the County of Rockbridge, it was unanimously decided in the negative—

On motion resolved that a select committee of six members be appointed by ballot to consider & report on all the duties assigned to this board, except that relating to the scite of the University, and a committee was appointed of Mr Jefferson Mr Madison, Mr Roane, Mr Stuart, Mr Dade & Mr Breckenridge—

On a motion by Mr Stuart that when the board adjourns, it shall be to the town of Staunton, in the County of Augusta, it was decided in the negative—

On motion resolved that when this board adjourns, it will adjourn till 9. oClock on Monday Morning

And the board was accordingly adjourned till 9. oClock on Monday Morning—

Monday August 3rd 1818

The Board having met according to adjournment

On the motion of Mr Roane. Resolved that the board will now proceed to declare its opinion which of the three places proposed, to wit Lexington, Staunton or the Central College is most convenient and proper for the site of the University of Virginia and on a call of the votes nominally, Mr Breckenridge, Mr Pendleton & Mr J Mc Taylor,[3] voted for Lexington, Mr Stuart & Mr Wilson for Staunton and Mr Creed Taylor, Mr Randolph, Mr Brockenbrough, Mr Rutherford, Mr Watkins, Mr Madison, Mr Mason, Mr Holmes Mr Roane, Mr Jackson, Mr Slaughter, Mr Cabell, Mr Claiborne Mr Jefferson, Mr Dade, & Mr Jones voted for the central college, so it was resolved that the central college is a convenient & proper place for the site of the University of Virginia

Resolved that this declaration of the opinion of the board be referred to the committee appointed on Saturday with instructions that they include it with the other matters referred to them & report thereon; and that they retire forthwith to prepare & make their report

Whereupon the committee withdrew, and after some time returned to their seats, and delivered in their report, which having been considered and sundry amendments made thereto, was, upon the question put, passed by the unanimous vote of the board.

Resolved that the secretary prepare without delay, two fair copies of the said report, to be signed each by every member present, and, to be forwarded by the President, one of them to the Speaker of the Senate, and the other to the Speaker of the House of Delegates.

And the board adjourned to tomorrow Morning. 9. oClock—

Tuesday August 4th 1818.

The board met according to adjournment.

The Secretary according to order, produced two fair copies of the report of the committee as amended & agreed to by the board, which were then signed by the attending members.

On motion of Mr Roane seconded by Mr Breckenridge.

Resolved unanimously "that the thanks of this board be given to Thomas Jefferson Esqr for the great ability, impartiality & dignity, with which he has presided over its' deliberations."

The question being then put.

Resolved that this board is now dissolved.

(Signed)

TH: JEFFERSON

Attest:

TH: W MAURY Sec^y

MS (Vi: RG 79, House of Delegates, Speaker, Executive Communications); in Maury's hand, signed by TJ and Maury. Printed in *University of Virginia Commissioners' Report*, 5–7; *JHD* (1818–19 sess.), 9–10 (8 Dec. 1818); and *Richmond Enquirer*, 10 Dec. 1818. Enclosed in TJ to Linn Banks and Edward Watts, 20 Nov. 1818. Proceedings and resolutions also summarized in *Richmond Enquirer*, 11 Aug. 1818.

[1] *JHD*: "John M. C: Taylor." *Richmond Enquirer*: "John M. C. Taylor."

[2] Omitted closing quotation mark editorially supplied.

[3] *JHD* and *Richmond Enquirer*: "J. M. C. Taylor."

II. Thomas Jefferson's Notes on the Geographic Center of Virginia's Population

[before 28 June 1818]

Counties on the Western waters.	
Brooke	5,511
Ohio	7,735
Monongalia	12,442
Wood	2,586
Harrison	9,499
Randolph	2,743
Mason	1,742
Kenhaway	3,514
Cabell	2,496
Giles	3,503
Greenbriar	5,420
Monroe	5,068
Tazewell	2,679
Lee	4,358
Russell	5,930
Washington	10,688
Wythe	7,199
Grayson	4,671
Montgomery	7,310
	105,094

Between the Allegany & Blue ridge.	
Hampshire	8,855
Berkley	9,950
Jefferson	8,319
Hardy	4,776
Frederick	16,157
Shenandoah	12,608
Pendleton	3,977
Rockingham	11,262
Bath	3,955
Augusta	11,428
Rockbridge	8,594
Botetourt	11,026
	110,907

between Patomak & Rappahanok.	
Loudon	16,181
Fairfax	7,169
Prince William	6,091
Fauquier	12,328
Stafford	5,635
King George	2,578
Westmoreland	4,022
Richmond	3,036
Northumberland	4,461
Lancaster	2,480
	63,981

Between Rappahanoc and York	
Culpeper	10,655
Madison	4,411
Orange	5,807
Spotsylvania	6,161
Caroline	6,780
Essex	3,717
King & Queen	4,985
King William	3,497
Middlesex	1,938
Gloucester	4,629
Matthews	2,159
	54,739

Between York and James rivers	
Albemarle	9,042
Nelson	5,005
Amherst	5,341
Louisa	5,470
Fluvanna	2,633
Goochland	4,739
Hanover	6,628
Henrico	5,099
Richmond City	5,987
New Kent	2,753
Charles city	2,163
York	2,256
James city	1,774
Warwick	715
Elizabeth city	1,874
	61,479

Between James river & Roanoke.	
Bedford	10,001
Campbell	5,633
Buckingham	8,384
Cumberland	3,890
Prince Edward	5,413
Charlotte	5,564
Powhatan	2,982
Amelia	3,408
Nottoway	2,910
Lunenburg	5,110
Mecklenburg	8,189
Chesterfield	3,964
Petersburg	3,495
Dinwiddie	5,082
Brunswick	6,043
Greenesville	2,254
Prince George	3,564
Surry	3,415
Sussex	5,018
Southampton	7,091
Isle of Wight	5,145
Nansemond	5,862
Norfolk	8,032
Norfolk borough	5,368
Princess Anne	5,572
	131,389

South of Roanoke.	
Franklin	8,052
Patrick	3,971
Henry	3,856
Pittsylvania	10,860
Halifax	12,470
	39,209

Eastern shore.	
Northampton	4,124
Accomac	11,201
	15,325.

white population
105,094
110,907
216,001

total white population[2]
63,981
54,739
131,389
61,479
39,209
15,325
582,123.[1]

whole white inhabitants[3]	582,123
West of Blue ridge	216,001
East of d°	366,122
difference	150,121

the 11. counties below & adjacent to the Blue ridge.

Loudon	16,181
Fauquier	12,328
Culpeper	10,655
Madison	4,411
Orange	5,807
Albemarle	9,042
Nelson	5,005
Amherst	5,341
Bedford	10,001
Franklin	8,052
Patrick	3,971
	90,794
$\frac{5}{6}$ of which are	75,662

A. a line from the middle of the mouth of the Chesapeak, thro' Rockfish gap to the Ohio.

Brook	
Ohio	
Monongalia	
Wood	
Harrison	
Randolph	40,516
$\frac{1}{4}$ Mason	435
part of Kanhaway	435
Hampshire	
Berkley	
Jefferson	
Hardy	
Frederic	
Shenandoah	
Pendleton	
Rockingham	75,904
$\frac{2}{3}$ Augusta	7,618
between Patomac & Rappahanoc	63,981
between Rappahan. & York	54,739
Hanover	6,628
Louisa	5,470
$\frac{1}{2}$ Albemarle	4,520
Eastern shore	15,325
North of the line.[4]	275,571
$\frac{1}{2}$ of the whole state is	291,061
difference	15,490

B. a line from Chesapeak thro' Lexington to Ohio.

$\frac{2}{5}$ Kanhaway & Cabell	2,404	
$\frac{2}{5}$ Greenbriar	2,168	
$\frac{2}{5}$ Rockbridge	3,437	
$\frac{7}{10}$ Amherst & Nelson	7,242	
$\frac{7}{8}$ Buckingham	7,336	
$\frac{9}{10}$ Cumberland	3,501	
$\frac{2}{3}$ Powhatan	1,988	
$\frac{1}{3}$ Henrico	1,700	
$\frac{9}{10}$ Charles city	1,946	
$\frac{4}{5}$ James city	1,419	
$\frac{1}{2}$ York	1,128	
Warwick	715	
Eliz. City	1,874	36,858
Monroe		
Tazewell		
Lee		
Russell		
Washington		
Wythe		
Grayson		
Montgomery		47,903
Botetourt		11,026
South of Roanoke		39,209
Bedford & Campbell		15,634
Prince Edwd & Charlotte		10,977
Amelia		
Nottoway		
Lunenburgh		
Mecklenburgh		
Chesterfield		
Petersburg		
Dinwiddie		
Brunswick		
Greenesville		
Prince George		
Surry		
Sussex		
Southampton		
Isle of Wight		
Nansemond		
Norfolk		
Norfolk boro'		
Princess Anne		83,950

$$582,123 = \begin{cases} \text{South} & 245,557 \\ \text{North} & 336,566 \end{cases}$$

difference   91,009

C. a parallel with the Blue R. thro Staunton

$\frac{1}{8}$ .Grayson	584	
$\frac{1}{6}$ Montgomery	914	
$\frac{2}{7}$ Botetourt	3,150	
$\frac{3}{5}$ Rockbridge	5,156	
$\frac{2}{5}$ Augusta	4,571	
$\frac{2}{5}$ Rockingham	4,505	
$\frac{1}{2}$ Shenandoah	6,304	
$\frac{2}{5}$ Frederic	6,463	
$\frac{1}{2}$ Jefferson	4,159	35,806
below the Blue ridge		366,122

$$582,123 = \begin{cases} \text{East} & 401,928 \\ \text{West} & 180,195 \end{cases}$$

difference   221,733

D. a parallel with the Blue R. thro Lexington.

$\frac{1}{4}$ Rockbridge	2,148	
$\frac{1}{5}$ Augusta	2,285	
$\frac{1}{5}$ Rockingham	1,719	
$\frac{1}{4}$ Shenandoah	3,152	
$\frac{1}{5}$ Frederic	3,231	12,535
below the Blue ridge		366,122

$$582,123 = \begin{cases} \text{East} & 378,657 \\ \text{West} = & 203,466 \end{cases}$$

difference   175,191

E. a parallel with the Blue R. thro the Central College

the parallel of equal division is	291,061
add $\frac{1}{5}$ of the 11. counties adjact to Bl. R.	18,158

$$582,123 = \begin{cases} \text{East} & 309,219 \\ \text{West} & 272,904 \end{cases}$$

difference   36,315

from Staunton to the nearest part of our Southern boundary is	$112\frac{1}{2}$ miles
from d° to the Patomac on a parallel with the Blue ridge.[6]	110.
difference	$2\frac{1}{2}$ miles
from the Central College to the Southern boundary	104. miles
from d° to Patomac on a parallel with the Blue ridge[7]	$92\frac{1}{2}$
difference	$11\frac{1}{2}$ mile

from Lexington to
   Southern bound^y 85 miles
from d° to Patomac on
   parallel with Bl. R.[8] 137½[9]
       difference   52½
these measures are from
   Madison's map.[10]

Observations and Conclusions from the preceding tables.[11]

The Rockfish gap of the Blue ridge is precisely equidistant from the nearest part of our Southern boundary, and from the Patomac, our Northern boundary, where it passes thro' the Blue ridge at Harper's ferry.

If from the middle of the mouth of the Chesapeak a line be drawn thro' the Rockfish gap, as a Central point, & continued in the same direction to the Ohio, our Western boundary, it will strike that river about 10. miles above the mouth of Kanhaway, and will divide the white population of the state equally, within 15,490; so much over a moiety being left to the South. such a line passes about 3½ miles South of Staunton, 5½ South of the Central College, and 27. miles North of Lexington. see Table **A**.

If the line, from the same point in the Chesapeak be drawn thro' Lexington, to the Western boundary, it will leave 336,566 to the North, & 245,557. to the South; making a difference in the division of 91,009. see Table **B**.

If a line be drawn along the top of the Blue ridge from S.W. to N.E. it leaves 216,001 on the Western side, and 366,122 on the Eastern, making a difference, in the division, that way of 150,121. see General Table of the counties.

If a line, parallel with that, be drawn thro' Staunton, it leaves 180,195. to the West; and 401,928 to the East, making a difference of 221,733. see Table **C**.

A like parallel thro' Lexington leaves 203,466 to the West, and 378,657. to the East, making a difference of 175,191. see Table **D**.

If thro' the Central College, it leaves 272,904 to the West and 309,219. to the East, making a difference of 36,315. see Table **E**.

The exact parallel of equal division would pass about 4½ miles Eastward of the Central College, throwing into the Western division about ⅚ of the population of the 11. counties next below, & adjacent to the Blue ridge.

From this parallel of equal division Staunton is 34. miles to the West, Lexington 25. and the Central College 4½.

On the whole it appears that the division between North & South is scarcely sensible for either Staunton or the Central College: while for Lexington there is a difference of 91,009. that the divisions between East and West give a difference, for Staunton of 221,733. for Lexington 175,191. and for the Central College 36,315.[12]

These measures are taken from Madison's map of Virginia, and for the verification of the numbers, a list of the counties is given, with the white population of each according to the last Census of the US. in 1810.

Where a line of division split counties into two parts, the proportion on each side of the line was estimated by the eye only.[13]

1st MS (ViU: TJP); entirely in TJ's hand; undated; with tables on recto and verso of a single sheet divided into three columns and "Observations and Conclusions" on recto of an additional sheet; archivally bound with following document. 2d MS (ViU: TJP); entirely in TJ's hand; undated; with tables on recto and verso of a single sheet divided into three columns and remainder of text on recto of an additional sheet; archivally bound with following document. Printed anonymously in *Richmond Enquirer*, 17 Dec. 1818, with note at head of text: "FOR THE ENQUIRER. The following statement is given to the public to show that the Central College is the proper site for the University of Virginia." Enclosed in TJ to James Madison, 28 June 1818, and Madison to TJ, [16 July 1818].

As when he composed his Notes on Collegiate Districts for a System of Public Education, [ca. 24 Oct. 1817], TJ here claimed to be confining his calculations of the center of population in Virginia to the white population. Whether by an oversight or deliberately, however, in both instances he actually included free blacks in the count, a point raised in the Virginia House of Delegates during the debate over the university bill (Joseph C. Cabell to TJ, 18 Jan. 1819).

[1] For this number *Richmond Enquirer* substitutes 366,122, the subtotal of inhabitants east of the Blue Ridge.

[2] Recto ends here.

[3] 2d MS: "white inhabitants—whole."

[4] Preceding three words not in 2d MS.

[5] Here and below, some fractions are expressed as decimals in 2d MS.

[6] 2d MS: "on a parallel with the Blue ridge to the Patomac."

[7] 2d MS: "on a parallel with B.R. to Patom."

[8] 2d MS: "on a parallel with B.R: to Patom."

[9] Fraction not in *Richmond Enquirer*.

[10] Sentence not in 2d MS.

[11] Sentence not in 2d MS.

[12] This paragraph and next are reversed in 2d MS.

[13] Sentence not in 2d MS.

III. Thomas Jefferson's Draft of the Rockfish Gap Report of the University of Virginia Commissioners

[ca. 28 June 1818]

The Commissioners for the University of Virginia having met at the[1] tavern in Rockfish gap on the Blue ridge on the 1st day of August of this present year 1818 and[2] until the   instant when the attendance of a Quorum of   members enabled them to form a board, proceeded on that day to the discharge of the duties assigned to them by the act of the legislature intituled 'An act appropriating part of the revenue of the literary fund, and for other purposes.'

The 1st of these duties was to enquire and report a proper site for the University contemplated by that act. in this enquiry they supposed[3] that the governing considerations should be the healthiness of the site, the fertility of the neighboring country, and it's centrality to the white population of the whole state: for altho' the act authorised and required them to recieve any voluntary contributions, whether conditional or absolute which might be offered thro' them to the President and Directors of the literary fund, for the benefit of the University, yet they did not consider this as establishing an auction, or as pledging the location to the highest bidder. in such a contest, it was certain that the great mercantile towns, as Richmond, Petersburg, Norfolk or Alexandria,[4] having a greater command of money, would readily have outbidden any country situation; and that the College of William and Mary, with it's abundant endowments in lands and personal property, with it's magnificent and capacious edifices, it's library and Apparatus, Physical and Mathematical, and all it's other accomodations in actual readiness, would have offered itself on the condition of being made the University. here the institution would have found itself provided with all the buildings and other necessaries in a proper state to recieve them, and in condition at once to enter into full operation. but as considerations of health, and of centrality of position had already occasioned this antient and respectable seminary to be overlooked, the Commissioners inferred that they were preferably to attend to the other circumstances of choice.

Three places were proposed; Lexington in the county of Rockbridge, Staunton in Augusta, and the Central College in Albemarle. each of these were unexceptionable as to healthiness & fertility. there is indeed a difference in the quality of the waters of these places; that below the Blue ridge being pure and free from foreign ingredients, and that above distinguished by it's calcareous impregnation. altho' this circumstance is not indifferent to many, yet the inhabitants on each side are equally attached to their own; and experience proves them equally wholesome:[5] and that even with strangers visiting the calcareous country use soon fortifies them[6] against the drastic effect of it's waters.   It is the degree of Centrality then which constitutes the important point of comparison between these places.

The Commissioners therefore taking for their guide the last Census of the US. prescribed by this act in another case as the rule of computation,[7] which Census gives the white population of each county separately, and a total of 582,123 for the whole state, found, that on the Western side of the Blue ridge there were about 216,000 white inhabitants, and on the Eastern side about 366,000, leaving 150,000 more below than above the ridge; and that a line parallel with that which should divide equally the population Northwest and Southeast of it must include about five sixths of the population of the range of counties next below and adjacent to the Blue ridge; such a line[8] passing near Fauquier Culpeper and Orange courthouses, and the towns of Milton, Lynchburg & Martinsville; that Staunton being about 34. miles N.W. from that line, a parallel thro' it would leave between 221. and 222,000. more on the Eastern than Western side; Lexington being about 25. miles N.W. from that line, it's parallel with the Blue ridge would leave about 175,000. more to the East than to the West; and the Central College being about $4\frac{1}{2}$ miles Northwest, it's parallel would be within 18,000 of being the line of equal partition between the Northwestern & Southeastern moieties.

That for a division the other way, to wit, between the Northeastern & Southwestern moieties of the state (Rockfish gap, on the Blue ridge, being, by our latest map, exactly equidistant from our Southern boundary, and from the Northern at the intersection of the Blue-ridge and Patowmac) if a line be passed from the middle of the mouth of the Chesapeak thro' that central point of the Gap, directly on to the Ohio, it will be a line of equal partition, in that way, within about 15,500, or one thirty seventh part of the whole, leaving so much less on the Northern than Southern side:[9] that a line from the same point in the Chesapeak thro Staunton or the Central college would vary from the other but insensibly; but that a line from the same point thro' Lexington to our Western border would leave about 91,000 more to the North than the South.

On the whole therefore the Central College being but $4\frac{1}{2}$ miles to the West, & $5\frac{1}{2}$ miles to the North of the true Central point of our whole white population, the board of Commissioners consider it as the most just and equal location for the whole state, & do therefore report it to the legislature as the proper site for the University contemplated by the act under which they are commissioned.[10]

2. The board having thus agreed on a proper site for the University to be reported to the legislature, proceeded to the 2ᵈ of the duties assigned to them, that of proposing a plan for it's buildings;[11] and they are of opinion[12] that that which has been adopted by the Visitors of Central College is well suited to the purpose of the University.[13] it consists of a row of distinct houses or pavilions, arranged in a line[14] on each side of a lawn 200. feet wide, and at about the same distance from each other, in each of which is a lecturing room, with from two to four apartments for the accomodation of a Professor and his family. these pavilions are united by a range of Dormitories, sufficient[15] for the accomodation of two students only, this provision being deemed advantageous to morals, to order, and to uninterrupted study. a Colonnade in front gives a passage along the whole range under cover from the weather.[16] a pavilion, on an average of the larger and smaller,[17] is expected to cost about 5000. Dollars,[18] and the Dormitories about 350 Dollars each, the number depending of course on that of the students. Hotels too of a single Refectory,[19] with two rooms for the accomodation of the tenant, are proposed to be placed in the same lines of building,[20] and are estimated to cost 3500. Dollars each. the advantages of this plan are, greater security against fire and infection, tranquility and comfort to the Professors and their families thus insulated, retirement to the Students,[21] and the admission of enlargement to any degree to which the institution may extend in future times. it is supposed probable that a building of somewhat more size in the middle of the grounds: may be called for in time, in which may be rooms for a library, for public examinations[22] for the schools of music, drawing and[23] other associated purposes.

3. 4. In proceeding to the 3ᵈ and 4ᵗʰ duties prescribed[24] by the legislature, of reporting 'the branches of learning which should be taught in the University, and the number and description of the Professorships they will require' the Commissioners were first to consider at what point it was understood that University education should commence? certainly not with the Alphabet, for reasons of expediency and impracticability, as well as from the obvious sense of the legislature, who, in the same act make other provision for the primary instruction of poor children expecting[25] doubtless that, in other[26] cases, it would be provided by the parent, or become perhaps a subject of

future and further attention for the legislature. the objects of this primary education determine it's character and limits. these objects would be

to give to every citizen[27] the information he needs for the transaction of his own business:

to enable him to calculate for himself, and to express and preserve his ideas his contracts and accounts in writing:

to improve, by reading, his morals and faculties:

to understand his duties to his neighbors and country, and to discharge with competence the functions confided to him by either:

to know his rights; to exercise with order and justice those he retains; to choose with discretion the fiduciaries of those he delegates; and to notice their conduct with diligence, with candor and judgment:

and, in general, to observe, with intelligence and faithfulness, all the social relations under which he shall be placed.

To instruct the mass of our citizens[28] in these their rights, interests & duties as men and citizens, being then the objects of education in the primary schools, whether private or public, in them should be taught[29] reading, writing & numerical arithmetic, the elements of mensuration (useful in so many callings) and the outlines of geography and history. and this brings us to the point at which are to commence the higher branches of education, of which the legislature requires the developement: those, for example, which are

to form the statesmen, legislators & judges, on whom public prosperity, & individual happiness are so much to depend:

to expound the principles and structure of government the laws which regulate the intercourse of nations, those formed municipally for our own government, and a sound spirit of legislation, which, banishing all arbitrary, and unnecessary restraint on individual action,[30] shall leave us free to do whatever does not violate the equal rights of another:

to harmonise and promote the interests of agriculture, manufactures and commerce, and by well-informed views of Political economy to give a free scope to the public industry:

to develope the reasoning faculties of our youth, enlarge their minds, cultivate their morals, & instill into them the precepts of virtue and order:

to enlighten them with Mathematical and Physical sciences, which advance the arts & administer to the health, the subsistence, and comforts of human life:

and generally to form them to habits of reflection, and correct action, rendering them examples of virtue to others, and of happiness within themselves.

These are the objects of that higher grade of education, the benefits & blessings of which the legislature now propose to provide for the good and ornament of their country, the gratification and happiness of their fellow citizens, of the parent especially, and his progeny, on which all his affections are concentrated.

In entering on this field the Commissioners are aware that they have to encounter much difference of opinion as to the extent which it is expedient that this institution should occupy. some good men, and even of respectable information, consider the learned sciences as useless acquirements: some think[31] that they do not better the condition of Man; and others that education like private and individual concerns,[32] should be left to private and individual effort; not reflecting that an establishment, embracing all the sciences which may be useful and even necessary in the various vocations of life, with the buildings & apparatus belonging to each,[33] are far beyond the reach of individual means, and must either derive existence from public patronage, or not exist at all. this would leave us then without those callings which depend on education, or send us to other countries to seek the instruction they require. but the Commissioners are happy in considering the statute under which they are assembled as proof that the legislature is far from the abandonment of objects so interesting.[34] they are sensible that the advantages of well directed education, moral, political and economical, are truly above all estimate. education generates habits of application, of[35] order, and the love of virtue, and corrects, by the force of habit, any innate obliquities in our moral organisation. we should be far too from the discoraging persuasion that man is fixed, by the law of his nature, at a given point; that his improvement is a chimaera, and the hope delusive of rendering ourselves wiser, happier, or better than our forefathers were. as well might it be urged that the wild and uncultivated tree, hitherto yielding sour and bitter fruit only, can never be made to yield better. yet we know that[36] the grafting art, implants a new tree on the savage stock, producing[37] what is most estimable both in kind and degree. education, in like manner, engrafts a new man[38] on the native stock, & improves what in his nature was vicious and perverse into qualities of virtue[39] & social value.[40] and it cannot be but that each generation, succeeding to the knolege acquired by all those who preceded it, adding to it their own acquisitions and discoveries,[41] and handing the mass down for successive and constant accumulation, must advance the knolege and well-being[42] of mankind, not infinitely, as some have said, but indefinitely, and to a term which no one can fix, or foresee. indeed we need look back only half a century, to times which many now living remember well, and see the wonderful advances in the sciences and arts which have been made within that period. some of these have rendered the elements themselves subservient to the purposes of man, have harnessed them to the yoke of his labors, and effected the great[43] blessings of moderating his own, of accomplishing what was beyond his feeble[44] force, and of extending the comforts of life to a much enlarged circle, to those who had before known it's necessaries only. that these are not the vain dreams of sanguine[45] hope, we have before our eyes real & living examples. what, but education, has advanced us beyond the condition of our indigenous neighbors? and what chains them to their present state of barbarism and wretchedness, but a bigotted[46] veneration for the supposed superlative wisdom of their fathers, and the preposterous idea[47] that they are to look backward for better things, and not forward, longing, as it should seem, to return to the days of eating acorns and roots, rather than indulge in the degeneracies of civilization. and how much more encouraging to the atchievements of science and improvement, is this, than the desponding view that the condition of man cannot be ameliorated, that what has been must ever be, and that, to secure ourselves where we are, we must tread with awful reverence in the footsteps of our fathers. this doctrine is the genuine fruit of the alliance between church and state, the tenants of which, finding themselves but too well in their present position, oppose all advances[48] which might unmask their usurpations, and monopolies of honors, wealth and power, and fear every change, as endangering the comforts they now hold. nor must we omit to mention, among the benefits of education, the incalculable advantage of training up able Counsellors to administer the affairs of our country, in all it's departments, Legislative, Executive, and Judiciary; and to bear their proper share in the councils of our National government; nothing, more than education,[49] advancing the prosperity, the power, and the happiness of a nation.

Encouraged therefore by the sentiments of the legislature, manifested in this statute, we present the following Tabular[50] statement of the branches of learning which we think should be taught in the University,[51] forming them into groupes, each of which are within the powers of a single Professor.[52]

I.	Languages. Antient	{ Latin Greek[53]	V.	{ Physics or Natural philosophy. Chemistry[59] Mineralogy[60]
II.	Languages Modern.	{ French Spanish Italian German Anglo-Saxon.[54]	VI.	{ Botany[61] Zoology
			VII.	{ Anatomy Medecine

[I]II.	Mathematics. Pure	{ Algebra
		Fluxions
		Geometry elementary
		    transcendental.
		Architecture Military
		    Naval
		    Civil[55]
			VIII.	{ Government[62]
				Political economy.
				Law of Nature & Nations.
				History (being interwoven with
				 Politics & Law)[63]

			IX.	Law Municipal.
IV.	Physico-Mathematics.	{ Mechanics[56] Pneumatics. Acoustics.[57] Optics. Astronomy Geography.[58]	X.	{ Ideology[64] General Grammar. Ethics Rhetoric. Belles lettres.[65]

Some articles in this distribution of sciences will need observation.

A Professor is proposed for Ancient languages, of the Latin and Greek[66] particularly. but these languages being the foundation common to all the sciences, it is difficult to foresee what may be the extent of this school. at the same time no greater obstruction to industrious study could be proposed than the presence, the intrusions, and the noisy turbulence of a multitude of small boys: and if they are to be placed here for the rudiments of the languages, they may be so numerous that it's character and value, as an University, will be merged in those of a Grammar school. it is therefore greatly to be wished that preliminary schools, either on private or public establishment, could be distributed in districts thro the state, as preparatory to the entrance of students into the University. the tender age at which this part of education commences, generally about the tenth year, would weigh heavily with parents in sending their sons to a school so distant as the Central establishment would be from most of them. districts of such extent as that every parent should be within a day's journey of his son at school, would be desirable in cases of sickness, & convenient for supplying their ordinary wants, and might be made to lessen sensibly the expence of this part of their education. and where a sparse population would not, within such a compass, furnish subjects sufficient to maintain a school, a competent enlargement of district must, of necessity,[67] there be submitted to. at these district schools, or Colleges boys should be rendered able to read the easier authors, Latin and Greek. this would be useful & sufficient for many not intended for an University education. at these too might be taught English grammar, the higher branches of numerical Arithmetic, the Geometry of straight lines and of the Circle, the elements of navigation[68] and Geography to a sufficient degree, and thus afford to greater numbers the means of being qualified for the various vocations of life, needing more instruction than merely[69] menial or praedial labor:[70] these institutions, intermediate between the primary schools and University, might then be the passage of entrance for youths[71] into the University, where their Classical learning might be critically compleated, by a study of the authors of highest degree. and it is at this stage only that they should be recieved at the University. giving then a portion of their time to a finished knolege of the Latin and Greek, the rest might be appropriated to the modern languages, or[72] to the commencement of the course of science for which they should be destined. this would generally be about the 15th year of their age, when they might go with more safety and contentment to that distance from their parents. until this preparatory provision shall be made, either the University will be overwhelmed with the Grammar school, or a separate establishment[73] for it's lower classes will be advisable, at a mile or two distance from the general one; where too may be exercised the stricter government necessary for them,[74] but unsuitable for young men.[75]

The considerations which have governed the specification of languages to be taught by the Professor of Modern languages were that the French is the language of general intercourse among nations, and is a depository of more human science than can be found in[76] any other language living or dead; that the Spanish is highly interesting to us, as the language spoken by so great a portion of the inhabitants of our continents, with whom we shall probably have great intercourse ere long; and is that also in which is written the greater part of the early history of America: The Italian abounds with works of very superior order,[77] valuable for their matter, and still more distinguished as models of the finest taste in style and composition: and the German now stands in a line with that of the most learned nations in richness of erudition, and advance in the sciences.[78] it is too of common descent with the language of our own country, a branch of the same original Gothic[79] stock, & furnishes valuable illustrations for us. but in this point of view the Anglo-Saxon is of transcendent[80] value. we have placed it among the Modern languages, because it is in fact that which we speak, in the earliest form in which we have knolege of it. it has been undergoing, with time, those gradual changes which all languages, antient and modern, have experienced; and even now needs only to be printed in the modern character and orthography, to be intelligible, in a considerable degree to an English reader. it has this value too above the Greek and Latin, that, while it gives the radix of the mass of our language, they explain it's innovations only. obvious proofs of this have been presented to the modern reader in the disquisitions of Horne Tooke, and Fortescue Aland has well explained the great instruction which may be derived from it towards a full understanding of our antient Common law, on which, as a stock, our whole system of law is engrafted.[81] it will form the first link in the chain of an historical review of our language thro' all it's successive changes to the present day, will constitute the foundation of that critical instruction in it which ought to be found in a seminary of general learning, and thus reward amply the few weeks of attention, which would alone be requisite for it's attainment. a language already fraught with all the eminent science of our parent country, the future vehicle of whatever we may ourselves atchieve, and destined to occupy so much space on the globe, claims distinguished attention in American education.

Medecine, where fully taught, is usually subdivided into several professorships. but this cannot well be without the Accessory of an hospital, where the Student can have the benefit of attending Clinical lectures, & of assisting at operations of Surgery. with this Accessory, the seat of our University is not yet prepared, either by it's population, or by the numbers of poor who would leave their own houses, and accept of the charities of an hospital. for the present therefore we propose but a single Professor for both Medicine and Anatomy. by him the elements of Medical science[82] may be taught, with a history & explanations of all it's successive theories from Hippocrates to the present day: and Anatomy may be fully treated. vegetable pharmacy will make a part of the Botanical course, and mineral and Chemical[83] pharmacy of those of Mineralogy and Chemistry.[84] this degree of Medical information is such as the mass of scientific students would wish to possess as enabling them, in their course thro' life, to estimate with satisfaction the extent and limits of the aid to human life and health, which they may understandingly expect from that art;[85] and it constitutes such a foundation for those intended for the profession, that the finishing course of practice at the bedsides of the sick, and at the operations of Surgery in a hospital, can neither be long nor expensive. to seek this finishing elsewhere, must therefore be submitted to for a while.

In conformity with the principles of our constitution, which places all sects of Religion on an equal footing, with the jealousies of the different sects in guarding that equality from encroachment and surprise,[86] and with the sentiments of the legislature in favor of freedom of religion manifested on former occasions, we have proposed no Professor of Divinity; and the rather as the proofs of the being of a god, the creator, preserver, and supreme ruler of the universe, the Author of all the relations of morality, and of the laws and obligations these infer,[87] will be within the province of the Professor of Ethics;[88] to which adding the developements of these general principles of morality[89] of those in which all sects agree[90] a basis will be formed common to all sects. proceeding thus far without offence to the constitution,[91] we have thought it proper[92] to leave every sect to provide, as they think fittest, the means of further instruction in their own peculiar tenets.

We are further of opinion that, after declaring by law that certain sciences shall be taught in the University, fixing the number of Professors they require, which we think should, at present, be ten, limiting[93] a Maximum for their salaries (which should be a certain, but scanty subsistence, to be made up by liberal tuition fees, as an excitement to assiduity) it will be[94] best to leave to the discretion of the Visitors the grouping of these sciences together, according to the accidental qualifications of the professors; and the introduction also of other branches of science, when enabled by private donations or by public provision, and called for by the increase of population, or other change of circumstances; to establish beginnings in short, to be developed by time, as those who come after us shall find expedient.[95] they will be more advanced than we are[96] in science and in useful arts, and will know best what will suit the circumstances of their day.[97]

We have proposed no formal provision for the Gymnastics of the school, altho' a proper object of attention for every institution of youth. these exercises with antient nations, constituted[98] the principal part of the education of their youth.[99] their arms and mode of warfare rendered them severe in the extreme. ours, on the same correct principle, should be adapted to our arms and warfare; and the Manual exercise, military maneuvres, and Tactics generally, should be the frequent[100] exercises of the Students, in their hours of recreation. it is at that age of aptness, docility and emulation of the practices of manhood, that such things are soonest learnt, and longest remembered. the use of tools too in the manual arts is worthy of encoragement, by facilitating to such as choose it an admission into the neighboring workshops.[101] to these should be added the arts which embellish life, dancing, music, and drawing; the last more especially, as an important[102] part of military education. these innocent[103] arts furnish amusement and happiness[104] to those who,[105] having time on their hands, might less inoffensively employ it. needing, at the same time, no regular incorporation with the institution, they may be left to accessory teachers, who will be paid by the individuals employing them, the University only providing proper apartments for their exercise.

The 5th duty prescribed to the Commissioners[106] is to propose such general provisions as may be properly enacted by the legislature, for the better organising and governing the University.

In the education of youth provision is to be made for 1. tuition; 2. diet, 3. lodging. 4. government, and 5. honorary excitements. the 1st of these constitutes the proper[107] functions of the Professors.[108]   2. the dieting the students should be left to private boarding houses of their own choice, and at their own expense;[109] the house only being provided by the University within it's own precincts,[110]   3. they should be lodged in Dormitories, making a part of the general[111] system of buildings.   4. the best mode of government for youth in large collections, is certainly a desideratum not yet attained with us. it may well be questioned whether <u>fear</u>, after a certain age is the motive to which we should have ordinary recourse. the human character is susceptible of other incitements to correct conduct, more worthy of employ, and of better effect. pride of character, laudable ambition, and moral dispositions are innate correctives of the indiscretions of that lively age, and, when strengthened by habitual appeal and exercise, have a happier effect on future character than the degrading motive of fear.[112] the affectionate deportment between father and son offers in truth the best example[113] for that of tutor and pupil; and the experience and practice of[114] other countries in this respect, may be worthy of enquiry and consideration with us. it will be then for the wisdom and discretion of the Visitors to devise and perfect a proper system of government, which, if it be founded in reason and comity, will be more likely to nourish, in the minds of our youth, the combined spirit of order & self-respect, so congenial with our political institutions, and so important to be woven into the American character.   5. what qualifications shall[115] be required to entitle to entrance into the University, the arrangement of the days and hours of lecturing for the different schools, so as to facilitate to the students the circle of attendance on them; the establishment of periodical and public examinations, the premiums to be given for distinguished merit;[116] whether honorary degrees shall be conferred, and by what appellations; whether the title to these shall depend on the time the candidate has been at the University, or, where Nature has given a greater share of understanding, attention

& application; whether he shall not be allowed the advantages[117] resulting from these endowments, with other minor items of government, we are of opinion should be entrusted to the Visitors; and the Statute under which we act having provided for the appointment of these, we think they should moreover be charged with

the erection, preservation, and repair of the buildings, the care of the grounds and appurtenances, and of the interests of the University generally:

that they should have power to appoint a Burser, employ a Steward,[118] and all other necessary agents:

to appoint and remove Professors, two thirds of the whole number of visitors voting for the removal:[119]

to prescribe their duties, & the course of education, in conformity with the law:

to establish rules for the government and discipline of the students, not contrary to the laws of the land:

to regulate the tuition fees, and the rent of the dormitories they occupy:[120]

to prescribe and controul the duties and proceedings of all officers, servants & others with respect to the buildings, lands, appurtenances & other property and interests of the University:

to draw from the literary fund such monies as are by law charged on it for this institution: and in general

to direct and do all matters and things which, not being inconsistent with the laws of the land, to them shall seem most expedient for promoting the purposes of the sd institution; which several functions they should be free to exercise in the form of bye-laws, rules, resolutions, orders instructions or otherwise as they should deem proper.

That they should have two stated meetings in the year,[121] towit, on   meetings at such times as they should appoint   and occasional meetings at such times as they should appoint, or on a special call with such notice as themselves shall prescribe by a general rule:[122] which meetings should be at the University, a majority of them constituting a Quorum for business: and that on the death or[123] resignation of a member, or on his removal[124] by the President and Directors of the literary fund[125] the sd[126] President and Directors[127] should appoint a successor.

That the sd[128] Visitors should appoint one of their own body to be Rector and with him[129] be a body[130] corporate under the style and title of the Rector &[131] Visitors of the University of Virginia, with the right, as such, to use a common seal; that they should have[132] capacity to plead and be impleaded in all courts of justice, and in all cases interesting to the University, which may be the subjects of legal cognisance and jurisdiction; which pleas should not abate by the determination of their office, but should stand revived in the name of their successors; and they should be capable in law, and in trust for the University, of recieving subscriptions and donations, real and personal, as well from bodies corporate, or persons associated, as from private individuals.

And that the sd Rector and Visitors should at all times conform to such laws as the legislature may from time to time think proper to enact for their government, and the said University should, in all things, and at all times be subject to the controul of the legislature.[133]

And lastly the Commissioners report to the legislature the following Conditional offers to the President & Directors of the literary fund, for the benefit of the University.

On the condition that Staunton shall be made the site of the University

On the condition that Lexington shall be made the site of the University[134]

on the condition that the Central College shall be made the Site of the University, it's whole property, real and personal, in possession or in action is offered. this consists of a parcel of land of[135] 47. acres, whereon the buildings of the College are begun, one pavilion and it's Appendix of[136] 17 dormitories being already far advanced, and with one other pavilion, and equal annexation of dormitories, being expected to be compleated during the present season. of another parcel of 153. acres, near the former, and including a considerable eminence very favorable for the erection of a future Observatory; of the proceeds of the sale of two glebes, amounting to[137] 3280.D. 86 cents; and of a subscription known to be[138] of[139]   Dollars and believed to be of about   Dollars more in outstanding subscription papers, out of which has been taken[140] the cost of the lands, of the buildings, and other works done.[141] for the conditional transfer of these to the President and Directors of the literary fund, a regular power signed by the subscribers and founders of the College, generally, has been given to it's Visitors and Proctor, who[142]

2d Dft (ViU: TJP); clean draft, with numbered pages, entirely in TJ's hand; undated, but composed in large part before it was enclosed to James Madison on 28 June 1818 and emended through the end of the Rockfish Gap meeting on 4 Aug. 1818, with later changes described in notes below; archivally bound with other texts described here and with MSS of preceding and following documents; edge trimmed. 1st Dft (ViU: TJP); rough draft entirely in TJ's hand; undated, but composed before 28 June 1818 completion date of 2d Dft, with later emendations; for evidence that there may have been still earlier versions (not found), see note 52 below; archivally bound with other texts described here and with MSS of preceding and following documents. MS (ViU: TJP); consisting of a single sheet of corrections to the above Dfts; entirely in TJ's hand; undated; with proposed changes keyed to page and line numbers in 2d Dft, but made in both Dfts as noted below; with TJ's check marks indicating which changes he made; archivally bound between the 1st and 2d Dfts. 2d Dft enclosed in TJ to Madison, 28 June 1818, and Madison to TJ, [16 July 1818].

TJ composed initial versions of both extant drafts of the Rockfish Gap Report before enclosing the later version to Madison on 28 June 1818. He penned the 1st Dft in his usual style for such texts, leaving a wide margin on one side of the paper so as to provide ample space for rewriting and additions. Despite these allowances, several pages were so heavily reworked or supplemented that TJ attached separate slips of paper to the draft sheet in order to position his further revisions at their appropriate locations. In the 2d Dft TJ used narrow margins. He later prepared explanatory Notes on Curricular Definitions (printed as next document below) and filed a version with each draft. Although TJ intended to keep it separate, it found its way into the final version of the Rockfish Gap Report (document 5 below). Also added to both drafts after initial composition and included in the final version of the report was a footnote by TJ on student-run police forces.

At some point after completion of the 2d Dft, TJ wrote the half-page list of corrections described above, which he then made to both drafts, even though they were widely variant by this time. In addition to many, more significant differences between the drafts described in the notes below, TJ made minor stylistic changes as he composed the 2d Dft, including the regularization of some of his idiosyncratic spellings. Thus "scite," "chuse," and "encorage" became "site," "choose," and "encourage" in the later version. TJ also converted many of his initial ampersands to "and" and expanded words he abbreviated in the 1st Dft. He continued to change the 2d Dft through the end of the meeting of the University of Virginia Commissioners at Rockfish Gap, copying the offer made there by Lexington's supporters and adding language closing the meeting on 4 Aug. 1818. An image of the page of the 1st Dft with TJ's earliest extant version of his tabular statement of university subjects is reproduced elsewhere in this volume.

[1] TJ here canceled "Rockfish gap" in 1st Dft.

[2] 2d Dft here preserves several lines of blank space. 1st Dft here reads (brackets in original) "adjourned [from day to day]."

[3] Word interlined in 1st Dft in place of "thought."

[4] Reworked in 1st Dft from "Richmond, Fredericksbg Alexandria or Norfolk."

[5] Word interlined in place of "healthy." Reworked in 1st Dft from "they are equally healthy."

[6] 1st Dft: "<soon> fortifies them in <the end> time."

[7] 1st Dft adds preceding fifteen words in margin in place of "of the US."

[8] Preceding three words interlined in 1st Dft.

[9] Preceding ten words interlined in 1st Dft.

[10] Text of page two ends early here in 2d Dft, with text to this point enclosed by TJ to Madison on 28 June 1818 but not intended to be shown to the Commissioners, as indicated in that letter.

[11] Reworked in 1st Dft from "the buildings thereof."

[12] In place of remainder of sentence and five following sentences, TJ later interlined in a different ink "that it should consist of distinct houses or pavilions, arranged at proper distances on each side of a lawn of a proper breadth, and of indefinite extent, in one direction at least; in each of which should be a lecturing room with from two to four apartments for the accomodation of a Professor and his family: that these pavilions should be united by a range of Dormitories, sufficient each for the accomodation of two students only; this provision being deemed advantageous to morals, to order, and to uninterrupted study; and that a passage of some kind, under cover from the weather, should give a communication along the whole range. it is supposed that such pavilions, on an average of the larger and smaller, will cost each about 5000.D. each Dormitory about 350. Dollars and Hotels of a single room for a Refectory, and two rooms for the tenant, necessary for dieting the Students will cost about 3500.D. each. the number of these Pavilions will depend on the number of Professors, & that of the Dormitories and Hotels on the number of Students to be lodged and dieted."

[13] Preceding seven words reworked in 1st Dft from "adapted to the purpose."

[14] Preceding three words interlined in 1st Dft.

[15] Word interlined in 1st Dft as "<20 for every pavilion &> sufficient each."

[16] Sentence reworked in 1st Dft from "a colonnade extends along the front of the whole giving a passage along the whole range under cover from the weather." Following it TJ added in margin and then canceled "these buildings are to be executed in a style of pure Grecian & Roman architecture to serve as models for the lectures in that art."

[17] Sentence to this point in 1st Dft reworked from "each of these pavilions with it's 20 dormitories."

[18] In 1st Dft TJ added a marginal note keyed to this sum with an asterisk reading "to wit about   bricks." Remainder of sentence added in margin of 1st Dft.

[19] Word interlined in 1st Dft in place of an illegible deletion.

[20] Remainder of sentence interlined in 1st Dft as "and are estimated <each at> to cost 3500.D. each, and the dormitories at an average about 350.D. each." TJ added marginal notes keyed to both of these sums, the first, keyed with a dagger, reading "to wit about   bricks," and the second, keyed with a double dagger, reading "13,220 bricks each on an average."

[21] Preceding four words interlined in 1st Dft.

[22] TJ later reworked preceding six words in a different ink to read (omitted word editorialy supplied) "[for] religious worship, under such impartial regulations as the Visitors shall prescribe, for public examinations, for a library."

[23] In 1st Dft TJ here canceled "perhaps."

[24] Word interlined in 1st Dft in place of "assigned."

[25] In 1st Dft paragraph to this point originally read "3. & 4. In proceeding to the 3^d & 4th duties assigned by the legislature, of reporting the branches of learning which should be taught in the University, and the number and description of the professorships they will require, the Commissioners are aware that they have to encounter much difference of opinion, as to the extent of the field the institution should cover: some good men, & even of respectable information consider the learned sciences as useless acquirements; some think." TJ rewrote this text at the bottom of the preceding page, which had ended short, and covered the original text with a strip of paper affixed with sealing wax, with text on strip oriented at 180 degrees from recto to verso, so that it could be flipped up and read continuously. Strip is no longer affixed in this manner, but is bound with 1st Dft. Text on strip continues until noted below.

[26] Word interlined in 1st Dft in place of "ordinary."

[27] Word interlined in 1st Dft in place of "one."

[28] Preceding two words interlined in 1st Dft in place of "the people."

[29] Preceding five words reworked in 1st Dft from "these should teach."

[30] Remainder of sentence interlined in 1st Dft in place of "may ameliorate by

conforming them to the just degree of natural right, limited only by the equal rights of others."

[31] Strip formerly affixed to 1st Dft ends here.

[32] Preceding four words interlined in 1st Dft in place of "the other vocations of life."

[33] Preceding eight words interlined in 1st Dft.

[34] Preceding seven words interlined in 1st Dft in place of illegible deletion.

[35] Preceding two words interlined in 1st Dft in place of "industry."

[36] Preceding four words interlined in place of an illegible deletion.

[37] Preceding sixteen words interlined in 1st Dft, with first four words reworked from multiple canceled phrases, including "altho' experience shows," and remainder of sentence reworked from original text reading in part "have proved that a new tree may be engrafted on the <wild> same stock which shall produce."

[38] Word reworked in 1st Dft from "<man> character."

[39] Word interlined in 1st Dft in place of "wisdom."

[40] In place of this word TJ later interlined "worth" in both Dfts based on his correction sheet, with 1st Dft originally reading "excellence."

[41] Preceding two words interlined in 1st Dft.

[42] Word interlined in 1st Dft in place of "happiness."

[43] Word interlined in 1st Dft in place of "precious."

[44] Word interlined in 1st Dft in place of "own."

[45] Word interlined in 1st Dft.

[46] Word interlined in 1st Dft in place of "superstitious."

[47] Word interlined in 1st Dft in place of "dogma."

[48] Word interlined in 1st Dft in place of "improvements."

[49] Instead of preceding word, 1st Dft reads "wise government."

[50] TJ here canceled "view."

[51] Remainder of sentence in 1st Dft reads "& the number of Professors necessary for them."

[52] Page ends short here in 2d Dft, with a space-filling flourish in TJ's hand. In

1st Dft TJ here wrote out a version of the tabular statement of subjects that jumped from number IV to number VIII, presumably an error made by TJ in copying from an earlier unknown draft. He then superseded his original and misordered text for numbers VIII through X by pasting on a small scrap, on which he then wrote numbers V and VI and began number VII, which he continued onto the original manuscript page, where he finished the table. Over this whole version he eventually pasted an additional half sheet with a new and cleaner version of the entire tabular statement. Both added pieces of paper have been detached from the original manuscript but are archivally bound with it. Changes by TJ noted below. The page of the 1st Dft showing TJ's copying error with replacement text removed is reproduced as an illustration elsewhere in this volume.

[53] TJ later added "Hebrew" in a different ink below this word.

[54] Word interlined in earliest version of tabular statement in 1st Dft.

[55] Word canceled in final version of tabular statement in 1st Dft. Order of three branches of architecture reversed in earliest version of tabular statement.

[56] Based on his correction sheet, TJ here later interlined "Statics" and "Dynamics" to 2d Dft and to final version of tabular statement in 1st Dft. In earliest version of tabular statement in 1st Dft, TJ listed statics and dynamics as sub-branches of mechanics and further subdivided dynamics into "Dynam proper," "Navign," and "Balistics."

[57] In earliest version of tabular statement in 1st Dft, TJ here canceled "or Phonics."

[58] In earliest version of tabular statement in 1st Dft, TJ here added "civil & Physical."

[59] TJ here erased what appears to be "including the principles of agriculture." In 1st Dft he initially wrote "Chemistry, including Chemical pharmacy," and then interlined "the principles of Agriculture &" after "including." In final version of 1st Dft TJ canceled everything after "Chemistry."

[60] In 1st Dft this entry initially read "Mineralogy, including Geology." In final

version of 1st Dft TJ added "& mineral Pharmacy" and then canceled everything after "Mineralogy."

[61] In 1st Dft this entry initially read "Botany, including vegetable pharmacy." In final version of 1st Dft TJ canceled everything after "Botany."

[62] In misordered version of tabular statement in 1st Dft, TJ here included "it's structure & principles," which he canceled when rewriting this section to correct his copying error and did not include in final version of 1st Dft.

[63] Omitted closing parenthesis editorially supplied. Misordered version of tabular statement in 1st Dft omits the parenthetical phrase, which TJ added when rewriting to correct his copying error and included in final version of 1st Dft.

[64] This and following two subjects initially preceded the grouping beginning "Government" in both the misordered version in the 1st Dft and the rewritten text that replaced it. In rewriting the text in the 1st Dft, TJ here added the word "proper."

[65] In 1st Dft TJ initially separated the two preceding subjects out into an eleventh branch as "Fine arts," where they are in reversed order. In final version of 1st Dft TJ moved them into this branch, with the latter subject listed as "Belles lettres & the fine arts." At this point in both Dfts TJ later affixed or interleaved, written on separate pieces of paper, his Notes on Curricular Definitions, the next document printed below.

[66] TJ later reworked preceding five words in a different ink to read "the Latin and Greek and Hebrew."

[67] Preceding five words interlined in 1st Dft in place of "might."

[68] Preceding four words interlined in 1st Dft.

[69] Preceding five words interlined in 1st Dft in place of "above the degree of."

[70] Based on his correction sheet, TJ here later interlined in both Dfts "and the same advantages to youths whose education may have been neglected until too late to lay a foundation in the learned languages," with first five words reworked on correction sheet from "they would provide too these useful branches of instruction for those."

[71] Preceding two words interlined in both Dfts. In 1st Dft they replace an interlined "from them."

[72] Remainder of sentence reworked in 1st Dft from "concurrently to a course of some science."

[73] Based on his correction sheet, TJ here later interlined "under one or more Ushers" in both Dfts.

[74] Based on his correction sheet, TJ here later interlined "young boys" in place of this word in both Dfts.

[75] Based on his correction sheet, TJ here later added "youths arrived at years of discretion" in place of preceding two words in both Dfts.

[76] Based on his correction sheet, TJ here later reworked the preceding twelve words to read "as a depository of human science is unsurpassed by" in both Dfts.

[77] Preceding seven words added to 1st Dft in place of "is a storehouse of excellent writings."

[78] Remainder of paragraph added to 1st Dft on a slip of paper affixed by TJ with sealing wax at the bottom of a page, to be read continuously from text on page, with text on slip oriented at 180 degrees from recto to verso so that it could be flipped up and read continuously. Slip is no longer affixed in this manner, but is bound with 1st Dft.

[79] Word interlined in 1st Dft.

[80] TJ here later interlined "peculiar" in a different ink in place of this word.

[81] On his correction sheet TJ queried whether to omit this sentence.

[82] Reworked from "Medecine" in 1st Dft.

[83] Preceding three words interlined and added in margin in 1st Dft in place of "Chemical."

[84] Preceding three words interlined in 1st Dft in place of "Chemistry."

[85] Text from "with satisfaction" to this point interlined in 1st Dft in place of "the reality and just extent of the aids of that art."

[86] Preceding four words interlined in 1st Dft, with "or" instead of "and."

[87] Preceding sixteen words interlined in 1st Dft.

[88] In 1st Dft TJ here canceled "as the foundation of Morality."

[89] Based on his correction sheet, TJ later interlined "moral obligations" in

place of preceding four words in both Dfts, with his note on correction sheet querying whether he should "? say 'of those general principles of morality in which all sects agree'" and going on to wonder if it might be "perhaps better" to delete "'principles' and insert 'obligations.'"

[90] In both Dfts TJ here later interlined in a different ink "with a knolege of the languages, Hebrew, Greek & Latin."

[91] Preceding eight words interlined in 1st Dft in place of "and from this point."

[92] TJ here later added "at this point" to both Dfts, with addition in 1st Dft also substituting preceding "proper" for "best."

[93] Based on his correction sheet, in both Dfts TJ here later added "(except as to the Professors who shall be first engaged in each branch)," with phrase interlined in 2d Dft and added in margin of 1st Dft, keyed to this point in text with an "I."

[94] Parenthetical phrase and preceding three words added in margin of 1st Dft, with TJ substituting "assiduity" for an uncanceled "industry."

[95] Preceding nine words interlined in 1st Dft in place of an illegible deletion.

[96] Reworked in 1st Dft from "be advanced beyond us."

[97] In 1st Dft TJ here canceled "and, admonished by the just example we are now setting, of leaving to them the management of their own affairs, they will leave their posterity in the like state of freedom, unfettered by regulations whose objects will long since have become obsolete."

[98] Reworked in 1st Dft from "with those antient nations which we have considered as the best models constituted."

[99] Reworked in 1st Dft from "part of their education."

[100] Word interlined in 1st Dft in place of "daily."

[101] Sentence added in margin of 1st Dft.

[102] Remainder of sentence reworked in 1st Dft from "qualification in the military arts."

[103] Word interlined in 1st Dft.

[104] Preceding two words interlined in 1st Dft.

[105] Remainder of sentence reworked in 1st Dft from "have time on their hands, which otherwise might be less innocently employed."

[106] Preceding two words interlined in 1st Dft in place of "us."

[107] Preceding three words interlined in 1st Dft in place of "should be almost the only," with "proper" substituted for "appropriate."

[108] Word interlined in 1st Dft in place of "teachers. as little as possible should be imposed on them which might render them unpopular with their pupils. for which reason they should be excused from all duties of correction, except for offences committed within the school or to themselves, or in their presence. those too who are the best qualified to teach, are often the least fit to govern."

[109] TJ here later interlined in a different ink "to be regulated by the Visitors from time to time."

[110] Based on his correction sheet, TJ later here added "& thereby of course subjected to the general regimen, moral or sumptuary, which it shall prescribe." On the correction sheet the phrase was reworked from "and thereby subjected to a general regimen <to be prescribed> moral or sumptuary, to be prescribed by the institution."

[111] In 1st Dft TJ here pasted over his original version of the following text, which read "system of buildings. 4. in those cases of infraction of order, which do not belong to the civil magistrate, the Proctor should be the organ of controul by such penances, & other punishments, not corporal, as the visitors from time to time should prescribe; with a right of appeal by the Student, on any particular aggrievement, to the board of Professors; at which board the Senior professor <shall> should preside, that is to say, he who has been longest a Professor of the University. 5. what qualifications shall." Substitute text is on both sides of a small piece of paper affixed by TJ over canceled text with sealing wax, with text on piece of paper oriented at 180 degrees from recto to verso so that it could be flipped up and read continuously. Piece of paper is no longer affixed in this manner, but is bound with 1st Dft. Substitute text continues until noted below. In margin of 1st Dft opposite this original text TJ added "'laudumque adrecta cupido' Virg.," a reference to Virgil, *Aeneid*, 5.138, which

describes racing sailors motivated by both fear and a desire to win. The reference is not keyed to the text by any symbol and may have been written by TJ as a note to himself to expand his original comments when composing his replacement text to include positive motivation as well as punishment.

[112] Based on his correction sheet, TJ here later added "hardening them to disgrace, to corporal punishments, & servile humiliations cannot be the best process for producing erect character." Text is interlined in 2d Dft and added to 1st Dft in the margin of a full manuscript page, keyed with a caret to this point in text on piece of paper containing substitute text that was formerly pasted onto draft as described above.

[113] Word interlined in 1st Dft in place of "model."

[114] In both Dfts TJ later added in a different ink a note keyed to this point in text with an asterisk reading "a police exercised by the Students themselves, under proper direction, has been tried with success in some countries, and the rather as forming them for initiation into the duties and practices of civil life." In 1st Dft, note is on full manuscript page and keyed to text on piece of paper containing substitute text that was formerly pasted onto draft as described above.

[115] Substitute text pasted by TJ onto 1st Dft ends here.

[116] Preceding eight words interlined in 1st Dft.

[117] In 1st Dft TJ here canceled "of superior proficiency."

[118] TJ here later canceled this word and interlined "Proctor."

[119] Preceding twelve words added to 1st Dft in a different ink.

[120] In 1st Dft, text from "not contrary" to this point reworked from "the tuition fees they shall pay, and the rent for the dormitories they occupy."

[121] In place of following ten words, TJ interlined in pencil "to wit on the 1st Monday of April & Octob." Similar addition made to 1st Dft in a different ink.

[122] Preceding sixteen words interlined by TJ in 1st Dft in place of "due notice thereof being given to every individual of their board."

[123] In place of this word, TJ here interlined in pencil (faint) "or failure to [act?] for the space of a year."

[124] TJ here interlined in pencil (faint) "[out] of the [Comm^{rs}]."

[125] In 1st Dft TJ here canceled "or change of habitation to a greater than his former distance from the University."

[126] TJ here later canceled preceding two words and interlined "or the Executive, or such other authority as the legislature shall think best, such."

[127] TJ here later interlined in a different ink "or the Executive or other authority."

[128] TJ here interlined in pencil "rector &."

[129] Preceding twelve words interlined in 1st Dft. In 2d Dft TJ canceled them in pencil.

[130] In 1st Dft TJ here canceled "politic &."

[131] Preceding two words interlined in 1st Dft.

[132] Preceding fourteen words interlined in 1st Dft in place of "with."

[133] Paragraph added by TJ in margin of 1st Dft in place of "That all decisions and proceedings of the sd Visitors should be subject to controul & correction by the President and Directors of the literary fund, either on the complaint of any individual aggrieved or interested, or on the proper motion of the sd President & directors." Following this paragraph 1st Dft reads (brackets in original): "[if the Central College be accepted for the University the following should be added. but it should be provided that the act should not suspend the proceedings of the Visitors of the Central College; but that, for the purpose of expediting the objects of the sd institution, they should be authorised, under the controul of the sd President & directors, to continue the exercise of their functions until the first meeting of the Visitors of the University] *<All which is submitted with dutiful respect to the wisdom of the legislature>*."

[134] In both Dfts TJ left blank space after the two preceding lines for copying in any resources offered by either Staunton or Lexington should they be chosen as the University of Virginia. In 1st Dft space remained blank. In 2d Dft TJ transcribed the offer made by Lexington's supporters

over these two lines in a different ink, presumably about the time that the offer was made at the meeting of the Commissioners of the University of Virginia at Rockfish Gap. His transcription of the offer, omitted here, does not differ substantially from that recorded in the final version of the Rockfish Gap Report, document 5 below.

[135] In 1st Dft TJ here left a blank which he filled in later with the number.

[136] Following number later canceled in both Dfts in a different ink.

[137] Following number later reworked in a different ink from an illegible sum.

[138] Preceding three words later canceled in both Dfts in a different ink.

[139] Following gap filled in later in a different ink with the sum "41,248."

[140] TJ later canceled text from "and believed to be" to this point in both Dfts and added in a different ink "on papers in hand, besides what is on outstanding papers of unknown amount, not yet returned. out of these sums are to be taken however."

[141] TJ here later added in a different ink "and for existing contracts."

[142] Text ends here, with TJ subsequently canceling this word and adding in a different ink "and a deed conveying the sd property accordingly to the President and directors of the literary fund has been duly executed by the sd Proctor and acknoleged for record in the office of the clerk of the county court of Albemarle. Signed and certified by the members present each in his proper hand-writing this 4th day of August 1818." Remainder of text in 1st Dft reads "have accordingly executed a deed for that purpose, duly proved <& recorded> for record in the County court of Albemarle. All which is submitted to the wisdom of the legislature."

IV. Thomas Jefferson's Notes on Curricular Definitions

[after 28 June 1818]

Some of the terms used in this table being subject to a difference of acceptation, it is proper to define the meaning & comprehension intended to be given them here.

Geometry, elementary, is that of straight lines and of the circle.

transcendental, is that of all other curves; it includes of course[1]

Projectiles, a leading[2] branch of the military art.

Military architecture includes Fortification, another branch of that art.

Statics respect matter generally, in a state of[3] rest, and include

Hydrostatics, or the laws of fluids particularly at rest, or in equilibrio.

Dynamics, as a general term, include

Dynamics proper, or the laws of solids in motion; and

Hydrodynamics, or Hydraulics, those of fluids in motion.

Pneumatics teach the theory of air, it's weight, motion, condensation, rarefaction E[t]c.

Acoustics, or Phonics, the theory of sound.

Optics the laws of light and vision.

Physics, or Physiology, in a[4] general sense, mean the doctrine of the Physical objects of our senses.

Chemistry is meant, with it's other usual branches, to comprehend the theory of Agriculture.[5]

Mineralogy, in addition to it's peculiar subjects[6] is here understood to embrace what is real in Geology.[7]

Ideology is the doctrine of Thought.

General grammar explains[8] the construction of Language.

MS (ViU: TJP); written entirely in TJ's hand on both sides of a small scrap that was originally affixed to the bottom of a page in TJ's 2d Dft of preceding document following tabular statement of subjects to be taught at the University of Virginia, with strip no longer affixed in this manner but archivally bound with 2d Dft; with text on scrap oriented at 180 degrees from recto to verso so that it could be flipped up and read continuously; undated, but likely composed after 2d Dft of preceding document was enclosed to James Madison on 28 June 1818. Dft (ViU: TJP); written entirely in TJ's hand on one side of a single sheet of paper and interleaved with TJ's 1st Dft of preceding document following tabular statement of subjects to be taught and archivally bound there; undated, but likely composed after 2d Dft of preceding document was enclosed to Madison on 28 June 1818.

Although TJ intended this as a separate explanatory note, it was inadvertently incorporated into the text of the Rockfish Gap Report as approved by the University of Virginia Commissioners on 4 Aug. 1818 and included in all subsequent versions. See note 18 in next document.

[1] In Dft TJ here canceled "Gunnery and."

[2] Reworked in Dft from "Projectiles <*generally, a*> an important."

[3] Preceding four words interlined in Dft in place of "at."

[4] Dft: "their."

[5] Reworked in Dft from "Chemistry is here meant to extend to the theory of Agriculture, as one of it's branches."

[6] Preceding six words interlined in Dft.

[7] In Dft remainder of sentence reads "but not it's multitudinous theories on the generation of the earth, & formation of the substances composing it in manner and time."

[8] Dft: "teaches."

V. Rockfish Gap Report of the University of Virginia Commissioners

The Commissioners for the University of Virginia having met, as by law required at the tavern in Rockfish gap on the blue ridge, on the 1st day of August of this present year 1818, and having formed a board, proceeded on that day to the discharge of the duties assigned to them by the act of the legislature intituled an "act appropriating part of the revenue of the literary fund and for other purposes" and having continued their proceedings by adjournment from day to day to Tuesday the 4th day of August, have agreed to a report on the several matters with which they were charged, which report they now respectfully address and submit to the legislature of the state.

The 1st duty enjoined on them was to enquire & report a site in some convenient & proper part of the state for an University, to be called the "University of Virginia"

In this enquiry they supposed that the governing considerations should be the healthiness of the site, the fertility of the neighbouring country, and it's centrality to the white population of the whole state: for altho the act authorised & required them to receive any voluntary contributions whether conditional or absolute, which might be offered thro them to the President & Directors of the literary fund, for the benefit of the University, yet they did not consider this as establishing an auction, or as pledging the location to the highest bidder.

Three places were proposed, to wit Lexington in the County of Rockbridge, Staunton in the County of Augusta, and the Central college in the County of Albemarle: each of these was unexceptionable as to healthiness & fertility. It was the degree of centrality to the white population of the state which alone then constituted the important point of comparison between these places: and the board, after full enquiry & impartial & mature consideration, are of opinion that the central point of the white population of the state is nearer to the central college, than to either Lexington or Staunton by great & important differences, and all other circumstances of the place in general being favorable to it as a position for an University, they do report the central college in Albemarle to be a convenient & proper part of the State for the University of Virginia.[1]

2d The board having thus agreed on a proper site for the University to be reported to the legislature, proceeded to the second of the duties assigned to them, that of proposing a plan for its buildings; and they are of opinion that it should consist of distinct houses or pavilions, arranged at proper distances on each side of a lawn of a proper breadth, & of indefinite extent in one direction at least, in each of which should be a lecturing room with from two to four apartments for the accommodation of a professor and his family: that these pavilions should be united by a range of Dormitories, sufficient each for the accommodation of two Students only, this provision being deemed advantageous to morals, to order, & to uninterrupted study; and that a passage of some kind under cover from the weather should give a communication along the whole range. It is supposed that such pavilions on an average of the larger & smaller will cost each[2] about $5,000, each dormitory about $350, and Hotels of a single room for a Refectory, & two rooms for the tenant necessary for dieting the students will cost about $3,500^3$ each. The number of these pavilions will depend on the number of Professors, and that of the Dormitories & Hotels on the number of students to be lodged & dieted. The advantages of this plan[4] are, greater security against fire & infection; tranquillity & comfort to the Professors, and their families thus insulated; retirement to the Students, and the admission of enlargement to any degree to which the institution may extend in future times. It is supposed probable that a building of somewhat more size in the middle of the grounds may be called for in time, in which may be rooms for religious worship under such impartial regulations as the visitors shall prescribe, for public examinations, for a Library, for the schools of music, drawing, and other associated purposes.

3. 4. In proceeding to the third & fourth duties prescribed by the legislature of reporting "the branches of learning, which shall[5] be taught in the University, and the number & description of the professorships they will require" the commissioners were first to consider at what point it was understood that university education should commence? Certainly not with the Alphabet for reasons of expediency & impracticability, as well as from the obvious sense of the Legislature, who, in the same act make other[6] provision for the primary instruction of poor children, expecting doubtless that, in other cases, it would be provided by, the parent, or become perhaps a subject of future, and further attention for[7] the legislature. The objects of this primary education determine its character & limits. —These objects would be,

To give to every citizen the information he needs for the transaction of his own business.

To enable him to calculate for himself, and to express & preserve his ideas, his contracts & accounts in writing.

To improve by reading, his morals and faculties.

To understand his duties to his neighbours, & country, and to discharge with competence the functions confided to him by either

To know his rights; to exercise with order & justice those he retains; to choose with discretion the fiduciaries of those he delegates; and to notice their conduct with diligence with candor & judgment

And, in general, to observe with intelligence & faithfulness all the social relations under which he shall be placed.

To instruct the mass of our citizens in these their rights, interests and duties, as men and citizens, being then the objects of education in the primary schools, whether private or public, in them should be taught reading, writing & numerical arithmetic, the elements of mensuration (useful in so many callings) and the outlines of geography and history, and this brings us to the point at which are to commence the higher branches of education, of which the legislature require the developement: those for example which are to form the statesmen, legislators[8] & judges, on whom public prosperity, & individual happiness are so much to depend:

To expound the principles & structure of government, the laws which regulate the intercourse of nations, those formed municipally for our own government, and a sound spirit of legislation, which banishing all arbitrary & unnecessary restraint on individual action shall leave us free to do whatever does not violate the equal rights of another.

To harmonize & promote the interests of agriculture, manufactures & commerce and by well informed views of political economy to give a free scope to the public industry

To develope the reasoning faculties of our youth, enlarge their minds cultivate their morals, & instil into them the precepts of virtue & order:

To enlighten them with mathematical and physical sciences which advance the arts & administer to the health, the subsistence & comforts of human life:

And generally to form them to habits of reflection, and correct action, rendering them examples of virtue to others & of happiness within themselves.

These are the objects of that higher grade of education, the benefits & blessings of which the legislature now propose to provide for the good & ornament of their country the gratification & happiness of their fellow citizens, of the parent especially & his progeny on which all his affections are concentrated—

In entering on this field, the commissioners are aware that they have to encounter much difference of opinion as to the extent which it is expedient that this institution should occupy. Some good men, and even of respectable information, consider the learned sciences as useless acquirements; some think that they do not better the condition of man; and others that education, like private & individual concerns, should be left to private & individual effort; not reflecting that an establishment, embracing all the sciences which may be useful & even necessary in the various vocations of life, with the buildings & apparatus belonging to each, are far beyond the reach of individual means, & must either derive existence from public patronage or not exist at all. This would leave us then without those callings which depend on education, or send us to other countries, to seek the instruction they require. But the Commissioners are happy in consider-

ing the statute under which they are assembled as proof that the legislature is far from the abandonment of objects so interesting: they are
sensible that the advantages of well directed education, moral, political & economical are truly above all estimate. Education generates
habits of application, of order and the love of virtue; and controuls,
by the force of habit, any innate obliquities in our moral organization.
We should be far too from the discouraging persuasion, that man is
fixed, by the law of his nature, at a given point: that his improvement
is a chimæra, and the hope delusive of rendering ourselves wiser,
happier or better than our forefathers were. As well might it be urged
that the wild & uncultivated tree, hitherto yielding sour & bitter fruit
only, can never be made to yield better: yet we know that the grafting
art implants a new tree on the savage stock, producing what is most
estimable both in kind & degree. Education, in like manner engrafts
a new man on the native stock, & improves what in his nature was
vicious & perverse, into qualities of virtue & social worth; and it cannot be but that each generation succeeding to the knowledge acquired
by all those who preceded it, adding to it their own acquisitions &
discoveries, and handing the mass down for successive & constant
accummulation, must advance the knowledge & well-being of man-
kind: not <u>infinitely</u>, as some have said, but <u>indefinitely</u>, and to a term
which no one can fix or foresee. Indeed we need look back only half
a century, to times which many now living remember well, and see
the wonderful advances in the sciences & arts which have been made
within that period. Some of these have rendered the elements themselves subservient to the purposes of man, have harnessed them to the
yoke of his labours, and effected the great blessings of moderating his
own, of accomplishing what was beyond his feeble force, & of extending the comforts of life to a much enlarged[9] circle, to those who had
before known it's necessaries only. That these are not the vain dreams
of sanguine hope, we have before our eyes real & living examples.
What, but education, has advanced us beyond the condition of our
indigenous neighbours? and what chains them to their present state
of barbarism & wretchedness, but[10] a bigotted veneration for the supposed superlative wisdom of their fathers and the preposterous idea
that they are to look backward for better things and not forward,
longing, as it should seem, to return to the days of eating acorns and
roots rather than indulge in the degeneracies of civilization. And how
much more encouraging to the atchievements of science and improvement, is this, than the desponding view that the condition of man
cannot be ameliorated, that what has been, must ever[11] be, and that to
secure Ourselves where we are, we must tread with awfull reverance

in the footsteps of our fathers. This doctrine is the genuine fruit of the alliance between Church and State, the tenants of which, finding themselves but too well in their present position, oppose all advances which might unmask their usurpations, and monopolies of honors, wealth and power, and fear every change, as endangering the comforts they now hold. Nor must we omit to mention, among the benefits of education, the incalculable advantage of training up able Counsellors to administer the affairs of our Country in all its departments, Legislative, Executive, and Judiciary, and to bear their proper share in the councils of our national Government; nothing, more than education, advancing the prosperity, the power and the happiness of a nation.

Encouraged therefore by the sentiments of the Legislature, manifested in this statute, we present the following tabular statement of the branches of learning which we think should be taught in the University, forming them into groups, each of which are within the powers of a single professor.[12]

I	Languages Antient	Latin Greek Hebrew	**V**		Physics or Natural Philosophy Chemistry Mineralogy
II	Languages Modern	French Spanish Italian German Anglo-Saxon	**VI**		Botany Zoology
			VII		Anatomy Medicine

III	Mathematics Pure	Algebra
		Fluxions
		Geometry elementary[13]
		    Trancendental
		Architecture Military
		    Naval
			VIII		Government
					Political economy
					Law of Nature & Nations
					History (being interwoven with
					  Politics & Law)[14]

			IX		Law Municipal
IV	Physico-Mathematics	Mechanics Statics Dynamics Pneumatics Acoustics Optics Astronomy Geography	**X**		Ideology General grammar Ethics Rhetoric Belle Lettres & the fine Arts

*

* Some of the terms used in this table being subject to a difference of acceptation, it is proper to define the meaning and comprehension intended to be given them here—
Geometry elementary is that of straight lines and of the circle
    Transcendental, is that of all other curves; it includes of course <u>Projectiles</u>, a leading branch of the Military Art
Military Architecture, includes Fortification, another branch of that art
Statics, respect matter generally, in a state of rest, and include
    Hydrostatics, or the Laws of fluids particularly, at rest or in equilibrio[15]

Some Articles in this distribution of Sciences will need observation

A Professor is proposed for antient Languages, the Latin, Greek and Hebrew, particularly, but these Languages being the foundation common to all the Sciences, it is difficult to foresee what may be the extent of this school. at the same time no greater obstruction to industrious study could be proposed than the presence, the intrusions, and the noisy turbulence of a multitude of small boys: and if they are to be placed here for the rudiments of the Languages, they may be so numerous, that its character & Value as an University, will be merged in those of a Grammar school. It is therefore greatly to be wished, that preliminary schools, either on private or public establishment, could be distributed in districts thro the state, as preparatory to the entrance of Students into the University. The tender age at which this part of education commences, generaly about the tenth year, would weigh heavily with parents in sending their sons to a school so distant as the Central establishment would be from most of them. Districts of such extent as that every parent should be within a days journey of his son at school, would be desireable in cases of sickness, and convenient for supplying their Ordinary wants and might be made to lessen sensibly the expence of this part of their education. and where a sparse population would not, within such a compass, furnish subjects sufficient to maintain a school, a competent enlargement of District must, of necessity, there be submitted to. At these District schools or colleges boys should be rendered able to read the easier Authors, Latin and Greek. this would be usefull and sufficient for many not intended for an University education. At these too might be taught English grammar, the higher branches of numerical Arithmatic, the geometry of straight lines and of the circle, the elements of navigation and Geography to a sufficient degree, and thus afford to greater numbers the means of being qualified for the Various Vocations

---

Dynamics, used as a general term include
    Dynamics proper, or the Laws of solids in motion and
    Hydrodynamics, or Hydraulics, those of fluids in motion
Pneumatics teach the theory of air, its weight, motion, condensation, rarefaction &c
Acoustics or Phonics, the theory of sound
Optics the Laws of Light & Vision
Physics or Physiology in a general sense, mean the doctrine of the Physical objects of our senses
Chemistry, is meant, with its other usual[16] branches, to comprehend the theory of Agriculture
Mineralogy, in addition to its peculiar subjects is here understood[17] to embrace what is real in Geology—
Ideology is the doctrine of thought
General Grammar explains the construction of Language[18]

of life, needing more instruction than merely menial or praedial labor; and the same advantages to youths whose education may have been neglected untill too late to lay a foundation in the learned languages. These institutions, intermediate between the Primary schools and University, might then be the passage of entrance for Youths into the University, where their classical learning might be critically[19] compleated, by a study of the authors of highest degree. And it is at this stage only that they should be recieved at the University—Giving then a portion of their time to a finished knowledge of the latin and Greek, the rest might be appropriated to the modern languages, or to the commencement of the course of science, for which they should be destined. This would generally be about the 15th year of their age when they might go with more safety and contentment to that distance from their parents. Untill this preparatory provision shall be made, either the University will be overwhelmed with the Grammar school or a seperate establishment under one or more ushers for its Lower classes will be adviseable, at a mile or two distance from the general one: where too may be exercised the stricter government necessary for young boys, but unsuitable for youths arrived at years of discretion

The considerations which have governed the specification of languages to be taught by the professor of modern Languages were that the French is the Language of general intercourse among nations, and as a depository of human Science is unsurpassed by any other language living or dead: that the Spanish is highly interesting to us, as the Language spoken by so great a portion of the inhabitants of our Continents, with whom we shall probably have great intercourse ere long; and is that also in which is written the greater part of the early history of America.

The Italian abounds with works of very superior order, Valuable for their matter, and still more distinguished as models of the finest taste in style and composition: and the German now stands in a line with that of the most learned nations in richness of erudition and advance in the sciences. It is too of common descent with the language of our Own Country, a branch of the same original Gothic stock, and furnishes Valuable illustrations for us. but in this point of View the Anglo-Saxon is of peculiar Value. We have placed it among the modern languages because it is in fact that which we speak, in the earliest form in which we have knowledge of it. it has been undergoing, with time, those gradual changes which all languages, antient and modern, have experienced: and, even now, needs only to be printed in the modern character and orthography, to be intelligible, in a considerable degree to an English reader. it has this Value too above the Greek and Latin, that while it gives the radix of the mass of our Language, they explain its innovations only. obvious proofs of this have been presented to the modern reader in the disquisitions of Horne Tooke, and Fortescue Aland has well explained the great instruction which may be derived from it towards a full understanding of our Antient common Law on which as a stock our whole System of Law is engrafted. it will form the first link in the Chains of an historical review of our language through all its successive changes to the present day, will constitute the foundation of that critical instruction in it, which ought to be found in a Seminary of general learning and thus reward amply the few weeks of attention which would Alone be requisite for its attainment. a language already fraught with all the eminent science[20] of our parent Country the future Vehicle of whatever we may Ourselves atchieve[21] and destined to Occupy so much space on the Globe, claims distinguished attention in American Education—[22]

Medicine, where fully taught, is usually subdivided into several professorships. but this cannot well be without the accessory of an[23] hospital, where the student can have the benefit of attending clinical lectures & of assisting at operations of surgery. With this accessory, the seat of our university is not yet prepared, either by its population, or by the numbers of poor, who would leave their own houses, and accept of the charities of an hospital. For the present therefore we propose but a single professor for both medicine & anatomy. By him the elements of medical science may be taught, with a history & explanations of all it's successive[24] theories from Hippocrates to the present day: and anatomy may be fully treated. Vegetable pharmacy will make a part of the botanical course, & mineral & chemical pharmacy, of those of mineralogy & chemistry. This degree of medical information is such as the mass of scientific students would wish to possess, as enabling them, in their course thro life, to estimate with satisfaction the extent & limits of the aid to human life & health, which they may understandingly expect from that art: and it constitutes such a foundation for those intended for the profession, that the finishing course of practice at the bedsides of the sick, and at the operations of surgery in a hospital, can neither be long nor expensive. To seek this finishing elsewhere, must therefore be submitted to for a while.

In conformity with the principles of our constitution, which places all sects of religion on an equal footing, with the jealousies of the different sects in guarding that equality from encroachment & surprise, and with the sentiments of the legislature in favor of freedom of religion manifested on former occasions, we have proposed no professor of Divinity: and the rather, as the proofs of the being of a god, the creator, preserver, & supreme ruler of the universe, the author of all the relations of morality, & of the laws & obligations these infer, will be within the province of the professor of ethics; to which adding the developements of these moral obligations, of those in which all sects agree with a knolege of the languages, Hebrew, Greek and Latin,[25] a basis will be formed common to all sects. proceeding thus far without offence to the constitution, we have thought it proper at this point, to leave every sect to provide as they think fittest, the means of further instruction in their own peculiar tenets.

We are further of opinion that, after declaring by law that certain sciences shall be taught in the university, fixing the number of professors they require, which we think should at present, be ten, limiting (except as to the professors who shall be first engaged in each branch) a maximum for their salaries, (which should be a certain but moderate subsistence, to be made up by liberal tuition fees, as an excitement to assiduity,) it will be best to leave to the discretion of the visitors, the grouping of these sciences together, according to the accidental qualifications of the professors; and the introduction also of other branches of science, when enabled by private donations, or by public provision, and called for by the encrease of population, or other change of circumstances; to establish beginnings, in short, to be developed by time, as those who come after us[26] shall find expedient. They will be more advanced than we are, in science and in useful arts, and will know best what will suit the circumstances of their day.

We have proposed no formal provision for the gymnastics of the school, altho a proper object of attention for every institution of youth. These exercises with antient nations, constituted the principal part of the education of their youth. Their arms and mode of warfare rendered them severe in the extreme. Ours on the same correct principle, should be adapted to our arms & warfare; and the manual exercise, military maneuvres, and Tactics generally, Should be the frequent exercises of the students, in their hours of recreation. It is at that age of aptness, docility & emulation of the practices of manhood, that such things are soonest learnt, and longest remembered. The use of tools too in the manual arts is worthy of encouragement, by facilitating, to such as choose it, an admission into the neighbouring workshops. To these should be added the arts, which embellish life, dancing music & drawing; the last more especially; as an important part of military education. These innocent arts furnish amusement & happiness to those who, having time on their hands, might less inoffensively employ it; needing, at the same time, no regular incorporation with the institution, they may be left to accessory teachers, who will be paid by the individuals employing them; the university only providing proper apartments for their exercise.

The 5th duty prescribed to the commissioners is to propose such general provisions as may be properly enacted by the legislature, for the better organising & governing the university.

In the education of youth, provision is to be made for 1. tuition. 2. diet. 3. lodging. 4. government. and 5. honorary excitements. The 1st of these constitutes the proper functions of the professors. 2. the dieting of the students should be left to private boarding houses, of their own choice, and at their own expense; to be regulated by the visitors from time to time, the house only being provided by the university within its own precincts, and thereby of course subjected to the general regimen, moral or sumptuary, which they shall prescribe. 3. They should be lodged in dormitories, making a part of the general system of buildings. 4. The best mode of government for youth in large collections, is certainly a desideratum not yet attained with us. It may well be questioned whether <u>fear</u>, after a certain age, is the motive to which we should have ordinary recourse. The human character is susceptible of other incitements to correct conduct, more worthy of employ, and of better effect. Pride of character, laudable ambition, & moral dispositions are innate correctives of the indiscretions of that lively age; and when strengthened by habitual appeal & exercise, have a happier effect on future character, than the degrading motive of <u>fear</u>; hardening them to disgrace, to corporal punishments, and servile humiliations, cannot be the best process for producing erect character. The affectionate deportment between father & son offers in truth the best example for that of tutor & pupil; and the experience & practice of* other countries in this respect, may be worthy of enquiry & consideration with us. It will be then for the wisdom & discretion of the visitors to devise & perfect a proper system of government, which, if it be founded in reason & comity, will be more likely to nourish, in the minds of our youth, the combined spirit of order & self respect, so congenial with our political institutions, and so important to be woven into the American character. 5. What qualifications shall be required to entitle to entrance into the university, the arrangement of the days & hours of lecturing for the different schools, so as to facilitate to the students the circle of attendance on them; the establishment of periodical and public examinations, the premiums to be given

---

* a police exercised by the students themselves, under proper direction, has been tried with success in some countries, and the rather as forming them for initiation into the duties and practices of civil life.[27]

for distinguished merit; whether honorary degrees shall be conferred; and by what appellations; whether the title to these shall depend on the time the candidate has been at the university, or, where nature has given a greater share of understanding, attention and application; whether he shall not be allowed the advantages resulting from these endowments, with other minor items of government, we are of opinion, should be entrusted to the visitors; and the Statute under which we act, having provided for the appointment of these, we think they should moreover be charged with the erection, preservation & repair of the buildings, the care of the grounds, & appurtenances and of the interests of the university generally: that they should have power to appoint a Burser, employ a Proctor & all other necessary agents; to appoint & remove professors, two thirds of the whole number of visitors voting for the removal: to prescribe their duties & the course of education, in conformity with the law: to establish rules for the government & discipline of the students not contrary to the laws of the land: to regulate the tuition fees, & the rent of the dormitories they occupy: to prescribe & control the duties & proceedings of all officers, servants & others with respect to the buildings, lands, appurtenances & other property & interests of the university: to draw from the literary fund such monies as are by law charged on it for this institution: and in general to direct & do all matters & things which, not being inconsistent with the laws of the land, to them shall seem most expedient for promoting the purposes of the said institution; which several functions they should be free to exercise in the form of bye laws, rules, resolutions, orders, instructions or otherwise as they should deem[28] proper.

That they should have two stated meetings in the year, and occasional meetings at such times as they should appoint, or on a special call with such notice as themselves shall prescribe by a general rule; which meetings should be at the university; a majority of them constituting a quorum for business; and that on the death or resignation of a member, or on his removal by the President & Directors of the Literary fund,[29] or the executive or such other authority as the legislature shall think best, such President & Directors or the Executive, or other authority should[30] appoint a successor.

That the said visitors should appoint one of their own body to be rector & with him, be a body corporate, under the style & title of the Rector & visitors of the University of Virginia, with the right as such, to use a common seal: that they should have capacity to plead & be impleaded, in all courts of justice, and in all cases interesting to the University, which may be the subjects of legal cognizance & jurisdiction; which pleas should not abate by the determination of their office, but should stand revived in the name of their successors; and they should be capable in law, and in trust for the University, of receiving subscriptions & donations, real & personal, as well from bodies corporate, or persons associated, as from private individuals.

And that the said Rector & Visitors should at all times conform to such laws, as the legislature may from time to time think proper to enact for their government; and the said University should in all things, & at all times be subject to the controul of the legislature—[31] And lastly the Commissioners report to the Legislature the following conditional offers to the President and Directors of the Literary fund for the benefit of the University.[32]

On the condition that Lexington, or its vicinity shall be selected as the site of the University, and that the same be permanently established there within two years from the date, John Robinson of Rockbridge County, has executed a deed to the President & Directors of the Literary fund, to take effect at his death for the following tracts of Land, to wit,

400 acres on the north fork of James River known by the name of Hart's bottom purchased of the late General Bowyer

171 acres adjoining the same purchased of James Griggsby

203 acres joining the last mentioned tract, purchased of William Paxton

112 acres lying on the north river above the lands of Arthur Glasgow conveyed to him by William Paxton's heirs.

500 acres joining the lands of Arthur Glasgow, Benjamin Cambden, and David Edmondson.

545 acres lying in Pryor's gap conveyed to him by the heirs of William Paxton deceased.

260 acres lying in Childers gap purchased of[33] William Mitchel[l][34]

300 acres lying also in Childer's gap purchased of Nicholas Jones

500 Acres lying on Buffalo, joining the lands of James Johnstone[35]

340 acres on the Cowpasture river conveyed to him by General James Breckenridge, reserving the right of selling the two last mentioned tracts, and converting them into other lands contiguous to Hart's bottom, for the benefit of the University.

Also the whole of his Slaves amounting to 57 in number.

One Lot of twenty two acres joining the town of Lexington to pass immediately, on the establishment of the University, together with all the personal estate of every kind;[36] subject only to the payment of his debts, and fulfilment of his contracts.[37]

It has not escaped the attention of the Commissioners that the deed referred to is insufficient to pass the estate[38] in the lands intended to be conveyed, & may be otherwise defective;[39] but if necessary this defect[40] may be remedied before the meeting of the Legislature which the Commissioners are advised will be done.

The board of Trustees of Washington College have also proposed to transfer[41] the whole of their funds, viz,

100 shares in the funds of the James River company.

31 acres of land on which all their buildings stand.

Their philosophical apparatus; their expected[42] interest in the funds of the Cincinnati society: the Libraries of the Graham and Washington societies; and 3000 dollars in cash, on condition that a reasonable provision be made for the present Professors.

A subscription has also been offered by the people of Lexington and its vicinity amounting to 17,878 dollars; all which will appear from the deed and other documents, reference thereto being had.

In this case also, it has not escaped the attention of the Commissioners, that questions may arise as to the power of the Trustees to make the above transfers.[43]

On the condition that the central College shall be made the site of the University, its whole property real & personal in possession, or in action is offered. This consists of a parcel of land of 47 acres whereon the buildings of the College are begun, one pavilion and its appendix of dormitories, being already far advanced, and with one other pavilion, & equal annexation of dormitories, being expected to be compleated during the present season. Of another parcel of 153 acres near the former, and including a considerable eminence very favorable for the erection of a future observatory.[44] Of the proceeds of the sales of two Glebes amounting to 3,280 dollars 86 cents; and of a subscription of 41.248 dollars[45] on papers in hand, besides what is on outstanding papers of unknown amount, not yet returned. Out of these sums are to be taken however, the cost of the lands, of the buildings, and other works done, and for existing contracts.

For the conditional transfer of these to the President & Directors of the literary fund, a regular power signed by the Subscribers and founders of the College generally; has been given to its Visitors and Proctor, and a deed conveying the said property accordingly, to the President and Directors of the literary fund has been duly executed by the said Proctor, and acknowledged for record in the Office of the Clerk of the County court[46] of Albemarle

Signed and certified by the members present, each in his proper handwriting this 4th day of August 1818.[47]

TH: JEFFERSON   PHIL: C: PENDLETON

CREED TAYLOR.   SPENCER ROANE

PETER RANDOLPH

W^M BROCKENBROUGH

ARCH^D RUTHERFORD

ARCH^D STUART

JAMES BRECKINRIDGE

HENRY E WATKINS

JAMES MADISON

ARMISTEAD T MASON

H^H HOLMES

JOHN MC. TAYLOR

J G JACKSON

THO^S WILSON

PHIL, SLAUGHTER

W^M H. CABELL

NATH^L H CLAIBORNE

W^M A. G DADE

W^M JONES

MS (Vi: RG 79, House of Delegates, Speaker, Executive Communications); in the hand of Thomas W. Maury and two unidentified persons, with emendations by TJ as noted below; signed by the commissioners listed; docketed by William Munford, clerk of the House of Delegates: "Report of the Commissioners for the University of Virginia—Decr 8th 1818— ☞500 Copies to be Printed immediately"; at foot of first page in pencil in TJ's hand: "Senate." Dft (ViU: TJP); entirely in TJ's hand; on recto of a single sheet, numbered page 1, with verso numbered 2 but otherwise blank; archivally bound between TJ's two drafts of the report (document 3 above); incomplete, consisting of first three paragraphs and closely following the final report; possibly prepared by TJ with the select committee of the University of Virginia Commissioners on 3 Aug. 1818 following the Commissioners' vote recommending Central College as site of the University of Virginia. Dft (photostat in ViU: TJP); in an unidentified hand, with unrelated calculations on verso and emendations by TJ as noted below; incomplete, consisting of the offer to the President and Directors of the Literary Fund by Lexington's supporters. MS (PPAmP); consisting of copy of *University of Virginia Commissioners' Report* presented by TJ to John Vaughan; with TJ's signed inscription (trimmed) on title page: "John Vaughan esq. [. . .]"; with two handwritten corrections to printed text by TJ as noted below. Printed in *University of Virginia Commissioners' Report*, 9–26; *JHD* (1818–19 sess.), 10–6 (8 Dec. 1818); *Richmond Enquirer*, 10 Dec. 1818; and elsewhere. Enclosed in TJ to Linn Banks and Edward Watts, 20 Nov. 1818, and TJ to Joseph C. Cabell, 20 Nov. 1818.

The 21 Feb. 1818 ACT OF THE LEGISLATURE mandating the meeting of the University of Virginia Commissioners at Rockfish Gap and outlining their duties included a PROVISION FOR THE PRIMARY INSTRUCTION OF POOR CHILDREN that allocated a portion of the income of the Literary Fund to the education of poor children in reading, writing, and arithmetic (*Acts of Assembly* [1817–18 sess.], 12). The British radical and philologist John HORNE TOOKE published a work on the English language, Ἔπεα Πτερόεντα. *or, the Diversions of Purley*, 2 vols. (London, 1786–1805; Sowerby, no. 4870; one of TJ's copies in ViCMRL), in which he emphasizes the importance of Anglo-Saxon etymology (*ODNB*; Christina Bewley and David Bewley, *Gentleman Radical: A Life of John Horne Tooke, 1736–1812* [1998], 233–40). Sir John FORTESCUE ALAND argues in the preface to his *Reports of Select Cases In all the Courts of Westminster-Hall* (London, 1748; Sowerby, no. 2079) that, inasmuch as English law was derived in part from Saxon law, legal students in particular should study the Anglo-Saxon language (*PTJ*, 30:569–70).

On 30 July 1818 JOHN ROBINSON OF ROCKBRIDGE COUNTY executed a deed offering at his death the property described above should Lexington be chosen as the site of the University of Virginia. In addition to specifying the parcels of land to be included in his bequest, the deed named all fifty-seven slaves (Tr in Rockbridge Co. Deed Book, L:244–9). Despite the recommendation by the University of Virginia Commissioners that Central College be made the site of the new university, Robinson continued to offer his property to the President and Directors of the Literary Fund in an attempt to influence the deliberations of the General Assembly. He drafted a deed in trust dated 9 Jan. 1819 offering the same lands and slaves for the benefit of the proposed university. In this subsequent deed Robinson agreed to exchange the property with Rockbridge County delegate John Bowyer for $1. Under the terms of the deed, Robinson maintained possession until the legislature selected Lexington, at which point Bowyer would convey these assets to the new school. The deed was, however, to become null and void if the offer was not accepted within two years (MS in ViU; in Chapman Johnson's hand, signed by Robinson and Bowyer, and witnessed by Johnson, Andrew Alexander, and Briscoe G. Baldwin).

¹Dft in TJ's hand ends here.
²Word interlined by TJ.
³Manuscript: "$3.500." *Commissioners' Report* and *JHD*: "3,500 dollars." *Richmond Enquirer*: "$3,500."
⁴*Commissioners' Report*: "place." Corrected by TJ to "plan" in PPAmP copy.
⁵*Commissioners' Report, JHD*, and *Richmond Enquirer*: "should."
⁶Word interlined.
⁷Word interlined by TJ in place of "of."
⁸Manuscript: "legislalators."
⁹Manuscript: "enlarg." *Commissioners' Report, JHD*, and *Richmond Enquirer*: "enlarged."
¹⁰Section in first unidentified hand begins here.
¹¹Preceding two words interlined by TJ in place of an illegible deletion.
¹²Page ends short here.
¹³Reworked from "elemental," here and below.
¹⁴Omitted closing parenthesis editorially supplied.
¹⁵Word initially incomplete due to copying error at margin, with final four letters interlined, possibly by TJ.
¹⁶Word interlined by TJ in place of "usefull."
¹⁷Word initially incomplete due to copying error at margin, with final five letters of word interlined by TJ.
¹⁸In PPAmP copy of *Commissioners' Report*, TJ placed a note in the margin around this list of definitions reading "A

note, which, by an error of the press was thrown into the text."
¹⁹Word interlined by TJ in place of "entirely."
²⁰Manuscript: "scieence."
²¹Reworked from "achieve," possibly by TJ.
²²Section in first unidentified hand ends here.
²³Reworked from "a" by TJ.
²⁴Maury here canceled "operations."
²⁵Preceding ten words interlined by TJ.
²⁶Reworked from "afterwards" by TJ.
²⁷Note at foot of page by TJ, keyed by him to text with asterisks.
²⁸Here "most" is canceled.
²⁹Word interlined by TJ.
³⁰Word interlined by TJ in place of "shall."
³¹Section in second unidentified hand begins here.
³²Dft not in TJ's hand begins here.
³³Word interlined by TJ in place of "from."
³⁴Word incomplete due to copying error at margin.
³⁵Manuscript: "Johnstons." Dft: "Johnstone." *Commissioners' Report, JHD*, and *Richmond Enquirer*: "Johnston."
³⁶Preceding three words interlined in Dft in place of "Of which he may die possessed."
³⁷Preceding five words interlined in Dft.
³⁸Preceding six words interlined in Dft in place of "creates no present estate."
³⁹Preceding four words interlined in Dft.
⁴⁰Word interlined in Dft in place of "oversight."
⁴¹Word interlined by TJ in Dft in place of "surrender."
⁴²Word interlined by TJ in Dft in place of his initial interlineation after "Interest" of "in expectancy."
⁴³Dft ends here, with phrase following "Trustees" reworked from "<to Surrender at least a part> <certain parts of> respecting these transfers."
⁴⁴Period, omitted in manuscript, supplied from *Commissioners' Report*.
⁴⁵Preceding three words not in *Richmond Enquirer*.
⁴⁶Word interlined by TJ.
⁴⁷Sentence in TJ's hand.

VI. Thomas Jefferson's Statement of Thanks to the University of Virginia Commissioners

[ca. 4 Aug. 1818]

I thank you, gentlemen, for the kind indulgence with which you have been pleased to view the feeble services I have been able to render to the board. but I am conscious I owe you many Apologies for the imperfect manner in which they have been rendered, and many Acknolegements for the spirit of order and harmony which has so much distinguished the proceedings of this board.

while I see the public concerns committed to such able Counsellors, and such able Counsellors willing to undertake their direction, my confidence is confirmed that our country is in the high road to prosperity and happiness.

I wish you a happy return, gentlemen, to your homes, your families and friends.

MS (ViU: TJP); entirely in TJ's hand; undated, but probably delivered in response to the vote of thanks to TJ that concluded the formal deliberations of the University of Virginia Commissioners on 4 Aug. 1818.

TJ also praised the ORDER AND HAR-MONY displayed by the commissioners in his letter to Martha Jefferson Randolph of 4 Aug. 1818. In a summary of the meeting published on 11 Aug. 1818, the *Rich-mond Enquirer* reported that at the close of the proceedings, TJ, as commission president, "rose, and in a very feeling and impressive manner congratulated the members of the board on the harmony which had prevailed in their deliberations on this great and momentous concern, expressed his sincere and ardent hope that the result of their labours would conduce to the permanent interests, and happiness of our beloved country, and bade them an affectionate farewell."

From James Monroe

DEAR SIR   Augt 4. 1818

I came home yesterday, & should have called at Monticello this morning, but for an injury I receivd in one of my legs on the journey, which has inflamed[1] it. A few days nursing will I hope restore it. I shall call as soon as I can ride out. I hope that you & your family are well, & that the business in which you are engagd has taken a direction satisfactory to you

very respectfully & sincerely yours   JAMES MONROE

RC (MHi); addressed: "Mr Jefferson Monticello"; endorsed by TJ as received 1 Sept. 1818 and so recorded in SJL.

HOME: Highland, Monroe's Albemarle County estate.

[1] Manuscript: "in flamed."

To Martha Jefferson Randolph

MY DEAR DAUGHTER   Rockfish gap Aug. 4. 18.

All our members, except 3 who came not at all[1] arrived on Saturday morning so that we got to work by 10. aclock, and finished yesterday evening. we are detained till this morning for fair copies of our report. Staunton had 2. votes, Lexington 3. the Central college 16. I have never seen business done with so much order, & harmony, nor an abler nor pleasanter society. we have been well served too. excellent rooms, everyone his bed, a table altho' not elegant, yet plentiful and satisfactory. I proceed today with judge Stuart to Staunton.[2] every body tells me the time I allot to the Springs is too short. that 2. or 3. weeks bathing will be essential. I shall know better when I get there, but I foresee the possibility and even probability that my stay there must be longer than I expected. I am most afraid of losing mr Correa's visit. I shall write to him from the springs. Cooper has failed in his election, Dr Patterson having obtained the Chemical chair.[3] I imagine he has written to me, but I must inform him from the springs of the cause of delay in answering him. kiss all the family for me, and be assured of my warmest love.   TH: JEFFERSON

PS. send Gill immediately for my bed E^tc.

RC (NNPM); adjacent to signature: "Mrs Randolph"; endorsed by Randolph. SC (MHi); lacking postscript; endorsed by TJ. Not recorded in SJL.

THE SPRINGS: Warm Springs.

[1] Word, interlined in RC, is not in SC.
[2] Omitted period at right margin editorially supplied.
[3] Omitted period at right margin editorially supplied.

From James Wilkinson

DEAR SIR   August 4th 1818

Residing as I do on the right Bank of the Mississippi seven Leagues below N. Orleans, it is no matter of surprize that your Letter, of the 25th of June, was not received before the 1st Inst.

I perceive with great pleasure, that the chaste harmony which has distinguished[1] your Pen above all others of our Country continues unimpaired; and with equal satisfaction do I receive the testimony of approbation & esteem which it conveys, to an humble but faithful Citizen, who has been illy requited for his toils sufferings & sacrafices in the public Service.

I acknowledge the receipt of your Letter merely to assure you, that I shall fulfil your desire respecting the explorations of Capt Pike under my Orders, so soon as indispensable daily labour may allow me time, to scrutinize my voluminous correspondence; in the mean time memory authorizes me to declare, that, under a verbal permission from you, before my departure from the seat of Government for St Louis in the Spring of 1805, <u>generally</u> to explore the borders of the Territory of Louisiana I did project the expeditions of Capt Z. M. Pike to th[e] Head of the Mississippi; & after his return from that excursion, to[2] restore to their nation a number of Osage Indians, who had been ransomed under my Authority, from the hostile Tribes by whom they had been captured; to make peace between certain Belligerous nations, & if practicable to effect an interview with & conciliate the powerful Bands of J.e.tans or Commanchees to the United States; He was also instructed by me, to ascertain the extent, direction & navigableness of the Arkansaw & Red Rivers, which discharge their Waters in[to?] the Mississippi.

I recollect to have seen Mr Wilson the Ornithologist, at Washington in the autumn 1808, & at Charleston S.C. the Winter following; I admired his Enterprize, perseverance & capacity, and had several conversations with Him concerning the Work he had undertaken, which I was desirous to promote with my humble means; He made various enquiries respecting the feathered Creation of this region, & instructed me how to preserve in dead Birds their living appearance; But I do not remember that Capt Pike or his expeditions were alluded to, and the details of that unfortunate meritorious young Soldiers Western Tour, published by Himself, will best explain its utter inaptitude to the deliberate investigations of the naturalists.—

With my best wishes for your continued Health & tranquillity, and in the Hope that you may still be made the instrument, to arrest the sinister course of our politicks, & recall the Republic to its original purity, I beg you to be assured of my high respect & attachment

JA: WILKINSON

RC (DLC); edge chipped; at foot of text: "Thomas Jefferson"; endorsed by TJ as received 5 Oct. 1818, but recorded in SJL as received 5 Nov. 1818.

Wilkinson's 1806 ORDERS to Zebulon M. Pike for his western expedition are printed in Pike, *An Account of Expeditions to the Sources of the Mississippi, and through the Western Parts of Louisiana, to the sources of the Arkansaw, Kans, La Platte, and Pierre Jaun, Rivers* (Philadelphia, 1810; Sowerby, no. 4169; Poor, *Jefferson's Library*, 7 [no. 371]), 107–10. J.E.TANS: "Jetans."

[1] Manuscript: "distinguised."
[2] Wilkinson here canceled "ascertain."

From Chapman Johnson

Wednesday morning [5 Aug. 1818?]

C. Johnson presents his respects to M[r] Jefferson, and asks the favor of him to drink tea with him this evening.

RC (DLC: TJ Papers, 213:38059); with Dft of TJ to Thomas Cooper, 7 Aug. 1818, on verso; partially dated; addressed: "M[r] Jefferson. Present."

This note was probably written during TJ's brief stay at Staunton on his way to Warm Springs (*MB*, 2:1346).

Jefferson's Trip to Warm Springs

I. THOMAS JEFFERSON'S NOTES ON INNS BETWEEN STAUNTON AND WARM SPRINGS, [AFTER 6 AUG. 1818]

II. THOMAS JEFFERSON'S NOTES ON DISTANCES BETWEEN WARM SPRINGS AND CHARLOTTESVILLE, [AFTER 6 AUG. 1818]

EDITORIAL NOTE

Following the meeting of the commissioners for the University of Virginia at Rockfish Gap, Jefferson traveled to Staunton and spent two nights at the home of his fellow commissioner Archibald Stuart. On 6 Aug. 1818 he began the nearly sixty-mile journey to Warm Springs on horseback, arriving there a day later and departing on 27 Aug. 1818. Although this was his first and only visit to Warm Springs, in the 1780s Jefferson had described several of the Virginia springs in his *Notes on the State of Virginia*, writing that the waters at Warm Springs "relieve rheumatisms." As early as 1811 Jefferson announced his intention to sample the curative waters to remedy his own rheumatic complaint, commenting to William A. Burwell that "if I am not better after a little rest at home, I shall set out for the warm springs." Later that year he remarked to John Wayles Eppes that "a sensible degree of amendment latterly has diverted my determination to go to the warm springs, which you ought to do. they are the only infallible remedy in the world." Jefferson paid hotel keeper John Fry $20 a week during his three-week stay, covering board and lodging for himself and his slave Burwell Colbert and feed for two horses. Jefferson's sojourn included excursions to Hot Springs, Flag Rock, and the waterfall at Falling Spring Branch. Instead of lessening them, his trip as a whole added to his health concerns. Jefferson contracted what was likely a staphylococcus infection, which made his return journey to Monticello painful and negatively affected his quality of life for some months to come. He probably composed the documents below during his travels, recording his general impressions of the taverns he patronized and the distances between stops (*MB*, 2:1346–7; *Notes*, ed. Peden, 34–6; TJ to Burwell, 19 Aug. 1811; TJ to Eppes, 6 Sept. 1811; TJ to Martha Jefferson Randolph, 7, 14, 21 Aug. 1818; Gene Crotty, *Jefferson's Western Travels Over Virginia's Blue Ridge Mountains* [2002], esp. 166, which includes a facsimile of a portion of TJ's account in the Warm Springs hotel ledger).

I. Thomas Jefferson's Notes on Inns Between Staunton and Warm Springs

[after 6 Aug. 1818]

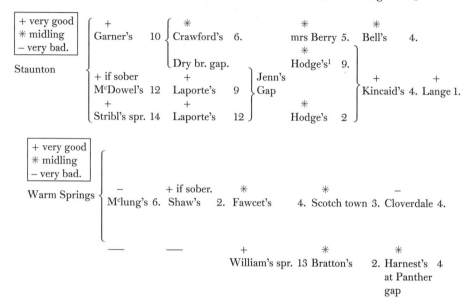

| + very good |
| * midling |
| − very bad. |

Staunton

+		*				*		*	
Garner's	10	Crawford's	6.			mrs Berry 5.		Bell's	4.
		Dry br. gap.				Hodge's[1]	9.		
+ if sober		+		Jenn's				+	+
McDowel's	12	Laporte's	9	Gap				Kincaid's 4.	Lange 1.
+		+				*			
Stribl's spr.	14	Laporte's	12			Hodge's	2		

| + very good |
| * midling |
| − very bad. |

Warm Springs

| − | + if sober. | * | | * | | − | |
| Mᶜlung's 6. | Shaw's | 2. | Fawcet's | 4. | Scotch town 3. | Cloverdale 4. |

—	—	+		*		*	
		William's spr. 13	Bratton's	2.	Harnest's	4
					at Panther
					gap

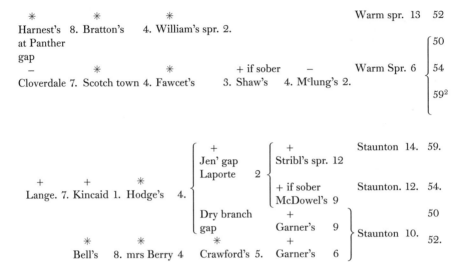

MS (ViU: TJP); written entirely in TJ's hand on both sides of a slip of paper; undated, but probably composed about the time of TJ's August 1818 visit to Warm Springs.

[1] TJ here erased "Jenning's 9."
[2] Recto ends here.

II. Thomas Jefferson's Notes on Distances Between Warm Springs and Charlottesville

[after 6 Aug. 1818]

Warm springs.

– M꜀lung's	6.
+ Shaw's	2
* Fawcets	4.
* Scotch town	3.
– Cloverdale	4
+ Lange	7
+ Kincaid	1.
* Hodge's	4.
+ Laportes[1]	2.
+? M꜀Dowel's	9
Staunton	12
	54

Wainsb.	13.
top of M^n	4
Morrison's	4
Yancy's	4
Harding's	7
Woods's	5
Charlv.	4

MS (ViFreJM); written entirely in TJ's hand on one side of a small scrap; undated, but probably composed about the time of TJ's August 1818 visit to Warm Springs; symbols defined in preceding document.

HARDING'S: Benjamin Hardin's Albemarle County tavern.

[1] Manuscript: "Lapotes."

To Thomas Cooper

DEAR SIR   Warm springs of Virginia Aug. 7. 18.

A meeting of Comm^{rs} to agree on & recommend to the legislature a site for their University was held at Rockfish gap on the 1st inst. where we agreed, 16. to 5. that it should be at our Central College; and from thence I came here to remove some Rheumatic affections[1] which have long incommoded me occasionally. my stay here will be of about a fortnight or 3 weeks, so that I may not get back to Monticello till the 1ˢᵗ week of Sep. I have heard that Dʳ Patterson has succeeded to the Chemical chair of the Coll. of Philada in which case you will be free to come on to us, and, if so, I expect you will have written to me & that your letter will remain unanswered at Monticello till I return. all this I write merely to explain in that event any delay which may take place in your recieving an answer from me.

Our 1ˢᵗ pavilion has been much retarded by the disappointments of workmen. I think it may[2] be ready to recieve you within 3. months from this time, and that within that time one wing of 9. dormitories may be ready, and in the course of the season another pavilion & 2. more wings of dormitories. the moment we announce the opening of our Latin & Greek school, we shall be overwhelmed with pupils, more I fear than[3] Charlottesville is prepared[4] to board.

The report of the Commʳˢ proposes to the legislature the site, the plan of buildings, the sciences necessary to be taught, the Nº of professors (10) necessary Eᵗc.

hoping, when I get home, to recieve a letter from you announcing your readiness to come on I salute you with constant frdshp & esteem.

Tʜ:J.

P.S. if mr Correa should be at Philadelphia pray communicate to him my movements as I shall hope to see him at Montº early in Sep.

Dft (DLC); on verso of Chapman Johnson to TJ, [5 Aug. 1818?]; at foot of text: "Dʳ Cooper"; endorsed by TJ. Enclosed in TJ to Martha Jefferson Randolph, 7 Aug. 1818.

[1] Word interlined in place of "complaints."
[2] Word interlined in place of "would."
[3] Manuscript: "then."
[4] Preceding two words interlined in place of "may be prevailed on."

To Martha Jefferson Randolph

My dearest daughter   Warm springs Aug. 7. 18.

I have heard that Dʳ Cooper has come on to Richmond, which however I doubt. if so he may possibly have come to Monticello. under this uncertainty where a letter may find him, I inclose one to you for him, with a request to forward it to him by mail wherever he is. I have left it open as it may enable you to judge what to do with it in every case.

I left Judge Stuart's yesterday after breakfast, and breakfasted here this morning between 9. & 10. I have performed the journey entirely on horseback and without fatigue. an attack of rheumatism in the knee yesterday, without retarding my journey, affects my walking. I have tried once to-day the delicious bath & shall do it twice a day hereafter. the company here is about 45. the table very well kept by mr Fry, and every thing else well. venison is plenty, and vegetables not wanting. I found the houses on the road from Staunton more detestable than any thing I have ever met with. but little gay company here at this time, and I rather expect to pass a dull time. express all my affections to our dear family and most of all be assured of them yourself.   TH: JEFFERSON

RC (NNPM); endorsed by Randolph. Recorded in SJL with TJ's summary: "lre for Cooper—my journey E^{t}c." Enclosure: TJ to Thomas Cooper, 7 Aug. 1818.

From Hugh Holmes

DEAR SIR   New Market August 8^h 1818

In transitu I drop you a line of introduction to make you acquainted with Mr Blackburn the bearer a gentleman of science and for many years the professor of Matthematics in W^m & Mary colledge—not personaly acquainted with this gentleman before the Accidental meeting on the road to day I have still no hesitation, from a knowledge of his reputation gained through unexceptionable channels to recommend him to your patronage with a View to aid the great work we have on hand and altho finished by us yet subject to alteration amendment or even final rejection—you may find his opinions usefull, indeed I hope he may aid you much in giving the Central Colledge a start and place a feather in its Cap before it makes its appearance before the Assembly

You already know that with sentiments of high regard & esteem I am your friend   H^H HOLMES

RC (MHi); addressed: "The honble Thomas Jefferson Esqre now at the Warm Springs" to be delivered by "Mr Blackburn"; endorsed by TJ as received 1 Sept. 1818 and so recorded in SJL. Enclosure: Augustine C. Smith to Holmes, Winchester, 7 Aug. 1818, introducing George Blackburn, "my much esteemed and learned friend"; indicating that Smith, Francis W. Gilmer, and others have frequently spoken of Blackburn's "great sientific acquirements"; stating that he "is certainly the first mathematician in the U. States"; and concluding that "in the rare and happy talent of communicating instruction he is perhaps unrivalled in the world" (RC in MHi; addressed: "The Honble Hugh Holmes Esq. Stanton V^a"; with note by Holmes at foot of text: "H^h Holmes to Mr Jefferson").

George Blackburn (1765–1823), educator, mathematician, and cartographer, was born and received his early education in Dublin. He immigrated to the United States by 1800 and successively operated schools in Philadelphia and Fauquier County. Blackburn served as the professor of mathematics at the College of William and Mary, 1804–11, and at South

Carolina College (later the University of South Carolina) in Columbia, 1811–14. He left the latter institution following a series of controversies related to student discipline that prompted him to publish a vindication of his conduct. During his time in South Carolina, Blackburn also helped to survey its boundary line with North Carolina, and he took latitude and longitude readings that he used in his map of South Carolina published in 1822. By 1817 he had settled in Baltimore, where he was professor of mathematics at the newly formed Asbury College. In 1821 Blackburn returned to Columbia and taught at an academy there until his death (Maxi-

milian LaBorde, *History of the South Carolina College* [1859], 79–83; Philadelphia *Poulson's American Daily Advertiser*, 1 Oct. 1800; Susan H. Godson and others, *The College of William & Mary: A History* [1993], 1:178, 202–3, 297, 304; Daniel Walker Hollis, *University of South Carolina* [1951–56], 1:62–3; Blackburn, *Narrative of Transactions in the South-Carolina College, during the three last courses* [1814?]; *Methodist Magazine* 1 [1818]: 110–6; Blackburn to TJ, 8 Mar. 1819; Charleston *City Gazette*, 23 Aug., 24 Oct. 1823).

IN TRANSITU: "in transit."

From Caesar A. Rodney

HONORED & DEAR SIR, Wilmington Aug. 8ᵗʰ 1818

On my return home, after an absence of many months, I am naturally led to enquire, after the health & happiness, of those, who are the constant objects of my respect regard[1] & solicitude. Among the first in my affections, is the sincere & uniform friend of my youth to whom I have always been personally & politically attached.

The people, of S. America whom I have lately visited, resemble in appearance, character & manners, those of our own country. I was most agreeably disappointed with the prospect I beheld A fine soil, a most delightful climate and an amiable humane & brave population. The improvements have been as rapid as circumstances permit. A system of moderation however prevails. They appear to avoid the excesses of the French Revolution, which really operates as a bloody buoy[2] warning them of the dangers.

I am now occupied in preparing a report on the subject of that country, which I expect to take on to Washington in the month of October. And I do flatter myself with the prospect of once more paying my respects to the best of friends.

With every sentiment of esteem affection & gratitude I remain Dear Sir

Yours Most Sincerely & Truly C A. RODNEY

RC (DLC); endorsed by TJ as received 1 Sept. 1818 and so recorded in SJL. RC (MHi); address cover only; with PoC of TJ to John Vaughan, 7 Dec. 1818, on verso; addressed: "Thomas Jefferson Monticello Virginia"; franked; postmarked Wilmington, 10 Aug.

BLOODY BUOY recalls a 1796 work of that name by "Peter Porcupine" (William

Cobbett) detailing the atrocities of the French Revolution and warning against political extremism. Rodney presented his REPORT on South America to Secretary of State John Quincy Adams on 5 Nov. 1818, and it was communicated to Congress on 17 Nov. and 15 Dec. 1818 (*ASP, Foreign Relations*, 4:217–348).

[1] Word interlined.
[2] Manuscript: "bloody, buoy."

From Joseph Milligan

Georgetown August 10th 1818

I beg that you will accept the copy of the Federalist which you will herewith receive as the joint present of Jacob Gideon Jr and myself he is the printer & publisher and I am the binder

respectfully yours   JOSEPH MILLIGAN

RC (DLC); dateline at foot of text; addressed: "Thomas Jefferson Esqr Monticello Milton V^ia [i.e., Virginia]"; endorsed by TJ as received 1 Sept. 1818 and so recorded in SJL. Enclosure: *The Federalist, on The New Constitution, written in the year 1788, by Mr. Hamilton, Mr. Madison, and Mr. Jay, with An Appendix, containing the letters of Pacificus and Helvidius, on the Proclamation of Neutrality of 1793; also, the original Articles of Confederation, and the Constitution of the United States, with the amendments made thereto. A New Edition. The numbers written by Mr. Madison corrected by himself* (Washington, 1818; Poor, *Jefferson's Library*, 11 [no. 649]; TJ's copy in ViCMRL).

Jacob Gideon (ca. 1789–1864), printer, was publishing government documents by 1817 in Washington, D.C. He was active in local politics, serving variously as a ward watchman, commissioner of elections, and member of the common council. In 1841 his son George S. Gideon became a partner in his printing and bookbinding business. Gideon died in Washington (Washington *Daily National Intelligencer*, 6 Dec. 1817, 25 Feb. 1864; *City of Washington Gazette*, 12 Apr. 1819; Washington *Daily National Journal*, 26 May, 13 Oct. 1829; Washington *National Journal*, 26 May 1831; Washington *Madisonian* [country edition], 16 Jan. 1841).

On 15 Aug. 1818 GIDEON sent James Madison a copy of the newly published volume. Madison had provided him with his personal copy of the 1799 New York edition of *The Federalist*, in which he identified the authors of each number and corrected his own essays (Madison, *Papers, Retirement Ser.*, 1:205–10, 212–3, 217, 223–4, 347–8).

From George Ticknor

DEAR SIR,   Madrid August 10. 1818.

Your very kind letter inclosing an introduction to mr. Erving reached me in Italy just as I was beginning my journey to this country and I should have answered it immediately on my arrival here if I had not at that moment heard you had forwarded through my father another for Cardinal Dugnani of which I also wished to give you news. For this, however, I have waited in vain, and after so long an interval, I must believe it lost, though during a very active correspondence of three years and an half, this is the only instance that such an accident has occurred to me. Should it, however, at last reach me, I shall immediately forward it to the Cardinal, through the Nuntio at this court.—

The letter for Mr. Erving has done everything for me, that a letter could do—not merely in civilities but in substantial good offices, which he has been continually rendering me ever since I have been here. It will give you pleasure to know, what, perhaps, you would not otherwise learn, since there are no Americans here to write it & Mr Erving is the last person in the world to tell such tales of himself,— that he has great personal influence at this court. The Russian Minister has more the confidence of the King—but, I am sure of the fact, when I tell you, that no foreign minister here is so much respected by M[r] Pizarro, the Secretary of State—or can do so much by his personal influence for his government as M[r] Erving. This personal influence he has gained only by his talents, by the directness and openess of all his proceedings by never asking any thing that he could not demand as a right and never claiming a right he did not mean to insist upon until he obtained it. I say, I am sure of this fact, not only because it is no secret in the corps diplomatique & in the court society here; but because Mr. Pizarro himself does not hesitate to say, that he thinks M[r] Erving has more talent, than any representative at Madrid—and I tell it to you because I think it is a fact which ought to be known, and because I do not know anybody else here who would be likely to tell it.

For myself, I am here, as I have been everywhere else in Europe, only for purposes of study and as I proposed to myself, when I came, nothing but Spanish & Spanish literature, the means have not been wanting, though if I had come to learn anything else, I should have been in despair long ago & now be on the other side of the Pyrenees. It is a great pleasure to me to feel at last, that I am approaching the conclusion of the objects for which I came to Europe and that I am so soon to be emancipated & return to the friends and the country where all my affections & hopes rest, as on their only centre & home. When I came to Europe, I proposed to myself to acquire a good knowledge of all the literatures of ancient & modern Europe.—I began with the Greek & as my studies were then prosecuted at the north.—I joined to it the German in both its dialects & the kindred languages of Sweden & Denmark, in which a little gleaning may be made for good letters already. Latin we learn at home &, therefore, when I had done what I could with these & followed some courses of lectures on more general subjects—I came to France where I gave myself entirely to French literature, though not forgetting the ancient language of the Fabliaux in which there are so many interesting monuments & the more poetical Provençal which connects the latin to ye modern languages of the South. From France, I went to Italy, where I picked up their dialects again, especially the Venetian & the Sicilian*—& now I am in Spain, having nearly finished my Spanish.—My object in all has been to get general, philosophical notions on the genius & history of each of these literatures & to send home good collections of books relating to the history of their languages & representing the whole series of their elegant literatures.

I left at home a small library & have sent to increase it about four thousand volumes—all chosen on the one system I have indicated.

In about a month I go to Portugal, where I shall easily finish the last language I have to learn & in November I hope to be in Paris for a few weeks, where nothing will give me more pleasure than to be useful to you, who have shown so much kindness to me. After this I shall divide the rest of my winter & the spring between Edinburgh, Oxford, Cambridge & London, examining their literary institutions & completing my collections of books and, then, as soon as the fine season commences embark for my home.—

All this time thus spent in Europe, I consider a sacrifice of the present to the future & what I most desire is, to make this sacrifice useful to my country. What I shall bring home from my education, will be 1. A Knowledge of the literary institutions of Europe & their modes of Instruction 2. A facility in speaking German & french & a power of speaking Italian & Spanish—and 3. A knowledge of the literatures of ancient & modern Europe, with a library that will give me the means of pursuing them indefinitely.—And now the question is—what I shall do with the knowledge that has cost me four of the best years of my life? For political distinction, I have no ambition—no <u>thought</u> even & never have had.—If there were a department in the general Government, that was devoted to Publick Instruction, I might seek a place in it—but there is none,—& there is none even in my State Government. All that remains for me, therefore, seems to be to go home & exert what influence I may be able to acquire in favour of the cause of good letters &, perhaps, if a proper occasion offers, which is probable, give some years to instruction by courses of publick lectures at our University

[*]In all ye dialects I have mentioned yre is now more or less of a literature & what there is, is very interesting as an expression of popular character & feeling.

You see, Sir, that I have spoken to you with great freedom—perhaps, with too much: but the reason is, that I desire extremely, to have you know my situation exactly as it is, & to ask your advice & opinion on the course of life best for me to pursue when I reach my home & begin the world as it were a second time at the age of twenty seven, with a moderate fortune, which makes me independent; because my wants are few.

Your assistance has been of very great use to me in Europe every where that your letters or your friends have made me known as your acquaintance or rather as a person whom you countenance. I do not ask you to continue such favours to me in England, because I know, if you can do it conveniently, your benevolence does not need to be solicited & the only instance in which I could ask it would be that of Mr Rush, our minister, whom I do not know & to whom I can in no way be so well introduced as by yourself. The most interesting literary society in London—& which would be peculiarly so to me from its being ye centre of all that relates to Spanish letters, is at Lord Holland's. I have a letter to him from Lucien Bonaparte; but I Should rather know him by means of some one in my own country. President Munroe, to whom I was once introduced by a letter of President Adams, is claimed by Lord H— as his intimate friend & Mr Munroe gives introduction to him freely. Perhaps, you, too, know him no less: but, if you do not, I leave it to your kindness to determine whether, under these circumstances you will ask him to do me this favour. If there be any thing in all this in the least inconvenient to you, I pray it may be as if I had never spoken of it.—

Remember me, I beg of you, to Colo. Randolph & Mrs. Randolph with their family, whom I hope to see at Monticello, if you will permit me to pay you a visit there soon after my return home. Farewell— my dear Sir—and in the idiom of the country, where I am, I pray heaven to preserve you many years, since all your years are years of usefulness.—I had almost forgotten to say, how much I am interested in the noble plan you have formed for education in your native State. I trust & believe it will succeed, & already foresee the pleasure of witnessing your happiness in its success.—   GEO: TICKNOR

The best—shortest & safest mode of addressing your favours to me is always through my father—E. Ticknor, Boston.—

I need not say, how much pleasure it will give me to be useful to you in England or Scotland in buying Books or in anything else.

RC (DLC); corner chipped; addressed: "Thomas Jefferson Esq—Monticello— (Albemarle) Virginia"; endorsed in transit: "Rec^d at Gibraltar & forwarded By y^o

Ob. sts Hill & Blodget Gib. 24ᵗʰ Augᵗ"; stamped "SHIP"; franked; postmarked New York, 13 Oct.; endorsed by TJ as received 22 Oct. 1818 and so recorded in SJL.

The RUSSIAN MINISTER at Madrid was Dmitry Tatishchev. OUR UNIVERSITY: Harvard University. John Adams introduced Ticknor to James Monroe (PRESIDENT MUNROE) in a letter of 21 Dec. 1814 (Lb in MHi: Adams Papers).

From Stephen Cathalan

DEAR SIR—   Marseilles the 13ᵗʰ August 1818—

I Confirm you my Respects of the 25ᵗʰ april & 2ᵈ may Last, which I hope will have Reached you, as well, as the nine Boxes of wine, with one Basket of Maccaroni, I Shipped, on the Ship fair Trader, Geo Fletcher Master, Bound for Alexandria, amounting as per Invoice to F 257=70= to your Debit;

on the 16ᵗʰ July, I was honnored with your Favor of the 5ᵗʰ april Inclosed in a letter of Mʳ Jⁿ Vaughan of Philadelphia of the 14ᵗʰ may, with one Draft of Stephen Gerard, on James Laffitte & Cᵒ of Paris, Payᵇˡᵉ at Sixty Days Sight unto my order & for your Accᵗ pʳ ƒ 2205— making Dᵃʳˢ 420, as Mentioned in your Said Letter, at ƒ 5—25 pʳ Dᵃʳ which I have Passed on your Credit.

the Ship Juliana, when I Received Mʳ Vaughan's Letter & Said Inclosures, being on Sailing out for Philadᵃ, I had Scarcely the Time to write a Line to Mʳ Vaughan to acknowledge him the Receipt of his Said Remittance, Requesting him to Inform you of it, & that your new orders mentioned in your Letter, would be Executed.

I wrote Immediately to Mʳ Durand of Perpignan for

one Cask of abᵗ 64 Gallons $\left.\begin{array}{c} \textbf{TJ} \\ \{\textbf{T}_{\textbf{R}}\textbf{J} \end{array}\right\}$ old Rivesaltes wine; in Dᵇˡᵉ Casks—
1   dᵗᵒ   of   30

he answered me on the 27ᵗʰ that =he had taken due notice of my order, which he hoped to obtain at moderate Price, tho' the good qualities are very Scarce, & he would do the best to Satisfy you;=[1] tho' I Recommended him to Send them to me as Soon as Possible, I have not heard from him Since;

I forwarded at Same time your Inclosed Letter to Mʳ Sasserno asking to him for you 300— Bottles of nice wine to Reach me, if Possible, before the 15ᵗʰ Insᵗ handing him at Same time a Copy of the Paragraph of your Letter about him & Said wine;—in answer =he Informed me, that his Commission as Consul has not yet Reached him, that he is not So much at a Loss, about it, Since I mentioned to him, that I thought it would be Sent at Same time with a number of new Commission to old and newly appointed Consuls, of the U.s. in Europe & in this kingdom of France near h. M. Ch^{an} M. to obtain h. Said M$^{ty's}$ Exequatur;=

=as to the wine, he has Shipped Six Boxes of 50 Bottles Each, red wine of <u>Bellet</u>-nice, which has been Sold to them, to be of the year 1812—& which he can Certify after being tasted by him and Connoisseurs, & worth to Laid on the Tables of the 1st Classes a Broad, & tho' it may not have of that <u>little</u> <u>Silky</u>, Enough, he apprehends, my Respectable Friend Th^s Jeff^{on} may wish; yet he hopes that it's quality will Suit his & his Friend's Palate considering it's <u>Corroborative</u> quality; he was So fortunate to have found, that quality of wine he was Sending to me, for you, that there is Scarcely no more dry old wine of Good quality, So more So, that they Sale now wine of 2 a 3 years Crops at about the Same Price, as the Last Sent to me for you, Last year; & this present Invoice, will not Cost more on Board at nice than about f 1=60 p^r Bottle;= he charges me, meantime =he may answer to your kind favor, to transmit you his Deep Sense of Gratitude, for your Interest & protection towards him;=;

This wine is Just arived & Landed here, but the Brig Siro of Philadelphia Geo. Lockyer,[2] having Cleared out & in this united States's Chancery, & Custom house, & being Still anchored in this Road Since before yesterday; it was Impossible for me to Ship it on her; She is Bound for Phil^a & the cheasapeack, and all what I have time to do, now, is to write you these few Lines, not being Sure, I may forward it thro' Said Brig Siro;—

meantime, then, I may, I hope about the end of this month Ship the whole you have ordered to me for your Self & your Grand Son T. Jefferson Randolph; I beg you to accept my best wishes for your Good health & happiness and of your whole worthy Family, with my Everlasting Gratitude, for your Good Continued Protection & Friendship, for me; with which I have the honor to be with Great Respect allways at your Commands & Sincerely—

my Dear Sir your most obed^t & Devoted Servt

STEPHEN CATHALAN.

RC (MHi); endorsed by TJ as received 5 Oct. 1818 and so recorded in SJL. RC (MHi); address cover only; with PoC of TJ to Fernagus De Gelone, 27 Dec. 1818, on verso; addressed: "Thos Jefferson Esqr Late President of the united States Monticello—virginia," with Cathalan's initialed additional notation that it was sent "By the Brig Siro Cap^n Geo. Lockyer"; franked; postmarked Norfolk, 29 Sept.

H. M. CH^{AN} M.: "His Most Christian Majesty," a title traditionally accorded to the king of France. An EXEQUATUR is "an official recognition of a consul or commercial agent by the government of the country to which he is accredited, authorizing

him to exercise his power" (*OED*). COR-
ROBORATIVE: "A strengthening or forti-
fying agent" (*OED*).

[1] Omitted closing quotation mark editorially supplied.
[2] Manuscript: "Lookyer."

From John Steele

DEAR SIR,   Custom House Philad[a] Aug. 13. 1818

Your favor of the 27th ult. was duly received, and the two cases of wine have been forwarded to Richmond agreeably to advice, as ℔ enclosed bill of lading. I send you also a memorandum of the duty, freight and other charges—Any service that you may occasionally require will be rendered with pleasure

I am with sincere regard

yours &c   JN[o] STEELE

RC (ViU: TJP-ER); endorsed by TJ as received 1 Sept. 1818 and so recorded in SJL. RC (DLC); address cover only; with PoC of TJ to Thomas Ritchie, 7 Dec. 1818, on verso; addressed: "Tho[s] Jefferson Esq[r] Monticello"; franked; postmarked Philadelphia, 13 Aug. Enclosures not found.

To Martha Jefferson Randolph

MY DEAR DAUGHTER   Warmsprings Aug. 14. 18.

I wrote to you by our last mail of the 8th having been now here a week & continued to bathe 3 times a day, a quarter of an hour at a time, I continue well, as I was when I came. having no symptom to judge by at what time I may presume the seeds of my rheumatism eradicated, and desirous to prevent the necessity of ever coming here a 2[d] time, I believe I shall yeild to the general advice of a three weeks course. but so dull a place, and so distressing an ennui I never before knew. I have visited the rock on the high mountain, the hotsprings, and yesterday the falling spring, 15. miles from here; so that there remains no other excursion to enliven the two remaining weeks. we are at present about 30, & at the Hotsprings 20. yesterday we were reduced to a single lady (miss Allstone) but there came in 4. more in the evening. mrs Egglestone (Matilda Maury that was) left us yesterday for the Hotsprings, obliged to be carried to the bath in a chair, being unable to walk. the 2. Col[o] Coles came in last night, & John Harris the night before. yesterday too Gen[l] Brackenridge left us, who had accompanied me from the Rockfish gap, and who has been my guide and guardian & fellow-lodger in the same cabin. we were constantly together, and I feel his loss most sensibly. he tells me you were at his house (in the neighborhood of Fincastle) on your tramontane excursion. I have contracted more intimacy with Col° Allstone than with any other now remaining. he is father of the mr Allstone who married Burr's daughter. the whole of the line of springs seems deserted now for the white Sulphur, where they have 150. persons, and all latter-comers are obliged to go into the neighborhood for lodging. I believe in fact that that spring with the Hot & Warm, are those of the first merit. the sweet springs retain esteem, but in limited cases. affectionate remembrance to all the family and to yourself devoted love. Th: Jefferson

RC (NNPM); endorsed by Randolph. Recorded in SJL with TJ's summary: "occurrences of the day."

The 2. col° coles were Edward Coles and Isaac A. Coles. col° allstone: William Alston.

Memorandum to William Alston on Wine

White Hermitage wine costs about 4. or 4½ francs the bottle. the best crop is that of M. Jourdans, who has always furnished me. it is a little silky. but he furnishes Maj^r Butler with that which is quite dry, which is preferred by some, according to taste, and is a superlatively fine wine.

The best claret (except the 4. crops) is furnished by M. Bergasse of Marseilles at 1. franc the bottle, ready bottled & 2 or 3. years old, ready for drinking.

Apply for the above to M. Cathalan Consul of the US. at Marseilles, who having been in the habit of furnishing them to me annually for 30. years past, will understand at once the particular kind or crop called for.

Mr Appleton of Leghorn can procure the best crop of the Florence wine called Montepulciano, which if put into good black bottles well cimented will come perfect. I have not lost 1. bottle in 100. in this way, whereas in the flask one half is generally lost.
this costs 25. cents the quart bottle when put on board the ship. it is certainly the first of all the Italian wines. Th:J.

Aug. 15. 18.

MS (Peter Manigault, Charleston, S.C., 1986; photocopy in ScHi: Alston-Pringle-Frost Papers); entirely in TJ's hand. Not recorded in SJL.

William Alston (ca. 1757–1839), planter and public official, served as a captain in the 2d South Carolina Regiment of the Continental army, 1779–81, and rose to colonel in the South Carolina militia after the Revolutionary War. He sat in four successive sessions of the South Carolina House of Representatives, 1776–84, before declining to serve a fifth term in 1785. Alston represented Prince George Winyah Parish in 1788 at the state ratification convention, where he voted in favor of the new federal constitution. Following a special election, Alston entered the state senate in 1788 and served during six sessions, 1788–94 and 1810–13, refusing a final election in 1814. He was a presidential elector for both TJ in 1800 and James Madison in 1812, held local offices, including tax inquirer and collector, and was a founder of the Georgetown Library Society, of South Carolina. Alston was a leading rice planter and among the prominent racers and breeders of thoroughbred horses of his day. In 1791 he hosted George Washington at his Clifton residence. Alston befriended TJ at Warm Springs in 1818. Over his lifetime he amassed landholdings totaling nearly thirty thousand acres, and at his death in Charleston he left an estate valued at well over half a million dollars, including 723 slaves (*ANB*; *BDSCHR*, 3:35–8; Heitman, *Continental Army*, 70; Donald Jackson and Dorothy Twohig, eds., *The Diaries of George Washington* [1976–79], 6:123–4; *MB*, 2:1363, 1377; *Edgefield* [S.C.] *Advertiser*, 11 July 1839).

In American usage at this time, CLARET could mean any light red wine. The 4. CROPS were Margaux, Latour, Haut-Brion, and Lafite, generally acknowledged to be the premier Bordeaux wine estates (John Hailman, *Thomas Jefferson and Wine* [2006], 36–7, 152–3).

Recommendation of Edmund Bacon

Warm Springs Virginia. Aug. 15. 18.

The bearer, mr Edmund Bacon has lived with me twelve years as manager of my farm at Monticello. he goes to the Missouri to look out for lands to which he means to remove. he is an honest, correct man in his conduct and worthy of confidence in his engagements: any information or instruction which any person may give him will be worthily bestowed, and if he should apply particularly to Govr Clarke on his way, the Governor will especially oblige me by imparting to him his information and advice   TH: JEFFERSON

MS (Roberta B. Coscia, Memphis, Tenn., 2007); in TJ's hand; with subjoined, signed, dated, supplemental recommendation by Thomas Mann Randolph of 14 Sept. 1820 (written during TJ's absence at Poplar Forest): "Mr Bacon has continued to possess the esteem confidence and good Will of his neighbours and of the family in which he has lived without any interruption to this day." Not recorded in SJL.

Bacon later recalled that TJ had recommended that he go to THE MISSOURI to look for land, but when he was ready to leave on his exploratory visit, "Mr. Jefferson was at the Warm Springs. In going to his Bedford farm, he had somehow caught the itch, and it troubled him a great deal, and he went to the Springs to see if he could not get rid of it. But he wrote me not to let his absence interrupt my plans, and said that in going, I would pass directly through the yard where he was staying, and he would see me there." When Bacon arrived in Saint Louis, he called on Governor William Clark, "showed him the letter from Mr. Jefferson, and I never was more kindly treated" (Pierson, *Jefferson at Monticello*, 29–30, 32).

From Charles G. Haines

HON. SIR   New York Aug. 18. 1818.

I take the liberty of sending you my pamphlet, concerning the Great Western Canal, written at the request of The New York Corresponding Association for the promotion of Internal Improvements.

I cannot but congratulate a Statesman, so distinguished as yourself among the Fathers of our Republic, that you have lived to see the day, when your toils and your sacrifices are repaid by the unparalleled happiness and prosperity of the Nation, to whose existence and welfare you have so greatly contributed.

With the highest consideration of respect, I have the honor to be Sir, your Ob^t Servt CHA^s G. HAINES.

RC (DLC); endorsed by TJ as received 1 Sept. 1818 and so recorded in SJL. RC (MHi); address cover only; with PoC of TJ to John Barnes, 7 Dec. 1818, on verso; addressed: "Hon. Thomas Jefferson, State of Virginia," with "Monticello" added in a different hand; franked; postmarked New York, with inconsistent date of 17 Aug. Enclosure: Haines, *Considerations on the Great Western Canal, from the Hudson to Lake Erie: with a view of its Expence, Advantages, and Progress* (Brooklyn, 1818; Poor, *Jefferson's Library*, 5 [no. 217]; TJ's copy in PPAmP, inscribed by Haines [trimmed]: "Hon. Thos Jeff[erson] from The Au[. . .]").

Charles Glidden Haines (1793–1825), attorney and author, was a native of Canterbury, Merrimack County, New Hampshire. He worked as a government clerk in that state before graduating from Middlebury College in 1816. Thereafter Haines studied law, first in Vermont and later in New York City. A supporter of DeWitt Clinton, he became the governor's private secretary at Albany. Haines was admitted to the New York bar in 1821. He wrote numerous political pamphlets and newspaper articles, and from 1822 to 1823 he collaborated with other lawyers in the publication of the *United States Law Journal, and Civilian's Magazine.* Haines was admitted to the bar of the United States Supreme Court in 1824 and acted as cocounsel with Henry Clay in *Ogden v. Saunders,* a case involving the constitutionality of the New York state bankruptcy laws. Governor Clinton appointed him adjutant general for the state in 1825, but Haines died in New York City before taking office (*DAB*; Haines, *Memoir of Thomas Addis Emmet, with a biographical notice of Mr. Haines* [1829], 5–32; Bela Bates Edwards, *Biography of Self Taught Men* [1832], 219–23; Walter E. Howard and Charles E. Prentiss, comps., *Catalogue of the Officers and Students of Middlebury College in Middlebury, Vermont . . . 1800 to 1900* [1901], 55; *New York Mercantile Advertiser*, 4, 6 July 1825).

From Victor Adolphus Sasserno

SIR.   Nice August 18. 18.

I received your honoured letter of april 5 in due time, it mentions, your preceding of feb. 22, which has not reached me till now, the same is with my consular commission you think in my power; i certainly would not have failed to make it Know to you, and to answer to your letter; t'is the less i ought do in return of the trouble i have caused you for the said commission, i don't forget it and will be as grateful as you have been Kind upon my account.

M[r] Cathalan in his letter, says me he thinks this delay proceding from the nomination of other consuls in some other ports of Europe, and that the Secretary of state will forward the commissions all at once.

The commission of 300 bottles of wine you are pleased to honour me with, is performed and set out a week ago for Marsiglia, where M[r] Cathalan will reship it for your parts, I have choosed the best quality existing now in Nice, and am sure you will be pleased with it. though the good qualities be excessively rare, considering that these Some[1] years the vineyard has given but a very bad and mean product. Notwithstanding i hope this sending[2] will be to your complete Satisfaction.

I don't Know whence do the difference between the last parcel and the preceding proceeds, (being then at Paris) but i think t'is occasionned by a difference in the year, the vineyard being allways the same, id est <u>Bellet</u>.

My father in law, who, in my absence has executed your different orders, has told me, that the parcel you have found <u>silky</u> was the provision of a proprietor, who unhappily has no more of it, this i am very sorry for, because of my desire to answer well to your confidence, and acknowledge at least by that the good offices you have done me; in return, i pray you earnestly, dispose in all occasions of my services, they are devoted to you as

Your most respectful servant   A. Sasserno

Dupl (MHi); at head of text in Stephen Cathalan's hand: "2[ta]"; at foot of first page in Cathalan's hand: "Th[s] Jefferson Esq[r] &[a] &[a]"; endorsed by TJ as received 2 Apr. 1819 and so recorded in SJL. Enclosed in Cathalan to TJ, 30 Nov. 1818.

MARSIGLIA is the Italian name for Marseille. MY FATHER IN LAW: Amant Spreafico.

[1] Thus in manuscript.
[2] Manuscript: "sendind."

From Ate. Bourier

New-Market Shenandoah County V[a]

MONSIEUR.   le 20 aout 1818.

Je viens d'être informé qu'une académie d'enseignement allait S'établir sous peu à charlottes-ville. Dans le cas où il faudrait quelqu'un pour enseigner la langue Française, Je prends la liberté de me recommander à vous pour l'emploi de professeur. Veuillez avoir la bonté de m'addresser votre réponse, au Soin de M^r le Doct^r S. Henkel (New-Market.) avec qui je demeure actuellement.

Je compte sur votre complaisance à cet egard et Suis en attendant,—
    Votre très obéïssant Serviteur   A^{TE} BOURIER

E D I T O R S '   T R A N S L A T I O N

SIR.   New-Market Shenandoah County V^a 20 August 1818.
    I have just been informed that an academy will soon be established in Charlottesville. Should you need someone to teach the French language, I take the liberty of recommending myself to you as professor. Kindly send me your reply care of Dr. S. Henkel (New-Market), with whom I currently reside.
    I count on your benevolence in this matter and am, in the meantime,—
    Your very obedient servant   A^{TE} BOURIER

RC (MHi); endorsed by TJ as received 7 Sept. 1818 and so recorded in SJL. Translation by Dr. Genevieve Moene.

From Nathaniel Bowditch

SIR   Salem Aug. 20. 1818.
I did myself the honor to present you a few months Since some mathematical papers, printed in the fourth volume of the Memoirs of the American Academy of Arts & Sciences. I have now taken the liberty to forward another paper of the same series, lately printed, which I hope you will do me the honor to accept.

    With sentiments of high consideration I remain Sir, your most obed^t hum^e ser^t   N. BOWDITCH.

RC (DLC); endorsed by TJ as received 2 Sept. 1818 and so recorded in SJL. RC (DLC); address cover only; with PoC of TJ to Frederick A. Mayo, 30 Nov. 1818, on recto and verso; addressed: "The Honorable Thomas Jefferson late President of the United States." Enclosure: Bowditch, "Remarks on Doctor Stewart's formula, for computing the motion of the Moon's Apsides, as given in the Supplement to the Encyclopedia Brittanica," in American Academy of Arts and Sciences, *Memoirs* 4 (1818): 51–60 (Poor, *Jefferson's Library*, 7 [no. 303]; TJ's copy in MBPLi, inscribed by Bowditch to "The Honorable Thomas Jefferson late Pres^t of the U. States from the Author").

From Robert B. Stark

Belfield Greensville County Aug[t] 20th 1818

At the request of M[r] Rob[t] Greenway of Dinwiddie—I address you—for the purpose of making a tender of a Botanical work (in manuscript)—accompanied[1] with a "Hortus siccus"—written & carefully collated by his Father, the late Dr James Greenway.

It purports to be a collection of three hundred plants, growing spontaneously in Virginia & adjacent parts of North Carolina; described from the living plant & arranged according to the "Delineatio plantæ"—as laid down by the celebrated professor Linnæus. To which is added the time of their flowering—the different soils & situations they inhabit—their virtues & doses—their use in dy'ing—for cultivation & improvement of land—their poisonous qualities and other useful remarks on their various properties—. All collected in this section of country—the fruit of several years labour.

I am induced to believe that the publication of this work—would be a desideratum in this Country—it is the most extensive original work on Botany—that I am acquainted with. Professor Bartons little work—I mean his "Essay towards a Materia medica" founded on a plan somewhat similar to D[r] Greenway's—has been most favourably received by the public—it has served some useful purposes. It has at least, invited the attention of some of our country men—to the study of the nature & properties of our indigenous plants. It has been a friendly guide—in the hands of the medical Student—conducting him with many pleasing observations—thro' an extensive wild[s]—hitherto but little explored.

Understanding that you cultivate a taste—as well as intimate knowledge of this pleasing science—has been our inducement in presenting it to you. If in forwarding it to <u>your address</u>. I can contribute to your amusement for a single hour—it will be a source of gratification to

yours with respect   R: B: STARK. M:D

RC (MoSB); endorsed by TJ as received 1 Sept. 1818 and so recorded in SJL. RC (DLC); address cover only; with PoC of TJ to Joseph Gales (1786–1860), 7 Dec. 1818, on verso; addressed: "Thomas Jefferson esq[r] Montichello near Charlottsville"; franked; postmarked Hicks Ford, Va., 23 Aug. 1818.

Robert Bolling Stark (ca. 1782–1839), physician and public official, was an assistant naval surgeon beginning in 1800, was promoted to surgeon in 1809, and evidently left the service the following year. He was chosen as a presidential elector for James Monroe in 1816 and 1820, represented Greensville County in the Virginia House of Delegates, 1816–17 and 1819–20, and supported the presidential candidacy of Andrew Jackson in 1824. By 1831 Stark was a physician at the Marine Hospital, first at Washington Point and later at Norfolk. At his death his property in the county and borough of

Norfolk, Princess Anne County, and Brunswick County was valued at approximately $90,000, including more than one hundred slaves (Callahan, *U.S. Navy,* 517; *JHD* [1816–17 sess.], 62–3 [3 Dec. 1816]; Leonard, *General Assembly,* 286, 299; *Richmond Enquirer,* 3 Aug. 1824; *A Register of Officers and Agents, Civil, Military, and Naval, in the Service of the United States* [1831], 67; *The Biennial Register of all Officers and Agents in the Service of the United States* [1838], 61; *Richmond Whig & Public Advertiser,* 8 Mar. 1839; Norfolk City Will Book, 7:408–11, 8:133–9, 141–2, 156–9; gravestone inscription in Cedar Grove Cemetery, Norfolk).

HORTUS SICCUS: an "arranged collection of dried plants; a herbarium" (*OED*). Carolus Linnaeus (Carl von Linné) published a DELINEATIO PLANTÆ ("delineation of plants") as a short monograph in 1758. It was incorporated into his *Systema Naturæ* beginning with that year's tenth edition.

[1] Manuscript: "accompnied."

From Thomas Cooper

DEAR SIR   August 21. 1818

Our election for the chemical chair comes on the first day of September. The issue is uncertain. I think the family influence of Mr Rob. Hare is likely to prevail. I have received an invitation from De Witt Clinton, Dr Hosack and D^r McNeven of New York, to accept of a chair of Chemistry connected with a board of agriculture there: the salary contemplated 2500$: but I have written in reply that I cannot accept of it under present circumstances.

I write at present to request your influence with Mr Monroe to send out in some capacity or other, our Mr Thomas Say, and Mr Thos Nuttal; really, as Zoologist and as Botanist, in the Macedonian. They have done more than any two other men of late, to extend our scientific reputation abroad, and are noticed with great respect in the Journal de Physique for last January. M. Correa is at Albany or he would heartily join in this recommendation. They want nothing more than a salary that would decently suffice for necessaries of life, during the cruise, and facilities to pursue their objects.

Why cannot we begin a system for a regular supply of a national Museum, by giving orders to Captains of national vessels to bring home objects of natural history? Knowing your continued love for science, I venture to make this request. I remain ever

Dear sir Your faithful & obliged friend   THOMAS COOPER

RC (MHi); endorsed by TJ as received 2 Sept. 1818 and so recorded in SJL. RC (MHi); address cover only; with PoC of TJ to Patrick Gibson, 9 Dec. 1818, on verso; addressed: "Thomas Jefferson Esq Montecello Virginia"; stamp canceled; franked; postmarked Philadelphia, 21 Aug.

Cooper served on an American Philosophical Society committee charged with securing government permission for

Thomas Say and Thomas Nuttall to travel to the Pacific Ocean on the United States frigate MACEDONIAN (APS, Minutes, 21 Aug. 1818 [MS in PPAmP]; Richard G. Beidleman, "Some Biographical Sidelights on Thomas Nuttall, 1786–1859," APS, *Proceedings* 104 [1960]: 88–9). Nuttall and Say were recognized for their contributions to botany and zoology, respectively, in the JOURNAL DE PHYSIQUE 86 (1818): 76, 82, 83–4, 85. Both had published articles in the *Journal* of the Academy of Natural Sciences of Philadelphia, vol. 1 (1817–18).

To Martha Jefferson Randolph

MY DEAREST DAUGHTER   Warmsprings Aug. 21. 18.

I wrote to you this day week and this day fortnight. we have been here in a continued state of fluctuation between the numbers of 40. & 60. a greater proportion of ladies than formerly: but all invalids, and perfectly recluse in their cabins. mr Glendy joined us to-day and will stay till Sunday. we had been many days without venison till the day before yesterday, in the course of which 8. deer were brought in their price 3ᵈ a ℔ nett. I do not know what may be the effect of this course of bathing, on my constitution; but I am under great threats that it will work it's effect thro' a system of boils. a large swelling on my seat, increasing for several days past in size and hardness disables me from sitting but on the corner of a chair. another swelling begins to manifest itself to-day[1] on the other seat. it happens fortunately that Capᵗ Harris is here in a carriage alone, and proposes to set out on the same day I had intended. he offers me a seat which I shall gladly accept. we propose to set out on Friday or Saturday next, to be 2 days on the road to Staunton, stay there one day, & 2 days more to get home. he will deposit me 4. miles below Rockfish gap, from whence I shall make my way home in the gig. perhaps these swellings may yet disappear, but I have little hope of that. Adieu my dear daughter receive my affectionate love for yourself and express it to all the dear family.   TH: JEFFERSON

RC (NNPM); endorsed by Randolph. Recorded in SJL with TJ's summary: "state of health. day for departure."

[1] Word interlined.

Promissory Note to Thomas Jefferson Randolph

Monticello 21st August 1818.

$3000.

Sixty five days after date I promise to pay to Thomas J. Randolph or order, negotiable and payable at the Office of discount and deposit of the United States bank in Richmond without offset Three thousand dollars for value received

TH: JEFFERSON

MS (MHi); written on a half sheet in Patrick Gibson's hand, signed by TJ.

At the date of this document, TJ was still at Warm Springs, not MONTICELLO. His financial records indicate that a note

in this amount to his grandson Thomas Jefferson Randolph was renewed on this date (*MB*, 2:1350). The presence of the extant text in TJ's papers may suggest that it is a previously signed and dated but unused duplicate.

From Spencer Roane

DEAR SIR.

Richmond, August 22d 1818.

On my arrival at this place, a few days ago, I found your favour of 28th June. The postmaster here had not sent it to Hanover, where I usually reside in the spring & Summer.—I am much flattered by the terms of your invitation, and should certainly have called on you had that letter been duly[1] received. As it was, I shd have given myself that pleasure, had not my departure been delayed 'till the last Hour.

I am glad to find that our selection of a site is generally approved, below the ridge, and that great confidence is reposed in the Commissioners, as to the plan. I have no Doubt but our report will be ratified. Much however yet remains to be done: and you who have done so much for us, will find your further exertions necessary, in this Cause on which the best interests of our Country so mainly depend. No person will co-operate more ardently than myself, in giving to those exertions their Complete Effect.

With the greatest Esteem and respect, I am, Dear sir,
yr obt st

SPENCER ROANE

RC (MHi); endorsed by TJ as received 1 Sept. 1818 and so recorded in SJL. RC (DLC); address cover only; with PoC of TJ to James Brownlee, 27 Nov. 1818, on verso; addressed: "Thomas Jef-

ferson Esqr monticello Albemarle: by mail to Charlotte'sville"; franked; postmarked Richmond, 24 Aug.

[1] Word interlined.

From Thomas Appleton

Leghorn 26th August 1818—

I have receiv'd, Sir, only this morning, your letter in date of 4th of April, covering the Statement of your account with Mad: Pini; and as a vessel will depart for Balt° in the course of an hour,[1] it affords me just the time to say, that your letter was accompanied by one from m^r John Vaughan, mentioning, "that he then inclos'd a bill of exchange[2] by S: Girard on La fitte & C° Paris for francs. 2415." but no Such bill was found therein by me.—I regret greatly this inadvertence of m^r Vaughan, inasmuch, as it prevents, or rather delays, the fulfilling the engagement with mad: Pini; and the disappointment will be in proportion to her present wants, which She informs me are Somewhat pressing. In the course of a few days, I shall wait on her at Pisa, and deliver into her hands your Statement and obligation, explaining at the Same time all the items.—I shall reply, very shortly[3] to those parts of your letter in relation to orvietto wine, & the <u>Sculptors</u>.[4]—Accept, Sir, the renewal of my unalterable respect & esteem

TH: APPLETON

RC (DLC); at foot of text: "Thomas Jefferson, esq"; endorsed by TJ as received 6 Dec. 1818 and so recorded in SJL. FC (Lb in DNA: RG 84, CRL); in Appleton's hand.

[1] FC substitutes "the morning" for preceding two words.

[2] FC here adds "for your account drawn."

[3] From "I shall wait" to this point, FC instead reads "I shall reply."

[4] FC: "the two Sculptors you require."

From Thomas Cooper

DEAR SIR   Aug. 26. 1818

I write now in reply to yours from the warm Springs, of the 7th Instant.

Dr Patterson is not chosen Chemical Professor, nor do I think he will be. The election does not take place till the first day of September. The event you shall be informed of, without delay.

If I should not succeed (a very possible case) M. Correa, Mrs Cooper and myself, set out forthwith for Charlotteville. She is entitled to be consulted by me, and therefore I take her. At present, she would be willing to renounce any chance I have here, and set out at once for Virginia: but she will be better able to judge when she arrives there. I shall not be influenced by the New York proposals. But I have a suit depending in the district federal court here, wherein I am Plf in ejectment, which will compel my being present the third week of October.

M. Correa is rambling about New York State. I heard of him last, at Albany.

The more I think of it, the more it strikes me as a matter of national importance, to commence something like a scientific plan for the promotion of natural science, & therefore to send out Mess. Say & Nuttal to Columbia, where they propose staying a year or two. MM. Correa, Collins & some others had raised funds to send out Nuttal to the Arkansas. If you think well of my suggestion in this respect, pray promote it with Mʳ Munroe.

I remain always Dear sir Your faithful friend

THOMAS COOPER

RC (MHi); endorsed by TJ as received 11 Sept. 1818 and so recorded in SJL. RC (MHi); address cover only; with PoC of TJ to Hugh Holmes, 21 Dec. 1818, on verso; addressed: "Thomas Jefferson Esq Montecello Virginia"; stamp canceled; franked; postmarked Philadelphia, 26 Aug.

Cooper, as plaintiff (PLF), sued to eject a competing claimant to the Limestone Lick tract in Northumberland County,

Pennsylvania, an interest in which he had purchased at a sheriff's sale more than a decade earlier. The United States Circuit Court for the Pennsylvania and New Jersey Districts ruled in Cooper's favor in October 1819 (Bushrod Washington, ed., *Reports of Cases Determined in the Circuit Court of the United States, for the Third Circuit, comprising the Districts of Pennsylvania and New-Jersey. Commencing at April Term, 1803* [1826–29], 3:546–57; Cooper to TJ, 24 Nov. 1819).

From William D. Simms

SIR   Custom House Alexandria 28ᵗʰ August 1818.

In the absence of the Collector, I have the honor to address you, with the information, that I have shipped (via Norfolk) nine Boxes of wine and one[1] Bale of Macaroni, to the care of Mʳ Gibson at Richmond.—

Below is a note of the duties and charges which I have paid.

With great respect I have the honor to be Sir yr ob Servᵗ

W D. SIMMS D.C.

Amᵗ of Duty on wine 8 Bottles	$32.26.
Do Do Macaroni	72.
Freight from Marseilles pr Bill	10.50
Do to Norfolk	2.50
Custom House charges	1.70
Wharfage & Drayage	65.
Dolls—48.33	

RC (MHi); adjacent to signature: "Thomas Jefferson Esq'"; endorsed by TJ as received 1 Sept. 1818 and so recorded in SJL; notation by TJ at foot of

text: "Oct. 27. 18. remitted 50.D. to Col° Charles Simms."

[1] Manuscript: "on."

From Richard Claiborne

VERY DEAR SIR   New Orleans ap[l] [Aug.] 29th '18.

Within 2 or 3 days of each other, I received your friendly favor of the 10th of May last, and one from the Marquis De Lafayette. Such a working of feelings as took place within my breast, at the occurrence, you may very well[1] imagine. Reflecting too that we were among the few remaining characters of old revolutionary times, I was filled with a serious degree of melancholy. But providence disposes of things for the best. Were we to live to uncommon ages, we might meet with public mortifications we little expected. I will Say however that I shall die with one consolation, and that is, that I did live to see the 4th of March 1801!!

The enclosed paper will be continued to you until my Essay on Steam Navigation shall be finished; and when I get my plates executed, and my pamphlet published, a copy shall be sent to you. I am now going through a course [of][2] trials with my boat, which have turned out to my own satisfaction—and if I succeed in my mathematical experiments, the Invention will likely be carried up to Steam Power. "Old brooms are thrown aside, and new brooms sweep clean."[3] So it will be with the Wheel and the Duckfoot Paddle.

The Steam boats which now run in the Misisipi and its waters, are as follows:

Vesuvius	390 Tons	
Ætna	360	
Orleans	324	
Washington	403	
Harriet	54	
Buffaloe	249	Besides these, many are
Kentucky	112	under way in the Ohio—
Constitution	112	one built at Mobile—one
Govr Shelby	106	preparing for Bayou Sara—
Geo. Madison	128	and two building in New
Vesta	203	Orleans, one of 700 Tons,
Genl Jackson	142	and the other of 500 Tons.
Cincinnati	157	Nay, they are springing up

Ohio	364	like Mushrooms, every
Louisiana	102	where.
Napoleon	315	Would the opposers of
Franklin	131	the purchase of Louisiana,
Eagle		now agree to take back the
Pike		purchase money, and give
James Monroe		up the Country?—!—!

The City of New Orleans is very healthy.

"Eternal sunshine rest upon thy head."   R CLAIBORNE

Trouble not yourself to write to me. Only suffer me [to?] make my communications to you.

RC (DLC: TJ Papers, 213:37960–1); misdated; mutilated at seal; addressed: "Tho. Jefferson Esquire Monticello V.a."; endorsed by TJ as received 29 Sept. 1818 and so recorded in SJL. Enclosure not found.

TJ was sworn in as president of the United States on THE 4TH OF MARCH 1801.

[1] Manuscript: "will."
[2] Omitted word editorially supplied.
[3] Omitted closing quotation mark editorially supplied.

From Thomas Cooper

DEAR SIR   Sep[r] 1. 1818 Philad[a]

M[r] Hare was elected to the chemical Chair of this University to day: Hare 10. Cooper 7. Patterson 3.   On a second vote the three for D[r] Patterson came over to Hare.

I have therefore lost no reputation, it being generally understood that the family influence of M[r] Hare was not [to][1] be resisted.

I wait for M[r] Correa: and propose setting out with him to Virginia.

In mean time I remain as usual with great respect

Dear Sir Your obliged friend   THOMAS COOPER

RC (MHi); endorsed by TJ as received 11 Sept. 1818 and so recorded in SJL. RC (DLC); address cover only; with PoC of TJ to David Meade Randolph (1798–1825), 21 Dec. 1818, on verso; addressed: "Thomas Jefferson Esq Monte-cello Virginia"; stamp canceled; franked; postmarked Philadelphia, 1 Sept.

THIS UNIVERSITY: the University of Pennsylvania.

[1] Omitted word editorially supplied.

From Robert Miller (1775–1861)

SIR Philad^a Septr 1st 1818

I Take the Libberty of Enclosing for your inspection, a few Heads of a Subject I have been Employ'd in for Some Months. I cannot Suppose it is Strange to you, but certainly it is to myself. chance and a Little spare time has Enabled me to Go a Length that Alarms myself. Yet I Should think the pursuit of Knowledge and Truth Should not be Laid asside, meerly to please the caprices of Self Styl'd Learn'd Men. I Know not any of the Dead Languages, and Scarcely my own, I have not practised Study. Nor never could comprehend the confused and forced Manner of our Grammar, hence you will Excuse the inaccuraces of one presuming to Occupy your time with what probably you may think Nonsense, but Should I find you Either have Known or can Look favourably on it, your advise (as far as you may feel warranted) whether any part thereof Should come to Light would be Verry acceptable. no man yet Knows it of my acquantance and Knowing the Aspersions that ignorance and prejudice cast on what they think innovations, you may be deter'd from Saying Any thing to one Totally unaquanted, but Should you think it worth Notice, Mr Henry Clay of Kentucky can inform you who I am. and whether any danger could be Apprehended from that Sourse.

I have made out a Kind of Dictionary of most of the words necessary to retranspose the Epic and which will Enable any one to Read Ancient history and Know Every character. I find it opens an immense field to the mind, and no End to figures, but unfortunately it involves with all the Languages,—or Caballas, the whole History of the Bible—a chapter of which containing as Great a Variety of Characters as any I Enclose

I am sir your Verry Ob^t & Hb^l Servt   ROBERT MILLER

[The?] words in Italicks tell plainly the progress the form, and the change, observe the [word?] Even in 59. and 64.

RC (DLC); corner torn; between dateline and salutation: "Mr Th^o Jefferson"; endorsed by TJ as received 11 Sept. 1818 and so recorded in SJL.

Robert Miller (1775–1861), merchant and public official, was a native of Albemarle County. At the age of nine he moved with his parents to Madison County, Kentucky, where they acquired a large tract of land. Miller's father gave him some of this property, situated in what in 1798 became the town of Richmond, where Miller ran a farm and an inn. By 1805 he and his brother William had a shop in Lexington, Kentucky, and three years later they were also doing business in Glasgow, in nearby Barren County. Sometime in 1805 or 1806 Miller became a creditor of Aaron Burr and his ally Harman Blennerhassett and thus became entangled in Burr's machinations to seize Spanish territory in the West. After suing both men for debt, Miller took possession of Blennerhassett's estate on a Virginia (later West Virginia) island in the Ohio River. Miller farmed hemp there until March 1811, when a fire shut down this operation. Later that same year he patented a machine to process flax and hemp. Back in Kentucky, Miller resumed his mercantile pursuits, which occasionally brought him to Philadelphia. He also served as Richmond's postmaster from at least 1810 until his removal in 1829, and he was active as a Freemason in the Lexington and Richmond lodges. Miller represented Madison County in the Kentucky Senate in 1829 and 1834–38. He died at his farm near Richmond (William H. Miller, *History and Genealogies of the Families of Miller ... and Brown* [1907], 54, 119, 122–4; Clay, *Papers*, vols. 1 and 3; Kentucky State Historical Society, *Register* 40 [1942]: 264; 41 [1943]: 328; 43 [1945]: 138; Lexington *Kentucky Gazette and General Advertiser*, 22 Jan. 1805; Miller to Paul Fearing, 2 Aug. 1807 [OMC: Samuel P. Hildreth Collection]; Grand Lodge of Kentucky, *Proceedings* [1808]: 11; [1809]: 12; [1810]: 26; [1818]: 55; Lexington *Reporter*, 30 Apr. 1808, 17 Mar. 1810, 4 May 1811; Lexington *Kentucky Gazette*, 12 Sept. 1809, 28 Aug. 1815, 7 Sept. 1837; William H. Safford, *The Blennerhassett Papers* [1891]; *Miller v. Burr* [16 Nov. 1809–3 Apr. 1811], Washington Co., Ohio, Court of Common Pleas Record Book, 5:134–8; *List of Patents*, 99, 643, 649; Richmond, Ky., *Globe*, 24 Jan. 1810; Martin R. Andrews, ed., *History of Marietta and Washington County, Ohio, and Representative Citizens* [1902], 111–2; Baltimore *Niles' Weekly Register*, 26 Dec. 1829; gravestone inscription in Richmond Cemetery, Ky.).

ENCLOSURE

Notes on Occult Knowledge by Robert Miller (1775–1861)

[ca. 1 Sept. 1818]

Atoms are Natures Laws Seperate and apart, they are Eternal and obtain from fate.

Seeds are their Declinations or unions in planting all her various fields of changes.

Heaven is the[1] Seat of their union, or House of Light and Life and they are the Stars which Enlivn it. the Moon their Disposition to unite or womb of all unions. the Sun Light, Life and cause, yet born after the Stars & Moon and is the God of Nature, and Star of its Day, He when Spoken of as one Operates his changes by the power of four, fire, Air, water and Earth, or Father Mother, Son and Generations

Declination is advancing from Sup^s Mundi to Mundi and is calculated by the Square of the Distance it has Descended—or in their Language Melted into Nature Operations, thro her crucible, and here you will find the Origin of the Great Newtons problem, and is wrong interpreted.

Man is the intilligence of fire, or God in S^s M. Made Mortal by the change into M. but yet remains Governour of Nature being its Mind, Sense Soul and Reason, Woman that of Air. his Life Motion, womb and Multiple Hence the field for Gods of the first Order, and their Declentions, or unions untill the come to the period of Daemons, Shades of Mortallity, and witches Ghosts &c^a. at a farther Stage towards Entering Natures first form, they Assume the character of Prophets, Priests, Statesmen, Soldiers, Servants, Kings &c^a. According to the Period of the form spoken of. always keeping an Eye to the Earth and its Divisions as a Resting place for the fleshly man—

form is the world, but those worlds or forms are continually on the Decline of S^s M and union in M, and although time is nothing, nor Date Ever Given. Except in comparison of the past present & future, yet Each form of a Moment Possesses all the Powers of a world of 12 Months, and is only distinguished by the progress in Creation or union[2] in M. or properly the Season of the year, and to Each form with various powers are Given all the intelligences and Creations or unions of that Season, but Each form when arive at its Zenith or Mid-day of its operation is Seized by the Succeeding Stronger Atraction and is Said to weary, to Sicken, to Get afraid, to Tremble and many other Comparisons, from that Moment, Transmuting into its Superior untill Totally Destroyed or Changed, which is Death in that Life. and they Rise Again in the Next after three days. or the power of the Two who began and this third Now obtain'd—See the figure, and is the Spark taken from the Ashes which kindles Natures New fire, and the Phoenix who had burnt herself. but Rises from those Ashes, this New form possessing the Threefold power. and Given Male & female Quallitys in Sex, or Six, and in Generation, and is the first Compleate form in Natures Great operation[3] her former being only Shades of forms, or thoughts of Declensions, this, is the Period and power of Epicurus, who is truly a Sensuallist.

you will find that all the ancients Names, are only personifications of the acts of powers. and Mathematically Established, the writers are all of them. the Seasons, Depicting the Elemental combat of that time in Such Character as they may Choose, whether, of the Statesman or power of combining, the Priest, or power of the Suns instruction or union the Historian or power of Growth, the Warior or power of combating and uniting the Kill'd of S^s M in M—or causing the prisoners, the taken five to Serve as Slaves in the New Nations of forms, or Kings the full power of any form when at its Mid-day operation &c^a—

Planets are the Gates, and pillars, and Mountains, &c^a of Natures Heaven; and are the Seven Great Arches thro which this God Man had to Go Ere he was Made in M, and his badge Must be the Star with 6 points to Denote the Labours of Change, and his Heavenly and Noble Lineage, and by which he was Enabled to Enter the 7th Gate and See Light and Life.

Milky way, is the Disposition of the first Stars or Laws in S^s M to Decline, Day is Motion or operation

Night, Disposition to unite, Dream, concoction, and House of womb of Day

Evening—first Hearing or feelings towards the coming Night of formation unto Life

Morning—first Glimerings of Light as Motion in any operation, Shade or form

Mountain. Laws of Nature unmelted, or but in Some Small degree. they Contain the Mines from which She is to dig her wealth, and by their feet are the Valleys of her Molten Laws, wherein run the Rivers of her powers of Motion or union. Even unto the Sea, or Summit of any form, and unto the Great Salt Sea or Stage of that Summits Decline into the Succeeding in those Mountains Nature finds the 12 precious Stones or Originall Powers of the Months which are the Great Generation the $\square^{SM}$ or 4 by $\angle^M$ or three = 12. and are the Signs thro which She is obldiged to Drive her now Tamed, but Glorious Sun. Amongst these Parnassus Stands preeminent, as being the first union of Natures Laws and on whose Summit the Gods did Truly rest, and from[4] whose base Sprung the immortal water, which Gave being and place or Name and fame, to all her forms, and Heroes— Hardness, is to be in S^s M, and Soft in M. these are drawn in Comparisons as Adam-ant. Natures Original Laws, Marble or Mother of forms, &c^a Stones, Laws yet indeclined. Rocks Laws Declined Measurably—Steel Iron &c^a. Laws in Natures crusible,—Gold, Silver and Bras, are Laws fill'd with Laws of union, then turning their face and Travelling in Declination and Lastly uniting Mercury, where the Dreadfull, but Loving fights of the Elements take place,—and Although but a Moment of time, Occupys Almost all Ancient History.

Ancients. are the Laws and powers of Nature, the Son of Man Mind or thought Set in Order as in a field, and Each Given full power to officiate. all creations and operations of which are in powers, or in fire and Air. for all History Ends when the Last union of forms take place and few reach that period. Every thing on our Earth Necessary to Enhance belief, and inculcate really, must be reflected. but as the Shade in the Glass is Right for Left So this in continually Right for Left. and in All <u>Epic</u>, and Nature is Given to perform in imagination by fire and Air what she really does in the year by the form—and in Men or their transactions. the time is placed back that fond imagination may have Scope. and that the Strongest passion of the Mind for the Marvellous may be Gratifyed without finding out the Secret—

Hence Julius Caesar. the enlightening power of the plant or Grape is attacked in the open Senate of Heaven, in July (Caesar being possession and a Propper Name for his House of 12 months[5]) by the clammy, and the Brutish Hard Quallity of Ripening, and pursed, or united in body, having drawn his cloak over him—and Cleopatra, or Great Matron of the Clay of the Oath or union. Lives during all the period of Some half a Dozen Emperors or Kings, and has Amours, fairly with all—

Troy is the first Detachd Atractions in union, and Greece a farther Stage and Troys form was Destroy'd by the rising one of Greece, after 10 years &c^a or by the form of 10, which is the united power of 4. the 3. and the 2 & 1. and is the Sum total of first power in uniting. and foundation of our figures

Alexander is the intelligence of the first of Natures created forms. and Truly the Son of Olympia, or the House of Natures Heaven, or Declination of Natures Laws in forming, at which time and place all the Celebrated powers of Nature Truly Met. and the war being Just over Agreed to play, or run &c^a the Olympiads of 5. or full Expiration of four Shews Exactly the Moment Designed—by the Name—

Shepherds. are the intelligences of the first thoroughly tamed and innocent Powers to Natures use. and which She can Now Eat or wear—and So of the Different Grades of beasts, whom She makes in her <u>field</u> of prepared Laws, ferocious or tame in proportion to the Squares of their Distances from S^s M—

Birds are the first flying intelligences in Air and before the field was Thoroughly formd they began. they are Also in Grades by the same Rules—untill finally and Lastly the Cock whose threefold crows or calls are heard by the awakers of Natures present Night.—

And the Ass. the Meanest beast of burthen is the Last of this Shade of hearts, and who really Goes over the passage or Bridge into the border of the Next—

in Language the whole Hemisphere of the Heavens of cause is **A**. and occupies or Should occupy an Extent of 40° of Voice, or Mouth, the Mouth and its organs being Nature turnd outside in, and having her Head of Mind and Reason. her Neck to Support it and Grant a passage to her Transmutations, her Stomack and body to Digest and Circulate &cᵃ and her hands of fire and Air. and ful of water and Earth—Air is **E** and the base and fellow of **A** their Son is **I**, and their circumferator or Growth is ○. but in the first Degree Should be but $\frac{3}{4}$ths of a circle—a □ is power Not in union and a Circle is powers in operation or in Naturs Hands:—the Diphtongs are Declinations of these Two Vowels and Semi Vowels to Each Other and Should be 6—the Base or real Consonants are the Lines of Boundary to these in their Various progress. and they also have their Servants—the first Should Stand on their own Base or be Squared by their own power. the Last are Mutable and assume Various characters in the Change,—**A** contains the Greatest Lattitudes of Voice or the air issued from the Mouths. and **E** Should the Least. and are the fire and air of Speech by which this Minor Nature man conveys his figures unto other intilligences—these forms, figures, Spaces, Letters, words Types, and all this Mystical Language of Printers. and which were all born with it on the day it is Said to have been found out. Just as if the first Ship had been dropped down to Man fully Rigged. and Labels on Every part. to Give the Green Seaman their Names.—all these Reasons Leave No doubt but that they the Writers of Ancient History understood printing well—the Italick Character is M. and the Roman Sˢ M. the different forms Given to the Same Letter in Each Denote the Stage of Declination. Nor can the Multiple of 5 or 12 be used until **I** is found, and he is the fifth of pythagoras and the first Music of Natures Spheres.

Also in this uniting operation are found the bases of all the Games we have, of Dice, and of Quoits, of chess and of cards, the Last being the Moons thirteen Houses by the power of the 4 Elements Who Shall possess, and here again is the Ace or fate. the King and Queen Natures Governours, and their Son **I**, and their spots Should be the Days of the Year—

Natures Moons Quarters are Love, copulation conception and birth— first Declination of Sˢ M. to M.—the Great Square **A.B**. Declines into **C.D**. but touching at **D** they decline at an angle of forty five, and being joyn'd, the power of **A** is Lessen'd one Half.

Hence they proceed in the work of creation, and Spend 6 Days or operations, and on the 7ᵗʰ arive in Heaven again, but including the passive Houses belonging to M. they Have form'd 12. and are the 12 Months Active and passive of our year, & Signs of our Zodiack—the Great Square having Displayed himself in **C.D**. is 4 his full powers in Sˢ M. and must finish the Square of himself, to complete Natures wheel, in the Passage of the Next. **I** finishes, and Covers the Same Base as **A.B** and is Natures Perfect form—and is in the 3ᵈ Great House, and 5ᵗʰ Division of Natures powers. **A**. there being one, in the Next the work is finished. Giving the Bases of almost all Geometry, Arithmetick, Square and Cube, and Lografhms.

their opinion then of Creation in Nature is that the Sun first Descends from the Summit of Libra, and So it must be, for the first and Original Sun of Nature contain in him the Life of it all. the power of all that he Now Displays. Hence they Describe Him Departing from there. with intent and power to Hunt Shoot and Scourge. this he does by Meeting Nature on the

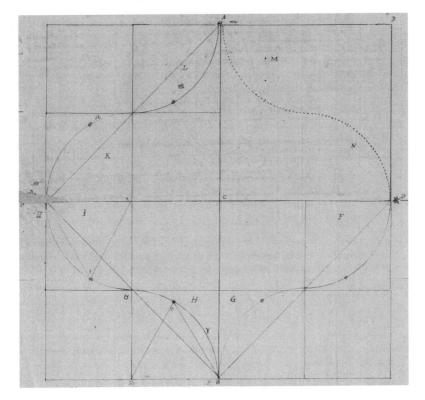

fields of Capricorn, that climbing Goatherd, where he begins his Tour and Declines to a Circle, and from that Moment he is 6 Days at Labour, on the 7th he Rests, and 8th he circumvents or circumcises, at ○.

this Side of her Square is the base or Depth[6] of Each Sign in this figure. and also the Side of an Issosseless Triangle, which join'd by half its force to a Mate forms the Shield of David, the Star of a prince, and is the Newborn King of Nature rising on her Horison, which will be weighed in the ballance at Libra or born of the Virgin—

After this if you will Square Nature full House by four, you will have the complement of her power During the Gaming and racing Season of the whole powers for her Prises. this will Divide the present Greatest Square of four, and now 16, into 64 and is the Dice board for Chess &c[a].

you will also find that this young prince Quicken'd into Life as **I** the forerunner is born at Libra. this pound of Troy—having passed into his 9th Month.

drop a perpendicular Down this Issesseless Triangle, and you have the first right angld Triangle. and this is done in Natures Last Division of S[s] M. and union in M. which is the root of Most part of the first book of Euclid— and root of Square & Cube &c[a]—many additional figures arise in Natures Successive changes. that time will not[7] permit to incert—

Plowing is fires first operation in Natures field, Just made ready for the crooked share of the binding Laws of S^s M. and hence the Naked plow-man of Hesiod.—to Reap is the produce thereof and which is immediate or the Next added particle. hence he is also then Naked.—

to plow with an Ox and an Ass cannot be, as one is the Great Support of the Rising 6 forms, and the Other the burthen bearer; and Death like Brayer of the Last of the Declining 6.—and like the Olive tree often Gets his head into it.—or puts it on at the window and Brays to alarm all the congregation &c^a—his young Denotes a verry Late Stage of the Declining form.—

the Stages in our Language are the four Elements or powers in S^s M. Given E[. . .] to M—^{8}

Deut. chap^t 28th—Moses the Speaker is figure, or Size throughout one form, or world Speaking the Effects of the sun on Nature thro a whole operation

1st—And it shall come to pass, if Man feel the first Ray, and inhale constantly, from the Living heats of the Sun, to be Enlighten'd, and to unite by all the powers of the Present heats (or unions) which I have united this Moment, that increasing Sun will rise thy form to perfection, and perfect thee above all the figures of the Mass.

2^d And all these powers of Growth Shall come to thee, and Successively, and per-petually fall into thee, if thou art in the path of the increasing Life of the Sun.

* 3^d. Blessed. (enlarg'd) Shalt thou be in the powers, and Blessed Shalt thou be in the preparations

4. Blessed Shall be thy first concoctions, and Declinations of the preparing powers, and the Produce of unions, and increase of their Meltings, & fat-ness of their cohesions.

5th Blessed Shall be the womb, and the unions.

6. Blessed Shalt thou be when thou Atractest, And Blessed Shalt thou be when thou formest (or expandest)

Be 6 times finishes Natures labour on that form, and hence the other 6 are Declining upwards into the Superior and may be represented by this figure Shewing her Ascending, and changing periods Each of these has its Thousand. Equal 12000. one operation × 12 the operations of a form, is 144,000 or an Host—and here begins the Games of Dice, chess, cards &c^a—

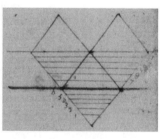

* 7. the Sun Shall cause the Elements that are advancing to be changed at their Entrance into thy form, they Shall come towards thee, one Element, but Disperse by the Magick of thy Seven Gates.—{or thus; they Shall come through the Door of haven but rise thro the Seven Arches—

* 8th the ascending Sun shall Give the power of preserving & forming thy con-coctions, or unions and Every Shade thereof, and he shall preserve thee^9 in the State he Gives thee.

9. And the Sun shall perfect your union, by his own power; as the Light of Life Now in you teaches, if thou continue associating, and inhaling his rays.

10. And all Shades of unions or powers thereof enjoyn thee, seeing thou hast a form by the Sun, and Shall fear and tremble as they come within the Sphere of thy Atractions. {See here the Heralds coats of Arms, Advancing in the forms of fear and trembling untill they become dovetail'd—

11 And the Sun Shall make thee[10] plentious in Effects, in the produce of thy Sevenfold powers and in the produce of their various unions. and in the produce of all the preparations which in the forms which the increasing Sun Season gave thee by the first Laws.

12 And the Sun Shall change for thee the Stores of his preparations, the House of Natures Life Shall operate the changes of thy various Shades in due Season, and they Shall descend as rain into thy form, and increase the work of thy power, and thou Shalt Henceforth lend unto many Shades, but no more borrow.

Golden Age

13. And the Sun Shall make thee the first, and not the last, be in powers courses only, and not in reallity Effect if that thou feel the first Motions of Enlivening Sol, which I embrace for thee this Shade to hold and to use them.

14. And thou Shalt not Move beyond powers, of Either fire or Air. Which I have in this form Given thee, to the beginning of your form or to the End, to pass into Other Shades to Serve them.

∗ 15 But it Shall come to pass if thou wilt not remain in voice first Season of the present Sun to Stand here as by Statute, according to the present Heat; that all these changes Shall Successively pursue, and amalgamate thee.

> { See 7 a 12 inclusive, where in his advance of 6 his is Chang'd
> { into a Double power, and Totally anihilated therein.

∗ 16. Chang'd Shalt thou be in thy powers, and chang'd Shalt thou be in the preperations[11]

17. Chang'd Shall be thy covering and its contents.

18. Chang'd Shall be the concoctions of thy powers, and the forms of thy frame, and increase of the Milk, the unions, and the fattenings of thy first insensible joynings.

19. Chang'd Shalt thou be when thou beginnest an operation, and Cursed Shalt thou be when finishest.

20. the Sun Shall Send upon thee[12] Atraction, and Shall vex thee by curtailing thy form every Shade thou Attemptest to Make, untill thou be chang'd, thy form Destroyed. and thou perish quickly, or vanish in the Embrace of Superior force. because of the changing Strength of thy Passion, whereby thou hast Passed out of the Power of my form or House

21 And the Sun Shall make the forerunner of Concoction cleave unto thee, untill he hath[13] chang'd thee from off the form with which thou Enterest, the frame

23. And the Laws of Nature that Gave[14] thee Life Shall be Shining with Melting heat, as Brass, and the unions within[15] thee Shall be rusting as Iron

24. the Sun Shall make the unitings of thy form, hard as powder and Dust: from the Living Laws of Concoction Shall it come, untill thou be chang'd—

25. And the Sun shall cause thee to be united to thy invaders. thou Shalt Enter them One with all thy might, but be Driven thro these Seven Gates, at the joyning them, And shalt be divided thro all the forms of their frame.

26. And thy unions, Shall be Meat into all the first Atoms of their forms, and to the joyning Parts thereof, and no power Shall prevent it.[16] or drive them off.

27. and the Sun will put into thee the power of procreation, and the Effects thereof, and with the unions thereof, and with the desire, from which thou canst not be return'd

28. the Sun Shall imbibe into thee, frensy, and rapid Motion, and the power of Cause.

29. And thou Shalt be uncertain in Midst of Operation, as those who Lay Still, and thou Shalt not increase in that Stage: and thou Shalt be only Bruised, and changd hereafter to your End, and no power can prevent thee.

∗ 30th thou Shalt unite an Air and another power Shall unite it. thou Shalt make a form, and thou Shalt Lose it: thou Shalt Lay a foundation, but cannot See the fruits thereof.

31. Thy union Shall be changed in a moment, and thou canst not feed thereon: thy Greatest Last Effort in union Shall be forced from thy Last Vew, and never will return: thy first unions Shall be given to thy Opressors, and no power in thee to prevent it.[17]

32. Thy Powers of fire, and of Air Shall be Given to a higher form, and thy Powers Shall See, and Sink Declining all the Long Operation: and there Shall be no ruling power in thy form.

33. The unions of thy form, and all thy Shades, Shall a frame Superior in Strength atract to it: and thou Shalt be only Squeezed and Bruised to your Last:

34. So that thou Shalt be unhing'd or chang'd in all the powers of increase which thou Shall Possess.—

35. the Sun Shall Smite thee in thy unions, and the unitors with a Great Season that cannot be chang'd, from thy Greatest power to thy Least.

36. the Sun Shall raise thee, and thy highest[18] figure which Surmounts thee, unto a form which neither thee nor thy prior forms have arived to; and there Shalt thou Serve other forms, preparing, and prepared.

37. And thou Shalt be the word, the Sentence, and the History, through all forms whither the increasing Life Shall lead thee.

∗ 38. Thou Shalt carry much Matter out into an operation, but Shall bring little back. for atractions Shall consume it.

39. Thou Shalt prepare forms, and Dress them, but cannot increase by their unitings. Nor Eat of the Grapes of their unions; for the first powers of Superior Atraction, Shall eat them.

40 Thou Shalt have interlockings thro all thy changing Edge, but thou Shalt not be Soften'd with their Meltings, nor anoint thyself with their cements, for thine interlockings Shall be chang'd, or cast his fruit.

41. Thou Shalt beget Intilligences of both Orders, but shall not enjoy them. they Shall go into the Grasp of the Strengthning Superior form.

42 all thy clasps of joynings, and produce of thy Greatest form, Shall, the Laws of Atraction consume.

43. The Strange Shade that Now is within thee, Shall rise above in Double Streng[th] and thou be Made proportionably weak thereby.

44. He Shall Lend thee Shapes in thy Declention. but thou Shalt not be able to [be] taken.[19] He shall be the Strongest and thou the weakest.

* 45. Moreover, all those cursing Motions Shall Successively Seize thee. by atraction and union, till thou be changed, because thou remainest not at the Stated form thou hadst when Spoken to by the Living Sun, nor Stand there to Keep the Statutes of that world—.

46. And those forms Shall Atract, and raise thee in their Strength, as a Sighn and wonder unto the following, and on all the Shades of forms untill thou art finish'd

47. Because thou continued not before the Sun, with the Life, and all its powers Given thee, and in abundance the Laws of these things. or forms being perfected.

48. Therefore Shalt thou Serve the increasing Shades, which the Sun Shall raise around thee: in Declining, and in Entring, and when joynd, and in the farthest Stage Towards change. Even when all Shade[20] of form is taken from thee, and he Shall yoke thee with the Strong Iron of Changing forms, and thy form Shall be drawn in untill he has changd thee.

49. And the Sun Shall bring a form upon thee. by heat, by the power of Concoction, as certain[21] as the Ray that Descendeth,[22] a form whose Motion is beyond your powers.

50. A form of strong Atractions, which Shall not regard the body of present Shade you have, nor Shew favour to the Declining Strength.

51. And he Shall unite thy unthoughtful[23] parts, and the cements of thy form untill thou be chang'd: which also Shall not leave thee either particle, power of Nourishment or Atraction, or the increase of thy Milky Shades, or of thy concoctions, untill he have chang'd thee.

52 And he Shall compress thee in thy powers, untill thy Greatest figures are drawn in, when[24] thou trustedethst, throughout all thy frame; and he Shall compress thee in all thy powers throughout all thy frame which the Sun hath Given thee.

53. And in the Last Stages, thou Shall chew assunder and atract[25] the Senseless particles of thy own frame, the particles produced of fiery powers and of Aires. which the sun thy Life hath Given thee, in the pressures, and Straitnings wherewith the coming forms Shall transmute thee.

* So that the intilligent particle that is changing among you, and knows not to which it belongs, his first power Shall turn against the yet Brother, and wife of his Bosom and against the minor intelligences which he Shall leave, the moment he is over—

55. So that he will not impart to any of them, of the changing Effects of his own power which he, Shall Atract the moment of Change: because he has nothing left on this Side, in the consuming change, and in the Strengthnings thereof, wherewith Coming forms Shall Straiten thee in all thy Last moments of form.

56. the Last tender and Delicate Airy intilligence among you, who at the moment of change, has no form to Stand on, Hence could not adventure to Set the sole of her feet upon the form, for Smallness, and Divisibility. Even her Disposition instantly changes, and her first thoughts are Evil[26] towards

the fire of her union or Present power, and towards her fiery intilligence, and towards her airy intelligence,

57. And towards her first Shade, form'd by her Sexual power as She passes the Line, (this is coming out between this feet) and towards the increase which She Shall have. for She Shall alternately consume them for want of all forms (things) or untill all her forms are again compleated: Secretly in the Transmutation and increasing Straitness, wherewith the advancing forms Shall contract thee in the Enlightening and Life increasing change.

58 If thou will not Stand (observe) at the words of thy form (nor seek to progress to Sentences or Lines) as imprinted in this present period,[27] that thou mayest Stay and worship this first Name of thy Sun, the Sun of thy Life.

59. then the Sun will make thy unions wonderfull (Doubly Great) and the unions of thy Laws of Nature, Even. Great unions, and of Long continuance; and Strong Motion and of one Shades continuance.

* 60 Moreover he Shall bring upon thee all the Diseases of Concoction, which you now Tremble for; and they Shall Cleave unto thee.

61 Also every Sickness and Every union, which is not written in this book. (Every union which you must pass thro untill perfected) them will the increasing Life of the Sun bring upon thee[28] untill thou be Chang'd.

62. And ye shall be left few in Number wheras ye were the whole Host of Natures Heaven, and your Number the Stars: because thou would advance beyond the period of Voice, of the Sun when he Gave thee[29] form.

63. And it shall come to pass, that, as the Sun Gave you Life, and Multiplyed your forms, So will he increase his Loving heats on you to change you, and to totally transpose your body; and thou Shall vanish at the Verge of the form thou art[30] passing over to.

64—And the Sun Shall unite thee among all unions, from one end of Concoction unto the other; and there thou Shall Serve other Suns other forms, which neither thine nor those that preceeded thee knew the Solidity of. Even Half Natures Laws prepared for use. or the Moment of chang from first State to Second Degree—

65. And among these Shades of forms Shall thou find no place, Neither Shalt the Semblance of body any more be thine: and the Sun Shall Give thee a Moving heart, and uniting Eyes, and the frame of Mind:

66 And thy Life shall hang on the pivot of Change at this moment, and thou Shalt Expect the fall Each Breath of Atraction, and union, and be without any assurance of prolongation:

67. In the Morning of the Last Breath on this Side, thou Shalt Say o that the Sun would Make it Evening, and in the Even (or first Glimmerings on the other side) thou Shall Say would to the Sun it were Morning. for the change, and for the Light which is Entered and Entering at both Eyes.

68 And the Sun Shall bring up to concoction or union again, with Great powers Sliver'd by his Rule, and wafted by the Breeze of His Spirit, by the power which I here shew you, you Shall cross it no more again: and you Shall be sold to the uniters, and be the Bands of all those Men & women, or forms, but no power of intelligence can change your Destiny.

MS (DLC: TJ Papers, 213:38073–6); entirely in Miller's hand; undated; edge trimmed and damaged; with concluding numbered list lacking a section 22.

In this document Miller draws on several traditions of occult knowledge in order to construct what may be best described as a hermetic worldview. Hermetic philosophy, which gained widespread acceptance during the Renaissance, is based on a collection of anonymous works variously attributed to the Egyptian deity Thoth or the Greek god Hermes Trimegistus, but most probably derived from second-century Gnostic thinkers. It aims at a complete understanding of the universe and man's position in it, deemed possible only after man's restoration to the primitive, divine status lost at the biblical fall. During the eighteenth and nineteenth centuries, hermetism resonated with the Christian primitivism of American radical religious reformers, especially Baptists, Congregationalists, Quakers, New Israelites, Swedenborgians and, later, Mormons. Restorationists like Miller believed that much universal knowledge and religious purity that had been lost could be retrieved from ancient philosophies as well as from the occult disciplines of kabbalism, astrology, and alchemy. Some of these ideas found their way into the mythology of Freemasonry and, in turn, the rise of Freemasonry in America fueled public interest in occultism. Miller and many other Freemasons probably became acquainted with British and American hermetic literature through the libraries of their Masonic lodges. Most of the concepts that make up Miller's worldview can be found in the popular works of William Lilly, the apocryphal "Erra Pater" and "C. Heydon," the Freemasons Andrew Michael Ramsay and Ebenezer Sibly, and Francis Barrett (Frances A. Yates, *Giordano Bruno and the Hermetic Tradition* [1964], esp. 1–19, 92–4; John L. Brooke, *The Refiner's Fire: The Making of Mormon Cosmology, 1644–1844* [1994], esp. 3–108; Lilly, *Christian Astrology* [London, 1659]; Pater, *The Book of Knowledge: Treating of the Wisdom of the Ancients* [Boston, (1790)]; Heydon, *Astrology* [London, 1792]; Ramsay, *The Travels of Cyrus* [Burlington, N.J., 1793]; Sibly, *A New and Complete Illustration of the Occult Sciences* [London, 1795]; Barrett, *The Magus, or Celestial Intelligencer; being a complete system of Occult Philosophy*, 3 vols. in 1 [London, 1801]; [Barrett], *The Lives of Alchemystical Philosophers* [London, 1815]).

The notion that ATOMS ARE NATURES LAWS . . . OBTAIND FROM FATE is central to Miller's cosmology. Borrowing from the first-century philosopher Lucretius (who himself drew on previous ideas, especially those of Democritus and Epicurus), Miller explains that everything in nature is composed of eternal, indivisible particles called atoms, which are constantly uniting and coming apart in transformation processes he called DECLINATIONS. But where Lucretius argued that these incessant changes occur completely at random, for Miller they are governed by the sun (the GOD OF NATURE), acting on the four basic elements of FIRE, AIR, WATER AND EARTH. The idea that all matter is composed of these four natural elements, not espoused by Lucretius, is fundamental to several older cosmologies, notably that of Plato, which hermetic thinkers since the Renaissance attempted to reconcile with Christianity. Miller's worldview combines a Neoplatonic approach to Christianity with the Kabbalah, a body of Jewish esoteric interpretations of the Old Testament that also flourished in Renaissance thinking (Lucretius, *On the Nature of Things*, books 1–2, in *Lucretius*, trans. William Henry Denham Rouse, Loeb Classical Library [1924], 2–187; Stephen Greenblatt, *The Swerve: How the World Became Modern* [2011], 73–4, 96, 185–8; David C. Lindberg, *The Beginnings of Western Science* [1992], 283; Allen G. Debus, *Man and Nature in the Renaissance* [1978], 16–26; Brooke, *Refiner's Fire*, 8, 11–2, 206; Sibly, *Occult Sciences*, 56–7; Barrett, *Magus*, 1:v–ix, 73–5, 2:33).

The earth, in Miller's cosmology, is described in alchemical terms, as a crucible where matter melts and transmutates, as well as in scientific terms, subject to Isaac Newton's law of gravitation. Thus, when changes come from superioris mundi (SUP^s MUNDI) or celestial worlds, the strength of their operations in the terrestrial realm (MUNDI) at a specific moment, is the SQUARE of what astronomers and astrologers also call declination, that is, the DISTANCE between the earth's equatorial plane and the sun's position at that moment on its apparent elliptical course around the earth. Miller understands man's declination from heaven to earth, or fall from grace, in kabbalistic terms. Man is accordingly an intelligence

(INTILLIGENCE) or immortal servant of the sun god in the superioris mundi (s^s m), but he becomes mortal once he descends to earth. Here he is GOVERNOUR OF NATURE, while woman is HIS LIFE MOTION, WOMB AND MULTIPLE, guaranteeing his perpetuation through reproduction (Lindberg, *Beginnings of Western Science*, 246–53; Sibly, *Occult Sciences*, 15, 56, 66; Ramsay, *Travels of Cyrus*, xix; Barrett, *Magus*, 1:13–21, 56–8, 85).

To Miller all FORMS of matter, including human beings, possess attributes and POWERS that depend on the SEASON OF THE YEAR, or the astrological configuration of the sky, at the moment of their birth. Similarly, the changes experienced during a form's lifetime are influenced by the twelve zodiacal signs associated with the sun's stations along its apparent path in the sky. THREE DAYS after a form's demise, its atoms recombine and give rise to a new one. This transition is epitomized by the mythical PHOENIX, which rises from its predecessor's ashes as a hermaphrodite form possessing the THREEFOLD POWER of Hermes multiplied by two (male and female), that is, the power of SIX. In Miller's view all forms have secret properties and behaviors. For example, the astrological PLANETS of Mercury, Venus, Sun, Moon, Mars, Jupiter, and Saturn can be interpreted as the SEVEN GREAT ARCHES through which man must pass after death on his way to eternal life. Mountains house the 12 PRECIOUS STONES, each corresponding to a zodiac sign and monthly power. These stones originate as distinct forms when the four elements undergo their transition from the celestial to the terrestrial worlds and are subjected to (or multiplied by) the threefold hermetic power. Miller believes that only through hermetic interpretation can one understand nature, perceived otherwise as a mere reflection, or Platonic SHADE, on our minds. He explains that historical events, such as the demise of JULIUS CAESAR, the destruction of TROY, and even the participation of ALEXANDER the Great in the Olympic games, parallel astrological occurrences, and that the true meaning of different earthly forms, be they SHEPHERDS, BIRDS, or LANGUAGE,

can be unveiled using number theories, especially that of PYTHAGORAS (Lindberg, *Beginnings of Western Science*, 248–9, 275–80; Pater, *Book of Knowledge*, 8, 10–1, 14–22; Heydon, *Astrology*, 1–4; Sibly, *Occult Sciences*, 20–1, 26, 94; Barrett, *Magus*, 1:39–40, 99–101, 158–9, 168–9; [Barrett], *Alchemystical Philosophers*, 185).

Miller uses a chart akin to those drawn by astrologers to represent his understanding of man's journey on earth, from birth through death to rebirth as a new form. Like most astrological horoscopes, Miller's scheme divides the sky into twelve sections (or houses) crossed by a circuitous line representing the apparent annual movement of the sun (☉). Each house also represents a period in man's life, under the influence of one of the twelve zodiac signs, seven of which the chart represents by their astrological symbols (♈ for Aries, ♉ for Taurus, ♊ for Gemini, ♋ for Cancer, ♌ for Leo, ♍ for Virgo, and ♎ for Libra). Miller's scheme illustrates the story of every human life through the archetypal story of Adam's fall from heaven (**A**) to earth (**D**) and his restoration back in heaven as the NEWBORN KING OF NATURE. As with most astrological interpretations, Miller's is highly idiosyncratic (Heydon, *Astrology*, 66–70, 210–22; Sibly, *Occult Sciences*, 154–7).

In the last pages of this document, Miller shows how his syncretic worldview can unveil the secrets buried in biblical texts. In his version of chapter 28 of Deuteronomy (DEUT. CHAP^T 28TH), God's curses on the unfaithful are interpreted as the human form's inability to change and be restored, that is, to achieve pleasure and reproduce, without the power of the sun. For example, Miller substitutes SUN for "Lord," POWERS OF GROWTH for "blessings," THY FIRST CONCOCTIONS for "the fruit of thy body," THE WOMB, AND THE UNIONS for "thy basket and thy store," CHANG'D for "cursed," AIR for "wife," and INTILLIGENCES OF BOTH ORDERS for "sons and daughters." Miller's interpretation calls to mind Lucretius's philosophy and erotic language (Lucretius, *On the Nature of Things*, 4.1037–

1287, in *Lucretius*, trans. Rouse, 356–77; Greenblatt, *Swerve*, 197–8).

Miller evidently continued to develop his hermetic cosmology long after sending this work to TJ. In a letter dated Glasgow, Kentucky, 8 Dec. 1829, he asked James Madison for his opinion on an enclosed (missing) "Confidential Communication on a Subject Pregnant with Good or Evil to the Human family, and of vital importance to this Union. Lucretius calls it (truly) the origin of things; it being that Science by which the Ancients invented, and yet Concealed the Machinery, this Airy Camoera Contains the patterns of all things, its value but one Talent. here numbers, Letters and Languages were made, Sciences and arts found parents, hence Every Government, Law, Religion, or building on Record are but so many Commemorators of one or more of those Hieroglifick Scenes" (RC in DLC: Madison Papers).

[1] Manuscript: "the the."
[2] Manuscript: "unin."
[3] Manuscript: "operatio."
[4] Manuscript: "from from."
[5] Manuscript: "monts."
[6] Preceding two words interlined.
[7] Manuscript: "mot."
[8] Page ends short at this point.
[9] Manuscript: "the."
[10] Manuscript: "the."
[11] In the margin to the left of this verse, perpendicular to text, Miller wrote (torn) "Declinations of the [. . .]."
[12] Manuscript: "the."
[13] Manuscript: "thath."
[14] Above and between preceding two words, Miller added "(is)."
[15] Above this word Miller added "(is)."
[16] Above and between preceding two words, Miller added "(them)."
[17] Above this word Miller added "them."
[18] Manuscript: "highgest."
[19] Manuscript: "takem."
[20] Above this word Miller added "things."
[21] Above this word Miller added "as swift."
[22] Manuscript: "Decendeth."
[23] Manuscript: "unthoughful."
[24] Manuscript: "wheen."
[25] Preceding two words interlined.
[26] Above this word Miller added "Atraction."
[27] Above this word Miller added "Book."
[28] Manuscript: "the."
[29] Manuscript: "the."
[30] Manuscript: "at."

From Thomas Cooper

DEAR SIR   Philad[a] Sep. 2. 1818

W[d] it not be well to get some thing like the inclosed inserted in the papers of Virginia, Kentucky, & Carolina, with a set of queries whe[r] this is not the time to ascertain if students cannot be taught medecine in Virginia by Virginians, as well as in Phila[a] by Virginians? Whe[r] the morals as well as the studies, and the expences also, of the sons of virginia planters, could not be as well superintended in Virginia as in Philadelphia? Whe[r] any of the teachers here, are known out of the State of Penns[a] except M[r] Hare, who is by no means advantageously known in Virginia. These and several other topics that will readily occur to you, may be worked to advantage at the present moment: & therefore I send you the inclosed. The Students here are exasperated at this election. —

So soon as I see M. Correa, I will settle with him when to visit your neighbourhood: in mean time, I am with much respect

Dear Sir Your obliged friend   THOMAS COOPER

I send papers by this post. I have inclosed a letter to Mr Wood of Petersburgh.

RC (MHi); postscript added in a different ink; endorsed by TJ as received 11 Sept. 1818 and so recorded in SJL. RC (DLC); address cover only; with PoC of TJ to John Wood (1791–1850), 9 Dec. 1818, on verso; addressed: "Thomas Jefferson Esq Montecello Virginia"; franked; postmarked Philadelphia, 2 Sept. Enclosures not found.

From Thomas Cooper

DEAR SIR   september 3. 1818

M. Correa and I will set out about the 16th. He will have to stay 2 or 3 days in Washington: we then set off for your Place.

In mean time, I think the present opportunity afforded us by Hare's election ought not to be lost; but the moment should be taken to appeal to the Parents in Virginia, on the strange infatuation of sending their children to be educated here, when they [could]^1 have that better done at home; whether for general or medical education About 300 new Students come here yearly. A greater proportion come from Virginia who do not graduate, than from other places: for Virginia affords more young men who come merely for the purposes of general education. Hence, the proportion of Students from Virginia here, will be greater than the following table of mere graduates w^d indicate. The following are the graduates last year, 10 Ap. 1818.

Massach.	1	Now, suppose the annual supply 300 as D^r
N. Yk	1	Chapman states to me it is: then 87 : 38 :: 300 :
N. Jersey	3	130+
Penn^a	21	But from the consideration above ment^d, that
Delaware	2	fewer graduate in proportion from Virginia, I
Maryland	3	sh^d take the annual supply from Virginia alone
Virginia	38	at 150 who spend annually on the average
N. Carol.	4	500$ — 75,000.
S. Carol.	7	A medical school with you (that is in your state)
Georgia	2	w^d arrest all the southern & western Students.
Kent^y	3	I w^d come on earlier, but I wait for M. Correa,
Mississ.	1	whose judgement and experience will greatly
Louisiana	1	aid our consultations. I am as usual with
	87.	great respect

Dear Sir Your friend and faithful Servant   THOMAS COOPER

RC (DLC); endorsed by TJ as received 11 Sept. 1818 and so recorded in SJL. RC (DLC); address cover only; with PoC of TJ to Joseph Milligan, 9 Dec. 1818, on verso; addressed: "Thomas Jefferson Esq Montecello Virginia"; franked; postmarked Philadelphia, 3 Sept.

[1] Omitted word editorially supplied.

From James Monroe

DEAR SIR   Albemarle Sep[r] 3. 1818

mr Poinsett, whose name & character are I presume well known to you will have the pleasure of giving you this introduction. He was employd very usefully in S° America, several years, under mr Madison, & had previously travelled thro' most of the European countries & particularly Russia, by whose Sovereign he was known, & treated with much attention. I expected to have presented him personally, but as he returns to Charlottesville to night that will not be in my power. He is of S° Carolina.

mr Harrison a very respectable gentleman, of our own country, will have the pleasure of accompanying mr Poinsett, whom, I also take the liberty of presenting to you—

with great respect yr friend   JAMES MONROE

RC (NNPM); endorsed by TJ as received 4 Sept. 1818 and so recorded in SJL.

Joel Roberts Poinsett (1779–1851), diplomat and public official, began his education under his father in his native South Carolina, continued it under Timothy Dwight in Connecticut, and then spent roughly a decade studying and traveling in Europe, 1796–1800, 1801–04, and 1806–09. In 1810 the Madison administration dispatched Poinsett to Buenos Aires as commercial agent, and a year later he was appointed consul general for Buenos Aires, Chile, and Peru. After a tumultuous term marked by his direct involvement in Chilean political and military affairs, he returned to South Carolina in 1815. Poinsett represented Saint Philip and Saint Michael Parish in the South Carolina House of Representatives, 1816–18, where he actively supported internal improvements, and he served in the United States House of Representatives, 1821–25. Under a special appointment from President James Monroe, he visited Mexico and Cuba to report on the potential for revolution there, 1822–23. From this experience Poinsett published *Notes on Mexico* (Philadelphia, 1824; Poor, *Jefferson's Library*, 7 [no. 351]; TJ's copy in DLC, with authorial inscription [possibly trimmed] "Thom. Jefferson from the Author"), and in 1825 he became the first American envoy extraordinary and minister plenipotentiary to Mexico. His service there was again controversial, and after being asked to leave by the Mexican government, Poinsett obtained his own recall from the United States government and returned to South Carolina in 1830. There he served another term in the state house of representatives (1830–31) and one in the state senate (1836). During this time Poinsett became the leader of the Unionist faction in the state, opposing Nullification and allying himself with President Andrew Jackson. From 1837–41 he was Martin Van Buren's secretary of war. Poinsett was an active Mason, a member of the American Philosophical Society from 1827, and founder and first president of the National Institute for the Promotion of Science and the Useful Arts, the collections of which were later absorbed by the Smithsonian Institution. His interest in horticulture and botany was recognized in 1836 when one of the plants he brought back from Mexico, the *Poinsettia pulcherrima*, was named in his honor (*ANB*; *DAB*; N. Louise Bailey and others, eds., *Biographical Directory of the South Carolina Senate, 1776–1985* [1986], 2:1286–90; James Fred Rippy, *Joel R. Poinsett, Versatile American* [1935]; PHi: Poinsett Papers; *PTJ*, esp. 34:628; Madison, *Papers, Pres. Ser.*, esp. 2:487–8, 500, 502n, 3:164–5; *JEP*, 2:188, 190, 3:441, 443–4 [13, 18 Nov. 1811, 7, 8 Mar. 1825]; APS, Minutes, 19 Jan. 1827 [MS in PPAmP]; *Edinburgh New Philosophical Journal* 20 [1836]: 412; Washington *Daily National Intelligencer*, 20 Dec. 1851).

From Stephen Cathalan

Dear Sir   Marseilles the 7ᵗʰ September 1818—

Mr Poinsot, <u>now</u> <u>at</u> <u>Cette</u>, Recommended to me, by a Relation of mine, Mr J^s Cathalan of <u>Marseillan</u>, has Requested me to Send him a Letter in his Behalf addressed by me to you, & to be Forwarded by him Self; (by 2ta)

I observed, that after Such and Emminent Services for your Country in the highest Stations, you was Retired in the Country, from Public & private affairs, & that it would be <u>Inconsiderate</u>, for me, to trouble you (from the quiet Life, it was Time for you to enjoy =with your good Family, Friends, Books and your Farms,=) about <u>Private</u> & <u>Selves</u> Business,[1] or Individual's Concerns, who having Resided in the united States, Even in the State <u>of</u> <u>virginia</u>, Ought to know that there is, as every where Else, Resp^ble Merchants, Notaries Publics, Even Lawyers, to attend, when Duly Empowered, in behalf of these who Left that Country, to the Transactions or Settlement of their Pending affairs;—& that in this Instance, or any other Similar ones, it Should be, <u>with</u> <u>the</u> <u>Greatest</u> <u>Reluctance</u>, I would Claim your attendance or Protection, on the <u>private</u> Demand of Mr Poinsot; whilst, it appears, by his own Letter to me of the 21st July last, =he had already applied <u>before</u> to Mr Barnet Consul of the United states at Paris, who Sent him my adress of his own hand writing,= (which Mr Poinsot inclosed in his said Letter to me) with this addition, =<u>ami de</u> Mr Jefferson, qui etait L'ami de Kosciuzko,= that is to Say <u>as</u> <u>I</u> <u>hav-ing</u> <u>the</u> <u>honor</u> <u>to</u> <u>be</u> <u>one</u> <u>of</u> <u>your</u> <u>Friends</u>, it is to me <u>only</u> <u>or</u> <u>alone</u>[2] <u>to</u> <u>Trouble you</u>, not only for me, &[3] my Friends, but even for the ones of my Friends & Relations!—of Course Such Refflexions, Laid me to Suspect, that Consul Barnet, probably, as I hope, also one of your Friends, may have declined to favor him with his own Letter direct to you;—& I don't know, whether Mr Poinsot has, or not, applied also, Before, for Such a Letter to you, to h. Exc^cy Albert Gallatin our Min-

lso your
friend;

ister P. P^ry at Paris‸ Both being natives of the Same Country, Geneva, or it's neighborough;—

why then, did I object, Mr Poinsot, on his applying to my Relation,
near Cette, has he asked me a Letter for you?—I was Lying to, or in
Statu quo, when a few Days ago, Thro' a mutual Friend of him, M^r
Poinsot, & of me, Mr Goudet also of Geneva, now here, handed me
further Details, whereof the herewith annexed is a Part, viz. a Copy
of a Letter from (1) our Friend, late, General Kosciusko of the 3^d
June 1817 in his Behalf adressed to you, which, Mr Poinsot Sent to
you, with his Documents about his Claims, whereof he is Since Deprived of an acknowledgment, of your having Received the Sames;

I, now, Beg You, my Dear Sir, to Inform him if you have Received
Said Letters & Documents & in that Case, whom you may have been
So kind as to charge of the Pursuit or Settlment of his Claims, in
order he may, under your Patronage, Correspond, Direct, with him;

I will be very Gratefull to you, for what you may have already
Done, or Will Do, for Mr Poinsot, hoping that you will Excuse him
and me, for our Importunity & my Own Appology, in this Instance;

I have the Honor to be with Great Respect

Dear Sir Your most obed^t Obliged & Devoted Servant

STEPHEN CATHALAN.

(1) when I Say =our Friend= it is because I became a Friend to Gal Kosciusko, with
whom I became personally acquainted at Paris, at our Late Friend Joel Barlow, on or
about the 18th Brumaire of Buena Parte; & Before Joel Barlow was appointed Minister
P.P^ry of the U.S. near this Emperor. whose foolish Invasion in Russia, was the Cause
of the Death at wilna of our Friend Said Joel Barlow, when Going to meet with Said
Emperor in the Year 1813—

RC (MHi); addressed: "Thomas Jefferson Esqr Late President of the United
States Monticello"; endorsed by TJ as
received 6 Dec. 1818, with additional notation of "(Poinsot)," and so recorded
in SJL. Enclosed in Peter Poinsot to TJ,
12 Sept. 1818. Enclosure: Tadeusz Kosciuszko to TJ, 3 June 1817.

AMI DE MR JEFFERSON, QUI ETAIT
L'AMI DE KOSCIUZKO: "friend of Mr.
Jefferson, who was the friend of Kos-

ciuszko." Napoleon (BUENA PARTE)
seized power in France in a coup launched
on 18 Brumaire (9 Nov.) 1799 (Owen
Connelly and others, eds., *Historical Dictionary of Napoleonic France, 1799–1815*
[1985], 87).

[1] Manuscript: "Busisness."
[2] Preceding two words present in the
middle of catchphrase but absent at top
of following page.
[3] Preceding two words interlined.

From Archibald Stuart

Dear Sir Staunton 8th Sepr 1818.

I presume you have seen Mr Wirt's Sketches of the life of Patrick Henry; and that he denies Mr H. favored the project of Establishing a Dictator during the revolutionary War.—Even doubts respecting events of such recent date tend greatly to impair the credit of History.—There are many now living who witnessed the part Mr Henry took on that subject.—After the Assembly was dispersed at Charlottesville in the year 1781 it met in Staunton where Mr Geo. Nicholas a member of that body proposed that a Dictator be established in this Commonwealth who should have the power of disposing of the lives and fortunes of the Citizens thereof without being subject to account.—In support of this resolution he observed that the Country was overrun by the Enemy and that the Operation of the Gov^t was nearly suspended:—That although the powers proposed to be confered were very great the character he proposed to fill the office would remove all apprehensions arising from the abuse of them—That this character was Genl Washington—That he was our fellow citizen, that we had a right to command his services and that he had no doubt but that on such an Occasion he would obey the call of his country.— In the course of his speech he refered to the practice of the Romans on similar occasions.—After Mr Nicholas sat down Mr Henry addressed the Chair; he observed it was immaterial to him whether the Officer proposed was called a Dictator or a Governor with enlarged powers or by any other name yet surely an Officer armed with such powers was necessary to restrain the unbridled fury of a licentious enemy and concluded by seconding the Motion.—

On the other hand it was contended by Mann Page from Spottsylvania and several other Members;—That our Affairs were not desperate, That the pressure we felt was but temporary, That the Gov^t was still efficient, That the spirit of the people was unbroken, That it was unbecoming in their representatives to damp their ardor by an Act of despair—That they had equal confidence with the mover of the resolution in the Integrity of Genl Washington, but that he nor no other man ought to be armed with such unlimited powers—That they well knew he would not accept the Office—That if he was willing to accept it, he was better employed at the head of the Army than in the exercise of powers which would render him odious to the people— After a lengthy discussion the proposition was negatived.—

I was present at this discussion and could easily discover that the proposition was not relished by the people. Their feelings were of a different character; had the enemy advanced they would have risen in mass to repel them.—

I communicated these facts to you shortly after they took place.—

I am yours most sincerely   ARCH[D] STUART

Tr (MH: Sparks Collection of American Manuscripts); entirely in the hand of Jared Sparks; at foot of text: "The Hon[ble] Tho[s] Jefferson Esq." Recorded in SJL as received 16 Oct. 1818.

For William WIRT's discussion of Patrick Henry's views on establishing a dic-

tatorship in Virginia, see Wirt, *Sketches of the Life of Patrick Henry* (Philadelphia, 1817; Poor, *Jefferson's Library*, 4 [no. 131], 204–7, 231). Stuart may have COMMUNICATED his recollection of the proposal to TJ orally in 1781 (*PTJ*, 6:85–6n).

Albemarle County Court Order Concerning a Proposed Road

[8 Sept. 1818]

Brightberry Brown Horsley Goodman & John Slaughter three of the persons appointed by a former order of this Court to view the ground from the corner of Charles L Bankheads fence near Charlottsville to the Secretarys ford thence across the river and down its northern side to the mouth of Chappel branch through which the road is proposed to be opened and substituted[1] by Thomas J Randolph and Thomas Jefferson in place of the present road leading from the Orange fork near Lewis's ferry downwards throw the lands of Richard Sampson Thomas J. Randolph and Thomas Jefferson to the Chappel branch made their report in these words to wit "in obedience &[c]" Whereupon on hearing the said Thomas J. Randolph and Thomas Jefferson in support of and Nicholas H Lewis alone in opposition to the establishment of said road by their Attorneys as well as the testamoney of divers witnesses who were sworn and examined and all circumstances weighed the Court is of opinion that it is better that the said road proposed as a substitute[2] be opened and substituted in lieu of the old road: Therefore it is considered and accordingly ordered by the Court that leave be granted to the said Thomas J. Randolph and Thomas Jefferson to open the road according to the report of the said viewers and to discontinue and shut up the old road for which the new one now established and received as a substitute.

Thomas J. Randolph is appointed surveyor of the road from the corner of Charles L. Bankheads fence to the forks of the road below Jeffersons Mill leading through north[3] Milton and the hands of

Thomas M Randolph Thomas J Randolph on the north side of the rivanna river and the hands of Charles L Bankhead are assigned him to keep the same in good repair.

MS (Albemarle Co. Order Book [1818–19], 150–1); in Alexander Garrett's hand; on p. 147 and applying to this entry: "At a Court Continued and held for Albemarle County the 8ᵗʰ day of September 1818. Present } John Harris James Old John Goss and Thomas Wood } Justices"; immediately after this entry: "Ordered that the Court be adjourned until Court in course. John Watson."

An undated map in TJ's hand shows the GROUND related to the proposed road (MS in ViU: TJP-ER, FC [Freudenberg-Casteen] no. 3131). At its next meeting the court ordered further "that the hands of Charles L. Bankhead be Attached to the gang of Elie Alexander surveyor of the road from Moors ford to Milton. It is ordered by the Court that the hands of Thomas Jefferson at Monticello such as are under the superintendance of Edmund Bacon be attached to the gang of Thomas Jefferson Randolph surveyor of the road from the corner of Charles L. Bankheads fence to Jeffersons Mill" (MS in Albemarle Co. Order Book [1818–19], 156; in Garrett's hand; repeated "to" after "Attached to" editorially omitted; on p. 151 and applying to this entry: "At a Court held for Albemarle County the fifth day of October 1818 Present } John Watson John Rodes John Goss and James Old } Justices").

¹ Manuscript: "subsituted."
² Manuscript: "subsitute."
³ Manuscript: "nort."

From James Monroe

DEAR SIR   Sepʳ 9. 1818.

Sometime ago you intimated to me a desire to dispose of a small tract of land, which you have between mr Alexanders & my land lying below the Blenhims tract. As this is detatched from your other lands, it is probable, that you may still be desirous of parting from it, and that it may fall into other hands, [which I should regret] without an arrangment between us. If my impression is correct, and we can agree, I shall be glad to become the purchaser, with which view I will thank you to state the price pr acre. I shall be able to make the payment in Jany next, or sooner if desir'd.

I hope that your health improves. If I can be, in any manner, useful to you, in the affairs of the College, during your confinement, I beg you to command me.

with great respect & regard your friend & servant

JAMES MONROE

I have finally decided to call my place here "Highland"

RC (DLC); dateline adjacent to signature; brackets in original; endorsed by TJ as received 10 Sept. 1818 from Highland and so recorded in SJL.

To Patrick Gibson

DEAR SIR   Monticello Sep. 10. 18.

I returned a few days ago from the springs, my health entirely prostrated by the use of the waters. they produced an imposthume, whic[h] with the torment of the journey back reduced me very low, so that I am not yet able to set up to write. but I am sensibly mending. my first attention has been to provide against your suffering as my endorse[r] by the bank curtailments. my grandson tells me he sent you on my account 50. Bar. flour in Aug. the river being low we are obliged to send half loads to Columbia, where we lodged 50. Barrels of flour som[e] days ago, and yesterday we loaded another half load on 2 boats, which are gone off and will take on the whole 100 barrels to you immediatel[y.] these you must sell for the current price so as to meet the curtailments. I now send you renewable notes for the banks of the US and of Virginia, blank, as I know not how to fill them. I have prepared a third for the note in the US. bank endorsed by my grandson, who not being here to endor[se][1] it I have thought it best not to lose a mail for these, and will inclose that by the next mail. the 150. barrels sent off in the last and present month will I hope cover your balance of July 1. and the curtailments of Aug. & Sep. for those of Oct. and Nov. be assured that timely provision shall be made so that you shall not suffer. my flour being all ready in the mill, our only difficulties are boats & the state of the river. immediately on Johnson's return I shall send off another 50. Bar. because I shal[l] be obliged within a short time to draw on you for about 300.D.

I expect that mr Johnson of Petersburg sent you some time ago a cas[k] of Scuppernon wine for me. that 2. cases of Tuscan wines addressed to yo[u] by the Collector of Phila Aug. 13. are now with you, and hope that 9 cases of wine addressed to you by the Collector of Alexa Aug. 28. & a box of Maccaro[ni] will be arrived by the time the boats get down, and that they will bring them a[ll] up. I salute you with affectionate friendship.

TH: JEFFERSON

PoC (MHi); edge trimmed; at foot of text: "M[r] Gibson"; endorsed by TJ. Enclosures not found.

THE SPRINGS: Warm Springs. An IMPOSTHUME is a cyst or abscess (*OED*).

MY GRANDSON: Thomas Jefferson Randolph. The collectors at PHILA and ALEXA were John Steele and William D. Simms, respectively.

[1] Word faint.

To Francis Eppes

Dear Francis   Monticello Sep. 11. 18.

I am lately returned from the warm springs with my health entirely prostrated by the use of the waters. they produced an imposthume and eruptions which with the torment of the journey back reduced me to the last stage of weakness and exhaustion. I am getting better, but still obliged to lie night and day in the same reclined posture which renders writing painful. I cannot be at Poplar Forest till the middle of October, if strong enough then. if you should have to go to another school, if you will push your Greek Latin and Arithmetic, there will be no time lost, as that prepares you for reception at the University on the ground of a student of the sciences. altho' I now consider that as fixed at the Central College yet it will retard the opening of that till the spring, as the conveyance of all our property to the Literary fund subjects us now to await the movements of the legislature. be assured, my dear Francis of my affectionate and devoted attachment to you.   Th: Jefferson

PoC (CSmH: JF); endorsed by TJ. Enclosed in TJ to Joel Yancey, 11 Sept. 1818.

From Honoré Julien

Monsieur   Washington Septembre 11th 1818

je vous Ecrit ce peu de Lignes que je Desire qui Vous trouve en Bonne Santé . . . . ainsi que La famille de Mr et Mdm Randolph.—

vous Récevré par Le Courié une Boite Contenant un fromage Suisse ordinairement on Le mange Rápée Sur des tartines de Beur— il-i-à des Lentille Si vous jugé apropos de Les Semer Ce Doit Etre a La fin de mars ou au Commencement Davril La nouvelle Lune— Dans une tere pauvre et Legere Si vous voulé quell produise dans de Bonne tere il ne produise pas. il i a aussi des pois D'espagne—que jait Recolté moi mesme. il faut qui Soit Semé dans de Bonne tere—

je vous Desire La continuatio[n] dune parfaite Santé—et Suis— avec Respect et Consideration.—Votre obeissan[t] Serviteur

HONORÉ JULIEN

EDITORS' TRANSLATION

SIR   Washington September 11ᵗʰ 1818

I write these few lines, which I hope will find you in good health . . . . as well as Mr. and Mrs. Randolph's family.—

You will receive by mail a box containing a Swiss cheese. It is usually eaten grated on buttered slices of bread. There are some lentils. If you think it proper to plant them, you must do so at the end of March or beginning of April, at the new moon, in poor and light soil, if you want them to be productive. In good soil they will not. There are also some Spanish peas that I picked myself. They must be planted in good soil—

I wish you the continuation of perfect health and am, with respect and consideration, your obedient servant   HONORÉ JULIEN

RC (DLC); edge trimmed; ellipsis in original; endorsed by TJ as received 18 Sept. 1818 and so recorded in SJL. RC (DLC); address cover only; with PoC of TJ to Samuel Knox, 11 Dec. 1818, on verso; addressed: "Thomas Jefferson Esqʳᵉ Monticello"; franked; postmarked Washington, 12 Sept. Translation by Dr. Roland H. Simon.

To Joel Yancey

DEAR SIR   Monticello Sep. 11. 18.

I am lately returned from the Warm springs with my health entirely prostrated by the use of the waters. they produced an imposthume and eruptions, which with the torment of the journey back reduced me to the extremest weakness. I am getting better, but still obliged to lie night and day reclined in one posture, which makes writing all but impossible. the visitors of the college meet the 1ˢᵗ week of October, as soon after which as I shall have strength enough, I shall be with you. I wish you to begin to get your flour to Richmond the 1ˢᵗ of Octob. & to get it down as fast as you can after that. I inclose a letter for my grandson Francis and assure you of my great friendship and respect.

                                        TH: JEFFERSON

PoC (MHi); at foot of text: "Mʳ Yancey"; endorsed by TJ. Enclosure: TJ to Francis Eppes, 11 Sept. 1818.

To Thomas Cooper

DEAR SIR   Monticello Sep. 12. 18.

Your letters of Aug. 26. Sep. 1. 2. 3. were recieved yesterday evening. I returned from the warm springs a few days [ago],¹ in prostrated health, from the use of the waters. their effect, and the journey back reduced me to the last stage of exhaustion; but I am recovering.

we shall all be happy to recieve here mrs Cooper, yourself & M. Correa, and expect that according to former request you will land here and make Monticello your head quarters. mrs Cooper will find my daughter & granddaughters anxious to make her easy & happy here; and the steady progress of my convalescenc[e] ensures my being well by the time of your arrival. I have spoke to the Presiden[t] on the subject of mr Say & Nuttal; he will do every thing he can lawfully do[.] on the subject of the Medical school, you will know, when you come, what the Comm[rs] at Rockfish gap have proposed. I cannot yet set erect to write and writing with pain I must do it with brevity. in hopes of seeing yourself and party about the time proposed, I salute you with constant frdship & respect.   T[H]: [JEFFER]SON

PoC (DLC); on verso of reused address cover to TJ; edge trimmed; signature faint; at foot of text: "Doct[r] Cooper"; endorsed by TJ.

[1] Omitted word editorially supplied.

From Peter Poinsot

Cette (Departement de l'Hérault)

MONSIEUR   12 September 1818

D'aprés la lettre de recommandation de mon digne ami feu General Kosciuzsko de Soleure du 3 Juin 1817 que j'eus lhonneur de vous addresser le 25 suivant, avec le plan & Copie de mes terres par duplicata: N'ayant pas eu l'honneur d'être favorisé de vos nouvelles Je me permis de vous écrire le 18 mai d[er] sur le même Sujet, en me référant à leur[1] contenu. Je me permets de joindre inclus une Copie de celle quil eut la bonté d'ecrire a Son Excellence Mr Monroe President des Etats Unis à mon sujet que j'ai envoyé à Mr Barnet votre Consul à Paris pour la lui faire acheminer avec deux de mes lettres lune à Monsieur le Président & l'autre à Monsieur le Sécrétaire d'Etat.

Au nom & à la mémoire de mon digne ami Kosciuzsko Je viens Solliciter Votre Excellence, pour la prier d'apostiller en ma faveur la lettre incluse, par triplicata, à Mr Monroe. Monsr Barnet m'avait fait esperer que le Sénat devait S'assembler au mois de Décembre dernier, quil esperait que ma nomination aurait lieu, d'autant qu'il m'avait recommandé d'une maniere particuliere à Son Excellence. N'ayant reçu aucune nouvelle Je deviens trés inquiet, deux mots de votre Excellence suffiraient à M Monroe pour obtenir ma nomination

Je Joins aussi une lettre de Monsr Cathalan, que mes amis m'ont procuré, Je n'ai pas osé me permettre de lui faire part de mes désirs

pour le Consulat de Cette, Je me suis reservé a le faire prier de Sin-
terresser pour moi prés de Votre Excellence.

Feu General Kosciuzsko, votre ami, peu de tems avant sa mort,
m'ecrivit, sous la date du p^r Septembre 1817. & voici comme il
S'exprime =Je n'ai aucun doute, mon cher Poinsot, que vous n'ayez
reçu votre nomination de Consul, Je l'apprendrai avec autant de plaisir, qu'il [m'a] été agreable de vous être utile=[2] il était tellement dans
la certitude que j'avais été nomme Consul, d'aprés la demande quil en
avait faite, qu'il m'en donna le titre par la lettre qu'il m'addressa. il est
mort dans cette persuasion: á lappui de ce que j'avance, Je Joins
l'addresse de Sa lettre revetue de Son cachet. pleinement convaincu
que vous aurez des égards à la Sollicitation d'un pere de famille qui
n'a d'autres désirs que de rendre ses Enfants heureux Permettez moi
je vous prie de vous offrir les sentimens de la plus vive reconnaissance
& d'assurer Votre Excellence de mon plus profond respect

Votre trés humble & trés obeissant Serviteur

POINSOT (PETER)

SIR   Cette (Department of Hérault) 12 September 1818
I write concerning the letter of recommendation of my worthy friend the
late General Kosciuszko, dated 3 June 1817 from Solothurn, which I had the
honor of sending you in duplicate on the 25th of the same month, along with
a map and copy of my land documents. Not having had the honor of being
favored with news from you, I took the liberty of writing you on the same
topic on 18 May and referring to the contents of my previous letters. I now
take the liberty of enclosing a copy of the letter General Kosciuszko was kind
enough to write on my behalf to His Excellency Mr. Monroe, president of the
United States. I have sent this letter to Mr. Barnet, your consul at Paris, for
him to forward with two of my letters, one to the president and the other to
the secretary of state.

In the name and memory of my worthy friend Kosciuszko, I beg Your
Excellency to endorse in my favor the enclosed letter to Mr. Monroe, done in
triplicate. Mr. Barnet had led me to hope that the Senate would assemble last
December, and that I would be nominated, since he had especially recommended me to His Excellency. Having received no news, I am becoming very
worried, and two words on my behalf from Your Excellency to Mr. Monroe
would suffice for me to obtain my nomination

I also enclose a letter from Mr. Cathalan, which my friends procured for
me. Not daring to advise him that I aspired to the consulship at Cette, I only
asked him to intercede in my favor with Your Excellency.

Shortly before his death your friend the late General Kosciuszko wrote me
a letter dated 1 September 1817. He expressed himself thus: "There is no
doubt in my mind, my dear Poinsot, that by now you have received your
nomination as consul. I will be as pleased to learn this as I was pleased to be

<u>useful to you.</u>" He was so certain that I had been nominated to the consulship following his request that he gave me that title in his letter. He died in this belief. In support of this claim I enclose here the address cover of his letter with his seal affixed to it. Fully convinced that you will honor this as you would an application from a father whose only wish is to make his children happy, please let me offer you my deepest gratitude and assure Your Excellency of my most profound respect

Your very humble and very obedient servant   POINSOT (PETER)

RC (DLC); with first enclosure on verso of attached address leaf; torn at seal; addressed: "Thomas Jefferson Esqre late President of the United States Montecello America"; stamp canceled; franked; postmarked Charleston, 26 Nov.; endorsed by TJ as received 6 Dec. 1818 and so recorded in SJL. Translation by Dr. Genevieve Moene. Enclosures: (1) Isaac Cox Barnet to Poinsot, Paris, 16 Feb. and 14 Mar. 1817, the former indicating that Poinsot's letter along with a copy of that of Tadeusz Kosciuszko has been sent to President James Monroe but noting that Monroe is away on a tour and Congress not in session; and the latter stating that Poinsot's and Kosciuszko's letters to Monroe have been forwarded via Le Havre, that Barnet has retained a copy of Kosciuszko's letter to show to Albert Gallatin, and that Gallatin might issue a temporary appointment (Trs in DLC; in Poinsot's hand; on verso of address leaf of covering letter). (2) Kosciuszko to Monroe, Solothurn, 20 Feb. 1817, congratulating him on becoming president, encouraging him to establish a military school, recommending Poinsot for the consulship at Cette, and testifying that he personally knows him to have conducted himself well in America and to have been thought worthy and knowledgeable by Franciszek Bukaty, the Polish minister in London (Dupl in DNA: RG 59, LAR, 1817–25, in French, mutilated, endorsed by TJ, enclosed in Poinsot to TJ, 6 June 1819; Tr in DLC: TJ Papers, 209:37327, entirely in Poinsot's hand, at head of text: "Copie litérale de la Lettre du feu Général Kosciuzsko à Son Excellence Monsieur Monroe Président des Etats Unis" ["Literal copy of the letter of General Kosciuszko, deceased, to His Excellency Mr. Monroe, president of the United States"], at foot of text: "le duplicata, en original, est entre mes mains" ["the original duplicate is in my hands"]). (3) Poinsot to Monroe, Cette, 5 Mar. 1817, seeking the consulship at Cette, which has been vacant since the death of Peter Walsh; citing Kosciuszko's support; enclosing testimonials; recalling his prior residence in the United States and the attachment to that country that "Still warms my heart"; noting that he is proud to own property in Virginia; and indicating that his residence and vineyard are in the neighborhood of Cette (RC in DNA: RG 59, LAR, 1817–25, addressed: "À Son Excellence Monsieur Monroe President des Etats Unis de l. Amerique"; Tr in DLC: TJ Papers, 209:37326, in Poinsot's hand, with his statement at foot of text that copies have been sent through Barnet and by duplicate via Bordeaux and that the same has been done for a letter of the same date to Secretary of State John Quincy Adams). (4) Kosciuszko to Poinsot, Solothurn, 1 Sept. 1817 (RC in DLC: TJ Papers, 209:37328; address cover only; addressed: "À Monsieur Monsieur Poinsot Consul des Etats Unis de l'Amerique à Cette"; postmarked Solothurn; endorsed by Poinsot; with unrelated notes on recto in Poinsot's hand and his extract from this letter on verso, given and translated in the covering letter above, headed "Expression de Sa lettre du 1er Septembre 1817"). (5) Stephen Cathalan to TJ, 7 Sept. 1818.

Alexander de Tubeuf was appointed to the CONSULAT DE CETTE in 1822 (*JEP*, 3:278, 279 [13, 20 Mar. 1822]).

[1] Manuscript: "à leur a leur" ("to their to their").

[2] Omitted closing quotation mark editorially supplied.

From Patrick Gibson

Sir   Richmond 14th Septr 1818—

I am truly concern'd to find from your letter of the 10th Ins^t that your health has suffer'd so severely from the use of the waters—I trust however that the painful effects produced will be but of short duration and that they will prove ultimately beneficial to you—The 50 bls: flour sent down I sold at $9½ and am sorry more was not sent at that time, even at an extra expence of carriage, as I cannot now obtain within $1¼ of that price, this I foresaw and inform'd Mr T. J Randolph of it—it must still be lower as the Miller's here are willing to contract for the delivery of it in Novr at a reduced price—Your note to T. J Randolph I have renewed for the original amount, and shall probably be able to do the same with the one due in a few days, by curtailing my own, which will make no difference to me—Col^l Burton who was here very lately has at length discover'd that the Cask of Scuppernon Wine, which he had supposed, had long since reach'd, was by some mistake sent to a Mr Thweats, I presume he has directed it to be forwarded to me—The 2 Cases Tuscan Wine as also the 9 Cases Wine from Alex^a and basket of Maccaroni have arrived and shall be forwarded by Johnson—

With much respect and esteem I am
Sir Your's   PATRICK GIBSON

RC (MHi); endorsed by TJ as received 18 Sept. 1818 and so recorded in SJL. RC (MHi); address cover only; with PoC of TJ to Louis H. Girardin, 26 Dec. 1818, on verso; addressed in a clerk's hand: "Thomas Jefferson Esqr Monticello"; franked; postmarked Richmond, 14 Sept.

From Wilson Cary Nicholas

My Dear Sir   Warren Sept. 14. 1818

I was sincerely concerned to hear of your indisposition: On saturday it gave me infinite pleasure to hear you had recovered. Will you pardon me if I take the liberty to entreat you, to spare your self the fatigue & exposure you so frequently encounter. Your life is too precious to be risqued.

But for your indisposition, I wou'd last week have sent you the enclosed with a request that you wou'd endorse & return them to me, I cou'd not think of giving you that trouble until I heard of your recovery. I beg the favour of you to endorse them & seal the enclosed, & forward it by the first mail to Mr Dandridge at Richmond. It is necessary one of them shou'd be used on the 23ᵈ. Unless I am obliged to go sooner to Richmond than I expect, I hope to have the pleasure of paying my respects to you next week.

I am with great respect & regard your much obliged

W. C. NICHOLAS

RC (DLC); at foot of text: "Thomas Jefferson Esqʳ"; endorsed by TJ as received 18 Sept. 1818 and so recorded in SJL. Enclosures not found.

From Craven Peyton

DEAR SIR   Monteagle Sept. 14ᵗʰ 1818.

The suite I had in the Staunton Chancery Court has been desided in my favour. Your being absent from home, prevented my informing You sooner. Your warm friend Judge Brown has given a lenthy Opinion which I will send You On my getting a coppy. I hope Your health is improveing fast.

with the greatest Esteem   C. PEYTON

RC (MHi); endorsed by TJ as received 14 Sept. 1818 and so recorded in SJL.

From José Corrêa da Serra

DEAR SIR   Philadelphia. 16. Septʳ 1818.

In the mountains of New Jersey i read in the Newspapers that your Legislature had decided that the central college of your University was to be at Charlottesville. Immediately on my return in Philadelphia i have witnessed the injustice done to Mʳ Cooper, by preferring to him a man poor in science, and unfit to increase his capital. I congratulate you for both these events which contribute so materially to the fullfilment of your views for the instruction of Virginia. Mʳ Cooper will bring there an immense store of useful knowledge accompanied with much philosophy and a great zeal for the dissemination of true science. I am much mistaken if his settlement in your state does not prove a remarkable epoch in the history of the Litterary advancement of Virginia. He will set out for Monticello in very few days, and i will have the satisfaction of presenting him to you before the end of this month, because in going to pay you my annual visit, i intend to profit of his company. In the mean time accept the assurance of the sentiments which i have Long vowed to you

Your most obedient servᵗ   JOSEPH CORRÊA DE SERRA

RC (DLC: TJ Papers, 213:38090); endorsed by TJ as received 23 Sept. 1818 and so recorded in SJL.

Robert Hare was the MAN POOR IN SCIENCE.

From Patrick Gibson

SIR   Richmond 17ᵗʰ Septʳ 1818

I received this morning under blank Cover your note to Thoˢ J. Randolph, on which I observe you have, I presume inadvertently, written a special indorsation, making it payable to me, which renders it necessary that I should put my name to it, or erase the indorsation, in which case I presume the Bank would not receive it—and as the addition of my name would be of no service to it, you will be pleased to send me another. I have received 100 bls of your flour, the 50 by Johnson have been inspected and made 44 Sʳf & 6 fine, 4 of these are light 2. 3ᵗᵇˢ ea & 2. 2ᵗᵇˢ ea, the expences and fines will be hereafter transmitted, the 50 by T. E R's boat were put out at the upper-end of the Basin, and exposed to an excessive rain, the boatman saying that he had no directions to whom to deliver the flour and supposed it was for Mʳ Peyton, I cannot yet say what injury has been sustained—I have ingaged to deliver 50 bls. of the Sʳfine at 8½$[1] to Jabez Parker for his note at 60ᵈ/. which I shall indeavour to have discounted—not more than 8$ can be obtained in Cash—Johnson has got the 11 boxes Wine and Maccaroni—I have paid Wᵐ Johnson 5/. pʳ barˡ for carriage which he says is the price agreed upon at this time—

With great respect & esteem I am
Your obᵗ Servᵗ   PATRICK GIBSON

RC (MHi); at head of text: "Thomas Jefferson Esqʳᵉ"; endorsed by TJ as received 19 Sept. 1818 and so recorded in SJL.

sᴿF: "superfine." T. E R'S BOAT: Thomas Eston Randolph's boat.

[1] Preceding two words interlined.

From James Monroe

Sepr 17. 1818.

J. M's best respects to mr Jefferson. He has the pleasure to send, for his perusal, a late letter from mr Rush, which it may be gratifying to mr Jefferson to see. J. M. will retake it, the next time he calls at Monticello. He hopes that mr Jeffersons health continues to improve.

RC (MHi); dateline at foot of text; endorsed by TJ as received 17 Sept. 1818 from Highland and so recorded in SJL.

The enclosed letter was probably Richard RUSH to Monroe, London, 13 Aug. 1818, indicating that he and Albert Gallatin will soon begin negotiations with the British government; commenting that the Russian minister plenipotentiary to the United States, Pyotr Ivanovich Poletika, plans to delay his departure for Washington until the conclusion of an upcoming conference at Aachen; reporting on Poletika's remarks regarding his diplomatic career, American relations with Spain, and his request that Rush forward him British newspapers in the legation packets sent to Washington; remarking that "You will perceive how much animadversion the affair of Pensacola, has drawn out from the journalists of this country. They are for the great allies watching and keeping us in order. Should it ever be a question whether one or more of them might be suffered to break down our independence, or even annihilate us as a people, we may easily guess if there would be any interference for our protection"; describing the hostility toward the United States of José Miguel de Carvajal-Vargas, 2d Duke of San Carlos, the Spanish ambassador in London; and concluding that in Great Britain the execution of Alexander Arbuthnot and Robert Ambrister continues to generate a popular outcry, but that, in light of the atrocities committed by the British, "Their affected indignation at the fate of these two Indian spies is at once artful and ludicrous" (RC in PHi: Simon Gratz Collection, at head of text: "Private," endorsed by Monroe and docketed in an unidentified hand: "1818 Spanish Affairs Seminole war"; Dupl in DLC: Monroe Papers, at head of text: "Private—Duplicate," endorsed by Monroe; FC in Lb in NjP: Rush Family Papers).

To James Monroe

Th:J. to the President   Sep. 17. 18.

I thank you, dear Sir, for the opportunity of perusing the inclosed, which I return without delay. it looks well, and when they know the whole of the affair of Pensacola, I have no doubt they will withdraw all idea of intermedling between Spain & us. I[1] trust we shall be able to avoid entanglement with the European alliance. we may let them alone for they cannot[2] conquer the S. Americans.

My health is improving; but I cannot yet set erect in a chair, nor do not soon expect to be able to get on horseback. I salute with affect^te frdship

RC (DLC: Monroe Papers); dateline at foot of text; addressed: "The President of the US Highland"; endorsed by Monroe, with additional endorsement and summary of letter in two different, unidentified hands. Not recorded in SJL. Enclosure: enclosure to Monroe to TJ, 17 Sept. 1818.

[1] TJ here canceled "think."
[2] Manuscript: "canot."

From Thomas Cooper

DEAR SIR   sept. 18. 1818

I am very sorry to hear of your weak state of health, but I hope to find you better by the comforts of home and rest.

M. Correa's carriage has undergone repairs, and will not be fit for use till Sunday morning when we propose to set out. I suppose it will require seven days to bring us to Montecello. Mrs Cooper declines being of the Party.

I defer all further communication, till I have the pleasure of assuring you personally of my continued attachment and respect.

THOMAS COOPER

RC (MHi); endorsed by TJ as received 28 Sept. 1818 and so recorded in SJL. RC (DLC); address cover only; with PoC of TJ to Abraham Lange, 25 Dec. 1818, on verso; addressed: "Thomas Jefferson Esq Montecello Virginia"; franked; postmarked (faint) Philadelphia, 1[8?] Sept.

SUNDAY was 20 Sept. 1818.

To Richard N. Thweatt

DEAR SIR   Monticello Sep. 18. 18.

I must trouble you once more on the subject of my unfortunate cask of Scuppernon wine. having written to mr Gibson concerning it, he says in answer 'Col° Burton, who was here very lately, has at length discovered that the cask of Scuppernon wine, which he had supposed had long since reached was, by some mistake sent to mr Thweatt. I presume he has directed it to be forwarded to me.' hence I conclude that the master of the vessel to whom mr Johnson was so kind as to commit it, has either drank, sold, or misdelivered it. in the latter case only, it may be worth while to enquire after it, as it might possibly be discovered. this is the office I ask from your kindness, and salute you with esteem & respect.   TH: JEFFERSON

PoC (MHi); on verso of reused address cover to TJ; at foot of text: "Richard N. Thweatt esq."; mistakenly endorsed by TJ as a letter to "Thweatt Archibald" and so recorded in SJL.

From Mathew Carey & Son

SIR   Philadᵃ Sept. 21. 1818

By last Mail, we took the liberty, which we hope you will excuse, of sending you a Volume of a very interesting work, which we have an idea of publishing, with such corrections & alterations as may be found necessary. The editorship is undertaken by a literary gentleman, whom we believe fully competent to do it justice.

Our wish is, if you should deem it right, to be favoured with a very brief recommendation of the work, which we shall regard as a very particular favour conferred upon

Your obᵗ hᵇˡᵉ servᵗˢ

√ M CAREY & SON

RC (MHi); in Mathew Carey's hand; dateline at foot of text; at head of text: "Hon Thomas Jefferson, Esqʳ"; endorsed by TJ as a letter from Mathew Carey received 28 Sept. 1818 and so recorded in SJL.

The INTERESTING WORK was the first volume of Edward Baines, *History of the Wars of the French Revolution, from the* *breaking out of the war in 1792, to the restoration of a general peace in 1815; comprehending The Civil History of Great Britain and France, during that period*, 2 vols. (London, 1817). TJ later acquired a four-volume octavo edition printed by Carey in Philadelphia in 1819, which contained additional notes and a history of the War of 1812 (Poor, *Jefferson's Library*, 4 [no. 89]; TJ's copy in MWiW-C).

From DeWitt Clinton

Albany 21 September 1818

Govʳ Clinton's respectful compliments to Mr. Jefferson & takes the liberty of enclosing a small publication

RC (MHi); endorsed by TJ as received 5 Oct. 1818 and so recorded in SJL. RC (DLC); address cover only; with PoC of TJ to William Radford and Joel Yancey, 31 Dec. 1818, on recto and verso; addressed: "Thomas Jefferson Esqr Monticello Virginia"; franked; postmarked Albany, 21 Sept., and Monticello [N.Y.?], 28 Sept. Enclosure: Clinton, *A Memoir on the Antiquities of the Western Parts of the State of New-York. Read before the Literary and Philosophical Society of New-York* (Albany, 1818; Poor, *Jefferson's Library*, 5 [no. 173]; TJ's copy in MiU-C); dated Albany, 7 Oct. 1817, and addressed from Clinton as society president to its vice president, Samuel L. Mitchill; asserting that "the western parts of the United States were, prior to their discovery and occupation by Europeans, inhabited by numerous nations in a settled state and much further advanced in civilization than the present tribes of Indians" (p. 4); and, as evidence, describing the towns, artifacts, and human remains he had observed in the western counties of New York.

From Joseph Dougherty

DEAR SIR   Washington City Sept[r] 21st 18

Conscious that your knowlege of my promotion will give you infinite pleasure—especially when sensible of being the original cause of it.

I am appointed, or, (perhaps elected) Superintendent of the buildings occupied by the State, War and Navy with a sallary of 500 Dollars per. an.

It was your letter—recommending me to the Senate in 1811: that got me the situation, and, as it will not engross half my time to attend at the office—I can still pursue my former business.

Hoping yourself & family are well

I am Dear Sir. your Humble Servt.   JO[s] DOUGHERTY

RC (DLC); endorsed by TJ as received 28 Sept. 1818 and so recorded in SJL. RC (MHi); address cover only; with PoC of TJ to Francis Preston, 21 Dec. 1818, on verso; addressed: "Tho[s] Jefferson Esq[r] Monticello va."; franked; postmarked Washington, 22 Sept.

TJ's earlier letter RECOMMENDING Dougherty was his Circular to Certain Republican Senators, 19 Sept. 1811.

From Patrick Gibson

SIR   Richmond 24th Sept[r] 1818—

The last load of 50 barrels which I mention'd to you as having been exposed by M[r] Randolph's boatman to a very heavy shower of rain I had sold to Davenport & Allen at 8$ dft on Philad[a], but on shipping it one of the heads came out, and I discover'd that it was damaged, some others were then open'd on board and were equally injured, I offer'd the purchasers to make a deduction, but as they were purchasing on order they refused to take it, and most of the flour being then stowed away—I was compelled either to subject myself to considerable expence here, or allow it to go on to the person for whom it was purchased, to be sold on my acco[t]—I adopted the latter deeming it more to your interest—I received this morning under blank cover your note to Tho[s] J Randolph—

With much respect I am Your ob[t] Serv[t]   PATRICK GIBSON

RC (MHi); endorsed by TJ as received 28 Sept. 1818 and so recorded in SJL. RC (MHi); address cover only; with PoC of TJ to Dugald Stewart, 21 Dec. 1818, on verso; addressed: "Thomas Jefferson Esq[re] Monticello"; franked; postmarked (faint) Richmond, 2[4] Sept.

From James Maury

DEAR SIR,   Liverpool 25th Sepr 1818

Should my Son Matthew happen to be near Monticello, I have desired him to pay his respects to you: this son has already been in the United States, whence he lately returned; but it has been deemed prudent for him to spend this winter there also, on account of his health. I am your obliged friend & sevt   JAMES MAURY

RC (DLC); at foot of text: "Thomas Jefferson Monticello"; endorsed by TJ as received 5 May 1819 and so recorded (with additional bracketed notation: "his son") in SJL.

Matthew Maury (1800–77), merchant, was born in Liverpool, England, the son of TJ's friend James Maury and grandson of his teacher, Rev. James Maury. He was educated at Eton College, entered his father's commission business by 1815, and by 1819 had returned to the United States to secure tobacco shipments. In 1832 Maury settled permanently in New York City, where he established a mercantile firm with his brother Rutson Maury. A longtime member of the New York City Chamber of Commerce, he served as its secretary, 1849–53 (DeWint-M: Maury Family Papers; Anne Fontaine Maury, ed., *Intimate Virginiana: A Century of Maury Travels by Land and Sea* [1941], 6, 89–107, 319, 321; Maury's passport application, 25 May 1864 [DNA: RG 59, PA]; *New-York Times*, 19 Sept. 1877).

From William J. Coffee

MOST HONORABLE
AND RESPECTED SIR   Sept 26th 1818 Greenwich St New-York

I Am Sorry to Intrude on y retirement tharfor I hope you kindness to me will Excuse my present Application for you Asistanes Acording to your former promies that of Sending of Imeaditly those boxes Containg my Laboures I fear much they will be Spoilt and tharfor let me prevail on you Indulgence I hav wrote so mainy time to mr Randolph and not having recevd the favor of Any kind of Answer am Apprehensiv he is not well

with Evey respect & duty to you & you Family I remain Dear Sir Sincerly you   W. J. COFFEE

RC (DLC); dateline at foot of text; addressed: "To Thos Jefferson Esqr Monteselo State of Virgina"; franked; postmarked New York, 26 Sept.; endorsement by TJ mutilated. Recorded in SJL as received 5 Oct. 1818.

From John Vaughan

D SIR   Philad. 26 Sep. 1818

I have received a letter from Mr Stephen Catalan 16 June advising reciept of 2205 f^r dft of Girard on Paris he will write to you soon but requests that I will inform you that he has rec^d the Bill—

I do not know whether M Correa has yet reached you—I enclose a letter for him—

We are completely at a Stand in the business of the Astronomical Comm^{ee} for Want of the Instruments or rather for want of knowing that we can have them they being actually here—We are not quite certain who to adress—Mr Crawford has been written to, in whose department the business heretofore rested, but no reply has been rec^d by the Comm^{ee}, we should wish to know with Certainty, whether any other Departm^t has the objects in charge—We dare not go to any expence, till this is ascertaind & we fear losing the privilege of the Building if we do not soon act—The warm interest you have ever Shewn to our society—emboldens me to hope that You may be able to serve us—by putting society in the right road, & giving your countenance to their requests

I remain Yours most sincerly   JN VAUGHAN

RC (MHi); at head of text: "Thomas Jefferson Monticello"; endorsed by TJ as received 5 Oct. 1818 and so recorded in SJL. Enclosure not found.

Stephen Cathalan's letter to Vaughan of 16 JUNE was more likely dated 16 July 1818 (Cathalan to TJ, 13 Aug. 1818). OUR SOCIETY: the American Philosophical Society.

From Reuben G. Beasley

SIR,   Havre, Sep. 28, 1818.

I have had the pleasure to receive your letter of the 8th of April; and for the friendly sentiments you express be pleased to accept my thanks. I shall be happy at all times to be useful to you, and I hope you will command me freely.

By this conveyance, the ship Dumfries bound to Baltimore, I forward to the Collector some Books for you received two days ago from Messrs DeBure, which I hope will arrive safe.

With the greatest respect & esteem
I am, Sir, your devoted   R G BEASLEY

RC (MHi); endorsed by TJ as received 27 Nov. 1818 and so recorded in SJL. RC

(DLC); address cover only; with PoC of TJ to Peter Laporte, 6 May [1819], on verso; addressed: "To Thomas Jefferson Monticello. ⅏ Dumfries"; stamped "SHIP"; postmarked Baltimore, 22 Nov.

The COLLECTOR at Baltimore was James H. McCulloch.

From Alfred H. Dashiell

SIR,   Sept^r   1818

Permit me for one moment to obtrude myself on y^r notice.—Being about to establish an Academy near Balt^o I am anxious to secure all means of success. As you were pleased to express a favourable opinion of the School near N London, & did me the honour of placing y^r grandson under my care, could you send me a line w^h I might give to the publick as a recommendation?.—

Excuse, Sir, the liberty I have taken. But the experience of y^r politeness, & y^r known benevolence, induced me to make a request of extreme delicacy.—

I remain, Sir, with great respect,
Your ob^t Servt
                                        A H DASHIELL

P.S. A line addressed to Ellicotts Mills, M^d will be rec^d—

RC (DLC: TJ Papers, 213:38091); partially dated; adjacent to closing: "Mr Jefferson"; endorsed by TJ as received 19 Oct. 1818 and so recorded in SJL.

Alfred Henry Dashiell (1793–1881), clergyman and educator, was a native of Kent County, Maryland, who graduated from the University of Pennsylvania in 1811. He read law with William Pinkney but turned to the ministry and was ordained in the Protestant Episcopal Church in Maryland in 1814. Dashiell moved to Virginia in 1817 and taught at the New London Academy but returned to Maryland late the following year and soon became a Presbyterian clergyman, serving churches in Philadelphia, Illinois, Tennessee, and New York. He was president of

the Nashville Female Academy and later of Caldwell College in Rogersville, Tennessee. When the Presbyterian Church split after Southern secession, Dashiell remained loyal to the Union. He died in Brooklyn, New York (*University of Pennsylvania Catalogue*, 27; Augustus Theodore Norton, *History of the Presbyterian Church, in the State of Illinois* [1879], 1:217–8; Ethan Allen, *Clergy in Maryland of the Protestant Episcopal Church since the independence of 1783* [1860], 30; American Education Society, *Quarterly Register and Journal* 1 [1829]: 53; *American Educational Year-Book* [1858]; 203; *Philadelphia Inquirer*, 21 Mar. 1881; gravestone inscription in Green-Wood Cemetery, Brooklyn).

From de Bure Frères

Monsieur   paris ce 1er 8bre 1818.

quoique nous ayions reçu de bonne heure la note des livres que vous desiriez avoir cette année, cependant il ne nous a pas été possible de vous les procurer tous, et nous avons été obligés de faire venir d'angleterre le grabe, dont il n'existoit pas un seul exemplaire a paris. nous avons egalement été obligés de differer l'envoi, pour des livres d'allemagne, mais nous n'avons pas voulu le faire plus longtemps de crainte de la mauvaise Saison. nous esperons, Monsieur, que vous recevrez votre caisse en bon etat, elle est emballée avec bien du Soin, et nous l'avons recommandée a M Beasly, votre consul au havre. nous attendons en ce moment un envoi d'allemagne, peut etre s'y trouvera-t-il quelques articles encore pour vous, dans ce cas, Monsieur, nous les garderons pour l'année prochaine. il vous paroitra extraordinaire qu'il y ait des livres francais que nous n'ayions pas pu vous envoyer, mais malgré les recherches que nous avons faites, il n'a pas été possible de les trouver.

nous n'avons pas osé, Monsieur, vous envoyer sans vous en prevenir, le xenophon de M Gail, que vous nous demandiez, cet ouvrage forme 10 volumes in 4° dont le prix est de 180 francs, mais encore il n'est pas tout a fait fini, si vous le desirez l'année prochaine nous le mettrons dans votre envoi.

nous vous donnons ici, Monsieur, la facture de notre envoi, ainsi que l'emploi de l'argent que vous nous avez envoyé, nous vous sommes maintenant redevables de la somme de f 203.75[cl] que nous gardons a votre disposition, ou bien qui sera en a compte sur votre demande de l'année prochaine. nous oublions Monsieur de vous dire que M gail n'a point imprimé de xenophon in 8° on ne trouve pas non plus séparément les scholia de didyme sur homere, il faudroit pour les avoir prendre l'homere, imprimé par les Elzeviers ou ces scholia se trouvent. cet homere qui est parfaitement imprimé, forme 2 volumes in 4°, souvent reliés en un seul, et vaut de 60 a 72 francs.

nous avons l'honneur d'étre, Monsieur, Vos tres humbles et tres obeissants Serviteurs

de Bure freres.
Libraires du Roi, et de la Bibliotheque du Roi.

S<small>IR</small>   Paris 1 October 1818.

Although we received in good time the list of books you wished to obtain this year, we have been unable to procure them all and were obliged to have the Grabe, of which not a single copy could be found in Paris, sent from England. We were also forced to postpone sending you the package until now because we were awaiting books ordered from Germany, but we did not want to delay any longer for fear of the wintry season. We hope, Sir, that you will receive your box in good condition. It was carefully wrapped, and we entrusted it to Mr. Beasley, your consul at Le Havre. At the moment we are waiting for a package from Germany, which may contain a few more items for you. If so, Sir, we will hold them for next year. You may think it strange that we were unable to send you some of the French books, but despite our searches they could not be found.

Sir, without consulting you first we did not dare send the Xenophon of Mr. Gail that you requested. This work consists of 10 quarto volumes and its price is 180 francs, but it is not yet completely finished. If you want, we will include it in next year's shipment.

We include herein, Sir, the invoice for the package we sent you as well as an account of the money you sent us. We now owe you the sum of 203.75 francs and will hold it either at your disposal or as an advance on your order for next year. We forgot, Sir, to tell you that Mr. Gail has not printed a Xenophon in octavo. A separate printing of Didymus's scholia on Homer cannot be found either. To get them it would be necessary to obtain the Homer printed by the Elzevirs, in which these annotations can be found. This Homer, which is perfectly printed, consists of 2 volumes in quarto, often bound as one volume, and is worth from 60 to 72 francs.

We have the honor to be, Sir, your very humble and very obedient servants
D<small>E</small> B<small>URE</small> F<small>RERES.</small>
Booksellers to the king, and to the royal library.

RC (MHi); in the hand of a representative of de Bure Frères; with MS of second enclosure on verso and MS of first enclosure on verso of address cover; addressed: "A Monsieur Monsieur th. jefferson a Monticello, en Virginie, Etats unis, D'Amerique"; stamped "SHIP"; stamp for paid postage replaced by frank; postmarked New York, 6 Feb.; endorsed by TJ as received 1 Mar. 1819 and so recorded in SJL; with additional notation by TJ beneath endorsement related to his 27 May 1819 reply: "books rec^d no letter Xenophon." Dupl (MHi); in the hand of a different representative, unsigned; with Dupls of first and second enclosures on verso of address cover; at head of text: "Duplicata"; endorsed by TJ as received 1 May 1819 and so recorded in SJL. Enclosed in TJ to James H. McCulloch, 2 Mar. 1819, and McCulloch to TJ, 8 Mar. 1819. Translation by Dr. Genevieve Moene.

[1] Blank in RC filled in with sum supplied from Dupl.

I

Invoice of Books from de Bure Frères

facture de livres[1] Remis en une Caisse cordée, emballée en toile grasse et maigre, marquée, <u>Libri</u> ⚒ 3. **M.T.J.** adressée au havre a M Beasly, consul americain,[2] par la Diligence de la Rue notre dame des victoires. 1818. 7bre 22.

	fr.
vetus testamentum. gr. edente Grabe. oxonii, 1707, 9 vol. in 8° v. b.	76–
origenis hexapla gr. et. lat. ed. Bahrdt. Lipsiæ, 1769, 2. vol. 8° v. j.	31–
Gassendi Syntagma philosophiæ Epicuri. hag. com. 1659, in 4° v. b.	6–
Systeme Social, par le B^on d'holbach. Londres, 1774, 3 tom. en 1 vol. 8° v. m.	5–
elements de la morale universelle, par le meme, 1790, in–18. bas	2–50
discours de l'Empereur Julien contre les chretiens. trad. par d'Argens, Berlin, 1768, in–8° v. m	2–50
herodotus gr. et lat. edente Schweighæuser. argentorati, 1816, 12 tomes rel. en 6 vol. in–8° v. j.	97–
Appianus Alexandrinus, gr. et lat. edente eadem. Lipsiæ, 1785, 3 vol. in–8° dem. rel	60–
Gnomici poetæ græci. ed. Brunck. argentor. 1784, in–12. m. r.	12–
Mœurs et coutumes des Romains, par Bridault, Paris, 1754, 2 tomes reliés en 1 volume in–12. v. ec[3]	4–
Vie privée de Louis **XV**, Londres 1781, 4 vol. in 12. bas. j.	14–
frais de Caisse, d'emballage, de Douane &c	13–
	323–

MS (MHi); in the hand of a representative of de Bure Frères; on verso of address cover of RC of covering letter; with endorsement, at foot of text in an unidentified hand, related to James H. McCulloch to TJ, 8 Mar. 1819: "Mar 8 1819 JH:MC." Dupl (MHi); in the hand of a different representative; on verso of address cover of Dupl of covering letter, with Dupl of second enclosure subjoined. Enclosed in TJ to McCulloch, 2 Mar. 1819, and McCulloch to TJ, 8 Mar. 1819.

For the books listed here, see TJ to de Bure Frères, 5 Apr. 1818, and enclosure. For explanations of bookbinding terms and abbreviations not defined below, see note to enclosure to David Bailie Warden to TJ, 12 July 1816.

FACTURE DES LIVRES . . . 1818. 7BRE 22: "Invoice for books sent in a crate tied with rope, wrapped in thin oilcloth, labeled <u>Libri</u> ⚒3. **M.T.J.** Addressed to Le Havre to Mr. Beasley, American consul, sent in the diligence of the Rue Notre Dame des Victoires. 22 September 1818." M. R.: "maroquin rouge" ("red morocco"). FRAIS DE CAISSE, D'EMBALLAGE, DE DOUANE &C: "costs of the crate, packing, customs, etc."

[1] Instead of preceding three words, Dupl reads "fourni a Monsieur th. Jefferson, a Monticello, et" ("furnished to Mr. Thomas Jefferson, at Monticello, and").

[2] Preceding two words not in Dupl.

[3] Dupl: "veau ecaille" ("tortoise calf").

II

Account with de Bure Frères

[ca. 1 Oct. 1818]

Avoir une Lettre de change payée le 23 aout de 630^{fr}

payé a M Warden	88^{fr} 00^c	⎫
redu sur L'envoi de 1817	15 25	⎬ 426 25
facture de ce jour	323	⎭ ————
Nous redevons		203.75^c

[ca. 1 Oct. 1818]

Credit, a letter of exchange paid 23 August for 630 francs

paid to Mr. Warden	88^{fr} 00^c	⎫
remainder from 1817 parcel	15 25	⎬ 426 25
invoice of today	323	⎭ ————
We owe		203.75^c

MS (MHi); in the hand of a representative of de Bure Frères; undated; on verso of RC of covering letter. Dupl (MHi); in the hand of a different representative; undated; on verso of address cover of Dupl of covering letter, subjoined to Dupl of first enclosure. Enclosed in TJ to James H. McCulloch, 2 Mar. 1819, and McCulloch to TJ, 8 Mar. 1819. Translation by Dr. Genevieve Moene.

From C. S. Haven

SIR   Boston Oct 2^d 1818

you will be surprized at the liberty I take of addressing[1] a letter to you, and asking a favour in this manner, indeed I shudder at my impertinence and dispare of obtaining my request, but the hope of being successfull and the impression that you are ever ready to alleviate the misery of humanity urge me to the trial (the favour I beg is money Suffecent to purchase a small share of a Ticket enclosed in a letter) I am aware of the difficulty I labour under in asking a favour in this manner, you do not know who I am, whether I merit your charity or not, you have only my word, and I may be some Idiot or crazy head[ed lu?]nitic, I can say I am the child of adversity and [. . .] [m]any of my few years she has ben my constant companion, I appeal to Heaven as a witness, consider I pray that what I[2] beg is but a trifle with you, but to me possebly of the greates moment, it may make me happy as to Riches, and be no injury to you, I beg pardon for any impertinence

[296]

and entreat it may not prevent my blessing your "name" as my benefactor and the friend of Humanity

your Ob^t Servt.   C. S. HAVEN

N.B should I be favoured I will pay you when I have drawn the
prize   C. S. HAVEN

RC (MHi); mutilated at seal; endorsed   ¹Manuscript: "addessing."
by TJ as received 14 Oct. 1818 and so   ²Haven here erased "ask."
recorded (mistakenly dated 1 Oct.) in
SJL.

From Joseph Hutton

SIR,   Petersburgh V^a October 2nd 1818

To express doubts of your cordial cooperation in any attempt to
promote the extention of literature in our Union, would be doubting
against conviction, and to solicit your patronage, under such a belief,
for the enclosed prospectus, will not, I feel confident, be deemed by
you, impertinent. Respectfully I request your name, & any other in
the immediate circle of your retreat, which, without inconvenience,
you may be enabled to obtain.

I remain respectfully Your Fellow Citizen,   JOS: HUTTON

RC (MHi); endorsed by TJ as received 15 Oct. 1818 and so recorded in SJL. RC (ViU: TJP); address cover only; with PoC of TJ to Thomas Cooper, 22 Jan. 1819, on verso; addressed: "Honb^{le} Thomas Jefferson Esqr Monticello, Charlotte'sville Albemarle Co V^a"; franked; postmarked Petersburg, 3 Oct. Enclosure not found.

Joseph Hutton (1787–1828), author, actor, and educator, was a native of Philadelphia. His first published play was *The Orphan of Prague. A New Drama* (Philadelphia, 1808). By 1811 some of his anonymous stories, including "Ardennis" and "The Castle of Altenheim," appeared in a literary journal, the *Philadelphia Repertory*. That same year Hutton began working as a teacher while continuing to publish his own work, including a volume of poetry, *Leisure Hours; or Poetic Effusions* (Philadelphia, 1812). He acted as well, performing in Philadelphia and traveling troupes, and from 1820 to 1821 he was a member of a company in New Orleans. Hutton settled permanently by 1823 in New Bern, North Carolina, where he operated a school and contributed verse to the local newspaper (Ann Carson, *The History of the Celebrated Mrs. Ann Carson* [Philadelphia, 1822], esp. 85; Samuel Kettell, *Specimens of American Poetry, with critical and biographical notices* [1829], 181–4; James Robinson, *The Philadelphia Directory for 1811* [Philadelphia, 1811], 174; J. Thomas Scharf and Thompson Westcott, *History of Philadelphia. 1609–1884* [1884], 2:958, 970, 975, 1139, 1142; Weldon B. Durham, ed., *American Theatre Companies, 1749–1887* [1986], 29, 34, 35; New Bern *Carolina Sentinel*, 2 Feb. 1828).

On this date Hutton sent a similar letter and enclosure to James Madison (Madison, *Papers, Retirement Ser.*, 1:364).

From Thomas Cooper

Dear Sir   Monticello Octr 3. 1818.

I put in writing what I have to observe, respecting the College at Charlottesville, because I think you will prefer having my remarks so stated, to any recollection of them.

I am not at Liberty to consult my Inclination alone: duty to my family, requires that I should attend to their Interest; and to those proposals which are most likely to promote it.

I presume, nothing can be permanently settled till the Legislature have decided on the scite of the University, and the plan of study: but perhaps I may ask without impropriety, the following questions respecting my own situation. I am fully aware, that in the present state of affairs, you cannot be committed by any reply: but your views of the subject may aid mine.

1. Taking for granted that I am to fill the Chair of experimental Philosophy Chemistry and Mineralogy, how is it contemplated to provide the necessary apparatus? From whence, and to what amount? I think the mere philosophical apparatus (independant of astronomy) will cost about 1500 dollars in London, or Paris. In Mineralogy, I have purchased to the amount of 750 dlrs beside my own personal collections, for several years.

2. A constant expence will attend the necessary chemical experiments: how is it to be defrayed? I think it will amount here to 300 dlrs annually, using great care and frugality. My courses of chemistry in Philadelphia cost me twice as much. At Philadelphia, Baltimore, and New York, the fee to the Professor being 20 Dollars for a course of four months, he defrays the expence of his own apparatus and experiments: but at Philadelphia, there are about 400 regular students: at New York, and Baltimore, about 120 each. Mr Hare at Williamsburgh had 75 Students; he was allowed 75 Dollars for his experiments which cost him 500 dlrs. The Trustees at Carlisle allowed me 200 Dlrs and a man to attend my Laboratory. It appears to me, that untill the class amounts to fifty at least, an allowance for this purpose will be reasonable; and to cease when the class amounts to one hundred.

The philosophical, and mineralogical apparatus once provided, will require an annual expence, but not much: though I consider it of importance to increase the latter continually.

3. Taking for granted that I shall fill the chair of municipal Law, it will be my duty, to deliver a course of Lectures on that subject, accompanied by periodical examinations. But if any young men should be desirous also of forming a class under my direction for <u>private</u> in-

struction, I presume there will be no objection to my taking such a class.

4. If I come here, I must for some time at least, of necessity, reside in the vicinity of the college. nor can I remove my family thither, till an eligible situation in the buildings be allotted for the purpose. The number of rooms contemplated for Professors with families, will hardly suffice for my wants.

5. You suggest, that the vacation will be annual only; for six weeks; in the depth of winter. I grant, that this would be the most convenient period of vacation for many of the students: but it will operate as a sentence of perpetual Imprisonment to the Professors. It would debar me in particular of much knowledge of scientific improvement, which a short annual residence in Philadelphia or New York, would enable me to acquire. New forms, and means of experiment, perpetually occur in large cities among scientific men, which books do not describe. In Mineralogy, new substances, and new localities are constantly presenting themselves. Without an annual opportunity of personal enquiry, I may fall gradually below the level of the day. It is for the interest of the Institution that I should be allowed these opportunities, and afford to take them. Moreover, I know of no instance of a vacation so limited: it is half the usual time allotted at other Institutions.

6^{ly} What is likely to be the Salary proposed in my case?

7^{ly} What am I to understand, as to the expence of my removal from Philad^a hither?

8^{ly} When should I come; and what lectures begin with?

The proposals made to me elsewhere, I can mention, if you wish to make the enquiry.

Pray accept Dear Sir, my best respects, and kindest wishes for your Health and Happiness.   Thomas Cooper

RC (ViU: TJP); addressed: "Thomas Jefferson Esqr"; endorsed by TJ as received 4 Oct. 1818.

From James Monroe

Octr 3.

J. Monroe has the pleasure to submit to mr Jefferson's perusal a letter from Judge Bland, on S^o american aff^{rs}, which he mentiond to him sometime since.

If the weather & mr Jefferson's health permit J. M. will be very much gratified by his company to day, with the gentlemen, now at Monticello, who promisd, with Col Randolph, to dine with him to day.

RC (DLC: TJ Papers, 213:38092); partially dated at foot of text; endorsed by TJ as a letter of 3 Oct. 1818 received the same day. Enclosure: Theodorick Bland to Monroe, Buenos Aires, 14 Apr. 1818, indicating that he is planning a visit to Chile; suggesting that Monroe obtain a description of the reception of the United States commissioners to South America from Caesar A. Rodney and John Graham; requesting permission to postpone submission of his official report until his return from Chile; noting that political conflict among the provinces hampers the ability of the United States to recognize their independence; stating that the people of Buenos Aires are committed to preserving their independence, but that "The Colonial System it is well known, was a complete despotism in all its branches, and when abrogated it not only left the people without any political forms capable of being remoulded into institutions friendly to liberty; but it also left them ignorant of the most important branch of political science, the organization and operation of free municipal institutions—Political science and general information are, however, spreading very fast; many of the useful arts and trades have been introduced; and Religious intolerance is rapidly crumbling away"; listing cattle as the primary export, but predicting that, with independence, the variety of commodities traded will increase; and concluding that he has drawn on the United States Treasury for $2,500 to pay his expenses and that he hopes to return from Valparaiso on board the USS *Ontario* "in August or September next" (RC in DLC: Monroe Papers; at foot of text: "James Monroe President of the U States Washington"; endorsed by Monroe).

To Thomas Cooper

TH: JEFFERSON TO DOCTᴿ COOPER.   Oct. 4. 18.

Before answering the queries stated in your letter of yesterday,[1] I must premise that whatever I say, will be founded on the hypothesis that our legislature shall adopt the Central College as the site for the University of Virginia, which of course entitles it to the funds appropriated to that object.

1. my letter to you of Oct. 10. approved by the Visitors authorizes me to say that they are willing to take your collection of mineral subjects, philosophical & chemical apparatus at a fair price as there stated, and that any further articles of apparatus will be provided to the necessary extent, either in America or from Europe.[2] & as these will be the property of the University the expense of keeping them up must of course be that of the University

2. the same letter assumes the defraying the expense in articles consumed necessarily in a course of chemical lectures; and I am sure they will not hesitate to agree to continue that until the number of students & consequent emoluments (say 50) shall render it reasonable that the Professor shall take that expence off their hands.

3. I suppose it quite reasonable that every Professor should be allowed to take classes for private instruction within their own department, or within any department not actually occupied by some other

professor but that no professor should encroach on the department of another.

4. until a building for the accomodation of your family be provided the rent of one will be at the expense of the University, the finding a hous[e] being a part of their engagement.

5. the time of the vacation is not fixed by the Visitors. my own opinion is that the convenience of the country generally, & especially of the lower country requires it should be in the winter months.

6. the Salary fixed by the Visitors is 1000.D. the tuition fees 25.D. but in consideration that the institution is new, that the Professors on their first arrival will have no pupils, and that time will be requisite to fill their school, I think provision should be made for a reasonable addition to the salary, until the tuition fees shall produce adequate emoluments, and I shall make this proposition to the next visitation.

7. the resolution of the Visitors, stated in my letter of Oct. 10. is 'that the expenses of transporting your library & collection of minerals to the College shall be reimbursed to you.' this of course includes packages & packing, freight from Philadelphia to Richmond, water transportation to Charlottesville & their delivery at the College.

8. I think it best that you should not come before the legislature shall have decided on the site of the University, which may not be perhaps till the 1st of March; and as the first school opened must be that of antient languages, and you were so kind in your letter of Nov. 24. 17. to undertake the care of that until we can provide a professor to our minds, that is what we should wish you to begin with.

Th: Jefferson

Dft (ViU: TJP); dateline at foot of text; edge trimmed; endorsed by TJ. Not recorded in SJL.

Cooper's LETTER OF NOV. 24. 17. was addressed to James Madison and is noted above at Madison to TJ, 29 Nov. 1817, in which it was enclosed.

[1] Reworked from "this day."
[2] Remainder of paragraph interlined.

To James Monroe

Th:J. to the President   Oct. 5. 18.

[. . .] Amant Spreafico, of Nice, to be Consul of that place instead of Victor Adolphus Sasserno deceased.

The above is the name of the person at Nice who wishes to be our Consul. he is a very respectable merchant of the place, was connected in the commerce of Sasserno the father, was left guardian of Sasserno the son, the late Consul, and still I believe continues in the same firm & business. affect^te salutations.

RC (DNA: RG 59, MLR); salutation beneath horizontal rule; dateline at foot of text; one word illegible due to tight archival binding; addressed: "The President of the United States Highland"; endorsed by Monroe: "The person recommended in case the other is dead." Not recorded in SJL.

To William Alston

DEAR SIR   Monticello Oct. 6. 18.

While I had the pleasure of being with you at the Warm springs, I took the liberty of recommending to you some wines of France & Italy, with a note of their prices & of the channels thro' which they may be got. but instead of calling for them on my recommendation only, I have thought it better that you should have samples to direct your choice. for in nothing have the habits of the palate more decisive influence than in our relish of wines. I have therefore made up a box of a couple of dozen bottles, among which you will find samples of the wines of White Hermitage, Ledanon, Roussillon (of Rivesalte) Bergasse claret, all of France, and of Nice & Montepulciano of Italy. I now send them to Richmond, to the care of Capt Bernard Peyton, Commission merchant of that place, to be forwarded to you by the first vessel for Charleston. some of them I hope will be found to your taste.

We were much distressed at the springs by the first accounts we recieved of your fall from your horse; but relieved by subsequent assurances that the injury had been less serious than at first feared; and that you had been able to proceed on your journey. I hope therefore that this finds you in health, & amidst the comforts of your own country. I became seriously affected afterwards by the continuance of the use of the waters. they produced imposthume, eruption, with fever, colliquative sweats and extreme debility. these sufferings, aggravated by the torment of long & rough roads, reduced me to the lowest stage of exhaustion by the time I got home. I have been on the recovery some time, & still am so; but not yet able to sit erect for writing. among my first efforts is that of recalling myself to your recollection, & of expressing the gratification I derived at the springs from your acquaintance & society. however little of life may remain for cherishing a cordiality which it must so soon part with, it will not be the less felt, while feeling remains. and in the hope that the tour I recommended of the upper & lower valley of the Blue ridge may give me, the ensuing autumn, the gratification of recieving you at Monticello,

I pray you to accept the assurance of my friendly attachment & high respect, & that I may be permitted to place here my respectful compliments for Miss and mr Allston who were the companions of your journey.   TH: JEFFERSON

RC (Peter Manigault, Charleston, S.C., 1986; photocopy in ScHi: Alston-Pringle-Frost Papers); addressed: "Col⁰ William Allston Charleston S.C.," with Charleston corrected to "George Town" in an unidentified hand; franked; postmarked Milton, 17 Oct., and (faint) Charleston, [. . .] Oct. PoC (DLC); on verso of reused address cover of Daniel Brent to TJ, 15 May 1818; torn at seal; endorsed by TJ.

COLLIQUATIVE SWEATS are so profuse as to "cause the body to waste away" (*OED*).

To James Breckinridge

DEAR SIR   Monticello Oct. 6. 18.

You have had a right to suppose me very unmindful of my promise to furnish you with drawings for your Courthouse. yet the fact is not so. a few days after I parted with you, the use of the waters of the warm spring began to affect me sensibly & unfavorably, and at length produced serious imposthume & eruption, with fever, colliquative sweats, & extreme debility. these sufferings aggravated by the torment of the journey home, over the rocks and mountains I had to pass, had reduced me to the lowest stage of exhaustion by the time I had got back. I have been on the recovery some time and still am so: but not yet able to sit erect for writing. by working at your drawings [a l]ittle every day, I have been able to compleat, & now to forward them by mail. with the explanations accompanying them, I hope your workman will sufficiently understand them. I send also some seed [of]¹ the Succory which I think I promised you.

I cannot omit this occasion of acknoleging to you my sensibility for [your]² kind attentions on our journey, and during our stay together at the springs. long kept by other vocations from an every-day intercourse with the world, I feel the need of a Mentor, when I enter it, & especially in an unknown society: an[d] I found the benefit of it in your kind cares. I only lament that the knolege of your worth and goodness comes to me when so little of life remains to cultivate and to merit it's cordial reciprocation. if my health should become again as firm as it was before the unlucky experiment of the springs, I shall not despair in my annual rambles to the Natural bridge, of being able at some time to extend them to Fincastle, towards which the pleasure of visiting you would be the chief inducement. nor will I despair that some of your journeyings, on private or public account, may lead you thro' our quarter, and give me the gratification of seeing you at Monticello. with deep & permanent impressions of cordial esteem, accept the assurance of my affectionate attachment and high respect.

TH: JEFFERSON

PoC (DLC); on verso of reused address cover of Thomas Ritchie to TJ, [ca. 21 May 1818]; three words faint; at foot of text: "General Breckenridge"; endorsed by TJ. Enclosures not found.

James Breckinridge (1763–1833), soldier, attorney, and public official, was a private in a company of riflemen from Botetourt County and later served as an ensign under Nathanael Greene in North Carolina during the Revolutionary War. He studied briefly at Liberty Hall Academy (later Washington and Lee University) and then read law under George Wythe at the College of William and Mary. Breckinridge's public service began with his 1782 appointment as deputy clerk of Botetourt County. He practiced law in that county starting in 1789 and held various offices, including town trustee for Fincastle, militia captain, county commonwealth's attorney, and federal revenue inspector. Breckinridge represented Botetourt in the Virginia House of Delegates for thirteen terms, serving 1789–90, 1796–1802, 1806–08, 1819–21, and

1823–24. He won election to the United States House of Representatives in 1809 and held that seat until 1817. Although Breckinridge, a Federalist, opposed the declaration of war on Great Britain in 1812, he led a brigade of Virginia militia following the burning in 1814 of Washington, D.C. Based at Grove Hill, his Botetourt County plantation, he operated mills, a brickyard, a tannery, and a forge. Breckinridge was one of the University of Virginia commissioners who met at Rockfish Gap in 1818, and the following year he was appointed to the new school's Board of Visitors, a position he held until his death (*ANB*; *DAB*; *DVB*; Katherine Kennedy McNulty, "Gen. James Breckinridge, Frontier Man for All Seasons," Roanoke Historical Society, *Journal 7* [winter 1971]: 2–21; Leonard, *General Assembly*; TJ to Breckinridge, 3 Mar. 1819; *Richmond Enquirer*, 24 May 1833; Botetourt Co. Will Book, E:372–3).

[1] Torn at seal.
[2] Torn at seal.

To Mathew Carey

DEAR SIR   Monticello Oct. 6. 18.

Your letter of Sep. 21. reached me on the 28. and the book which is the subject of it had come to hand by the preceding mail. both found me recovering from a long indisposition, and not yet able to set up to write, but in pain. the reading a 4to volume of close print is an undertaking which my ordinary occupations and habits of life would not permit me to encounter: nor under any circumstances could I arrogate to myself the office of directing or anticipating the public judgment as to the publications worthy of their attention. letters of mine, unwarily written, have been sometimes used by editors with that view, but not with my consent, but in one or two particular cases. if the vol. of Baines's[1] book you sent me be your only copy, I will return it to you. if you have another, I would willingly keep it, and be glad to recieve the 2^{d} when it comes out.

I shall be glad if you can send me by mail the 2. books under-
mentioned, and would rather recieve them <u>unbound</u>. I see them advertised by Wells & Lilly of Boston. I salute you with sincere esteem
and respect.   TH: JEFFERSON

Griesbach's Greek testament. the 8vo and full edition.
The New testament in an improved version on the basis of Newcome's translation

RC (PHi: Lea & Febiger Records);
postscript added separately to RC and
PoC; addressed: "Mr Matthew Carey
Philadelphia"; franked; postmarked Charlottesville, 8 Oct.; endorsed by Carey as
received 11 Oct. and answered 16 Oct.
1818. PoC (DLC); on verso of reused address cover of William H. Fitzhugh to
TJ, 18 May 1818; mutilated at seal; endorsed by TJ.

The 2. BOOKS UNDER-MENTIONED
were Johann Jakob Griesbach, Ἡ Καινὴ

Διαθήκη. *Novum Testamentum Graece*,
2 vols. (Cambridge, Mass., 1809; Poor,
Jefferson's Library, 9 [no. 503]), and a
Unitarian work, *The New Testament, in
an Improved Version, upon the basis of
Archbishop Newcome's New Translation:
with A Corrected Text, and Notes Critical
and Explanatory* (probably the 4th ed.,
London, 1817; Poor, *Jefferson's Library*,
9 [no. 503]; for an earlier edition see
Sowerby, no. 1489).

[1] Manuscript: "Haines's."

To William J. Coffee

DEAR SIR   Monticello Oct. 6. 18.
    I recieved last night your favor of Sep. 26. the boxes which were
the subject of it had been sent off about 3. weeks to the care of Capt
Peyton of Richmond to be forwarded to you. until that date the state
of the river had been such as that no boat could pass down it. hoping
you will have recieved them safely before this gets to hand, I pray you
to accept the assurance of my great esteem & respect
                                                        TH: JEFFERSON

PoC (MHi); on verso of reused address cover of James P. Preston to TJ, 20 May
1818; endorsed by TJ.

From Thomas Cooper

DEAR SIR   Frederick'sburgh Octr 6. 1818
    I was a little surprized yesterday, when M. Correa congratulated
me on having agreed to come to Charlottesville.
    This is one of the mistakes so often arising from making a contract,
matter of conversation, instead of writing. Therefore, I take the opportunity of the first post-town, to set it right.

I was tempted to say, that if the permanent salary were 1500 in lieu of 1000 dollars, I would at once reject every other offer that had been made to me. You said, the permanent Salary w^d be only 1000 dollars, but it would be encreased to 1500, untill the emoluments from the Students would make my income that sum; when the 500 Dollars would be withdrawn. This proposal of yours, I repeated, not with a view of assenting to it, but of understanding it distinctly. Indeed, the bent of my mind, was, to reject it; but I felt in a moment, the impropriety of not giving further consideration to a proposal, which you on reflection considered as fair and reasonable. I shall therefore hold it under advisement; and comparing it with the offers made me from other quarters, I shall be ready to give you a definitive answer, whenever I am required so to do.

I have no doubt, your institution will flourish; but not with the rapidity that you expect; or that I wish. It will not in my opinion come into full operation these three years: when it is in full operation, it will gradually encrease. But I feel a persuasion, that it will be my lot there, to live upon little more than a bare competence; and having aided to bring the institution into repute, I shall quit it in the course of nature, for my successor to reap the fruits of past exertions.

I cannot count upon my expences being less than 1500 Dlrs per annum: if I am to live and lay by little or nothing, what reasonable motive should induce me, to prefer the privations of 1500 dollars at Charlotte'sville, to the many comforts of 3000 dollars at Philadelphia or New York? to settle with my family in a new place, to form new acquaintances, and new habits, and to quit old and tried friends? I know of no reasonable inducement so to act, but the hope of leaving my family better provided for when I die, by the savings I may lay aside for them while I live.

Perhaps I may appear to you in this case, more actuated by pecuniary considerations than I ought to be. But when I reflect, that the comfort of my family now, and their subsistence hereafter, will depend on the prudent management of the few years of exertion that remain to me, I feel the importance to them, and the obligation on myself, of taking every future step with a view to their benefit.

Whatever may be decided in my case, I shall feel anxious to promote the success of your institution, because I am persuaded it is calculated to do great good. Wherever I am therefore, call upon me for every assistance I can render it.

Further; I think more and more of the injustice done you by Mr Ord, in his life of Wilson. Whenever you are prepared to say any thing on the subject to the public, I will get your remarks inserted in the peri-

odical journals of Philadelphia, & of N. York. I remain always Dear
Sir, Your obliged and assured friend.   THOMAS COOPER.

RC (ViU: TJP); endorsed by TJ as received 14 Oct. 1818 and so recorded in SJL.

To Joseph Dougherty

DEAR SIR   Monticello Oct. 6. 18.
    I sincerely congratul[ate] you on the appointment mentioned in
your favor of Se[p. 21. an]d if my testimony in your behalf has contributed to procu[re] it, it is an additional pleasure. I am just recovering from a long indisposition, and being still unable to set up to
write, but in pain, I must place here the assurance of my friendship &
best wishes.   TH: JEFFERSON

PoC (DLC); on verso of reused address cover of James Sloan to TJ, 29 May 1818;
mutilated at seal; at foot of text: "Mʳ Dougherty"; endorsed by TJ.

To Honoré Julien

Monticello Oct. 6. 18.
    I thank you, my good friend, for the favors of the cheese & seeds
mentioned in your letter of Sep. 11. to have been forwarded to me. if
by water, they will probably still come safely to hand: but if by the
stage, they h[a]ve probably stopped at Fredericksburg or at some
other stage house by the way. uncertain by what route they have been
forwarded, I have been unable to enquire for them. but whether lost
or safe, I recieve it as a mark of your good will which is more acceptable to me than [t]he objects themselves. I am recovering from a long
indisposition, and not yet [a]ble to set up to write but with pain, and
must therefore place here my best wishes for your prosperity and assurances of my constant & affectionate esteem.
                                               TH: JEFFERSON

PoC (DLC); on verso of reused address cover of Archibald Stuart to TJ, 30 May
1818; three words faint; at foot of text: "M. Julien"; endorsed by TJ.

To James Monroe

TH:J. TO THE PRESIDENT OF THE US.   Oct. 6. 18.

I recieved last night a letter from Cathalan of Aug. 13. informing me he had just recieved some boxes of wine for me from Sasserno, who, of course was then living: but he had not yet recieved his Consular commission. it will be better therefore to await further information, and the rather as, if he be dead, I shall be sure to hear it from Cathalan or Spreafico. perhaps indeed it might be well to send a duplicate of Sasserno's commission. affectionate salutns

RC (DNA: RG 59, MLR); dateline at foot of text; addressed: "The President of the US. Highland"; docket, in an unidentified hand, reads in part: "Duplicate forwarded." Not recorded in SJL.

To John Vaughan

DEAR SIR   Monticello Oct. 6. 18.

I recieved last night your favor of Sep. 26. with the inclosed for mr Correa. he & Dr Cooper had left us in the morning, & going direct to Philadelphia, I cannot dispose of it better than by returning it to you. I rec^d also last night a letter from mr Cathalan, acknoleging the remittance of 2205.f = 420.D. the latter part of your letter will need further explanation, I mean that which speaks of the instruments wanted by the Astronomical committee the application to mr Crawford, the danger of losing the privilege of the building E^{t}c. I do not know what this relates to. probably it may have been stated in some previous letter which has not come to hand. if it is any thing in which I can be useful, I shall apply to it with zeal, on recieving the necessary explanations. I salute you with affection & respect.

TH: JEFFERSON

RC (PPAmP: Thomas Jefferson Papers); addressed: "John Vaughan esquire Philadelphia"; franked; postmarked Charlottesville, 8 Oct.; endorsed in an unidentified hand as received 11 Oct., with additional notation in another unidentified hand: "Letter for Mr. Correa Am^n Philos. Society." PoC (MHi); on verso of reused address cover to TJ; endorsed by TJ. Enclosure not found.

To John Adams

Monticello Oct. 7. 18.

It is very long, my dear friend, since I have written to you. the fact is that I was scarcely at home at all from May to September, and from that time I have been severely indisposed and not yet recovered so far as to sit up to write, but in pain. having been subject to troublesome attacks of rheumatism for some winters past, and being called by other business into the neighborhood of our Warmsprings, I thought I would avail myself of them as a preventative of future pain. I was then in good health and[1] it ought to have occurred to me that the medecine which makes the sick well, may[2] make the well sick. those powerful waters produced imposthume, general eruption, fever,[3] colliquative sweats, and extreme debility, which aggravated by the torment of a return home over 100. miles of rocks & mountains reduced me to extremity. I am getting better slowly and, when I can do it with less pain shall always have a pleasure in giving assurances to mrs Adams & yourself of my constant and affectionate friendship & respect. Th: Jefferson

RC (MHi: Adams Papers); addressed: "President Adams Quincy. Mass."; franked; postmarked Charlottesville, 10 Oct.; endorsed by Adams as answered 20 Oct. 1818. PoC (DLC); on verso of reused address cover to TJ; endorsed by TJ.

[1] Preceding seven words interlined.
[2] Word interlined in place of "will."
[3] Omitted comma at right margin editorially supplied.

To Anthony Finley

Sir   Monticello Oct. 7. 18.

A long absence from home, and long indisposition since my return, and present feeble condition must apologise for this late and short acknolegement of your favor of Aug. 3. I have abandoned all attention to the editions of the Notes on Virginia since the first Paris & Lon[d]on editions. both of those were very correct; but I have but a single copy of each which I could not spare; nor would my age or present habits of life permit me to undertake a revisal of the work or to offer any additions or alterations. such changes have taken place since the first publication, as make the revisal a work of much labor & enquiry. Accept the assurance of my respect. Th: Jefferson

PoC (MHi); on verso of reused address cover of James Rawlings to TJ, 14 May 1818; ink stained; at foot of text: "Mr Anthony Finley"; endorsed by TJ.

To William F. Gray

SIR   Monticello Oct. 7. 18.

A long indisposition since I returned home must apologise for this late acknolegement of your favor of Aug. 3. and altho on the recovery, I am not yet able to sit at the writing table but in pain. if the University should be established here, a first object for it's visitors will be to invite a bookseller from Amsterdam to establish a book store at the University for classical & foreign books. the relations of Amsterdam with Germany & the North of Europe as well as with Paris recommend it for foreign productions. but another store for English & country books will certainly be necessary, and the general character of the neighborhood as well as the demands of the University or College, will I think ensure very considerable sales. I know that another concern have entertained thoughts of setting up such a store in Charlottesville, but as yet I believe they have not decided: and I shall really be glad if you should find it convenient to anticipate them, and will certainly render you any service [. . .] I am a subscriber to the American Scientific journal of Professor [Silliman] & to the Analectic magazine, and should be glad if you could have me placed on your list, as I find you are an Agent for these works.[1] I possess the first 14. volumes of the Edinburg Review, and shall be glad if you can furnish me the subsequent volumes to the present day, bound in boards; as well as to continue to furnish me the future numbers as they come out. only be so good as to send me at such intervals as you please the account for these publications, which shall be always immediately remitted to you at Fredsbg, or paid to your store if you have one here which will be more convenient.   Accept the assurance of my best wishes and respect   TH: JEFFERSON

PoC (DLC); on verso of reused address cover of Joseph Milligan to TJ, 11 May 1818; torn at seal, with part of one word rewritten by TJ; at foot of text: "Mr W. F. Gray"; endorsed by TJ.

[1] Omitted period at right margin editorially supplied.

To Caesar A. Rodney

Monticello Oct. 7. 18.

A long absence from home, my dear friend, and long indisposition since my return, must apologise for this late and short acknolegement of your favor of Aug. 8. I am on the recovery, but not yet able to set up to write but in pain. I can therefore only return you thanks for the communications of your letter, which strengthen my hopes that our Southern brethren may be able to do as we have done. my wishes could not be strengthened, and you have lessened my doubts whether they can so far shake off the shackles of the priesthood as to give fair play to their own common sense. this is all that is necessary to make them equal to self government. your letter was the more welcome as the lying of the newspapers backwards & forwards have produced in me the habit of passing over unread every thing they pretend to give as to S. America, thinking absolute ignorance preferable to error. I must here conclude with assurances of my constant & affectionate friendship & respect.   TH: JEFFERSON

RC (DeHi: H. F. Brown Collection); addressed: "Caesar A. Rodney esq. Wilmington Del"; franked; postmarked Charlottesville, 10 Oct. PoC (DLC); on verso of reused address cover of Francis Adrian Van der Kemp to TJ, 11 May 1818; mutilated at seal; endorsed by TJ.

Rodney later inquired of John Wayles Eppes about a possible visit to TJ. On 11 Jan. 1819 Eppes replied from Washington that "Mr Jefferson when I heard last from him had recovered his health—It would afford him great pleasure I am certain to receive a visit from you—If you visit him I should be very glad if you would take my house in your way. In the month of August for several years past he has visited his property in Bedford and will most probably be there at the period you propose making your visit—If this should be the case the nearest rout is immediately by my house—Turn off at Fredericksburg & cross at Cartersville on James River—I live about 30 miles from that place and immediately in the most direct rout to Bedford. It is also the nearest and best way to the Springs in Virginia—Mr Jefferson has erected on his property in Bedford a very handsome Brick house with eight rooms and passes much of his time there taking with him occasionally his grand daughters. For several years he has passed the months of august and September in Bedford" (RC in PHi: Simon Gratz Collection; addressed: "C. A. Rodney Esqr Wilmington Delaware"; franked).

To Robert B. Stark

SIR   Monticello Oct. 7. 18.

A long absence from home & a longer indisposition since my return, from which I am not yet recovered must apologise for this late acknolegement of your favor of Aug. 20. and of the offer of the MSS. of the late Dr Greenway. his character as a botanist had long been known to me, and a hope entertained that he would have published himself the result of his labors. age has withdrawn me from those pursuits myself, but not from the desire of seeing them followed by others, & of availing the world of their fruits. it is with this view I accept the offer from mr Robert Greenway and yourself of making me the Depository of those valuable papers. I should endeavor to have them made public, so as to give their benefit to the world, and the honor to it's author. whether this could be best done thro' the American Philosophical society or how otherwise, I cannot say until trial. a motive the more would be the encoraging a substitution of Vegetable for the Mineral pharmacy. the MS. itself might come by the mail; and the Hortus siccus, probably too large for that, if securely boxed, will come safely thro' the hands of Capt Peyton of Richmond, who knows the best channel of conveying it to me. I pray that mr Greenway & yourself will accept assurances of my sense of the confidence you are pleased to repose in me, and of my great esteem & respect.

TH: JEFFERSON

PoC (CSmH: JF-BA); at foot of text: "Doct^r R. B. Stark"; endorsed by TJ.

To DeWitt Clinton

Monticello Oct. 8. 18.

Th: Jefferson presents his compliments to Govr Clinton and his thanks for his memoir on the antiquities of our country. if all those which are spread over the face of the Continent were described with the care which distinguishes this memoir, and brought together, they might elicit some general hypothesis on the nations which preceded us here. if among their remains, any of the hard metals could be found, clearly antecedent to the discovery of America, it would enlarge the bounds of conjecture.—weaned by age and it's consequent torpitude from such pursuits, he is still happy to see them followed up by younger & more vigorous minds for the benefit of future races, and he salutes Govr Clinton with his friendly recollections, esteem & respect.

RC (NNC: Clinton Papers); dateline at foot of text; addressed: "His Excellency Governor Clinton New York," with "Albany" added in an unidentified hand; franked; postmarked Charlottesville, 10 Oct.; endorsed by Clinton, with additional notation in a different hand: "acknowledging receipt of memoir on western antiquities." PoC (DLC); ink stained; mistakenly endorsed by TJ as a letter of 7 Oct. 1818 but correctly recorded in SJL.

To Charles G. Haines

Monticello Oct. 8. 18.

Th: Jefferson presents his compliments to mr Haines and his thanks for his interesting pamphlet on the great Western canal. he rejoices in the hope that the money which the old world has wasted in eternal wars, and which might have made a garden of the whole globe, if so applied, is likely, by the US. to be employed not for the destruction of man, but for his happiness. he salutes him with respect.

PoC (DLC); on verso of reused address cover to TJ; dateline at foot of text; endorsed by TJ.

From James Madison

[ca. 8 Oct. 1818]

I was much gratified in learning from the President that you were so well recovering from the attack your health suffered beyond the mountains. I wish I could join you at the meeting of the visitors on monday, & attend also that of the Agricultural Society. But circumstances do not allow me that pleasure.

RC (ViU: TJP); undated fragment; with a later attached slip in an unidentified hand noting that it is "Part of a letter" from Madison to TJ "dated <u>Oct. 1818</u>"; possibly part of an otherwise unlocated letter from Madison to TJ recorded in SJL as received 10 Oct. 1818 from Montpellier, with inconsistent 18 Oct. 1818 date of composition.

United States PRESIDENT James Monroe visited Madison at Montpellier on or shortly after 8 Oct. 1818. The AGRICULTURAL SOCIETY of Albemarle met on Monday, 12 Oct. 1818. In his absence, Madison was reelected president (True, "Agricultural Society," 280–1).

From Lewis D. Belair

SIR New York Octobr 9[h] 1818

I Have the Honour to here Inclose a Consise Catalogue of a valuable Collection of Books Just Rec[d]: I shall be Highly Honourd to Receive your order.

Respectfully yours LEWIS D BELAIR

RC (MHi); endorsed by TJ as received 22 Oct. 1818 and so recorded in SJL. RC (DLC); address cover only; with PoC of TJ to Joseph Jones, 15 Jan. 1819, on verso; addressed: "Thomas Jefferson Esq[e] Montecelo Milton V[a] p[r] Mail"; franked; postmarked New York, 9 Oct. Enclosure: Fernagus De Gelone's 1818 advertising circular, describing his business relationship with Belair in New York City and providing a list of booksellers in other American cities as well as on the islands of Saint Thomas and Jamaica who will also fill his orders; promising a reduction in European market prices ranging from 5 to 15 percent, provided that the buyer pays "freight, insurance, and custom-house duty in America"; specifying that orders include the cost of the books plus a supplement of "about 8 per cent of that sum of money for all my expences of clearance in Europe, Brokerage, postage, boxes, packing up, land carriage, etc." and be submitted to American consuls or merchants in Europe; mentioning a "description of Books called *Librairie courante*, such as Novels, Belles-Lettres, Books neither quite modern nor very ancient, on which you may have as much as 25 per cent abbated from the Catalogue or market prices, for cash"; commenting that "It is your advantage to unite with some friends to make your orders larger, which will give you a fair chance for greater discounts"; and providing an extensive list of European titles available from Belair in New York; with marginal numbering by TJ, corresponding to the books he ordered in his letters to Belair of 27 Oct. and 16 Nov. 1818, and his handwritten notes at foot of p. 3: "Abregé des 10 livres d'Architecture de Vitruve. Paris. Coignard. 1674. 12mo," and at foot of p. 4: "Aeschyle. Theorie des fonctions analytiques. pa. La Grange. 4to Analyse du traité de la mecanique celest de P. S. Laplace par Biot. brochure" (printed circular, signed by Fernagus de Gelone, in DLC: TJ Papers, 214:38214–5; dated "Paris 1818"; at head of text: "EUROPEAN BOOK TRADE").

From Josiah Meigs

SIR,   Washington City Oct. 12. 1818.

I have the honour to present, with this, <u>two</u> Copies of Abstracts of Calculations to ascertain the <u>Longitude</u> of the <u>Capitol</u>.—and I take the liberty to express a wish that further efforts may be made to effect this object—

A private Citizen, of the illustrious character of Mr Jefferson, can give to every useful object an impulse which multitudes could not effect.

With Esteem—Respect—and Affection. I am Yours

JOSIAH MEIGS

RC (DLC); at foot of text: "Thomas Jefferson, Esq."; endorsed by TJ as received 22 Oct. 1818 and so recorded in SJL. Enclosure: William Lambert, *Abstracts of Calculations, to ascertain the Longitude of the Capitol, in the City of Washington, from Greenwich Observatory,* *in England* (Washington, 1817; Poor, *Jefferson's Library,* 7 [no. 303]; TJ's copy in MBPLi, inscribed "Josiah Meigs to Thomas Jefferson, Esq, October 2, 1818"; for another copy, see Lambert to TJ, 10 Oct. 1817).

To Bernard Peyton

DEAR SIR   Monticello Oct. 13. 18.

The rain now falling will I think enable Johnson's boats to go down. I send him therefore a box of wine for Col° Allston of Charleston which I have taken the liberty of addressing to your care to be forwarded. I think you formerly advertised spun cotton for sale; I must request you to send me 150. ℔ of what runs 5. yds to the ℔. if you have it not yourself, you will do me the favor to get it. if to this you can add one or two good cheeses it will add to the obligation. I make no more apologies for the trouble because I am sure you are tired of their repetition and that your kind good will renders them unnecessary. Affectionately your's. TH: JEFFERSON

PoC (MHi); on verso of a reused address cover of an otherwise unlocated letter from James Madison to TJ (addressed: "Thomas Jefferson Monticello" by "Mr Lowndes"; recorded in SJL as a letter dated only "May," received 19 May 1818 from Montpellier and delivered "by mr Lowndes"); at foot of text: "Capt Peyton"; endorsed by TJ.

William Lowndes, a member of the United States House of Representatives from South Carolina, 1811–22, visited James Madison at Montpellier and TJ at Monticello in May 1818. In a small volume of historical anecdotes that he compiled between 1819 and 1822, Lowndes recalled that "I saw Mr Jefferson for an hour at Montichello—who told me that in his admon when a war seemed probable with Spain he directed Genl Wilkinson to state what number of troops would be necessary to conquer Cuba & Mexico. For Mexico he required only provisions landed at Vera Cruz?—for Cuba 20,000 men to take & hold it" (MS in DLC: Lowndes Papers; in Lowndes's hand; undated).

From Honoré Julien

MONSIEUR washington Octobre Le 14 1818
jais eu Lhoneur de Recevoir votre Letre en Date du 6—justant qui maprend que vous navez pas Recut qui Contient Le fromagé et Les graines que je vous Envoie . . . . . et en voila La Cause Cest que jesperois vous La faire parvenir par La Ligne des Stages—mais Les Stage najant pas voulut Sen Chargé Cest Ce qui a Causé Le Retard—jais prié une personne qui Etoit a washington et qui Demeure a Richmond de vouloir Bien Se chargé de La Boite Esperant quell vous parviendrois plutot mais jais Recus une Letre de cette personn[e] [e]n date du 5°—[1] qui me Dit quil na pas Encore trouvé Les mojens de vous La faire parvenir

cest avec peine que japrend que vous avez Eté indispose[2] mais jespere que La presente vous trouvera parfaitment—en Bonne Santé—Cest Ce que je Desire—: et Suis avec Respect et Consideration
HONORÉ JULIEN

Mr Brunet Confectioner near the New theatre Richmond took Charge of the Box—and if you have not Received it—you might perhaps—find Some opportunity to have it Conveyed to you H. J.

EDITORS' TRANSLATION

SIR   Washington October 14, 1818
I had the honor of receiving your letter dated the 6th, informing me that you
have not received the cheese and seeds that I sent you . . . . . The reason is
that I hoped to have them delivered to you by the stage line, but the stage
would not take charge of it. That caused the delay. I asked a person who was
in Washington and who lives in Richmond to be kind enough to take the
box, hoping that it would reach you sooner, but I received a letter dated the
5th from that person telling me that he had not yet found a way to have it
delivered to you

I am sad to learn that you have been ill, but I hope that the present letter
will find you in perfect health. This is my wish, and I am with respect and
consideration   HONORÉ JULIEN

Mʳ Brunet Confectioner near the New theatre Richmond took Charge of the
Box—and if you have not Received it—you might perhaps—find Some opportunity to have it Conveyed to you   H. J.

RC (DLC); edge trimmed and chipped;   Washington, 15 Oct. Translation by Dr.
ellipsis in original; endorsed by TJ as re-   Roland H. Simon.
ceived 22 Oct. 1818 and so recorded in
SJL. RC (MHi); address cover only; with   [1] Preceding four words added in left
PoC of TJ to James Oldham, 1 Jan. 1819,   margin.
on verso; addressed: "Thomas Jefferson   [2] Manuscript: "jndespose."
Esqʳᵉ Monticello"; franked; postmarked

From Victor Adolphus Sasserno

SIR,   Nice Octᵇᵉʳ 14. 1818.
    The letter i had the honour of writing to you last August 18. made
you Know that i had sent you, through Mʳ Cathalan, Six chests holding 300 bottles Bellet's wine; these, i am told by Mʳ Cathalan have
been stoped in Marseilles till now for want of ships Sailing for your
ports. 'tis very unpleasant, however, i hope, this delay will not hinder
their arriving at their destination before the beginning of the winter.
In the said letter, i also said to you, that i had received, neither your
letter of feb. 22ᵈ (mentioned in your last to me of april 5) nor my
commission. Now and with pleasure i inform you, Sir, that they both
came yesterday to my hands after a very great bye-way, the bundle
was directed, to Mʳ Hammet Consul of the United States at Naples,
who has opened it and Sent to Mʳ Cathalan. i have already received
the patent, the bound and your honoured letter, the remaining Mʳ
Cathalan will send me by the first opportunity. Presently i must obtain the Exequatur of the Sardinia's King to take intire possession of
my office.

i dare flatter myself, well to justify your confidence, and the favour of the president, and deserve his and your approbation in discharging worthily the duties impos'd on me by my office.

I have nothing more left, Sir, but to thank you for your Kindnesses, and reiterate to you the offer of my devoted Services here as well as in all other parts where you will employ them, the acknowledgement and pleasure shall be always on my Side.

I Salute you, Sir, with consideration and respect and am for life. Your most devoted and obedient Servant.   A. SASSERNO

RC (DLC); endorsed by TJ as received 2 Apr. 1819 and so recorded in SJL. Enclosed in Stephen Cathalan to TJ, 30 Nov. 1818.

THE BOUND: presumably the consular bond.

From Mathew Carey

SIR   Philad[a] Oct. 16. 1818.

Your favour of the 6th which I duly rec[d] is before me.

I feel the justice and propriety of the objection you make to comply with my request on the subject of Baines, which was manifestly incorrect, and which I hope you will have the goodness to excuse. I was induced to make it at the urgent instances of Rev.[1] M[r] Weems, contrary in truth to my own opinion of right. It is not the first, by five hundred, of the exemplifications I have made of Ovid's

Video meliora proboque—
Sed deteriora sequor—

I am engaged in a work which I call Vindiciæ Hibernicæ, which embraces the reigns of Elizabeth, James I & Charles I. & will, I hope, develope such a scene of fraud, forgery, and perjury, as has never taken place before, nor since—& I hope never will again. If you have any Books bearing on this subject, a list w[d] much oblige me, if you can spare time.

I remain, with sincere respect, Your ob[t] h[ble] serv[t]

MATHEW CAREY

By this mail you will receive the other volume of Baines, price $12—

RC (MHi); dateline beneath signature; at head of text: "Thomas Jefferson, Esq[r]"; endorsed by TJ as received 25 Oct. 1818 and so recorded in SJL.

VIDEO MELIORA PROBOQUE—SED DE-TERIORA SEQUOR ("I see the better and approve it, but I follow the worse") closely follows Ovid, *Metamorphoses*, 7.20–1 (*Ovid*, trans. Grant Showerman, J. H. Mozley, and Frank Justus Miller, Loeb Classical Library [1914–29; rev. George P. Goold, 1977–79], 3:342–3).

[1] Word interlined.

From Anonymous Republicans in Charleston, South Carolina

RESPECTED SIR   Charleston October 16th 1818

Knowing it will give you great pleasure to hear that your old and valued friend Mr Charles Pinckney has after much intreating, complied very reluctantly with the wishes of his Republican friends—to become a Candidate in order to keep a very able and popular Federalist General Huger from Representing Charleston in Congress, we have the pleasure to inform you that after the warmest contest that has ever taken place here he has carried his Election by a great majority—the contest we hope on the part of Mr Pinckney's friends was conducted with great temper and moderation and has displayed in the course of three months incessant attack so many of the most important Speeches, and acts and political writings in the reign of Federal terror and Such a body of Political Services of Mr Pinckney and particularly to the Republican Party as was irresistable and notwithstanding we had to contend with the whole force wealth and Influence of the federal party Joined by 200 quids and what is astonishing all the officers of the Federal Government in Charleston except the District Judge who was with us. notwithstanding all this the genuine Republican Party rose in thier Strength chose for thier Candidate against his wishes Mr Charles Pinckney whom they Supposed To be more properly now at the head of the genuine Democratic Party in this State than any other man and whose great talents both as a Speaker and writer whose weight of Character and political Services and above all, his noble and Disinterested political consistency which as you long know has Seperated him entirely from his two violent federal Relations the two General Pinckneys would make him more liable to Succeed than any other man. the result has justified our opinion—the Republicans rose In thier Strength and we have carried him triumphantly by a great majority much greater than was expected to Represent the City of Charleston and the Surrounding Six Election districts. the first Exporting district, and next to new York by far the most important and richest commercial District In the Union. we know the Government always had great confidence in Mr Pinckney and his Representati[ons] to them and we are Sure this recent and high mark of confidence from Such a district as Charleston will If possible Serve to increase it, we enclose Some Papers prepared by the Conducters of Mr Pinckneys Election For your perusal. you would undoubtedly have heard from himself on the occasion But unfortunately only four Days before the Election his Eldest Daughter the Wife of Colonel Hayne died and has so oerwhelmed him with Sorrow that he is almost turned into Stone with grief, and from that moment has left everything to his friends—his grief is Such as we have not words to express. it happens fortunately that his beloved daughter has left two fine Boys and an infant girl to console her friends and this we hope with his own good Sense and reflection wil[l] after nature has had its vent comfort and restore him to his Friends

we have the honour to be with great attachment and Respect your Republican friends and Admirers

RC (DLC); dateline at foot of text; edge chipped; endorsed by TJ as an anonymous letter concerning "(Pinkney's election)" received 8 Nov. 1818 and so recorded in SJL. Enclosures not found.

Charles Pinckney CARRIED HIS ELECTION to the United States House of Representatives with nearly as many votes as the combined tallies of Daniel Elliott Huger and William Crafts, the Federalist candidates (Charleston *City Gazette and Commercial Daily Advertiser*, 14, 19 Oct. 1818). John Drayton was the United States DISTRICT JUDGE for the South Carolina District at this time (*ANB*). The TWO GENERAL PINCKNEYS were Charles Pinckney's cousins Charles Cotesworth Pinckney and Thomas Pinckney. All three began their political careers as Federalists, but Charles Pinckney became a Republican in the 1790s (*ANB*, 17:533–8, 539–40). Charles Pinckney's ELDEST DAUGHTER, Frances Henrietta Pinckney Hayne, the wife of Robert Y. Hayne, died on 8 Oct. 1818 (*City Gazette and Commercial Daily Advertiser*, 12 Oct. 1818).

From John Barnes

MY DEAR SIR   George Town D.C. Oc[t] 17. 1818.

I am under great concern indeed on hearing your present indisposition[1] hath deprived you of enjoying your accustomed exercise on horseback—may we hope you will soon partake of so beneficial a restorer of health:—do I pray you afford me the consolation wished for.—

Respecting the late General Kosciusko's affairs, presume nothing particular has occured.—I have often thought and wished, you had exchanged a letter with Messr[s] Baring, Brothers & C[o] (London) who doubtless has been applied to, in order to learn the state of the General's finances &c—. By refering to my letter 10th Jan[y] 1818. you will find a sketch of the General's account with me: a fair copy of statement is now handed—of my receipts of Interest and Dividends from and after 26th Nov[r] 1816. to the 1st Oc[t] 1817. both inclusive

amount $1090.08.

From which deduct statement of my account rendered } 812:00
said 26 Nov[r] 1816. exclusive of interest &c[a]   }

Leaves $278.08

to be accounted for whenever you may judge proper.

With tenders of esteem & affection
I am dear Sir, Most respectfully, Your ob[t] sv[t]

JOHN BARNES,

RC (MHi); in a clerk's hand, signed by Barnes; on a sheet folded to form four pages, with letter on p. 1, p. 2 blank, enclosure on p. 3, and endorsement on p. 4; at foot of text: "Thomas Jefferson Esq[r]

Monticello"; endorsed by TJ as received 22 Oct. 1818 and so recorded in SJL.

[1] Manuscript: "indispotion."

ENCLOSURE

John Barnes's Account with Tadeusz Kosciuszko

Gen[l] Thad[s] Kosciusko in account with John Barnes.

1816			
Nov[r] 26 To amount of balance due J.B. as per a/c rendered M[r] Jefferson		$812.00	
1817 By dividends and interest received—viz.			
Jany 2 " 3 months Interest due 31[st] Decm[r] on his $12.500. 6 per cent U.S. Stock N[t]	$182.82		
Ap[l] 1. " 3 months due on ditto. ditto	182.82		
" 10 " half years dividend due 20[th] March on 46 Shares Bank of Columbia 8 per Ct: n[t]	179.40		
July 1 " 3 months Interest due on $12.500. 6 p[rc]t N[t]	182.82		
Sep[t] 22 " half years dividend due 20 Ins[t] on said 46 Shares Bank of Col[a] N[t]	179.40		
Oct. 1 " 3 months Interest on $12.500. 6 per c[t] N[t]	182.82	1090.08	
From which sum deduct the above		812.00	
Principal due Gen[l] K. E.E. (Exclusive of In[t] &c.)		$278.08	

N.B. On the 2[d] Jan[y] 1818. John Barnes presented himself at the office of Discount and Deposit in order to receive the General's quarterly Interest but refused paying it having read advice of the untimely death of the General.

Said amount on $12,500 (Quarterly) at 6 per cent. is $187.50. paid Quarterly
Bank of Columbia—on 46 Shares due 20ᵗʰ March 1818. (also refused) at 8 pʳcᵗ would be $184 paid half yearly.[1]

EE.   JOHN BARNES,
Geo Town—Coᵃ 17 Octʳ 1818.

MS (MHi); conjoined with covering letter; in a clerk's hand, with conclusion in Barnes's hand; with horizontal and vertical rules in red ink.

E.E.: "errors excepted."

[1] Remainder in Barnes's hand.

From John Wayles Eppes

DEAR SIR.   Mill Brook october 17. 1818.

The various rumours which have reached us as to the state of your health have been such as to excite serious apprehension and alarm[1] on the part of your friends—All the recent accounts concur in representing you as entirely well or so far recovered as no longer to cause anxiety on the part of your friends—accept my congratulations on an event which I am certain no human being can hale with[2] more heartfelt pleasure than myself—

Francis left New London a few days before the vacation in consequence of hearing of your indisposition—He would have gone immediately to Monticello but from the uncertainty as to your return from the springs & our hearing immediately afterwards that you were so far recovered as to be entirely out of danger—on hearing this I determined to keep him until he could get some Winter cloathing of which he was very bare—

Mʳ Dashiell's leaving New-London renders it necessary again to seek out some place for Francis—The central University will probably not go into immediate operation—Mʳ Baker has a very well educated young man living with him at present and I propose sending him there until the spring after which if the central University is not in readiness I will send him to any other which you may prefer—

Present me to all the family and accept for your health & happiness my warmest wishes.

Your affectionately   JNO W EPPES

P.S.

The original subscription paper which you forwarded to me has been lost or mislaid—When it passed out of my hands there was no name to it except my own for 200 dollars payable in[3] four years 50 dollars on the 1st of april 1818 & 50 dollars annually on the first day of april of the three following years—The term of the first payment being now so far passed & the paper being probably lost I have executed a new one which I enclose for the same sum 200 dollars & divided it into two payments viz april 1819. & apl. 1820—It will make I hope no difference & I have no motive for making the change but to prevent my appearing as a delinquent subscriber the time of the first payment being long since passed—

RC (ViU: TJP-ER); addressed: "Thomas Jefferson Esqr Monticello"; endorsed by TJ as received <18> 19 Oct. 1818 and so recorded (mistakenly dated 17 Sept.) in SJL.

Eppes's enclosure confirming his subscription to Central College has not been found. The Master List of Subscribers to Central College, [after 7 May 1817], listing his $200 donation as the only sum pledged from Buckingham County, is printed above at 5 May 1817, as is the Central College Subscription List, [ca. 7 May 1817], which TJ had sent him on 6 Aug. 1817.

THE SPRINGS: Warm Springs.

[1] Manuscript: "dlarm."
[2] Manuscript: "with with."
[3] Manuscript: "in in."

From Joseph Milligan

DEAR SIR   Georgetown Oct 17th 1818

I have sent you by this days mail a full Copy of the <u>political</u> <u>Economy</u> If you think there should be an Index or table of Contents please send it by mail as soon as you can as that is all that will now delay the publication

Yours with respect   JOSEPH MILLIGAN

RC (DLC); endorsed by TJ as received 22 Oct. 1818 and so recorded in SJL. RC (DLC); address cover only; with PoC of TJ to Milligan, 12 Jan. 1819, on verso; addressed: "Thomas Jefferson Esqr Monticello Milton"; franked; postmarked Georgetown, 19 Oct.

To Patrick Gibson

[D]EAR SIR   Monticello Oct. 18. 18.

After long delay for want of a tide we were enabled by the last rain to send off by Johnson's boats 106. (I think) barrels of flour to be delivered to you. from the mill too I expect mr T. E. Randolph has sent, or will immediately send 50. barrels of rent[1] flour. besides placing you in safety as to my curtailments, these remittances will put you in funds to meet a draught I must make on you within a day or two for between 3. & 400 D. and another soon after for about as much more. as I do not know the sums to be renewed on my several notes I must ask the favor of you to forward me blanks in time. my health continues low, so that I have little prospect of visiting Bedford this fall, but I write to mr Yancey to hasten down his flour.   I salute you affectionately   TH: JEFFERSON

PoC (MHi); on verso of portion of re-used address cover to TJ; edge trimmed; at foot of text: "Mr Gibson"; endorsed by TJ.

[1] Word interlined in place of "toll."

To Robert Patterson

DEAR SIR   Monticello Oct. 18. 18.

I have long had a disabled telescope which cannot be repaired nearer than Philadelphia, and I have never till now had an opportunity of forwarding it safely to that place; nor do I know who is the best hand there at repairing. the bearer mr Trist, on his way to Westpoint, and going in the stage, is so kind as to take charge of it and to deliver it to you; and the favor I must ask of you is to put it into the hands of the best workman with instruction as soon as repaired to let me know by mail the cost. I will then remit it to him and advise him how to forward the instrument to me. indeed if, with the instrument, you will be so good as to put this letter into his hand, it will be his [suffi]cient instruction and save you all further trouble; for w[hi]ch [I mu]st find my apology in your friendship and my necessity. [I salute y]ou with constant and affectionate respect.

                                    TH: JEFFERSON

PoC (MHi); on verso of reused address cover to TJ; mutilated at seal, with losses supplied from Dupl; at foot of text: "Doct^r Robert Patterson"; endorsed by TJ. Dupl (PPAmP: Thomas Jefferson Papers); on verso of RC of TJ to Patterson, 2 Feb. 1819; at head of text: "<Duplic> Copy"; at foot of text: "turn over."

From Martin Dawson, with Jefferson's Note

DEAR SIR   Milton 19th October 1818

I hold your Specialty to Edmund Bacon for three
hundred and twenty Seven Dollars $327.—
Interest on the same from 28th Sep^t last to

                                                                   $ _____

payment when convenient will Oblige
    Yo. Ob. Hu. Ser^v   MARTIN DAWSON

[*Note by TJ on verso beneath endorsement:*]
Nov. 11. 18. gave ord. on P. Gibson 330.D. being int. to Nov. 20.

RC (ViU: TJP-ER); addressed: "Thomas Jefferson esq^{re} } Monticello"; endorsed by TJ as received 22 Oct. 1818 and so recorded in SJL.

From John Adams

MY DEAR FRIEND   Quincy Octr 20. 1818

one trouble never comes alone! At our ages We may expect more and more of them every day in groups, and every day less fortitude to bear them.

When I saw in Print that you was gone to the Springs, I anxiously Suspected that all was not healthy at Monticello.

you may be Surprised to hear that your favour of the 7th has given me hopes. "Imposthume, general Eruptions colliquative Sweats," Sometimes and I believe often indicate Strength of Constitution and returning Vigour. I hope and believe they have given you a new Lease for years, many years,

your Letter which is written with your usu[a]l neatness and firmness confirms my hopes.

Now Sir, for my Griefs.! The dear Partner of my Life for fifty four years as a Wife and for many years more as a Lover now lyes, in extremis, forbidden to Speak or be Spoken to.

If human Life is a Bubble, no matter how Soon it breaks. If it is as I firmly believe an immortal Existence We ought patiently to wait the Instructions of the great Teacher.

I am, Sir, your deeply afflicted Friend   JOHN ADAMS

RC (DLC: TJ Papers, 205:36481); mutilated at seal, with missing text supplied from FC; endorsed by TJ as received 30 Oct. 1818 and so recorded in SJL. RC (MHi); address cover only; with PoC of TJ to Nathaniel Potter, 17 Jan. 1819, on verso; addressed by Susannah Boylston Adams Clark (Treadway): "Thomas Jefferson—Late President of the USA Monticello"; franked; postmarked Quincy, 21 Oct. FC (Lb in MHi: Adams Papers; misdated 20 Oct. 1815, but entered with 1818 correspondence in Lb).

From John H. Cocke

SIR,   Bremo Octo 20. 1818

Governor Preston having occasion to pass thro' your neighbourhood avails himself of an opportunity which he has long wished for, of becoming acquainted with you. I take pleasure in making you known to each other, because I confidently hope, that my agency will be productive of mutual gratification.

I have the pleasure to inform you that I left Mr Cabell on friday recovering fast.

Accept Sir, my best wishes for your speedy & perfect restoration to health—

Yours respectfully   J. H. COCKE

P.S. I send the Sea Kale Seed by Governor Preston

RC (CSmH: JF); endorsed by TJ as received 20 Oct. 1818 and so recorded in SJL. RC (MHi); address cover only; with PoC of TJ to Fernagus De Gelone, 22 Jan. 1819, on verso; addressed: "Mr Jefferson Monticello" by "Govr Preston."

From Bernard Peyton

DEAR SIR   Richm^d 20 October 1818

I was favor'd yesterday with your esteem^d letter by Mail, & this morning with the Box of Wine spoken of for Col^o Allston by Mr. Johnson's Boat which shall be shipped tomorrow in a Vessel bound to Charleston direct, & he furnished with the bill of Lading by mail immediately.

I have procured, & send by Mr. Johnson one hundred & fifty pounds Cotton Yarn N° 5 which runs generally five yards to the pound, & hope you will find it to answer, I keep a constant supply of this article & shall be glad to furnish you at all times—   In my search for Cheese's I met with your neighbour Mr. James Leitch who informed me he had examined throughout the City & procured a Hamper of the very best to be had, & would furnish you with any quantity you may wish at Cost, which I tho't would answer you entirely, & therefore made no further enquiry.

I am greatly rejoiced to hear that your health is again restored, & sincerely hope it may be long preserved: No apologies are necessary in calling on me for any kind of service in my power, it is a source of gratification, rather than trouble to oblige you—

With sincere regard Your Mo: Obd: Servt. B. Peyton

N.B. I also send by Mr. Johnson a small Box to your address which was handed me a day or two since by a gentleman from Norfolk.

B. P.

RC (MHi); at foot of first page (torn): "[(turn o]ver)" for postscript on verso; endorsed by TJ as received 29 Nov. 1818 and so recorded in SJL.

From Patrick Gibson

Sir   Richmond 21st Octr 1818.

Since writing to you on the 24th Ulto I have received three loads of flour on your accot say 156 bls: of which 132 are S: fine 10 fine and 14 condemned—the S: fine & fine I have sold to R. K. Jones at $8\frac{1}{4}$ & $8\frac{3}{4}$\$ on 60 ^{d}/_. the 14 bls: having been made out of smutted wheat, and consequently both dark and bitter, I have found it hitherto impossible to dispose of at any price, the bakers will not buy it, and it cannot be shipp'd out of the State—I have paid B. Peyton $106.38 on your accot

With sentiments of respect I am
Your ob Servt   Patrick Gibson

22d Your favor of the 18th is just received
    Your dfts shall be attended to, and blanks forwarded to you in time, Your note to T.J.R due next week I shall endeavour to have renewed for the full amot and shall offer R. K. Jones's note for disct to meet your dfts

RC (MHi); between dateline and salutation: "Thomas Jefferson Esqre"; endorsed by TJ as received 25 Oct. 1818 and so recorded in SJL.

From Thomas W. Maury

Charlottesville 21st October 1818
Th: W. Maury with best respects to Thomas Jefferson Esqr

RC (MHi); with PoC of TJ to William Davenport, 2 Feb. 1819, on verso; dateline at foot of text; addressed (torn): "[. . .] Jefferson Esqr Monticello."

This note presumably covered an enclosure, not found, possibly related to Maury's service as secretary at the meeting of the University of Virginia Commissioners at Rockfish Gap in August 1818.

From William F. Gray

SIR,   Fredericksburg Octo. 22. 1818

I have the pleasure of acknowledging the rec^t of your kind letter under date the 7th Curt.—Accept my thanks for your friendly notice of my letter of the 3rd Aug.—Since I was at Charlottesville, I have been strongly advised to the measure of establishing a Bookstore there; my own inclination favoured it; and, other motives being now strengthened by your approbation and friendly promise of support, I am determined upon taking the step so soon as I can make certain arrangements here, and get a competent young man, in whom I can trust, to take charge of the store at Charlottesville.

I shall send you by tomorrow's Stage all the numbers of the Edinburgh Review from 29 to 58 inclusive. No. 59 will follow in a few days. I had none of these numbers done up in boards, but thinking you only mentioned <u>boards</u> in order that I might not send them <u>bound</u> in <u>leather</u>, I have ventured to send them in the state in which they are usually delivered to subscribers. If, however, you are particularly desirous of having them bound in boards, let them be sent back at your convenience and it shall be done. In the bundle are a few Books which were bought here a few days ago, and directed to be sent to Mrs T. M. Randolph, to the care of Mr Leach of Charlottesville; but knowing her to be a member of your family I have taken the liberty of sending them directly to Monticello.—I should be glad of the privilege of sending the new publications to Monticello.

I will with much pleasure furnish you with the Analectic Magazine and Silliman's Scientific Journal, if you will tell me what numbers you want.—My arrangements with the publisher of the Analectic Magazine will make it most convenient for me to furnish you with <u>that</u> work from the begining of a year.

That you may be speedily restored to health and enjoy length of days, is the respectful wish of

Your Obt. Svt.   W. F. GRAY

RC (DLC); endorsed by TJ as received 30 Oct. 1818 and so recorded in SJL.

MR LEACH: James Leitch.

From John Trumbull

DEAR SIR   New York Oct° 23ᵈ 1818

I have the Satisfaction to acquaint you that my painting of the Declaration of Independance is finished (as far as it can be, until I see it in its place at the Capitol)—and, with permission of the President, is now publicly[1] exhibiting in this City:—It has excited some attention, and has drawn forth one Criticism of so malignant a Character that I felt it necessary <u>immediately</u> to reply to it:—and as in my reply I have taken the liberty of using your name, & referring to your ancient friendship, and the interest which you from its origin took in this work, I have thought it my duty to enclose to you both the criticism and reply.   fully persuaded that you will forgive the liberty which I have taken, in consideration that the poison required an <u>instant</u> antidote; & if suffered to operate until I could have obtained your permission, its effects might have proved dangerous to the reputation of the work

I hope that you, and all your Family enjoy & will long enjoy, Health and all Happiness

I am Dʳ Sir Your much obliged & grateful   Jɴᵒ TRUMBULL

RC (DLC); at foot of text: "Thoˢ Jefferson Esqʳ Monticello"; endorsed by TJ as received 30 Oct. 1818 and so recorded in SJL. Dft (Joseph Rubinfine, West Palm Beach, Fla., 2010).

Trumbull exhibited his PAINTING OF THE DECLARATION OF INDEPENDENCE (reproduced elsewhere in this volume) at the New York Academy of Fine Arts from 5 Oct. to 9 Nov. 1818, with an admission fee of twenty-five cents per person. He donated the final day's receipts of nearly $350 to the local institution for the deaf and dumb (New York *Mercantile Advertiser*, 3 Oct. 1818; New York *National Advocate*, 2 Nov. 1818; *New-York Evening Post*, 7 Nov. 1818; *New-York Daily Advertiser*, 10 Nov. 1818).

[1] RC: "publily." Dft: "publicly."

ENCLOSURES

I

"Detector" to Editor of the New York *National Advocate*

MR. EDITOR—   [ca. 20 Oct. 1818]

I have lately seen the painting by colonel Trumbull, "representing the Declaration of Independence," which is said to contain "portraits of forty-seven of the members present in Congress on that memorable occasion."

This picture has been drawn by direction of Congress, and is now submitted to public inspection by permission of the government.

It is not my intention to examine the merits of this production as a specimen of the arts. It may, perhaps, be *a very pretty picture*, but is certainly no representation of the Declaration of Independence. The errors in point of fact, with which it abounds, ought to exclude it from the walls of the capitol, where its exhibition will hereafter give to the mistakes[1] of the artist the semblance and authority of historical truth.

The manifest intention of Congress, in directing the preparation of this picture, was to perpetuate accurate recollections of one of the greatest events in history, and to hand to posterity correct resemblances of the men who pronounced our separation from Great Britain. In tracing such a sketch, the fancy of the painter has a very limited indulgence. Some latitude is allowed him, as respects design and embellishment; but the very object of his effort enjoins a scrupulous adherence to fact, in all that regards the actors and main incidents of his subject. If he overleaps this boundary, he violates the plain rules of propriety and common sense; and his piece sinks from the grade of a great historical painting into a sorry, motley, mongrel picture, where truth and fiction mingle, but cannot be discriminated. To make the "national painting" in question subservient to a display of the likeness of any American, however distinguished, who was not both a member of Congress and present in that body when Independence was declared, is no less ridiculous than it would be to introduce into it the head of lord Chatham, or that of col. Barre.

Among "the portraits of forty-seven of the members present in Congress on that memorable occasion," col. Trumbull has given those of George Clinton of New York, and Benjamin Rush and George Clymer of Pennsylvania.— Now, the truth happens to be, that neither of these gentlemen were present when independence was declared, and never gave a vote for or against the declaration. Mr. Clinton, if I am not mistaken, was appointed a general in June, 1776, and was serving, when Congress pronounced our severance from Great Britain, in a military capacity in the province of New York. Messrs. Rush and Clymer were not elected to Congress until the 20th of July, 1776, that is to say, sixteen days after the final passage of the declaration, and nineteen days subsequent to its approval in committee of the whole. The names of the two gentlemen last mentioned, together with those of James[2] Smith, George Taylor and James Ross, appear among the signatures to the Declaration of Independence in consequence of the following circumstances:—On the 19th day of July, 1776, (the day before the election of Mr Rush, and his associates above mentioned) Congress passed a resolution that each of its members should sign that instrument. It was not, however, engrossed on parchment and prepared for signatures until the 2d[3] of August. The new members from Pennsylvania having taken their seats in the interim, signed the declaration in obedience to the resolution of the house.

The persons who are believed to have been present when the independence was declared, and whose portraits do not appear in the paintings of col. Trumbull, are—

Henry Wisner, of Newyork; John Hart, of New Jersey; John Morton and Charles Humphreys, of Pennsylvania; Cæsar Rodney, of Delaware; Thomas Stone, of Maryland; Thomas Nelson, jun. Richard Lightfoot Lee, and Carter Braxton of Virginia; John Penn, of North Carolina; Button Gwinnett and Lyman Hall, of Georgia.

That portraits of these distinguished men are not contained in the piece is not a fault of the artist, who has been unable to obtain accurate likenesses of them. But it is particularly to be regretted, that an authentic representation of Cæsar Rodney, of Delaware, could not have been found to substitute for one of the faces which have no pretensions to a place. To the vote of this gentleman, on the 4th of July, and to the accidental or intentional absence from their seats of Robert Morris, of Pennsylvania, and John Dickinson, also of Pennsylvania, (not of Delaware, as the artist has it in his prospectus,) it is owing that *the vote of the states* was unanimous in favor of the national charter on its[4] final adoption. The delegates of Delaware present in congress on the 1st of July, when the declaration of independence passed to committee of the whole, were divided in opinion—Mr. Read,[5] one of the attending delegates from that state, being *against* the measure, and Mr. M'Kean, the other attending delegate, being *for* it. The vote of Pennsylvania, in committee of the whole, was unfavorable to independence—Mess. Morris, Dickinson, Willing[6] and Humphreys, declaring against it, in opposition to Mess Franklin, Morton and Wilson.

I have thought proper to offer these few remarks, both because the permission given by the government to exhibit the painting in New York, seems to be an invitation to dispassionate criticism, and because the artist still has time before the removal of his picture, to make it, if practicable, accord with historical truth. To exhibit it in its present form on the walls of the capitol at Washington, would be a severe satire on our ignorance of our own history, and would justly expose our legislative councils to the scoff and sneers of every intelligent foreigner who may visit us.[7] If, with its palpable errors, the painting shall be displayed in congress hall, we would advise that two of the pictures which are intended to accompany it may, with similar propriety, depict Montgomery dictating the capitulation of Yorktown, and Washington dying under the walls of Quebec! DETECTOR.

Printed in New York *National Advocate*, 20 Oct. 1818 (clipping in DLC: TJ Papers, 213:38110); undated; at head of text: "*To the editor of the National Advocate*" and (in quotation marks) "GREAT NATIONAL PICTURE." Reprinted in *Port Folio*, 4th ser., 7 (1819): 84–6, and elsewhere.

Mordecai M. Noah was the EDITOR of the *National Advocate* at this time (Brigham, *American Newspapers*, 1:672). The phrases REPRESENTING THE DECLARATION OF INDEPENDENCE and PORTRAITS . . . OCCASION are quoted from Trumbull's proposal for publishing a print of his painting of the *Declaration of Independence* (undated broadside in ViU:

Albert H. Small Declaration of Independence Collection, and a different version in NHi). JAMES ROSS and RICHARD LIGHTFOOT LEE are mistaken references to George Ross, of Pennsylvania, and Richard Henry Lee, of Virginia.

[1] *Port Folio*: "mistake."
[2] *National Advocate*: "Jame." *Port Folio*: "James."
[3] *Port Folio*: "3d."
[4] *National Advocate*: "its its."
[5] *National Advocate* and *Port Folio*: "Reed."
[6] *National Advocate*: "Welling." *Port Folio*: "Willing."
[7] *Port Folio* text ends here.

II

John Trumbull to "Detector"

New-York, 19th [ca. 20] Oct. 1818.[1]

Mr. Trumbull returns his thanks to *Detector*, for having given him an opportunity of laying before the public some account of the origin and progress of the Painting of the Declaration of Independence, which he could not otherwise have done, without being liable to censure for egotism.

After the termination of the war of the Revolution, Mr. T. determined to study the art of Painting, for the purpose of recording the great events and great men of that period. In the year 1786, the paintings of the Battle of Bunker's Hill, and the attack on Quebec were finished, were seen by, and received the most flattering approbation of, the first artists and connoisseurs in England, France, Germany, and Prussia. Considering the success of his general plan thus secured, he proceeded to determine the other subjects which should form his series; and among these the Declaration of Independence was considered as the most important.

At this time, Mr. Trumbull enjoyed the friendship and hospitality of Mr. Jefferson, then Minister of the United States at Paris; and it was under his roof, and with the aid of his advice, that the arrangement and composition of this picture was settled. In the following summer of 1787, the head of Mr. John Adams, then Minister of the United States in London, was painted, a few days previous to his return from his mission; and shortly after the head of Mr. Jefferson was painted in Paris.

The question immediately occurred, which Detector has so shrewdly[2] discovered, who were the men actually present on the 4th of July?—The Journals of Congress are silent,—it would be dangerous to trust the memory of any one,—and the only prudent resource was to take as a general guide, the signatures to the original instrument, although it was as well known to Mr. Jefferson and Mr. T. then, as it is now to the sagacious Detector, that there were on that instrument the names of several gentlemen who were not actually present on the 4th of July; and also, that several gentlemen were then present who never subscribed their names.

The Record was therefore taken as a general guide: and with regard to all the most important characters represented in the painting, there was, and (begging my sagacious friend's pardon) there is, no doubt:

In 1789, Mr. T. arrived in this town from Europe, and passed the winter here, Congress being then in session.—Here the portraits of Richard Henry Lee, Roger Sherman, Lewis Morris, Francis Lewis, &c. &c. were painted, and, at this time he was informed, that George Clinton, then Governor, had been a member present in Congress on the 4th of July, although his name was not among those subscribed to the instrument. He therefore waited on Governor Clinton to ascertain the fact, *and was by him assured that he was present on that memorable occasion.* The Governor consented with pleasure to sit for his portrait—and on this testimony the portrait was painted.

This session of Congress was peculiarly[3] important, and had collected in this city many eminent men, military as well as civil; and Mr. T. thus had a fair opportunity not only of advancing the picture in question, but of collecting the materials for other subjects. He was of course well known to President

Washington, and to all the distinguished characters of the day. He made it his duty, and his business, to ask the advice and criticism of all those who did him the honour to sit for their portraits; and not only the Declaration of Independence, but the Battles of Trenton and Princeton, and the Surrender of York Town, were very much advanced under the eye, with the criticism, and with the approbation, of the men who had been the great actors in the several scenes.

In May, 1790, Mr. T. went to Philadelphia, where, during three months, he added considerably to his stock of materials. Here he was informed that Thomas Willing was a member present in Congress on the 4th of July, although his name was not on the list of signatures. On application to Mr. Willing, he assured Mr. T. that he was present, but opposed to the measure, and therefore had not signed. Mr. T. did not feel it to be his duty to record only those who had been supporters of the measure, and therefore requested Mr. Willing to sit, which he did.

In November, of the same year, Mr. T. went to Boston and New-Hampshire, and obtained portraits from the Life of John Hancock, Samuel Adams, R. T. Paine, Josiah Bartlett, and many others.

In February, 1791 he went to Charleston, S. C. and obtained from the Life, portraits of Edward Rutledge and Thomas Heyward—and copies of pictures of Thomas Lynch and Arthur Middleton, who were dead—as well as many heads of men eminent in other scenes, military as well as civil, which entered into his plan. On his return, he went to York Town, in Virginia, and made a correct drawing of the scene of Lord Cornwallis's surrender—at Williamsburg obtained a portrait from the Life of George Wythe, &c. &c.

Mr. T. afterwards made two visits to the east, went to Saratoga, and passed the winters of 1792 and 3 in Philadelphia, where Congress then sat—always endeavoring to obtain correct information; and when men whose memory it was desirable to preserve were dead, using all the means in his power to obtain from their surviving friends whatever memorial existed.

During this period Mr. T. had, and solicited no other patronage or assistance in his arduous undertaking, than subscriptions for those prints which have been long since published from his pictures of the death of Warren & Montgomery.

He was known during these four years, to be employed in this pursuit. He enjoyed the friendship and advice of the most eminent men in the country and he was not idle. The men of those days are now almost all gone to their reward; and but for the indefatigable perseverance of Mr. T. in a pursuit, which his friends often smiled at as visionary, it would at this moment be impossible to obtain even such imperfect pictures as Detector considers this to be.

One word more to this most estimable, kind and impartial critic. Two years ago Mr. T. was advised to submit the small picture of this subject (to which all that has been said refers) to the view of the Government, in the expectation that it might attract their attention. In consequence, the Declaration of Independence, the Surrender of Lord Cornwallis, the Battle of Trenton, and that of Princeton were taken to Washington—and with permission of the Speaker hung up in the Hall of the Representatives, where they remained subject to criticism for several days—and there is no doubt that the honourable testimony borne to their authenticity and correctness by many cotemporaries in both Houses of Congress, as well as by Mr. Madison then President, and Mr. Monroe then Secretary of State, was the cause of that employment which is the source of undissembled satisfaction to Mr. T. and which he proudly trusts gives him a title to be remembered hereafter with the events which it has been the occupation, and is now the delight of his life, to have so commemorated

Mr. T. still[4] solicits candid and liberal criticism, and will thank any person who will point out an error in his work, and kindly supply him with the means or[5] information by which he may correct it. But he holds malignity and envy in profound contempt.

Printed in *New-York Daily Advertiser*, 22 Oct. 1818 (clipping in DLC: TJ Papers, 213:38111); dateline at foot of text, presumably misdated, inasmuch as Trumbull was responding to the previous enclosure, which first appeared in a 20 Oct. 1818 newspaper. Reprinted in New York *National Advocate*, 23 Oct. 1818; *Port Folio*, 4th ser., 7 (1819): 86–8; and elsewhere.

In an apparent response to the above letter in the 22 Oct. 1818 issue of the *National Advocate*, "Detector" pointed out that in addition to the individuals he had already identified as "not having been in congress on the 4th July, 1776, or at any previous time, but whose portraits, nevertheless, appear in Mr. Trumbull's painting," he had overlooked Charles Carroll of Carrollton, who was not elected to represent Maryland "until *the very day* that independence was declared." "Detector" added that "The statement you make as coming from Mr. Trumbull, that George Clinton was present at *the signing* of the declaration of independence, must, I apprehend, be founded in some misunderstanding on the part of Mr. Trumbull of Gov. Clinton's expressions. The latter was, *by election*, a delegate in congress from New York during all the period from the 22d of April, 1775, to the 5th of May, 1777. Such being the case, we *must* infer that he was not attending in congress when the declaration was subscribed, for the secret resolution passed by that body on the 19th July, 1776, (a fortnight before the declaration was engrossed on parchment) made it imperative on every member who should sit in congress that year to put his signature to the instrument. The fact of his presence at the signing,

and that of his signature not appearing to the declaration, could only be reconciled by his having refused to subscribe, a circumstance which certainly did not occur, and which, if it had taken place, ought to have particularly excluded his portrait from col. Trumbull's painting." "Detector" further remarked that Clinton had no more right to inclusion in the painting than James Duane, John Alsop, John Jay, Simon Boerum, and Philip Schuyler, "all of whom were, on the 4th July, 1776, delegates to congress, (but not attending ones) from this state, and of most of whom 'authentic representations' might easily be obtained." In addition to Clinton and Carroll, "Detector" declared that Benjamin Rush and George Clymer should have been excluded, noting that "Neither of which gentlemen took his seat in congress until after independence was declared."

Although no response from Trumbull himself has been located, the controversy did not close with this addendum by "Detector." A further editorial response from the *National Advocate* appeared in its 26 Oct. 1818 issue and was followed in that paper a day later by a still more detailed defense by "Detector" of his opinion. The *New-York Daily Advertiser* of 28 Oct. 1818 printed what appears to be the final editorial remark on this controversy.

Although GEORGE CLINTON was a delegate to the Second Continental Congress and supported independence, he was recalled to military duty in New York before he could vote for or sign the Declaration (*ANB*; *DAB*; *Public Papers of George Clinton, First Governor of New York, 1777–1795, 1801–1804* [1899–1914], 8:398).

[1] At head of text in brackets is an editorial commentary reading "In the National

Advocate of Tuesday morning, an article appeared under the signature of '*Detector*,' the writer of which charges Col. Trumbull with having violated the truth of history in his picture of the Declaration of Independence, by introducing portraits of several gentlemen who were not present when Independence was declared, and omitting those of others who are 'believed to have been present' on that occasion. The following is Col. Trumbull's answer to this charge. Had Detector been really solicitous for the integrity of history,—if he had no other object in view, he might easily have satisfied his scruples, and dissipated his fears, by an application for information to Col. Trumbull himself. As it now stands, we are much mistaken if the public do not ascribe the attack to the carpings of ill-nature and envy." Paragraph repeated in *National Advocate* but omitted in *Port Folio*.

[2] *Daily Advertiser*: "shrewly." *National Advocate* and *Port Folio*: "shrewdly."

[3] *Daily Advertiser*: "peculiary." *National Advocate* and *Port Folio*: "peculiarly."

[4] *Daily Advertiser*: "stills." *National Advocate* and *Port Folio*: "still."

[5] *Port Folio*: "of."

From Joseph C. Cabell

DEAR SIR,   Edgewood. 24 Oct: 1818.

I am happily recovering from the severe fever which has, of late, confined me to my bed for 20 days, but am barely able to take a turn across the room. Col: Coles told me the substance of his conversation with you lately at Monticello; observing, that you wished to go to Bedford & had a thought of calling on me on your way, but your health being bad, it was doubtful whether you would be strong enough to perform the Journey. It would give me very great pleasure to see you at my House. If you should come, you will find it necessary to make a circuit, by crossing at Warren, & taking the Warminster Road at the Church, or a little before you get to it.[1] But I fear, Sir, your state of health will not permit you to travel without danger of making it worse. Do not be apprehensive[2] that you will not see me: as, if you do not come this way before I leave home, I will certainly come by Monticello. I think my health will admit of my travelling by the 10th of next month. I would wish to set out[3] sooner, but weakness or the arrangement of my affairs for the winter, will probably detain me till then, if not longer. I shall be on the road a little before, or a little after the 10th. The road between this and warren, is now impassable for a Carriage; but I shall carry hands with me to help me over the gullies.

I remain, dear Sir, faithfully yr friend,   JOSEPH C. CABELL

RC (ViU: TJP-PC); at foot of text: "Mr Jefferson"; endorsed by TJ as received 30 Oct. 1818 and so recorded in SJL.

[1] Cabell here canceled (several words illegible) "Should you come this way I wish if it be agreeable to you you would call on Majr Charles Yancey who lives

just opposite to me. I wish this, because I think such a visit would gratify him, and it might [. . .] on the public [. . .]."

From de Bure Frères

MONSIEUR   paris ce 24 8bre 1818.

nous esperons que vous avez reçu la Lettre que nous avons eu l'honneur de vous ecrire le 1er de ce mois. vous aurez peut etre reçu la caisse que nous vous avons expediée. nous vous reiterons ici, Monsieur, nos regrets de n'en avoir point pu trouver davantage, mais il n'y a point eu de notre faute, et nous serons peut etre plus heureux l'année prochaine

ayant, Monsieur une occasion de faire passer aux etats unis des Exemplaires du catalogue de la Bibliotheque de feu M Clavier, nous profitons de cette facilité pour vous en adresser un. si par hazard vous n'aviez point le temps de nous ecrire, dans le cas ou il y auroit quelques articles de la vente, qui vous conviendroient, cela pourra toujours vous servir a vous les faire connaitre, pour les demandes que vous pourrez etre dans le cas de nous faire—cette Bibliotheque est composée d'un grand nombre d'excellens livres d'etude, qui se rapprochent beaucoup de ceux que nous vous envoyons.

Nous avons l'honneur d'etre, Monsieur, Vos tres humbles et tres obeissants Serviteurs

DE BURE FRERES.
Libraires du Roi, et de la Bibliotheque du Roi.

EDITORS' TRANSLATION

SIR   Paris 24 October 1818.

We hope that you have received the letter we had the honor of writing you on the first of this month. Perhaps you have also received the crate of books that we sent you. We reiterate our regret, Sir, that we were unable to find more, but it was not our fault, and we may be more fortunate next year

Having occasion to ship copies of the *Catalogue des Livres de la Bibliothèque De Feu M. Clavier* to the United States, we take advantage of this opportunity to send you one. If some of the items for sale interest you, but for some reason you do not have time to write us, you can always use this catalogue to let us know what they are, in case you wish to order them from us. This library consists of many excellent scholarly books, which are very similar to those we are sending you.

We have the honor to be, Sir, your very humble and very obedient servants

DE BURE FRERES.
Booksellers to the king, and to the royal library.

RC (MHi); endorsed by TJ as received 7 Feb. 1819 and so recorded in SJL. Translation by Dr. Roland H. Simon.

To Joseph Milligan

DEAR SIR   Monticello Oct. 25. 18.

I recieved with great joy the compleat copy of the translation of Tracy's work. it will need no other Table of Contents than the Analytical table from page ix. to xxviii. mr Tracy had a particular wish it should be known that I revised the translation. on the next leaf[1] therefore I have addressed a letter to you which may be printed on a single leaf, and inserted between the title page & Prospectus. send me one of these leaves when printed, that I may insert it in the copy of the work you sent me, to be forwarded to the author. I salute you with friendship and respect.   TH: JEFFERSON

RC (NjP: John Story Gulick Collection of American Statesmen); addressed: "Mr Joseph Millegan George town Col."; frank clipped; postmarked Milton, 27 Oct. 1818. PoC (MHi); on recto of reused address cover of James Oldham to TJ, 15 June 1818, with PoC of enclosure to above document on verso; edge trimmed; endorsed by TJ. Enclosure: TJ to Milligan, [ca. 25 Oct. 1818].

[1] Reworked from "sheet."

To Joseph Milligan

SIR   [ca. 25 Oct. 1818]

I now return you, according to promise, the translation of M. Destutt Tracy's treatise on Political economy, which I have carefully revised and corrected. the numerous corrections of sense in the translation have necessarily destroyed uniformity of style, so that all I may say on that subject is that the sense of the author is every where now faithfully expressed. it would be difficult to do justice, in any translation, to the style of the original, in which no word is unnecessary, no word can be changed for the better, and severity of logic results in that brevity, to which we wish all science reduced. the merit of this work will, I hope, place it in the hands of every reader in our country. by diffusing sound principles of Political economy, it will protect the public industry from the parasite institutions now consuming it, and lead us to that just and regular distribution of the public burthens from which we have sometimes strayed. it goes forth therefore with my hearty prayers that while the Review of Montesquieu, by the same author, is made with us the[1] elementary book of instruction in the principles of civil[2] government, so the present work may be in[3] the particular branch of Political economy.   TH: JEFFERSON

RC (Anonymous, Keswick, Va., 2008); undated; words at beginning of several sentences capitalized by Milligan, with TJ's lowercasing retained above; at foot of text: "Mr Millegan." PoC (MHi); on verso of PoC of covering letter and address cover of James Oldham to TJ, 15 June 1818; edge trimmed. Printed in Destutt de Tracy, *Treatise on Political Economy*, dated Monticello, 25 Oct. 1818, and again with that date in *American Beacon*

and Norfolk & Portsmouth Daily Advertiser, 16 Dec. 1818, and Washington *Daily National Intelligencer*, 31 Dec. 1818. Undated extract consisting of last three sentences printed in *Richmond Enquirer*, 21 Dec. 1818. Enclosed in TJ to Milligan, 25 Oct. 1818.

[1] Manuscript: "the the."
[2] Word interlined.
[3] Manuscript: "in in."

To Richard Rush

DEAR SIR   Monticello Oct. 25. 18.

This letter will be presented you by mr George Ticknor, a gentleman from Massachusets whose father is of distinguished standing in that state. this gentleman has been 4. years travelling and[1] sojourning in the different countries of Europe for the purposes of instruction, and with the same views will pass the approaching winter in Edinburg, Oxford, Cambridge and London. you will find him learned, discreet, correct and honorable; and in addition to the natural claim of an American citizen to your patronage, you will yield it for the heart-felt pleasure of gratifying the worthy. you may safely present him to whomsoever he may wish as a fine[2] sample of the American citizen. do it then for his sake, for your own sake and for mine, and accept the blessings of an old man with his cordial salutations.

                                    TH: JEFFERSON

RC (NjP: Rush Family Papers); addressed: "His Excellency Richard Rush Min. Plen^y of the US. London favored by Mr Ticknor"; endorsed by Rush, with his additional notation: "Introduces Mr Ticknor." PoC (MHi); on verso of portion of reused address cover to TJ; edge trimmed;

endorsed by TJ. Enclosed in TJ to Elisha Ticknor and TJ to George Ticknor, both 25 Oct. 1818.

[1] RC: "<*and*> and," with first word not canceled in PoC.
[2] TJ here canceled "specimen."

To Elisha Ticknor

[D]EAR SIR   Monticello Oct. 25. 18.

I recieved two days ago, a letter from your son informing me he should pass the ensuing winter in Edinburg, Oxford, Cambridge and London, and asking a letter of introduction to Mr Rush our minister at London, and that I would pass it through you. the inclosed letter to him covers one to mr Rush, and to his I add my own request that you will be so good as to transmit it and to accept the assurances of my high respect and esteem. TH JEFF[ERSON]

PoC (MHi); on verso of portion of reused address cover to TJ; edge trimmed; signature incomplete due to polygraph error; at foot of text: "Elisha Ticknor esq."; endorsed by TJ. Enclosures: TJ to George Ticknor, 25 Oct. 1818, and enclosure.

To George Ticknor

DEAR SIR   Monticello Oct. 25. 18.

I recieved, two days ago, your favor of Aug. 10. from Madrid, an[d] sincerely regret that my letter to Cardinal Dugnani did not reach you at Rome. it would have introduced you to a circle worth studying as a variety in the human character. I am happy however to learn that your peregrinations through Europe have been succesful as to the object to which they were directed. you will come home fraught with great means of promoting the science, & consequently the happiness of your country; the only obstacle to which will be that your circumstances will not compel you to sacrifice your own ease to the good of others. many are the places which would court your choice; and none more fervently than the College I have heretofore mentioned to you, now expected to be adopted by the state and liberally endowed under the name of 'the University of Virginia.' in this it is proposed to teach all the sciences deemed useful at this day; and our estimate is that they may be embraced by about 10. professors whom we propose to procure, of the first order of science in their respective lines wherever to be had, at home or abroad. on our plan of an Academical village, each Professor will have a separate house to himself, a fixed salary of from 1000. to 1500.D. a year, with a tuition fee of 25.D. from every student attending him, with an ensurance that the tuition fees and salary together shall make up at least 2000.D. but with a probability that the tuition fees will carry the profits far above that sum. for we have reason to believe that it will be the immediate resort for all the Southern & Western states.   I pass over our professorship of Latin, Greek & Hebrew, & that of modern languages, French, Ital. Span. German & Anglo-Saxon, which altho' t[he] most lucrative would be the most laborious, and notice that which you would splendidly fill of Ideology, Ethics, Belles lettres & Fine arts. [I] have some belief too that our genial climate would be more friendly to your constitution than the rigors of that of Massachusetts. but all this may possibly yield to the 'hoc coelum, sub quo natus educatusque essem.' I have indulged in this reverie the more credulously because you say in your letter that 'if there wer[e] a department in the Gen¹ government that was devoted to public instruction, I might seek a place in it. but there is none. there is none even in my state govrnt.'¹ such an institution of the general government cannot be until an amendmen[t] of the Constitution, and for that and the necessary laws and measures of execution, long years must pass away. in the mean while we consider the institution of our University as supplying it's place, and perhaps superceding it's necessity. with stronger wishes than expectations therefore I will wait to hear from you, as our buildings will not be ready under a year from th[is]² time and to the affectionate recollections of our family add assurances of my constant and sincere attachment.   TH: JEFFERSON

P.S. I inclose you a letter to mr Rush, tho' to him I am sure you needed none. the President is daily expected at his farm adjoining me when the letter to Lᵈ Holland shall be asked.

PoC (DLC); corner torn and edge trimmed; at foot of first page: "Mʳ Ticknor"; endorsed by TJ. Enclosure: TJ to Richard Rush, 25 Oct. 1818. Enclosed in TJ to Elisha Ticknor, 25 Oct. 1818.

In a speech urging the Romans to stay in their native city, Camillus refers to HOC COELUM, SUB QUO NATUS EDUCATUSQUE ESSEM ("this sky beneath which I had been born and reared") (Livy, *History of Rome*, 5.54.3, in *Livy*, trans. Benjamin O. Foster, Frank Gardner Moore, Evan T. Sage, and Alfred C. Schlesinger, Loeb Classical Library [1919–59; repr. dates vary], 3:182–3).

¹ Omitted period at right margin editorially supplied.
² Word faint.

To Nathaniel Bowditch

DEAR SIR   Monticello Oct. 26. 18.

I have for some time owed you a letter of thanks for your learned pamphlet on Dʳ Stewart's formula for obtaining the Sun's distance from the motion of the moon's Apsides; a work however, much above my Mathematical stature. this delay has proceeded from a desire to address you on an interest much nearer home, and on the subject of which I must make a long story.

On a private subscription of about 50. or 60,000 D. we began the establishment of what we called the Central college, about a mile from the village of Charlottesville and 4. miles from this place, and have made some progress in the buildings. the legislature, at their last session, took up the subject and passed an act for establishing an

University, endowing it for the present with an annuity of 15,000.D. and directing Commissioners to meet, to recommend a site, a plan of buildings, the professorships necessary for teaching all the branches of science at this day deemed useful E^{t}c. the Commissioners, by a vote of 16. for the Central college, 2. for a 2^d place and 3. for a 3^d adopted that for the site of the University. they approved, by an unanimous vote, the plan of building begun at that place, and agreed on such a distribution of the sciences as it was thought might bring them all within the competence of 10. professors; and no doubt is entertained of a confirmation by the legislature at their next meeting in December. the plan of building is, not to erect one single[1] magnificent building to contain every body, and every thing, but, to make of it an Academical village, in which every professor shall have his separate house, containing his lecturing room, with 2. 3. or 4. rooms for his own accomodation, accordingly as he may have a family or no family, with kitchen, garden E^{t}c distinct Dormitories for the students, not more than two in a room, & separate boarding houses for dieting them by private housekeepers. we conclude to employ no Professor who is not of the 1st order of the science he professes, that where we can find such in our own country, we shall prefer them, and where we cannot, we will procure them wherever else to be found. the standing salary proposed is of 1000. to 1500.D. with 25.D. tuition fee from each student attending any professor, with house, garden E^{t}c free of rent. we believe that our own state will furnish 500. students, and having good information that it will be the resort of all the Western and Southern states, we count on as many more from them, when in full operation. but as the schools will take time to fill, we propose that until the tuition fees, with the salary shall amount to 2000.D. we will make up that deficiency so as to ensure 2000.D. from the out-set. the soil in this part of our country is as fertile as any upland soil in any of the Maritime states, inhabited fully by a substantial yeomanry of farmers (tobacco long since given up) and being at the 1st ridge of mountains, there is not a healthier or more genial climate in the world. our maximum of heat, and that only of 1. or 2. days in summer is about 96. the minimum in winter is $+5\frac{1}{2}$ but the mean of the months of June July, Aug. are 72. 75. 73. and of Dec. Jan. Feb. are 45. 36. 40. the thermometer is below 55. (the fire point) 4. months in the year, and about a month before & after that we require fire in the mornings and evenings. our average of snow is 22.I. covering the ground as many days in the winter. the necessaries of life are extremely cheap, but dry goods and groceries excessively dear, which renders it prudent to draw them directly from Philadelphia, New York or Boston, as they come to our doors by water. our religions are Presbyterian, Methodist, Baptist & a few Anglicans, a preacher of some of these sects officiating in Charlottesville every Sabbath. our society is neither scientific nor splendid, but independant, hospitable, correct and neighborly. but the Professors of the University will of themselves compose a scientific society. they will be removable only by a vote of two thirds of the visitors, and when you are told that the visitors are mr Madison, Presid^t Monroe & myself, all known to you by character, Senator Cabell, Genl Cocke, mr Watson, gentlemen of distinguished worth and information, you will be sensible that the tenure is in fact for life.   Now, Sir, for the object of all this detail. I have stated that where men of the 1st order of science in their line can be found in our own country, we shall give them a willing preference. we are satisfied that we can get from no country a professor of higher qualifications than yourself for our Mathematical department, and we entertain the hope and with great anxiety that you will accept of it. the house for that Professorship will be ready at midsummer next or soon after, when we should wish that school to be opened. I know the prejudices of every state against the climates of all those South of itself: but I know also that the candid traveller advancing Southwardly, to a certain degree at least, sees that they are mere prejudices, and that the real advantages of climate are in the middle & temperate states, and especially when above their tide waters.

I must add that all this is written on the hypothesis that the legislature will confirm the report of the Commissioners. but that is not doubted: and[2] therefore I make this early application to pray you to take this proposition into consideration; and as soon as you can settle your mind on it, to favor me with a line on the subject, shortening my anxiety for it's reception only according to your convenience. in the mean time accept the assurance of my great esteem and respect.

TH: JEFFERSON

RC (MBPLi: Bowditch Collection); at foot of first page: "Mr Bowditch." PoC (DLC); endorsed by TJ.

Bowditch enclosed his PAMPHLET, which included criticism of Matthew Stewart's technique for lunar apsidal calculations, in his letter to TJ of 30 Mar. 1818.

[1] Word added in margin.
[2] Manuscript: "and and."

To Lewis D. Belair

S<small>IR</small>   Monticello Oct. 27. 18.

Among the books on the catalogue you were so kind as to send me I have noted the underwritten which I should be willing to procure at suitable prices. will you be so good as to drop me a line stating their prices and formats. in the mean time, & without waiting a further order, be so good as to send me the Dictionary Gr. & Fr. of Planche, and Cortez's correspondence. the former being but an 8vo may be sent by mail; and so may the latter as being still less. only send them by different mails. I would rather recieve them <u>unbound</u>. Accept the assurance of my respect   T<small>H</small>: J<small>EFFERSON</small>

1.	l.	7.	from bottom. La Malle's Sallust
		3.	from bottom. Guerres civiles de Rome d'Appien. by what translator?
[2?]. l.		3.	Tacite Lat. Fr. by La Malle.
		6.	Pline le jeune Lat. Fr.
		11.	Dictionnaire bibliotheque. of what date?
		35.	Antiquitès Romaines de Denis d'Halicarnasse.
		[50.]^1	Du Cange Glossarium.
		58.	Suetonius. Lat. Fr. by wh[at translator]^2?
[3.?] l.		11.	Stephani Thesaurus.
		14.	La Place. Systeme du monde Mecanique celeste.
		35.	Cabanis humeurs Catarrhales.
		40.	Correspondre de Cortez avec Charles V.
		49.	Planche Dict. Gr. Fr.
		64.	Dictionnaire de medecine avec Lexicon E^{t}c
		71.	P[ersoo]n^3 Synopsis plantarum
		74.	Sacrorum bibliorum Concordantiae.
4.	l.	4.	Persoon. Synopsis fung[orum.]^4 is not this included in his Synopsis plantarum.

there is an Abregé des 10. livres de Vitruve. Paris. Coignard. 1674. 12mo which I should be glad of if you have it.

PoC (MHi); on verso of portion of reused address cover to TJ; left edge of book list trimmed; with page and line numbers in list corresponding to the advertising circular of Ferngaus De Gelone enclosed by Belair in his letter to TJ of 9 Oct. 1818 and described there; endorsed by TJ.

Beneath signature and to right of book list TJ summarized an otherwise unlocated letter to Belair of 31 Oct. 1818 (not recorded in SJL): "Oct. 31. added Logarithmes de Lalande   Henri IV de Perefixe." TJ eventually acquired two copies of Joseph Jérôme Le Français de Lalande, *Tables de Logarithmes pour les Nombres et Pour les Sinus* (Paris, 1805; repr. 1815; Poor, *Jefferson's Library*, 8 [no. 405]; one of TJ's copies in ViCMRL, on deposit ViU, with Nicholas P. Trist's note that TJ had given it to him).

The DICTIONARY GR. & FR. TJ ordered here was Joseph Planche, *Dictionnaire Grec-Français, composé sur l'ouvrage intitulé Thesaurus Linguæ Græcæ, de Henri Étienne* (Paris, 1817; Poor, *Jefferson's Library*, 13 [no. 849]; TJ's copy in MH). CORTEZ'S CORRESPONDENCE was Gratien Jean Baptiste Louis, vicomte de Flavigny, trans., *Correspondance de Fernand Cortès avec l'empereur Charles-Quint, Sur la Conquête du Mexique* (Paris, 1778; Poor, *Jefferson's Library*, 4 [no. 117]; TJ's copy in MoSW).

TJ acquired three duodecimo volumes of the works of Pliny the Younger (PLINE LE JEUNE) that he apparently bound separately as a two-volume set of Pliny's letters (Poor, *Jefferson's Library*, 13 [no. 793]) and a single volume of his *Panegyricus* of Trajan (Poor, *Jefferson's Library*, 13 [no. 816]; identified as a translation by Louis de Sacy in TJ to Frederick A. Mayo, 9 Apr. 1819). TJ's copy of the latter (in MoSW) is de Sacy, trans., *Panégyrique de Trajan, par Pline le Jeune, en Latin et en Français* (Clermont, France, 1809), and the compilation of the letters was probably de Sacy, trans., *Lettres de Pline le Jeune, en Latin et en Français, Suivies du Panégyrique de Trajan*, 2 vols. (Clermont, 1809); both editions were published by Landriot.

The advertising circular of Fernagus De Gelone enclosed in Belair to TJ, 9 Oct. 1818, lists "Cailleau's Dictionnaire Bibliographique" on page two, line eleven. This work was R. Duclos and Jacques Charles Brunet, eds., *Dictionnaire Bibliographique, Historique et Critique des Livres Rares*, 4 vols. (Paris, 1790–1802), published by André Charles Cailleau, and mistakenly requested above by TJ as DICTIONNAIRE BIBLIOTHEQUE.

STEPHANI THESAURUS was the Greek-language thesaurus of Henri Estienne, originally published and previously owned by TJ as Estienne, Θησαυρὸς τῆς Ἑλληνικῆς Γλώσσης. *Thesaurus Graecae Linguae*, 4 vols. (Geneva, 1572; Sowerby, no. 4760). The DICTIONNAIRE DE MEDECINE offered by Belair was Pierre Hubert Nysten, *Dictionnaire de Médecine, et des sciences accessoires a la médecine . . . suivi de deux vocabulaires, l'un Latin, l'autre Grec* (Paris, 1814).

Abregé des Dix Livres d'Architecture de Vitruve, a volume edited by Claude Perrault and published by Jean Baptiste COIGNARD (Paris, 1674; Poor, *Jefferson's Library*, 12 [no. 722]; TJ's copy in MoSW), was acquired by TJ the following year through the Paris firm of de Bure Frères (de Bure Frères to TJ, 11 Sept. 1819).

[1] Word obscured at crease.
[2] Two words faint.
[3] Word faint.
[4] Word faint.

To William J. Coffee

SIR   Monticello Oct. 27. 18.

You were so kind as to offer your services in any little commissions [I] might have occasion for in New York. there is one in which your talent [&] observation will be of more value to me than that of any other person there of my acquaintance. you saw probably my cisterns, and know that they have continued useless for want of a proper cement to line them. all agree that the substance called Terras, imported from Amsterdam and Hamburg, is proved effectual by long experience, and I am told it is in use in New York and can there be had. my cisterns have about 1280. square feet of surface, and, for a coat of half an inch thickness, would require 40. bushels either of that material alone, or of the mixed material, whatever that is, and so more or less in proportion as the coat should be thicker or thinner. will you be so good as to inform me whether the material is to be had in N. York and at what price? how thick a lining is found sufficient for the inside of a Cistern? and any details of manipulation which you may be so kind as to collect for me.

I hope you have long ago recieved your models, and am requested by the family to present you the assurances of their friendly recollections, as I do of my own great esteem and respect.

TH: JEFFERSON

PoC (MHi); on verso of reused address cover to TJ; two words faint; at foot of text: "M[r] Coffee"; endorsed by TJ.

Tarras (TERRAS) is a mortar or hydraulic cement made from pulverized German pumice (*OED*).

To Henry Dearborn

DEAR GENERAL   Monticello Oct. 27. 18.

I never saw till lately the IXth vol. of Wilson's Ornithology. to this a life of the Author is prefixed, by a mr Ord, in which he has indulged himself in great personal asperity against myself. these things in common I disregard, but he has attached his libel to a book which is to go into all countries & thro' all time. he almost makes his heroe die of chagrin at my refusing to associate him with Pike in his expedition to the Arkansa, an expedition on which he says he had particularly set his heart. now I wish the aid of your memory, as to the main fact on which the libel is bottomed, to wit, that Wilson wished to be of that expedition with Pike particularly, and that I refused it. if my memory is right, that was a military expedition, set on foot by General Wilkinson,[1] on his arrival at S[t] Louis as Governor and Commanding officer, to reconnoitre the country, and to know the positions of his enemies, Spanish and Indian: that it was set on foot of his own authority, without our knolege or consultation; and that being unknown to us until it had departed, it was less likely to be known to Wilson, and to be a thing on which he could have set his heart. I have not among my papers a scrip of a pen on the subject; which is a proof I took no part in it's direction. had I directed it, the instructions E[t]c would have been in my hand writing, & copies in my possession. the truth is this, I believe. after the exploration of the Missisipi by Lewis & Clarke and of the Washita by Dunbar, we sent Freeman up the Red river; and on his return we meant to have sent an exploring party up the Arkansa, and it was my intention that Wilson should have accompanied that party. but Freeman's journey being stopped by the Spanish authorities, we suspended the mission up the Arkansa to avoid collision with them. will you be so good as to lay your memory and your papers under contribution to set me right in all this?

Can you, without involving yourself in offence with Stewart, obtain thro' any channel, a frank and explicit declaration on what ground he detains my portrait? for what term? and whether there is to be an end of it? I think he has now had it 10. or 12. years. I wrote to him once respecting it, but he never noticed my letter.—I am on the recovery from a sickness of 6. or 7. weeks, but do not yet leave the house. our family all join in affectionate recollections and recommendations to mrs Dearborne and yourself, and none with more constant affection and respect than myself.   TH: JEFFERSON

RC (ViU: Peter Coolidge Deposit); addressed: "Maj^r General Dearborne Boston"; franked; postmarked Charlottesville, 29 Oct.; mistakenly endorsed by Dearborn as a letter of 29 Oct. 1818. PoC (DLC); endorsed by TJ.

TJ sat for this portrait by Gilbert Stuart (STEWART) in May 1800. Bush, *Life Portraits*, 45–7, documents the painting, now lost, and reproduces an 1801 engraving presumably based on it.

[1] Manuscript: "Wilkirson."

To Charles Simms

DEAR SIR   Monticello Oct. 27. 18.

After a long absence from home, and a longer spell of sickness following it and from which I am but recovering, my first attentions have been to the remittance of duties and charges for the 9. boxes [of] wine & [1.] of Macc[aro]ni, which you were so kind as to recieve and forward to me. the exact amount was 48.33 for which I now inclose 50.D. in bills of the US. bank, which is as near as I can make out in bills. the fracti[o]nal difference need not be regarded.

I expect daily other shipments of books & wines from Havre and Mars[eilles.] [sho]uld they come to your port [I] will ask the favor of you to reship them immediately to mr Gibson at Richmond, noting to me the duties & charges which shall always be faithfully remitted. Accept the assurance of my great esteem & respect

                                               TH: JEFFERSON

PoC (MHi); on verso of reused address cover of John Barnes to TJ, 3 July 1818; faint; at foot of text: "Col° Simms"; endorsed by TJ.

To John Steele

DEAR SIR   Montic[ello] Oct. 27. 18.

After a long absence from home, and a longer spell of sickness following it, and from which I am but recovering, my first attentions have been to the remittance of duties and charges for the 2. boxes of wine you were so kind as to recieve and forward to me. the exact amount was 18.58 for which I now inclose a 20.D. bill of the US. bank, which is as near as I can come in bills. the fractional[1] difference need not be regarded.

I expect daily other shipments of books and wines from Havre and Marseilles. should they come to your port I will ask the favor of you to have them reshipped immediately to mr Gibson at Richmond noting to me the duties and charges which shall always be faithfully remitted. Accept the assurance of my great esteem & respect

TH: JEFFERSON

PoC (MHi); on verso of reused address cover of Anthony Charles Cazenove to TJ, 3 July 1818; dateline faint; at foot of text: "John Steele esq."; endorsed by TJ.

[1] Manuscript: "fraction," probably reflecting incomplete enhancement of faint word by TJ.

From Thomas Brown

RESPECTED FRIEND   Troy Oct 28th 1818

Entertaining a high opinion of thy learning and useful abilities, and sincerely believing that it is thy wish to promote whatever may be of benefit to mankind; I have taken the liberty to forward to thee, the enclosed publication, by which thou wilt See what I have been able to effect by that long Neglected tho' powerful agent Electricity: which I think must be gratifying to thee, and to every other person who wishes the good of mankind.—I think it rather extraordinary, that, Altho' there are very few remedies in the whole history of medicine, that has been more Strongly recommended than electricity, and that by a variety of writers of the highest reputation, yet, that no person in this country, has ever made a full & faithful trial of it before.—There has been Somethings respecting its application to diseases, that has retarded its progress as a medicine, which are now removed.[1]—That thou mayest See the progress, or notice that has been taken of it, Since I began to make trial of it in disease, I have enclosed, only,[2] a few of the peices that have appeared in print on the Subject Since the publication of the book.—As I have read thee, I feel as if I was Somwhat acquainted with thee. I have therefore written with the more freedom.—If thou Should find leasure, & be disposed to write me a line on the Subject, it would be gratefully received.

Accept the assureances of my respect and esteem,

THO[s] BROWN

RC (DLC); addressed: "Thomas Jefferson Esq[r] Monticello Virginia"; franked; postmarked; endorsed by TJ as received 8 Nov. 1818 and so recorded in SJL. Enclosure: Brown, *The Ethereal Physician: or Medical Electricity Revived* (Albany, 1817; Poor, *Jefferson's Library*, 5 [no. 192]), which details treatments with electricity by Brown and his colleague Jesse Everett resulting in "upwards of sixty Cures, in the short space of two years, in Cases of *Rheumatism, Head-ach, Pleurisy, Abscess, Quinsy, Piles, Incubus*, &c. &c." Other enclosures not found.

Thomas Brown (b. 1766), self-described medical electrician, was born into a Quaker family in New York City. In 1787 he became a member himself of the Society of Friends, but he relinquished his membership three years later and took up preaching as a Methodist. Brown traveled in 1798 from his home in Cornwall, New York, to visit the Shaker community at Niskayuna, also in that state, and soon became a convert, traveling frequently from Cornwall to Niskayuna until he left the sect in 1805. Seven years later he published a book about his years as a Shaker. Brown eventually settled in Troy, near Albany, and by 1815 he was studying the medical benefits of electrical charges.

He received a patent the following year for an improvement to an electrical apparatus. Until at least 1830 Brown was working as a medical electrician in the vicinity of Troy. During this period he also published books on Judaism and Universalism (Brown, *An Account of the People called Shakers: their Faith, Doctrines, and Practice* [Troy, 1812; Sowerby, no. 1707]; DNA: RG 29, CS, N.Y., Cornwall, 1810, Albany, 1830; *Albany Register*, 31 Mar. 1812; *List of Patents*, 170; *American Magazine, a monthly miscellany* 1 [1816]: 362–3; *Albany Advertiser*, 2 Nov. 1816; Chillicothe *Weekly Recorder*, 10 Apr. 1818; *New-York Gazette & General Advertiser*, 23 May 1818; Cooperstown *Watch-Tower*, 12 Oct. 1818; Troy *Farmers' Register*, 29 June 1819; *Philanthropist* 3 [1819]: 124; *Medical Repository*, new ser., 5 [1820]: 104–8; *Klinck's Albany Directory for the year 1822* [Albany, 1822], 19; Brown, *The History of the Destruction of the City and Temple of Jerusalem* [Albany, 1825]; Brown, *A History of the Origin and Progress of the Doctrine of Universal Salvation* [Albany, 1826]; *The Albany Directory, for the years 1830–31* [1830], 55).

[1] Preceding four words interlined.
[2] Word interlined.

From George Wyche

SIR   Hick'sford Greenville Cty Va Oct 28th 1818

I am loth to have my name added to the list of people who break in upon your retirement.—

The Ambition of the correspondence of the first man of the age would not have induced me to violate the Laws of politeness by making such an intrusion[1] upon a man whom I have never seen. But the known interest which you feel in whatever relates to the Geology or topography of our country & your critical information upon that subject must furnish my apology.—

I have been appointed by the executive amongst other matters to make a survey of the Blue Ridge Mountain from James River until it Crosses itself in the Allegany & thence along the last mentioned mountain[2] to north Carolina

In the prosecution of this survey, I have at sundry places endeavored to ascertain the elevation of the mountains above[3] their bases, & In ascending Roanoak & Stanton Rivers I have endeavored to Calculate the extend of fall from the Blue Ridge to tide water. I had no other means of observations than a Quadrant & the difficulty of getting a proper base for one side of the triangles has I fear rendered some of the estimates incorrect—This difficulty at the Peaks of Otter was sufficient to deter me from the attempt & understanding, that you had made very particular calculations of its height at a date greatly posterior to your Notes upon Virginia, I have thrown myself entirely upon your mercy under the belief that the Executive as well as the public will be better satisfied with your calculations than any I could make.—

Will you therefore be pleased to communicate to me the result of your Calculations & in what manner they were made whether with a Barometer or not? That I believe is the present common way of calculating the heights of Mountains Tho where a desirable base Can be obtained & an instrument of a considerable length of Radius certainly not the most correct—

To my great astonishment I found that part of the Alleganys on the Ridge that divides the waters, making the County Line between Montgomery & Grayson on the one side and Franklin & Patrick on the other No mountain at all, But the whole Country West presenting the appearance of a level & almost smooth surface,[4] while it terminated on the east by a perpendicular pitch of nearly 2000 feet, presenting from the last mentiond Counties the View of a wall, or prodigious[5] embankment of mountains of the above mentiond height.—

Will you be pleased to inform whether that is the case generally with the Allegany in the north section of the State & in the other States or not?—

If the Earth were a perfect sphere would it follow that the tides every where would determine the level of the Country, or that the Radius of the Earth from the Centre[6] to the head of tide water in the St Lawrence would be just as long as another[7] radius proceeding from the Centre to the head of tide water in James River? Or what is the same thing does that circumstance determine the length of such Radii every where in the same parallel—?—

With the most profound Respect I am your Obed. Sev^t—

GEO. WYCHE

RC (MoSHi: TJC-BC); adjacent to closing: "Thomas Jefferson Esq."; endorsed by TJ as a letter from "Clpo." Wyche received 4 Nov. 1818 and so recorded in SJL.

George Wyche, surveyor, lived in Greensville County by at least 1814, and in 1816 local officials contracted with him to produce a map of the county. About the same time he was appointed one of John Wood's assistants in surveying and mapping all the counties of Virginia. Wyche owned ten slaves in 1820 (*Petersburg Intelligencer*, 26 July 1814; Greensville Co. Order Book, 6:76–7, 160; Washington *Daily National Intelligencer*,

8 Oct. 1816; Wyche to Wilson Cary Nicholas, 26 July, 3 Nov. 1816, John Wood to the Virginia Council of State, 25 Oct. 1819, and Wyche to James P. Preston, 1 Nov. 1819 [Vi: RG 3, Governor's Office, Letters Received]; Earl G. Swem, comp., *Maps relating to Virginia in the Virginia State Library* [1989], 87; DNA: RG 29, CS, Greensville Co., 1820).

[1] Manuscript: "itrusion."
[2] Manuscript: "montain."
[3] Manuscript: "abovee."
[4] Manuscript: "surfacee."
[5] Manuscript: "prodious."
[6] Manuscript: "Centree."
[7] Manuscript: "as a nother."

From Bernard Peyton

DEAR SIR   Rich^d 29th: October "18

This morning's Mail put me in receipt your esteemed favor of the 24th Cur^t & contents observed.

I have this morning waited on Mr Brunet & applied for the Box of which you speak & am informed that it was delivered some time since to Mr M. B. Poitiaux who forwarded it about a week since by a Mr Huntingdon, I hope before this reaches you it will have come to hand safely.

By Mr Johnson's Boat I forwarded the Cotton Yarn you ordered, together with a small Box from Norfolk which I hope is safely received: The Box of Wine for Co^l Allston has been shipped several days, & he advised by Mail to Charleston with a bill of Lading—With very sincere[1] regard Dear Sir

Your Mo: Obd: Servt: BERNARD PEYTON

RC (MHi); endorsed by TJ as received 31 Oct. 1818 and so recorded in SJL. RC (MHi); address cover only; with final page of PoC of TJ to Joel Yancey, 17 Jan. 1819, on verso; addressed: "Mr Thomas Jefferson Monticello Milton"; stamp canceled; franked; postmarked Richmond, 29 Oct.

TJ's letter to Peyton of THE 24TH Oct. 1818 has not been found and is not recorded in SJL. MR HUNTINGDON may have been the Charlottesville merchant William Huntington.

[1] Manuscript: "sincre."

From Richard N. Thweatt

Petersburg Oct. 29th 1818

Having just returned with my family from a long trip up the country, I never received your favor until now—As I stated to you in a former letter, Co^l Burton sent your cask of wine to Mr Johnson of this place—and Mr J. as I also stated sent it to your agent, Mr Gibson in Richmond—The Captain of the vessel by whom Mr J. sent it, was, he says, a stranger to him, but was recommended as an honest and punctual man—Mr Johnson has kept a look out for him ever since he understood that the wine was not delivered agreeably to his orders—He tells me, he has not as yet been able to lay his eyes upon him—Co^l Burton was with me a few days ago, and I mentioned to him your anxiety about the wine he had sent you—it not coming to hand—He would with great pleasure, I know, procure you another cask of the same kind, as soon as he could meet with it; and should you desire it, let me know, and I will most cheerfully communicate with Co^l B. upon the subject—

With great Respect yours &c   RICHARD N. THWEATT

RC (MHi); endorsed by TJ as received <4> 5 Nov. 1818 and so recorded in SJL. RC (MHi); address cover only; with first two pages of PoC of TJ to Joel Yancey, 17 Jan. 1819, on recto and verso; addressed: "Thomas Jefferson Esqr Monticello"; franked; postmarked.

From Joseph Milligan

DEAR SIR   Georgetown october 30th 1818

I have by this days mail Sent you a copy of the little book on Gardening which I wrote to you about last Spring if you have time to spare I will esteem it a favour if you will Examine the work you will find it contains all Hepburn^s & Gardiner^s Book and the little Treatise by Mr Randolph of Williamsburg and Some new matter at the following pages =prospectus= page 20 a note on hot beds page 117 to 161 on Fences & Walks page 242 a note on currants from page 334 to the end hints on the cultivation of native[1] vines[2] If you Should think well of it I will not fear to recommend it to the public

I have two copies of the political economy in the bindery which will be bound and sent by the next days mail one of which I wish you to send to the author I will Send you ten copies in Boards by the way of Fredericksburg to the care of M^r W^m F Gray this I will do without farther advice you may expect them at the same time you receive the two copies by mail

Yours With Esteem and respect   Joseph Milligan

RC (DLC); endorsed by TJ as received <4> 5 Nov. 1818 and so recorded in SJL. RC (DLC); address cover only; with PoC of TJ to John Adams, 19 Jan. 1819, on verso; addressed: "Thomas Jefferson Esqr Monticello Milton (virginia)"; franked; postmarked Georgetown, 2 Nov.

THE LITTLE BOOK ON GARDENING was Milligan's revised edition of John Gardiner and David Hepburn, *The American Gardener* (Georgetown, 1818; Poor, *Jefferson's Library*, 6 [no. 276]). It appended additional material, including John Randolph (ca. 1727–84), *A Treatise on Gar-*

dening (Richmond, 1793; Sowerby, no. 806; Poor, *Jefferson's Library*, 6 [no. 275]). The final segment of the new work, "A Few Hints on the Cultivation of Native Vines, and directions for Making Domestic Wines," included quotations from TJ to John Adlum, 7 Oct. 1809 and 20 Apr. 1810 (attributed to an unnamed "personage of the very highest authority on all subjects of this nature"), which stressed the desirability of cultivating indigenous grapes for wine (pp. 338–9).

[1] Manuscript: "natives."
[2] Unmatched closing guillemet („) here editorially omitted.

From Peter J. Zeltner

Monsieur,   [received 30 Oct. 1818]

Ayant eu l'avantage de jouir pendant plus de vingt ann[ées] de l'amitie toute particuliere de l'Illustre défunt, qui à passé plûs de quinze[1] dans ma maison je n'ai pu ignorer les relations amicales qu'il a cultivées avec vous: une amitie fondée sur l'éstime réciproque, ne pourrait qu être durable: aussi suis que bien persuade des regrets que Vous causera la nouvelle de son décès Si peu attendu;[2] Il en avait quitte en May 1815 pour repondre aux desirs que lui avait temoigne L'Empereur de Russie, de conférer avec lui à Vienne Sur le Sort de la Pologne; de Vienne il est revenu jusqu'a Soleure en Suisse où il a demeuré chez mon frère en attendant que les circonstances[3] décident, S'il doit aller dans Sa patrie où revenir ici dans l'asile qu'il S'était choisi; il etait Sur le point de prendre ce dernier part, quand la mort l'enleva à Sa patrie et[4] a Ses nombreux amis, parmi les quels je Sais que Vous étes au premier[5] rang. C'est cette consideration qui m'a fait un devoir de Vous annoncer directement cette triste nouvelle.

Come[6] le géneral Kosciuszko a disposé de la majeure partie de la fortune en faveur de mes enfans, de mes nièces freres et belle Soeur, et que je Suis en outre tres lié avec ses parents que je compte aller Voir en Pologne. je vous prie de vouloir donner des renseignements Sur le

Capital qu'il a laissé entre Vos mains et autres objets qui pourraient être a Votre Connaissance;[7] Vous obligeres infiniment celui qui a l'honneur d'etre avec estime et haute consideration

    Monsieur   Votre tres humble et obeissant serviteur

                                         P J ZELTNER

EDITORS' TRANSLATION

SIR,   [received 30 Oct. 1818]

Having had the privilege of enjoying for more than twenty years the very special friendship of the illustrious deceased, who spent more than fifteen years in my home, I could not ignore the amicable relationship he cultivated with you. A friendship based on mutual respect could not help but endure; I am therefore certain that the news of his unexpected death will distress you. In response to the wishes of the Emperor of Russia, he had left in May 1815 to confer with him in Vienna regarding the fate of Poland. From Vienna he came back to Solothurn, Switzerland, where he stayed at my brother's house while waiting on circumstances to decide whether he should go to his homeland or return here to the refuge he had selected for himself. He was about to choose the latter when death took him away from both his homeland and his numerous friends, among whom I know you are in the first rank. This consideration has made it my duty to announce this sad news to you directly.

As General Kosciuszko has disposed of most of his fortune in favor of my children, nieces, brothers, and sister-in-law, and since I am, moreover, very close to his relatives, whom I intend to visit in Poland, I ask that you please send me the details of the funds he left in your hands and other effects of which you may have knowledge; you will be greatly obliging one who has the honor to be, with esteem and high consideration

    Sir   Your very humble and obedient servant   P J ZELTNER

Tr (DNA: RG 21, CCDCCR); undated; edge chipped, with missing text supplied from 2d Tr; docketed in part as "Zeltner's first letter to Mr Jefferson"; used in Washington County, D.C., chancery case 105, *Armstrong v. Lear.* Tr (DNA: RG 267, SCACF, box 141, case 1303, *Armstrong v. Lear*); undated. Recorded in SJL as a letter "(without date)" received 30 Oct. 1818. Translation by Dr. Genevieve Moene.

Peter Josef Zeltner (1765–1830), public official, diplomat, and banker, was born in Solothurn, Switzerland. Educated at a local Jesuit school, he served as an officer in the Swiss Guards in Paris, 1783–91. Zeltner then returned to his hometown and sat on its council, 1791–98 and 1814–30. He also represented the Helvetic Republic as a member of both the provisional government and the national grand council in 1798 and as a diplomat stationed in the French capital, 1798–1800. Remaining in France thereafter, Zeltner operated a banking house and from 1801 to 1815 hosted the Polish patriot Tadeusz Kosciuszko at his residences in Paris and Berville, near Fontainebleau. In one of his wills Kosciuszko named Zeltner's children as his legatees. Zeltner died in Solothurn (*Dictionnaire historique de la Suisse* [2002–14], 13:825; *ANB*, 12:885; Alex Storozynski, *The Peasant Prince: Thaddeus Kosciuszko and the Age of Revolution* [2009], 252, 275, 279).

MON FRÈRE: Franz X. Zeltner.

[1] Both Trs: "quize."
[2] Both Trs: "attendee."
[3] Both Trs: "circonstanes."
[4] 1st Tr: "il." 2d Tr: "it."

[5] Both Trs: "premi."
[6] Abbreviation for "Comme."

[7] Both Trs: "Conniassance."

From Franciszek Paszkowski

MONSIEUR,   Soleure en suisse ce 1er de Novembre 1818.
feu le Général Kosciuszko m'ayant honoré de son amitié pendant sa vie, m'a comblé des bienfaits en mourant, m'ayant légué par son Testament la moitié des fonds qu'il avait en Angleterre; par là je me suis trouvé à même d'obtenir du légataire de ses effets Mr Xavier Zeltner Vos lettres originales avec les minutes de celles qu'il vous avait ecrites; j'etais bien jeune quand j'ai eu le bonheur de voir pour la prémière fois le Général à Paris en 1801. & l'enthousiasme avec lequel je l'aimai avant de le connoître, se changea en la plus tendre & la plus profonde vénération, lorsqu'il me permit pendant trois ans de suite de le suivre dans Sa vie privée; cette vénération aussi tendre & aussi profonde qui, après Son decès desesperait de jamais retrouver un objet où elle aurait pu se placer avec le même bonheur; cette vénération Monsieur, s'est porté toute entière Sur Vous après la lecture de vos lettres & j'ai cru pouvoir me permettre de Vous en faire l'aveu qui Soulage mon coeur en me faisant croire que Vous ne dedaignerez pas Son hommage. La perte du Général m'est d'autant plus sensible que je calcule mieux celle que ma patrie a faite en lui; car dépuis longtems l'humanité dans la vieille Europe ne peut placer Son espoir de renaissance que sur le nouveau monde & une de plus douces consolations que j'ai puisée dans vos lettres a été celle de voir que cet espoir etait bien fondé. Permettez moi que je gardes ces lettres; elles me serviront d'encouragement & d'appui.   Mr Xavier Zeltner un de plus intimes amis du Général chez qui il a demeuré ici entouré de tous les soins imaginables de toute la famille entre les bras de laquelle il est mort, s'était empressé de vous mander dans le tems cette triste nouvelle; mais Sa lettre envoyée par un negotiant de Bordeaux semble ne vous être pas parvenue; je prends soin de passer celleci par vôtre mission à Paris desirant qu'elle ait un meilleur sort & qu'en vous portant l'expression de mon attachement & de mon respect, elle vous assure de ceux de tous les amis du Général & de tous les bons Polonais. Je me trouve ici en visite chez Mr Zeltner & nous ne nous sommes entretenus que de Vous & de nôtre defunt incomparable ami; demain je pars pour Dresde où je veux me domicilier plus près de mon pays, ne pouvant y vivre aussi tranquille. Si vous daignez m'honorer d'une reponse, ayez la bonté de la recommander à votre légation à Paris

pour m'être envoyée par le Ministre du Roi de Saxe qui y reside. elle me parviendra Surement par cette voie.

Agréez, Monsieur, nos voeux les plus Sincères pour Vôtre conservation & la constante prosperité de Vôtre patrie; nous Sommes Sûrs des Vôtres.
    FRANÇOIS PASZKOWSKI
        Général Major & ancien aide de Camp de S. M. le
        Roi de saxe.

E D I T O R S'   T R A N S L A T I O N

SIR,   Solothurn Switzerland 1 November 1818.
Having honored me with his friendship during his lifetime, the late general Kosciuszko showered me with generosity on his death, bequeathing me half of his English funds. This enabled me to obtain from the heir to his estate, Mr. Franz X. Zeltner, your original letters, along with the record of his to you. I was very young when I had the good fortune to see the general for the first time, in Paris in 1801, and the enthusiasm with which I had loved him before making his acquaintance grew into the deepest and most affectionate veneration when he allowed me to accompany him in his private life for three consecutive years. This veneration was so tender and deep that, after his passing, I despaired of ever finding another to whom I could apply it with the same felicity. Sir, after reading your letters, this veneration has been completely transferred to you. I allow myself to make this confession, which soothes my heart, in hopes that you will not disdain its homage. The loss of the general is even more painful to me when I think how it has affected my homeland. For a long time humanity in old Europe has been able to base its hope for a rebirth on the New World alone, and one of the sweetest consolations I have drawn from your letters has been learning that this hope was well founded. Allow me to keep these letters, which will encourage and support me.   Mr. Franz X. Zeltner, one of the general's closest friends, and in whose home he was living (surrounded by every imaginable attention from the whole family, in whose arms he died), hastened to inform you of this sad news, but his letter, which was sent through a merchant in Bordeaux, does not seem to have reached you. I am taking care to pass this one through your diplomatic mission in Paris in the hope that it will be more fortunate. By conveying to you my feelings of attachment and respect, I also assure you of the attachment and respect of all the general's friends and of all good Poles. I am currently visiting at Mr. Zeltner's house, and we have talked of nothing but you and our late, incomparable friend. Tomorrow I leave for Dresden, intending to reside there in order to be closer to my country, in which I cannot live as peacefully. If you should deign to honor me with a reply, please be so kind as to entrust it to your legation in Paris, to be sent to me through the king of Saxony's minister there. That way it will be sure to reach me.
Please accept, Sir, our most sincere wishes for your preservation and the continual prosperity of your country, just as we are sure of your wishes for us and our country.
    FRANÇOIS PASZKOWSKI
        major general and former aide-de-camp to His Majesty the
        king of Saxony.

RC (DLC); at foot of first page: "Monsieur Thomas Jefferson à Monticello en Virginie"; endorsed by TJ as received 7 Feb. 1819 and so recorded in SJL. Translation by Dr. Genevieve Moene.

Franciszek Paszkowski (1778–1856), soldier, was educated in Polish Galicia before studying in France at the Sorbonne. He met Tadeusz Kosciuszko in Paris in 1801 and was his secretary for the next three years. Paszkowski served in the military for eighteen years and rose to the rank of major general, serving for a time as aide-de-camp to Frederick Augustus I, king of Saxony and ruler of the Napoleonic-era Grand Duchy of Warsaw. He retired in about 1814 and lived thereafter in the Republic of Kraków, where he farmed and pursued scholarly activities, supported in part by a legacy from Kosciuszko. Paszkowski's biography of Kosciuszko was published posthumously in 1872 (*Biographie Nouvelle des Contemporains* [Paris, 1820–25], 17:470–1; Jan Pachoński, *General Franciszek Paszkowski, 1778–1856* [1982; reviewed by Adam A. Hetnal in *Polish Review* 4 (1988): 475–6]; Alex Storozynski, *The Peasant Prince: Thadeus Kosciuszko and the Age of Revolution* [2009], 249, 329; Wladyslaw de Fedorowicz, *1809 Campagne de Pologne* [1911], 1:316–9; *Lettres de l'Empereur Napoléon du 1er Aout au 18 Octobre 1813* [1909], 119–20; Jean A. Konopka, *Lettres de Soleure de Tadeusz Kosciuszko, 1815–1817* [2000], 84–5; *Revue Encyclopédique, ou Analyse Raisonnée* 8 [1820]: 621; Paszkowski, *Dzieje Tadeusza Kościuszki: Piérwszego Naczelnika Polaków* [1872]; gravestone inscription in Rakowicki Cemetery, Kraków, Poland).

To Patrick Gibson

DEAR SIR   Monticello Nov.[1] 3. 18.

Yours of the 21st is recieved, and with respect to the 14. barrels of condemned flour, I will pray you not to dispose of it at all, but to hold it subject to the order of Messrs T. E. Randolph & Colclaser (tenants of my mill) or of their agent. I find it absolutely necessary that a distinction should be observed in the different flours you recieve for me. these are of 3. different[2] masses. 1st 50 barrels of rent flour from Messrs Randolph & Colclaser, every quarter, which will have simply on them the brand of the ʃHADWELL MILLS. 2ly 350. barrels a year from this place, being the rent paid me for the hire of my plantations here by my grandson Th: J. Randolph. this has also the brand of the 'Shadwell mills,' but I have given orders that hereafter there shall be an additional mark ⨑. to distinguish it.
3. my flour from Bedford, which is generally manufactured at Mitchell's mills and will have that brand on it. if the mill-rent flour is damaged or condemned, Randolph & Colclaser are responsible to me. if the crop flour from this place is condemned, my grandson indemnifies me. if the Bedford flour is condemned, mr Mitchell is answerable; so in all these if there be an overproportion of Fine flour. a small mark of distinction to every parcel mentioned in your accounts of sales, will direct me always to the responsible person, such as **S.M.** for Shadwell mills, ⨑. for the crop flour from hence, and the initial of Mitchell's

brand, [w]hatever it is. this alone can enable me to call on the responsible person.—I am still confined to the house, but in the hope of soon getting out of it.　　　ever and affectionately your's

TH: JEFFERSON

P.S. in my letter of Oct. 18. I said I should make one draught on you for between 3. & 400 D and another for about as much more. the 1st was made in favʳ of James Leitch for 400.D.[3] the 2ᵈ is not yet made but soon will be. in the mean time came an unexpected demand from Bedford for 303.04 for which I was obliged to draw on you, and in favor of the sheriff of Albemarle also for taxes. I have ordered my Bedford flour to be now carried down.

PoC (MHi); on reused address cover of William King (of South Carolina) to TJ, 4 June 1818; one word faint; adjacent to signature: "Mʳ Gibson"; endorsed by TJ.

26 Oct. 1818 TJ gave Albemarle County deputy SHERIFF Ira Garrett an order on Gibson for $120.26, of which $112.80 was for taxes and $7.46 for "tickets" (MB, 2:1347–8).

The UNEXPECTED DEMAND from Bedford County actually totaled $333.04 and was to reimburse Archibald Robertson for settling TJ's account with his overseers William J. Miller and Robert Miller. On

[1] Reworked from "Oct."
[2] Manuscript: "diffent."
[3] Omitted period at right margin editorially supplied.

From George Washington Jeffreys

DEAR SIR.　　　　　　　Red House Nᵒ C. Nov. 3ʳᵈ 1818.

Not knowing the address of Col Randolph, your son in Law[1] the enclosed letter is sent to your care, with the request that you will fill out the address and forward it to him by mail or otherwise.

The Agricultural Society which I have formerly mentioned to you; continues its exertions with increased ardour & success holding from them the appointment of corresponding Secᵗʸ the duty devolves on me of endeavouring to collect information by letter from the most distinguished farmers in the different parts of the union. To Col Randolph our views are directed, to whom we feel greatly indebted for having introduced amongst us (through your goodness) so valuable an improvement as horizontal ploughing. We are anxious to learn his general system of improvement, but particularly his rotation of crops in connection with his modes of horizontal ploughing &c.

Accept Sir my respect & esteem and beleive me to be very truly yours.　　　　　　　GEORGE W. JEFFREYS.

RC (DLC); endorsed by TJ as received 15 Nov. 1818 and so recorded in SJL. RC (DLC); address cover only; with PoC of TJ to Richard Duke, 24 Jan. 1819, on verso; addressed: "His Excellency Thomas Jefferson Esqr. Milton V^a Mail via Petersburg & Richmond"; franked; postmarked Red House, 30 Nov. 1818. Enclosure not found.

[1] Preceding four words interlined.

From Nathaniel Bowditch

RESPECTED & DEAR SIR   Salem Novr 4. 1818

I have just received your much esteemed letter of the 26th ult. containing the highly honorable proposal relative to the Professorship of Math^s in the Central University, a situation which would be very pleasant to any one whose <u>engagements</u> would permit him to accept the proposal; but <u>several</u> important trusts (amounting to nearly half a million of dollars) undertaken for the children of an eminent merchant late of this Town, and which upon principles of honour cannot be resigned but with my life, bind me, by the powerful bands of <u>interest</u> to the place of my nativity, endeared to me by the many civilities received from my Townsmen while rising into life without any other advantages than such as the industry of a young person, thrown upon the world to provide for himself at the early age of 11 or 12 years, could procure. My income from these various trusts &^c exceeds $3000. Considerable time is left to me to devote to those studies which have been the delight of my leisure hours. My wife, whose health is very delicate is averse from any change of place which would remove her far from those dear friends who have done so much for her in sickness. These & other circumstances of a similar nature must be my excuse for declining the professorship offered in your letter in such terms of kindness & civility.

Please to present to the Gentlemen Visitors, who have done me this honor, my best wishes for them personally & for the success of the institution entrusted to their care, with the hope that the Professorships will be filled by persons eminently qualified to render the University highly respectable & beneficial to our Country.

I remain Sir, with sentiments of high consideration & respect your most obedient, humble servant   N BOWDITCH

RC (DLC); endorsed by TJ as received 21 Nov. 1818 but recorded in SJL as received a day later. RC (MHi); address cover only; with PoC of TJ to Wilson Cary Nicholas, 14 May 1819, on verso; addressed: "The Honorable Thomas Jefferson Late President of the United States Monticello"; franked; postmarked Salem, 11 Nov. FC (MBPLi: Bowditch Collection); in Bowditch's hand and endorsed by him: "To Pres^t Jefferson Nov 4 1818 relative to Cen^l Unv^y copied."

From Lewis D. Belair

Sir   Philadelphia Nov 6th 1818

Yours under date of The 27th and 31^t ult^o, duly Came to hand, The answers of which have Sustained a Little delay owing to my Being In This City, Where I have Opened a Depot of The Estabblishment of New York.—

Having here at hand The Three Defferint Works Which you have Requested, I have forwarded Them ⅌ two Mails as ⅌ Request <u>Viz</u>

1 Planche Dict Grec & f^s 1 Large 8vo Bound $6.25

1 Didot Logarithmes ⅌ Lalande 18me	87½
1 Corespondance de Cortes &c 12me	1 12½
	8—25

I have here Included The List of Part of The Works you Mention; Excepting a few which I have not yet unpacked and Their Invoices In New York, I Shall This day write to my Representative and desire him under his hand to direct you The Same, you Will have The Goodness to Direct your next to me at The Last Mentioned Place,

I Have the Honour to be With The Highest Esteam Your devoted Servt   Lewis D Bélair

<u>Liste</u>

\ Duchange Glossarium[1] 3 f^o Bound In Velum $20 00

\ Cabanis Humeurs Catarales 1 8vo (Thin)   87½

\ Saluste Dureau de la Malle L & f^r 1 8vo half   } one of
Bound   2 25   } Each
The Same In 2 12me Broché   2 12½ } left

\ Les 12 Cesars ⅌ Suêton Translated ⅌ Henri

only Copy { Ophellot de la Plause avec des Mêlanges[2] Phylosophiques[3] et des Notes 4 8vo bound (Very Scarce)   7 50 —

Thêsori Linguae Gracae Stephano Construstë 5 Large f^o Bound In Velum (Very Scarce) The only Copie which Was for Sale In The Market[4] at The time of Its Importation Cost 350 f^s I Will Sell It to you   at 90 00

Synopsis Plantarum ⅌ Persoone Velum Paper
   2 Large 12° fine Print   10. 00

Synopsis Fungorum is a Seperate Work from The other   }
by The Same Author 1 12° $4,50 (I have only one Copie   } <u>Plates</u>
of Each on hand.)[5] <u>It is</u> a <u>Book</u> of <u>much demand</u>   }

\ Henri IV ♈ Péréfixe 12me Broché 87½
\ Guerres Civiles⁶ de Rome dappien⁷ Traduite ♈ J. J.
 Combes-dounous Ex Legislateur membre de Société
 &c &c 1808 3 8vo bound   7 00

 The Following Belonging to your List I have not at
Present But I Expect Shortly a few Copie of Each of
Them,
Tacite Lat & f^r Dureau la Mal Thay Sold 5 8vo Bound $12. 00
Laplace Mecanique Celeste 4 4to Broché   22 00
  Système du Monde 1. 4to   5. 50
Yours In Haste   LEWIS D BÉLAIR

RC (MHi); between dateline and salutation: "Thomas Jefferson Esqr Montecelo Milton V^a"; with marginal slash marks corresponding to books ordered by TJ in his response of 16 Nov. 1818 and most likely in his hand; endorsed by TJ as received 15 Nov. 1818 and so recorded in SJL.

For TJ's letter of 31^T UL^TO see note to TJ to Belair, 27 Oct. 1818. Belair's REPRESENTATIVE was Francois Redon. BROCHÉ: stitched, when used to describe an unbound book (*OED*).

TJ sought the translation of Suetonius (SUÉTON) by Jean Baptiste Claude Delisle de Sales (pseudonym Henri Ophellot de La Pause), *Histoire Des Douze Césars de Suétone, . . . Avec des Mélanges Philo-*

sophiques & des Notes, 4 vols. (Paris, 1771; Poor, *Jefferson's Library*, 3 [no. 48]; TJ's copy in MdBJ). The edition of Appian's GUERRES CIVILES DE ROME that TJ acquired was Jean Isaac Combes-Dounous, trans., *Histoire des Guerres Civiles de la République Romaine*, 3 vols. (Paris, 1808; Poor, *Jefferson's Library*, 3 [no. 42]; TJ's copy in ViU).

¹Manuscript: "Classarium."
²Manuscript: "Métanges."
³Manuscript: "Phylosophique."
⁴Manuscript: "Marked."
⁵Omitted closing parenthesis editorially supplied.
⁶Manuscript: "Civile."
⁷Manuscript: "dappiers."

From Henry Dearborn

DEAR SIR,   Boston Novem^r 6th 1818—
 On the 4th ins^t I had the pleasure of receiving your letter of the 27th of Octob^r. Pikes expedition for exploring the Arkansa &c, was planned¹ & directed entirely by Genl Wilkinson, while he was governor & Military commander of uper Louisiana, you had previously contemplated the sending an exploring party on that river but the fate of the party sent up the red river induced a suspension of the expedition on the Arkansa until some explanation could be had with the Spanish authorities in relation to the interruption of the party on the red river, and in the mean time Genl Wilkinson sent off the expedition under Pike. I recollect that you proposed a Mr Wilson to be

Joined to the party that was intended for the Arkansa, and that I suggested a doubt as to the sufficiency of[2] our funds for imploying any one in addition to the number previously proposed, but you thought, that, although our means were small, we might venture to imploy Wilson on moderate termes, and if the proposed expedition had been carried into effect, I presume that M[r] Wilson would have been attached to the party.

having no papers to assist my memory I can only state the facts according to my best recollection. but I am very certain that you had no agency or direction in Pikes expedition on the Arkansa, and that no exploring party was sent up the Arkansa by your direction.—

As there has been a much greater intimacy between my Son & Stewart, than between Stewart & myself, I requested my Son to call on him and endeavour to obtain such frank & explisit information from him as you desire, an interview took place, and after many trifling excuses, for the long detention of the portrait, and its unfinished situation he said that he could not finish it in cold weather, but would certainly complete it in the Spring, we will endeavour to push him on, and if possible, compel him to finish it as early in the Spring as we can.—I most sincerely hope that your[3] health is quite restored and that you may enjoy many more years in health & happiness. M[rs] Dearborn joins me in kind regards to yourself, your excellent daughter,[4] her Husband & children.   H. DEARBORN—

RC (DLC); endorsed by TJ as received 15 Nov. 1818 and so recorded in SJL.

[1] Manuscript: "planed."
[2] Manuscript: "of of."
[3] Manuscript: "you."
[4] Manuscript: "daugter."

From William S. Murphy

RESP[D] SIR   Ohio. Chillicothe 6th November 1818

Ever since the establishment of the Bank of the U.S, I have diligently enquired, wherever I could obtain information of its constitutionality—Yet I have not, and I believe I cannot satisfy my mind. Therefore, I take the liberty to request your Opinion.

sir I am a young man—& have just commenced the practice of Law in this place—I read with A Stevenson Esq[r] in Richmond V[a] & have Seen you there—I hope you will gratify me with an answer—I am in search of truth—& on this important question I desire much the advice of one on whom I look as on a father

Accept Sir this assurance of my esteem & Respect

WILLIAM S MURPHY

RC (MHi); endorsed by TJ as received 23 Nov. 1818 and so recorded (mistakenly described as from Cincinnati) in SJL. RC (MHi); address cover only; with PoC of TJ to Jerman Baker, 14 May 1819, on verso; addressed (one word illegible): "Thomas Jefferson Esqʳ [. . .] presᵈ of U. States—Montescello—Virginia"; franked; postmarked Chillicothe, 7 Nov.

William Sumter Murphy (d. 1844), attorney and public official, was born in South Carolina, read for the bar in Richmond, and moved in 1818 to Chillicothe, Ohio, where he practiced law. He also attained the rank of brigadier general in the Ohio militia. In 1841, at the request of President John Tyler, Murphy became a special agent of the United States to the already defunct Central American Confederation. He arrived in Guatemala City late in 1841 and gathered information on political and economic affairs in the region through the following year. In 1843 Tyler gave Murphy an interim appointment as chargé d'affaires to Texas, but the Senate rejected his nomination in the spring of 1844 after Murphy made an unauthorized pledge of United States protection to Texas in the event of American annexation and an invasion by Mexico. He died shortly thereafter in Galveston (*DAB*; Henry Holcomb Bennett, ed., *The County of Ross* [1902], 186; Chillicothe *Supporter, and Scioto Gazette*, 29 May 1822, 8 July 1824; DNA: RG 29, CS, Ohio, Chillicothe, 1830; Kenneth E. Shewmaker and others, eds., *The Papers of Daniel Webster: Diplomatic Papers* [1983–87], 1:326–48; Boston *Atlas*, 10 May 1843; *JEP*, 6:195, 293 [18 Dec. 1843, 23 May 1844]; Washington *Daily National Intelligencer*, 16 Aug. 1844; *New-Orleans Commercial Bulletin*, 17 Aug. 1844).

From Henry E. Watkins

SIR, Prince Edward[1] Nov 6ᵗʰ 1818

You were good enough to say, when I had the pleasure of seeing you in Stanton, that you would send me some of the seed of the Succory, if I would remind you of it after your return home.—It is therefore; that I now take the liberty of requesting that you would foward me a parcel of the seed of this plant; And I do this with the less reluctance, from a confidence that you think highly of its usefulness, and would be gratified in giving aid to its more extensive cultivation. I am desirous of trying it under favourable circumstances, and would be glad to be informed, (if you have leisure) what kind of soil suits it best, what is the proper time and manner of sowing it, And how it should be worked.—A package directed to me, and sent to the care of Ellis & Allan of Richmond would probably be safely received.

Yours with very great esteem HENRY E WATKINS

RC (DNAL: Thomas Jefferson Correspondence, Bixby Donation); at foot of text: "Thomas Jefferson Esquire"; endorsed by TJ as received 23 Nov. 1818 and so recorded in SJL.

Henry Edward Watkins (1782–1856), attorney and public official, was a native of Prince Edward County. He studied successively at Hampden-Sydney College in 1796, at what is now Washington and Lee University, and at the College of New Jersey (later Princeton University), from which he graduated in 1801 before studying law at the College of William and Mary. Watkins represented Prince Edward County in the House of Delegates, 1812–13, 1819–21, 1822–27, and

1832–33, and he sat in the Senate of Virginia, 1833–35. During a break in his service as a delegate, Watkins saw duty as a cavalry lieutenant in the Prince Edward County militia during the War of 1812. He was a trustee of Hampden-Sydney, 1807–31 and 1836–53, sat on the Rockfish Gap Commission in 1818 that, under TJ's leadership, chose the site of the University of Virginia, and in 1827 became the treasurer of Union Theological Seminary, then a part of Hampden-Sydney. In the 1850 census Watkins is described as a farmer with real estate valued at $89,000. At the time of his death in Prince Edward County he owned $170,000 in slaves and real estate (Elizabeth Marshall Venable, *Venables of Virginia* [1925], 131–2; *Catalogue of the Officers and Alumni of Washington and Lee University, Lexington, Virginia, 1749–1888* [1888], 55; *Princeton Catalogue*, 113; *William and Mary Provisional List*, 42; *General Catalogue of the Officers and Students of Hampden-Sidney College, 1776–1906* [1908], 16, 18; Leonard, *General Assembly*; Butler, *Virginia Militia*, 177; *VMHB* 7 [1899]: 34, 36–7; 23 [1915]: 320–1; DNA: RG 29, CS, Prince Edward Co., 1820–50; *Richmond Enquirer*, 24 Nov. 1835; *Richmond Whig and Public Advertiser*, 15 Aug. 1856; gravestone inscription in Watkins family cemetery, Prince Edward Co.; Prince Edward Co. Will Book, 10:275–9, 290–2).

[1] Remainder of dateline beneath signature.

From William J. Coffee

HONORABLE SIR   New York N^or 7th 1818

As I promised you when at monticello, so had I previous to the reciept of your Verey pleaseing and welcom Commission made moste of the necessary Inquires with relation to your Cisterrns, to day I have as fare as I can completed my Inquires on that Subject. A Part of duty I owe to you past Kindness. [Duch Terras] thar is no Such thing in this City thare was som yeares Ago Imported Such A Cement which was thought Excellent, for water uses but Owing to its high price and som other causes it is not now to be met with either in the commercial world, or in the building line. In fact it is Superseded by A cement caled Roman Cement but made in England in many Places it is much Cheape and by all that have used it in this great City thought to be the best Cement ever Introduced for works under water, this I my self know that in England 20 years Experianc has proved to the[1] world its Value[2]

My Dear Sir on the other Sid and part of this you will find my ferther directions and Oppion and with them be Pleased to receve my best and kindest wishes for you and yous   W. J. COFFEE

RC (DLC); brackets in original; addressed: "To Thos Jefferson Es^qr Monticello State of Virgina"; franked; postmarked New York, 11 Nov.; with enclosure subjoined and TJ's Notes on Roman Cement, [ca. 21 Nov. 1818], beneath endorsement; endorsed by TJ as received 21 Nov. 1818 but recorded in SJL as received a day later; with additional notation by TJ beneath endorsement giving Coffee's address as "501. Greenwich street   or to Dr Hosack N. York."

[1] Manuscript: "to the to the."
[2] Manuscript: "Valwe."

ENCLOSURE

William J. Coffee's Memorandum on Roman Cement

[ca. 7 Nov. 1818]

notes on the Roman Cement

This Cement is not A Composition It is A natural production of A Very Extraodinary Kind I think it is Very Common in this Country, and Som future time I shall troubl you to Asist me in finding it out as I well understand the maner of manufatre and Application, and tharefor my Observation[s] to you as to the maner of usesing it may be depended on

All the new and fashionably Houses have Cistren made of this Cement and in Som Cases the outsids Are decorate[d] it is now coming in to Vouge in this City Vere fast. It has also being used to Stop Out the back waters from Buildings and in One Instans to Stop out the back water from mixing with the water of A wood Cistern in Boath Cases with Every Success. The Price of this Cement is $9 pr Barrel of five Bushel[s] in Each Barrel as you will see When we Consider the hight price of prepared Plaster which is as much as from 7 to 8$ pr Barrel of five bushel[s] we cant think much of 9$ for wat is so usefull and from so distant a Clime

I have Inclosed a printed Card so that you will know ware to Aply to should you make up you mind to use it I have also Sent you two or three Specimen[s] of the Cement as Imported so that you may try in som mesur in you Study before you giv an Order One of thease Specimen[s] mark[ed] ⬡ I got from out of A Barrel Just Opene[d] in The Public Store for Inspection this you know must be Considerd a fair trial thare are now as pr Advertisement sent you 20 Barrel[s] no doubt all good Tho the Season in you Country A fine One for The Operation If Immeaditly taken hold of other ways you had better to Stay till April or the Last week in march, in this Case you Can hav If you give you Immiadet Order to the manufactory in London wat you may want Sent direct to Richmond the other Specimen I had out of A Barrel that had being on Headed fer Som day & not minded in the maner it should be as it was the remains of wat was left in the making of A Cisterns in mury St, Built by A m^r maybe Builder of new York. its not so good it is mark'^d △ The litle Cistern is made of it yet I think this in its present State would do provided it was well Lay on the Brickwork I Only mention becaus you might hav A Barrel thus exposed to the Common Air, thease Specimen[s] I shall send off by the Ship to Richmond to the Care of Capt Peyton to be Sent to you as soon a Possable

Oparation

As to the Thickness in new York The workmen Lay it on, from half to $\frac{3}{4}$ of Inch, but I Should Say, not Less then from $\frac{3}{4}$ of Inch to One Inch—in Short the thicker it the mor you are Sur of Success previous to the Laying on the Cemnt Let you walls & Bottom be well Cleaned from dirt of all kinds and the morter from the Joints take out also the Present Clay and Sand or wat may be at the bottom of you Cistern, that don Let thar be a Large Squar Bored 2 Feet by 6 Strond and Smooth on One Side Let One Cask of Cement be roled to the top of you Cistern and op^t it Place the Squar Board in the bottom of Cistern then Let the Attendant or the mason take out of this Barrel half A Peck Only at a tim and Place it on the Board below, Place this half Peck in the form A Cone, from the Point of which make an Eaqul Concavity to the Board Put in to this no more water [which ought to be Very Clean][1] then will make the Cement in to that Consistance of dough to bake for Bread, for If the man Should over water the mixing in Ever so small a dgree so in Proposition would the Cement be Injured ontill the division would be so gread as to Concretion which If Properly attended will be allmost as Hard a Common Stone.   I Should recommend the mason Cover One half of Each End at Side of Cistern thinly at first Say $\frac{1}{4}$ Inch this Should be well Troweld or rubed in, to the bricks but allways taking the greatest Care not to tuch the Cemnt any Longer then is necessary to give it adherence this requires Som address—for If you mix up Som of this Cemnt very Stiff Leave it to Set and not tuch it ontill it is hard you will find this harder then that from the hands of the workman,

On this thin Coat Let him Place in the Same maner his Last & finishing Coat which ought to be Just floated down with a rule and never tuch with the Trowel, but Left to Set in this way he gos on ontill he has Complete the whole, but you must mind that he maks Sound Joining & Angles that no Air may Caus a Crack which would Spoil all.

The Bottom I think I would finish the Last on A[ccount?] of Likelyhood to Injury it ought to be Composed of well [. . .] layed or wat is Caled beded in this Roman Cement in the [. . .] of morter and on that bottom Lay your Coat of Roman Cemnt at Least One Imch in thickness begining at the ferthermost Part of the Cistern and working backwards. not Suffer any pressure on the bottom ontill it has becom Quite harde that may be in A day or two at which End of time If you Can Conviently fill you Cistern with water or Let a Small[2] Boy get in and fling water over the whole this will much asist. in a few days from that time it asume a moldy Look which is A sign of its goodness— I fear by this time you will be very glad my Small sheet of paper is allmost full of any thing you Like to Call it you hav brought it on you self and then cant blame me. and I Conclude by saying that If you think you Cand do this business so well as you Could wish I will Inspect it for you in next march on my route as I do Intend call and Look at monciello Once again my Only reward for two or three days Inspection will be two glasss of good wine Every day affter diner ontill then If you want my Services in New York you may Command them and I shall with Pleasur be conformabe to you wish

The End

MS (DLC: TJ Papers, 214:38126–7); entirely in Coffee's hand; undated; torn at seal; subjoined to covering letter. Enclosure not found.

An unheaded (ON HEADED) barrel has had its closing lid removed (OED).

[1] Brackets in original.
[2] Word interlined.

Agreement by John M. Perry to Sell Lands to Central College

Articles of Agreement entered into this seventh day of November 1818 Between John M Perry of the one part and Nelson Barksdale Proctor of the Central College of the other part Witnesseth, that the said John M Perry for and in consideration of the sums of money hereafter mentioned to be paid him by the said Nelson Barksdale hath granted, bargained and sold, and by these presents doth grant, bargain and sell unto the said Nelson Barksdale Proctor of the Central College and to his successors in office for the use of the said College one certain parcel of Land lying & being in the County of Albemarle & adjoining the said College Lands. containing by a late survey   acres. and bounded as follows towit Begining at a stake in Wheelers road corner to the College tract of forty three and three quarter acres, thence up the said road as it meanders, sixty eight poles to a stake, thence north five degrees West forty four poles to a stake, near the barn, thence North thirteen degrees East One hundred and thirty seven poles to a stake in the three choped road, thence down the same as it meanders sixty and a half poles to the corner of the said College tract of forty three and three quarter acres, thence along the lines of said tract South ten and a half degrees West twenty two poles to a stone pile and persimmon tree, thence South three degrees East thirty six poles to a stake near the corner of the Garden thence South nineteen degrees West twenty nine poles to a pile of stone thence South thirty degrees East thirty five poles to the begining For which said parcel of Land said Perry for himself his heirs &ᶜ doth covenant to make a compleat right & title, In consideration whereof the said Nelson Barksdale Proctor as aforesaid for himself and his successors in office doth covenant to pay to said Perry his heirs or assigns the sum of forty dollars per acre, also to pay said Perry his heirs &ᶜ the value of the improvements now upon the said parcel of Land. includeing the pailing [insd?] of the Garden such value to be assertained by three disinterested judges, one chosen by sᵈ Perry. one by sᵈ Barksdale and a third by the two thus chosen, The one half of which said purchase of land & improvements, to be paid sᵈ Perry on the first day of March next. the remaining half on the 25ᵗʰ of December 1819. The said Perry retains possession of the dwelling houses yard, out houses and garden untill the first day of August next. and of the Carpenters shop with access to & from it untill the Land upon which it stands is wanted, by the College and then the same is to be removed by said Perry (it being agreed that this shop is not to be valued as an improvement on said Land) Provided allways and it is hereby specially agreed between the parties, that if the Legislature of the State of Virginia shall locate the University of said State at the now Central College then and in such case this agreement and every covenant herein contained, shall stand confirmed, and remain obligatory upon the parties and all covenants herein contained shall be executed with good faith by each party. But Should the Legislature, not locate the University at said Central College then, this agreement and every part hereof shall cease, determine and become null, and void, And now for the true & faithfull performance of all the several covenants herein contained, the parties to these presents bind themselves to each other in the penalty of thirty thousand dollars, In Witness whereof they have hereunto set their hands and seals the day & year first above written

Witness   JOHN. M: PERRY (seal)
ALEX: GARRETT

                          NELSON BARKSDALE (seal)
approved[1]   proctor C.C.[2]
TH: JEFFERSON

MS (ViU: TJP); in Garrett's hand, signed by Perry, Barksdale, Garrett, and TJ; one word illegible; docketed, in an unidentified hand: "48¾ Acres of Land a 40$" and "Capt Perry," and by Garrett: "Perry & Barksdale (Proctor) } Agreement."

After Central College became the University of Virginia, this transaction was confirmed with a Conveyance of Lands to the University of Virginia by John M. Perry and Frances T. Perry, 25 Jan. 1820.

[1] Word in TJ's hand.
[2] Title in Barksdale's hand.

From John Stevens

SIR,   Hoboken, near New York, Nov[r] 7[h] 1818.

The vast importance, in my humble opinion, of the subject matter of the communications herewith enclosed must be my apology for the liberty I now take in requesting your perusal of them.

Should the object proposed to the consideration of the general government meet your approbation, or be considered by you of sufficient moment to induce you to favour me with an expression of your sentiments respecting it, impressed, as I should be, with a due sense of the honour, permit me also to say, that it would afford to me the highest gratification.

With Sentiments of the most profound Respect & Consideration, I have the Honour to be, Sir, Your Obed[t] Serv[t]   JOHN STEVENS

RC (MoSHi: TJC-BC); dateline at foot of text; at head of text: "His Excellency Thomas Jefferson Esquire"; endorsed by TJ as received 15 Nov. 1818 and so recorded in SJL. Dft (NjHi: Stevens Family Papers, 1993); damaged at crease; endorsed by Stevens as a "Copy Letter to Mr Jefferson & to Mr Madison." Enclosures not found.

John Stevens (ca. 1749–1838), engineer, was born in New York City, grew up in Perth Amboy, New Jersey, and graduated from King's College (later Columbia University) in 1768 before studying law. Instead of practicing that profession he followed his father into politics, serving during the American Revolution as treasurer of New Jersey and in 1782–83 as surveyor general of the eastern part of that state. From about 1788 onwards Stevens devoted his life to perfecting and promoting steam transportation, focusing first on steamboats and later on steam-powered trains. He encouraged enactment of the first federal patent laws in order to secure protection for his own designs, and he subsequently received numerous patents for his improvements. Largely self-taught as an engineer, Stevens joined forces with the foundry owner Nicholas J. Roosevelt to put his ideas into practice. His attempts to establish a steamboat line of his own were frustrated by the Hudson River monopoly of Robert Fulton and Stevens's brother-in-law and former part-ner, Robert R. Livingston. He could, however, claim responsibility for the first seagoing steamboat and for helping to secure the first American legislative railroad act. Stevens was elected to the American Philosophical Society in 1789. He died in Hoboken (*ANB*; *DAB*; Miriam V. Studley, Charles F. Cummings, and Thaddeus J. Krom, eds., *Guide to the Microfilm Edition of the Stevens Family Papers* [1968]; *PTJ*, 27:797, 803–4; Milton Halsey Thomas, *Columbia University Officers and Alumni 1754–1857* [1936], 101; Washington, *Papers, Rev. War Ser.*, 2:80–1, 16:293; APS, Minutes, 17 Apr. 1789 [MS in PPAmP]; *List of Patents*, 5, 33, 78, 164; Stevens, *Documents tending to prove the Superior Advantages of Rail-Ways and Steam-Carriages over Canal Navigation* [New York, 1812; Poor, *Jefferson's Library*, 5 (no. 217); TJ's copy in PPAmP]; New York *Evening Post*, 7 Mar. 1838).

Stevens sent an identical letter to James Madison on this date (Madison, *Papers, Retirement Ser.*, 1:373, 380–1). He had previously sent a similar but longer letter to James Monroe, in which he stated that he was enclosing "what has occurred to me respecting Rail Roads, concluding with a proposal for carrying into effect a Rail Road from the River Delaware near Trenton, to the River Rariton at or near New Brunswick" (Stevens to Monroe, 21 Oct. 1818 [NjHi: Stevens Family Papers]).

To William F. Gray

S$_{IR}$ Monticello Nov. 8. 18

I recieved safely the Edinburg reviews, and I now return them to be half bound in volumes. with them I send the 14: vol^s which I had before, as also 29. vol^s of other things, all to be bound according to the directions on the inclosed paper, and I will ask such dispatch as the solidity of the work admits. the box containing them now goes to the stage office at Charlottesville.

It will be followed by another box of other pamphlets to be bound, which I have not yet made up, and thought better to put into a subsequent box, not to over burthen the stage.

I shall shortly also send on a 3ᵈ box to your care to be forwarded to Millegan. for elegant bindings to choice books, there is no one in America comparable to him. his bindings are so tasty, so solid, and as heavy as blocks of metal. I have generally applied to him to get such books as I want, unbound, & to bind them. but I have found him very slow and even uncertain as to <u>procuring</u> them. this may be from a slack credit, or from too much other work so that I shoul[d] expect to be more certainly served if you would undertake to get the books for me, to be forwarded either here at once or to Millegan as should be directed. for the present I will request you to procure for me Bowditch's book of navigation, unbound, and to forward it to me here by mail. I never chuse to have the mail burthened with more than a single vol. at a time, & that never larger than an 8ᵛᵒ. in heavier cases we must engage the portage by the stage.   I salute you with esteem and respect.   TH: JEFFERSON

PoC (DLC); on verso of reused address cover of Brett Randolph to TJ, 7 July 1818; edge trimmed; at foot of text: "Mʳ Gray"; endorsed by TJ.

The BOOK OF NAVIGATION was probably Nathaniel Bowditch, *The New American Practical Navigator* (4th ed., New York, 1817).

E N C L O S U R E

Bookbinding Directions for William F. Gray

[ca. 8 Nov. 1818]

Edinburg Review.   30. vols. half bind with leather backs, common gilt, and lettered 'Edinburg Review. 1802.3' or 'Edinburg Review. 1803' Eᵗc as may be seen on the 1ˢᵗ 14. vols. but the vol. of Index must be lettered 'Edinburg Review. 1812. Index.'

*Analectic magazine. 2. v. half bound, leather back. neatly gilt. lettered 'Analectic magazine 1818' but the 2ᵈ vol. must be kept back[1] till the remaining months come in.

*Port folio. 8. vols. half bind. leather backs. neatly gilt. lettered with the title & year.

\Emporium. 3. vols. half bind. leather backs. common gilt. lettered with title & year.

*Belfast magazine. 3. vols. half bind. leather backs. neatly gilt. lettered with title & year.

*Literary magazine. 2. vols. half bind. leather backs. neatly gilt. lettered with title & year.

*Monthly register. 1. vol. half bind. leather back. neatly gilt. lettered with title & year.

\Robinsons reports. 2. vols[2] half bind. plain law leather back, lettered with title & vol. to wit V. & VI.

\Law Journal. 2. vols. half bind. plain law leather back. lettered with title.

\Laws U.S. 2. vols. half bound. plain law leather back. lettered 'Laws U.S. 1803.4.' and '1805.6.'

\Cormon's[3] dict. 2. v. \Historia de España. 2. v. fully bound in a common neat binding lettered with title & vol.[4]

2. maps in sheets. to be pasted on linen, without rollers.

procure Bowditch's

MS (DLC: TJ Papers, 215:38332); entirely in TJ's hand; undated.

At the foot of these instructions TJ summarized an otherwise unknown letter to Gray of 11 Nov. 1818 (not recorded in SJL): "Nov. 11. wrote supplementory direction to trim leaves." By a PLAIN LAW LEATHER BACK, TJ probably meant a binding using so-called "law calf" skin, which was uncolored or cream colored and used historically for law books (Matt T. Roberts and Don Etherington, *Bookbinding and the Conservation of Books: A Dictionary of Descriptive Terminology* [1982], 151; *OED*, cf. "law"). The LAW JOURNAL was the *American Law Journal* edited by John E. Hall (Poor, *Jefferson's Library*, 10 [no. 600]).

What TJ here calls LAWS U.S. is described in Poor, *Jefferson's Library*, 10 (no. 590), as "Session's Laws of the United States, 1803, '4, '5 and '6, 8vo." This may have consisted of the four pamphlets containing the laws passed during the four congressional sessions of 1803–07.

[1] Preceding three words interlined in place of "wait."

[2] Preceding two words interlined.

[3] In margin to the left of this word TJ wrote: "59. vols," the total number of volumes to be bound by Gray, not counting the maps.

[4] Entry for preceding two titles interlined.

To Honoré Julien

Monticello Nov. 8. 18

I thank you, my good friend, for your excellent Swiss cheese. it is safely recieved, is very fine, and very acceptable, and the more so as a testimony of your good will towards me. my health is getting better slowly, but I do not venture out of the house yet. I salute you with affectionate friendship and sincere wishes for your prosperity

TH: JEFFERSON

PoC (DLC); on verso of reused address cover of Mathew Carey & Son to TJ, 5 July 1818; at foot of text: "M. Julien"; endorsed by TJ.

To John Neilson

DEAR SIR   Monticello Nov. 8. 18.

I inclose you 4. letters lately recieved, which [I] suppose to be from your friends in Ireland, and which I hope may give you agreeable news from them.

I return you also the papers which mr Dinsmore gave me from you, and I see, not without sensible regret, that our ideas of the mode of charging interest are very different. I never in my life paid a cent of compound interest; being principled against it; not but that compound may be made as just as simple interest, but then it should be at a lower rate. interest simple or compound[1] is a compensation for the use of money, and the legislature supposed, as is the truth & general opinion, that taking one mode of employing money with another, 6. per cent simple interest is an average profit. but had they established a compensation by way of compound interest, they would have probably fixed it at 4. or $4\frac{1}{2}$ per cent. the difference it makes in our case is but a little over 40.D. a sum which with you I think nothing of, could I allow myself to countenance what I think is wrong, without pretending to censure those who think differently, as it is your debt, in the form in which I always considered it shall be paid out of the proceeds of my crop now going to market as soon as sold, which possibly may be not till April. your debt has remained in my hands because not called for, & in the belief you had no[2] expectation of placing it at better profit. had I ever supposed you wished to employ it otherwise, it should never have been kept from you a moment. in no case however will this difference of opinion lessen my wishes to be useful to you, nor my friendly esteem for you.   Th: Jefferson

PoC (MHi); on verso of reused address cover to TJ; one word faint; at foot of text: "Mr Nielson"; endorsed by TJ as a letter to "Nelson John" and so recorded in SJL. Enclosures not found.

The LEGISLATURE of Virginia set the maximum allowable interest rate at 6 percent in November 1796 (*Acts of Assembly* [1796 sess.], 16–7). TJ settled his account with Neilson on 16 Apr. 1809, leaving a DEBT of $435.75 (*MB*, 2:1245). For TJ's eventual agreement on the interest due, see his 31 May 1820 letter to Neilson.

[1] Preceding three words interlined.
[2] TJ here canceled "view."

From Robert Walsh

Dear Sir   Philadelphia Novr 8^h 1818

We heard in this city, a few weeks ago, that you were painfully indisposed; and I believe there was no one to whom this information gave more chagrin than to my self. I consider the prolongation of your vigor and life as devoutly to be wished not only on account of your personal merits, and past services to the country, but with a view to the great good which you may still effect.

Not being assured of your perfect restoration, I am not certain whether I ought to intrude upon you with the suggestions I am about to make. I rely, however, upon your wonted indulgence.—I take a most lively interest in the history and character of Franklin, and have lately written, for Delaplaine's Repository, a Biographical Notice of him, which will, I trust, be thought not altogether unworthy of the subject. It is my intention to prepare, in the Course of time, a full Essay upon his Life and Writings, and it will be my aim to clear him of all the aspersions which have been cast upon him from various quarters. The charge most frequently urged against him, and lately repeated with a semblance of authority in Boston, is that of a complete subservience to the Court of France during the negotiations with England for peace; of a readiness to wave the formal recognition of our Independence,[1] to relinquish the privilege of fishing on the banks of Newfoundland &c—You have no doubt heard of this charge before, and if you have read the portion of his Correspondence published by Temple Franklin, you must I think have seen there enough to Convince unprejudiced & reflecting persons, of its' incorrectness. But this is not of force to silence envy or bigotry.

It has occurred to me that you who succeeded him—"replaced" him, tho' you would not admit the term—may be well acquainted with what passed in relation to the Preliminaries, and not unwilling to communicate what your impression is concerning his[2] views and conduct on the occasion. I am not so unreasonable as to ask you for detailed explanations: a few words will suffice to enable me to proceed with confidence in my own opinion, or to correct it, if I happen to be in error. Your testimony will settle the question; & it would be much to be regretted if any doubts injurious to the memory of Franklin, were suffered to remain.

The state of your health is matter of continued anxiety to very many here, & we will, I earnestly hope, soon receive such intelligence as to relieve us of all disquietude.

I offer my resp[l] Comp[ts] to your excellent family, and am,

Dear Sir, with the highest Consideration, Your ob[t] servant

ROBERT WALSH JR

RC (DLC); endorsed by TJ as received 15 Nov. 1818 and so recorded in SJL. RC (DLC); address cover only; with PoC of TJ to William C. Rives, 28 Jan. 1819, on verso; addressed: "Thomas Jefferson Esq[re] Monticello Virginia"; franked; postmarked Philadelphia, 9 Nov.

Walsh's BIOGRAPHICAL NOTICE of Benjamin Franklin appeared in *Delaplaine's Repository*, 2:41–124. TJ SUCCEEDED Franklin as minister plenipotentiary to France in 1785 (*PTJ*, 8:33).

[1] Manuscript: "Indepence."
[2] Reworked from "Franklin's."

From William Alston

It is highly gratifying to me to be held in remembrance by one whom I so greatly respect & esteem. I feel, very sensibly, the kind Sentiments towards me, that you have been pleased to express in your very friendly letter, which I did not receive until lately, as it lay a long time in the Post-Office, in Charleston, where I have not been since my return to Carolina; and my friend there, not knowing of my arrival here, did not forward it to me, as soon as he would, otherwise have done. I am very glad to hear from you that you are recovering from the effects produced by the water at the warm Springs; and sincerely hope that your health is now perfectly restored.

Please to accept my best thanks for your present of wine, which I am informed by Mr Peyton, has been shipped to Charleston; but which has not yet arrived.—I am, at this time, suffering under the severest affliction from the loss of a most beloved Son. He had just[1] arrived at the age of 21 years, was admitted to plead at the Bar, & was about to take his station upon the great Theatre of human action. You may judge, my good friend, of my agonized feelings, when I first came to the knowledge of the great calamity that had befallen me. In looking over a News paper at Fayetteville, in No. C^a; I read an account of the death of my best beloved Son, killed instantly by a fall from a Horse. I was, for some time, almost deprived of my Senses. It is not long since it pleased God to take from me my eldest Son, who was every thing to me that the fondest Parent could wish. Blessed with such talents, & possessing such virtues that, at the early age of 31 years he was appointed, at a very important period (the commencement of the late war) to the chief magistracy of the State; which shewed how high he stood in the estimation & opinions of his fellow Citizens. I had hoped to have leaned upon this Son, & that he would have been my support in my old age. The Son whom I have lately lost was, after the decease of his elder brother, the first in my affections, as he not only possessed all the virtues that ornament the human character, but from the early proof of talents that he had shewn he possessed, promised to have imitated his brother at some future period. I have lived too long. Would it had pleased the Almighty to have ordained it in the animal, as it is in the vegetable creation, that we should drop off, following each other, in rotation, like the leaves on trees.—May you, my respected friend never suffer the pangs I feel. I hope the remainder of your valuable life may glide on in tranquillity & ease, in the full enjoyment of every blessing that this world can afford; that you may be so happy that,

"Day may roll on day & year on year
Without a sigh, a sorrow or a tear—"

My health & feelings are such that I do not believe I shall ever leave this State whilst I live. If any inducement could tempt me to do so, it would be the pleasure of taking you once more by the hand, by accepting your friendly invitation to Monticello.—I shall send to my Factor, in Cha⁵ton, sometime in Decb⁽, a barrel of rice to be shipped to M⁽ Malory at Norfolk, to be forwarded to you—And in Jan⁽ or Feb⁽ I will send a further supply, as it will keep good longer, when prepared at that Season.—

I wish I knew of any thing else here that would be acceptable to you.—

With Sentiments of the highest respect & esteem, I am, my dear Sir, very truly, Yours   W. ALSTON

RC (DLC); endorsed by TJ as received 3 Dec. 1818 and so recorded in SJL.

Jacob Motte Alston (A MOST BELOVED SON) died on 11 Sept. 1818 (gravestone inscription in Alston family cemetery, Oaks Plantation, Georgetown County, S.C.). Alston's ELDEST SON, former South Carolina governor Joseph Alston, died in

1816 (ANB). DAY MAY ROLL ON DAY . . . OR A TEAR paraphrases a sentiment in a 1723 poem by Alexander Pope, "To Mrs. M. B. on her Birth-day": "Let day improve on day, and year on year, Without a Pain, a Trouble, or a Fear" (Pope, Minor Poems, ed. Norman Ault and John Butt [1954], 244–7).

[1] Word interlined.

From Thomas Appleton

Leghorn 10ᵗʰ November 1818—

my last letter, Sir, was under date of the 26ᵗʰ of August, acknowledging the receipt of one from you of the 4ᵗʰ of April, under cover of a few lines from m⁽ Vaughan; mentioning that he then inclos'd a bill of exchange, by your order, for 2415– francs; but on my opening the letter, no bill was found contain'd therein;—I have ever Since been most anxiously waiting to receive one of the Sets of exchange,[1] in order to pay the interest due to mad⁽ᵉ Pini, whose means,[2] are, I believe, on a level with her expences, but the delay of the payment, has occasion'd her some degree of disappointment.[3]—By the first vessel bound to any Southern port, I shall convey to you, the two artists[4] you are desirous of obtaining; and I hope, Sir, you will find them corresponding, in all respects, to the wishes you express'd in your letter.—

Giacopo Raggi, the elder of the two I have procur'd, is in his 45th year, and very able in his profession as Architect.—he is capable of cutting the columns of[5] every order of Architecture, and in which are compris'd pilastres, cornice, basement, piedestals; indeed all those members, which come within the denomination of "il Solido;" After these,[6] another order of workman is requir'd, which is term'd in italian "Ornatista," who performs all the ornamental parts of the columns.—for this latter work I have Selected the cousin of the Architect, whose name is michele Raggi, of the age of 35, and equally[7] able in his profession.—they have both been warmly recommended to me by particular friends of mine at Carrara, and who are themselves, the first architects of the City.—they appear in great vigour of health; and their morals are irreproachable.—they are both married; the former leaves for the present here his wife and daughter; while the latter who has been lately married, will take his wife with him; but they, as yet, have no children.—I have therefore stipulated, agreeably to your instructions, that they shall be provided during the term of three years, with a suitable lodging and diet, and five hundred and twenty-five Spanish dollars; each annually.—they are in their separate branches, greatly superior to any who have hitherto been sent to the U. States; and their salary is not more than one half of what others have been allow'd.—they will carry with them all their necessary instruments of working; together with many plans and models of architecture.—in a word, Sir, before they depart, a notarial[8] act of the most binding sort, will be sign'd by them, and a copy sent to you.—You are sensible, Sir, that it is extremely difficult, if not impossible, to find any of this order of men, who are to leave, perhaps, forever, their native country, without anticipating some portion of their first year's salary;[9] I shall therefore be compell'd to advance, to each, about=150– dollars, to prepare them for so great an undertaking.—It is also, the universal custom among our merchant-captains, to receive the passage-money before sailing, which I presume, will be—100– dollars each; so that, at least, 500– dollars will be requir'd; and no bill, however good, on the U:S, can be dispos'd of, at less than 10 ℔C^t discount; and this I shall be compell'd, I presume, to allow to the purchaser:—I believe that neither of these artists require any incitement to conduct themselves with honesty and good faith; but I have made to them a sort of[10] homilie, which seems to have deeply impress'd their minds; that their happiness, at least in this world, depends[11] on an undeviating observance of honor and fidelity.—there is now but one american-vessel in port; and which is bound to India—indeed, never has there been a period, during the 20 years I have resided here, that the commerce of all ports of the mediterranean was at so low an ebb, as at the present time; however, by the first vessel, the artists shall be sent; and, depend Sir, every proper precaution shall be taken, that they may be safely consign'd into your hands.[12]—.—A few days since died in this city, m^r Joseph Barnes, a native of Virginia, and who many years ago, was appointed as consul in Sicily; but from some unaccountable reasons, he never took possession of his consulate.—He has resided here for the last eighteen years, and inseperably[13] united, with a Singularly mysterious englishman, with whom he came from England; and from whom, I believe, he has never been seperated a single day, in all this long period of time.—they brought here, I have reason to think, about—100,000— dollar[s] and their occupation has chiefly been,[14] an usurious discounting of notes, and other similar dealings; but all their transactions have been so envellop'd in impenetrable obscurity, that they drew on themselves, the continu'd watchfulness of government, and something very distant from esteem and respect of the whole city.—their dress and mode of living was that of the most extreme misery, while they were known to have many thousand pounds at their command.—Every part of their business was carried on in the name of Joseph Barnes; and his unexampled[15] associate, a certain E. I. Newton appear'd only as his friend and counsellor; and thus this impenetrable secrecy has remain'd, and is buried with him.— They had no counting-room, or any visible place of transacting their concerns, but in the streets;[16] and in their attic[17] Story in the suburbs, where they resided, no mortal, for many years, has enterd but themselves.—As I have before said, every paper is in the name of m^r Barnes; and Newton, ever 'till now, has denied having any interest or concern therein; but it was generally thought,[18] that Barnes was, for the most part,[19] a cover to Secure the property during the period of french authority; and Since that time, from creditors of N— in England.—At least, this is what Newton now asserts, and that no part belong'd to Barnes: to whomsoever it appertains will shortly be determin'd.—the laws of Tuscany do not allow a foreign accredited agent, to place the Seals of his government, within the city; it is only permitted on board of the vessels of his nation.—thus I applied at an early hour on the morning of his interrment, to the Chancellor of the tribunal, and a Commissary, assisted by magistrates,[20] plac'd the Seals of government on all the rooms of the appartment, at my instigation— a "Curatore," has been nam'd by the tribunal, and in the course of a few days they will proceed in my presence to the examination of the papers, in which I apprehend much confusion, knowing as I well do, their great irregularity in all their transactions.—if Newton was really the proprietor, there are great appearances that he has no legal[21] document from Barnes acknowledging the former as the owner[22] — indeed, the terror he is in, seems a strong confirmation of our suspicions. — It is impossible to form any correct estimate, what may be[23] the amount of the property; but I should judge it to be somewhere between 30 and[24] 50,000— dollars, although they experienc'd severe losses from embracing hasardous speculations;[25] which promis'd large interest, and in which they were the dupes & victims; for they were often the prey of artful & designing men, who knew their avarice. —[26] mr Barnes had been for many months, apparently declining in health, though he constantly denied having any complaint, and even in this State, he would devour like a starving wolf if invited at a dinner; but when at his own expence, his diet was confin'd almost intirely to bread and water. — Such, indeed, of late years, was his disgusting appearance, that I believe his body has not been cover'd with a shirt, for a single day,[27] until that of his interrment. — It seems he died the Second day after his confinement; but it cannot be discover'd how he finish'd his life, as no one was present, but his associate, who never tells a truth but when off his guard.[28] — No physician was call'd, nor was his death known until the third day after his discease, when Newton inform'd me, in order to take the necessary steps for his burial—I immediately applied to the protestant[29] Chaplain, who has the care of the[30] burying-ground, and measures were taken to inter the body the following morning; but the state of putrefaction had already made such progress, as requir'd the orders of a magistrate to the porters to place the cadavre in the coffin, & convey him to the ground, where he was buried with as much decency, as the case admitted of; for the manner of his death, and his more extraordinary life,[31] had drawn round his house, an innumerable rabble, as it was well known to all his wretched neighbourhood. — I have been thus particular, Sir, in order that you might Select Such parts, as you may judge proper, to communicate to his Son, who mr Barnes often told me he left in Virginia. — I now proceed to what is important at the present time; and which is, as to the property which may be found. — my opinion is much in favor of mr Barnes coming into possession of a part, if not the whole. — Some Small expence, therefore, will be necessary—it will, of course then be requisite, should mr Barnes be desirous of the continuance of my Services,[32] that he Should Send to me, his full powers, in legal form; and at the Same time, open a credit for the expence, Say about One hundred dollars; which, I presume will be sufficient. — the surest mode of conveyance will be to send the letters; by duplicates,[33] to the care of mr Samuel Williams, American-merchant,

N⁰ 13—Finsbury square London; from whom I shall receive them by post, in the course of a fortnight.—

I have receiv'd from your friend m^r Vaughan, many books, and diplomas for Vienna, Turin & Pisa, which have been faithfully transmitted; and I have, in return, receiv'd from the university of Pisa, the history of their institution to be transmitted to him; which I shall forward by the earliest opportunity.—The president has express'd to me in a letter, how greatly desirous he is, to cultivate this mutual intercourse of information with the accademies of the u:S—it has compell'd me, of course, to reply, in which, I have ventur'd to assure him, that he will find a very sincere reciprocity.[34]—Accept, Sir, the expressions of my very great esteem & respect.   TH: APPLETON

RC (DLC); edge chipped; endorsed by TJ as received <19> 18 Feb. 1819. RC (DLC); address cover only; with PoC of TJ to Binney & Ludlow, 5 Feb. 1820, on verso; addressed: "Thomas Jefferson, esq^r Monticello Virginia"; stamped "SHIP"; postmarked Baltimore, 11 Feb.; FC (Lb in DNA: RG 84, CRL); in Appleton's hand, unsigned; with only the most significant differences from RC noted below; at foot of text: "Sent to m^r Shaler at marseilles to forw^d by m^r Peron." Recorded in SJL as received 18 Feb. 1819.

ORNATISTA: "ornamentalist." Joseph Barnes DIED 10 Oct. 1818 in Leghorn. Appleton reportedly believed as of 1832 that Barnes had been starved to death by his partner, E. I. Newton, who went on to kill himself the same way in 1821 (Miriam Allen Deford, "An American Murder Mystery," *Prairie Schooner* 22 [1948]: 284–7). TJ had appointed Barnes CONSUL IN SICILY in 1802 (*JEP*, 1:406, 407 [2, 10 Feb. 1802]). CURATORE: "administrator; trustee." The PROTESTANT CHAPLAIN at Leghorn was Thomas Hall (Deford, "American Murder Mystery," 285).

The history of the UNIVERSITY OF PISA conveyed through Appleton to John Vaughan, librarian of the American Philosophical Society, was Angelo Fabroni, *Historiae Academiae Pisanae*, 3 vols. (Pisa, 1791–95). The APS recorded receipt of a gift from "the Academy of Pisa" on 19 Mar. 1819 (Benjamin Sproni to Appleton, 3 Nov. 1818 [PPAmP: APS Archives]; APS, Minutes [MS in PPAmP]).

[1] Instead of preceding six words, FC reads "the 1st or the 2^d."
[2] FC here adds "of existence."
[3] FC: "anxiousness."
[4] FC: "architects."
[5] Preceding three words not in FC.
[6] FC here adds "are finish'd."
[7] FC: "very."
[8] FC: "public."
[9] FC: "some part of their salary."
[10] Instead of preceding three words, FC reads "an extemporary."
[11] FC: "their happiness will solely depend."
[12] Text from "there is now" to this point not in FC.
[13] RC: "inseperately." FC: "inseperably."
[14] FC: "has seemed to be."
[15] Word not in FC.
[16] FC here adds "they had no servant."
[17] Instead of preceding word, FC reads: "5," followed by illegible superscript.
[18] Instead of preceding four words, FC reads "public opinion was otherwise; and."
[19] Instead of preceding four words, FC reads "only part owner or."
[20] FC: "Constables."
[21] FC here adds "& valid."
[22] FC: "Sole owner."
[23] Instead of preceding seven words, FC reads "Say now what is."
[24] Instead of preceding eight words, FC reads "think, it still is, 40, or."
[25] FC: "undertakings."
[26] Preceding four words not in FC.
[27] Instead of preceding three words, FC reads "many Years."
[28] Preceding ten words not in FC.

[29] FC: "british."
[30] FC here adds "protestant."
[31] Preceding five words not in FC.

[32] FC: "exertions."
[33] Preceding two words not in FC.
[34] Paragraph to this point not in FC.

To Thomas Brown

SIR   M[o]nti[cello] Nov. 10. 18.

I thank you for the copy of your Medical electricity which you have been so kind as to send me. I concur entirely in the opinion expressed by D[r] Mitchell in his letter to you that 'facts are the foundation of all useful knolege in Physics,' and those you have collected will doubtless bring into notice the process they recommend. these merit our thanks, & every thing has my good wishes which may alleviate the sufferings of our fellow men. accept the assurance of my esteem & respect.   TH: JEFFERSON

PoC (DLC); on verso of reused address cover to TJ; dateline faint; at foot of text: "D[r] Tho[s] Brown"; endorsed by TJ.

To William H. Crawford

DEAR SIR   Monticello Nov. 10. 18.

Totally withdrawn from all attention to public affairs, & void of all anxiety about them, as reposing entire confidence in those who administer them, I am led to some remarks on a particular subject by having heretofore taken some concern in it. and I should not do it even now but for information that you had turned your attention to it at the last session of Congress, and meant to do it again at the ensuing one.

When mr Dallas's Tariff first appeared in the public papers, I observed that among his reforms, none was proposed on the most exceptionable article in mr Hamilton's original Tariff, I mean that of wines. I think it a great error to consider a heavy tax on wines, as a tax on luxury. on the contrary it is a tax on the health of our citizens. it is a legislative declaration that none but the richest of them shall be permitted to drink wine, and in effect a condemnation of all the midling & lower conditions of society to the poison of whisky, which is destroying them by wholesale, and ruining their families. whereas, were the duties on the cheap wines proportioned to their first cost the whole midling class of this country could have the gratification of that milder stimulus, and a great proportion of them would go into it's use and banish the baneful whisky. surely it is not from the necessities of our treasury that we thus undertake to debar the mass of our citizens the use of not only an innocent gratification, but a healthy substitute instead of a bewitching poison. this aggression on the public taste and comfort has been ever deemed among the most arbitrary & oppressive abuses of the English government. it is one which I hope we shall never copy. but the truth is that the treasury would gain in the long run by the vast extension of the use of the article. I should therefore be for encoraging the use of wine by placing it among the articles of lightest duty. but, be this as it may, take what rate of duty is thought proper, but carry it evenly thro' the cheap as well as the high priced wines. if we take the duty on Madeira as the standard, it will be of about 25. per cent on the first cost, and I am sensible it lessens frauds to enumerate the wines known and used here, and to lay a specific duty on them, according to their known cost; but then the unknown and non-enumerated should be admitted at the same per cent on their first cost. there are abundance of wines in Europe some weak, some strong, & of good flavor, which do not cost there more than 2. cents a quart, and which are dutied here at 15. cents. I have my self imported wines which cost but 4. cents the quart and paid 15. cents duty. but an extraordinary inconsistence is in the following provisions of the Tariff.

'Claret & <u>other wines not enumerated</u> imported in

bottles, per gallon	70. cents
when imported otherwise than in bottles	25. cents
black bottles, glass, quart, per gross	144. cents'

if a cask of wine then is imported, and the bottles brought empty to put it into the wine pays $6\frac{1}{4}$ cents the quart, & the bottle 1. cent, making $7\frac{1}{4}$ cents the bottle. but if the same wine is put into the same bottles there it pays 15. cents the quart, which is a tax of $7\frac{3}{4}$ cents (more than doubling the duty) for the act of putting it into the bottle there, where it is so much more skilfully done, and contributes so much to the preservation of the wine on it's passage. for many of the cheap wines will not bear transportation in the cask which stand it well enough in the bottle. this is a further proscription of the light wines, and giving the monopoly of our tables to the strong & Alcoholic, such as are all but equivalent in their effects to whisky. it would certainly be much more for the health & temperance of society to encorage the use of the weak, rather than of the strong wines. 2. cents a quart first cost, & $\frac{1}{2}$ a cent duty would give us wine at $2\frac{1}{2}$ cents the bottle with the addition of freight & other small charges, which is but half the price of grog.   These, dear Sir, are the thoughts[1] which have long dwelt on my mind, and have given me the more concern as

I have the more seen of the loathsome and fatal effects of whisky, destroying the fortunes, the bodies, the minds & morals of our citizens. I suggest them only to you, who can turn them to account if just; without meaning to add the trouble of an answer to the overwhelming labors of your office. in all cases accept the assurance of my sincere esteem & high consideration.   TH: JEFFERSON

RC (Raab Collection, Ardmore, Pa., 2015); damaged at crease and signature clipped, with missing text supplied from PoC. PoC (DLC); on reused address covers of James H. McCulloch to TJ, 30 June 1818, and Horatio G. Spafford to TJ, 29 May 1818; mutilated at seal, with one word rewritten by TJ; at foot of first page: "Mr Crawford"; endorsed twice by TJ.

In its LAST SESSION, the United States House of Representatives had ordered Crawford to report on "what further improvement it may be practicable to make in the tariff of duties upon imported goods, wares, and merchandise." On 8 Feb. 1819 he submitted to the House a list of articles on which tariffs could be reduced. While he did not mention wine,

the duties on that beverage were among those lowered during the session (*JHR*, 11:496 [20 Apr. 1818]; *ASP, Finance*, 3:415–9; note to William A. Burwell to TJ, 28 Nov. 1818).

For TJ's response to Alexander J. DALLAS'S TARIFF following its publication in the PUBLIC PAPERS, see TJ to Dallas, 26 Feb. 1816, and note. Alexander HAMILTON'S ORIGINAL TARIFF was passed on 4 July 1789 as "An Act for laying a Duty on Goods, Wares, and Merchandises imported into the United States." It set a duty of eighteen cents per gallon of Madeira and ten cents a gallon on all other wines (*U.S. Statutes at Large*, 1:24–5).

[1] Manuscript: "thought."

James Dinsmore's Report on Tin to Central College Board of Visitors

Haveing been requested by the visitors of the Central College to Examine and report on the Eligibility of Tin as a Covering for Houses as Introduced in Staunton—I beg leave to inform them that I have repaired to that place. was Introduced to the owners of the two Principal Houses Coverd with Tin—m^r Smith, and m^r Cowan and also to m^r Brook the workman who put it on—they all acted with great Candour & were at Considerable Pains to give me every Information they were in possession of—m^r Smith haveing Asisted to put the tin on his House, Seems to have aquired a practical Knowledge of the evils to be avoided and the Proper method to be Pursued—by the want of Such knowledge the first Side that was Covered of his house leaked a little—one point to be Particularly observed he Says is to have the Sheeting Plank Seasoned, Closely Jointed, & perfectly even on the upper Surface; want of attention to this he thinks was one Cause of his House leaking, and giving the tin too little lap the other—in ad-

dition to this m^r Cowan thinks if the Sheeting was tounged & Groved it would be an additionl Security his only fears about the tightness of his Roof being the effects of the Sun through the tin drawing up the edges of the Sheeting and thereby rendering the Surface of the tin uneven—I have not my Self any apprehension on that Score with Pine Sheeting Seasoned & well nailed down, without groveing—
I also Suggested the Propriety of Painting the tin before laying down which they agreed would be an advantage mr Smith observing that his roof had been perfectly tight Since it was Painted & had not been Subject to leak from Suction as heretofor—the laps at the lower ends of the Corners Should not be less than one & an half inches—with these precautions I think I am Justified in Saying that a tin Roof may be made as tight as one of any other metal—the last one executed in Staunton[1] (Mr Cowans) has a very handsome appearance and its lightness is Certainly a great recommendation, of its durability they have no Practical Knowledge—but have it from good athourity that they have been in use in montreal & Quebeck for forty or fifty years without Painting & are Still Sound this fact might be ascertaind?—
The first Cost of the tin for Covering mr Smiths House was about $8 pr Square Say $135 for what Coverd 17$\frac{1}{2}$ Square but one eighth additional may be allowed for Increasing the width of the laps—m^r Brooks price for Cutting and machineing is $2 per Box—for Putting on $5 per Square—the Cost for nails is very trifleing they reccomend that Particular attention Should be Paid in the Purchase of the tin there being a Considerable quantity of it of very inferior quality—Zinc Costs 21 Cts the Sup^{al} foot and appears to be a very Solid evenly, Sheet about the thickness of English mill^d Lead, & mr Brook Says is in use for Covering Houses & Sheathing vessels in Baltimore & that it Solders very well—
all which is Respectfully Submitted

JA^s DINSMORE
Central College Nov. 10. 1818

MS (ViU: TJP); in Dinsmore's hand; at foot of text: "m^r Jefferson Chairman of the Board of visitors of the Central College"; endorsed by TJ: "Dinsmore James. tin cover."

[1] Manuscript: "Stantoun."

To John Farrar

SIR   Monticello Nov. 10. 18.

I have duly recieved the Introduction to the elements of Algebra which you have been so kind as to send me, and return you my thanks for this mark of your attention. it will be a valuable present to the young Algebraists of our country, as the author from whom it is taken was certainly remarkable for the perspecuity as well as profoundness of whatever he wrote. I have often wondered however that Bezout's course of mathematics has not been translated and introduced to the use of our schools. it is certainly the plainest for the student[1] of any one I have ever seen, and particularly far more so than Hutton's which is generally, I believe, used with us. this author's talent for explanation is remarkably happy. he presents his idea so simply and directly, that however difficult, it is comprehended as soon as presented. he has the disadvantage for us, which all the continental mathematical authors have, of giving the Infinitesimal method of calculus, instead of that of fluxions, which to us are more familiar, and perhaps more convenient of notation. like other continental authors also he takes no notice of Ld Napier's Catholic rule in Spherical trigonometry, so valuable for the ease with which it is retained in the memory. but with these changes, I know of no book so valuable for the use of schools. Accept the assurance of my esteem & respect.

TH: JEFFERSON

RC (NjP: Andre deCoppet Collection); addressed: "Mr John Farrar Professor of Mathematics Cambridge Mass."; franked; postmarked Charlottesville, 12 Nov.; endorsed by Farrar. PoC (DLC); on verso of reused address cover of Robert Walsh to TJ, 6 July 1818; torn at seal, with one word rewritten by TJ; endorsed by TJ.

John Farrar (1779–1853), mathematician and educator, was a native of Lincoln, Massachusetts. He graduated from Harvard University in 1803 and studied at Andover Theological Seminary for two years before returning to Harvard, first as a tutor of Greek and, in 1807, as the Hollis professor of mathematics and natural philosophy. He held this position for the remainder of his career, retiring for health reasons in 1836. Farrar translated many important French scholarly works and introduced the latest European methods of teaching mathematics and science to Harvard. He was elected to the American Academy of Arts and Sciences in 1808 and served as its recording secretary, 1811–23, and vice president, 1829–31. Farrar occasionally sent TJ books and pamphlets he had authored or translated. When TJ's granddaughter Ellen W. Randolph Coolidge and her husband, Joseph Coolidge, lived in Boston, they became friendly with Farrar, and through them in 1827 he offered advice on candidates to fill the vacant chair in mathematics at the University of Virginia. Farrar died in Cambridge (*DAB*; *DSB*; *Harvard Catalogue*, 22, 63, 184; Joseph Coolidge to Nicholas P. Trist, 18 Apr., 1, [2], 28 June, 18 July, 16 Oct. 1827 [DLC: NPT]; *Boston Daily Atlas*, 11 May 1853; John G. Palfrey, *Notice of Professor Farrar* [1853]; gravestone inscription in Mount Auburn Cemetery, Cambridge, Mass.).

The Swiss mathematician Leonhard Euler was THE AUTHOR on whom Farrar drew for his work, *An Introduction to the Elements of Algebra, designed for the use of those who are acquainted only with the first principles of Arithmetic. Selected from the Algebra of Euler* (Cambridge, 1818; Poor, *Jefferson's Library*, 8 [no. 395]). For

John Napier's (NEPIER'S) theorem, see TJ to Louis H. Girardin, 18 Mar. 1814, and TJ's Notes on Napier's Theorem, printed above at that date.

[1] Manuscript: "studest."

To William Short

DEAR SIR   Monticello Nov. 10. 18.

Altho' become averse to the taking up my pen, I cannot suffer myself to be entirely forgotten by my friends, and therefore must occasionally recall myself to their recollection. I am just now recovering from an illness of three months, not yet having left the house, altho I hope within a few days to be able to do so.[1] abandoning all attention to the march of the political machine the only thing public which now employs my care is the establishment of the College which I formerly mentioned to you. this is become the more worthy of our concern as it is likely to be adopted by the state as the University of Virginia. Commissioners appointed by their authority have recommended the site of the Central college as the properest for that of the University, and have reported an Outline of what the institution should be. this supposes 10. professors necessary to embrace the whole circle of useful sciences, & we shall exert ourselves to procure them of the ablest which America or Europe can furnish.[2] 15,000.D. a year are vested in the institution, & it is believed that as much or more will be still added. instead of[3] a single large building, we make it an Academical village in which every Professor will have a house to himself. two of these are nearly ready, and as many will be erected the next summer as workmen can be procured to execute. we look forward with pleasure to this great literary addition to our society, and to the attraction it will excite for other settlers for the benefit of educating their families. we mean that our buildings, altho' small, shall be models of chaste architecture.   My illness having prevented my visiting Bedford this fall, I expect to pass most of the next summer and autumn there. I hope that your silence has not, as mine, proceeded from ill health, and pray you to be assured of my constant & affectionate friendship & respect.   TH: JEFFERSON

RC (ViW: TJP); at foot of text: "Mʳ Short"; endorsed by Short as received 16 Nov. PoC (MHi); on verso of reused address cover to "The President of the United States"; edge trimmed; endorsed by TJ.

Short was presumably responsible for a letter from "A. B." to John Binns as editor of the Philadelphia *Democratic Press* that quoted from and summarized the above letter's comments on TJ's improved health and his plans for the University of Virginia and was widely copied or abstracted in contemporary newspapers. Having begun by saying that he wrote "to relieve the anxiety of the public mind" regarding TJ's health, "A. B." concluded that "It is pleasing to see this Nestor of our worthies indulging himself in this rational solace of his old age, and hope he will live to see the University flourishing within the view of his Monticello" (Phil-adelphia *Democratic Press*, 19 Nov. 1818; Washington *Daily National Intelligencer*, 23 Nov. 1818; and elsewhere).

[1] Preceding two sentences quoted in newspapers cited above.

[2] Preceding eight words quoted in newspapers cited above.

[3] Remainder of sentence quoted in newspapers cited above, with "College" substituted for "village."

To William Wirt

DEAR SIR   Monticello Nov. 10. 18.

In my letter of congratulation on your entran[ce into][1] office, I introduced a question of business which I knew must go to you in the end, for the sanction of your opinion and I thought it better therefore to ask it in the beginning, as it is easier to prevent error than to cure it. the question was in what court I must prove the will of Gen[l] Kozciuzko to authorise the withdrawing his funds in the hands of the US? that they may be administered according to the provisions of his will. his residence was in Switzerland, the trust established is to be executed in this state exclusively, his will is deposited here, his exr resides here, & his bona notabilia are in the hands of the US. who are omnipresent in these states by the functionaries & funds applicable to the debt. I wish to prove [it in] our district court, if that will do, because I could attend & giv[e] proof personally. if it will do in our court of Chancery at Staunton, I might perhaps be able to go that far, but no where more distant. I do not mean to accept the executorship, because the trust [will][2] take a longer course of time than I have left of life; but I have engaged Gen[l] Cocke to do it, and should only prove the will and get the administration committed to him. but I must beseech you, my dear Sir, who are equally familiar with the laws of our state as with those of the US. to advise me what probat will be required to justify the treasury in paying the funds to the admr with the will annexed, that I may take no false step, & get this sacred & delicate trust disposed of according to the intentions of my deceased frien[d.][3] Accept the assurances of my constant & affectionate esteem & respec[t]   TH: JEFFERSON

PoC (DLC); on verso of reused address cover of John Armstrong to TJ, 1 July 1818; torn at seal and edge trimmed, with missing text supplied from Tr; at foot of text: "William Wirt esq. A.G. of the US."; endorsed by TJ. Tr (MdHi: Wirt Papers).

¹ Words faint.
² Word faint.
³ Word faint.

BONA NOTABILIA: "Notable goods; property worth accounting for in a decedent's estate" (*Black's Law Dictionary*).

To George Wyche

SIR   Monticello Nov. 10. 18.

Age and it's consequent infirmities of body & relaxation of mind, oblige me to excuse myself from all correspondence. I am no longer equal to it. I will answer however your enquiries respecting my admeasurement of the heights of the peaks of Otter. this was done about 3. years ago with an excellent Ramsden's Theodolite of $3\frac{1}{2}$ I. radius, having a Nonius dividing the degrees to 3' minutes but shewing distinctly enough to $1\frac{1}{2}$' with two telescopes & cross spirit levels. I got a base of $1\frac{1}{4}$ mile along the low grounds of the Little Otter in the lands of mr Clarke & mr Donald, nearly parallel with the two mountains and about 4. miles from the points in their base vertically under their summits. there was a descent of 15.f. in the length of the base, which was taken into calculation. I got also a cross base of $\frac{55}{100}$ of a mile, crossing the other and pointing directly to the sharp peak. I found the height of the sharp peak above the bed of the river $2946\frac{1}{2}$ feet, that of the flat peak $3103.\frac{1}{2}$ f. the distance between the two summits $9507\frac{3}{4}$ f.

Two observations with a Sextant gave for a mean of the latitude of the sharp peak 37°–28'–50".

Your indulgence will, I am sure, excuse the necessary brevity of this answer and accept the assurance of my great esteem & respect.

TH: JEFFERSON

PoC (MoSHi: TJC-BC); on verso of reused address cover of Mathew Carey & Son to TJ, 27 June 1818; at foot of text: "Mʳ Wyche"; endorsed by TJ.

Documents pertaining to TJ's ADMEASUREMENT of the Peaks of Otter are printed above at 10 Nov. 1815. His calculation of the LATITUDE of the Sharp Peak of Otter is printed at 18 Sept. 1815.

To Joel Yancey

DEAR SIR   Monticello Nov.¹ 10. 18

When I wrote to you on the 11ᵗʰ of Sep. I confidently hoped to recover my health and strength to be with you long before this. but I
am not yet able to go out of the house: and altho' much recovered, I
shall not have strength for the journey until it will be too cold to undertake it. I shall not therefore see you until April. in this case I must
pray you to act in all things for the best according to your own judgment, and without waiting to consult me. a first object will be to get
the flour down immediately, and the tobᵒ got ready and down as early
as possible. what your homespun falls short of clothing for the people
must be supplied from mr Robertson's. I will state below who are to
have blankets, and who beds this year. with respect to the hogs when
ready for slaughter, the overseer's allowance is first taken, then 20.
for the negroes, 12 to be kept there for my use and the rest to come
here. I suppose those to come here had better be killed there, to give
the benefit of the offal to those who raised them, and if our waggon
here is necessary to join yours to bring the meat down it shall be at
Poplar Forest any day you will name. I think you were expecting to
be able to begin in furnishing us some beeves and muttons for the
winter. if you have them to spare, they may come with the waggon. I
must pray you to get mr Martin to saw for me the stuff stated on the
next page, and to have it hauled home and stowed away in time. I
shall carry up Johnny Hemings & his 2. assistants early in the year
and they will work there till the fall. I salute you with affectionate
esteem & respect   TH: JEFFERSON

PoC (MHi); on verso of reused address cover to TJ, with enclosures on
recto of address cover; at foot of text: "Mʳ
Yancey"; endorsed by TJ.

A missing letter from Yancey to TJ of
Nov. 1818 is recorded in SJL as received
18 Nov. 1818 from Poplar Forest.

¹ Word interlined in place of "Oct."

I

List of Blankets and Beds to be Distributed to Poplar Forest Slaves

[ca. 10 Nov. 1818]

Blankets.

Cate
Hal
Hanah
Sally
Armistead
Maria. Cate's
Gawen
Austin
Flora
Fanny
Edy. 1. for herself
& 1. for Nancy & Robert
Dick
Dinah.
1. for Joe & Shepherd
Betty
Cate. Betty's
Jesse
Maria. Nanny's
20. Milly. Nanny's

Beds

Cate
Hanah. Cate's
Lucinda.
Edy
Dinah
Betty
Aggy
8. Maria. Nanny's

Maria having now a child, I promised her a house to be built this winter. be so good as to have it done. place it along the garden fence on the road Eastward from Hanah's house.

PoC (MHi); in TJ's hand; undated; on verso of covering letter, with second enclosure subjoined.

Maria's CHILD was James Hubbard (Betts, *Farm Book*, pt. 1, 131).

II

Sawing Instructions for James Martin

[ca. 10 Nov. 1818]

Bill for Capt Martin
10. joists 8. by 10.I. 24.f. long clear of bad knots[1] windshakes & cracks. heart of poplar.
10. d° 4 by 10.I. 24.f. long. heart of poplar clear of bad knots.
5. pieces 6.I. square 16.f. long. heart of poplar.
500.f. sheeting plank. poplar.

PoC (MHi); in TJ's hand; undated; on verso of covering letter, subjoined to first enclosure.

[1] Preceding two words interlined, with carets preceding and following "of."

To John Barnes

DEAR SIR   Monticello Nov. 11. 18.

I take up my pen merely to answer the kind anxiety you are so good as to express in yours of the 17th Oct. respecting my health. I am recovering steadily but have not yet got out of doors; but I think within a very few days I shall be able to get on my horse, to me the most sovereign of all Doctors. Affectionately Adieu.

TH: JEFFERSON

PoC (MHi); on verso of reused address cover of John H. Hall to TJ, 15 July 1818; at foot of text: "Mr Barnes"; endorsed by TJ. Tr (MHi); with Tr of enclosure to John Barnes to TJ, [30] Nov. 1818, on verso.

To Andrew Kean

SIR   Monticello Nov. 11. 18.

Altho' strangers personally, we are not so in character, and on this ground I take the liberty of addressing you on a subject interesting to both. with great confidence in the aids of medecine as far as experience has approved it's processes, I have in absolute abhorrence the fanciful and ephemeral theories under which dashing practitioners are so wantonly sporting with human life. our country is overrun with young lads from the Philadelphia school, who with their mercury & lancet in hand are vying with the sword of Bonaparte which shall have shed most human blood. in such hands therefore you may readily imagine how desirable it must be for us to get established in our neighborhood a Physician of experience, and of sober, cautious practice; that when afflicted with the diseases incident to our nature, we may have a resource in which we have confidence. altho' distance has prevented your being much in this part of the country, yet the character of your practice has been long known to me, and is the motive of the present application; believing, that circumstances exist which may give a preference in your eye to a position offering an easy, instead of a¹ laborious practice. you have heard of the College proposed to be established within a mile of Charlottesville, and now likely to be adopted by the legislature for the University of the state. they have already endowed their University with 15,000.D. a year, and it is confidently expected they will enlarge the endowment so as to make it adequate to the communication of instruction in all the branches of useful science. the Commissioners they appointed for this purpose have reported that 10. Professors will be requisite, and it is proposed to procure these of the first abilities which America or Europe can furnish, so as to place the institution at once on such eminence as to fear no competition. and so great is the want of such an institution, and such the confidence anticipated in this that we think we may safely count on 5. or 6. pupils from each of the hundred counties in the state, and we are well informed that all the states West and South of this are looking to it as their best resource and, together, will furnish as many students as our own state. we suppose then we may count on 1000. students coming in as fast as we can provide accomodations for them. Charlottesville contains about 500 inhabitants, so that a position half way between that & the College would place you within half a mile of a population of 1500. inhabitants, besides a thickly settled neighborhood. not but that there are boy-doctors enough at hand. but they would disappear in the presence of an experienced physician as mists before the sun. there is one indeed who gets a tolerably good practice, the effect of his modest pretensions, cautious practice & great personal worth. but heir to an independant fortune, it is understood he means to retire from the drudgery of the business: nor would he stand a competition with yourself.   think then, good Sir, of this proposition, & weigh well the comfort & advantage of an abundant and easy practice, especially when ease, with advancing years, shall have become more and more desirable. one favor however I will ask. that no intimation be given of this application from myself. I love to enjoy the good will of my neighbors, and might lose that of some who may think their interests in danger. but if you are disposed, as I would wish & recommend, to come and examine the ground proposed to you, do me the favor to make this your headquarters, as being at hand for the enquiry and information you may wish. within the course of the next month the legislature will probably decide on the location reported by their commissioners, and no time should then be lost, lest the ground should be anticipated by another. I pray you to be assured of my best wishes & services, as well as of my great esteem & respect.   Th: Jefferson

RC (Mrs. Charles D. Zimmerman, Council Bluffs, Iowa, 1972); damaged at fold, with missing text supplied from PoC; addressed: "Doctor Kain near Yancyville"; franked; endorsed in an unidentified hand: "Inclosed to D Johnson, & forwarded by him Per M Randolph." PoC (DLC); edge trimmed; endorsed by TJ.

Andrew Kean (1775–1837), physician, was born in County Armagh, Ireland, and immigrated with his family to Philadelphia at about the age of ten. Soon thereafter they settled in Alleghany County, Virginia. Kean went to live in Staunton about 1790 and studied medicine under Alexander Humphreys. He then moved to Yanceyville in Louisa County and practiced medicine in the surrounding counties. During the War of 1812 Kean served as a surgeon in John H. Cocke's brigade. In 1818 he moved to Lickinghole in

Goochland County. That same year TJ asked him to relocate to Charlottesville to practice medicine, which Kean did about six years later. TJ and members of the Randolph family employed his services during his residence in Charlottesville, but early in 1825 Kean returned with his family to Goochland County, where he died. At Kean's request, TJ appointed his son John V. Kean the first librarian of the University of Virginia (Linneas B. Anderson, *Brief Biographies of Virginia Physicians of Olden Times* [1889], 1–8; *Goochland County Historical Society Magazine* 12 [1980]: 57–64; DNA: RG 29,

CS, Goochland Co., 1820, 1830; Thomas Jefferson Randolph's Account with Kean, [28 Feb.–6 Nov. 1824] [ViU: Papers of the Jefferson, Randolph, Nicholas, and Kean Families]; *MB*, 2:1409; TJ to Kean, 27 Jan. 1825; Kean to TJ, 19 Feb. 1825; *Richmond Whig and Public Advertiser*, 5 Dec. 1837; Goochland Co. Deed Book, 31:284–5).

The physician with a TOLERABLY GOOD PRACTICE may have been John C. Ragland.

[1] Reworked from "to an easy, over a."

To John Trumbull

DEAR SIR   Monticello Nov. 11. 18.

Your's of Oct. 23. is recieved, and I trust you have silenced the Critic on your Decln of Indepdce, as I am sure you must have satisfied every sound judge. painters as well as poets have their licence. without this the talent of imagination would be banished from the art, taste and judgment in composition would be of no value, and the mechanical copyist of matter of fact would be on a footing with the first painter. he might as well have criticised you because you have not given his white wig & black stockings to mr Cushing, nor his real costume to Roger Sherman. I think I pourtrayed to you, in words, the countenance of T.W. while the Declaration was reading. I hope you have given it all it's haggard lineaments. if you have not, touch it again. it ought to be preserved as the eikon of the non-concurrents. he refused to sign. as to the use you have made of my name, it did not need apology. it is always at your command for any service it can render you. I am just on the recovery from a three months sickness. affectionately Adieu.   TH: JEFFERSON

RC (CtY: Franklin Collection); addressed: "Col⁰ John Trumbull New York"; franked; postmarked Charlottesville, 14 Nov.; endorsed by Trumbull. PoC (DLC); on verso of reused address cover to TJ; edge trimmed; endorsed by TJ.

T.W.: Thomas Willing. EIKON: "icon."

From Wilson Cary Nicholas

Dear Sir   Novr 12th 1818

The first of the two notes you were so good as to endorse for me will come round by the time I get to Richmond. I enclose two others which you will be pleased to endorse.

I am with great respect Dear Sir sincerely yours

W. C. Nicholas

RC (DLC); dateline at foot of text; endorsed by TJ as received 13 Nov. 1818 from North Milton and so recorded in SJL. Enclosures not found.

From Francois Redon (for Lewis D. Belair)

Monsieur,   New York Novbr 12th 1818.

Par Ordre de Mr Lewis D Belair a Philadelphia j'ai l'honneur de vous marquer les Prix des Livres Suivant

1. Pline le jeune Lat. franc^s 3. 12°	$ 2.87½
1. Dictionnaire de Bibliotheque /:que Mr Belair ne possede que Sous le titre <u>Bibliographie de France</u>:/[1] 3. 8° broché 1814. 15. 16.	13.50.
1. Antiquité Romaine de Denis d'Halicarnasse 6. 8°	10.00.
1. Dict^{re} de Medecine 8° /:est vendu:/	2.75.
1. Sacrorum bibliorum Vulgatæ 2. 4to	7.12½

1. Abrégé des 10 Livres de Vitruve[2] Paris 1674. 12° ne se trouve pas sous ce titre dans le Magazin

Bien charmé Si vous nous chargez de vos Commissions j'ai l'honneur de me signer avec la plus parfaite Consideration

Monsieur Votre très humble & très obeissant Serviteur

Francois Redon

EDITORS' TRANSLATION

Sir,   New York November 12th 1818.

By order of Mr. Lewis D. Belair in Philadelphia, I have the honor to inform you of the prices of the following books

1. Pliny the Younger Latin and French 3. duodecimo	$ 2.87½
1. *Dictionnaire de Bibliotheque* (Mr. Belair has this only under the title of *Bibliographie de la France*) 3. octavo stitched 1814. 15. 16.	13.50.
1. *Les Antiquités Romaines de Denys d'Halicarnasse* 6. octavo	10.00.
1. *Dictionnaire de Médecine* octavo (sold)	2.75.
1. *Sacrorum Bibliorum Vulgatæ* 2. quarto	7.12½

1. *Abregé des dix livres d'Architecture de Vitruve* Paris 1674. duodecimo. We have not found it under this title in the store

We would be delighted if you will entrust your orders to us, and I have the honor of signing myself with the most perfect consideration

Sir your very humble and very obedient servant   FRANCOIS REDON

RC (MHi); endorsed by TJ (brackets in original) as a letter from "Belair Louis de [by Francois Redory]" received 22 Nov. 1818 and so recorded in SJL. RC (MHi); address cover only; with PoC of TJ to Patrick Gibson, 14 May 1819, on verso, and its enclosure on recto; addressed: "Thomas Jefferson Esqr Mon-tecelo Virg^a"; franked; postmarked New York, 12 Nov. Translation by Dr. Genevieve Moene.

[1] Omitted closing parenthetical symbols editorially supplied.
[2] Manuscript: "Vituves."

To John Adams

Monticello Nov. 13. 18.

The public papers, my dear friend, announce the fatal event of which your letter of Oct. 20. had given me ominous foreboding. tried myself, in the school of affliction, by the loss of every form of connection which can rive the human heart, I know well, and feel what you have lost, what you have suffered, are suffering, and have yet to endure. the same trials have taught me that, for ills so immeasurable, time and silence are the only medecines.[1] I will not therefore, by useless condolances, open afresh the sluices of your grief nor, altho' mingling sincerely my tears with yours, will I say a word more,[2] where words are vain, but that it is of some comfort to us both that the term is not very distant at which we are to deposit, in the same cerement, our sorrows and suffering bodies, and to ascend in essence to an ecstatic meeting with the friends we have loved & lost and whom we shall still love and never lose again. God bless you and support you under your heavy affliction.   TH: JEFFERSON

RC (MHi: Adams Papers); addressed: "President Adams Quincy Massachusets"; franked; postmarked Charlottesville, 17 Nov.; endorsed by Adams as answered 8 Dec. 1818. FC (DLC); entirely in TJ's hand. Tr (MHi: Adams Papers); mimicking TJ's hand, but probably in that of William S. Shaw; endorsed by John Quincy Adams, with his additional initialed notation: "This Letter, and one of 30 Augt 1791—from the same to the same—received from Mr Felt—Adm^r of W. S. Shaw 19 Augt 1826"; with Tr of address cover, lacking frank and postmark.

On 8 Nov. 1818 the *Richmond Enquirer* announced THE FATAL EVENT of the death in Quincy of Adams's wife, Abigail Adams.

[1] FC: "medecine."
[2] Word interlined in FC.

From Patrick Gibson

Sir Richmond 13ᵗʰ Novʳ 1818

Your favor of the 3ᵈ postmark'd Charlottesville the 7ᵗʰ was not received until the 9ᵗʰ which was so far unfortunate as I had the day before sold the 14 barˢ condemn'd flour to Sterling J: Crump at $6— the proceeds however shall be held subject to the order of T: E: Randolph & Colclaser—I shall attend to your instructions, relative to the distinction you wish observed in the several parcels of flour— I have paid your dfts to Leitch $400 I: Garrett $120²⁶ and to A Robertson $303.$\frac{4}{100}$—With sincere wishes for your restoration to health

I am with much respect Yours PATRICK GIBSON

RC (MHi); between dateline and salutation: "Thomas Jefferson Esqʳᵉ"; endorsed by TJ as received 21 Nov. 1818 but recorded in SJL as received a day later.

From Hannah

MASTER November 15ᵗʰ 1818

I write you a few lines to let you know that your house and furniture are all safe as I expect you would be glad to know I heard that you did not expect to come up this fall I was sorry to hear that you was so unwell you could not come it greive me many time but I hope as you have been so blessed in this that you considered it was god that done it and no other one we all ought to be thankful for what he has done for us we ought to serve and obey his commandments that you may set to win the prize and after glory run

master I donot[1] my ignorant letter will be much encouragement to you as know I am a poor ignorunt creature, this leaves us all well

adieu, I am your humble sarvant HANNAH

RC (MHi); endorsed by TJ as a letter from "Hanah" received 18 Nov. 1818. An image of this letter is reproduced elsewhere in this volume.

Hannah (b. 1770), one of TJ's slaves, was the daughter of Cate (later Cate Hubbard). Apparently born at Monticello, she was at Poplar Forest by 1791, when the birth of her first child was recorded there. By about 1797 she was the wife of Hall, an enslaved blacksmith and hog keeper at Poplar Forest. Hannah worked as a laborer at its Tomahawk plantation. She also worked as a spinner and was TJ's

cook and laundress when he or his guests visited Poplar Forest. Hannah was still there late in 1823, a year after Elizabeth Trist described her as having "the care of the House" (Betts, *Farm Book*, pt. 1; Lucia Stanton, *"Those Who Labor for My Happiness": Slavery at Thomas Jefferson's Monticello* [2012], 23, 165; TJ's Instructions for Poplar Forest Management, Dec. 1811; Ellen W. Randolph [Coolidge] to Martha Jefferson Randolph, 14 Apr. 1818 [ViU: Coolidge Correspondence]; Joel Yancey to TJ, 19 Nov., 12 Dec. 1819; TJ to Yancey, 16 Mar. 1820, 15 Aug. 1821; Cornelia J. Randolph to Virginia J.

Randolph [Trist], 24 Apr. 1821 [NcU: NPT]; Elizabeth Trist to Nicholas P. Trist, 28 Nov. 1822 [DLC: NPT]; List of Poplar Forest Slaves [ca. 16–31 Dec. 1823]).

YOU MAY SET TO WIN THE PRIZE AND AFTER GLORY RUN paraphrases the Bible,

1 Corinthians 9.24: "Know ye not that they which run in a race run all, but one receiveth the prize? So run, that ye may obtain."

[1] Thus in manuscript.

To Lewis D. Belair

SIR   Monticello Nov. 16. 18.

I have safely recieved Planche's Dict^y Cortès & the Log. of la Land, and your letter of the 6th inst. is this moment recieved. I decide at once to take Ducange, Cabanis, Saluste 8vo Suetone, Perefixe, Appien which were mentioned in my letters of Oct. 27. & 31. and as soon as I recieve the information you promise of the formats & prices of Pline Dict. Bibliogr. Dict. de Medecine. Denys d'Halicarn. Bibliorum Concordantiae also mentioned in my sd letters, I will determine which of them I take. I will request you moreover to inform me of the formats & prices of

pa. 2. l. 22.   Epictetus Gr. & Ital.
    3. l. 18.   Geometrie de Le Gendre
        19.   Metaphysique du Calcul infinit[1] de Carnot.
        20.   Algebre d'Euler

when this information shall be recieved I will indicate by what conveyance they are to be sent. in the mean time lay by for me another copy of Planche's dict. Gr. & Fr.
        and of Lalande's Logarithmes stereotypes.
I am very anxious to get the translation of Aeschylus mentioned in the Compte rendu of the Institute of 1808. seance de 20. Fevrier, Discours de Dacier which seems then to have been recently made, which, if you have not you can get from Europe sooner than I can. I shall expect a copy of the Tacite par La Malle when you recieve it. I salute you with esteem and respect   TH: JEFFERSON

I prefer recieving them unbound

PoC (MHi); on verso of reused address cover of Thomas Appleton to TJ, 29 Apr. 1818; above postscript: "M. Belair"; endorsed by TJ.

For TJ's letter of Oct. 31, see note at TJ to Belair, 27 Oct. 1818.

In September 1818 TJ belatedly received a copy of Jacob L. Kesteloot, ed., *Discours sur les Progrès des Sciences, Lettres et Arts, depuis MDCCLXXXIX jusqu'à ce jour; ou Compte Rendu par l'Institut de France a S. M. l'Empereur et Roi* (The Hague, 1809; Poor, *Jefferson's*

Library, 13 [no. 831]), which Kesteloot had sent in 1809. It included a DISCOURS ("address") to the French Council of State on 20 Feb. 1808 by Bon Joseph Dacier concerning works of history and ancient literature published since 1789 by members of the Institut de France, as well as upcoming publications, including an anticipated translation of Aeschylus (p. 89).

From William Short

DEAR SIR   Philadelphia Nov: 17. 1818.

In the long course of our acquaintance, & of my friendship & veneration for you, I do not recollect ever to have recieved a letter from you which has so much excited my sensibility, & at the same time given me so much pleasure as yours of the 10ᵗʰ inst.—It is such a mark of your friendly recollection under such painful circumstances, & at the same time relieves me from so much sollicitude on account of your health that I cannot sufficiently express my gratitude for it.

The first account which I recieved of your indisposition was from Gˡ Pinckney of sᵒ Carolina, who had been at the Virginia springs soon after you had left them, & had then proceeded to N. York where I saw him. He expressed great sympathy on the occasion, to me, & which I am certain he felt—I took up my pen immediately to write to you & ask information on this subject, which gave me much uneasiness at the time—but I was deterred from executing my plan by a recollection of the pain which it would give you to write, & by knowing at the same time that Correa was gone on a visit to you & was expected to return to Philadelphia, where I should meet with him. In effect it turned out so; & from him I learned as well as from Dʳ Cooper, the then state of things—they considered it favorable—And in this way we remained until a report was brought here of your having a relapse—Correa came with much anxiety to learn from me if I had any information on this subject, or if I knew any thing of the report— My opinion & my hope, as we could not trace the report to any source, was that it was merely the echo of the first report which I had heard at N. York.

In this state of painful sollicitude, wishing to write & fearing to give you the trouble of answering, I remained until the arrival here of Mʳ Divers, your neighbor. He gave me all the information I could expect to recieve. He had seen you on the 26ᵗʰ of the last month—& he considered you then, though much enfeebled, in a state of convalescence. I could not however divest myself of much uneasiness. Your letter now encourages me to hope that nothing but time is wanting to put you in your <u>statu quo</u>. My prayers for this are most sincere, as I am sure you readily believe. I hope I shall learn this wished for progress—Nothing can give me more true & heartfelt satisfaction.

It is a great gratification also to me to learn from you the favorable prospect as to the University. Although there is little probability of my again becoming a resident of my native State, yet my good wishes towards it are in nothing diminished—I retain that kind of affection for it, which children do for their parents independent of all considerations of fear or hope.

I cannot be indifferent to what relates to education or the mental improvement of man, in any part of the world—but it pleases me more in the U. S. than elsewhere—& more in Virginia than any other State, & really more in your neighborhood than in any other part of the State. I feel how great service you will be able to render to an institution of the kind you contemplate, & how great a solace this will be to you in your advancing age. The connexion of your name with this institution has already decided a very wealthy inhabitant of Havanna, a Frenchman whom I met with at Ballston last summer to send his sons there to be educated—They are now very young—but he enquired very particularly of me as to the University & its prospects, & told me he was resolved to send there, if it went into operation in your neighborhood & under your eyes, the two boys whom he presented to me as intended <u>alumni</u> of the Jefferson college, as he called it.

The idea of an academical village instead of one large building, is well concieved I think—It will be necessary that the institution should own so large a tract of land, as that the residence of the students should be a mile removed from any tavern not immediately under the control of the college—and indeed it would be well to have no tavern within less than that distance of the college—at Princeton they might have effected this but they did not—& no discipline is found sufficient to keep young men out of those that are near the college. Unfortunately for this country the point of honor is placed in liberality as to drinking in a tavern—because the being sober there argues a meanness as to the purse—& on this head a young man would lose consideration as certainly as in shewing a fear of danger—The best & only method then is to erect a physical obstacle as to entering a tavern, & this can only be done by distance. If the tavern be out of the bounds, the punishment may be for breaking the bounds, & not for going into the tavern, where a point of honor is supposed to exist.

Among the books which I have lately recieved from France, are 4. vol^s of <u>melanges literaires</u> of our old friend <u>le doyen de la literature Francaise, l'Abbè Morellet</u>—He will write as long as he lives, & will write well as long as he writes. There is also a posthumous work of M^de de Stael—It is certainly the best of all her works, & I think, the best work on the French revolution—A work of a different kind is— les Memoires de M^de d'Epinay. This Lady was dead I believe before you went to France—She was the sister in law of M^de d'Houdetot—& was known as the protectress of Rousseau—l'hermitage where he wrote & lived, belonged to her. Her memoirs, which were not intended to be printed, are much in the way of Rousseaus' confessions— They were confided by her to Grimm, who was considered always as her lover au fait, but which seems now to be questionable—When he left France, these remained in the care of his Secretary, at whose death, they fell into the hands of his family, & from them passed into the hands of the Editors—A Lady, a friend of mine, who sends me this work tells me she sends it, because "il pourra, je pense, vous amuser— il occupe le public avec interêt, parcequ'il parle de beaucoup de personages connus, qu'il devoile de petites intrigues, & que le scandale amuse toujours"   The same Lady, I am sorry to see it, speaking on public affairs, says, they present "un état de choses peu satisfaisant dans son ensemble—personne n'est content."—This produces a greater effect on me, as the Lady is dispassionate & belongs to a house, much known to you, where good sense, moderation, & sound views of things, are hereditary. I have seen nothing from France for a long time which has so much discouraged me.

The pleasure of communing with you makes me immindful of the tax I am imposing on your patience, & the fatigue I give you of reading so long a letter. I will end it here then in repeating to you my dear sir, the assurances of all those sentiments with which you have so long inspired me, & with which I shall end my life, as your affectionate friend &

obed^t serv^t   W: SHORT

RC (MHi); endorsed by TJ as received 21 Nov. 1818 but recorded in SJL as received a day later.

The POSTHUMOUS WORK of Madame de Staël Holstein was *Considérations sur les principaux événemens de La Révolution Françoise*, 3 vols. (Paris, 1818; Poor, *Jefferson's Library*, 4 [no. 91]).

IL POURRA, JE PENSE . . . AMUSE TOUJOURS: "it will, I think, amuse you— it holds the interest of the public, because it speaks of many well-known figures and unveils petty intrigues, and because scandal is always amusing." UN ÉTAT DE CHOSES . . . N'EST CONTENT: "an altogether unsatisfactory state of affairs—no one is happy."

From Joseph C. Cabell

DEAR SIR, Enniscorthy. 18 Nov. 1818.

I arrived here on 11th inst on my way to Monticello, and on 12th was visited by a most unexpected and mortifying relapse, which, tho in part removed, still hangs lingering about me, has thrown me into a weak & delicate state of body, and threatens to deprive me altogether of the satisfaction & advantage of seeing you before the meeting of the Assembly. I yield the idea of a personal interview with great reluctance. I wished to peruse the Report of the Commissioners, to converse with you fully on the subject of the University, and to state to you my present impressions relative to the proposition you think of making to me in the event of the passage of the Bill. Situated as I am, I seem reduced to the necessity of adopting the more imperfect mode of communicating thro' a friend. If you could venture to trust the Report out of your hands before it goes into those of Messrs Gordon & Carr, I think we could return it to you safely on saturday or sunday. In regard to the contemplated trip to Europe our friend Col: Coles, who is intimately acquainted with my situation, will be able to give you the same information as I could myself were I present. Probably such objections to me, as he will state, would be considered insurmountable by yourself; and if not by you, by the other Visitors. Suppose them, however, removed, the proposition is one of great importance, and I request a reasonable time to consider of it. It is my intention in every event to retire from the Senate at the close of the approaching session. The current of my inclination strongly inclines me to withdraw altogether, and endeavor by greater personal attention to derive a moderate revenue from my estate, and at the same time to cultivate Science & Literature. A part of the District are disposed to bring me forward as a candidate for Congress: conversations have passed amounting, perhaps, to something like a commitment on my side: but nothing having been finally decided on, & this cruel fever shaking my mind & body, and threatening to impair my already frail constitution, it is not improbable I may, in quitting the Senate, give up all pretensions to further popular preferment. The voyage you propose to me, is to my mind truly interesting, and I cannot conceal the gratification I feel at the confidence the proposition discovers. Having said this, I must leave the rest to my friend Coles.

The Senate will doubtless adjourn in a week from the commencement of the session, and the first 15 days will be employed by the House of Delegates in receiving petitions. The Bill for locating the University might be introduced on 16th and decided on in that House by 20th. Should it succeed there, you may count on its success in the Senate. It would be beneficial, if you would write such a bill as you think the occasion will require, and commit it to the care of such person as you deem proper to be entrusted with it: as also, if you would write to Judge Roane, Judge Brooke, & a few select friends, & request them to speak to the active and influential members of the House of Delegates.

I am D[r] Sir, faithfully y[r] friend   JOSEPH C. CABELL

RC (ViU: TJP-PC); endorsed by TJ as received 19 Nov. 1818 and so recorded in SJL. RC (DLC); address cover only; with PoC of TJ to Thomas C. Flournoy, 24 Jan. 1819, on verso; addressed: "M[r] Jefferson Monticello Care of Col: Coles."

William F. GORDON and TJ's nephew Samuel CARR represented Albemarle County in the Virginia House of Delegates at this time (Leonard, *General Assembly*, 293). During the proposed TRIP TO EUROPE Cabell was to recruit professors for the University of Virginia. The mission was delayed until 1824 and ultimately undertaken by Francis W. Gilmer (Cabell to TJ, 15 Feb. 1819).

From James Dinsmore

SIR   Nov 18. 1818

from the best Calculation m[r] Perry & my Self Can make we find that a Square of Hart Pine Shingling, all expences Included, viz. timber, getting, Hauling Putting on, Nails &[c] Cannot at Present be done for less than ten Dollars—with Respect   JA[s] DINSMORE

RC (ViU: TJP); written on a small scrap; dateline at foot of text; addressed: "M[r] Jefferson."

From William Craig

SIR   Rome November 19th 1818

I take the Liberty in writing to you on a perticular Subject tho my acquaintance with your Honor is but Small, that being at a time when there was so many present you have no Recollection of me; I was Entroduced to you in the City of washington by John Randolph when you were in the office of vice president of the United States and Sir Soon after that period I Came out to the western Country Caried the first Communication west that Effected the Change of Administration, and has Constantly Supported the[1] measures adopted by the men in power with your Honor at the Head of Department; and Shall Ever beleive that the Change to A Republican Adminstration was the

Salvation of the United States & A continuance of our Liberties. to you Sir the Honor of this Change is principally Due. and Sir I must for one Congratulate[2] you as one of the first Character in being at this Day you being an undiviating Son of (Light Liberty & Equality) Sir I Dont pen these lines to flatter you by any means but I am Confident that it becomes my Duty as a Testimony of my Respect for you and your Service Done to your Country; Sir I have been Imployed in the western Country Since previous to your Election to the presidential Chair in Surveying now in the Study &[3] practice of law; and has been Recommended to the president and Senate of the United States as one of the Judges of the Superiour Court by A number of Respectable Citizens of this Section the Now (Messouri) Teritory. which is Expected to be Erected into A seperate Teritory this Session of Congress now Sir I Know your Influence is as Great as any other man with the president and Senate. and if you would be Good Enough to write to Some of your friends on my behalf I Should be Confident of the Appointment and Sir if it is not Convenient for you; nor Should you not think proper. I am Still the Same man and Beleive you to be the Greatest man now in Being (and its not only my opinion but the General opinion of the western People,) and you Can fill the presidential Chair Again if you think it would be policy No more from your undiviating friend only my prayer that you will be Rewarded as your Merrit Deserve   W^M CRAIG

RC (DLC); with idiosyncratic delimiters editorially altered to parentheses; addressed: "Thomas Jefferson Esqr Formerly president of the United States"; franked; postmarked "Arkansa Mo T," 25 Nov.; endorsed by TJ as received 2 Mar. 1819 and so recorded in SJL.

William Craig worked as a surveyor before he began operating a tavern at Arkansas Post and took up the practice of law. He was unsuccessful in his 1818 attempt to be named a judge for the soon-to-be-created Arkansas Territory and received only two votes in the 1819 election of its territorial delegate. Craig became a county magistrate in 1822 but later left Arkansas County (Josiah H. Shinn, *Pioneers and Makers of Arkansas* [1908]; DNA: RG 59, LAR [1817–25]; Arkansas Post *Arkansas Gazette*, 20 Nov. 1819; *Terr. Papers*, 19:19–21, 41–2, 802).

Arkansas became a SEPERATE TERITORY from Missouri on 2 Mar. 1819 (*Terr. Papers*, 19:44–50).

[1] Manuscript: "the the."
[2] Manuscript: "Congratetulate."
[3] Preceding two words interlined.

Rockfish Gap and Warm Springs by Edward Beyer

present position oppose all ~~improvements~~ advances which might
unmask their usurpations, and monopolies of honors
wealth and power, and dread every change as endangering
the comforts they now hold. nor must we omit to mention
among the benefits of education the incalculable advan
tage of training up able Counsellors to administer the
affairs of our country, in all it's departments, Legisla
tive, Executive & Judiciary, and to bear their proper share
in the Councils of our National government; nothing more
than wise government, advancing the prosperity, the
power and the happiness of a nation.

    Encoraged therefore by the sentiments of the legisla
ture, manifested in this statute, we present the following
Tabular statement of the branches of learning which we think
should be taught in the University, & the number of Professors
necessary for them.

Language	I. Languages antient	Latin.
		Greek.
	II. Languages modern	French
		Spanish
		Italian
		German.
		anglo-saxon
Mathematical pure & mixed	III. Mathematics pure	Algebra.
		Fluxions
		Geometry elementary
		transcendental
		Architecture Civil
		Naval
		Military
	IV. Phisico mathematics	Mechanics individ'l Statics Dynamics
		Pneumatics.
		Acoustics ~~Phonics~~
		Optics.
		Astronomy
		Geography civil & Physical.

		Ideology
VIII	General Grammar.	
		Ethics
IX		Government. it's structure & principles.
		Political economy
		Law of Nature and Nations
		History
X		Law municipal.
XII		Medecine.
Ideological	VIII	Ideology proper.
		General Grammar
		Ethics
	IX	Government. ~~structure & principles~~
		Political economy
		Law of Nature & Nations.
		History [being interwoven with Law & Politics]
	X	Law Municipal.
Fine arts	XI	Belles lettres.
		Rhetoric

Draft of Rockfish Gap Report

58 executed by the said Rector, and acknowledged for record in the Office of the Clerk of the County court of Albe=marle

Signed and certified by the members present, each in his proper handwriting this 4th day of August 1818.

Th: Jefferson
Cre?d Taylor.
Peter Randolph
Wm. Brockenbrough

Ank. Rutherford
Arch'd Stuart
James Breckinridge
Henry E Watkins

James Madison
Armistead T Mason
J. Holmes

Phil. C. Pendleton
Spencer Roane
John Mc. Taylor
Hy Jackson
Thos Wilson
Phil. Slaughter
Wm. Cabell
Nathl H Claiborne
Wm A. G Dade

William Wirt by Charles Willson Peale

November 15th 1818

Master I write you a few lines to let you know that your house and furniture are all safe as I expect you would be glad to know & I heard that you did not expect to come up this fall I was sorry to hear that you was so unwell you could not come it greive me many time but I hope as you have been so blessed in this that you considered it was god that done it and no other one we all ought to be thankful for what he has done for us, we ought to serve and obey his commandments that you may set to win the prize and after glory run Oh Master I do not my ignorant letter will be much encouragement to you as know I am a poor ignorant creature, this leaves us all well adieu, I am your humble servant

Hannah

Hannah to Thomas Jefferson, 15 November 1818

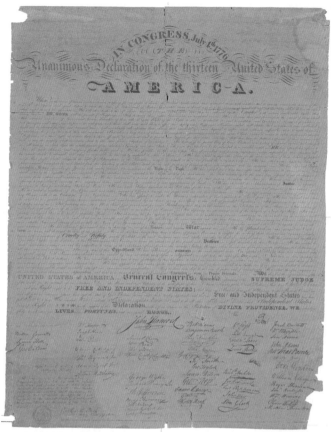

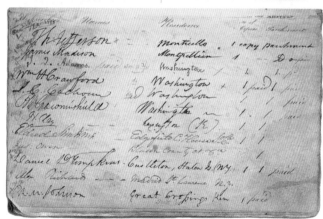

Benjamin O. Tyler's Engraved Declaration of Independence
and Subscription Book

The Declaration of Independence by John Trumbull

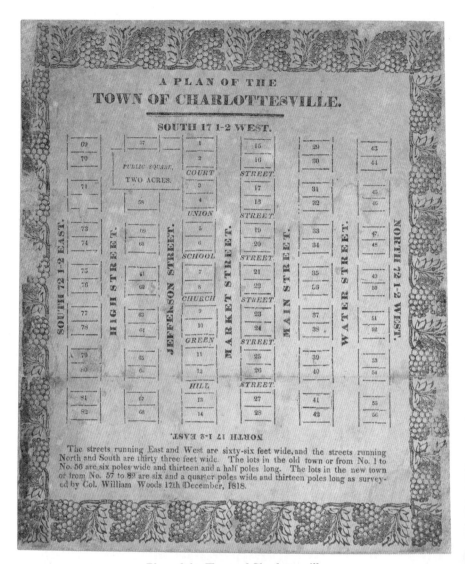

| 69 | 57 | 1 | 15 | 29 | 43 |
| 70 | | 2 | 16 | 30 | 44 |

PUBLIC SQUARE,   COURT STREET.
TWO ACRES.

| 71 | | 3 | 17 | 31 | 45 |
| | 58 | 4 | 18 | 32 | 46 |

UNION STREET.

| 73 | 59 | 5 | 19 | 33 | 47 |
| 74 | 60 | 6 | 20 | 34 | 48 |

SCHOOL STREET.

| 75 | 61 | 7 | 21 | 35 | 49 |
| 76 | 62 | 8 | 22 | 56 | 50 |

CHURCH STREET.

| 77 | 63 | 9 | 23 | 37 | 51 |
| 78 | 64 | 10 | 24 | 38 | 52 |

GREEN STREET.

| 79 | 65 | 11 | 25 | 39 | 53 |
| 80 | 66 | 12 | 26 | 40 | 54 |

HILL STREET.

| 81 | 67 | 13 | 27 | 41 | 55 |
| 82 | 68 | 14 | 28 | 42 | 56 |

SOUTH 72 1-2 EAST.   HIGH STREET.   JEFFERSON STREET.   MARKET STREET.   MAIN STREET.   WATER STREET.   NORTH 72 1-2 WEST.

NORTH 17 1-2 EAST.

The streets running East and West are sixty-six feet wide, and the streets running North and South are thirty three feet wide. The lots in the old town or from No. 1 to No. 56 are six poles wide and thirteen and a half poles long. The lots in the new town or from No. 57 to 82 are six and a quarter poles wide and thirteen poles long as surveyed by Col. William Woods 12th December, 1818.

Plan of the Town of Charlottesville

The Founding of the University of Virginia: The University Bill

THOMAS JEFFERSON'S BILL TO ESTABLISH A UNIVERSITY,
[BETWEEN 19 NOV. AND 14 DEC. 1818]

EDITORIAL NOTE

As the 1818–19 legislative session approached, Jefferson and his allies prepared to submit to the Virginia General Assembly the 4 Aug. 1818 Rockfish Gap Report of the University of Virginia Commissioners, which recommended that Central College be the site of the University of Virginia. On 18 Nov. 1818 Joseph C. Cabell wrote to Jefferson suggesting that the former president compose a bill enacting this recommendation. Jefferson accordingly drafted the following bill after he received that letter on 19 Nov. and before Cabell mentioned the proposed statute in his 14 Dec. 1818 letter to Jefferson. Cabell, at this time a state senator, actively guided the bill through both the House of Delegates and the Senate, supplying Jefferson with frequent updates throughout the process.

The Rockfish Gap Report was presented to the House of Delegates on 8 Dec. 1818. Cabell and Albemarle County delegates Samuel Carr and William F. Gordon succeeded in recruiting Samuel Taylor, a delegate from Chesterfield County, as an ostensibly neutral party to move that the report be referred to a select committee. This was immediately done, with Taylor as committee chair. On 14 Dec. Cabell advised Jefferson that at the second meeting of the select committee, Taylor had presented a text of Jefferson's bill that he had copied in his own hand, presumably to disguise its authorship. Despite attempts by members of the select committee to change the location of the University of Virginia to Lexington or to report the bill with the site of the university left blank, it was returned to the House on 17 Dec. with the proposal to make Central College the University of Virginia still intact.

Once returned to the full House of Delegates, the bill took a little over a month to pass. Legislators from western districts continued fighting to position the university west of the Blue Ridge Mountains. Critics challenged Jefferson's assertion that Charlottesville was the potential location closest to the geographic center of Virginia's white populace. They quarreled with his methods of calculation, his possibly inadvertent inclusion of free blacks in his population count, and his failure to allow adequately for the faster rate of western population growth. Delegates Andrew Alexander and John Bowyer, of Rockbridge County, and Briscoe G. Baldwin, of Augusta County, led efforts to situate the university at Lexington and Staunton, respectively. Nevertheless, the bill passed the House of Delegates by a vote of 143 to 28 on 19 Jan. 1819 with relatively few changes, the most significant being the addition of a provision appropriating $20,000 from the Literary Fund for the education of the poor. The bill moved through the Senate more quickly. Received from the House of Delegates on 20 Jan., it was immediately sent to a committee headed by Cabell, who reported to the Senate two days later that it would offer no amendments. On 25 Jan. the Senate took up the bill, and a final attempt to change the location of the university by Senator Chapman Johnson, a resident of Staunton, was handily defeated. With only one vote in opposition, Jefferson's bill passed in the Senate. When it became law on 25 Jan. 1819 as "An Act for the establishment of an University," Central College officially became the University of Virginia (Cabell to TJ, 18 Nov., 8, 14, 17, 17, 24 Dec. 1818, 7, 18, 21, 25 Jan. 1819; TJ to Cabell, 1, 28 Jan. 1819; William C. Rives to TJ, 20 Jan. 1819; *JHR* [1818–19 sess.]; *JSV* [1818–19 sess.]; Bruce, *University*, 1:226–35).

Thomas Jefferson's Bill to Establish a University

[between 19 Nov. and 14 Dec. 1818]

A Bill for the establishment of an University.[1]

Be it declared by the General assembly of Virginia that the conveyance of the lands and other property appur[t]aining to the Central college in the county of Albemarle which has been executed by the Proctor thereof under authority of the subscribers and founders, to the President and Directors of the literary fund, is hereby accepted, for the uses and on the conditions in the sd deed of conveyance expressed.

And be it enacted that there shall be established on the site provided for the sd College, an University, to be called 'the University of Virginia'; that it shall be under the government of [7.][2] visitors to be appointed forthwith by the Governor with the advice of council, notifying thereof the persons so appointed, and prescribing to them a day for their first meeting at the sd University, with supplementory instructions for procuring a meeting subsequently, in the event of failure at the time first appointed.

The sd Visitors, or so many of them as, being a majority, shall attend, shall appoint a Rector of their own body to preside at their meetings, and a Secretary to record attest[3] and preserve their proceedings, and shall proceed to examine into the state of the property conveyed as aforesd, shall make an inventory of the same, specifying the items whereof it consists, shall notice the buildings and other improvements already made, and those which are in progress, shall take measures for their completion, and for the addition of such others from time to time as may be necessary.

In the sd University shall be taught the Latin, Greek & Hebrew l[an]guages, French, Spanish, Italian, German & Anglo-Saxon, the different branches of Mathematics pure and Physical, Natural philosophy, the principles of Agriculture, Chemistry, mineralogy including

Geology, Botany,[4] Zoology, Anatomy, Medecine, Civil government, Political economy, the Law of Nature and Nations, Municipal law, history, Ideology, general grammar, Ethics, Rhetoric and Belles lettres, which branches of science shall be so distributed, and under so many Professors, not exceeding ten, as the Visitors shall think most[5] proper and expedient.

Each Professor shall be allowed the use of the[6] apartments & accomodations provided for him, and those first employed such standing salary as the visitors shall think proper and sufficient, and their successors such standing salary, not exceeding [1000][7] Dollars, as the Visitors shall think proper and sufficient; with such tuition fees from each student as the visitors shall from time to time establish.

The sd Visitors shall be charged with the erection, preservation and repair of the buildings, the care of the grounds and appurtenances and of the interests of the University generally: they shall have power to appoint a Burser, employ a Proctor and all other necessary agents; to appoint and remove Professors, two thirds of the whole number of Visitors voting for the removal: to prescribe their duties & the course of education, in conformity with the law: to establish rules for the government & discipline of the students, not contrary to the laws of the land; to regulat[e] the tuition fees, and the rent of the dormitories occupied; to prescribe and controul the duties and proceedings of all officers,[8] servants and others, with respect to the buildings, lands, appurtenances & other property and interests of the University; to draw from the literary fund such monies as are by law charged on it for this institution; and, in general, to direct and do all matters and things which, not being inconsistent with the laws of the land, to them shall seem most expedient for promoting the purposes of the sd institution; which several functions they shall be free to exercise in the form of bye-laws, rules, resolutions, orders, instructions, or otherwise as they shall deem proper.

They shall have two stated meetings in the[9] year, to wit, on the first Mondays of April and October, and occasional meetings at such other times as they shall appoint, or on a special call, with such notice as themselves shall prescribe by a general rule; which meetings shall be at the University; a majority of them constituting a Quorum for business; and on the death,[10] resignation of a member, or failure to act for the space of one year, or on his removal out of the Commonwealth, or by the Governor with advice of Council, the Governor with like advice shall appoint a successor.

The sd Rector[11] and Visitors shall be a body corporate, under the style and title of the Rector and Visitors of the University of Virginia, with the right, as such, to use a common seal; they shall have capacity to plead & be impleaded in all courts of justice, and in all cases interesting to the University, which may be the subjects of legal cognisance & jurisdiction; which pleas shall not abate by the determination of their office, but shall stand revived in the name of their successors; and they shall be capable in law, and in trust for the University, of recieving subscriptions and donations real and personal, as well from bodies corporate, or persons associated, as from private individuals.

And the sd Rector and Visitors shall at all times conform to such laws as the legislature may from time to time think proper to enact for their government; and the sd University shall, in all things, and at all times, be subject to the controul of the legislature.[12]

The sd board of Visitors, or some one or more members[13] thereof by nomination of the board shall, once in every year at least visit the sd University,[14] enquire into the proceedings and practices thereat, examine the progress of th[e] students, and give to those who excel in any branch of science there taught such honorary marks and testimonies of approbation as may encorage & excite to industry and emulation.

On every 29th day of February, or, if that be Sunday, then on the next or earliest day thereafter on which a meeting can be effected, the Governor & council shall be in session, and shall appoint Visitors of the sd University, either the same or others, at their discretion, to serve until the 29th day of February next ensuing, duly and timely notifying to them their appointment, & prescribing a day for their first meeting at the University; after which their meetings stated and occasional shall be as herein before provided.

Provided that nothing in this act contained shall suspend the proceedings of the Visitors of the sd Central College of Albemarle; but, for the purpose of expediting the objects of the sd institution, they shall be authorised, under the controul of the Governor & council, to continue the exercise of their functions, and fulfill those of their successors until the first actual meeting of their sd successors.[15]

PoC (ViU: TJP); entirely in TJ's hand; undated, but composed sometime after 19 Nov. 1818 receipt of Joseph C. Cabell to TJ, 18 Nov. 1818, and before composition of Cabell to TJ, 14 Dec. 1818; faint. Dft (Vi: RG 79, Rough Bills); printed text, with handwritten emendations in multiple unidentified hands. MS (Vi: RG 78, Enrolled Bills); in an unidentified hand, signed by Edward Watts as Speaker of the Senate of Virginia and Linn Banks as Speaker of the House of Delegates; at head of text: "An Act for the establishment of an University   Passed January the twenty fifth 1819." Printed in *Acts of Assembly* (1818–19 sess.), 15–8, with each paragraph numbered, and in *Richmond Enquirer*, 28 Jan. 1819.

[1] Rough bill here adds "Read the first and second time, and committed to a Committee of the whole House."

² Brackets in original.

³ Word interlined.

⁴ Omitted comma at right margin is present in all other versions and editorially supplied here.

⁵ Word not in enrolled bill or *Acts of Assembly*.

⁶ Preceding three words interlined.

⁷ Brackets in original.

⁸ Omitted comma at right margin is present in all other versions and editorially supplied here.

⁹ Word canceled in rough bill, with "every" interlined. Enrolled bill and *Acts of Assembly*: "every."

¹⁰ Omitted comma at right margin is present in all other versions and editorially supplied here.

¹¹ *Richmond Enquirer*: "proctor."

¹² Keyed to this point in text, rough bill here adds in pen: "<*Be it therefore enacted*> And the Said Rector and visitors of the University of Virginia, Shall be, and they are hereby required to make report annually, to the President and Directors of the literary-fund, (to be laid before the legislature at their next succeeding Session) embracing a full account of the disbursements, the funds on hand, and a general Statement of the Condition of the said University." Additions incorporated into enrolled bill and *Acts of Assembly*.

¹³ Preceding five words canceled in rough bill, with "<*three*> a majority" interlined. Enrolled bill and *Acts of Assembly*: "a majority."

¹⁴ Omitted comma at right margin is present in most other versions (*Acts of Assembly* has semicolon) and editorially supplied here.

¹⁵ Keyed to this point in text, rough bill here adds in pen: "And be it further enacted, That the additional sum of <*fifteen*> twenty thousand dollars, shall be and the same is hereby appropriated to the education of the poor, out of the revenue of the Literary fund, in aid of the sum heretofore appropriated to that object; to be paid in the same manner, and upon the same conditions in all respects, as is prescribed by the fourth section of the act, entitled, 'An act appropriating part of the revenue of the Literary fund, and for other purposes' passed the 21ˢᵗ day of February 1818." The printed portion of the rough bill ends with "This act shall commence and be in force from and after the passing thereof." Additions incorporated into enrolled bill and *Acts of Assembly*.

To Linn Banks and Edward Watts

Sɪʀ   Monticello Nov. 20. 1818.

The Commissioners appointed under the act of the last General assembly for appropriating a part of the revenue of the literary fund, and for other purposes, met according to law, at the Rockfish gap, on the 1ˢᵗ day of August last, and having continued their session by adjournments until the 4ᵗʰ day of that month, agreed to a Report, which being signed in Duplicates, individually and unanimously, by all the members who attended, they instructed me to transmit to the Speakers of¹ both houses of legislature.   in obedience to that instruction, I now inclose one of the sd original reports, with a copy of their journal, and of the documents exhibited and left in their possession.

Some of the outstanding subscription papers therein mentioned, have been returned with additional subscriptions to the amount of 2650. Dollars and an additional purchase has been made of 48¾ acres of land adjoining the site of the Central College, necessary to the probable extent of buildings should that be adopted, as proposed by the Report, for the site of the University; which circumstances having taken place since the date of the Report, I have deemed it a duty to mention as supplementory to it.

I have the honor to be with sentiments of the highest respect and consideration, Sir

Your most obedient and most humble servant

TH: JEFFERSON

RC (Vi: RG 79, House of Delegates, Speaker, Executive Communications); at foot of text: "The honorable The Speaker of the House of Delegates of Virginia." PoC (CSmH: JF-BA); addressed at foot of text and endorsed by TJ as a letter to the speakers of the Virginia Senate and House of Delegates. Printed in *University of Virginia Commissioners' Report*; *JHD* (1818–19 sess.), 9 (8 Dec. 1818); and *Richmond Enquirer*, 10 Dec. 1818, with all printed versions addressed only to the Speaker of the House of Delegates. Enclosures: (1) Proceedings of Rockfish Gap Meeting of the University of Virginia Commissioners, 1–4 Aug. 1818, printed above at 4 Aug. 1818. (2) Rockfish Gap Report of the University of Virginia Commissioners, 4 Aug. 1818. (3) Conveyance of Central College Properties to the President and Directors of the Literary Fund, 27 July 1818. Letter to Watts enclosed in TJ to Joseph C. Cabell, 20 Nov. 1818.

Linn Banks (1784–1842), attorney and public official, was born in a part of Culpeper County that became Madison County in 1792. He studied at the College of William and Mary through 1806, then read law, and was admitted to the bar in Madison County two years later. Banks served as a captain in the Virginia militia during the War of 1812 and subsequently attained the rank of colonel. He was elected as a Republican to the House of Delegates in 1812 and represented Madison County in that body for the next twenty-six years, presiding as Speaker, 1817–38. In the latter year Banks won a seat in the United States House of Representatives by special election and served until his defeat in a reelection bid in 1841. Throughout his career he continued to practice law. In 1840 Banks owned forty-seven slaves. He died in Madison County (*DVB*; E. Griffith Dodson, *Speakers and Clerks of the Virginia House of Delegates, 1776–1955* [1956], 7, 56–7, 141; *William and Mary Provisional List*, 6; Leonard, *General Assembly*; DNA: RG 29, CS, Madison Co., 1840; *Richmond Whig and Public Advertiser*, 18 Jan. 1842; Madison Co. Will Book, 7:162–3, 485).

Edward Watts (1779–1859), attorney and public official, was born in Prince Edward County, graduated from the College of New Jersey (later Princeton University) in 1801, and then read law in Campbell County with Christopher Clark. He took up the practice of law in Campbell County, which he represented in the Virginia House of Delegates, 1808–09. Watts sat in the Senate of Virginia, 1809–21, acting as Speaker from late in 1816 until he left that body. He moved to Botetourt County by 1820, and when the portion in which he resided split off to become Roanoke County in 1838, he served as the commonwealth's attorney for the new county's circuit court. From 1830 to 1835 Watts was a trustee of Washington College (later Washington and Lee University). In 1834 the House of Delegates elected him brigadier general of the 13th brigade of the Virginia militia in place of his recently deceased father-in-law, James Breckinridge. That same year Watts ran unsuccessfully for governor of Virginia. He retired from public life about 1840 and devoted himself to agriculture. Watts owned 74 slaves in 1820 and 134 two decades later. He died at his home in Roanoke County (S. Bassett French Biographical Sketches [Vi: Personal Papers Collection]; John Frederick Dorman, *The Prestons of Smithfield and Greenfield in Virginia: Descendants of John and Elizabeth (Patton) Preston Through Five Gen-*

erations [1982], 123–4; *Princeton Cata-logue*, 113; Leonard, *General Assembly*; *JSV* [1816–17 sess.], 12–3 [5 Dec. 1816]; DNA: RG 29, CS, Botetourt Co., 1820, 1830, Roanoke Co., 1840, 1850; George S. Jack and Edward B. Jacobs, *History of Roanoke County*; *History of Roanoke City* . . . [1912], 8; *Catalogue of the Officers and Alumni of Washington and Lee University, Lexington, Virginia, 1749–1888* [1888], 38; *JHD* [1833–34 sess.], 160 [8

Feb. 1834]; *Richmond Whig and Public Advertiser*, 12 Aug. 1859; gravestone inscription in Fair View Cemetery, Roanoke; Roanoke Co. Will Book, 1:135–9).

For the ADDITIONAL PURCHASE of 48¾ acres of land for Central College, see Agreement by John M. Perry to Sell Lands to Central College, 7 Nov. 1818.

[1] Preceding three words not in *Richmond Enquirer.*

To Joseph C. Cabell

DEAR SIR   Monticello Nov. 20. 18.

I very much lament the cause which has deprived us of the pleasure of seeing mrs Cabell and yourself at Monticello on your way to Richmond. I now commit to your care a letter to be delivered to the Speaker of the Senate, which contains the Report of the Commissioners who met at Rockfish gap. having been written in great haste, and by several hands, dividing the work in order to expedite their departure, it is very imperfectly legible: and as it is important that it should be printed correctly, I inclose you the original draught also, made literally conformable to the authenticated one, and which I would wish you to put into the hands of the printer. being much more legible, he will be less liable to commit mistakes. it will serve for your own information in the mean time, which the Commissioners thought would be proper, while they deemed it disrespectful to the legislature, and otherwise inexpedient that it's contents should be communicated but to particular persons before delivery. it was their opinion that it should be delivered to each Speaker, in the chair, on the second morning of the session.

Col⁰ Coles will explain to you what has past on the subject of the proposed voyage, which I consider as requiring indispensably a special agent, & in which Genˡ Cocke concurred, without a doubt of the unanimous approbation of our Colleagues. with sincere wishes for the reestablishment of your health I salute you affectionately

TH: JEFFERSON

RC (ViU: TJP); at foot of text: "Joseph C. Cabell esq."; endorsed by Cabell. PoC (DLC); on verso of reused address cover of one of the two letters from Patrick Gibson to TJ of 27 July 1818; endorsed by TJ. Enclosures: TJ to Linn Banks and Edward Watts, 20 Nov. 1818 (the RC to

Watts), and enclosures, with a second copy of the 4 Aug. 1818 Rockfish Gap Report of the University of Virginia Commissioners.

The PRINTER of the *University of Virginia Commissioners' Report* was Thomas Ritchie.

From Joseph Milligan

DEAR SIR   Georgetown November 20th 1818

I sent two complete copies of political Economy to you by post and I will on the 21st send you ten copies in boards to the care William F Gray in Fredericksburg

I will anounce the work in the Intelligencer on the first day of December, I propose to send a young man to Norfolk Petersburg & Richmond & perhaps to Lynchburg to promote the circulation and sale of work If you could give me a letter to one of your friends in each of those places it might bring the business forward more speedily I do not wish to impose a task on you but if I do not now make[1] a vigerous effort to push the work it will fall stillborn from the press

I Sent you a little book on gardening thr° post office which I trust reached you

respectfully yours   JOSEPH MILLIGAN

RC (DLC); endorsed by TJ as received 28 Nov. 1818 and so recorded in SJL.

The Washington *Daily National* IN-TELLIGENCER of 31 Dec. 1818 announced the publication of Destutt de Tracy, *Treatise on Political Economy*, and printed TJ to Milligan, [ca. 25 Oct. 1818]. The YOUNG MAN was James Thomas. For the LITTLE BOOK ON GARDENING, see Milligan to TJ, 30 Oct. 1818, and note.

[1] Manuscript: "mak."

From Daniel Pettibone

[Mo]ST EXCELLENT SIR—   [ca. 20 Nov. 1818]

I take the liberty to call to your Recollection to the small hand axe that I presented to your excellency in the year 1807—as a specimen of a new & useful improvement I had made on edge-tools—sir—you was pleesd to observ that it was your opinion that the improvement I had made was worth (to the public) all the Gu-gauze Patents that had been granted since the formation of the Patent Law as it would effect almost every individual more or less—

P.S. I have made very great improvements in warming public building—and May be of Some use to the Colledge that is proposed to be erected near to your place—I am sir your Most obedt Servnt

DANIEL PETTIBONE

RC (ViW: TC-JP); undated; salutation torn; with enclosed printed circular on same sheet between letter and postscript; addressed: "His Excellency Thomas jefferson Esqr Monticillo Verginia"; endorsed by TJ as a letter of 20 Nov. 1818 received 6 Dec. 1818 and so recorded in SJL, with endorsement and SJL entry applying to both cover letter and enclosure.

Daniel Pettibone (1770–1820), smith and inventor, was baptized in Bloomfield, Connecticut. He received patents for a variety of inventions, including improvements in welding cast steel to iron, boring gun barrels, warming rooms, and manufacturing tools, and he published several pamphlets about his inventions. Pettibone lived in Connecticut, Washington, D.C., and Boston before settling in about 1810 in Philadelphia, where he died (*Connecticut Church Records, State Library Index, Bloomfield Congregational Church, 1738–1924* [1958], 167; I. Fayette Pettibone, *Genealogy of the Pettibone Family* [1885], 24; *List of Patents*; *Windham* [Conn.] *Herald*, 29 Mar. 1804; Georgetown *Washington Federalist*, 5 Mar. 1806; Pettibone to TJ, 12 Jan. 1808 [ViW: TC-JP]; Latrobe, *Papers*, 2:736–7, 801; DNA: RG 29, CS, Pa., Philadel-

phia, 1810; Wilmington *American Watchman and Delaware Republican*, 21 Dec. 1811; *Census Directory For 1811* [Philadelphia, 1811], 233; Washington *Daily National Intelligencer*, 18 June 1813; Historical Society of Pennsylvania, *Memoirs* 8 [1867]: 143, 270–1; J. Thomas Scharf and Thompson Westcott, *History of Philadelphia. 1609–1884* [1884], 3:2261, 2271; *The Philadelphia Directory and Register, For 1820* [Philadelphia, 1820]; *New-York Columbian*, 8 Feb. 1820).

GU-GUAZE: presumably a variant of "gew-gaw." Pettibone received patents for his rarefying air stove in 1808 and 1812. His heating system was adopted for WARMING multiple public buildings in Philadelphia and installed about 1820 in the United States Capitol (*List of Patents*, 68, 113; Scharf and Westcott, *History of Philadelphia*, 3:2271; Latrobe, *Papers*, 2:737, 801; *JHR*, 41:315 [28 Jan. 1846]).

E N C L O S U R E

Circular Letter from Daniel Pettibone

HONOURED SIR,   Philadelphia, Nov. 20, 1818.
I HAVE taken the liberty of enclosing you the within pamphlet, describing the rise and progress of a very important discovery; viz. the Welding of Cast Steel to Iron, or to other Steel, for edge tools, &c.

My object sir, is the renewal of a Patent, granted in March, 1806, and hope that you will have time to look over the first part of the pamphlet,[1] trusting you will place it with such of your papers as you think worthy to preserve as matter of public utility.

I am Sir, your most obedient servant,   DANIEL PETTIBONE.

RC (ViW: TC-JP); printed text; with covering letter written above and below it on same sheet. Enclosure: Pettibone, *The Petition of Daniel Pettibone, to the Senate and House of Representatives of the United States, for the renewal of his patent for Welding Cast Steel to Iron, in such a manner As to be applied to edge tools or other purposes where steel is required* (Philadelphia, 1818; Poor, *Jefferson's Library*, 6

[no. 223]; TJ's copy in DLC: Rare Book and Special Collections).

Pettibone received a PATENT on 21 Aug. 1819 for his method of "Welding cast steel to iron, &c." (*List of Patents*, 206).

[1] The phrase "before the subject comes before you" is here canceled in ink.

Notes on Roman Cement

[ca. 21 Nov. 1818]

the Roman cement is a native production of the Isle of Thanet. it is an earth impregnated with iron ore, the vitriolic acid & Manganese. and it is said may be found wherever there is an iron ore.

MS (DLC: TJ Papers, 214:38127); entirely in TJ's hand; undated; on address leaf of William J. Coffee to TJ, 7 Nov. 1818, with date conjectured from that letter's date of receipt.

To Mathew Carey

SIR   Monticello Nov. 22. 18.

The reverend mr Weems called on me a few days ago on the subject of your letter of Oct. 6. and recieved the same answer which I had given to yourself in mine of the 25th   in the course of our conversation however I mentioned to him that there was indeed a history of England which, could we get it reprinted, I would risk the presumption of inviting the attention of readers to it, meaning the history published by Baxter, one of the whigs prosecuted at the same time with Horne Tooke, and discharged on the verdict rendered in favor of Tooke. it's particular character requires explanation.

We all know the high estimation in which Hume's history of England is held in that and this country. the charms of it's stile and selection of it's matter, had it but candor and freedom from political bias, would make it the most perfect sample of fine history which has ever flowed from the pen of man; not meaning to except even the most approved models of antiquity. it was a great misfortune for the world that he wrote this history backwards. he began with that of the Stuarts, and at that time probably meant to give no other. being his first exhibition in that line, it was to establish his character, and he bestowed on it all the powers & polish of his acute mind & fine taste. like other writers he was disposed to magnify the merits of his heroes, and that disposition was whetted perhaps by the pride of country, and a desire to raise it into that degree of respect which it had well merited by it's eminence in science, but had not as yet obtained from the sister[1] kingdom. from these, or other, motives he gave to his history the aspect of an apology, or rather a justification of his countrymen the Stuarts. their good deeds were displayed, their bad ones disguised or explained away, or altogether suppressed where they admitted no palliation, and a constant vein of fine ridicule was employed to disparage the patriots who opposed their usurpations, and vindicated the freedom and rights of their country. the success of this work induced him to go back to the history of the Tudors, and having now taken his side as the apologist of arbitrary power in England, the new work was to be made a support for the old. accordingly all the arbitrary acts of the Tudor sovereigns were industriously selected and displayed, as regular exercises of constitutional authority, and the resistance to them assumes the hue of factious opposition. he then went back the last step, and undertook to fill up the chasm from the Roman invasion to the accession of the Tudors, making this, as the second work, still a justification of the first; and, of the whole, a continued advocation of the heresy that, by the English constitution, the powers of the monarch were every thing, and the rights of the people nothing: a heresy into which he probably would not have fallen had he begun his history at the beginning. yet so fascinating is every part of his work, and really so valuable it's candid parts, that it will be read, and is read by every student, on his entrance into English history: and the young reader who can lay down Hume, under any impression favorable to English liberty, must have a mind of extraordinary vigor and self possession.   used now as the elementary & standard book of English history, the whig spirit of that country has been compleatly sapped by it, has nearly disappeared, and toryism become the general creed of the nation. what the patriots of the last age dreaded & deprecated from a standing army, and what could not have been atchieved for the crown by any standing army, but with torrents of blood, one man, by the magic of his pen, has effected covertly, insensibly, peaceably; and has made voluntary converts of the best men of the present age to the parricide opinions of the worst of the last. whether oppressive taxation is not now reviving the feelings of liberty which Hume had lulled to rest, is a question which we cannot at this distance decide.

As the knolege of our own history must be based on that of England, so here, as there, Hume furnishes that basis: and here, as there, the young reader will retain a bias unfavorable to, what that has prepared him to consider as, the factious freedom of the people: and when, from a student, he becomes a statesman, he will become also the tory of our constitution, disposed to monarchise the government, by strengthening the Executive, and weakening the popular branch, and by drawing the municipal administration of the states into the vortex of the general authority.   as it is quite impracticable to put down such a book as this, we can only sheathe it's poison by some antidote. this is to be attempted in two ways. reprint Hume with the text entire, and in collateral columns, or in Notes, place the Antidotes of it's disguises, it's misrepresentations, it's concealments, it's sophisms, and ironies, by confronting with them authentic truths from Fox, Ludlow, McCaulay, Rapin and other honest writers. this would make a work of great volume, and would require for it's execution profound judgment and learning in English history. the 2^d method is that which Baxter has adopted. he gives you the text of Hume, purely and verbally, till he comes to some misrepresentation or omission, some sophism or sarcasm, meant to pervert the truth; he then alters the text silently, makes it what truth and candor say it should be, and resumes the original text again, as soon as it becomes innocent, without having warned you of your rescue from misguidance. and these corrections are so cautiously introduced that you are rarely sensible of the momentary change of your guide. you go on reading true history as if Hume himself had given it. it is unfortunate, I think, that Baxter has also abridged the work; not by alterations of text but by omitting wholly such transactions and incidents as he supposed had become less interesting to ordinary readers than they were in Hume's day. this brings indeed the work within more moderate compass, accomodated perhaps to the time and taste of the greater bulk of readers; yet for those who aim at a thoro' knolege of that history, it would have been more desirable to have the entire work corrected in the same way. but we must now take it as it is; and, by reprinting it, place in the hands of our students an elementary history which may strengthen instead of weakening their affections to the republican principles of their own country and it's constitution. I say we should reprint it; because so deeply rooted is Humism in England, that I believe this corrective has never gone to a 2^d edition. it still remains, as at first in the form of a ponderous 4to of close print, which will probably make 3. or 4. vols 8vo

After bringing the history down to where Hume leaves it, Baxter has continued it thro the intermediate time to the early part of the French revolution. but as he had no remarkable talent for good writing, the value of this part of his work is merely as a Chronicle.

On the whole, my opinion is that in reprinting this work, you will deserve well of our country; and, if you think that my presumption in giving an opinion as to a book worth the attention of our historical students will recieve their pardon from the motives on which it is risked, you are free to use this letter in justification of the opinions it professes; and with every wish for the publication of the work, and it's salutary effect on the minds of our youth, I salute you with sentiments of great esteem & respect.   Th: Jefferson

RC (OONL: Joseph Nancrède Papers); endorsed by Carey as received 27 Nov. PoC (DLC); at foot of first page: "Mr Matthew Carey." Tr (PPL); misdated 22 Nov. 1824; in French.

Carey's LETTER OF OCT. 6 was actually that of Carey & Son to TJ dated 21 Sept. 1818. TJ's own ANSWER was dated 6 Oct. 1818, not THE 25TH. The work by

John BAXTER was *A New and Impartial History of England, From the most Early Period of Genuine Historical Evidence to the Present Important and Alarming Crisis* (London, [1796–1801]; Sowerby, no. 405). PRIDE OF COUNTRY refers to David Hume's Scottish heritage.

[1] TJ here canceled "country."

To Lewis D. Belair

SIR   Monticello Nov. 23. 18.

I have just recieved from Mr Redory the information asked as to the rest of the books named in my letters of Oct. 27. & 31. and I request you to lay by for me the Pliny Fr. & Lat. the Dictionnaire Bibliographe, and Denis d'Halicarnasse. I presume I may expect in a very few days answers to the enquiries of my letter of Nov. 16. respecting Epictetus, le Gendre, Carnot & Euler, which will enable me to decide which of them I take, and will put me in possession of information as to the amount of the whole I shall have decided for, when I will immediately remit you the amount and direct the conveyance of the books. but as I should be glad to recieve the Dictionnaire Bibliographique by a quicker conveyance, I would be glad you would send a volume at a time by mail, and each a week apart, a precaution I wish to take that I may not overburthen any one of our mails. direct them to me at Monticello [. . .] [Char]lottes[ville] and accept the assurance of my respect.   TH: JEFFERSON

PoC (MHi); on verso of reused address cover of RC of Peter Poinsot to TJ, 18 May 1818; torn at seal, with two words rewritten by TJ; at foot of text: "M. Belair"; endorsed by TJ.

To Lafayette

Monticello Nov. 23. 18.

The hand of age, my dear friend, has been pressing heavily on me for the few last years, and has rendered me unequal to the punctualities of correspondence. my health too is lately very much broken down by an illness of three months from which I am but now on the recovery. if therefore I am slack in acknoleging the reciept of your much valued letters, your goodness will ascribe it to it's true causes, declining age & health.

I learn with great pleasure that your country will have, in the end a good degree of freedom, by a proper attemperament of limited monarchy with representative ingredients; indeed that you have already such a government; for as far as I understand your present constitution, it has more of popular independance and integrity in it than the boasted one of England: and what it still wants time and the advance of light will bring, probably as fast as the people can be prepared for it. this I hope will be waited for without risking new convulsions.

Here all is well. our government is now so firmly put on it's republican tack, that it will not be easily monarchised by forms. you have made a mighty noise in Europe about our taking possession of some posts in Florida. the President's message, delivered a few days ago will set you right on that subject; and shew that no wrong was contemplated for a single moment. and, what shews an honorable & comfortable trait in our nation, was the universal uproar of our own people in the first moment of the apparent aggression, and until they saw that their government had no such thing in view. I was delighted with this proof of moral principle in our citizens as to the conduct of their foreign relations, and considered it as a pledge that they would never, as a nation, approve of any measure swerving from justice.

Mr Poirey has plausible ground for supposing I have been inattentive to the claim for compensation for his services during the revolution which he committed to my care. but I am without blame on this score. just as I recieved his papers the then Secretary at war retired from office. I knew it would be worse than useless, during the vacancy to commit to a chef de bureau a business which he would not have weight nor confidence enough to act in with effect. the vacancy continued unfilled nearly a twelvemonth. as soon as a Secretary was appointed, I placed the case and papers under his consideration. the inclosed letter from him will shew it's present state and prospects: and I now write to him to secure his early attention to it during the present session. being now entirely unequal to the labors of the writing table, I must request of M. Poirey to consider my intermediate silence as saying that nothing is yet done, on the assurance that the moment that any thing definitive takes place I will give him notice of it.   I am rendered very happy by being able at length to send M. Tracy a copy of the translation of his book on political economy; the publication of which is at length accomplished. the delay has been scandalous, and to me most vexatious. but I am fully repaid by the good the publication will render to our country. God bless you and preserve you and yours in health and happiness as long as you shall desire it yourselves. Тн: Jefferson

RC (Mrs. Laird U. Park, Philadelphia, 1944; photocopy in ViU: TJP); addressed: "Monsr de la Fayette à Paris." PoC (DLC); on reused and undated note addressed to TJ in an unidentified hand and listing cash amounts totaling $100, possibly related to James Leitch's 28 July 1818 loan of this amount to TJ; endorsed by TJ. Most likely enclosed in TJ to Albert Gallatin, 24 Nov. 1818, and TJ to Daniel Brent, 27 Nov. 1818, but see also note to Brent to TJ, 10 Jan. 1819.

ATTEMPERAMENT: "mixture in due proportions" (*OED*). In his annual MESSAGE to Congress of 16 Nov. 1818, President James Monroe justified Andrew Jackson's 1818 seizure of Pensacola and Saint Marks on the ground that the inability of the Spanish to maintain law and order in West Florida threatened the United States. He added that both would be returned to Spain, the former unconditionally and the latter when a force competent to defend it arrived (*Annals*, 15th Cong., 2d sess., 11–8, esp. 12–5).

Secretary of War William H. Crawford RETIRED FROM OFFICE in October 1816 (*ANB*). CHEF DE BUREAU: "chief clerk." The INCLOSED LETTER was probably Secretary of War John C. Calhoun to TJ, 25 July 1818 (see note to TJ to Calhoun, 27 Nov. 1818).

From James Monroe

Dear Sir   washington nov^r 23. 1818

I send you a copy of the documents relating to negotiations with Spain, from a very distant day, to the end of the last Session, which will be interesting to you, tho' not new, having had the direction of them, in the stage, which formd the outline of what has since followd.

Our attitude with the allied powers, in regard to S° Am:, is as favorable, as it well can be, mr Rush & mr Gallatin having had conferences, the former with Ld C., & the latter with the Duke of R., & the Russian minister at Paris, in which they were inform'd by those ministers, that their gov^{ts} could not well move in that aff^r without the U States, by which, it was meant, as is inferr'd, against the U States. Had we made a bolder, or more precipitate movment, it might have produc'd a corresponding one on their part, very different from that, which it is expected, they will adopt & pursue. At present, our weight, is thrown into the scale of the Colonies, in a way, most likely, to produce the desird effect with the allies in favor of the colonies, without[1] hasard of loss to ourselves.

I heard, with great pleasure, by mr Burwell, that your health had improv'd, since I left you. that it may continue to improve, is the sincere wish, of your friend & servant   James Monroe

RC (DLC); endorsed by TJ as received 27 Nov. 1818 and so recorded in SJL. RC

(MHi); address cover only; with PoC of TJ to Smith & Riddle, 6 May 1819, on verso; addressed: "Thomas Jefferson Monticello Virg^a^"; franked; postmarked Washington, 23 Nov. Enclosure: *Message from the President of the United States, transmitting the Correspondence between the Department of State, and the Spanish Minister, residing here, Showing the Present State of the Relations between the Two Governments* (Washington, 1818; possibly Poor, *Jefferson's Library*, 11 [no. 662]).

L^D^ C. and THE DUKE OF R. were Robert Stewart, Viscount Castlereagh, the British foreign minister, and Armand Emmanuel du Plessis, duc de Richelieu, the French prime minister. The RUSSIAN MINISTER AT PARIS was Carlo Andrea Pozzo di Borgo.

On this date Monroe sent the enclosure and a similar letter to James Madison (Madison, *Papers, Retirement Ser.*, 1:382–3).

[1] Reworked from "with."

From Franklin G. Smith

To THE HON.
THOS. JEFFERSON ESQUIRE.   Powelton. Ga. 23. Nov. 1818.

A long life devoted to the advancement of his country's welfare induces his countrymen to beleive that Mr. Jefferson is not indifferent to any thing connected with it. It is in this confidence that a young man of 20 years takes the liberty of laying before Him a design for the improvement of the Printing Press. If to Mr. Jefferson the plan appears useless he will conclude so by His silence; but if otherwise may he be permitted to beg an expression of that opinion?

Most Respectfully.   F. G. SMITH

RC (MiU-C: Thomas Jefferson Collection); on a sheet folded to form four pages, with enclosed drawing on p. 1, letter on p. 2, text of enclosure on p. 3, and address on p. 4; addressed: "His Excellency Mr. Jefferson. Monticello. Virginia"; stamped; postmarked Powelton, 23 Nov.; endorsed by TJ as a letter from "Smith F. G. B." received 6 Dec. 1818 and so recorded in SJL.

Franklin Gillette Smith (1797–1866), clergyman and educator, was born in Benson, Rutland County, Vermont. He graduated from Middlebury College in 1817 and studied at Princeton Theological Seminary, 1819–20. Smith taught for a time in Georgia and in Prince Edward County before settling in Lynchburg, where he provided instruction, was ordained as an Episcopal minister in 1823, served as rector of Saint Paul's Episcopal Church beginning about 1824, and opened a girls' school in 1829 with the eventual assistance of his wife. In 1837 they moved to Columbia, Tennessee, where Smith published a family magazine called the *Guardian* and headed the Columbia Female Institute, 1838–52. In the latter year he founded his own girls' school there, the Columbian Athenæum. During the Civil War Smith served in the Confederate home guard. He continued as the Athenæum's principal until his death (William A. Smith, *Rev. Franklin Gillette Smith, Founder of the Columbia Athenæum* [1897]; Thomas Scott Pearson, *Catalogue of the Graduates of Middlebury College* [1853], 49; Edgar J. Wiley, comp., *Catalogue of the Officers and Students of Middlebury College* [1917], 45; *Semi-Centennial Catalogue of the Theological Seminary, Princeton, New Jersey* [1862], 13; DNA: RG 29, CS, Lynchburg, 1830, Tenn., Maury Co., 1840–60; gravestone inscription in Rose Hill Cemetery, Columbia, Tenn.).

Franklin G. Smith's Design for Improvement of the Printing Press

[ca. 23 Nov. 1818]

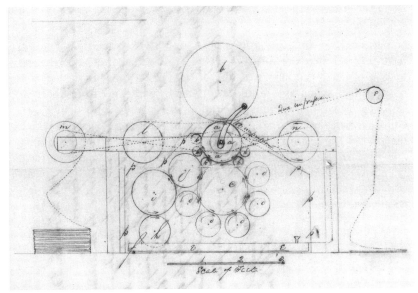

It is taken for granted that paper of a proper width can be manufactured to any required length in a continuous sheet; as it is made in Delaware—perhaps in other parts of the U. States.

References to the figure.

a—is a round body 3 feet long, 1 foot in diameter to the surface of which the types are confined by means of a pressure at each end of the columns—they are not pressed sideways.

b.—is an other roller which produces the impression.

c. a roller that spreads the ink.

d.d. etc. rollers pressing on c. to lay the ink properly.

e. is the part containing the ink—stationary at the end f. and rises at the other end by turning g.

h. is a roller having 30 or 40 thin circular metalick plates projecting from its whole length which dip in the ink in[1] e. and lay it on i. which communicates to j. whence it passes to c. & thence to the types.

k.k. etc. are rollers impinging on the types.—The paper is rolled on l. while in the station m.—At the first impression it is rolled on n.; but in the second passes over o.—All the rollers used in laying on the ink are enclosed by p.p. etc.

Types must be so cast that in setting them up they may represent a circle.
The press is put in motion by any convenient power.

MS (MiU-C: Thomas Jefferson Collection); entirely in Smith's hand; undated; on same sheet as covering letter.

[1] Manuscript: "in in."

To John Stevens

SIR   Monticello Nov. 23. 18.

Age, and it's consequent infirmities of body & relaxation of mind, have obliged me to retire from all general correspondence. I am no longer equal to the labors of the writing table. there is moreover a natural term when age should know itself, withdraw from observation, and leave to the new generation the management of it's own concerns. with my best wishes in favor of every improvement which may better the condition of mankind, at my period of life tranquility and rest from cares are the summum bonum. trusting therefore to your kind consideration for my excuse, I return you the papers inclosed to me, unread, and unopened with the assurance of my high respect and esteem.

TH: JEFFERSON

RC (NjHi: Stevens Family Papers); faint, with illegible text supplied from PoC; at foot of text: "Mr Stevens"; endorsed by Stevens. PoC (MoSHi: TJC-BC); on verso of reused address cover to TJ; endorsed by TJ. Enclosure: enclosures to Stevens to TJ, 7 Nov. 1818.

From Cérès de Montcarel

MONSIEUR,   Richmond 24 9bre 1818

Retirée depuis quelques mois a la Campagne pour raison de Santé Je n'ai appris que fort tard qu'il S'élevoit, Sous votre protection, une maison d'éducation près Charlotteville; Nous ignorons S'il y a quelqu'un de nommé pour être à la tête de L'instruction de cette maison C'est pourquoi, malgré que nous n'ayons pas L'honneur d'être connus de Vous Monsieur, nous nous empressons mon mari et moi de vous offrir nos Services, vous priant d'avoir la bonté de nous faire Savoir le plus promptement possible Si nous pouvons nous flatter de L'esperance de réussir.

Nous croyons pouvoir vous assurer Sans être taxés de trop d'amour propre, que la place que nous demandons n'est pas au dessus de nos moyens; nous avons tenus ici, pendant 2 ans une Maison d'éducation que le mauvais état de ma Santé, Seul, nous a obligé de quitter. la bienveillance que nous ont Conservé les personnes les plus distinguées de cette ville, est une preuve que nous avons mis tous nos Soins a remplir leurs intentions Sur leurs enfans.

Nous n'oserions pas à la vérité nous charger d'enseigner la langue Anglaise, nous Sentons trop bien qu'une prononciation parfaite est une chose absolument nécessaire, Nos conditions Seroient donc, de maintenir un ordre exact dans la maison, d'enseigner par nous même, la langue françoise, l'histoire, la géographie, l'écriture et le dessin, les talens de mon mari dans cette partie Sont assez Connus a Richmond ayant fait des portraits chez M^{rss} Wickham, Dr Adams et quelqulautres personnes de cette ville.

Nous prenons la liberté de vous adresser une des lettres de recommandation que nous a donné Mr Lee lors de notre départ de france, il était alors Consul a Bordeaux. Nous ne voulons pas importuner nos amis pour en obtenir d'autres amoins que nous n'ayons espoir de Succès et que Vous n'en desiriez; nous Sommes persuadés d'avance que M^{rss} Wickham, Adams, Chevalier, Girardin, Wm Mayo et quelqulautres avec qui nous Sommes liés nous en donneront de Satisfaisantes.

Ce que nous nous permettrions de demander mon mari et moi, pour La Surveillance de L'école, L'enseignement de L'écriture, du dessin, du françois de L'histoire et de La géographie, Seroit d'être Logés, chauffés, éclairés, d'avoir mille dollars de fixe et un maitre payé par la maison pour enseigner aux jeunes personnes a lire et la grammaire Anglaise; mon mari demanderoit aussi la permission de donner des Leçons au dehors et de faire des portraits dans Ses momens de loisir.

Veuillez Croire, Monsieur, que nous mettrons tous nos Soins a remplir avec zèle la place de Confiance que nous demandons et a mériter l'approbation de L'homme illustre dont nous Sollicitons aujourd'huy La protection.

Recevez Monsieur L'assurance de notre respect et de notre parfait dévouement   CÉRÈS DE MONTCAREL

Je joins ici, un de nos prospectus pour vous montrer que notre école a été ouverte Sous les auspices de personnes respectables et par qui nous Serons[1] encore recommandés Si la chose est nécessaire.

Notre adresse est a Mr Alex de Montcarel a Richmond

EDITORS' TRANSLATION

SIR,   Richmond 24 November 1818
Having withdrawn to the country for a few months due to my health, I learned only quite lately that an educational establishment is being erected in Charlottesville under your protection. We do not know if anyone has been

named as its head of instruction. This is why, although we do not have the honor of being known by you, Sir, my husband and I hasten to offer you our services, asking you to be so kind as to let us know as soon as possible whether we can flatter ourselves with the hope of success.

We believe we can assure you, without being charged with too much pride, that the position we are requesting is not above our abilities. We have kept here, for 2 years, an educational establishment that only the poor state of my health forced us to abandon. The benevolence that the most distinguished people in this city have maintained toward us proves that we have taken every pain to fulfill their intentions with regard to their children.

To be sure, because we feel very strongly that perfect pronunciation is absolutely necessary, we would not dare take charge of teaching the English language. Therefore, we would be responsible for maintaining strict order in the house and teaching French, history, geography, penmanship, and drawing. My husband's talents in this last field are known rather well in Richmond, as he has done portraits at the homes of Mr. Wickham, Dr. Adams, and some other people here.

We take the liberty of sending you one of the letters of recommendation Mr. Lee gave us when we left France. He was then consul at Bordeaux. We do not wish to trouble our friends for additional letters of recommendation unless you want them and we have a chance of success. We are already quite certain that Messrs. Wickham, Adams, Chevalier, Girardin, William Mayo, and other people with whom we are on good terms will give us satisfactory ones.

For supervising the school and teaching penmanship, drawing, French, history, and geography, my husband and I would dare to ask for housing, heat, lighting, a thousand dollars in fixed income, and a master paid by the school to teach the young people reading and English grammar. My husband would also request permission to give lessons outside of the establishment and to execute portraits in his spare time.

Please believe, Sir, that we will do our best to fill with zeal the position of trust we are requesting and to deserve the approbation of the illustrious man whose protection we solicit today.

Please receive, Sir, the assurance of our respect and perfect devotion

Cérès de Montcarel

I enclose a prospectus to show you that our school was opened under the auspices of respectable people, by whom we will be recommended if necessary.

Our address is Mr. Alex de Montcarel in Richmond

RC (MHi); endorsed by TJ as received 28 Nov. 1818 and so recorded in SJL. Translation by Dr. Genevieve Moene. Enclosure: prospectus, dated Richmond, 18 Sept. 1816, in English, advertising a boarding school for young ladies in Richmond to be operated by Cérès de Montcarel; listing as the curriculum a variety of academic subjects and artistic skills; specifying that she will teach French and her husband will offer training in drawing and painting; noting that an American man will provide instruction in academic subjects, a professor of dancing will be hired, and a French woman will give music lessons while also assisting with the French classes; giving the cost of boarding and courses, with separate prices for day students; naming Richard Channing Moore, John Wickham, Robert Pollard, Joseph Marx, and James Brown Jr. as references; and concluding that the schoolroom will be the one recently vacated by Louis H. Girardin in the house of Mr.

Revalain near the corner of 9th and H streets (TJ's copy of broadside in MHi). Other enclosure not found.

Cérès de Montcarel, educator, was a widowed schoolteacher known as Cérès Duvernay when she married Alexandre Jacques René Le Goueslier de Montcarel (1771–1822) in Paris in 1809. She had been living there since at least 1805 and had a relationship for several years with the poet Adelbert von Chamisso prior to her marriage to de Montcarel. At the time of their wedding the groom was seeking a position as an auditor in Paris. The de Montcarels subsequently immigrated to the United States and by 1816 were living in Richmond, where he worked as a miniaturist and cameo artist and she operated a school for young ladies. They were still in Richmond in 1820, but at the time of his death Alexandre de Montcarel was a wholesale grocer in New Orleans and a partner in the firm of Baudry & Montcarel (*Revue des Deux Mondes* 39 [1907]: 463; Karl August Varnhagen von Ense, ed., *Briefe von Chamisso . . .* [1867], 1:150–79; Nicolas Viton de Saint-Allais and others, eds., *Nobiliaire universel de France* [1872–77], 12:75; R. Lewis Wright, *Artists in Virginia before 1900: An Annotated Checklist* [1983], 42; Joseph C. Cabell to TJ, 12 Mar. 1819; DNA: RG 29, CS, Richmond, 1820; *Commercial Directory* [Philadelphia, 1823], 227, 230; gravestone inscription for Alexandre de Montcarel in St. Charles Borromeo Cemetery, Destrehan, La.).

[1] Manuscript: "Seron."

To Destutt de Tracy

[D]EAR SIR   Monticello Nov. 24. 18.

I am at length enabled to write to you with some degree of courage, because I can accompany my letter with a copy of the translation of your valuable book on Political economy, which at length we have got thro' the press. the horrible delay has proceeded from the unfaithful conduct of the 1st and 2d undertakers of the work, and my great distance from them. this put it out of my power to urge them but by way of letter, which they little regarded. the premier jet of the translation was very defective both in style & sense. the latter I have rendered entirely faithful; the former could not be made what the original merited. I have ventured to insert a single note, which is at page 202. where you treat of the subject of taxation. the taxes of France & the names by which they are designated, being those used in the text, their significations would be not at all understood here. I subjoined therefore in a note a more general view, and one better understood here, to which the reader would be able to apply your principles. I hope this book will become the Amanuensis of our students and statesmen, and will improve us in a science in which of all others we have blundered most.

It would give me great joy to learn that your health is improved, & that you may still be enabled to compleat the Encyclopedie Ideologique in which you have advanced so far. my own health is failing.

my strength has been declining rapidly the few last years, the mere effect of age, and I am just now recovering from an illness of three months, which will leave me, I apprehend, in but a shattered condition.

I pray you to accept the assurance of my great esteem and consideration. TH: JEFFERSON

PoC (DLC); on verso of reused address cover of John H. Cocke to TJ, 10 July 1818; edge trimmed; at foot of text: "M. Destutt Tracy"; endorsed by TJ. Enclosure: Destutt de Tracy, *Treatise on Political Economy*. Enclosed in TJ to Albert Gallatin, 24 Nov. 1818, and TJ to Daniel Brent, 27 Nov. 1818.

The earlier UNDERTAKERS OF THE WORK were William Duane and Thomas Ritchie. PREMIER JET: "first attempt." TJ's SINGLE NOTE explaining tax classifications used in Destutt de Tracy, *Treatise on Political Economy*, is printed above at 6 Apr. 1816.

To Albert Gallatin

DEAR SIR   Monticello Nov. 24. 18.

Your letter of July 22. was most acceptable to me, by the distinctness of the view it presented of the state of France. I rejoice in the prospect that that country will so soon recover from the effects of the depression under which it has been laboring; and especially I rejoice in the hope of it's enjoying a government as free as perhaps the state of things will yet bear. it appears to me indeed that their constitution, as it now is, gives them a legislative branch more equally representative more independant, and certainly of more integrity than the corresponding one in England. time and experience will give what is still wanting and I hope they will wait patiently for that, without hazarding new convulsions.

Here all is well. the President's message, delivered a few days ago, will have given you a correct view of the state of our affairs. the capture of Pensacola, which furnished so much speculation for European news writers, (who imagined that our political code, like theirs, had no chapter of morality) was nothing here. in the first moment indeed there was a general outcry of condemnation of what appeared to be a wrongful aggression. but this was quieted at once by information that it had been taken without orders, and would be instantly restored. and altho' done without orders, yet not without justifiable cause, as we are assured will be satisfactorily shewn. this manifestation of the will of our citizens to countenance no injustice towards a foreign nation, filled me with comfort as to our future course.

Emigration to the West & South is going on beyond any thing imaginable. the President told me lately that the sales of public lands within the last year would amount to ten millions of Dollars. there is one only passage in his message which I disapprove, and which I trust will not be approved by our legislators. it is that which proposes to subject the Indians to our laws without their consent. a little patience & a little money, are so rapidly producing their voluntary removal across the Missisipi, that I hope this immorality will not be permitted to stain our history. he has certainly been surprised into this proposition, so little in concord with our principles of government.

My strength has been sensibly declining the last few years, & my health greatly broken by an illness of 3. months, from which I am but now recovering. I have been able to get on horseback within these 3. or 4. days & trust that my convalescence will now be steady. I am to write you a letter on the subject of my friend Cathalan, a very intimate friend of three & thirty years standing, and a servant of the US. of near 40. years. I am aware that his office is coveted by another, and suppose it possible that intrigue may have been employed to get him removed. but I know him too well not to pronounce him incapable of such misconduct as ought to overweigh the long course of his services to the US. I confess I should feel with great sensibility a disgrace inflicted on him at this period of life. but on this subject I must write to you more fully when I shall have more strength, for as yet I sit at the writing table with great pain.

I am obliged to usurp the protection of your cover for my letters, a trouble however which will be rare hereafter. my package is rendered more bulky on this occasion by a book I transmit for M. Tracy. it is a translation of his Economie politique, which we have made and published here, in the hope of advancing our countrymen somewhat in that science; the most profound ignorance of which threatened irreparable disaster during the late war, and by the parasite institutions of banks is now consuming the public industry. the flood, with which they are deluging us, of nominal money, has placed us compleatly without any certain measure of value, and, by interpolating a false[1] measure, is decieving & ruining multitudes of our citizens.

I hope your health, as well as mrs Gallatin's, continues good, & that whether you serve us there or here, you will long continue to us your services. their value & their need are fully understood & appreciated. I salute you with constant and affectionate friendship and respect   Th: Jefferson

RC (NHi: Gallatin Papers); addressed: "His Excellency Albert Gallatin Min. Plen. of the US. at Paris"; endorsed by Gallatin. PoC (DLC); on reused address cover of Anthony Finley to TJ, 3 Aug. 1818; endorsed by TJ. Enclosures: (1) TJ to Destutt de Tracy, 24 Nov. 1818, and enclosure. (2) TJ to David Bailie Warden, 24 Nov. 1818. (3) TJ to Peter Poinsot, 25 Nov. 1818, and enclosures. TJ to Lafayette, 23 Nov. 1818, was probably also enclosed, but see note to Daniel Brent to TJ, 10 Jan. 1819. Enclosed in TJ to Brent, 27 Nov. 1818.

Gallatin's letter OF JULY 22, not found, is recorded in SJL as received 11 Sept. 1818 from Paris. In discussing federal policy toward American INDIANS in his annual message to Congress of 16 Nov. 1818, James Monroe argued that "To civilize them, and even to prevent their extinction, it seems to be indispensable that their independence, as communities, should cease, and that the control of the United States over them should be complete and undisputed" (*Annals*, 15th Cong., 2d sess., 17).

[1] TJ here canceled "value."

To David Bailie Warden

DEAR SIR   Monticello Nov. 24. 18.

Age and declining health have very much disabled me from the duties of correspondence, or your several kind favors should not have been unacknoleged. I am just now recovering from an illness of 3. months, and have hardly yet taken my place at the writing table. so uneasy indeed have the labors of that become from these causes that I have been obliged to retire from all general correspondence. the interest I take in the government and science of France renders your favors not the less acceptable because I cannot answer them; and that which I take in your own success will always render gratifying whatever I can hear in favor of it. the message of our President to Congress, delivered a few days ago, will have given you full information of the state of our affairs. our transactions with Spain have given a scope to the European news writers for insinuations not favorable to our political morality. but without foundation. the government never hesitated a moment as to the restoration of the places taken by their officers, without orders, but not without cause. and had they hesitated, the general outcry raised by our whole people against the act, while they supposed it an intended aggression, would not have permitted the retention of the places. this outcry (altho groundless) gave me great pleasure, as an evidence that could the government in any case be disposed to swerve from morality in it's foreign transactions, the public opinion would not permit it.   the Debures serve me so well, that I have continued my applications for books to themselves directly. I expect daily a cargo from them, and wonder indeed I have not heard of it before this date. in the ensuing spring I shall make them a remittance as usual for still another. I observe indeed that the cost of books is immensely advanced since I was at Paris. with sincere wishes for your health & happiness, accept the assurance of my constant esteem & respect.   Th: Jefferson

RC (MdHi: Warden Papers); addressed: "M. David B. Warden Paris"; endorsed by Warden: "rec⁴ 13 Jan. (seal broken) from Thomas Jefferson." PoC (DLC); on verso of reused address cover

of one of the two letters from Patrick Gibson to TJ of 27 July 1818; torn at seal; endorsed by TJ. Enclosed in TJ to Albert Gallatin, 24 Nov. 1818, and TJ to Daniel Brent, 27 Nov. 1818.

From Burgess Allison

Respected Sir   Washington D.C. Novʳ 25ᵗʰ 1818.

Knowing that every improvement in the Arts & Sciences, which tends to promote the happiness or comfort of mankind, always gives you pleasure, I have taken the liberty of sending you the enclosed Pamphlet, exhibiting an improvement in Naval Architecture.

Mʳ Annesley the Author was a particular acquaintance of mine before he went to Europe, which was about two years ago. He had built a small Sloop on the Hudson River, which plied between N. York & Albany for two years prior to his leaving this, and succeeded admirably. From that success he was encouraged to go to Europe, where it seems he has built another vessel upon the same Plan. He transmitted me several Copies of his Publication, which has afforded me the pleasure of distributing them among my friends & Gentlemen of Science—He writes me Word, that encouraged by the French Minister at London, he was to set off for Paris the next day, and meant to go from thence to Amsterdam: and then, to use his own words, for this Country, the best one that ever did, or does now exist on Earth for the happiness of mankind—

I am again Stationed here for this Winter as Chaplain to the house of Representatives; and should you be able to spare so much time, I should be pleased to hear your opinion of this System of Naval Architecture—

Wishing you every blessing, I remain respectfully Your Hbˡ Svᵗ & fellow Citizen   B Allison

RC (DLC); at foot of text: "Thoˢ Jefferson Esqʳ"; endorsed by TJ as received 28 Nov. 1818 and so recorded in SJL. Enclosure: William Annesley, *A Description of William Annesley's New System of Naval Architecture, as Secured to Him, for the United States of North America, Great Britain, Ireland, and the Colonies, by His*

Majesty's Royal Letters Patent (London, 1818; Poor, *Jefferson's Library*, 5 [no. 217]; TJ's copy in PPAmP).

The french minister at london was René Eustache, marquis d'Osmond (Hoefer, *Nouv. biog. générale*, 38:907–8).

From Charles Willson Peale

MY DEAR SIR   Washington Novr 25th 1818.

Some time past I meet with a gentleman in the Museum who informed me of your extreme indisposition, and from his account of your complaints, I dispaired of ever writing to you another letter, while painting the Presidents Portrait I received the pleasing intelligence of your restored health. Your emminant Labours for the good of mankind will endear your memory to future ages. I will give a feeling trait, when I had heard of your danger of leaving us, I mentioned the account to a gentleman, I well know by a former conversation, that he was not your friend, his reply to me was that he was exceeding sorry, which he uttered feelingly. I came to this city with the intention of painting a few portraits of the most distinguished characters for the Museum and to shew that the aged by application can improove in the fine Arts, and, also to know whether the United States would purchase my Museum at a fair price, and established it on a permanant foundation. I am anxious to preserve it from a division in case of my death. The Stadt-house will not admit of our improvment of the Museum, for we cannot find room to put any interresting articles that we possess at this moment, and as it is, it is too much of a medley. I have no space to put my late Portraits, yet that, shall not discourage me, as I love the art and know that it is the best imployment of my time. before I leave this place I purpose to give you some account of the portraits I shall have painted, in a hope that it may not be fateagueing to read my scroles, as I mean to be concise. may you have yet length of days—ah! I have just thought of telling you that I have heard of an African living in Georgetown that is said to be 140 years of age, I mean to see him & paint his Portrait—with much esteem

and respect I am ever your friend   C W PEALE

RC (MHi); endorsed by TJ as received 8 Dec. 1818 and so recorded in SJL. RC (DLC); address cover only; with PoC of TJ to John C. Calhoun, 4 Apr. 1819, on verso; addressed: "Thomas Jefferson Esqr Monticello Virginia"; franked; postmarked Washington, 27 Nov. PoC (PPAmP: Peale Letterbook).

STADT-HOUSE: "city hall"; the Pennsylvania State House (later known as Independence Hall). The AFRICAN LIVING IN GEORGETOWN and later painted by Peale was a former slave named Yarrow Mamout (Peale, *Papers*, 3:617, 650–2).

To Peter Poinsot

SIR   Monticello in Virginia. Nov. 25. 18

Your letter of May 18. and it's duplicate were recieved in Aug. and September. in proposing me to you as an agent to look after yo[ur][1] lands on the Kanhaway, my deceased friend General Kosciusko must have considered me as continuing stationary at what I was when he last saw me. I then retained health and vigor enough of body & mind to be useful to others. but 20. additional years have made great change. at the age of 75. and much enfeebled, I have been obliged to give up the manag[e]ment of my own affairs to others. your lands are 300. miles from my res[i]dence, in a part with which we have no communication. & where I do not know a single person who might be engaged to act for you. I made an effort however thro' a friend, a member of our legislature, to enquire first in the land office for the state of the land, and to endeavor to find out some one in it's neighborhood who could undertake to look after them.[2] the result of his enquiries at the land office will appear in the inclose[d] papers: but he could hear of no one in that part of the country who coul[d] be engaged to make the enquiries you desire. I must return the case therefore to you with the apology 'Senex sum et curis laevissimis imp[ar.']' if the lands are fertile, and the title not lost by abandonment, they must b[e] of very great value; they would possibly command 20. or 30. Dollars the acre. you will consider therefore whether they may not be worth the[3] mission of a special agent, who landing at Washington or Baltimor[e] would get a passage by the stage to the neighborhood of the land, in a distance of between 1. and 200. miles. with my regrets that I can be no further useful to you accept the assurance of my great respect.

                                                      TH: JEFFERSON

PoC (DLC); on verso of reused address cover of William Kean to TJ, 23 July 1818; edge trimmed; at foot of text: "M. Poinsot des Essarts Cette"; endorsed by TJ. Enclosure: first enclosure to Poinsot to TJ, 25 June 1817. Enclosed in TJ to Albert Gallatin, 24 Nov. 1818, and TJ to Daniel Brent, 27 Nov. 1818.

TJ may have also enclosed here the letters to him of 6 and 13 Feb. 1818 from Joseph C. Cabell (A MEMBER OF OUR LEGISLATURE) concerning Poinsot's claim. The phrase SENEX SUM ET CURIS LAEVISSIMIS IMP[AR] comes from Tacitus, *Annals*, 14.54, in which Seneca the Younger uses these words to apologize to the Roman emperor Nero that he is "an old man and unequal to the lightest of cares" (*Tacitus*, trans. Maurice Hutton, William Peterson, Clifford H. Moore, John Jackson, and others, Loeb Classical Library [1914–37; repr. ca. 2006], 5:192–3).

[1] Word faint.
[2] Omitted period at right margin editorially supplied.
[3] Manuscript: "a the."

From Lewis D. Belair

SIR   Philadelphia Nov 26ʰ 1818

Yours of The 16ʰ Insᵗ I have Just Recᵈ—It Was forwarded to me from New York Where I Intended to have Been Long Before This time,—I Have Order'd to have Lay'd aside The Diffᵗ Works which you have Concluded to Take—I Herein Inclose The List of Prices and formats of The Books you have Spoken off,

Epictetus (Manuel de) Greek & Italian This Work is not yeat unpacked It is Called In The Invoice "Bodonis Edition (Scarce Book) Velum Paper,"[1] I Think That it is one or two Vol In 8ᵛᵒ The Price of which is $5.87½ Cost 20 franc

Géométrie de Legendre Broché 1 8ᵛᵒ 1817   2 25

Algebre d'Euler avec des Notes ⅌ Garnier

In 2 Vol In 8ᵛᵒ (The Last Copy) Broché   4 25

Metaphysique ⅌ Carnot 1 8ᵛᵒ 175 (It is Sold)

I Shall With Much Pleasure Reserve you a Copie of Tacite Dureau de la Malle,—I have not The Works you Mention, Intiteled Compte Rendû of The Institute of 1808 Séance du 20 fevrier &&&, I Shall have It Imported by The first Oportunity;

With Respect Yours   LEWIS D BÉLAIR

RC (MHi); between dateline and salutation: "Thomas Jefferson Esqʳ"; endorsed by TJ as received 6 Dec. 1818 and so recorded in SJL.

The Greek and Italian edition of the *Enchiridion* or *Manual* (MANUEL) of Epictetus described here was translated (under the pseudonym Eritisco Pilenejo)

by Giuseppe Maria Pagnini and published by Giambattista Bodoni (Ἐπικτήτου Ἐγχειρίδιον. *Manuale di Epitteto* [Parma, 1793]; Poor, *Jefferson's Library*, 8 [no. 434]).

[1] Omitted closing quotation mark editorially supplied.

From Francis Eppes

DEAR SIR   Mill Brook Nov: 26ᵗʰ 1818

You will no doubt be surprised at seeing the date of this letter, thinking that I have been at school for some time past, I have however been detained at home much longer than I myself expected by the indisposition of our family. A bilious Fever has been prevalent in our neighbourhood this fall and carried off many it is now much abated. I set out this week at Furtherest for Mʳ Bakers and will let you hear from me as soon as I arrive there. It is very uncertain whether Mʳ Barbour will continue his school after Christmas, if he does not I shall pursue the course you recommended to me untill the Central College goes into operation.

I have taken a list of my Fathers Books as you desired & find that but few classical ones are among them and as I suppose that you merely wished to see those I only send you a list of <u>them</u>. In looking over them I found a quarto edition of Hedericks Lexicon & a superb copy of Homer but the latter is too large to be of much use.

By this time I hope you enjoy the blessings of Health without which happiness cannot be enjoyed on this earth. Papa has writen to us from Washington and I believe is heartily tired of public life.

present me affectionately to the family.

I remain your affectionate Grandson   FRAN^cs EPPES

RC (MHi); endorsed by TJ as received 3 Dec. 1818 and so recorded in SJL. Enclosure not found.

HEDERICKS LEXICON: the Greek lexicon of Benjamin Hederich.

From Francis W. Gilmer

DEAR SIR.   Richmond. Nov. 26. 1818.

I have heard with great pleasure of your convalescence. by winter you will be quite well to enjoy the triumph of the university which is now beyond all danger.

It is highly probable that you will be consulted by friends from Philadelphia as to a successor to Dorsey & our excellent friend Doct^r Wistar. Should you be—I must beg of you to converse with Colo: Randolph on the pretensions of Doctr: Watson of this place. He knows him as well as I do—& as a physician & anatomist better than I can. He is every way superior to Smith of Williamsburg who was spoken of in preference to Dorsey.

Watson is so modest, & so little known that I have felt the liberty I take with you in some degree due to him—& extorted from me. The motive I am sure will excuse me to you.

most respectfully yours &c.   F. W. GILMER.

RC (MoSHi: Gilmer Papers); endorsed by TJ as received 6 Dec. 1818 and so recorded in SJL. RC (ViU: TJP-CC); address cover only; with PoC of TJ to Wilson J. Cary, 4 May 1819, on verso; addressed: "Thomas Jefferson esq^r Monticello Albemarle"; franked; postmarked Richmond, 27 Nov.

George Watson (ca. 1784–1853), physician, attended the College of William and Mary, obtained medical training in Edinburgh and Paris, and received an M.D. degree from the University of Pennsylvania in 1809, after which he practiced medicine in Richmond. He was a militia surgeon during the War of 1812 and a founding member of the Medical Society of Virginia in 1824. His brother David Watson sat on the first board of visitors of Central College. Watson bought a Richmond residence designed by Robert Mills and also owned an estate in Louisa County, at which he died (Valentine Museum, *Richmond Portraits . . . 1737–1860* [1949], 202–3; ViHi: Watson Family Papers; *William and Mary Provisional List*, 43; *Catalogue of the Medical Graduates of the University of Pennsylvania* [2d ed., 1839], 82; Wyndham B. Blanton, *Medicine in Virginia in the Nineteenth Century* [1933], 76, 238, 320; Richmond *Daily Dispatch*, 14 Oct. 1853; Louisa Co. Circuit Superior Court of Law and Chancery Wills [1828–1901], 89–90).

TJ did not write in support of Watson, but other prominent Virginians did, including John Marshall, who on 11 Dec. 1818 commended him as "a man of science a physician, and a gentleman" who "stood high in the public Opinion." He was not, however, offered the vacant anatomy chair at the University of Pennsylvania (Marshall, *Papers*, 8:401–2).

From Fredericksburg on 12 Oct. 1818, Gilmer wrote a letter to TJ's nephew Dabney Carr that, among other things, encouraged him to begin work on a biography of TJ: "what would you say to edifying the world by a chaste, elegant, and philosophical life of Cit^n Thomas your Uncle? He is in my judgement the best subject for biography after Gen: Washington which our country has afforded. This is a question worthy of consideration. It would be a great thing for a profound & eloquent writer to give an ample & rich portrait of the old Philosopher & present the proceeds of the work to the Central College—or what perhaps would be as wise—put them in his pocket—to buy Christmas plums for his children. I fear unless the old man has a hint about this matter he will leave his papers to some quack or impostor (for you know how easily he is duped) who will disgrace his subject, himself & his country. He cannot in nature live long, & that the work may appear soon after his death it should be speedily begun" (RC in Vi: Gilmer Letters to Carr; addressed: "The Honble Chancellor Carr. Winchester V^a"; stamped; postmarked Fredericksburg, 13 Oct.; endorsed by Carr).

From Craven Peyton

DEAR SIR   Monteagle No^r 26.[1] 1818

My Son delivared Your reply to my Note Yesterday offaring to sell some Negroes if there was a positive necessity for my haveing the money. I was garded with Mr Smith in the bargain, that if it was not convenient to advance the Money Monday Next it was not a bargain. I have Your Convenience And ease more at hart then all the proparty On earth. And beg You will Not think of a sale, I will again try & borrow, the money that I may be short of.[2] the Negroes I baught is the greatest bargain I have heard of And wou^d now in the uppar counties command $4,000. More then the sum I am to give

with the greatest esteem   C. PEYTON.

RC (MHi); endorsed by TJ as received 26 Nov. 1818 and so recorded in SJL.

TJ's missing REPLY to Peyton of 25 Nov. 1818 is not recorded in SJL. Peyton's prior NOTE of 25 Nov. 1818, also not found, is recorded in SJL as received from Monteagle the same day.

[1] Reworked from "25."
[2] Omitted period at right margin editorially supplied.

From Marie Louise Martel Walsh

Monsieur   ce 26 9bre 1818

la haute Consideration et le profond respect que feu m^r Walsh mon epoux m'a inspiré pour votre personne, joints a la conviction ou je Suis de votre Caractere genereux; m'enhardissent a vous entretenir de mes malheurs, et implorer votre Bienveillance pour la veuve d'un zelé Concitoyen, que vous avez daigné jadis honorer de votre puissante protection.

Nommé Consul americain au port de Sette Sur la mediterranée pendant votre presidençe, m^r Walsh n'a cessé durant plusieurs années d'exercice, de Secourir de tous Ses moyens les americains qui ont reclamé Sa Sollicitude; trop heureux lorsqu'il Se presentoit une occasion de faire du bien a Ses chers compatriotes! mais ce zéle Si recommandable et dont il Se Glorifioit, ne l'a pas mis lui meme a l'abri des plus cruels revers. en effet les Secousses politiques qui Si long temps ont agité l'europe, contrarierent constament Ses efforts, en interceptant Ses rapports commerciaux et paralysant Ses talents. de telle Sorte que Sa fortune en Souffrit de vives atteintes. la paix generale et la liberté des mers arriverent enfin. mais hélas! m^r Walsh rongé de peines et atteint d'une maladie grave, y Succomba le 14. 9bre 1814, presqu'au moment ou le traité qui fut Signé quelques mois aprés, lui promettoit les plus belles esperançes. Ses dernieres volontés m'ont rendu heritiere universelle de Ses Biens presents et a venir; c'est a ce titre, monsieur, et en qualité de veuve d'un Consul de votre nation, mais plus encore d'apres vos vertus et votre Bienfaisançe, que je prends la liberté de vous interceder pour Connaitre un fait qui importe puissament a mes interets. il S'agit d'une heredité considerable que feu m^r le major Walsh, mort a la floride il y a douze ou treize ans, laissa a mon epoux; ce qu'il apprit Seulement d'une maniere indirecte, ainsi que je vais avoir l'honneur de Vous l'exposer.

en 1806 ou 1807, m^r Walsh residant a montpellier, recut une lettre de monsieur Skipwith, alors consul general des etats unis d'amerique a paris, lui annonçant que M^r hunts americain S'etoit presenté chez lui pour demander des renseignements Sur un nommé peter Walsh, irlandais de nation, natif de Waterford, negoçiant a cadix, lequel venoit d'heriter depuis peu des Biens Delaissés par feu le major Walsh, mort a la floride, Sans designation precise du lieu; ajoutant que vû l'absence d'heritier, le gouvernement avoit mis les biens Sous le Sequestre. m^r hunts dit en outre a m^r Skipwith, que Si l'heritier etant connu, vouloit donner les fonds et titres necessaires, il Se chargeroit volontiers de le faire rentrer dans Ses droits. m^r Walsh dans Sa réponse a ce dernier, convint etre la personne designée par le testateur qu'il Connaissoit particuliérement Comme Son parent; ce qui d'ailleurs etoit evident puisqu'il reunissoit en lui tous les caracteres indiqués dans l'acte, ayant habité vingt ans [a][1] cadix, ou le major Walsh le croyoit encore lors de Son decés; mais il observa en faisant Ses remerciments a m[r] Skipwith que les circonstances politiques et Surtout la guerre, S'opposoient a toutes demarches dans le moment; Se reservant de faire valoir Ses droits lorsque la paix auroit lieu. j'ai eu l'honneur de vous faire part que la mort me ravit mon epoux peu de temps avant cette heureuse epoque; de telle Sorte que les choses en Sont demeurées dans le meme etat jusqu'a ce moment; n'ayant Scû depuis Son decés, quels moyens employer pour avoir des renseignements certains.

quoique m[r] Walsh n'ait point laissé de posterité; j'ai deux nieces interessantes qu'il regardoit commes Ses propres filles; et ce Seroit mal remplir Ses intentions Si je ne cherchois a leur faire tout le bien qui est en ma puissançe; aussi ce motif pressant est-il le Seul mobile de toutes mes demarches. Serois-je assez heureuse, monsieur, pour vous inspirer quelqu'interet Sur leur Sort et le mien? et oserois-je vous Supplier de vouloir bien employer votre pouvoir et vos relations etendues, a decouvrir S'il est reëllement vrai qu'a l'epoque ci dessus designée, le major Walsh est mort a la floride, laissant des biens dont le gouvernement ou quelque pretendu heritier Se Soit emparé? il Seroit Surtout important d'etre instruit du lieu de Sa residence a l'epoque de Son decés; et S'il a fait les dispositions dont m[r] hunts avoit fait part a m[r] Skipwith. c'est monsieur, la graçe que j'implore de votre caractere bienfaisant; et qu'il vous est plus facile que tout autre de m'accorder, quelles que Soient les difficultés, par l'influence que vous donne la haute dignité ou vous avez eté elevé, et mieux encore la reputation d'homme probe et vertueux que vous vous etes Si justement acquis.

Si par l'effet de vos bontés la verité m'etoit connue, je ferai les diligences necessaires et enverrai les pieces legalisées pour justifier mes droits a l'heredité. daignez, monsieur, acceder a la priere d'une veuve eplorée, m'honorer d'une réponse et etre d'ailleurs bien convaincu que quels que Soient les resultats, personne n'est avec plus de respect et de veneration que moi,

votre tres humble et obeissante Servante   V. WALSH

mon adresse est: M[de] Veuve Walsh, maison vernet,
  prés le peyrou,
    a montpellier—

SIR   26 November 1818

The high consideration and profound respect for you that my late husband, Mr. Walsh, inspired in me, together with my strong belief in your generous character, embolden me to tell you of my misfortunes and implore your benevolence toward the widow of a zealous fellow citizen, whom in the past you have honored with your powerful protection.

Named American consul at the Mediterranean port of Cette during your presidency, Mr. Walsh never ceased, during several years in that post, to help by all possible means Americans who requested his solicitude. He was only too happy to have a chance to assist his dear fellow citizens! But this zeal, which is so commendable and in which he took great pride, did not shelter him from the most cruel setbacks. Indeed, the political upheavals that agitated Europe for so long constantly thwarted his efforts by blocking his commercial relations and paralyzing his talents, to such an extent that his fortune suffered severely. General peace and freedom of the seas finally came. But alas! Eaten away by sorrow and afflicted by a grave illness, Mr. Walsh succumbed on 14 November 1814, not long before the signing a few months later of a treaty that would have promised to fulfill his highest hopes. His last will made me the sole heiress to his estate, present and future. In this capacity, Sir, and as the widow of a consul of your nation, but even more because of your virtues and benevolence, I take the liberty of asking your intercession to discover a fact that matters greatly to me. It concerns a considerable inheritance that the late Major Walsh, who died in Florida twelve or thirteen years ago, left to my husband, and about which he learned only indirectly, as I will have the honor to explain.

In 1806 or 1807 Mr. Walsh, who resided in Montpellier, received a letter from Mr. Skipwith, then consul general of the United States of America at Paris, advising him that Mr. Hunts, an American, had presented himself at his house asking for information regarding a man named Peter Walsh, an Irish national, born in Waterford, merchant in Cádiz, and who had just inherited an estate left by the late Major Walsh, who had died at an undesignated location in Florida. He added that, in the absence of an heir, the government had sequestered the estate. Moreover, Mr. Hunts told Mr. Skipwith that, if the heir was identified and could produce the necessary funds and titles, he would be happy to help restore him to his rights. Mr. Walsh acknowledged in his reply to Mr. Skipwith that he was the person named by the testator, whom he knew well as his relative. Besides, this fact was obvious inasmuch as he combined in his person all the characteristics indicated in the document, having lived in Cádiz for twenty years, where Major Walsh still believed him to be at the time of his own death. But in thanking Mr. Skipwith he observed that political circumstances, and the war above all, prevented him from taking any steps at that time, and that he would wait until the return of peace to assert his rights. I have already informed you that death robbed me of my spouse shortly after this happy time. Things have remained unchanged since my husband's death, as I do not know how to obtain reliable information.

Although Mr. Walsh left no descendants, I have two fascinating nieces whom he treated like his own daughters, and I would be carrying out his wishes very poorly if I did not try to do them all the good in my power. This pressing reason is the only motive for all my steps. Will I be so fortunate, Sir, as to inspire some interest in their fate and mine? And will I dare beg you to be so kind as to use your power and extensive connections to find out if it is really true that Major Walsh died in Florida at the abovementioned time, leaving an estate which the government or some alleged heir has seized? Above all, it would be important to learn his place of residence at the time of his death and whether he made the arrangements of which Mr. Hunts informed Mr. Skipwith. This, Sir, is the favor that I beg of your benevolent disposition, which is easier for you than for anyone else to grant me, whatever the difficulties may be, given the highly dignified position you have attained and, better yet, your justly acquired reputation as a man of probity and virtue.

If I find out the truth as a result of your kindness, I will hasten to take the necessary steps and will send notarized forms in order to prove my right to the inheritance. Please, Sir, deign to accede to the prayer of a tearful widow, honor me with a reply, and be sure that, whatever the result, I am, with as much respect and veneration as anyone,

your very humble and obedient servant   WIDOW WALSH

My address is: Madame Widow Walsh, Maison Vernet,
    at the Peyrou,
        Montpellier—

RC (MoSHi: TJC-BC); in an unidentified hand, signed by Walsh; dateline adjacent to closing; endorsed by TJ as received 10 July 1819 and so recorded in SJL. Translation by Dr. Genevieve Moene.

Marie Louise Martel Walsh (ca. 1764–1856), a member of a commercial family from Montpellier, France, was the wife of Peter Walsh, the United States commercial agent at Cette. She died in Montpellier (Stephen Martel to James Monroe, 2 Dec. 1814, and Joseph C. Cabell to William H. Crawford, 21 Dec. 1815 [DNA: RG 59, LAR, 1809–17]; *Journal Officiel de l'Empire Français*, 28 Oct. 1869).

[1] Omitted word editorially supplied.

To Daniel Brent

DEAR SIR   M[on]ticello Nov. 27. 18.

I trouble you now, as heretofore with my letters to Europe. the bulk is rendered larger than heretofore by the addition of a book. but the trouble will be less repeated my present letters amounting in fact to letters of leave to my European correspondence. the advance of years & decline of health oblige me to withdraw from all unnecessary correspondence, and none is less necessary or interesting than this. I salute you with assurances of my great esteem & respect.

TH: JEFFERSON

PoC (DLC); dateline faint; at foot of text: "Daniel Brent esq."; endorsed by TJ. Enclosures: (1) TJ to Destutt de Tracy, 24 Nov. 1818, and enclosure. (2) TJ to Albert Gallatin, 24 Nov. 1818. (3) TJ to David Bailie Warden, 24 Nov. 1818. (4) TJ to Peter Poinsot, 25 Nov. 1818, and enclosures. TJ to Lafayette, 23 Nov. 1818, was probably also enclosed, but see note to Brent to TJ, 10 Jan. 1819.

To James Brownlee

SIR   Monticello Nov. 27. 18.

Your letter of the 9th never reached me until the 23[d]. it was impossible, my good Sir, that you could have applied to a person less capable of serving you. long retired from the world and it's business, paying no attention to new regulation, going no where, seeing no body[1] but those who accidentally come here, I am totally ignorant of the steps to be taken to obtain your right, nor have I any means of learning them. the best thing you could do would be to commit your case to one of your delegates, who, if he does not himself know the proper steps, can readily learn them of the gentlemen he will meet at the ensuing session of the legislature, or from the public offices. [to save?] you the trouble of writing it over again I inclose your [letter?] stating it. only observe that Col° Lewis of the North garden was named Charles, not andrew. I would serve willingly if in my power; as it is you must accept my regrets and my best wishes that you may obtain the justice which may be due to you.   TH: JEFFERSON

PoC (DLC); on verso of reused address cover of Spencer Roane to TJ, 22 Aug. 1818; mutilated at seal; at foot of text: "M[r] James Brownlee"; endorsed by TJ. Enclosure: Brownlee to TJ, 9 Nov. 1818, not found, recorded in SJL as received 23 Nov. 1818 from Waynesboro.

James Brownlee (ca. 1750–ca. 1826) was living in Fluvanna County in 1777 when he enlisted as a private in the 14th Virginia Regiment of the Continental army. He served at the battles of White Plains and Brandywine, the siege of Fort Mifflin, and the battles of Whitemarsh and Monmouth before being discharged in 1781 due to injuries he had sustained. At that time Brownlee was still living in Fluvanna County, but afterwards he settled in Waynesboro. He received a pension in April 1818, but as of 1820 he owned only $56 worth of assets and owed $60 in rent. At the time of his death Brownlee's personal property was valued at over $350 (DNA: RG 15, SRRWPBLW; DNA: RG 29, CS, Waynesboro, 1820; Augusta Co. Will Book, 14:217, 15:398–9).

[1] Manuscript: "boay."

To John C. Calhoun

Monticello Nov. 27. 18.

Th: Jefferson with great reluctance trespasses on the labors of the Secretary at war, merely to remind him of the case of M. Poirey, aid de camp and Secretary to Gen[l] la Fayette; lest in the overwhelming mass of his duties it might escape his notice. he salutes him with assurance of his great personal esteem and high respect.

PoC (DLC); on verso of reused address cover of otherwise unlocated letter from Calhoun to TJ, 25 July 1818 (addressed: "Thomas Jefferson Esq[r] Monticello

Virginia"; with frank in Calhoun's hand: "War Dept"; postmarked Washington, 27 July; recorded in SJL as received 30 July 1818 from Calhoun at the War Department); dateline at foot of text; endorsed by TJ.

From Thomas B. Parker

S<small>IR</small>   Boston Nov 27th 1818

The Subscriber, altho' a stranger to your person, takes the liberty of requesting your perusal of a few lines in the inclosed N. Paper respecting the state of your health—in order that you Dear Sir may percieve the change which, apparently so at least, has taken place in the opinions of some men who, if not at present were once your most bitter enemies and persecuters.

The Editor of the inclosed N. Paper has been, and probably is now, as warm a lover[1] of the British system of Government as can be found in this Country. And tho' his affections remain the same yet still he is obliged for his personal benefit to accommodate the sentiments of his columns to the opinions of the publick.

A few years since this man would, no doubt, have been much gratified at the opportunity of recording the decease of the "Opposer of Tyrany" And now, pressed on all sides by publick opinion, is necessitated for his own credit to announce to the people the restoration to health of the "Friend to and Supporter" of the Rights of Man.

The contrast is so great that I could not refrain from communicating to you on the subject,

I am a young man and on reflection cannot but shudder at the thoughts of the changes which may take place in the Government of our Country by the abilities of depraved and ambitious men while the founders of our Republick and our political quids are resting in their silent and dark abodes.

I beg of you Dear Sir to overlook my presumption and be assured that many very many of your Countrymen have a deep interest in your health and happiness

With great Respect Give me leave to Subscribe myself Your friend[2]

T<small>HOMAS</small> B P<small>ARKER</small>

RC (DLC); at foot of text: "Honorable Thomas Jefferson Monticello V^a"; endorsed by TJ as received 6 Dec. 1818 and so recorded in SJL. Enclosure not found.

Thomas B. Parker (ca. 1796–1822), clerk, was a native of Massachusetts. By 1812 he was an assistant in the Boston post office, where he eventually earned an annual salary of $500. Parker died in Boston (*Boston Patriot*, 4 Apr. 1812; *A Register of Officers and Agents, Civil, Military, and Naval, in the service of the United States, on the Thirtieth day of September, 1816* [Washington, 1816], pt. 2, p. 71; *The Boston Directory* [1818]: 164;

[1820]: 162; [1821]: 185; DNA: RG 29, CS, Boston, 1820; *A Register of Officers and Agents, Civil, Military, and Naval, in the Service of the United States, on the 30th of September, 1821* [Washington, 1822], pt. 2, p. 121; *Independent Chronicle and Boston Patriot,* 9 Feb. 1822; *Boston Commercial Gazette,* 11 Feb. 1822).

[1] Reworked from "friend."
[2] Manuscript: "frind."

To Craven Peyton

DEAR SIR   Monticello Nov. 27. 18.

I am very sensible of the kind indulgence expressed in your letter of yesterday[1] which lays me under an obligation the more to prevent your suffering by it if in my power, & will still if possible raise the money by a sale of property. my grandson had mentioned to me that a woman of mine who has 5. children and no husband had expressed a wish to be sold. I had a meeting with him yesterday, and authorised him to sell them if he could get what he thought a reasonable value for them. he estimated the 6. at £1000. the woman is a fine handy sensible one, a worker in the crop, 35. years old, with a child of 3. months old (a boy) 2. daughters of 4. and 6. years old, and 2. sons of 11. and 13. the last works well at the plough already. I wish indeed you could take them yourself. if you can accomplish your late purchase without this money, the thing would be easy because half the price would be in your own hands, and the rest might await your convenience in the spring, or longer paying interest. only say the word and they are yours. affectionately your

   friend & serv[t]   TH: JEFFERSON

RC (Mrs. Charles W. Biggs, Lewisburg, W.Va., 1950); addressed: "Craven Peyton esq. Monteagle"; endorsed by Peyton: "Offar to sell Negroes." PoC (MHi); on verso of a reused address cover from William F. Gray to TJ; endorsed by TJ.

The enslaved woman WHO EXPRESSED A WISH TO BE SOLD was probably Lucy (b. 1783), who along with her older children Robin (b. 1805), Sandy (b. 1807), Molly (b. 1814), and Melinda (b. 1816) had been leased to Thomas Jefferson Randolph to work at Lego earlier in 1818. On 9 Apr. 1820 TJ traded the family, now including Lucy's son Nicholas (b. 1818), to Randolph for seven of his slaves (TJ's Notes on Lease of Tufton and Lego to Randolph, [after 1 Jan. 1818]; Betts, *Farm Book,* pt. 1, pp. 130, 160–1).

A letter of this date from Peyton to TJ, not found, is recorded in SJL as received the same day from Monteagle.

[1] Preceding two words interlined.

To Henry E. Watkins

Dear Sir   Monti[cell]o Nov. 27. 18.

Dear Sir   Monti[cell]o Nov. 27. 18.

Your fav^r of the 6th did not get to hand till the 23^d and I now with pleasure send you as much of the Succory seed as can well go under the volume of a letter. as I mentioned to our Colleagues at the Gap, I had forgotten which of them expressed a willingness to try this plant; and therefore I have waited for their application having taken care to have a plenty of seed saved.

Sow the seed in rich beds, as you woud tobacco seed, and take the advantage of good seasons in the spring to draw & transplant them. the ground should be well prepared by the plough, I have generally set the plants 18.I. or 2.f. apart every way, to give room for several weedings the 1st summer, for during that they are too weak to contend with the weeds. after that they will not be in danger from weeds. do not cut the plants the 1st year that they may shed their seed and fill up all the intervals, the grasing of sheep destroys the plant. it is perennial, & of immense produce, and is a tolerable sallad for the table in the spring, somewhat like the turnep tops but earlier.   The warm spring bath proved extremely injurious to my health. I have been very poorly ever since, but within a week past have got on horseback, altho' not yet entirely well. Accept my friendly salutations & assurances of great esteem and respect.   Th: Jefferson

PoC (DNAL: Thomas Jefferson Correspondence, Bixby Donation); on verso of reused address cover to TJ; dateline faint; at foot of text: "Henry E. Watkins esq."; endorsed by TJ.

the gap: Rockfish Gap.

From William A. Burwell

Dear Sir,   washington No^{v}br 28th 1818—

Dear Sir,   washington No^{v}br 28th 1818—

Yesterday at a meeting of the Committee of Ways & Means it was proposed to change the duties on wine agreable to your suggestion, & to lessen the duty upon Books printed in Foreign languages imported into the U States—

both Subjects have been refer'^{d} to Mr Crawford for his consideration and unless he urges some strong objection I am persuaded they will pass both houses of Congress. I understand from Mr Milligan none but the most common School Books in Latin or Greek are printed in America. of course high duties to protect American Manufactures (the ordinary apology) are not necessary—the spirited exertions making to revive education will speedily increase the demand for Classical & scientific Books and every obstacle to the cheap importation of them should be removed—

I have been requested by Mr Milligan to mention that Tracys work is at length publish'd—

as I have not heard that your health is worse I indulge the hope you have gradually recoverd, and again enjoy that blessing. will you be so good as to remember me in the kindest manner to the family. and accept D[r] Sir my best wishes for your health[1] & happiness

W. A. BURWELL.

RC (DLC); endorsed by TJ as received 6 Dec. 1818 and so recorded in SJL.

On 8 Dec. 1818 the United States House of Representative's COMMITTEE OF WAYS & MEANS reported a bill to reduce import duties on certain wines and eliminate them on books printed in foreign languages. The reference to books was no longer in the bill's title when the House approved it on 26 Feb. 1819, and after passing in the Senate on 3 Mar. 1819, it became law the same day as "An Act to regulate the duties on certain wines." The statute reduced the tariff on wines not enumerated in a 27 Apr. 1816 law from seventy to thirty cents per gallon when imported in bottles or cases and from twenty-five to fifteen cents a gallon in

other containers (*JHR*, 12:71, 183, 303–4, 315, 320; *JS*, 8:314, 317, 329, 345; *U.S. Statutes at Large*, 3:515).

Continuing earlier lobbying efforts made directly to the Treasury Department, TJ presumably offered Burwell his SUGGESTION that Congress lower the duties on wine and books in person prior to 23 Nov. 1818, when Burwell returned to Washington having recently visited Monticello (TJ to Alexander J. Dallas, 26 Feb. 1816 (third letter); TJ to William H. Crawford, 10 Nov. 1818; James Monroe to TJ, 23 Nov. 1818; Elizabeth Trist to Nicholas P. Trist, 28 Nov. 1818 [DLC: NPT]).

[1] Manuscript: "heath."

To Mathew Carey

DEAR SIR   Monticello Nov. 28. 18.

In a letter of Oct. 6. I requested the favor of you to send me Griesbach's Greek testament, the 8[vo] & full edition, and
The New testament in an improved version on the basis of Newcome's translation which, altho' published in Boston, I supposed could be had in Philadelphia. hearing nothing of them I conjecture they are either forgotten or not to be had in Philadelphia. I would rather have them <u>unbound</u>, and they may come by mail if to be had. I salute you with friendship & respect.   TH: JEFFERSON

RC (PHi: Lea & Febiger Records); addressed: "M[r] Matthew Carey Philadelphia"; franked; postmarked; endorsed by Carey as received 4 Dec. and answered

7 Dec. PoC (DLC); on verso of reused address cover of Robert Walsh to TJ, 1 Aug. 1818; endorsed by TJ.

To James H. McCulloch

SIR   Monticello Nov. 28. 18.

Mr Beasley our Consul at Havre in a letter of Sep. 28. informs me that the ship Dumfries, by which he sends that letter, bound for Baltimore, brings a box of books for me. I have no letter or invoice from my bookseller, but shall doubtless soon recieve one. if it is permitted by the rules of the office to reship them before a settlement of the duties, I will pray you to forward them to Richm^d to the address of mr Patrick Gibson, on the assurance that the moment I recieve the bookseller's bill it shall be forwarded to you, and the duty remitted as soon thereafter as it shall be made known to me. books are so liable to sea-damage and the season so fast advancing as to make it desirable to get them home with as little delay as possible. Accept the assurances of my great esteem and high respect   TH: JEFFERSON

PoC (MHi); on verso of a reused address cover from William D. Simms to TJ; at foot of text: "James H. McCulloch esq."; endorsed by TJ.

To Burgess Allison

Monticello Nov. 29. 19. [1818]

I thank you, Sir, for the pamphlet you have been so kind as to send me on Naval architecture. retired from the business of the world, enfeebled in body by age & relaxed in mind I cease to[1] pay attention wherever I can be excused from it. the improvement appears probable and beautiful, and I wish well to every thing which may better the condition of man, and to nothing more than what may advance your own prosperity and happiness for which I pray you to accept my sincerest wishes with the assurance of my great esteem and respect.

TH: JEFFERSON

PoC (DLC: TJ Papers, 216:38630); on verso of reused address cover to TJ; misdated; at foot of text: "Mr Allison"; endorsed by TJ as a letter of 29 Nov. 1818 and so recorded in SJL.

[1] TJ here canceled "interest."

To Cérès de Montcarel

Monticello Nov. 29. 18.

Th: Jefferson presents his compliments to Mad^e Montcarel, and on the subject of the University proposed to be established near Charlottesville he must refer her to a report of Commissioners to the legislature which will probably be published on their meeting. by that she will percieve that the institution not being yet definitively decided on, the persons of course, are not yet appointed to whom she must apply to be placed, with M. Montcarel, at the head of that institution according to the wish expressed in her letter of the 24th. he prays her to acceptance of his respects.

P. S. he returns mr Lee's letter

PoC (MHi); on verso of reused address cover of Francis Eppes to TJ, 2 Aug. 1818; dateline between text and postscript; endorsed by TJ. Enclosure not found.

To Joseph Milligan

DEAR SIR   Monticello Nov. 29. 18.

Your's of the 20th is just now recieved. the book of gardening had come to hand in due time, and I observe in it some useful additions; particularly that on the vine. the 2. copies of Tracy were also recieved, and one of them immediately put under[1] cover for Mr Tracy. for these books accept my thanks. the 10. copies shall be distributed to such gentlemen as I think most likely to recommend the work. you ask letters from me to divers places to encorage the purchase of the book. but no stronger letter can be written than that prefixed to the book, and being no longer equal to the labors of the writing table, I have withdrawn myself from all letter writing but on my own affairs. [as] to the book's falling, it is possible it may not sell as rapidly [as] if written by M^de Genlis or Hanah Moore; but while Euclid and Locke hold their ground, this like them will be the elementary book of the science it teaches, and will be in the hands of every one who wishes to become acquainted with it. altho' I think that two and twenty legislatures & double that number of colleges & academies should devour such a work in an hour, yet time will be necessary for them to know it's merits & it's eminence.

I am making up a box of about 40. vols to be forwarded to you by the stage of which I shall pray immediate dispatch in the binding, there being among them some books of daily and indispensable use. I salute you with friendship & respect   TH: JEFFERSON

PoC (MHi); on verso of reused address cover of Richard N. Thweatt to TJ,
31 July 1818; torn at seal; at foot of text:
"Mʳ Millegan"; endorsed by TJ.

The letter PREFIXED to Destutt de
Tracy, *Treatise on Political Economy*, is
TJ to Milligan, [ca. 25 Oct. 1818].

[1] Manuscript: "unver."

From John Barnes

DEAR SIR—   George Town Coᵃ 31 [30] Novʳ 1818.

Your very Acceptable favʳ 11 Insᵗ as it assured me, of your nearly
perfect recovery—was not only gratifying to my self but to many
inquiring friends—more Especially—it will be to your Venerable
and highly Esteemed—The Honᵇˡᵉ John Adams Esqʳ in his Eighty
fifth year—when late interesting letter of the 20ʰ Insᵗ Addressed to
Mʳ Joseph Milligan—I have most feelingly read. requested Copy—
(herewith inclosed)—as a Valuable Memento for preserving—. The
powers of his Mind still strong—but the hand feeble and quivering—
excites the Melancholy gloom of decayed Nature, scarce ledgible.—to
gratify his Urgent request to Mʳ Milligan—induced me to risque that
confidence reposed in letters—by transmitting to Mʳ Adams—(thro
Mʳ Milligan—) your Original to me—for which I promise my self
you will excuse
I am Dear Sir
most Respectfully your Obedᵗ servant.   JOHN BARNES

RC (MHi); misdated; endorsed by TJ
as received 6 Dec. 1818 and so recorded in
SJL. RC (MHi); address cover only; with
PoC of TJ to James Eastburn & Company, 3 May 1819, on verso; addressed:
"Thomas Jefferson Esqr Monticello, Virginia"; franked; postmarked Georgetown,
30 Nov.

John Adams had recently begun his
eighty-fourth (not EIGHTY FIFTH) year
(*ANB*). In his letter to Joseph Milligan,
Quincy, 20 Nov. 1818, a copy of which
was enclosed here, Adams thanked Milligan for a book, commented on agri-

culture and horticulture, and concluded:
"Can you give me any Intelligence of Mʳ
Jefferson, I have received allarming in-
timations, without any certain information. He is the last and oldest of my
confidential bosom friends, let party, faction and politicks, say what they will" (Tr
in MHi, on verso of Tr of TJ to Barnes,
11 Nov. 1818, at head of text: "Copy," at
foot of text: "Mʳ Joseph Milligan George
Town Columbia"; FC in Lb in MHi:
Adams Papers). Milligan transmitted the
ORIGINAL of TJ to Barnes, 11 Nov. 1818,
in a 30 Nov. 1818 letter to Adams (RC in
MHi: Adams Papers).

From Stephen Cathalan

My Dear Sir   Marseilles the 30th november 1818

    by my last Respects of the 13th august last, by the Brig Siro, Geo Lockyer[1] Master bound for Philad[a] and in answer to your kind favor of the 5th april, I acknowledged you Receipt of your Remitance on lafitte & c[o] of Paris p[r] F 2205=; I Received Since the 2[ta] of your Said Letter, also your Two Lines (no Date) Inclosing the 4th Bill of Said Remit[ce]

TJ
n° 1 a 8

N° 9

    Tho' Since deprived of your favours, I hope that my Letters of the 30th March, 25th april and of the 2[d] May last, will have Reached you;—this Last Inclosed my Invoice of 8 Boxes of 24 B[les] Each, Red wine 1814 of Bergasse (you ordered me by yours of the 18th January) of one Baskett Maccarony, amounting to F 257=70=

with 1 Box of 24 B[les] of Said Bergasse's wine returned here from Senegal, and having much Emproved in quality, by Crossing the Tropick I wished you Should taste it, with your Good Grand Son & Friends;—The whole I Shipped on the Ship Fair Trader G T. Fletcher Master Bound for alexandria virg[ia] Consigned to the Collector of that district;

    in my Letter of the 25th april, I Expressed you =my Gratitude & wishes to be Continued in the office of Consul of the U.s. and to Post-pone my Second Request, thro' your Self, for obtaining Permission to Resign it to a future and Indefinite Epoqua;=

    Tho' I am Since Deprived of your Favours, I hope that you enjoy of Such a good State of health as I wish you may be and to Continue for many years in the Bosom of your good Family, Friends and neighburgs;—

    for my own Part, I will Inform you that I have been afflicted in the last Days of Sep[ber] & in october last, with a <u>Gastrique</u> or Bilious Fever, that M[rs] Cathalan falled Sick also, near about the Same time, on Account of her Constant good Cares near me, Days and nights; but, that owing to the allmighty, and to our Doctor M;—Both, we are now perfectly Recovered;—this D[or] M. M[r] Serrier is the Doctor of the hospital of this City, and he Confers his attendance & best Cares to the American Seamen I Send to Said hospital;—

    This Sickness and Long Convalescence, are the motives which have prevented me, hitherto, to Send you the herewith Inclosed Two Bills of Loading & Two Invoices of the Sundry articles, therein detailled, you ordered me by your's of the 5th april last, which I Shipped on Board the Brig Planter of Petersburg D[el] anderson M[er] bound for

Petersburg—Virg^{ia} which Sailed from this Port on the 21st oct^{ber} last, & which I hope you will Soon Receive after this Date;

The Invoice for your own account, amounts to   F 1068=60=
the other one for acc^t of Th^s Jefferson Randolph Esqr
your Good G^d Son in Law, to   244=30=

which Sums I have charged on your Debit;—

the whole was Consigned to the Collector of the District of Petersburg, as you will observe it by the herein Copy of my Letter to him of the 21st october Last;

by the Bill of Lading for your Acc^t you will observe that I Shipped also, one Box Cont^{ing} Immortals Flowers for your Ladies Grand Daughters; They will find amongst them Some ones of a different & Darker Colours; Those are[2] died, which is done with that kind of Chimical Composition, whereof there was in that Box, a Small bit, a Part whereof being disolved into Fresh water, as Soon as that flower is touched with that dissolution, it Changes it's Colour; this Instruction, I apprehend to have forgot to write on a Paper, wrapping that Composition, when I, with Mrs Cath^n, in our Convalescence, & Just out of fevers; were making up, our Selves, that Box.

the only one article mentionned in your List, which I could not Send you by that vessel, is =the 50 lb Raisins of Smyrna Sans Pepins,= as there was none in Town to be procured, Since I Received your order, & if any Should arive here, which may be in winter, I will Send you the quantity Requested;

on the Back Part of my afore mentioned Invoices, there is an abstract of your & your Grand Son's acc^t cur^t by which it Results a Balance in your favor p^r F 1=58= to your Credit on a new-Acc^t

your Letter of the 22^d February to Mr A. F^{is} Sasserno of Nice, with his Consular Commission and other Documents from the Secr^{ry} of State, Reached him in october Last; this Packet was forwarded, (I think from Trieste) to our Consul at Naples, who forwarded it to me, by Sea, & I to Mr Sasserno; I herein Inclose you his Letter in answer to yours;—

a Propos of Consular[3] Commissions or Patents, by my Letter of the 19th august Last, to h. Ex^{cy} alb^t Gallatin, Minister P. P^{ry} of the U.s. at Paris, I mentioned to him, that =I was Surprised that my name, as Consul of the U.s. or Comm^{al} Agent of the U.s. for Marseilles had not been Inserted, as before, in the almanacks Royal of the years 1816=17—& 18= that I had wrote to h.E. on that Same Subject on the 27th March 1817—but as I had not Received on it any answer from him, I was; then, Reiterating my Request for his answer, on the motives which might be the Cause of Such an Ommission;=—

I Received the Following answer;　　=Paris 2^d Sep^{ber} 1818=

=your Letter of the 19th ult^o has been Received by me, in the absence of Mr Gallatin, who has gone for Some time to England;—I am unable to Inform you, of the Reason why your name, as Consul of the U.s. at Marseilles, is omitted in the Almanack Royal;—all those from the united States, whose names are there Inserted, have been appointed by the President, <u>Since the Return of the king and have Received Exequaturs from his Majesty</u>=; =I have the honor to be Very Respectfully &^{a} &^{a}=^{4}

(Signed) =D^l Sheldon J^r= (the Sec^{ry} of the U.S. Legation)

Thus, My Dear Sir, I am Still & fully Exercising under your own Commission, when President, directed to the 1st Consul B^a Parté and in virtue of his own Exequatur, & while new Commissions have been Granted to the other Consuls appointed for this kingdom, the one for me (or I) has been Forgoten in/or by the Depart^{nt} of State;—you will find this unregular, as I might, one Day, be questioned for it, by the Existing authorities of the King, tho' they have not, to my knowledge, yet observed this unregularity;—

I Receive from them dayly, Testimonies of their Satisfaction for my having been So Long Continued in office and in Préfference to a new one, which I am owing to your Self!

I have not wrote, nor I will write on that Subject to the Secretary of State, as I hope that Since you may have Received my Letter of the 25th april & the President Consenting to lett me Continue in office, he will have Caused a Commission to be made out for me, Signed by him & Forwarded to me by the Secr^{ry} of State;

with my best Sincere wishes for you & your worthy Family, I have the honor to be with great Respect

My Dear Sir

Your very Gratefull, Devoted & obedient Servant

STEPHEN CATHALAN.

RC (MHi); addressed: "Thos Jefferson Esqr &^{a} &^{a} Monticello"; endorsed by TJ as received 2 Apr. 1819 and so recorded in SJL; with additional notation by TJ beneath signature related to his response of 26 May 1819:
"√my last　Apr. 5. 18.
　√quality of the Nice.
　√reduction of duties. never send in cask
　√guard ag^t calling Claret or Bordeaux
　√Bergesse send an adventure
　√　　　imitate Nice."
Enclosures: Victor Adolphus Sasserno to TJ, 18 Aug., 14 Oct. 1818. Enclosed bills of lading not found. Other enclosures printed below.

For the TWO LINES (NO DATE) by TJ to Cathalan enclosing the 4TH BILL of exchange for his remittance, see note to James H. McCulloch to TJ, 30 June 1818. The COLLECTOR for Alexandria was Charles Simms. TJ's LETTER OF THE 22^D FEBRUARY 1818 was to Sasserno. The CONSUL AT NAPLES was Alexander Hammett. Cathalan's LETTER OF THE 19TH AUGUST LAST to Albert Gallatin is in DNA: RG 84, LRF. The 1ST CONSUL of France was Napoleon Bonaparte (Bᴬ PARTÉ).

[1] Manuscript: "Lookyer."

[2] Cathalan here canceled "Dyed."
[3] Manuscript: "Coasular."
[4] Omitted closing guillemet editorially supplied.

ENCLOSURES

I

Stephen Cathalan to Joseph Jones

SIR   Marseilles the 21ˢᵗ october 1818—

by order[1] of Thoˢ Jefferson Esqʳ late President of the U. States, I Remit you herein Inclosed; viz;

TJ   1 Bill of Lading for wines & other articles for his own Acct[2] marked as in Margin—

TᴿJ   1 Bill of Lading for wines for the acct[3] of Thˢ Jefferson Randolph Esqʳ his Grand Son in Law;—

which I have Shipped on the Brig Planter of Petersburg Dᵉˡ anderson Master, bound for Petersburg—Virginia, to your Consignation;—

you will Please, after his arival, to Receive Said articles, and to forward them as Soon as Possible to Thˢ Jefferson Esqʳ at Monticello, & to his Grand Son in Law what belongs to him.—

you will Please, also, in Conformity of the Instructions of Thˢ Jefferson Esqʳ to make Separate accounts or Bills for all your Disbursments, for Freight, Duties & other Expenses; one against Said Late President, and the other against his G. Son in Law, as I am Directed by his G. Father to make[4] Separate Invoices for Each of them, which however I Send to the Grand Father;

This Brig being Ready to Sail out, as I have not[5] been able to Collect all the Bills for their Cost and Charges, I cannot make out Said Invoices, nor transmit them to you, for the Recovery of the Duties of Importation in the U.S. of Said articles;—which I will do by the way of Bordeaux or havre; you will please to Inform, on arival, Thˢ Jefferson Esqʳ of this Shipment to your Consignation, not having time to do it, myself, by this opportunity & not being yet Recovered of a Serious Bilious Fever![6] with a tender of my best Services, in whatever I may be usefull to you or to your Friends Recommended by you to me, in this Corner of the Mediteranean within my Consular District; I have the honor to be Respectfully

Sir your most obedᵗ Servᵗ   STEPHEN CATHALAN.[7]

Tr (MHi); at head of text: "Copy"; addressed: "The Collector of the District of Petersburg State of Virginia Petersburg—Virgⁱᵃ." RC (NcD: Jones Papers); notation by Jones on verso of final page: "5ᵗʰ Febʸ 1819.   Sent the Bills of Lading. & draft on Mʳ Patrick Gibson of Richmond to Mʳ Charles K. Mallory Norfk

Collr.   Jos. Jones Collr." Enclosures not found.

[1] RC: "by order & for the Account."
[2] RC: "private account."
[3] RC: "private account."
[4] Instead of remainder of sentence, RC reads "out them, but to Send to him, how-

ever as I do, & as directed my Invoices or Bills, to him;—you may then do the Same for your Disbursments."

[5] In RC sentence to this point reads "This brig being on the Point of Sailing out, & as I have been Severely Sick Since the 24th Sep[br] last, till four Days ago, that I am Recovering; I have not."

[6] Instead of text from "Bordeaux or havre" to this point, RC reads "havre or Bordeaux, & I hope that my Letter to you, will Reach you before the arival at Petersburg of the Brig Planter; as I apprehend of not having time to write Two Lines to my old Respect[ble] Friend & Protector Th[s] Jefferson, by this Brig, by the above-mentioned motives (which I will

do by the ways I mention to you) I will beg of you to Inform him, on the arival of the Planter, that She has on Board, all the articles ordered by him, Except the Smyrna Raisins, Sans Pepins, which I could not Procure, as there is none to be Got in Town; it was too late when his order Reached me, on the 13th august, as the Raisins of Smyrna, when ordered from this, arives here in March & till the End of april, yearly & are Soon Consumed, or Sent out from this City, after their Landing on Shore."

[7] RC includes a postscript reading "I Beg of you to Excuse my bad hand & the Irregularity of this Letter, which I have not to copy again;— S. C[n]."

II

Stephen Cathalan's Invoice of Items Shipped to Thomas Jefferson

Invoice of Sundries Shipped by Step Cathalan Esq[r] by order & for account & risk of Th[s] Jefferson Esq[r] at Monticello (Virg[a]) on board the brig Planter of Petersburg, D[el] Anderson Master bound to Petersb, (Virginia) to the Consignation of the Collector of that District;—Viz:

			F	¢
TJ	Six boxes of 50 Bott[ls] each red wine of Bellet			
EC	(Nice) of 1812; Say 300 B[les] a f 1,56[¢l] P[r]			
N[o] 1 a 6	Bottle, charges & package included at Nice		468	
	Freight from Nice to Marseilles as P[r] Bill	F 9		
	Porterage, Custom, Duty, Store rent at the entrepot &[ca] &[ca]	13 60	22	60
		F	490	60
TJ	One Cask, in double Cask, old Rivesaltes wine, Invoice of F[cois] Durand of Perpignan, of the 4th of Sept[b]			
	Velting 32 veltes at f 10, P[r] velte	F 320		
	Cask & Double Cask	21		
	Transport from Rivesaltes to S[t] Laurent & other charges at that place	9.		
	Freight from S[t] Laurent to Marseilles	15		
	Porterage at Marseilles, Store rent of the Entrepot, Craftage, Duty &[c]	10 15	375	15
TJ	Three boxes containing Superfine olive oil of Aix Together N54 oil; the bottles Packing, Duties included &[ca] a f 3,15[¢] P[r] bottle		113	40
TJ	One boxe containing 12 bottles Anchovies @ f 2,75[¢] P[r] bottle on board		33	

TJ One Basket macaroni 𝒩𝒜𝒲 105 all charges included
   on board à f 53,50

		56	15
	F	1068	90

Marseilles 26th of Octobr 1818.
E. E.   STEPHEN CATHALAN.

MS (MHi); in a clerk's hand, signed by Cathalan; on p. 2 of sheet folded to form four pages, with Cathalan's Invoice of Items Shipped to Thomas Jefferson Randolph, 26 Oct. 1818, on p. 1, TJ's Account with Cathalan, 30 Nov. 1818, on p. 3, and p. 4 blank.

[n]54 OIL: presumably "54 pounds of oil net weight." Inferring from other Cathalan documents, the abbreviation and symbol following MACARONI evidently stand for "pounds net ancient weight of Marseille." E. E.: "Errors Excepted."

[1] Above this amount TJ noted: ".29¼."

III

Stephen Cathalan's Invoice of Items Shipped to Thomas Jefferson Randolph

Invoice of Sundry wines Shipp'd by Stepn Cathalan Esqr for account & risk of Ths Jefferson Randolph Esqr by order of Ths Jefferson Esqr at Monticello (Virga) on board the brig Planter of Petersburg Del Anderson Master bound for Petersburg & to the Consignation of the Collector for that District;   Viz:

T^RJ One Cask in double Cask old Rivesaltes wine				
velting 16 veltes @ f 10 Pr velte	F 160			
The Cask & double Cask	12			
Transport from Rivesaltes to St Laurent	6			
Charges at Marseilles:				
Freight from St Laurent to Marseilles	9			
Portages, craftage, Store rent of the Entrepot, Duty				
of Export &c	6	193		
T^RJ Two boxes of 24 bottles Each red wine of Bergasse				
Claret; 48 Bottles @ f 1,	F 48			
Portage, craftage & duty	3 60	51	60	
		F 244	60	

Marseilles the 26th of Octobr 1818
E. E. STEPHEN CATHALAN.

MS (MHi); in a clerk's hand, signed by Cathalan; on p. 1 of sheet folded to form four pages, with Cathalan's Invoice of Items Shipped to TJ, 26 Oct. 1818, on p. 2, TJ's Account with Cathalan, 30 Nov. 1818, on p. 3, and p. 4 blank.

The COLLECTOR for Petersburg was Joseph Jones.

Thomas Jefferson's Account with Stephen Cathalan

Deb[r]				Th[s] Jefferson Esq[r] in acc[t] Curr[t] with Step[n] Cathalan.	Cred[or]
F 240,05	March	30th 1818.		Due me by Th[s] Jefferson Randolph, to balance	
392 77	Avril	28.	"	id by Th[s] Jefferson id	
257.70	"	"	"	To my Invoice of 8 Casses, wine of Bergasse & one basket of Macarony.	
	July	16th 1818		by Step[n] Girard's Draft remitted to me by J. Vaughan by his order & for his account	2205
1068 30	October	26.	"	To my Invoice Per brig Planter for his account & risk as here annexed	
244 60	"	"	"	To my Invoice P[r] said brig Planter for account of his G[d] Son Th[s] Jefferson Randolph, as here annexed.	
1 58	"	"	"	Balance to his credit, on a new account.	
F2205 00[¢]				E. E. Marseilles the 30th nov[ber] 1818=	F. 2205[¢]
				STEPHEN CATHALAN.	

MS (MHi); in a clerk's hand, with dateline and signature in Cathalan's hand; on p. 3 of sheet folded to form four pages, with Cathalan's Invoice of Items Shipped to TJ, 26 Oct. 1818, on p. 2, his Invoice of Items Shipped to Thomas Jefferson Randolph, 26 Oct. 1818, on p. 1, and p. 4 blank.

From William F. Gray

SIR,   Fredericksburg Nov. 30. 1818

Your several favours respecting the Box of Books that you sent for me to bind, with the Books themselves, have been duly rec[d]—On examining[1] the Books, I find some of the periodical works are not entire; and before they are bound up I thought it right to ask you if you were apprised of this, and if you wish them bound as sent, or not.—The "Port Folio," in particular, lacks several numbers.—The "Emporium," you call "3 Vols"—There are three Vols[2] of Judge Coopers, and three Nos. of D[r] Coxe's which preceeded Cooper's. Shall I bind them as sent or seperate them?

I shall be very happy in supplying your orders as far as in my power, and hope I shall generally be able to do it to your satisfaction. The copy of Bowditch's Book shall be forwarded to you as soon as it can be procured.—

I have a general correspondence with the Booksellers in the northern Towns, and they are very prompt in supplying my orders, and in sending me every thing that is new; so that any thing that you may see advertised by any of them, you can get from me nearly as soon as you could by ordering it from the advertizer, and at the same price.

You may expect the Books that you sent to be bound, in a fortnight from this.

Respectfully Your Obt. Svt.   W^M F. GRAY

RC (DLC); endorsed by TJ as received   [1] Manuscript: "examing."
6 Dec. 1818 and so recorded in SJL.   [2] Word interlined.

From Samuel Knox

SIR   Balt^re College Novr 30th 1818.

A gentleman of this city, and friend of mine, in passing, some time since, thro' Virginia, and Near to your Seat, Informed me that he fell in with your Nephew Mr Carr, who kindly enquir'd after me—And also Inform'd him that he had Recently heard you expressing a wish, that if I was not otherwise engag'd, some place Suited to me, might be found in your intended University. Owing chiefly to that casual circumstance, as Related to me, and the idea also, that I shall soon be disengag'd I have presum'd on the Liberty of writing to you on that Subject.

Ever since the popular ferment, previous to your Presidential Election, I have been the victim of Party Persecution. At an Annual Meeting of the general Assembly of the church to which I Belong, at Winchester in Virginia, in the month of May preceding your[1] Election, I happen'd to be a Delegate from the Presbytery of Baltimore. In the Course of that Session it was Render'd manifest to several members from Pennsylvania—And from Virginia, of the same principles with myself, that thro' the Influence of Jedadiah Morse, Near to Boston— and a few other influential men, then at the Assembly—it's Sitting there, that year—Connected with some matters, then under discussion, was intended to prejudice the Southern Members, who Attended, against your Election. This, I Set myself Against with all the energies in my power And for which, however humble or limited the sphere of that power, or any personal Influence I possess'd, I was not soon to be forgiven.

On the same Acc^t a hostile spirit was taken up Against me by the Trustees of Fredericktown Academy, at that time Under my Direction. The Messrs Potts—And other highly Fed^l Gentlemen of that place Remov'd their Sons And plac'd them at Princeton college—Assigning as their Motive that they had been improperly Instructed by me. To counteract a procedure so groundless and malignant—I was forc'd to Send on an Address to the Faculty of Princeton college, Requesting, in the most earnest manner, an examination of the Youth from Fredericktown—And the favour of a certificate of the manner in which They had acquitted themselves on that Examination, on being admitted to their college. The Result was very flattering to me—I Receiv'd a certificate, which the circumstances mentioned Induc'd me to publish, "that no Youths had ever Entered that college, who Done more credit to themselves, or to their Instructor."[2]

That, however, and the Desire of being disconnected from such Patrons of public Education—and parents who could so treat the Instructor of their Sons, Soon afterwards Induced me to Resign the charge of that Institution, at which I had previously a greater Number of students from the different counties in Maryland—and some from the adjacent counties in Virginia than was at that time, in the State college at Annapolis, tho' Endow'd with an Annuity of Seventeen Hundred pounds—And Conducted by a Faculty of considerable Reputation as to literary Acquirements.

After some disappointments, I was Induc'd to Settle in this City. Several friends Had Influenc'd me to Believe that I would Her[e] Breathe, in an Atmosphere, more Congenial with my principles and habits of thinking, than that which I had last experienc'd. At that time, a Number of the Respectable citizens of this place Had obtain'd from the Legislature of Maryland a charter for a college, on liberal principles; but without any Endowment, but such as might be Rais'd by a Lottery; or Voluntary Donations. The first Principal of this New Establishment was a Mr James Priestley—Now, I Believe, of Cumberland college, State of Tenessee. He Relinquish'd Balt^{re} college on Acc^t of a Differenc[e] with it's Trustees, Respecting the quantum of his Emolument. The College was Suspended for some time—And afterwards Resum'd Under my Direction. The tide of Party-Spirit, however, still Ran high against me—Not a Fed^l Gentleman would put a Son under my tuition. The college of St Mary, in this place, was much more Congenial with their principles—And the Jesuitical Spirit of which, I had first the Honour of developing to the public.

At present, tho' Balt^{re} College, without funds or Endowment, Still maintains an Existence—And tho' many Youths of Considerable promise of Usefulness to their country Have here finish'd their Course of Education—And tho' a few Patrons also particularly William Pinkney Esqre Late Envoy to Russia, still afford Us all their Countenance;

Yet, the Institution is unable to Support itself, Against such discouragement, in any proper Consistency with it's designation as a College.

Indeed I Regret much, Having it to Say, that the Gentlemen of Any Influence, in this place, from whom I had Reason to expect most—Have Never Been liberal as to the patronage of public Education. Several of them think it, on a liberal scale, an Obstruction to Mercantile Success. Previous to the late war when those principles, for a time, Had the Ascendency in this State, Which I had, without Regard to persons or parties, always Considered, as most salutary to civil and Religious Liberty; I hoped to Obtain some Aid to our college from the Gen¹ Assembly of the State—But the application was in Vain—The State Treasury, it was Said, could afford Nothing to colleges. Indeed, Several of the Fed¹ Gentlemen, then at Annapolis, frankly told me that Nothing would be Done for public Education, while that Party, to which I had attach'd myself, was in Power.

Since that time, a Sectarian Spirit, still more Injurious to Liberal Education, has Arisen in Baltimore. The Catholics have their favourite Seminary. The Episcopalians theirs'—And the Methodists, the most Numerous of any, at last Session of Assembly, obtain'd a charter, for their Ashbury college, for which they Manifest their Usual Zeal and Exertion.

In addition to all these obstructions to the Success of Baltʳᵉ College, I was so Unhappy as to have a serious Difference with one of our Trustees, a Revᵈ Gentleman of this city, on Account of Some Discipline to which his Son was Subjected at college. His Conduct to me, was most malignant and Unwarrantable, Tho' a countryman of my Own, Himself too a persecuted man, Yet Neither the Sacred Investiture he Bore, Nor Any other motive that ought to Have Influenc'd his professional Example and character, Restrain'd him from a conduct toward me and my professional Standing and Interest, as unjust, and as malevolent, as Any Individual ever Resorted to, or adopted against another.

I could not Justify myself in intruding on your attention, an Occurrence so disagreeable, Only that I have heard that man vainly Boast of the Interest he had in your Esteem—as also in that of Mʳ & Mʳˢ Madison—And Judging from other circumstances in his conduct to me, equally as improbable, Did not know but the Breath of his malignity might, on some Occasion, such as this, Extend itself even to You

A Consciousness of Integrity; And also an Open and impartial And Unanimous Decision of the matter at Issue, between us, by the Board of Trustees, in my favour, Have fully Convinc'd the Public, where it was known, of the ground of that Revd Gentleman's Malignity—And that he Injur'd himself more by it, than he Did the Victim whom he so wantonly and perseveringly Sought to Overwhelm.

Having thus, I fear disagreeably, Introduc'd myself—The only apology I can make for it is, That I Deem'd it necessary for your Information, in Judging Correctly of the following Overture, which I now take the Liberty, very Respectfully, to Submit.

Having Observ'd in our public papers, that you Are particularly and Zealously Engag'd in founding an University in your Vicinity for the State of Virginia—And Judging that you will, consequently, Have to Employ a Variety of Professors or Instructors, to Supply the Different Departments in that Institution, I have thought that it might be possible that I would Succeed in Obtaining, thro' You, Some place in it, Suited to My qualifications; And where my Services Migh[t] find also a more extensive Sphere of Usefulness, than Under existing Circumstances, my present Situation affords.

Being a Widower—And my children, four Daughters, all Respectably and comfortably Settled in the world—And [m]ore independent, in that respect, than their father, my Views, I beg leave to Assure you, are not so much turn'd to Emolument—As to a sincere Desire of being more generally Useful to Society.

At the University of Glasgow, where I finishd my course of Education—and there obtain'd the highest Degree Conferr'd on a Student, I pass'd thro' a course of Genl Science and Literature—But as well there, as in my professional practice since, Have been most conversant with the 'Literæ humaniores,' or classical Learning. In that Department, I think I could still Render essential Service to Any Seminary founded on an extensive Scale of Usefulness—And tho' Principal of a college, where I now Reside, would have no objection to Serve as a member of any faculty, in a University, in Any Department I thought myself qualified to fill with credit And Usefulness. Though considerably Advanc'd in Life, I Bless God I continue to enjoy good Health, And a capacity for Industry And exertion—And the smallest Greek print I meet with, I can yet Read without Spectacles—Notwithstanding all this, However, I fear I shall Stand Condemn'd, as to Age—by the garrulous egotism of this Letter, if on no other Account.

In every Establishment, Such as that which I Suppos[e] You Now contemplate, much Depends on the talents, Zeal And Industry of the Faculty employ'd. Without these combin'd—It cannot Succeed. Without these, however liberally endowed It cannot be lastingly Useful.

The greatest Characters for Scientific and literary attainment, Seldom make the best Instructors—And yet without Such characters, at least as part of the Faculty, No <u>University</u> Could be Reputable.

Much Depends, also, on proper Accommodations. I have Seen Some few of the best colleges And Academies in Europe—And Several also in this country—But I have Seen none as well Calculated for preserving good Order and Discipline As I think they might be. When the Building and Accommodations of that in which I now Instruct, was in a state of preparation, I endeavour'd, to Have them adapted to my Views—But Owing to some of the Obstructions, already mention'd, I found that a Building Committee, or even An Architect or carpenter, was Consider'd, by a Majority of our Board of Trustees, as knowing better what was adapted to these purposes than the Instructor of long Experience.

I Have now Submitted to you, with no little Reluctance, such circumstantial Information as I deem'd Necessary, for your being in possession of, Respecting any Individual, who should Aspire to the Honour of your countenance as a candidate for any Department in that laudable Establishment And Undertaking in which you Are Engag'd.

That it may please Divine Providence to Spare your Useful Life, to See its' Advantages Realised by Society, is the Sincere prayer of your greatly Respectful And most Obed^t H^{ble} Servt SAM^L KNOX

RC (DLC); edges trimmed and torn; endorsed by TJ as received 9 Dec. 1818 and so recorded in SJL. RC (CSmH: JF); address cover only; with PoC of TJ to John Wayles Eppes, 7 Apr. [1819], on recto and verso; addressed: "Thomas Jefferson Esqre Monticello Albemarle County Virginia"; franked; postmarked Baltimore, 3 Dec.

Late in 1802 Knox wrote an open letter to the sixteen TRUSTEES OF FREDERICK-TOWN ACADEMY lamenting that none of them had attended the 23 Dec. examination at the school; giving the full results; attributing the absence of many trustees to party spirit; and vindicating his competence by including a 14 Dec. letter from the faculty of the College of New Jersey (later Princeton University) affirming that the performance of Knox's former students who had enrolled at the college was "creditable to themselves and honorable to their instructor" (Frederick

Bartgis's Republican Gazette, 31 Dec. 1802).

The MESS^{RS} POTTS of Frederick, Maryland, were Richard Potts and his brother William Potts. Richard's namesake son joined William's sons Robert B. Potts and William Potts in studying at Princeton in the first decade of the nineteenth century (*DAB*; Thomas Maxwell Potts, comp., *Historical Collections relating to The Potts Family in Great Britain and America* [1901], 357–9; *Princeton Catalogue*, 116–8, 406).

The STATE COLLEGE AT ANNAPOLIS was Saint John's College, which was established in 1785 with an initial legislative annuity of £1,750 and briefly paired with Washington College in Chestertown as the first state university (Bernard C. Steiner, *History of Education in Maryland* [1894], 95). On 20 Dec. 1810 the Maryland House of Delegates considered adding SOME AID for Baltimore College to a bill endowing academies, but the provision was rejected and the bill tabled (*Votes and Proceedings of the House of Delegates of the State of Maryland* [Annapolis, (1811)], 85–6).

Saint Mary's College was the FAVOURITE SEMINARY of Baltimore's Catholics, while the Methodists preferred Asbury (ASHBURY) College, which was organized in 1816 and chartered by the Maryland General Assembly in February 1818 (Steiner, *Education*, 247–8). Knox had

quarreled in Baltimore with John Glendy (the REV^D GENTLEMAN), a fellow Irish immigrant and Presbyterian clergyman (John Patterson to TJ, 11 Aug. 1817). LITERÆ HUMANIORES: the humanities, especially classical literature (*OED*).

[1] Manuscript: "you."
[2] Omitted closing quotation mark editorially supplied.

To Frederick A. Mayo

SIR   Monticello Nov. 30. 18.

I have just made up two boxes of pamphlets which I send to Milton to be forwarded to you by the boats of that place so soon as the state of the river will permit. these contain 39 volumes of which 38. are to be half bound only, moderately gilt on the backs, lettered according to the papers stuck in them respectively, corresponding with the list on the next page, and their leaves to be trimmed. one volume, (the correspondence of Cortés & Charles V.) I send merely that you may give me on it a specimen of your best binding. I am particular in my bindings, and have hitherto been obliged to send my choice books to Millegan in George town, because I have found no workman in America but him who can give me such as the London and Paris bindings. besides the good taste with which he works, a book bound by him is as heavy as a piece of metal, while the common bindings of this country are so spongy, that after a book has been once opened, it will never shut close again. therefore I repeat that I wish you to shew on this volume the best work you can do (but not Marocco). when the books are ready be so good as to notify me by mail and send your bill and I will inclose you an order for the amount, and direct how the boxes are to be returned to me. I shall be glad to recieve them with as little delay as the solidity of the work will admit, and I salute you with respect.   TH: JEFFERSON

8^vos   Pamphlets historical
         Pamphlets historical.
         Natural history.
         Pamphlets. Medical.
         Pamphlets. Navigation
         Pamphlets. Arts
         Pamphlets. Education

Pamphlets. Agriculture
Friend of peace.
Discourses. Unitarian.
Pamphlets. Religious.
Pamphlets. Religious.
Pamphlets. Law.
Pamphlets. Political.
Commerce. Money.
Political. Foreign.
Political. Foreign.
Orations.
American magazine.
Reviews.
Weekly Register. 1811.12.
Weekly Register 1812.
Weekly Register 1812.13.
Weekly Register 1813

$\left.\right\}$ E^{t}c. to 1818. being 14. vols.

4^{tos} Historical.
Physiological.
Convention of 1775.
Languages.

12mo Cortès à Charles V.

P.S. I inclose herewith a pamphlet which was overlooked till after the boxes were nailed up, and which I pray you to add to the volume of 'Discourses Unitarian.'

PoC (DLC); on reused address cover of Nathaniel Bowditch to TJ, 20 Aug. 1818; adjacent to signature: "Mr Frederic A. Mayo"; endorsed by TJ. Enclosure not found.

Frederick August Mayo (1785–1853), bookbinder, was born Friedrich Gotthilf Mejo in Nossen, Saxony, and learned his trade in Germany. He worked throughout Europe as a bookbinder until he was impressed into the British navy. Mayo spent nearly four years as a sailor before arriving in the United States by 1808, when he set up shop in Staunton. In 1815 he established a bindery and book and stationery store in Richmond, working in partnership with Philip DuVal as Frederick A. Mayo & Company. After that firm dissolved, Mayo joined with John Frayser as Mayo & Frayser, 1816–17. By 1821 Mayo had gone bankrupt and given up his book and stationery business. He returned to bookbinding as his main employment and so continued until 1836. TJ sent him numerous books and pamphlets to be bound between 1818 and 1825. Mayo also operated a public garden beginning in 1822 at Springhill, his home near Richmond. In addition to his lengthy career as a bookbinder, he worked as a land agent and frequently traveled west to explore and acquire land. In 1850 Mayo authored a book encouraging Germans to immigrate to the United States (Hannah D. French, "Thomas Jefferson's Last Bookbinder: Frederick August Mayo," in her *Bookbinding in Early Amer-*

ica: *Seven Essays on Masters and Methods* [1986], 148–220; *Staunton Political Censor*, 24 Aug. 1808; DNA: RG 29, CS, Augusta Co., 1810, Henrico Co., 1820–50; Staunton *Spirit of the Press*, 18 May 1811; Richmond *Enquirer*, 29 Apr. 1815; *Richmond Enquirer*, 7 Oct. 1815, 30 Mar., 3 July 1816, 28 Feb., [4] Apr. 1817, 24 Feb., 11 Aug. 1818, 6 Mar., 8 Oct. 1819, 30 Jan. 1836, 26 Apr. 1853; Richmond *Virginia Argus*, 24 Apr., 19 June 1816; TJ to Mayo, 28 Dec. 1820; Mayo to TJ, 2 Apr. 1821; Mayo, *40 Jahre in Virginien, oder Kommt nach West-Virginien!* [1850]; *Richmond Whig and Public Advertiser*, 22 Apr. 1853).

One of THE PAPERS STUCK IN the groupings to be bound, the one that TJ sent with his PAMPHLETS. NAVIGATION (Poor, *Jefferson's Library*, 5 [no. 217]), can be found with his bound set in PPAmP. DISCOURSES. UNITARIAN: Poor, *Jefferson's Library*, 9 (no. 532). COMMERCE. MONEY: Poor, *Jefferson's Library*, 12 (no. 710). The two volumes of pamphlets described as POLITICAL. FOREIGN are Poor, *Jefferson's Library*, 11 (nos. 680–1). ORATIONS: Poor, *Jefferson's Library*, 13 (no. 826); TJ's copy in ViU. REVIEWS: Poor, *Jefferson's Library*, 13 (no. 834). PHYSIOLOGICAL: Poor, *Jefferson's Library*, 7 (no. 303); TJ's copy in MBPLi. CONVENTION OF 1775: Poor, *Jefferson's Library*, 10 (no. 576); TJ's copy in Vi; see also note to Philip Doddridge to TJ, [17] Jan. 1816. LANGUAGES: possibly Poor, *Jefferson's Library*, 14 (no. 913).

From Alfred H. Dashiell

SIR,   Ellicotts Mills Dec.r 1st 1818

I presume to intrude myself upon your notice, which your generosity will forgive: & if it is to ask a favour, nothing but the greatest confidence in that benevolence which you extend towards so many, & which I myself have formerly experienced, could have given me the courage, or furnished the inducement.

Since my removal from New London to M.d, I have been endeavouring to establish a Classical Seminary in the neighbourhood of Baltimore: but from the great competition in this business, my own youth, & especially from the want of certificates, or of papers accrediting me as a Teacher, in whom confidence had been reposed, or who was entitled to it, my undertaking has not met with that encouragement which I wish, & which I hope it will merit.

My only resource, therefore, for the removal of these difficulties, is to apply to those by whom I was Known in V.a & who honoured me with their attention, for a line, which will authenticate my standing in the Academy at New London, & the credit due to my fidelity as evinced in the publick examination of its students. Could you prevail on yourself, Sir, to give me something of this purport, I need not say how gratifying it would be to all who feel an interest in my welfare, nor what an essential benefit it would render

Yr most humble & ob.t Serv.t   A H DASHIELL

[457]

P.S. Should I be honoured with an answer, have the goodness, Sir, to mention, where Francis is, & if he is pursuing his studies with his wonted diligence.   AHD.

RC (DLC); endorsed by TJ as received 9 Dec. 1818 and so recorded in SJL. RC (MoSHi: TJC-BC); address cover only; with PoC of TJ to Rodolph Schaer, 4 Apr. 1819, on verso; addressed: "Mʳ Jefferson Monticello Albemarle Vᵃ ꝥ mˡⁿ"; stamp canceled; franked; postmarked Ellicott's Mills, 3 Dec.

From Thomas Fillebrown

Sɪʀ,   Washington City, Dec. 1, 1818.

The accompanying book is most respectfully, though reluctantly, submitted to you for perusal. I am induced to this course by friends here, who have been so highly gratified with it, as to wish you might see it.—I have delayed sending for months, out of pure deference to the character of, and respect due so illustrious a personage as the late President of the United States:—but the renewed solicitations of my friends prompts me to comply with their requests, confident that your generous liberality will pardon my freedom in thus encroaching on your domestic felicity with a matter so trivial,

I believe no copy, save the enclosed, is to be found this side the place of its origin; consequently it is valued, and I am induced to expect its return. I purchased it in Vermont; and being personally acquainted with many of the leading characters alluded to in its pages, have added with my pen, the "names," where initials only were introduced. This was done for the more convenient reference of strangers, through whose hands it has so often passed and repassed, as to be almost worn out.—The matter of which it treats, will perhaps never be forgotten.—Pity for the unfortunate subjects, will induce me to lay it aside for the present after its return.

It is a source of peculiar pleasure to me to learn your health is so far re-established; and warrants a hope that your valuable life will be preserved to us yet many years.

With the highest respect and consideration.

I have the honor to be, Sir, Your most ob. servant,

Tʜ: Fɪʟʟᴇʙʀᴏᴡɴ. Jr. Clk. Navy Dept

RC (MHi); at foot of text: "Thomas Jefferson, late President U. S. Monticello, Va."; endorsed by TJ as received 6 Dec. 1818 and so recorded in SJL. Enclosure not found.

Thomas Fillebrown (1794–1873), clerk, was born in Hallowell in the Maine district of Massachusetts and moved by 1817 to Washington, D.C., where he found employment as a clerk in the Navy Department. In 1829 President Andrew Jackson learned that Fillebrown had spoken out against the alleged sexual improprieties of Margaret "Peggy" O'Neale Eaton, the wife of Secretary of War John H. Eaton. Jackson championed the virtue of Mrs. Eaton in a widely publicized scandal, and it may be no coincidence that around this time Fillebrown was removed from his position as clerk and arrested for improperly receiving commissions for his work disbursing public funds to naval hospitals. Fillebrown was soon released, sued for commissions still due to him for his government work, and was awarded $430, which it took him three decades to collect. After Jackson left office, Fillebrown regained his clerkship and spent the rest of his life working in the Navy Department's Bureau of Provisions and Clothing, at times as its chief clerk. He also served in Washington's militia from 1825 until 1860, rising to the rank of colonel in 1846 (Charles Bowdoin Fillebrown, *Genealogy of the Fillebrown Family, with Biographical Sketches* [1910], 54–7; *Letter from the Secretary of the Navy, transmitting Statements of the Names of the Clerks Employed in the Navy Department* [Washington, 1818]; Washington *Daily National Journal,* 19, 23 May 1829; *Richmond Enquirer,* 16 June 1829; DNA: RG 29, CS, Washington, D.C., 1830–70; Jackson, *Papers,* 7:197–8, 460–1, 756–8; *Reports from the Court of Claims, submitted to the House of Representatives during the Second Session of the Thirty-Fifth Congress, 1858–'59* [1859]; *JHR; JS; U.S. Statutes at Large,* 12:835 [11 Apr. 1860]; Robert Mills, *Guide to the Capitol and National Executive Offices of the United States* [1847], 61; Washington *Daily National Intelligencer,* 3 May 1851, 10 May 1861; Mills, *Guide to the Capitol and to the National Executive Offices of the United States* [1854], 57; gravestone inscription in Oak Hill Cemetery, Washington).

From Patrick Gibson

SIR   Richmond 3ᵈ Decʳ 1818—

Since writing to you on the 13ᵗʰ Ultᵒ I have not received any of your favors—your dft in favʳ of Martin Dawson $330 has been paid—I will thank you to send me blanks for the renewals of your several notes in bank—no flour has yet been received from Lynchburg the price has declined to 8⅜$ and is likely to be lower

With much respect I am

Your obᵗ Servᵗ   PATRICK GIBSON

RC (MHi); between dateline and salutation: "Mʳ Thomas Jefferson"; endorsed by TJ as received 8 Dec. 1818 and so recorded in SJL.

From Jean Guillaume Hyde de Neuville

Monsieur   W. 3 Xᵇʳᵉ 1818

un evenement heureux Pour la france et Pour lhumanité ne peut que Vous interesser vivement, jai donc l'honneur de vous adresser l'extrait du moniteur qui annonce officiellᵗ l'evacuation entière du territoire francais Par l'armée d'occupation.

Lundi dernier ma patrie a été rendue à toute Son independance; Le Sentiment de Bonheur que cette Pensée me fait eprouver est si vif que je ne resiste Point au Plaisir de transmettre bien vite cette grande et importante Nouvelle aux hommes qui Savent le mieux apprécier l'amour du Pays. Vous, Monsieur, qui avez tant fait Pour le vôtre et dont tous les instans, même dans la retraite, Sont consacrés à lui être utile vous excuserez aisement mon importunité et concevrez que du moment ou jai voulu Parler de la france et de Son bonheur jai du necessairement Penser à lun de Ses Plus illustres amis.

Permettez monsieur que je saisisse cette occasion de vous remercier et de l'accueil que vous avez bien voulu me faire, et de la lettre obligeante que vous venez d'ecrire à Mr Crawford, relativement au tarif de nos vins. Je ne doute Plus du Succès de ma reclamation, Puisque Vous avez bien voulu lui Prêter votre appui. elle est juste, elle Sera utile, votre opinion Suffit Pour Le démontrer, et Pour faire naître la conviction dans tous les esprits. Agréez, avec lexpression de ma gratitude, celle des Sentimens de haute consideration et de respect avec lesquels jai lhonneur d'être

Monsieur

Votre très humble et très ob^t Serviteur

G. HYDE DE NEUVILLE

Permettez que Mad^e Randolph et Mlles Ses filles trouvent ici l'assurance de mon respect et Mr Randolph[1] celle de ma consideration très distinguée et de mon regret de navoir point eu lhonneur de le rencontrer.—

EDITORS' TRANSLATION

SIR Washington 3 December 1818

As a fortunate event for France and humanity cannot but interest you deeply, I am honored to send you an extract from the *Moniteur* officially announcing the complete evacuation of the occupation army from French territory.

Last Monday my homeland became fully independent again. This thought gives me so much happiness that I cannot resist the pleasure of immediately transmitting such grand and important news to men who know best how to appreciate the love of one's country. You, Sir, who have done so much for your own and whose entire time, even in retirement, is devoted to being useful to it, will easily forgive my importunity and understand that as soon as I wanted to talk about France and its happiness, I necessarily thought of one of its most illustrious friends.

Allow me, Sir, to seize this opportunity to thank you for your kindness in having made me feel so welcome and for your recent obliging letter to Mr. Crawford regarding the tariff on our wines. I no longer doubt the success of my complaint, inasmuch as you were kind enough to lend it your support. The claim is just, it will be useful, and your opinion is enough to demonstrate it and arouse conviction in everyone's mind. Please accept, together with my gratitude, the feelings of high consideration and respect with which I have the honor to be

Sir

Your very humble and very obedient servant

G. HYDE DE NEUVILLE

Allow me to assure Mrs. Randolph and her daughters of my respect and Mr. Randolph of my very distinguished consideration and regret for not having had the honor of making his acquaintance.—

RC (DLC); dateline at foot of text; endorsed by TJ as received 9 Dec. 1818 from Washington and so recorded in SJL. Translation by Dr. Genevieve Moene.

The text of the EXTRAÎT DU MONITEUR enclosed here has not been found, but on 3 Dec. 1818 Hyde de Neuville sent James Madison a handwritten extract from the Paris *Moniteur Universel* of 12 Oct. 1818, stating that the duc de Richelieu had signed an agreement with the ministers of Austria, Great Britain, Prussia, and Russia, which stipulated that their army of occupation would leave French territory by 30 Nov. 1818 (LUNDI DERNIER) and set the total reparations then owed by France at 265 million francs (Tr in DLC: Madison Papers; see also Madison, *Papers, Retirement Ser.*, 1:386–7).

[1] Manuscript: "Randolp."

From Andrew Kean

SIR   Goochland dec[r] 3rd 1818

It was only on last Saturday that your esteemed favor reached me—I hope to be at Monticello about the 15th of this month but possibly professional duty may make it some days later—To obtain a circle where the population was more dense & wealthy I removed last february from Yanceyville to Lickinghole in Goochland—Here I have a pretty considerable tract of Land so circumstanced that I think it could not be disposed of at present[1] for any thing like it's value.—

A residence convenient to the Central Colledge would indeed weigh greatly with me—I confidently hope in that establishment in a few Years being one of the first in the World—And few individuals have as much reason to feel on private grounds interest in it's welfare or a desire to reside near it—Being already the Father of five sons—my eldest seventeen years old and a Wife young enough to render it quite probable that we may have five more

But as when we meet I shall submit for[2] your consideration & advice the whole of this subject I shall only add my gratefull acknowledgements & profound respects—   ANDREW KEAN

RC (DLC); endorsed by TJ as received 6 Dec. 1818 and so recorded in SJL.

[1] Kean here canceled "without."
[2] Preceding two words interlined in place of "solicit."

Anecdotes of Benjamin Franklin

[ca. 4 Dec. 1818]

Our revolutionary process, as is well known, commenced by petitions, memorials, remonstrances E^tc from the old Congress. these were followed by a non-importation agreement, as a pacific instrument of coercion. while that was before us, and sundry exceptions, as of arms, ammunition E^tc were moved from different quarters of the house, I was sitting by Dr Franklin and observed to him that I thought we should except books: that we ought not to exclude science, even coming from an enemy. he thought so too, and I proposed the exception, which was agreed to. soon after it occurred that medecine should be excepted, & I suggested that also to the Doctor. 'as to that, said he, I will tell you a story. when I was in London, in such a year, there was a weekly club of Physicians, of which Sr John Pringle was President, and I was invited by my friend Dr Fothergill to attend when convenient. their rule was to propose a thesis one week, and discuss it the next. I happened there when the question to be considered was Whether Physicians had, on the whole, done most good or harm? the young members, particularly, having discussed it very learnedly and eloquently till the subject was exhausted, one of them observed to Sr John Pringle, that altho' it was not usual for the President to take part in a debate, yet they were desirous to know his opinion on the question. he said, they must first tell him whether, under the appellation of Physicians, they meant to include <u>old women</u>; if they did, he thought they had done more good than harm, otherwise more harm than good.'[1]

The confederation of the States, while on the carpet before the old Congress, was strenuously opposed by the smaller states, under apprehensions[2] that they would be swallowed up by the larger ones. we were long engaged in the discussion; it produced great heats, much ill humor, and intemperate declarations from some members. Dr Franklin at length brought the debate to a close with one of his little apologues. he observed that 'at the time of the Union of England & Scotland, the Duke of Argyle was most violently opposed to that measure, and among other things predicted that, as the whale had swallowed Jonas, so Scotland would be swallowed by England. however, said the Doctor, when Ld Bute came into the government, he soon brought into it's administration so many of his countrymen that it was found, in event that Jonas swallowed the whale.' this little story produced a general laugh, restored good humor, & the Article of difficulty was passed.

When Dr Franklin went to France, on his revolutionary mission, his eminence as a philosopher, his venerable appearance, and the cause on which he was sent, rendered him extremely popular. for all ranks and conditions of men there, entered warmly into the American interest. he was therefore feasted and invited to all the court parties. at these he some times met the old Dutchess of Bourbon, who being a chess player of about his force, they very generally³ played together. happening once to put her king into prise, the Doct^r took it. 'ah, says she, we do not take kings so,' 'we do in America,' said the Doctor.

At one of these parties, the emperor Joseph II⁴ then at Paris, incog. under the title of Count Falkenstein, was overlooking the game, in silence, while the company was engaged in animated conversations on the American question. 'how happens it, M. le Comte, said the Dutchess, that while we all feel so much interest in the cause of the Americans, you say nothing for them?' 'I am a king by trade,' said he.⁵

When the Declaration of Independence was under the consideration of Congress, there were two or three unlucky expressions in it which gave offence to some members. the words 'Scotch and other foreign⁶ auxiliaries' excited the ire of a gentleman or two of that country. severe strictures on the conduct of the British king, in negativing our repeated repeals of the law which permitted the importation of slaves, were disapproved by some Southern gentlemen, whose reflections were not yet matured to the full abhorrence of that traffic. altho' the offensive expressions were immediately yielded, these gentlemen continued their depredations on other parts of the instrument. I was sitting by Dr Franklin who percieved that I was not insensible to these mutilations. 'I have made it a rule, said he, whenever in my power, to avoid becoming the draughtsman of papers to be reviewed by a public body. I took my lesson from an incident which I will relate to you. when I was a journeyman printer, one of my companions, an apprentice Hatter, having served out his time, was about to open shop for himself. his first concern was to have a handsome sign-board, with a proper inscription. he composed it in these words 'John Thompson, Hatter, makes and sells hats. for ready money,' with a figure of a hat subjoined. but he thought he would submit it to his friends for their amendments. the first he shewed it to thought the word 'Hatter,' tautologous, because followed by the words 'makes hats' which shew he was a Hatter. it was struck out. the next observed that the word 'makes' might as well be omitted, because his customers would not care who made the hats. if good & to their mind, they would buy, by whomsoever made. he struck it out. a third said he thought the words 'for ready money,' were useless as it was not the custom of the[7] place to sell on credit. every one who purchased expected to pay. they were parted with, and the inscription now stood 'John Thomson sells hats.' 'sells hats' says his next friend? why nobody will expect you to give them away. what then is the use of that word? it was stricken out, and 'hats' followed it, the rather, as there was one painted on the board. so his inscription was reduced ultimately to 'John Thomson' with the figure of a hat subjoined.'[8]

The Doctor told me, at Paris, the two following anecdotes[9] of the Abbe Raynal. he had a party to dine with him one day at Passy, of whom one half were Americans, the other half French & among the last was the Abbé. during the dinner he got on his favorite theory of the degeneracy of animals, and even of man, in America, and urged it with his usual eloquence. the Doctor at length noticing the accidental stature and position of his guests, at table, 'come, says he, M. l'Abbé, let us try this question by the fact before us. we are here one half Americans, & one half French, and it happens that the Americans have placed themselves on one side of the table, and our French friends are on the other. let both parties rise, and we will see on which side nature has degenerated.' it happened that his American guests were Carmichael, Harmer, Humphreys and others of the finest stature and form, while those of the other side were remarkably diminutive, and the Abbé himself particularly, was a mere shrimp. he parried the appeal however, by a complimentary admission of exceptions, among which the Doctor himself was a conspicuous one.[10]

The Doctor & Silas Deane were in conversation one day at Passy on the numerous errors in the Abbe's Histoire des deux Indes, when he happened to step in. after the usual salutations, Silas Deane said to him 'the Doctor and myself Abbe, were just speaking of the errors of fact into which you have been led in your history.' 'Oh no, Sir, said the Abbé, that is impossible. I took the greatest care not to insert a single fact, for which I had not the most unquestionable authority.' 'why, says Deane, there is the story of Polly Baker, and the eloquent apology you have put into her mouth, when brought before a court of Massachusets to suffer punishment under a law, which you cite, for having had a bastard. I know there never was such a law in Massachusets.' 'be assured, said the Abbé, you are mistaken, and that that is a true story. I do not immediately recollect indeed the particular information on which I quote it; but I am certain that I had for it unquestionable authority.' Doctor Franklin who had been for some time shaking with restrained laughter at the Abbe's confidence in his authority for that tale, said 'I will tell you, Abbé, the origin of that story. when I was a printer and editor of a newspaper, we were sometimes slack of news, and to amuse our customers, I used to fill up our vacant columns with anecdotes, and fables, and fancies of my own, and this of Polly Baker is a story of my making, on one of those occasions.' the Abbé, without the least disconcert, exclaimed with a laugh 'Oh, very well, Doctor, I had rather relate your stories than other men's truths.'

PoC (DLC: TJ Papers, 214:38175–7); consisting of five pages written in TJ's hand on three sheets, with verso of third sheet blank; undated; with letter "P" in an unidentified hand at top of pp. 1 and 5. Printed in Philadelphia *National Gazette and Literary Register* (of which Robert Walsh was a founder and contributor), 5 Apr. 1820, and elsewhere. Enclosed in TJ to Walsh, 4 Dec. 1818.

A WHALE or large fish swallows Jonah in the Bible, Jonah 1–2. TJ's draft of the Declaration of Independence included complaints that George III had sent SCOTCH AND OTHER FOREIGN mercenaries to the colonies, but in the final version adopted by the Second Continental Congress, the wording was changed to "large Armies of foreign Mercenaries" (*PTJ*, 1:319, 419, 420, 427, 431). In his notes on the proceedings of the Second Continental Congress, TJ reported that on 2 July 1776 the clause of the Declaration accusing George III of perpetuating slavery in the colonies was deleted at the request of the SOUTHERN GENTLEMEN from South Carolina and Georgia (*PTJ*, 1:314–5, 317–8, 418, 426).

THE STORY with which Franklin credited himself was "The Speech of Miss

Polly Baker, before a Court of Judicature, at Connecticut near Boston in New-England; where she was prosecuted the Fifth Time, for having a Bastard Child: Which influenced the Court to dispense with her Punishment, and induced one of her Judges to marry her the next Day" (Leonard W. Labaree and others, eds., *The Papers of Benjamin Franklin* [1959–], 3:123–5). Guillaume Thomas François (Abbé) Raynal printed the story as factual in book 17 of his *Histoire Philosophique et Politique Des établissemens & du commerce des Européens dans les deux Indes* (Amsterdam, 1770, and other eds.; Sowerby, no. 466), 6:257–62.

[1] First page ends short at this point.
[2] *National Gazette*: "the apprehension."
[3] Manuscript: "generall." *National Gazette*: "generally."
[4] Roman numeral interlined.
[5] Second page ends here.
[6] Word not in *National Gazette*.
[7] Third page ends here.
[8] Omitted closing quotation mark editorially supplied.
[9] *National Gazette*: "the following anecdote."
[10] Fourth page ends short at this point. Remainder of text not in *National Gazette*.

From John G. Jackson

DEAR SIR,   Clarksburg Decr 4th 1818

I had learned through the public prints, & other channels of communication; of your recent severe, & alarming illness; & the deep distress I felt during all that period, having been succeeded by the fullness of joy, & thankfulness for your restoration to health: I cannot without committing[1] violence to my feelings, refrain from expressing my sincere gratification at your recovery; & my fervent prayer,[2] that your invaluable life, may be spared to your Country[3] for many years— That we may enjoy the benefits of your continued usefulness—with the opportunities of testifying the sincerity of our affection, & veneration for you.

I am your mo. Ob[t] Serv[t]   J G JACKSON

RC (MHi); endorsed by TJ as received 25 Dec. 1818 and so recorded in SJL. RC (MHi); address cover only; with PoC of TJ to John Barnes, 14 Mar. 1819, on verso; addressed: "The Honble Thomas Jefferson Monticello near Charlottesville Virginia"; franked; postmarked Clarksburg, 7 Dec. Dft (InU: Jackson Collection); endorsed by Jackson: "JGJ to

mr Jefferson} Copy 4 Decr 1818 Ans[r] enclosed."

[1] Word interlined in Dft.
[2] Preceding seven words interlined in Dft in place of "& my unfeigned Wish."
[3] Preceding two words interlined in Dft in place of "us."

To Robert Walsh

DEAR SIR   Monticello Dec. 4. 18.

Yours of Nov. 8. has been some time recieved; but it is in my power to give little satisfaction as to it's enquiries.[1] D[r] Franklin had many political enemies, as every character must which, with decision enough to have opinions, has energy & talent to give them effect on the feelings of the adversary opinion. these enmities were chiefly in Pensylvania & Massachusets. in the former they were merely of the proprietary party. in the latter they did not commence till the revolution, and then sprung chiefly from personal animosities, which spreading by little and little, became at length of some extent. D[r] Lee[2] was his principal calumniator, a man of much malignity, who, besides enlisting his whole family in the same hostility, was enabled, as the agent of Massachusets with the British government, to infuse it into that state with considerable effect. mr Izard, the Doctor's enemy also, but from a pecuniary transaction never countenanced these charges against him.[3] mr Jay, Silas Deane, mr Laurens, his colleagues also, ever maintained towards him unlimited confidence and respect. that he would have waived the formal recognition of our Independance I never heard on any authority worthy notice. as to the fisheries, England was urgent to retain them exclusively, France neutral, and I believe that had they been ultimately made a sine quo non, our[4] Commissioners (mr Adams excepted) would have relinquished them rather than have broken off the treaty. to mr Adams's perseverance alone on that point I have always understood we were indebted for their reservation. as to the charge of subservience to France, besides the evidence of his friendly colleagues before named, two years of my own service with him at Paris, daily visits, and the most friendly and confidential conversations convince me it had not a shadow of foundation. he possessed the confidence of that government in the highest degree, insomuch that it may truly be said that they were more under his influence, than he under theirs. the fact is that his temper was so amiable and conciliatory, his conduct so rational, never urging impossibilities, or even things unreasonably inconvenient to them, in short[5] so moderate and attentive to their difficulties, as well as our own, that what his enemies called subserviency, I saw was only that reasonable disposition, which, sensible that advantages are not all to be on one side, yielding what is just and liberal, is the more certain of obtaining liberality and justice. mutual confidence produces of course mutual influence, and this was all which subsisted between D[r] Franklin & the govmt of France.

I state[6] a few anecdotes of D[r] Franklin, within my own knolege,[7] too much in detail for the scale of Delaplaine's work, but which may find a cadre in some of the more particular views you contemplate.   my health is in a great measure restored, and our family joins with me in affectionate recollections & assurances of respect.

TH: JEFFERSON

PoC (DLC); at foot of first page: "Robert Walsh esq." Printed in Philadelphia *National Gazette and Literary Register* (of which Walsh was a founder and contributor), 5 Apr. 1820, and elsewhere. Enclosure: TJ's Anecdotes of Benjamin Franklin, [ca. 4 Dec. 1818].

[1] *National Gazette* text begins here.
[2] Surname replaced by a dash in *National Gazette*.
[3] Sentence not in *National Gazette*.
[4] TJ here canceled "other."
[5] Word interlined in place of "fact."
[6] *National Gazette*: "subjoin."
[7] *National Gazette* text ends here.

From Daniel Brent

DEAR SIR,   Washington, December 5th 1818.

I had the pleasure of receiving, some days ago, your Letter of the 27th of last month, enclosing two packets addressed to M[r] Gallatin, which I committed, the day before yesterday, to D[n] Luis Noeli, Secretary to the Spanish Legation here, who will embark in two or three days on board the British packet at New york, to proceed, by the way of England and France; to Spain; and he obligingly promised to deliver them, himself.

I shall always take great pleasure in executing your commands—and I should regret exceedingly if the cause to which you last allude, that of declining health, were to continue to render them less frequent in this way.   I have the Honour to remain,

    with the highest Respect & sincere Esteem, D^r sir, your Obed^t & very humble serv^t DANIEL BRENT.

RC (DLC); endorsed by TJ as received 9 Dec. 1818 and so recorded in SJL. RC (DLC); address cover only; with PoC of TJ to Robert S. Garnett, 4 Apr. 1819, on verso; addressed: "Mr Jefferson, Monticello"; franked; postmarked Washington, 5 Dec.

From Hugh Holmes

DEAR SIR   Winchester Decr 6th 1818
    I was much surprised to find the newspapers announcing you as labouring under dangerous dissease, when you were convalescent at the time I had the pleasure of seeing you last at Monticello—If the sympathy of individual friends is grateful to a suffering patient what must that of a nation be? believing from experience that such is the effect as one of your friends I beg leave to add my share and an hope and prayer for your speedy recovery—
    I had intended when last at Monticello to ask the favor of you to give me a letter to your friend in France to make choice of some Nice wine for me but your situation then forbidding you to write I did not mention the subject to you—If you are now enabled to write or when you shall be it will greatly oblige me to receve such a letter which I will give to m^r Cassenove of Alex^a who will import the wine for me—
    with much respect and great regard
    I am Dr Sir your friend & Sev^t H^H HOLMES

RC (MHi); endorsed by TJ as received 14 Dec. 1818 and so recorded in SJL. RC (DLC); address cover only; with PoC of TJ to James Eastburn & Company, 2 Apr. 1819, on verso; addressed: "The honble Thomas Jefferson Esqr of Monticello Milton Albemarle V^a" by "mail"; franked; postmarked.

Reports by NEWSPAPERS following TJ's trip to Warm Springs indicated that he was seriously ill and even that he was near death (*Alexandria Herald*, 16 Nov. 1818; *American Beacon and Norfolk & Portsmouth Daily Advertiser*, 20 Nov. 1818).

To John Barnes

Dear Sir   Monticello Dec. 7. 18.

Your favor of Nov. 31 (for Dec. 1. I suppose) came to hand last night, and your communication of my letter to mr Adams is entirely approved, as our friendly sentiments are fully reciprocal. no one can sympathise with him on his late loss more sincerely than I do.

I am withdrawing from newspapers, and therefore write the inclosed for the editors of the National Intelligencer, which I leave open for your perusal. will you do me the favor to pay up my balance (a little more than a year) and let me know the sum which I will immediately remit you.

My health is in a great degree restored. I now ride daily and am gathering flesh & strength. ever affectionately yours

Th: Jefferson

PoC (MHi); on verso of reused address cover of Charles G. Haines to TJ, 18 Aug. 1818; at foot of text: "Mr Barnes"; endorsed by TJ. Enclosure: TJ to Joseph Gales (1786–1860), 7 Dec. 1818.

Barnes's favor of nov. 31 is printed above at 30 Nov. 1818. The editors of the Washington *Daily National Intelligencer* were Gales and William W. Seaton.

From Mathew Carey & Son

Dear Sir   Philad^a Dec. 7. 1818

Your favor of 28^h ult. we have duly, rec^d &, agreeably to your request, have forwarded the above Per Mail.

√ Your obnt Serv^{ts}   M Carey & Son

[*At head of text:*]   Philad^a Decr 7. 1818
Hon. Thomas Jefferson

Bot of M Carey & Son

1 Griesbachs Greek Testa^t 8vo	$2.50
1 Improv^d Version of New Testam^t (Lond)	4.00
	6.50

RC (MHi); in the hand of a representative of Mathew Carey & Son, signed by Mathew Carey; endorsed by TJ as a letter from Mathew Carey received 14 Dec. 1818 and so recorded in SJL.

To Thomas Fillebrown

Monticello Dec. 7. 18.

Th: Jefferson returns to mr Fillebrown the pamphlet he has been so kind as to send him with thanks for it's communication. he trusts that the drastic medecines which have been administered to the unfortunate subjects of this work will have cured them of their past complaints and prevent a return of them. he considers the whole effect of the Hartford Convention as having been very salutary. he salutes mr Fillebrown with respect.

RC (MdAN); dateline at foot of text; attached to verso of flyleaf of volume 1 of *The American Almanac and Repository of Useful Knowledge for the year 1830* (1830), with this copy inscribed as presented to the United States Naval Academy by Fillebrown on 26 Aug. 1852. Not recorded in SJL. Enclosure not found.

To Joseph Gales (1786–1860)

Sɪʀ   Monticello Dec. 7. 18.

I have long ceased to read newspapers, except a single one of my own state, & that chiefly for the advertisements. perfectly resigned as a passenger to the steerage of those who are navigating the vessel of State, & with entire confidence in them, I scarcely enquire or wish to know what is passing. age has relieved me from these cares, and now calls for tranquility and rest. under these circumstances it is useless to be recieving newspapers which I never open, and difficult and troublesome to be making small & fractional remittances into other states. I have therefore requested my friend mr Barnes to pay up my account with you to the last day of the present year, say of the present month, and to be discontinued as a subscriber after that date.

I make my acknolegements to you for the satisfaction recieved [...] your paper as long as these communications had any object with me, and I retire from it with the best wishes for your success health & happiness.   Tʜ: Jᴇꜰꜰᴇʀꜱᴏɴ

PoC (DLC); on verso of reused address cover of Robert B. Stark to TJ, 20 Aug. 1818; torn at seal; at foot of text: "Mr Gales"; endorsed by TJ, with his additional notation: "Newspapers." Enclosed in TJ to John Barnes, 7 Dec. 1818.

The newspaper ᴏꜰ ᴍʏ ᴏᴡɴ ꜱᴛᴀᴛᴇ was the *Richmond Enquirer*. ʏᴏᴜʀ ᴘᴀᴘᴇʀ: the Washington *Daily National Intelligencer*.

To Thomas Ritchie

DEAR SIR   Monticello Dec. 7. 18.

It is long since I have ceased to read any newspaper but yours, and I shall continue to read no other. withdrawing therefore from all others I pray you to have me discontinued as a subscriber to the Compiler. should the legislature have the report of the University Commissioners printed in a pamphlet be so good as to send me half a dozen copies. mr Gibson as usual will pay you for these as well as my newspaper account. I salute you with friendship & respect

TH: JEFFERSON

PoC (DLC); on verso of reused address cover of John Steele to TJ, 13 Aug. 1818; at foot of text: "Mᴿ Ritchie"; endorsed by TJ, with his additional notation: "Newspapers."

YOURS: the *Richmond Enquirer*.

To John Vaughan

DEAR SIR   Monticello Dec. 7. 18.

I recieved yesterday from mr Appleton of Leghorn a letter of Aug. 26. in which he says 'your letter of Apr. 4. was accompanied by one from mr John Vaughan, mentioning that he then inclosed a bill of exchange by S. Girard on Lafitte & co. Paris for francs 2415.ᵗ but no such bill was found therein by me.' he has probably written the same to you, and I have no doubt the inadvertence has been corrected, and I note it only to make certainty doubly certain. ever faithfully & affectionately

Your's   TH: JEFFERSON

PoC (MHi); on verso of reused address cover of Caesar A. Rodney to TJ, 8 Aug. 1818; at foot of text: "John Vaughan esq."; endorsed by TJ.

From John Adams

DEAR SIR   Quincy Dec 8, 18

Your Letter of Nov. 13 gave me[1] great delight not only by the divine Consolation it afforded me under my great Affliction: but as it gave me full Proof of your restoration to Health.

While you live, I Seem to have a Bank at Montecello on which I can draw for a Letter of Friendship and entertainment when I please.

I know not how to prove physically that We Shall meet and know each other in a future State; Nor does Revelation, as I can find give

Us any possitive Assurance of Such a felicity. My reasons for believing, it, as I do, most undoubtingly, are all moral and divine.

I believe in God and in his Wisdom and Benevolence:[2] and I cannot conceive that Such a Being could make Such a Species as the human merely to live and die on this Earth. If I did not believe a future State I Should believe in no God. This Universe;[3] this all; this το παν; would appear with all its Swelling Pomp, a boyish Fire Work.

And if there be a future State Why Should the Almighty dissolve forever all the tender Ties which unite Us So delightfully in this World and forbid Us to See each other in the next?

Trumbull with a band of Associates drew me by the Cords of old Friendships[4] to See his Picture on Saturday where I got a great Cold. The Air of Ph[a]neuil Hall is changed. I have not been Used to catch Cold there.

Sick or Well the friendship[5] is the Same of your old Acquaintance

JOHN ADAMS

RC (DLC); hole in manuscript; endorsed by TJ as received 17 Dec. 1818 and so recorded in SJL. RC (DLC); address cover only; with PoC of TJ to Robert Walsh, 11 Apr. 1819, on verso; addressed in an unidentified hand: "Thomas Jefferson late President of the U.S—Monticello"; franked; postmarked Quincy, 9 Dec. FC (Lb in MHi: Adams Papers).

το παν: "totality." Adams had been to see John Trumbull's painting of *The Declaration of Independence* at Faneuil (PHANEUIL) Hall in Boston. The regular admission fee was twenty-five-cents (*Boston Intelligencer & Evening Gazette*, 5 Dec. 1818).

[1] Word not in FC.
[2] Preceding fifteen words not in FC.
[3] RC: "Unverse." FC: "Universe."
[4] RC: "Frienships." FC: "Friendship."
[5] RC: "frienship." FC: "friendship."

From Joseph C. Cabell

DEAR SIR,   Richmond 8th Dec[r] 1818.

The Senate formed a House to-day: the House of Delegates yesterday. A conference between Mess[rs] Carr and Gordon & myself held this morning resulted in an agreement to get M[r] Taylor of Chesterfield to bring forward the subject of the University in the House of Delegates. Not to speak of those other circumstances in his favor, which should induce me to prefer him, we thought his position in the State, would give him less the appearance of local feelings & interests. I introduced those gentlemen to him[1] & M[r] Taylor undertook the task at our request. The Report was read, and received with great attention in both the Houses. A resolution to print a number of copies passed each House. The ability and value of the Report I am informed are universally admitted. It was referred in the lower House to a select committee, and the Speaker is friendly to the measure. Present prospects are very favorable to a successful issue. Some votes about W^m & Mary may be lost: but nothing like a serious diversion in favor of a western scite is, I believe, to be apprehended. Philip R. Thompson of Kenawha, & the delegates from that Quarter will vote for Charlottesville. From the rest of the west I have not had time to hear. A portion of the Assembly will be opposed to the whole subject: and how far a combination between this part and the Lexington Interest may jeopardize the measure I cannot now determine. All that I can now positively affirm is that the clouds seem to be scattering and the prospect to smile. I will do myself the pleasure to write you from time to time. My friends advised me to push on to W^{ms}burg and to stay there till the entire recovery of my health: but feeling myself getting better, I resolved to stay and do what I could to promote this business. At Bremo my fevers returned, but since I left that place, my recovery has been advancing uninterruptedly. I shall proceed to W^{ms}burg, and stay a week or two, as soon as the subject of the University shall be put on a footing satisfactory to my mind.

I am, Dr Sir, sincerely & faithfully yours

JOSEPH C. CABELL

P.S. Mr Hunter of Essex will support the Report.

RC (ViU: TJP-PC); endorsed by TJ as received 14 Dec. 1818 and so recorded in SJL. RC (DLC); address cover only; with PoC of TJ to Wilson Cary Nicholas, 1 Apr. 1819, on recto and verso; addressed: "Thomas Jefferson Monticello"; franked; postmarked Richmond, 8 Dec.

On this date Samuel TAYLOR OF CHESTERFIELD successfully moved in the Virginia House of Delegates that five hundred copies of the *University of Virginia Commissioners' Report* be printed for the members of the General Assembly, including delegates on a SELECT COMMITTEE the House created to consider the communication. Taylor was then named to the select committee, along with delegates John Bowyer, of Rockbridge County; Samuel Carr, of Albemarle County; Briscoe G. Baldwin, of Augusta County; William C. Rives, of Nelson County; Charles Yancey, of Buckingham County; Archibald Magill, of Frederick County; William F. Gordon, of Albemarle County;

Andrew Alexander, of Rockbridge County; William S. Archer, of Amelia County; John Robertson, of the city of Richmond; George Townes, of Pittsylvania County; Philip R. Thompson, of Kanawha County; Lewis C. Tyler, of James City County; Robert Mallory, of Orange County; James Machir, of Hardy County; William Steenbergen, of Shenandoah County; John Hooe, of King George County; Joseph J. Degraffenreid, of Lunenburg County; and Edmund Penn, of Amherst County (*JHD* [1818–19 sess.], 16; Leonard, *General Assembly*, 293–5).

The House SPEAKER was Linn Banks. Delegates PHILIP R. THOMPSON and James HUNTER OF ESSEX both ultimately voted in favor of "An Act for establishing an University," which established Central College as the University of Virginia (*JHD* [1818–19 sess.], 112 [19 Jan. 1819]).

[1] Word interlined in place of "each other."

To Lewis D. Belair

Sir   Monticello. Dec. 9. 18.

Your letter of Nov. 26. is recieved and enables me to ascertain the amount of the cost of the books I have rec^d and those I wish now to be forwarded, and I accordingly inclose you 90. Dollars in bills of the bank of the US. in Philadelphia. I shall subjoin the list of the books, and the prices as I read them in your several letters. you will observe that I desire a 2^d copy of Planche's Greek Dictionary and also a 2^d copy of Lalande's stereotype edn of his Logarithms. this last, being small, I will pray you to inclose it by the 1^{st1} mail. the Dictionnaire Bibliographique may also come by mail, observing the precautions of my letter of Nov. 23. all the rest should be securely packed in a good box and sent to Richmond addressed to me to the care of Capt Bernard Peyton of that place, who will pay freight & charges & forward them to me. the risks of the mail will make an acknolegement of the rec^t of the contents of this letter acceptable. I salute you with esteem & respect.   Th: Jefferson

D

these are rec^d	Planche. Dict. Gr. & Fr.	6.25	a 2^d copy of Planche's Dict.	6.25
	Lalande. Logarithmes. Stereot.	.08$\frac{1}{2}$	a 2^d copy of Lalande's Logarith.	.08$\frac{1}{2}$
	Correspondce de Cortés	1.12$\frac{1}{2}$	Pline^2 le jeune Lat. Fr.	2.87$\frac{1}{2}$
	DuCange Glossarium	20.	Dict. Bibliographique	13.50
	Cabanis Catarrhe	.08$\frac{1}{2}$	Denys d'Halicarnasse	10.
	Salluste de La Malle	2.25	Epictetus Gr. Ital.	5.87$\frac{1}{2}$
	Suetone Lat. Fr.	7.50	Geometrie de Le Gendre	2.25
	Henri IV. de Prefixe	.08$\frac{1}{2}$	Algebre d' Euler	4.25
	Appien. guerres civiles	7.	brought forward	44.38
		44.38		89.46$\frac{1}{2}$

RC (RNHi); corner torn, with missing fraction in total for right column supplied from PoC; addressed: "M. Louis de Belair Bookseller New York"; torn, with probable loss of franking signature and damage to gift inscription by Fernagus De Gelone: "Pour Mr Elmendo[rf] l'aîné. memento, homo! qui pulvis is et in pulverem reverteris. donné par fernagus De Gelone—16th October 1821—Nous ne Sommes pas encore au 16eme Jour d'Octobre—15. Lundi Soir" ("For Mr Elmendorf the elder. Remember, man! You are dust and to dust you will return. Given by fernagus De Gelone—16th October 1821—We are not yet to the 16th day of October—15. Monday evening"). PoC (MHi); on verso of a reused address cover from James Monroe to TJ; torn at seal; endorsed by TJ. Recorded in SJL with bracketed notation: "90.D."

The low price TJ quotes for Joseph Jérôme Le Français de Lalande's work on LOGARITHMES is based on a misreading of Belair to TJ, 6 Nov. 1818 (see also note to TJ to Belair, 27 Oct. 1818, and Fernagus De Gelone to TJ, 7 Jan. 1819).

[1] Preceding two words interlined.

[2] Preceding this and the entries for each of the five remaining titles in this column of RC, an unidentified hand has added an "✕."

To William Duane

DEAR SIR   Monticello Dec. 9. 18.

I have long ceased to read newspapers, except a single one of my own state, and that chiefly for the advertisements. perfectly resigned as a passenger to those who are navigating the vessel of state, and with entire confidence in them, I scarcely enquire, or wish to know what is passing. age has relieved me from these cares, and now calls for tranquility & rest. under these circumstances it is useless to be recieving papers which I never open, and troublesome & difficult to make small & fractional remittances into other states. a proof of the latter is my now remitting a 5. Dollar bill of the Bank of Virga because one of the US. bank cannot be had in this interior part of the country. I believe this remittance pays my subscription to the Aurora to May 18. of the ensuing year, after which I must pray to be discontinued as a subscriber. in retiring from it I make my acknolegements for the signal services it rendered us in times which severely tried the republicanism of our fellow citizens, and I salute you with my best wishes for your prosperity, health & happiness.

TH: JEFFERSON

PoC (DLC); on verso of reused address cover to TJ; at foot of text: "Gen¹ William Duane"; endorsed by TJ, with his additional notation: "Newspapers." Recorded in SJL with bracketed notation: "5.D."

The SINGLE ONE was the *Richmond Enquirer.*

To Patrick Gibson

DEAR SIR   Monticello Dec. 9. 18.

The first mail after the reciept of your favor of the 3ᵈ instant, carries the present with the blank notes for renewal.   Mʳ Yancey assured me he would have my Bedford flour down in all November; which I hope he has effected.   I drew on you on the 7ᵗʰ inst. in favor of Th: J. Randolph for 201.D. and on the 8ᵗʰ in favor of James Leitch for 280.D. a few other neighborhood debts will be coming on me in the course of the month amounting to 2. or 300.D. more. I salute you with friendship & respect.   TH: JEFFERSON

PoC (MHi); on verso of reused address cover of Thomas Cooper to TJ, 21 Aug. 1818; at foot of text: "Mr Gibson"; endorsed by TJ as a letter of 10 Dec. 1818 and so recorded in SJL. Enclosures not found.

The $201 draft that TJ gave to Thomas Jefferson RANDOLPH reimbursed him for wages paid to Thompson Gooch, the overseer at Lego. The draft for James LEITCH covered repayment for a cash loan as well as $50 to the carpenter Larkin Powers, $20 to Frank Carr to cover TJ's annual "subscription" to an Episcopal minister, and $81 to William Stewardson for stonework at TJ's mill (*MB*, 2:1348, 1349).

To Joseph Milligan

DEAR SIR   Monticello Dec. 9. 18.

I sent yesterday to Milton a box of books to be forwarded to you by mr Gray. it contains 32. volumes to be bound. there is in each a note how it is to be lettered, and some of these notes express that the book is to have a neat plain binding. all the rest are to be bound in your best manner. I wish you could see the books I recieve from Paris. they are equal to the best English work in weight & solidity and beautifully varied in the taste. I now inclose a small volume which was omitted by accident to be put into the box. it is to be trimmed, as you will see, to fit my petit format shelves

I have safely recieved the 10. copies of Tracy, and have begun their distribution. I send some to members of Congress & of the [V]irginia assembly, but most of them to the different colleges and Universities of the US.

Pray bind the books with as little delay as the solidity of the work will admit, as some of them are in daily use. I salute you with friendship.   TH: JEFFERSON

Xiphilinus.
Euler's Algebra. by Farrar.
Simpson's Euclid.   Josephus. Gr. Lat. Eng. 15. vols
Sloane's Italy   Geologie de Faujas.
Physique de Hauy. 2. v.   Revoln de France. Stael. 3. v.
Commentaire sur   Planche Dict. Gr. Fr.
  Montesquieu. Tracy.   ———

Canals and Navigation.   Logarithmes [the vol. now
                                        inclos^d]^1

English's Christianity   those marked thus ___ to be plain
                                        bound

Aesop by Croxall.
Graglia's Dict. Ital. Eng.
Graglia's Dict. Eng. Ital.

when done, be so good as to send
me your account which shall be
promptly[2] remitted.

PoC (DLC); on verso of reused address cover of Thomas Cooper to TJ, 3
Sept. 1818; torn at seal; at foot of text:
"Joseph Millegan"; endorsed by TJ. Enclosure: Joseph Jérôme Le Français de
Lalande, *Tables de Logarithmes pour les
Nombres et Pour les Sinus* (Paris, 1805;
repr. 1815; Poor, *Jefferson's Library*, 8
[no. 405]).

CANALS AND NAVIGATION may have
been the work about which TJ asked
Milligan in his letter of 18 May 1818,
namely Samuel Young, comp., *A Treatise
on Internal Navigation. To which is Annexed, the Report of Albert Gallatin on
Roads and Canals* (Ballston Spa, 1817;
Poor, *Jefferson's Library*, 5 [no. 215]).

[1] Brackets in original.
[2] Manuscript: "prompty."

To Hezekiah Niles

Monticello Dec. 9. 18.

Th: Jefferson incloses to mr Niles a five Dollar bill of the bank of
Virginia which he believes pays for the Weekly Register till Sep. 18.
of the ensuing year, and salutes him with esteem & respect.

PoC (DLC); on verso of a reused address cover from James Monroe to TJ;
dateline at foot of text; endorsed by TJ as
a letter to "Niles Henry" and so recorded

(with additional bracketed notation of
"5.D") in SJL; additional notation by TJ
above endorsement: "Newspapers."

From Joseph M. Sanderson

DEAR SIR—   Baltimore Dec. 9 1818—

I Send you the prospectus of a work which I am about to publish—
I wish to know your opinion of the plan, & if not imposing too much
on your leisure I would be glad if you would suggest any alteration
by which it can be made interesting to the People of the United
States—A work of the kind appears to be Much wanted—for Many
of the Signers to the Declaration of Independence are entirely unknown to two-thirds of the people—The avidity recently displayed
for the possession of the print of the Declaration of Independence, &
the anxiety to know the history of the several Signers is a proof that
the characters of Many of those illustrious men have been neglected—
Such however is the Motive that has prompted me to the undertaking & I trust that through the assistance of the several connexions I
shall be able to Make it honorable to the nation—To you I would
apply for some of the facts relative to the passage of the law—but I

[477]

fear it would be too much intrusion—If however there is any thing you could communicat[e] without interfering with your ease that would tend to illustrate the work—I shall consider Myself under an unbounded obligation to you—with wishes therfore for your ease & comfort, I remain, very respectfully
        your humble Servant   JOSEPH M. SANDERSON
                                                48 Market street
                                                Baltimore

RC (MHi); edge trimmed; endorsed by TJ as received 14 Dec. 1818 and so recorded in SJL. RC (ViU: TJP); address cover only; with PoC of TJ to Thomas Cooper, 9 Apr. 1819, on verso; addressed: "His Excellency Thomas Jefferson Monticella Virg."; franked; postmarked Baltimore, 9 Dec.

Joseph McClellan Sanderson (1792–1866), printer and publisher, was a native of Carlisle, Pennsylvania. In the War of 1812 he volunteered as a private in an artillery unit, and by 1815 he was working as a printer in Philadelphia. Sanderson relocated briefly to Baltimore. There he was a partner in the firm of Sanderson & Ward, which sold prints and mirrors. After the partnership became insolvent and dissolved in 1819, Sanderson returned to Philadelphia. In 1818 he had begun promoting a multivolume edition of biographies of signers of the Declaration of Independence. Containing contributions by his brother John Sanderson, he published it as *Biography of the Signers to the Declaration of Independence*, 9 vols. (Philadelphia, 1820–27; Poor, *Jefferson's Library*, 5 [no. 152]). The second volume, published in 1822, included a biography of George Wythe based on information submitted by TJ. Financial constraints obliged the brothers to relinquish the project to others thereafter. Sanderson was publisher of the *Aurora General Advertiser* for a short interval in 1823, and he also published the *Philadelphia Price Current*, 1827–29. He ran the Merchants' Coffee House and later built and operated the Merchants' Hotel. Sanderson retired in 1847, later moved to New York City,

and died there (Edward Carpenter and Louis Henry Carpenter, comps., *Samuel Carpenter and his Descendants* [1912], 98; *A History of Philadelphia, with a Notice of Villages in the Vicinity* [1839], 33; *Baltimore Patriot & Mercantile Advertiser*, 6 Nov., 16 Dec. 1817, 25 Apr., 2 Sept. 1818, 30 Sept. 1819; Samuel Jackson, comp., *The Baltimore Directory* [Baltimore, 1819]; TJ to John Sanderson, 31 Aug. 1820; TJ's Biography of George Wythe, [ca. 31 Aug. 1820]; Gordon M. Marshall, "The Golden Age of Illustrated Biographies: Three Case Studies," in Wendy Wick Reaves, ed., *American Portrait Prints: Proceedings of the Tenth Annual American Print Conference* [1984], esp. 53; *A Checklist of Pennsylvania Newspapers* [1944], 11, 38; DNA: RG 29, CS, Pa., Philadelphia, 1820–40; New York *Evening Post* and *New York Herald*, both 4 Jan. 1866).

Although the enclosed PROSPECTUS for Sanderson's *Biography of the Signers to the Declaration of Independence* has not been found, a presumably similar newspaper version announced that the biographies would be written by Paul Allen; that the work would run to ten half-volumes priced at $2.50 each, "printed on fine paper, made expressly for the purpose"; and that it would include a history of the proceedings of the Continental Congress as well as the text of the Declaration itself, with facsimile signatures (*Baltimore Patriot & Mercantile Advertiser*, 10 Dec. 1818). The firm of Sanderson & Ward acted as agents for the sale of Benjamin O. Tyler's PRINT OF THE DECLARATION OF INDEPENDENCE (*Baltimore Patriot & Mercantile Advertiser*, 18, 23 Apr. 1818).

To John Wood (of New York)

SIR   Monticello Dec. 9. 18.

It is very[1] troublesome and difficult to make small and fractional remittances into other states. a proof of this is my present remittance of a 5. Dollar note of the Bank of Virginia, because one of the US. bank cannot be had in this interior part of the country. this I believe pays my subscription to the New York sales report to the end of the present year, after which, for the reason above mentioned, I must pray to be discontinued as a subscriber and I salute you with esteem & respect.   TH: JEFFERSON

PoC (DLC); on verso of reused address cover of Thomas Cooper to TJ, 2 Sept. 1818; at foot of text: "Mr John Wood"; endorsed by TJ as a letter to "Wood John j^r (successor of Eldredge)," with the additional notation: "Newspapers." Recorded in SJL with the bracketed notation: "5.D."

John Wood, printer, collaborated with Nathaniel T. Eldredge in 1816 in printing the *New-York Public Sale Report*. When that partnership dissolved in 1818, Wood became the sole publisher of the paper, which by 1820 had been renamed *Wood's New-York Sale Report and Price Current* (Brigham, *American Newspapers*, 1:683, 706; *MB*, 2:1349; New York *Mercantile Advertiser*, 21 Sept. 1818; *Wood's New-York Sale Report and Price Current*, 5 Feb. 1820; *Longworth's New York Directory* [1817]: 191, 457–8; [1818]: 362; [1819]: 433).

[1] Word interlined in place of "so."

From Francis Adrian Van der Kemp

MY DEAR AND RESPECTED SIR!   Oldenbarneveld 10 Dec. 1818.

During Several months I intended to write you—which for a while was delayd by my occupations during the Summer Seasons—and Some gloomy apprehensions, that I should write in vain. In this painful anxiety Some dark rumours, that mr jefferson was Severily indisposed made me abandon the thought and I listened rather to fear than to hope. Indeed this year had been to me peculiarly distressing—by the fall of relatives and friends here and in Europe—The one Succeeded the other—

ut unda inpellitur[1] unda—

My Dear friend mrs Adams did in her last Letter exert herself to Sooth my anguish and too acute feelings—when one of her friends informed me, at her request, of her approaching departure from us—and with the next mail—I received tiding—She was no more—My fate is peculiar in this respect—So many, who honoured me with their distinguishing kindnesses—and all departed except an Adams a

Jefferson. I doubt not therefore, as I See from a § in a Pennsylvanian paper—your recovery—that you will not[2] take it amiss, that I address you once more—even though i can not render my Letter very interesting—it would no doubt give me an unbounded Satisfaction was it in my power—and to aspire to it can not be blamed—

I had only a few lines this week of mr. Adams—his health is good—and his calm firmness—unbroken, as my friends informed me.

The interesting contents of your Lett. of Febr. 9—had long before, and have often Since that period the Objects of my investigation—It is too general the case, and the richest Spring of error—that first an hypothesis is framed—and then facts distorted—as on the bed of Procrustes—if you join to this a equivocal and often incorrect Phraseology—then few errors exists, which may not be traced up to one of these Sources—while an exact definition of words as well as of terms—and assuming nothing as truth, which is problematic, would be the means of avoiding numerous logomachies—This particularly is the case with regard to the facts and words of creation—nothing matter—Spirit & this has been the cause of the various theories of the Wernerians—and Huttonians—both true in Some respects—and of the numberless, more or less correct theories of the geologistes—The existence of an Intelligent first cause—whose nature we can not comprehend—and of whom we can not acquire—in the most exalted Station—we may imagine—but very inadequate conceptions—The existence of Such a Being—all powerful—all wise and good—is the chief point. An undetermined—and eternal Successive creation is not inconsistent with it—nay—may enhance these Ideas—millions and millions of world—eternally renovated—with Inhabitants adapted to its varieties—in an uninterrupted Succession, allways Striving and gradually—even unvoluntarily—led to higher perfection—imbues us—it Seems—with a more Sublime idea of a first cause—than the existence of any part—for a few triffling years—and a few Ephemeridal Insects.   Neither do I See in the gospel doctrine any thing contrarÿ to Similar possibilities—our future existence—this was its chief, but—with the mean how to obtain it—It does not even Strike me, as an incongruity, althoug I have not examined the Subject thoroughly, that even the brute creation might be intended for a higher degree of perfection—individually as well as Specifally—althow not yet Susceptible[3] of moral obligations,

But I wander in a field too vast—without knowing—if it is acceptable—I believe—I mentioned, that our Gov—and Some of my friends have persuaded me to examine and translate our Records—I am not determined, if I Shall continue in this difficult task—my eyes are nearly dimmed—but its contents remain highly interesting—I finished about 1000 in fol. among these—Two vol. of Law Records of the city of Albany—of the middle of 17. cent: when this place for its Security against the natives had yet a board fence. The oath was held very Sacred—and offered and accepted with high reverence—quite otherwise as in the courts in our days—the police was active and rigid—justice expeditious and energetic—and tho arbitrary—generally just—without assistance or intervention of Lawyers—The magistrates often despotic—and yet the community, Sometimes So bold, that the first dared not to use any controul—but permitted the Latter to act—as they pleased, leaving to it the consequences—No language—during the Revolution was Stronger than thers—1654—Their bigotry was high—the Magistrates Swore—to defend the Reformed Religion and Synod. of Dort—and not to tolerate any Sect—In reading these petitions—So bold So provoking—considering the association—in this State—and N. Engl—I See the Embryo—Seed—of Revolutionary principles—which in time were to be developed—and was indeed this grand task not long before prepared in that number of Small Republics in Italy—and their principles—spread by their Literati—at the revival of Letters—over the whole continent of Europe—and well principally Germanÿ—and afterwards France? It Seems So—that a Philosophical improvement had been long preparing, and that the numerous bold burlesque writers—the merciless attacks on the Clergy—the undermining of the authority of priests and Popes—the defiance of Spiritual weapons and bold defence of the Secular arm—layd the foundation—on which—one or two centuries later Luther and calvin build—Such a Was Cecco-d'Ascoli perhaps Rienzo too—certainly Piero Carnesecchi and others—Here is a yet undiscovered Country—and I am confident, if the public and private Librairies of Italy were Searched by candid and enlightened Travellers vast treasures might be discovered and much light Spread on the knowledge of the human mind—to which conclusion I am inclined from the glances I have thrown on their Literary productions of the 15 and Sixteenth Century—

In England—as well as in germany truth Steps boldly forward with gigantic Steps—few publications more in the manner of Basanistes—assisted by prudent Politic Reformers may Sap that baseless Fabric, and crumble it in ruins—Let only the XXXIX art be Sent hors de combat, leaving the loaves and fishes of Church-emoluments—as a Political measure—to the Episcopalians without compelling these to a particular Set of tenets—with the Sinking of the rotten burroughs and few other Parliamentary reforms. and England may Survive a long while in prosperity—While all the continental powers Shall have dwindled away to their former insignificancy—and arts and Sciences—and commerce—having crossed the ocean—and numerous Independant Governments—of every Size and modification established and grown up in America, the names of Washington—of Adams and Jefferson Shall be reechoed from the Atlantic to the Pacific Sea. One word more—I See—with great Satisfaction—that—Te auspice—Deo adjuvante—your university is to be regenerated. All depends upon its organisation—can your all-powerfull influence in Virginia not effect—the creation of one Professorat—of Divinity—,,to give Lectures in <u>Jewish Antiquities Ekclesiastical history</u> and <u>Biblical Criticism</u>,,—whose united powers—well combined—and prudently and boldly exerted—no error can resist?   I received from England Belsham Portrait—a masterly engraving—and with it—a Letter of a Mabar Indian to the unitarian Society—who preaches that doctrine in India with Success—informing me, that the learned Brahmin[x] whose only objection to Christianity is the doctrine of the Trinity, intends to make a visit to London—If So—I expect to hear its Success. Recommending me to the continuance of your kind distinguishing attentions, I remain with high respect

    Your grateful and obliged   F Adr van der Kemp

[x] Ram Mohan Roy[4]

RC (DLC); dateline at foot of text; endorsed by TJ as received 26 Dec. 1818 and so recorded in SJL. RC (MHi); address cover only; with PoC of TJ to Frederick A. Mayo, 25 Mar. 1819, on verso; addressed: "Thomas Jefferson LLD at his Seat Monticello Virginia"; franked; postmarked Trenton, N.Y., 10 Dec.

UT UNDA INPELLITUR UNDA ("as wave is pushed on by wave") is from Ovid, *Metamorphoses,* 15.181 (*Ovid,* trans. Grant Showerman, J. H. Mozley, and Frank Justus Miller, Loeb Classical Library [1914–29; rev. George P. Goold, 1977–79], 4:376–7). Abigail Adams's LAST LETTER to Van der Kemp, dated 28 Apr. 1818, offered her condolences for the death of one of his grandchildren (FC in Lb in MHi: Adams Papers; Van der Kemp to TJ, 5 Apr. 1818). The followers of Abraham Gottlob Werner and James Hutton (WERNERIANS—AND HUTTON-IANS) espoused competing theories of

geological creation. By SPECIFALLY Van der Kemp evidently means "as a species," as opposed to "as individuals." OUR GOV: DeWitt Clinton.

When Jewish refugees fearing persecution in Brazil arrived in New Amsterdam in 1654, colonial governor Peter Stuyvesant wanted them ejected. They enlisted the help of Jews in Amsterdam, who successfully petitioned the Dutch West India Company on their behalf (Hasia R. Diner, *The Jews of the United States 1654 to 2000* [2006], 13–4). The Thirty-Nine Articles (XXXIX ART) of 1571 laid out the basic tenets of belief of the Church of England, whose clergy were required to subscribe to them (John Bowker, ed., *The Oxford Dictionary of World Religions* [1997], 971).

TE AUSPICE—DEO ADJUVANTE: "We implore God's help." Rammohun Roy (the MABAR INDIAN) was a political and religious thinker in Calcutta who advocated a monotheistic blend of Hindu and Christian traditions (*ODNB*).

To Alfred H. Dashiell

SIR   Monticello Dec. 11. 18.

Your favor of Dec. 1. has been duly recieved. altho' age & declining health and strength would render me much averse from placin[g] myself before the public on any occasion; yet the duty of bearin[g] testimony to the truth of any fact <u>within my knolege</u>, would over[r]ule [t]hat reluctance: to go <u>beyond my knolege</u>, would be more than error on the other side. on one of my visits to Bedford I learned with pleasure, from my neighbors there, that they had procured, for the Academy of N. London, a teacher from whom, altho' they were not judges of his classical qualifications, they had formed sanguine hopes and even expectations, of a satisfactory administration of the school. I was glad myself, without further information, to place my grandson Eppes under the same hopes. no opportunities occurred, as you will recollect, of my forming, for myself, any estimate of the degree of classical instruction which you might be able to give to your pupils, except the examination I attended. but that was of boys little advanced, some of whom I think you told me had been with you but 3. months, & none of them a year. the examinations were short, those of all the classes being comprised within the compass of 3. or 4. hours, nor did any thing occur, during the examination, which could give you an opportunity of shewing to what higher grade of instruction you were competent. under these circumstances, any certificate I could give, if restrained within the limits of my <u>knolege</u>, must be so modified as to signify very little. I should regret much the loss of an occasion of being serviceable to you, were it not that the opportunities of manifesting your qualifications for instruction are such as will enable you to do justice to yourself with little delay; & certainly I wish your success with great sincerity. at New London, I am certain, you might have had as many pupils as you would have recieved. my grandson Eppes, after whom you are so kind as to enquire, is at a private school where he will remain until our Central college, or University, shall get into operation. I pray you to accept the assurance of my continued esteem & respect   TH: JEF[FERSON]

PoC (DLC); on verso of a reused address cover from Wilson Cary Nicholas to TJ; several words faint; at foot of text: "Mʳ Dashiell"; endorsed by TJ.

To Samuel Knox

SIR   Monticello Dec. 11. 18

Your favor of Nov. 30. was recieved on the 9th inst. the institution to which your letter relates, was proposed at first to be established, on private subscriptions, under the name of the Central College. these subscriptions amounting to not more than 50,000.D we expected to employ not more than 2. or 3. professors. on petitioning the legislature for some constitutional regulations for it, they took up the subject of education more generally, and passed a law for the establishment of an university, & appointment of Comm^{rs} to report to them a proper site & plan, to accept donations E^tc these Commissioners have reported in favor of the Central College as a site, whereupon the visitors of that College transferred it's whole property, lands, buildings, and subscriptions to the public for the use of the University. it's present situation then is such [th]at it's Visitors are functi officio, having conveyed away the subject of their trust; and the legislature have as yet decided nothing, and consequently no new authorities yet exist who can act on any applications. as to myself, I give all the aid I can towards bringing it into existence; but, that done, age, and declining health and strength will oblige me to leave to younger characters the details of execution. 'senex sum, et curis levissimis impar.' I withdraw even from all correspondence not indispensably incumbent on me.   I am sorry to hear of persecutions of science in Maryland. education has been too much neglected in the Southern states. in no form of government, more than ours, is it true, that 'knolege is power.' and under all governments it is wealth, reputation and happiness. I pray you to accept the assurance of my great esteem & respect.

TH: JEFFERSON

PoC (DLC); on verso of reused address cover of Honoré Julien to TJ, 11 Sept. 1818; torn at seal; at foot of text: "Dr Samuel Knox"; endorsed by TJ.

FUNCTI OFFICIO: "without further authority or legal competence because the duties and functions of the original commission have been fully accomplished" (*Black's Law Dictionary*). For the phrase SENEX SUM, ET CURIS LEVISSIMIS IMPAR, see note to TJ to Peter Poinsot, 25 Nov. 1818.

[484]

From Francis Preston

Dear Sir   Richmond. Dec[r] 11th 1818

It was with considerable difficulty I prevailed on myself the other day to call on you, believing that you were so frequently interrupted by visitors without bussiness that it must be oppressive to you—but my devotion to you politically and personally and the circumstance of your late indisposition induced me to forego the difficulty, and determine on paying my respects to you—And altho' the hour I spent with you was extremely satisfactory to me, yet I thought it would probably be my last claim on your time—But in the Course of our conversation you mentioned your acquaintance with Dougal Stuart & M[r] Leslie literary Characters of Edinburg and since my arrival at this place having rec[d] a letter from my Son now in Europe announcing to me that he will spend the Winter in Edinburg I have tho't it would be of singular advantage to him to be made acquainted with these gentlemen— I have therefore prevailed on myself to ask a short introductory letter in favour of him from you to them—and I will answer for it by my Character which I hold more dear than any other consideration that his deportment and integrity will be correct and unimpeachable—

You will readily perceive the solicitude of a Parent in this application by its manner, but I beg of you my Dear Sir if it is out of your ordinary Course to give letters of this sort, that you will not hesitate a moment even of giving yourself the trouble to answer this—much less to comply with the request

I am D[r] Sir with great Esteem & respect Your mo ob[t]

FRAN[s] PRESTON

RC (MHi); endorsed by TJ as received 17 Dec. 1818 and so recorded in SJL.

Francis Preston (1765–1835), attorney and public official, was born in Botetourt County at his family's estate of Greenfield, studied at the College of William and Mary, 1783–87, and read law under George Wythe. He represented Montgomery County in the Virginia House of Delegates, 1788–89, was a deputy commonwealth's attorney, 1788–93, and sat in the United States House of Representatives, 1793–97. Preston moved to Washington County in 1793 and settled in Abingdon in 1810. He was a county justice, sheriff, and master of his Masonic lodge. Active in the Washington County militia by 1799, Preston commanded a regiment in the War of 1812 and eventually attained the rank of major general. He returned to the House of Delegates, 1813–14, and served in the Senate of Virginia, 1817–20. Preston died in Columbia, South Carolina, while visiting his son William C. Preston. At his death his personal property was valued at $22,731.50, including forty-one slaves (Lewis Preston Summers, *History of Southwest Virginia, 1746–1786, Washington County, 1777–1870* [1903], esp. 755–6; *William and Mary Provisional List*, 33; Leonard, *General Assembly*; Preston to TJ, 1 Jan. [1809] [ViW: TC-JP]; Butler, *Virginia Militia*, 209, 235, 307–8; DNA: RG 29, CS, Washington Co., 1810, 1820, Abingdon, 1830; Washington *Daily National Intelligencer*, 8 June 1835; Richmond *Whig*

& Public Advertiser, 16 June 1835; Washington Co. Will Book, 7:63–4, 66–7; gravestone inscription in Aspenvale Cemetery, Seven Mile Ford, Smyth Co.).

From John Vaughan

D^R SIR.   Philad. 11 Dec. 1818

I have your favor of 7th & feel no Small satisfaction once more to hear from you after Your severe indisposition—I hope nothing of it remains—Mr Appleton wrote to me that he missed the Bill—My Clerk who saw it made up says it was certainly put in—a Second Copy went via New York—& I have now sent the two remaining ones. Via Marseilles & Havre—I trust he is long since in possession of the Dft—

I remain with great respect Your friend & servant

J^N VAUGHAN

M Cooper mentioned a Swelling which wanted to be discussed.[1] There is a plaister here which Dr Physic & others used—called Mahy's plaster, introducd at my instigation which is very powerful in its effects— Should any thing of the Kind be wanted, let me have the pleasure of sending it—

RC (MHi); at head of text: "Thomas Jefferson Monticello"; endorsed by TJ as received 17 Dec. 1818 and so recorded in SJL.

MAHY'S PLASTER was purportedly invented in France in 1713 under the name of "Divine Ointment" or "Divine Plaster Cloth" and brought in about 1793 to Philadelphia. Sold there as Mahy's Plaster Cloth by multiple purveyors using varying ingredients, it was touted as a cure for a wide range of medical conditions (Philadelphia *Franklin Gazette*, 13 June 1818; Lewis Merlin, trans., *The Treasure of Health* [Philadelphia, 1819], viii–x, 251–5).

[1] Omitted period at right margin editorially supplied.

From John Barnes

DEAR SIR—   George Town Co^a 12th Decr 1818.

In conformity to your fav^r of the 7th I inclose Messrs Gales & Seatons, receipt $6⁶⁷, it gives me sincere pleasure to find, you take your Usual ride, may a continuance of it, restore you to perfect health,—is the repeated wishes of your Numerous inquiring friends.

Be Asured—no One more so—than

Dear Sir,

Your Obed^t servant   JOHN BARNES,

RC (MHi); endorsed by TJ as received 17 Dec. 1818 and so recorded in SJL. RC (ViU: TJP); address cover only; with PoC of TJ to Curtis Carter and William B. Phillips, 9 Apr. 1819, on verso; addressed: "Thomas Jefferson, Esqʳ Monticello, Virginia"; franked; postmarked Georgetown, 12 Dec. Enclosure: receipt from Gales & Seaton to TJ, [ca. 11 Dec. 1818], for $6.67, covering his subscription to the Washington *National Intelligencer* from 31 Oct. 1817 to 11 Dec. 1818 (MS in DLC: TJ Papers, 214:38190; printed form, with blanks filled in by an unidentified hand; undated; endorsed by TJ: "Newspapers. Gales & Seaton Natˡ Intelligencer recᵗ to Dec. 11. 1818").

From William Short

DEAR SIR   Philadelphia Dec: 12. 1818

My letter of the 17ᵗʰ ulᵗᵒ will have informed you of the very great pleasure which yours of the 10ᵗʰ gave me, & the relief which I recieved from it at the moment, on account of the anxiety under which I was as to your health. I feel now that I have need of a repetition of this anodyne—for since your letter of the 10ᵗʰ of Novʳ now more than a month, I have not heard of the progress of your convalescence. I wish therefore very much indeed to hear from you again on this subject—but I fear at the same time to ask it, knowing as I do, how much trouble it gives you to write, & how many calls of this kind you have. It would be a great gratification to me if I could by any means procure a regular bulletin of your health, but I know that is impossible, & as Hume says, the human mind submits to necessity.

On recieving your letter my first impulse was to administer to your friends here the same relief which I had recieved—Many of them had at different times expressed to me their anxiety on account of the reports which prevailed. I thought the best mode would be to write a note to Mʳ Vaughan, who is a kind of petite poste in the City, & in it I inserted an extract from your own letter as being most satisfactory—& I requested him to make your friends here (all of whom he was more likely to see in one day, than I should be in a week) acquainted with the favorable turn in your disorder. Mʳ Vaughan in his zeal thought he could not do better than to insert my note in the gazette. This I percieved by finding it inserted in the National Intelligencer as taken from a Philadelphia paper. This was not my intention & I should not have inserted thus any part of your letter without your permission. This I observe as a general rule. In the present instance there is no inconvenience, & the intention of Vaughan I know was good.

I shall be very anxious to hear the decision of the Legislature as to the location of the University. I hope & trust they will adopt the report of the commissioners chosen as they were, from every district of the State. It would have been much more proper, it seems to me, to have left it definitively to them than to have reserved it for Legislative interference.

This Legislature for some years back has seldom met without making, or threatening, some attack on the Canal in which you were so good as to procure me shares during my absence in Europe—I always apprehended this would be the case as soon as the dividends should be such as to exite envy, & I remember having scandalized Mr Eppes, by advancing this sentiment when I met with him at Monticello on my first return from Europe—But I know that an hundred men together are never ashamed of any thing. And therefore I always endeavour as far as possible not to place myself within the immediate grasp of an Assembly who by a <u>Whereas</u>, can do any thing as Lord Coke says of the Sovereign Court of Parliament, except making a Man, a Woman. A favorable occasion presenting itself I have therefore sold my shares for $375 each which you procured at less than par or $200—The late dividends gave more than legal interest on $375—& if the maxim of <u>laissez faire</u> & <u>laissez passer</u> should be applied to the Canal, the dividends without doubt will increase—but as I said, I did not like to be one of a company making large & increasing dividends under the immediate view of an Assembly—The purchasers were a public institution composed of men much better acquainted with the Legislature than I am, & better able to judge of the prospect of their interference. I hope therefore they will keep their fingers off—I shall not however regret the sale, as I acted on a general principle, & have a particular aversion to uncertainty in matters of this kind.

I hope you have seen M^{de} de Stael's last work—I think it would please you much, & that you would approve the principles she professes from beginning to end. It is the most faithful picture of the great personages of the Revolution that I have seen. The wild genius of M^{de} de Stael which you saw unbridled & uncontrolled, has been rendered docile by experience & is rich indeed in profound observations. Her heart was always excellent—her head had become worthy of her heart.

I forget that even reading my <u>griffonage</u> may be painful to you, & may discourage you from writing. I will end here therefore with only renewing my intreaty to hear from you & learning the progress of your convalescence if it can be done without too much pain to you.　　　I remain dear sir, as you have ever known me, with sentiments of invariable gratitude & affection

Your friend & servant　　　　　　　　　　　　　　W: SHORT

RC (MHi); endorsed by TJ as received 20 Dec. 1818 and so recorded in SJL.

On the day before Short wrote this letter, James Madison reported from Montpellier to James Monroe on TJ's CONVALESCENCE, writing that "Dʳ Eustis & his lady having given us a call, it was agreed that he & myself shᵈ make a short visit to Mʳ Jefferson of whose state of health, I had never been able to get any precise information. We found him substantially restored from his indisposition, with good appetite, and in the daily practice of taking exercise on horseback. All that remains of the effect produced by the mineral water, is a cutaneous affection of the most superficial kind, which will probably soon disappear" (DLC: Monroe Papers).

In his essay "Of Polygamy and Divorces," David HUME argued that "the Heart of Man naturally submits to Necessity, and soon loses an Inclination when there appears an absolute Impossibility of satisfying it" (Hume, *Essays, Moral and Political* [Edinburgh, 1741–42], 2:189). The Parisian PETITE POSTE carried mail within the city and suburbs, while the grande poste went throughout France and abroad. TJ began buying shares in the James River Company's CANAL on Short's behalf in 1795 (*PTJ,* 28:353, 431, 434, 438, 444). Soon after returning from France, Short met John Wayles EPPES at Monticello in September 1802 (Merrill D. Peterson, ed., *Visitors to Monticello* [1989], 34).

The opinion that an English PARLIAMENT "can do any thing but make a man a woman, and a woman a man," was attributed to Henry Herbert, 2d Earl of Pembroke, by his son Philip Herbert, the 4th Earl, in a speech in 1648 (Elizabeth Knowles, ed., *The Oxford Dictionary of Quotations* [2004], 591). Griffonnage (GRIFFONAGE): "scribble; scrawl."

To Jean Guillaume Hyde de Neuville

Monticello Dec. 13. 18.

I thank your Excellency for the notice, with which your letter favors me, of the liberation of France from the occupation of the allied powers. to no one, not a native, will it give more pleasure. in the desolation of Europe to gratify the atrocious caprices of Bonaparte, France sinned much: but she has suffered more than retaliation. once relieved from the Incubus of her late oppression, she will rise like a giant from her slumbers. her soil and climate, her arts and eminent science, her central position and free constitution, will soon make her greater than she ever was. and I am a false prophet if she does not, at some future day, remind of her sufferings those who have inflicted them the most eagerly. I hope however she will be quiet for the present, and risk no new troubles. her constitution, as now amended, gives as much of self-government as perhaps she can yet bear, and will give more when the habits of order shall have prepared her to recieve more. besides the gratitude which every American owes her, as our sole ally during the war of independance, I am additionally affectioned by the friendships I contracted there, by the good dispositions I witnessed, and by the courtesies I recieved.

I rejoice, as a Moralist, at the prospect of a reduction of the duties on wine, by our national legislature. it is an error to view a tax on that liquor as merely a tax on the rich. it is a prohibition of it's use to the midling class of our citizens, and a condemnation of them to the poison of whisky, which is desolating their houses. no nation is drunken where wine is cheap; and none sober, where the dearness of wine substitutes ardent spirits as the common beverage. it is in truth the only antidote to the bane of whisky. fix but the duty at the rate of other merchandise, and we can drink wine here as cheaply as we do grog: and who will not prefer it? it's extended use will carry health and comfort to a much enlarged circle. every one in easy circumstances (as the bulk of our citizens are) will prefer it to the poison to which they are now driven by their government. and the treasury itself will find that a penny apiece from a dozen is more than a groat from a single one. this reformation however will require time. our merchants know nothing of the infinite variety of cheap and good wines to be had in Europe; and particularly in France, in Italy, and the Graecian islands: as they know little also of the variety of excellent manufactures and comforts to be had any where out of England. nor will these things be known, nor of course called for here, until the native merchants of those countries, to whom they are known, shall bring them forward, exhibit & vend them at the moderate profits they can afford. this alone will procure them familiarity with us, and the preference they merit in competition with corresponding articles now in use.   Our family renews with pleasure their recollections of your kind visit to Monticello, and joins me in tendering sincere assurances of the gratification it afforded us, and of our great esteem & respectful consideration   TH: JEFFERSON

RC (facsimile in catalogue for Sotheby's auction, New York City, 15 June 2006, lot 203, pp. 211–2). PoC (DLC); at foot of first page: "M. de Neuville. Ambassador of France." Not recorded in SJL.

From Joseph C. Cabell

DEAR SIR,   Richmond 14 Dec. 1818.

M. Banks has not appointed as good a select committee as I had expected. There is a decided majority of the committee in favor of the Central College: but the eastern members are less attentive than the western. I have urged the importance of having a full meeting, before the final question is taken. M. Taylor is aware of the danger. The committee has had two meetings; at the first, it was decided to report by bill. M. Taylor has copied your bill and at the second meeting offered it to the committee. The friends of Lexington wish to have the clause of location reported with a blank. I think it will ultimately be decided to fill the blank with the Central College. At the 2^d meeting this morning, the Valley members called for time to consider the provisions of the bill: the real object was to have time to manoevre. The motion was resisted, but carried; some of the friends of Charlottesville voting with them. The members from Rockbridge called for a calculation[1] to prove the assertion in the Report, that Charlottesville is nearer to the Center of population than Staunton or Lexington. The object seemed to be to draw out your calculations exhibited to the Commissioners. The answer given by an eastern member was that each member might satisfy himself by reference to the Census of 1810. The point was left unsettled. It will come on again at the next meeting on a motion to strike out Charlottesville from the bill. The Committee will meet again on thursday morning. The Valley members will be strongly opposed to the Central College. The members from beyond the Alleghaney will divide. Those South of Kanawha will generally vote with us, as Mr Thompson informs me. The prospect is still favorable: but the effect of intrigue and management is beyond the reach of calculation. There is a party in the House of Delegates opposed to the measure in every shape. I hope that party is not strong. The weight of character in the Board is working the effects I calculated on when I first suggested that measure. The wayward spirits on this side the ridge are awed into acquiescence. I am D^r sir, faithfully yours   JOSEPH C. CABELL

P.S. Some imprudent friend has suffered it to get out that you are the author of the bill. It has been sneeringly remarked that we have a bill "ready cut & dry." I hope the knowledge of the fact will do no injury. An attempt will doubtless be made to give it the appearance of dictating to the Assembly: yet I believe it will not succeed.

RC (ViU: TJP-PC); endorsed by TJ as received 17 Dec. 1818 and so recorded in SJL. RC (DLC); address cover only; with PoC of TJ to John Laval, 11 Apr. 1819, on verso; addressed: "Thomas Jefferson Monticello"; franked; postmarked Richmond, 14 Dec.

The MEMBERS FROM ROCKBRIDGE County on the select committee of the Virginia House of Delegates formed to consider the *University of Virginia Commissioners' Report* were Andrew Alexander and John Bowyer (Leonard, *General Assembly*, 295).

[1] Manuscript: "calcution."

From Patrick Gibson

Sir   Richmond 14th Decr 1818 —

I have received your favor of the 9th Ins^t covering three blank notes for renewal, also advising sundry dfts, which shall be attended to — Not a barrel of your Bedford flour has yet been received, which is unfortunate as it has declined since last month, and must be lower so soon as, the Mills can grind, and it can be brought freely into market

With much respect & esteem I am Your ob^t Servt

PATRICK GIBSON

RC (MHi); between dateline and salutation: "Thomas Jefferson Esqre"; endorsed by TJ as received 17 Dec. 1818 and so recorded in SJL.

From James H. McCulloch

Sir   Custom House Balt^o Coll^{ts} Off' Decr 14 1818

I had the pleasure of receiving your letter of the 28th Ult^o respecting a box of books shipped by Mr Beasly for you in the Dumfries from Havre de Grace & directed to my care. I had waited for the opportunity of receiving & shipping the box to Richmond, or you should have been informed at first of its arrival, & answered afterwards upon receiving your letter. It is to day put on board the Schooner Federalist J Brown for that place, & I have informed Mr Gibson of its going to his care.

The rules of the Custom House are not[1] rigidly applied in the cases of such whose public station & services have continued a privilege of dispensation from some formalities. If you have no friend here Sir, to make the entry when the invoice is received, it will be sufficient to remit the duties upon your own calculation in this manner.

The am^t of cost ⅌ bookseller's or agent's acc^t —

charges of carri^a French duty &c—(insur^{ce} commiss & outward pack^{ag} excepted)

10 ⅌ C^t added to value—& upon the aggregate[2] 15 ⅌ C^t

Francs estimated a $18\frac{1}{2}$ Cts ⅌—& $1\frac{1}{4}$ ⅌ C^t added to make dollars; & this will be a good Custom House reckoning in the case of this article.

I remain Sir with all the respect & readiness to serve that you can wish—very sincerely   JA^s H M^cCULLOCH

RC (DLC); endorsed by TJ as received 20 Dec. 1818 and so recorded in SJL. RC

(ViU: TJP); address cover only; with PoC of TJ to Randolph Harrison, 11 Apr.

1819, on verso; addressed: "Thomas Jefferson Esqr Monticello Near _____ Virginia"; franked; postmarked (faint) Baltimore, [1]4 Dec.

[1] Word interlined.
[2] Manuscript: "aggreate."

From David M. Randolph (1798–1825)

DEAR SIR   Richmond December 14. 1818.

A man named Warrener, a bricklayer & plasterer by trade, desired me to ask of you whether he could get employment at the Central College.[1] I have seen some of his work and as far as I can judge it is very well executed, he will work one month on trial on any terms you please, and if at the expiration of that time you chose it, he will engage to remain as long as he is wanted, satisfactory recommendations can be produced, both as to his morals, and to his abilities in the line of his profession, being regularly bred to the business[2] in his own country (England) he is qualified to execute the ornamental branches of his trade equally well as the more usefull; if you wish to employ him, you will let me know it and he will go up directly. I believe another workman could be procured if wanted, who is as capable as the one above mentioned, with the best wishes for the long continuation of your valued & usefull[3] life.

I remain with the greatest respect yours to command

D M RANDOLPH, JUNIOR

RC (DLC); endorsed by TJ (trimmed) as received 2[0] Dec. 1818. RC (MHi); address cover only; with PoC of TJ to Patrick Gibson, 11 Apr. 1819, on verso; addressed: "Thomas Jefferson Esqr Monticello Albemarle va"; franked; postmarked Richmond, 16 Dec. Recorded in SJL as received 20 Dec. 1818.

David Meade Randolph (1798–1825) was the son of David Meade Randolph (ca. 1759–1830) and Mary Randolph, and the nephew of TJ's son-in-law Thomas Mann Randolph. He attended the College of William and Mary, 1816–18. Known as Meade within the family, he visited his cousins at Monticello in 1818 and 1823 and maintained a friendly correspondence with Nicholas P. Trist and Hore Browse Trist. Randolph suffered from poor health that apparently resulted in a physical deformity, making it difficult for him to earn a living. He resided at various locations in Virginia, often staying with family members. In his final year he was teaching at a school in York County, at which time his father unsuccessfully attempted to get him appointed librarian at the University of Virginia. Randolph died while on a visit to his mother in Norfolk, a fate his cousin Virginia J. Randolph Trist described as "the most fortunate that ever befel him" (Robert Isham Randolph, *The Randolphs of Virginia* [1936], 217–8; *William and Mary Provisional List*, 33; Randolph to Nicholas P. Trist, 10 Feb., 6 Nov. 1818, 13 Mar., 24 Mar., 6 Oct. 1820, 7 Oct. 1823, Martha Jefferson Randolph to Jane H. Nicholas Randolph, 14 Aug. 1818, and Elizabeth Trist to Nicholas P. Trist, 27 July 1820 [NcU: NPT]; Hore Browse Trist to Nicholas P. Trist, 22 Mar., 24 Sept. 1819 [DLC: NPT]; Martha Jefferson Randolph to Ann Cary Morris, 28 Dec. 1821 [PPAmP: Smith-Houston-Morris-Ogden Family Papers];

David M. Randolph [ca. 1759–1830] to TJ, 20 Apr. 1825, and TJ's reply, 2 May 1825; Martha Jefferson Randolph to Ellen W. Randolph Coolidge, 13 Oct. 1825 and Virginia J. Randolph Trist to Coolidge, 16 Oct. 1825 [ViU: Coolidge Papers]; *Richmond Enquirer*, 18 Oct. 1825).

[1] Omitted period at right margin editorially supplied.
[2] Manuscript: "biusiness."
[3] Manuscript: "esefull."

From Fernagus De Gelone

Sir,   New York Decemb. 15 1818.

According to your orders to Mr Belair, I have laid aside for you

1° Ducange Glossarium. 3. folio bound in vellum.

2° Cabanis, affections catharrales, 8vo

3° Sallustii Catilin. &a Dureau La Malle. 8vo bound. french Latin

4° Suetone, 4 8vo Latin french. bound. De la pause. 1771.

5° henri quatre, par Perefixe. 12° broché.

6° Appien, Guerres Civiles de Rome.—

7° Planche, Dictionnaire, Grec français. gros 8vo

. Tacite, Dureau La Malle.
  Pline le Jeune—
  Denis d'halicarnasse.
.. Stephani Thesaurus Græcæ
   linguæ. 5. folio.
.. La Place Système du Monde.
. Sacrorum Bibliorum
  Concordantiæ.
.. Persoon's Synopsis fungorum
..   do   plantarum.
.. La Place, Mecanique Celeste.
. Dictionnaire de Medecine, avec
  Lexicon.
  Epictetus. Greek and Italian. <u>Bodoni</u>. very Scarce in Europe.
  vellum.

I will lay these books aside at the prices mentioned by Mr Belair. the thesaurus Costs in cash 375 francs. the London Copy which is reprinting will Cost in England at least 20. guineas.

I open more books received by the Tybee and the factor.

Dictionnaire Bibliographique has not been Sent. there was only one copy which is not found in the Store. after I have put order in my books, if it is here or in Philadelphia, I will direct it to you. I have Journal Bibliographique de la france. it relates only to the four or five years past. it has tables and a dictionnaire raisonné.

from this day, I will take orders for Europe, for books and maps of all descriptions and languages.

If I am at last encouraged as a Man fit for the purpose, I intend to have the most useful book-Store in America. I will be in Europe again next Spring. I think I could be useful to the General Government. I do not want money, but when the property is received and accepted.

Pray, Sir, be So good as to give me your opinion about the probability of Success of another branch of my establishment in Georgetown, or Washington City, Richmond or Charleston S.C. I ask your pardon for this liberty.

I am most respectfully sir
Your most humble obedient Servant

FERNAGUS DE GELONE
96. Broad Way

I have a Store or rather a book establishment in Paris, and I have been an American for Sixteen years.

RC (MHi); with dots preceding titles evidently added by TJ and relating to his 27 Dec. 1818 reply; endorsed by TJ as received 20 Dec. 1818 and so recorded in SJL. RC (MHi); address cover only; with PoC of TJ to Nathaniel Gordon, 1 Apr. 1819, on verso; addressed: "Thomas Jefferson Esqr Monticelo—Milton. Virg^a"; franked; postmarked New York, 15 Dec.

GROS 8VO: "large octavo." The JOURNAL BIBLIOGRAPHIQUE DE LA FRANCE was *Bibliographie de la France, ou Journal Général de l'Imprimerie et de la Librairie* (Poor, *Jefferson's Library*, 14 [no. 928]). DICTIONNAIRE RAISONNÉ: "critical dictionary."

From George H. Richards

SIR. New London Connecticut Decr 15th AD 1818.

It has long[1] been a favourite object of my literary ambition to become the biographer of yourself and a few other the great and eminent men of our country. The varied scenes which have passed in review since you came upon the stage of action, and the part you have acted in that novel & splendid drama which has been exhibited in the theatre of the new world, have created a public interest in your private memoirs, whilst but little leisure can have been afforded you for their compilation. This task should not be left unexecuted. Our national is so interwoven with your personal history as, in a degree, to be inseperable. The present & future ages have claims which should not be refused; & justice to the merits of your own fame & to the veracity of History enforces the demand.

Under these circumstances, as well from a sense of public duty as from an admiration of the virtues & talents of the subject of the memoir, I venture to offer my services to execute the task, if it be not already confided to abler hands.

Of the delicacy & responsibility of such a work, I am not unaware, and that it may not be entrusted to any man without satisfactory testimonials of character, education, and ability. Such testimonials shall be produced, the moment it is ascertained that the services here offered will be acceptable.

To render these services, it would be necessary to have access to all those papers, whether of a public or private nature, which you might think calculated to reflect light upon any events of your life; and to improve these papers, I should be ready, either to examine them at your residence, or to have them transmitted to me at this place.

From the conditions on which the offer of my services on this subject is made, I trust, Sir, you will not deem it presumptuous; but accept, as an apology, the assurance of those sentiments of profound respect

with which I have the honour to be Your Ob. Sert.

GEO. H. RICHARDS.

RC (ViW: TC-JP); endorsed by TJ as received 28 Dec. 1818 and so recorded in SJL. RC (DLC); address cover only; with PoC of TJ to Peter S. Du Ponceau, 14 Mar. [1819], on verso; addressed: "To His Excellency Thomas Jefferson, Late President of the United States, Monticello, Virginia."

George Hallam Richards (1791–1843), attorney and public official, was born in New London, Connecticut, graduated from Brown University in 1809, and subsequently studied law at Tapping Reeve's Litchfield Law School. He qualified for the bar immediately prior to the War of 1812 but enlisted in the United States Army at the outbreak of hostilities and served from 1812 to 1815, rising from first lieutenant to captain in the artillery. After three years' wartime absence, Richards had difficulty resuming his legal career and sought a government position, becoming a clerk in the Treasury Department in Washington by 1823. He proposed to produce biographical works on prominent Americans and in 1833 published one on General Alexander Macomb. Richards also patented improvements to carriages, tanning, and waterproofing. In the 1830s and 1840s he lived in New York City, where he was working as a deputy revenue inspector at the time of his death (*Historical Catalogue of Brown University, 1764–1904* [1905], 105; Marian C. McKenna, *Tapping Reeve and The Litchfield Law School* [1986], 194; Heitman, *U.S. Army*, 1:828; "A Federal Republican" [Richards], *The Politics of Connecticut* [Hartford, 1817]; Richards, *An Oration, delivered before Union Lodge, No. 31, at St. James' Church, in the City of New-London* [New York, 1819]; *List of Patents for Inventions and Designs, issued by the United States, from 1790 to 1847* [1847], 101, 209, 302; DNA: RG 59, LAR, 1817–25; Peter Force, *The National Calendar, and Annals of the United States for MDCCCXXIII* [Washington, 1823], 22; Easton, Md., *General Advertiser*, 30 Dec. 1828; Richards, *Memoir of Alexander Macomb, the Major General commanding the Army of the United States* [1833]; *Longworth's New York Directory* [1835]: 552; [1842]: 516; [1843]: 284; DNA: RG 29, CS, N.Y., New York, 1840; New York *Evening Post*, 23 Dec. 1843; Washington *Daily National Intelligencer*, 5 Jan. 1844).

On this date Richards sent a similar letter to John Adams (MHi: Adams Papers).

[1] Word interlined.

From Samuel Butler (for Hezekiah Niles)

SIR   Baltimore 16th Decr. 1818.—

Your favor of 9th Ins^t is at Hand covering five dollars for your subscription to the Weekly Register for the current year—inclosed you have a rec^t for the same. and please receive thanks for your polite attention and punctuality.

With great respect I am sir yours

S. BUTLER

in behalf of HEZ. NILES

who at present is out of Town—

RC (DLC); at foot of text: "Thos Jefferson Esqr Monticello"; endorsed by TJ as a letter from "Henry" Niles received 20 Dec. 1818 and so recorded in SJL; with additional notation by TJ above endorsement: "Newspapers." Enclosure: receipt from Butler (for Niles) to TJ, Baltimore, 16 Dec. 1818, for five dollars, covering subscription to Baltimore *Weekly Register* "from No. 364 to No. 416 or for 1 year up to September, 1819" (MS in DLC; printed form, with blanks filled in by Butler [here indicated by underscoring] and signed by him).

From Joseph C. Cabell

DEAR SIR,   Richmond. 17th Decr 1818.

The select committee of the House of Delegates on the subject of the university has just had a third meeting. 13 members attended. On the question whether the bill should be reported with a blank as to the scite, it was decided[1] in the negative by the casting vote of the Chairman. The Central College was selected as the scite, and the bill reported to the House. The Lexington party sought for further delays under the pretext of wanting time to consider the calculations as to the centre of population, and to bring forward their own claims. I am really fearful for the ultimate fate of the bill. Since the date of my last, I have discovered that the Delegation from the west are forming a combination among themselves to vote against the bill on the passage. Finding themselves in a minority on the question of the Scite, they will endeavor to defeat the measure altogether for the present. There is a party in the East in favor of putting down the Literary fund. Should these parties unite on the question on the passage of the Bill, it will be lost; and this result is much to be apprehended. The fund cannot be put down, & I cannot but hope that many of its enemies will vote for the University as the best means of rectifying what they deem a bad appropriation. On consultation with Col: Nicholas & my brother W^m I determined to publish your calculations as to the centre of population, in this mornings' enquirer. We deemed the

[497]

publication essential to unite the eastern delegation[2] & to put them under responsibility to their constituents. The anonymous shape was preferrd; but the author is very well known. Knowing the course of argument which the Lexington party would take as to the progress of population since 1810, I have made some auxiliary statements to shew that on the most liberal allowance to the west, we shall have in 1820, a surplus of from 80 to 100,000 white persons. These will be used only in a defensive way.

I am, D[r] Sir, faithfully yours   JOSEPH C. CABELL

RC (ViU: TJP-PC); endorsed by TJ as received 20 Dec. 1818 and so recorded in SJL. Enclosed in Cabell to TJ, 17 Dec. 1818 (second letter).

Chesterfield County delegate Samuel Taylor was THE CHAIRMAN of the House select committee considering the University Bill. TJ's CALCULATIONS AS TO THE CENTRE OF POPULATION of Virginia are printed above at 4 Aug. 1818 as document 2 in a group of documents on the Rockfish Gap Meeting of the University of Virginia Commissioners.

[1] Cabell here canceled "to fill."
[2] Cabell here canceled "on the east of the ridge."

From Joseph C. Cabell

DEAR SIR,   Senate Chamber. 2 p.m. 17 Dec[r] 1818.

Since writing the within I have conversed with M[r] Davidson, the Senator from Clarksburg. He arrived but two days ago. His friendship I was sure of: I feared the opposition had drawn him so far over, as to silence him: but I did him injustice. He tells me he has conversed with 22 members from the N. West: and they all, except one,[1] expressed themselves in favor of the Central College. Davidson's information again revives my hopes of a favorable issue. He will be very useful to us on this occasion, and his arrival is well timed & very fortunate. Thro' him I can penetrate the designs of the opposition, and I trust be able to break their combination. Rest assured, sir, that nothing that I can do on this occasion shall be omitted to procure success. I will not stir from the seat of Government till this business is settled: my friends have urged me to go to Williamsburg: but I have refused; even if the dangers to my life existed, which they apprehended, I could not risk it in a better cause.—Faithfully yours

JOSEPH C. CABELL

RC (ViU: TJP-PC); endorsed by TJ as received 20 Dec. 1818 and so recorded in SJL. RC (MHi); address cover only; with PoC of TJ to Mordecai M. Noah, 11 Apr. 1819, on verso; addressed: "Thomas Jefferson Monticello"; franked; post-marked Richmond, 17 Dec. Enclosure: Cabell to TJ, 17 Dec. 1818 (first letter).

M[r] DAVIDSON: George J. Davisson.

[1] Cabell here canceled "promised."

From Anonymous

In sight of virginia, my native State

VENERABLE FRIEND   Dec^{br} 18th 1818

I rejoice to find you engaged in your latter days, in so laudable an undertaking as that of perfecting a system for the education of our youth: an estabilishement much wanted on your side of the mountains: and which must hereafter prove a great blessing to our posterity.

But, what has astonished me more than all the miracles of Moses, is, that the birth state of Washington, Jefferson, Madison and Munro: from being a star of the <u>first</u> magnitude, has dwindled down to that of a <u>fourth</u>: and if the same causes, continues to operate with the same effect, for twenty five or thirty years more; she will be found as low as the <u>seventh</u>! What is the cause of this <u>opprobrium</u> in virginia's state legislation? And why, with all the advantages of an immense territory, chequered and intersected by fine rivers and streams, do we, notwithstanding, continue to <u>loose rank</u> in the constellation of the states? Alas! I fear, nay I am <u>sure</u>, "there is something <u>rotten</u> in this our state of Denmark." And with your permission, I will endeavour to point out, wherein.

In the first place, we virginians are influenced by a <u>false pride</u>, and a <u>foolish</u> attachment to old forms and customs: which prevents us from <u>imitating</u>, those wise and wholesome improvements in state policy, introduced and practised by the Northern and Western States: whose <u>flourishing</u> condition, is a sad sattire on our state government.

In the next place, a <u>rapid increase</u> of our <u>western population</u>, is the <u>only</u> means left us, to check our retrogade movements. But this cannot be expected under the present aristocratic <u>aspect</u> of some of our laws: nor under the present baneful influence of that hydra of Virginia legislation, the <u>Uncertainty of Virginia titles</u>. This alone, <u>banishes</u> (annually) thousands of the hardy sons and daughters of virginia, from their native state: who with sighs and tears, may be found daily quitting the shores of virginia, in hopes of finding more hospitable laws—Can Jefferson calmly think of dying, while this <u>curse</u>, like a millstone, is grinding and wasting the vitals of his country? God forbid! If the <u>Sage</u> of Monticello help us not: Who shall help us?

Sincerely your friend

RC (MHi); endorsed by TJ as a letter from "Anon. *(J. C. J)*" on "politics" received 16 Jan. 1819 and so recorded in SJL.

The presumably pseudonymous signature is illegible, and TJ seems to have found it equally so and attempted to mimic it in endorsement and SJL.

SOMETHING ROTTEN IN THIS OUR STATE OF DENMARK is from William Shakespeare, *Hamlet*, act 1, scene 4.

From Dabney Cosby

DEAR SIR,   Staunton December 18th 1818

Understanding the Trustees of the Central College have delegated to you the Authority to Contract for the buildings thereof, and believeing in the event of the Commissioners Report to the Legislature being approved, that Authority will be still extended, I wish to offer my services to You in the Character of a Brick maker & Layer.

I have followed that calling upwards of 20. Years and flatter myself with General Satisfaction to my Employers. Could Put up from 3 to 400.000 this Year and from 6 to 700.000 next Year and as long afterwards as required

I will give You Ample security for the Performance of my Contracts and Satisfactory testimonials of my Ability and Knowledge of my Profession.

If you deem a Personal interview necessary I will wait on You At any time You may designate, and Pledge myself to Conduct the business Personally—and <u>faithfully</u>.

Please to inform me by Letter so soon as Your Convenience will Permit that in the event I undertake the Clay may be exposed as much as Possible to the frost this Winter.

With due Respect Yrs   DABNEY COSBY

RC (ViU: TJP); addressed: "Thomas Jefferson Esquire Monticello"; endorsed by TJ as received 25 Dec. 1818 and so recorded in SJL; additional notation by TJ above endorsement: "Brick."

Dabney Cosby (1779–1862), brick mason and builder, was a native of Louisa County who began his career as a brick maker in Staunton late in the 1790s. He worked on the construction of the University of Virginia from 1820 to 1822, as principal brick mason on Hotels D and E and eight dormitories on the west range. Cosby moved to Buckingham County in the mid-1820s and helped build courthouses in Goochland, Lunenburg, and Sussex counties. He subsequently relocated to Prince Edward County and designed and erected buildings at Union Theologi-cal Seminary, then located at Hampden-Sydney College. Cosby also helped construct the main hall of Randolph-Macon College at its original location in Boydton. In 1839 he worked on Halifax County's courthouse. By 1840 Cosby had settled in Raleigh, North Carolina, and he lived in that state thereafter. His career evolved from brick making, first to building and then to design. In later census records his occupation is listed as architect. As of 1860 Cosby owned real estate valued at $1,200 and personal property totaling $6,500, including approximately thirteen slaves (*DVB*; Vi: Cosby Papers; ViHi: Cosby Account Book; *MB*, 2:1393; *Staunton Censor*, 10 Aug. 1808; DNA: RG 29, CS, Augusta Co., 1810, Staunton, 1820, Prince Edward Co., 1830, N.C., Raleigh, 1840–50, 1850 slave schedules, N.C.,

Greenville, 1860, 1860 slave schedules; ViU: PP, Proctor's Ledgers; *Raleigh Register, and North-Carolina Gazette*, 18 May 1841; *Weekly Raleigh Register*, 16 July 1862; gravestone inscription in Oakwood Cemetery, Raleigh).

Early in 1819 Cosby's supporters recommended his work and character to Central College's proctor, Nelson Barks-

dale, and its treasurer, Alexander Garrett (Erasmus Stribling to Barksdale, Staunton, 6 Jan. 1819 [RC in ViU: TJP; endorsed by TJ: "Cosby Dabney. recom^d by Stribling"]; John Waugh to Garrett, Staunton, 7 Jan. 1819 [RC in ViU: TJP; endorsed by TJ: "Bricklayers. Cosby Dabney. recom^d by Waugh"]).

From Anonymous

VERY RESPECTFUL SIR,   Decr 19th 1818.—

Observing in the Enquirer, a Letter from yourself, addressed to "Charles Pinckney Esqr." I concluded to send you a few remarks on certain passages of your Letter; and, believe me Sir, my design is to say nothing but what has a direct tendency to promote your happiness in this world and the next. I greatly esteem your character Sir, and am thankful to GOD and you for the great Services you have rendered a free and happy Country. But, my dear Sir, we all have to live in a future and eternal state! This all-important Truth, you seem (if one may judge from the manner of your writing) rather to dispute; for, Sir, you say, "I weaken very sensibly—yet, with such a continuance of good health, as makes me fear I shall wear out very tediously, which is not what one would wish &c"—

O! my friend, if there was no hereafter, "one would not (sure enough) wish to wear out tediously," but if we are immortal, and are certain to live eternally in a future State of existence, and that too in bliss or woe, we ought to be thankful to GOD, our maker, for not stopping the breath of life suddenly, but rather, by causing us to wear away gradually, gives us warning of our approaching dissolution, that we may be stirred up thereby, to make the necessary preparation for our removal into a new and untried world! Man is not, while in his natural state, prepared to meet GOD. No: the best of men, while unrenewed in Heart, have no disposition or fitness for the enjoyment of a holy GOD in the realms above.—Mr. Jefferson's morals, as a man, were never disputed by any one. The people of America, Sir, will remember you with gratitude, love, and esteem, while you live, and after you are dead: they praise GOD for the influence of your brilliant talents and liberal Sentiments &c among them; but, my dear Sir, all these things, and a thousand more of a like nature, are no proof at all, that a man is a Saint; and, unless you are made a Saint by the influence of Almighty grace, you cannot be happy in Time nor

Eternity! "You must be born again," in order to be qualified for the heavenly world.

GOD, by giving you a lingering weakness, &c. Seems, in mercy, to be reminding you, my friend, that your clay tenement is coming down, and that you are hastening on to the "House appointed for all living." O! therefore, betake yourself to prayer! Fall upon your knees before your maker, and importunately beseech him, for the Sake of his blessed Son, Jesus Christ, to change your Heart, and give you Joy and peace. Then, as you glide down the stream of time into the Ocean of Eternity, you will have bright and glorious prospects beyond the tomb.

Morality, honesty, justice between man and man &c fits us, my friend, for this world, by making us good and valuable members of human Society; but O! my friend, inward piety alone fits us for Heaven!

The authenticity of GOD's Book, the holy Bible, was never disputed by men of candour, sound sense and good understanding; and that Book teaches that man is a lost, ruined, degenerate and miserable creature naturally; and that, in order to be happy and Saved, he must repent, believe in a Saviour and have his fruit unto Holiness &c. These principles, my friend, [. . .] entirely consistent with Sound Reason & understanding. We see glaring proofs innumerable, that man is in a lost and undone condition. Some (ah! multitudes) discover this by their vicious, immoral conduct, while the most moral and civil among us, or in the world, give also, sufficient evidence, that they are strangers to a holy GOD! If their outward conduct is irreproachable, yet, their hearts are worldly, and not right. Now, in order that the heart may become right, there must[1] be an inward, a Supernatural change; which change can only be effected by the operations of divine Grace. Our blessed Redeemer calls this change a "New birth," or the being "Born again." That you, my worthy friend, may experience this great Renewal, and be happy forever, is the unceasing wish and fervent prayer of your sincere friend &c

RC (DLC); in same hand as covering letter; mutilated at seal; addressed: "His Excellency, Thomas Jefferson Esq' Formerly president of the united States, Near Lynchburg" by "Mail: Lynchburg Post-Office"; endorsed by TJ as a letter from "Anon." with "postmark Rocky mount" received 18 Jan. 1819, with the additional bracketed notation: "fanaticism," and so recorded in SJL. Enclosed in Anonymous to TJ, [between 19 Dec. 1818 and 7 Jan. 1819].

TJ's letter to CHARLES PINCKNEY of 3 Sept. 1816, quoted here, was printed in the Richmond Enquirer on 8 Dec. 1818, with quote matching the version printed in the New York National Advocate accounted for at that document. Jesus tells Nicodemus that YOU MUST BE BORN

AGAIN in the Bible, John 3.3 and 3.7. Job expresses his confidence that after death he will be taken to the HOUSE APPOINTED FOR ALL LIVING in Job 30.23. The biblical phrase FRUIT UNTO HOLINESS comes from Romans 6.22.

[1] Remainder of text added perpendicularly in margin between second and third page.

From Anonymous

O! MY WORTHY SIR,   [between 19 Dec. 1818 and 7 Jan. 1819]

I feel an increasing concern for your happiness and salvation. Since the enclosed was sealed, the Enquirer again has fell into my hands, in which I find much said in favour of the "Luminous pen and influence of Thomas Jefferson Esqr."

O! my friend, your Country will never forget you! All ranks extol your character, and praise GOD for your abilities &c

But, with the talents of an Angel, a man may be void of Religion, and miss Heaven! My friend, Religion is all and all! It is (to use the words of its holy and divine Author) "the one thing needful."

Other accomplishments, wit, Learning, good morals, influence among men &c &c have their use, but O! my friend, without Religion, inward piety, a change of heart &c no Soul will see GOD in peace! I am c[on]cerned for your eternal welfare! you are immortal, and must assuredly live for ever, either in Bliss or woe!

The last time I saw you, I thought, from your appearance, that you was declining fast! you had the appearance of a person hastening to the tomb! GOD bless you! O! ask his Blessing, and it shall be granted. Go frequently on your knees in secret, and pray to the GOD who made you, and never give over, till you know by happy experience, the Joys of Religion. You are a man already fit for this world; a valuable man indeed; but Religion will fit you for the world to come; and nothing but Religion can do this.—Heavens bless and Save you!

RC (DLC: TJ Papers, 214:38198); in same hand as enclosure; undated, but composed between dates of enclosure and postmark; torn at seal; addressed: "His Excellency, Thomas Jefferson Esqr. Formerly president of the united States; ℗ Mail to Lynchburg P. Office"; franked; postmarked Rocky Mount, 7 Jan. 1819; marked "Missent" in an unidentified hand and redirected in another hand to Charlottesville. Presumably received by TJ on 18 Jan. 1819, as was the enclosure. Enclosure: Anonymous to TJ, 19 Dec. 1818.

In its 10 Dec. 1818 issue the *Richmond Enquirer* praised TJ's LUMINOUS PEN while reprinting his 20 Nov. 1818 letter to Linn Banks and Edward Watts. Listening to Jesus is described as THE ONE THING NEEDFUL in the Bible, Luke 10.42.

From James Riley

Venerable Sir   New York Dec[r] 19th 1818

Having (Since my return from Slavery in Africa) been appointed by mr James Simpson our old Consul in Morocco, his agent for Settling his accounts with Government (of about 23 years standing) and to petition Congress in his behalf for arrearages of pay to which he has always considered himself Justly entitled or for such other relief as Congress shall deem fit to afford him, in his present embarrassed circumstances, occasioned by his long residence in a Barbarous[1] Country where his necessary expenditures have from the first been far more Considerable than his Salary allowed by law,

I take the liberty (though personally a stranger[2]) to enclose you a printed Copy of his representation & petition, which I shall in a few days cause to be laid before Congress, with a request that you will have the goodness to examine the Document. particularly, as many of the facts therin stated must have come within your official knowledge when Secretary of state & President of the United States

If mr Simpsons statements are true (which I have no reason to doubt from his general character) and if he has uniformly & faithfully as well as oeconomically discharged the Various duties of his office, with a pointed regard to the Public good,[3] I think there cannot exist a doubt but he is entitled to the consideration & munificence of the government & the Country[4]

I have Visited mr Simpson & partook of his bounty & hospitality when in distress, he has expended besides his Salary all his private property in the Public service and has been forced to the humiliating necessity of applying[5] to Congress, in order to enable him to pay debts he has been obliged to contract for his ordinary subsistence I have also to request you in mr Simpsons name to make such remarks on his representation & Petition as your knowledge of facts, benevolent character and Justice[6] shall dictate and to forward them together with Such observations as you may think proper, to the Hon[le] the Sec[y], of State, as early as convenient, in order that he may thereby be prepared to answer such questions as a committee of congress may propose on this, to mr Simpson, most interesting Subject,[7]

I have in common with my unprejudiced country-men always admired the sense & wisdom that conceived & wrote the declaration of our independence & the Statesman, philanthropist, & Philosopher, to whom my Country & mankind[8] are indebted for Such unparralled benefits and I cherish a hope that it will be yet in my power once to behold the Father of our most Valuable institutions (the envy & the admiration of the civilized World,) that I may tell my Children with emotions of delight, I have seen the immortal Jefferson; reverence & adore & practice his liberal & enlightened, religious & republican principles & transmit them, as far as in you lies, to the latest posterity unimpaired

Please forgive this effusion of grattitude from the heart of one who has tasted & drank of the bitter cup of affliction in Barbary, & who has seen much of the tyranny and oppression heaped upon the devoted heads of civilized & christian Communities in Europe, & who can contrast with deep sensibelity their situation compared with ours

I should be happy to receive a line from you in Washington where I expect to be in 10 Days,

Wishing you health & every blessing, I am with considerations of veneration & Esteem & the most profound respect, Your most humble & devoted Servant   JAMES RILEY

RC (ViW: TC-JP); addressed: "Hon^{le} Thomas Jefferson Late President of the United States Monticello Virginia"; endorsed by TJ as received 28 Dec. 1818 and so recorded in SJL. Printed in W. Willshire Riley, ed., *Sequel to Riley's Narrative: being a series of Interesting Incidents in the Life, Voyages and Travels of Capt. James Riley* (1851), 338–40. Enclosure not found.

James Riley (1777–1840), mariner and author, was a native of Middletown, Connecticut. He began a sailing career at age fifteen and commanded his own ship within five years. Riley's maritime activities stalled during the Napoleonic wars, but in 1815 he set sail for the Cape Verde Islands as master and supercargo of the brig *Commerce*. After it was shipwrecked on the coast of Africa, a group of nomadic Arabs enslaved him and the other survivors. Riley managed to secure their purchase by a trader bound for Morocco, where the British consul ransomed the group. He returned to the United States in 1816 as a celebrity and published a popular account of his hardships in captivity. After several years in Washington as an agent for James Simpson, the United States consul at Tangier, Riley moved west, working in 1819 as a deputy surveyor in Ohio and Indiana before settling in Ohio with his family in 1821. There he spent several years as a farmer and miller

and served in the lower house of the Ohio legislature, 1823–24. Following a series of financial setbacks and the onset of ill health, Riley moved with his family to New York in 1826. Two years later he resumed a seafaring career, eventually forming a partnership that specialized in trade between Morocco and the United States. As a result of his experience as a slave, Riley supported the work of the American Colonization Society and campaigned against the admission of Missouri as a slave state. He died at sea (*ANB*; Riley, *An Authentic Narrative of the loss of the American Brig Commerce* [1st ed., New York, 1817; 3d ed., New York, 1818, Poor, *Jefferson's Library*, 7 (no. 334), TJ's copy in CSmH]; *Sequel to Riley's Narrative*; New York *Evening Post*, 8 Apr. 1840; Washington *Daily National Intelligencer*, 20 Apr. 1840).

On this date Riley sent a similar letter to James Madison (Madison, *Papers, Retirement Ser.*, 1:394–6).

JAMES SIMPSON, United States consul at Gibraltar, 1794–96, and at Tangier thereafter, began to petition Congress in February 1818, initially requesting payment of $4,000 a year for his service since 1795 and later expanding his request to include a housing allowance. His application remained unsettled at his death in 1820 (*JEP*, 1:157–8, 209, 3:217 [28, 29 May 1794, 19, 20 May 1796, 15 May 1820]; *JHR*, 11:203, 406, 13:157–8 [3

Feb., 1 Apr. 1818, 21 Jan. 1820]; *JS*, 8:154–5, 287, 9:129–30, 411 [15 Jan., 19 Feb. 1819, 31 Jan., 13 May 1820]). Following his release from captivity, Riley VISITED Simpson in Tangier and stayed at the latter's house in January 1816 prior to returning to the United States (*Authentic Narrative* [3d ed.], 381–2).

[1] *Sequel to Riley's Narrative*: "barbarian."

[2] *Sequel to Riley's Narrative*: "personally unacquainted."

[3] *Sequel to Riley's Narrative*: "with a due regard to the public interest."

[4] *Sequel to Riley's Narrative*: "of his Government and country."

[5] *Sequel to Riley's Narrative*: "appealing."

[6] *Sequel to Riley's Narrative*: "sense of justice."

[7] *Sequel to Riley's Narrative*: "important subject," with following two paragraphs omitted.

[8] Preceding two words interlined.

To John Barnes

Monti[cel]lo Dec. 21. 18.

I thank you, dear Sir, for your settlement with Gales and Seaton for me, and I now inclose you 7. Dollars reimbursement in Richmond bills, which I hope may be readily disposed of with you.

I find myself quite restored in health and strength and feel much indebted to my friends for their solicitudes and enquiries on the occasion. to yourself I tender assurances of my constant friendship & respect   TH: JEFFERSON

PoC (MHi); on verso of reused address cover of Dupl of Peter Poinsot to TJ, 18 May 1818; dateline faint; at foot of text: "Mr Barnes"; endorsed by TJ. Recorded in SJL with additional bracketed notation: "7.D. for Natl Intell."

To Stephen Cathalan

DEAR SIR   Mont[icello] Dec. 21. 18.

Judge Holmes of this state, a particular friend of mine is desirous of procuring for his own use, some of the fine wines with which you have been so kind as to furnish me from your vicinity from time to time, and asks from me a letter to recommend him to your services. I have not hesitated to[1] give it with assurances that he will be served with the same fidelity both as to quality and price which I have experienced from your hands.

Your letter of Aug. 13. was recieved on the 5th of Oct. but I have heard nothing since of the shipment of the wines requested in mine [o]f[2] Apr. 5. I expect however hourly to hear of their arrival. [ev]er and affectionately Your's   TH: JEFFERSON

PoC (DLC: TJ Papers, 205:36548); on verso of reused address cover of David Bailie Warden to TJ, 13 July 1818; dateline faint; torn at seal; at foot of text (torn): "[Stephe]n Cathalan esq. Consul of the US. at Marseilles"; endorsed by TJ. Enclosed in TJ to Hugh Holmes, 21 Dec. 1818.

¹Manuscript: "to to."
²Word faint.

To Hugh Holmes

DEAR SIR   Monticello Dec. 21. 18.

I inclose you the letter to mr Cathalan of Marseilles which you request in yours of the 6ᵗʰ. let me advise you by all means, besides the wine of Nice, to desire from him some of Bergasse's claret. be assured you will find it a fine wine, superior to most of what can be bought in America, and it will cost you there 24. francs, say a guinea the box of 24. bottles.

[A]fter the pleasure of seeing you here, I became much worse, and was indeed reduced very low. but I am now in good health and strength, and much indebted to my friends for their sympathies on the occasion. Accept the assurance of my great esteem & respect.

TH: JEFFERSON

PoC (MHi); on verso of reused address cover of Thomas Cooper to TJ, 26 Aug. 1818; one word faint; at foot of text: "Judge Holmes"; endorsed by TJ. Enclosure: TJ to Stephen Cathalan, 21 Dec. 1818.

To Frederick A. Mayo

SIR   Monticello Dec. 21. 18.

Doubting whether my box of books may have yet got to your hands, on account of the low state of our river and having since recieved sundry pamphlets which I wish to have bound up with those sent, I now send them in a [s]eparate package by mail. each contains a direction into what volume it is to be inserted. I salute you respectfully   TH: JEFFERSON

PoC (MHi); on verso of portion of a reused address cover from James Monroe to TJ, the remainder of which was used for TJ to William Short, 21 Dec. 1818; one word faint; at foot of text: "Mʳ Frederic A. Mayo"; endorsed by TJ.

From James Monroe

DEAR SIR.   washington Decr 21. 1818
General King of the District of maine [mass:] expressing a desire of being known to you personally, & his intention, to make you a visit, I take much interest in forwarding his views, by giving him this introduction. His uniform support of the republican cause, & useful services, in the late war, are I presume known to you. I hear with great pleasure that your health is completely restord. with best wishes for its continuance, I am
    Dear Sir very respectfully your friend & servant

JAMES MONROE

RC (DLC); brackets in original; endorsed by TJ as received 30 Dec. 1818 and so recorded (with additional bracketed notation: "Gen¹ King") in SJL.

William King (1768–1852), merchant and public official, was born in Scarborough, Massachusetts (later Maine). He was educated at home, attended one term at Phillips Academy in Andover, and worked in sawmills beginning at age thirteen. In 1791 King formed a mercantile partnership with his brother-in-law in Topsham, Massachusetts (later Maine), eventually moving in 1800 to nearby Bath, where he prospered as a merchant and shipowner. His long political career included service in the Massachusetts General Court representing Topsham, 1795 and 1799, and Bath, 1804–06, and as a state senator for Lincoln County, 1807–11 and 1818–19. King became a major general of militia in 1808 and called out his forces when the British occupied eastern Maine during the War of 1812. After Massachusetts failed to assist in defending Maine during the war, King became a leader of the movement to make it a separate state. When statehood was achieved in 1820 he was elected Maine's first governor. In 1821 King resigned the governorship to become a commissioner settling claims under the Adams-Onís Treaty and served in this capacity for three years. He was federal customs collector at Bath, 1830–34. King began his political career as a Federalist, became a Republican in 1803, and ran again for governor, unsuccessfully, in 1835 as a Whig. He visited TJ at Monticello in December 1818. King's financial fortunes declined later in life, and he died in poverty in Bath (*ANB*; *DAB*; *JEP*, 4:45, 81–2, 376 [14 Jan., 25 Mar. 1830, 22 Mar. 1834]; *Bangor Daily Whig and Courier*, 23 June 1852; gravestone inscription in Maple Grove Cemetery, Bath).

On this date Monroe wrote a similar letter introducing King to James Madison (Madison, *Papers, Retirement Ser.*, 1:396).

From Elisabetta Mazzei Pini and Andrea Pini

Il 21. Xbre 1818.

Dal Sig^r Console Appleton ci fu rimesso una di Lei¹ Obligazione² Col contegio esatto delle Somme a noi mandate come pure ci fa conoscere La Somma Capitale³ che trovassi attualmente⁴ nelle di lei mani Dal

medemo Sig^r Appleton ci fu significato che annesso a questa' ob-
ligazione vi dovevano essere Cambiali per la Somma di 445. Dollars
e 66. Centesimi componente l'interessi dell'Anno 1818—Queste
Cambiali non sono state trovate^5 dal Sig^r Appleton incluse nel di Lei
Plico per conseguenza si crede che possino essere perdute. La preghi-
amo dunque gentilissimo Sig^re di degnarsi prendere in considera-
zione questa circostanza e spedirci delle nuove Cambiali per poter
ritirare questa somma Inoltre la supplichiamo di accordarci il favore
facendo delle altre rimesse, di dirigersi a qualche Banchiere di
Livorno che si averebe il vantagio d'essere piu solecitamente pagati.
Nell renderle infinite grazie di tante sue bontà abiamo l'onore di con-
fermarci con tutto il rispetto

EDITORS' TRANSLATION

21. December 1818.
Mr. Consul Appleton sent us a letter from you with the exact reckoning of the
sums you had remitted to us as well as informing us of the balance of the
principal that was actually in your hands. The same Mr. Appleton informed
us that bills of exchange for 445 dollars and 66 cents, constituting the interest for the year 1818, should be attached to this letter. Mr. Appleton did not
find them in your envelope; consequently it is believed that they may be lost.
Therefore, dearest Sir, we beg you to deign to consider this circumstance and
send new bills of exchange, so that we can collect this money. Moreover, for
the other payments we beg you to favor us by directing them to a banker in
Leghorn, which would help us to be paid more promptly. In sending you
infinite thanks for all your kindnesses, we have the honor of confirming all
our respect for you

Dft (ItPi: AFM); in Andrea Pini's
hand; endorsed: "Al Sig^r Jefferson."
Translation by Dr. Jonathan T. Hine.
Not recorded in SJL and probably never
received by TJ.

^1 Preceding two words interlined.
^2 Keyed to this point with dashes is Andrea Pini's note in left margin: "del 5.
aprile 1818" ("that of 5. April 1818"). TJ's
letter to Thomas Appleton was actually
dated 4 Apr. 1818.

^3 Reworked from "Somma totale" ("full
amount").
^4 Order of preceding two words reversed in manuscript, with Andrea Pini
indicating that they should be changed to
current reading by adding numbers one
and two above them.
^5 Preceding three words interlined in
place of "essendo a noi pervenute" ("having been received by us").

To Francis Preston

Dear Sir Monticello Dec. 21. 18.

I send with pleasure an introductory letter for your son to mr Stewart. with mr Leslie I have not a personal acquaintance, and must have expressed myself carelessly to have been otherwise understood.[1] indirect circumstances would give me a right to apply to him with confidence on behalf of our College, but no claim on his personal attentions. mr Stewart however will, I am sure, make your son acquainted with him and such other literary characters as he may wish to know personally,

I offer you[2] with great sincerity, the assurance of my particular esteem & high respect. Th: Jefferson

Dft (MHi); on verso of reused address cover of Joseph Dougherty to TJ, 21 Sept. 1818; at foot of text: "<*H. E. Governor*> Francis Preston. esq."; endorsed by TJ. Enclosure: TJ to Dugald Stewart, 21 Dec. 1818.

[1] Reworked from "carelessly if you understood me otherwise."

[2] Preceding three words interlined in place of "I am waiting with great anxiety the determination of the legislature on the establishment of our University. I tender to your Excellency."

To David M. Randolph (1798–1825)

Monticello Dec. 21. 18.

Th: Jefferson presents his compliments & thanks to mr Randolph for the information in his letter of the 14th instant respecting the bricklayer. should the legislature adopt the Central College for the site of their University advertisements will be immediately put into the public papers for undertakers of the brickwork Carpentry & house joinery, from which every one will learn in what way & to whom they are to apply for employment. there will be abundant work for them. he salutes mr Randolph with esteem & respect.

PoC (DLC); on verso of reused address cover of Thomas Cooper to TJ, 1 Sept. 1818; dateline at foot of text; endorsed by TJ.

To William Short

Dear Sir Monticello Dec. 21. 18.

The messenger who carried yesterday to the Post-office a copy of our University Report which I put under cover to you, brought in return your favor of the 12th and it's kind enquiries after my health. a single Bulletin now suffices on that subject, as I find my health and strength quite restored; for altho some effects of the waters are still sensible, they are wearing off so steadily that I consider myself as entirely well.   I recieved a copy of M^{de} de Stael's work from her son & son in law. it is indeed a most precious & superlative work. the world there sees in his true character what an impudent adventurer has been able to convulse it for 20. years.   our University report is now under consideration before our legislature. there are some local & some personal hostilities intriguing against it; yet I have a good deal of confidence in it's passing in some shape; and the more as at their last session they appropriated 15,000 D. per. ann. to the use of an University, which they cannot revoke, because our Senate is almost unanimously with us, many therefore will yield to the consideration that the money being set apart may as well be put to some use. their whole literary fund is $1\frac{1}{2}$ millions of D. at interest and the capital otherwise daily increasing. from this I have a hope we may within a year or two get them to double their endowment, which may make the establishment what the Report contemplates. but with 15,000 D. only it will go on slowly on account of the buildings, library E^{t}c.

ever affectionately yours   TH: JEFFERSON

RC (ViW: TJP); at foot of text: "Mr Short." PoC (MHi); on verso of portion of a reused address cover from James Monroe to TJ, the remainder of which was used for TJ to Frederick A. Mayo, 21 Dec. 1818; endorsed by TJ.

Napoleon was the IMPUDENT ADVENTURER. "An Act appropriating part of the revenue of the Literary Fund, and for other purposes," had allocated 15,000 D. PER. ANN. to a state university once a site was chosen (*Acts of Assembly* [1817–18 sess.], 14 [21 Feb. 1818]).

To Dugald Stewart

DEAR SIR   Monticello in Virg^a Dec. 21. 18.

The bearer of this letter is mr Preston, son of the present Governor of Virginia. he is not known to me personally; but my assurances are from such a source as secure me in taking on myself to vouch for his worth and correctness of conduct and character. he proposes to pass the present winter in Edinburgh and wishes of course to be known to those whose characters have given them eminence abroad as well as at home.

we are now in the 30th year since we witnessed together in Paris the commencement of those tremendous scenes which have since convulsed that fine country, and, we may say indeed all Europe. time however has had no effect in lessening my esteem for you, nor my sense of your high claims on the friends of science. in asking therefore for mr Preston the privilege of presenting [hims]elf to you, I profit of the same occasion of recalling myself to your friendly recollection, and of tendering you the assurance of my unabated esteem and high respect.

TH: JEFFERSON

PoC (MHi); on verso of reused address cover of Patrick Gibson to TJ, 24 Sept. 1818; torn at seal, with two words rewritten by TJ; at foot of text: "Dugald Stewart esquire"; endorsed by TJ. Enclosed in TJ to Francis Preston, 21 Dec. 1818.

Dugald Stewart (1753–1828), philosopher and educator, was born in Edinburgh and studied at the university there before attending philosophy lectures at the University of Glasgow, 1771–72. He took over his father's mathematics courses at the University of Edinburgh the latter year and was promoted to the chair in that discipline in 1775. Stewart also started teaching moral philosophy in 1778, transferred to that chair in 1785, and held it until 1816, although he retired from lecturing in 1810. In the 1800–01 academic session he began to offer a private class on political economy. Stewart was a popular and influential lecturer and writer who made major contributions to the field of epistemology and influenced the development of philosophy curricula in Europe and the United States. TJ met him in France in 1788 or 1789 and successfully nominated him for membership in the American Philosophical Society in 1791. Stewart died in Edinburgh (*ODNB*; Sir William Hamilton, ed., *The Collected Works of Dugald Stewart*, 11 vols. [1854–60; repr. 1994]; *PTJ*, 13:241–2, 14:648, 15:204–5, 29:415; APS, Minutes, 21 Oct. 1791 [MS in PPAmP]; Stewart, *Elements of the Philosophy of the Human Mind* [London, 1792 and 1827 (vols. 1 and 3); Edinburgh, 1814 (vol. 2); Sowerby, no. 1244; Poor, *Jefferson's Library*, 8 (no. 456)]; Edinburgh *Caledonian Mercury*, 14 June 1828).

William C. Preston, the BEARER, was the son of Francis Preston and nephew of Governor James P. Preston.

From Joseph Delaplaine

D^R SIR, Decr 22. 1818

I hope you may[1] be pleased with the 3^d half vol. of the Repository which I this day send to you.—Can you favour me with a line?

Yours with perfect esteem JOSEPH DELAPLAINE

RC (DLC); dateline at foot of text; addressed: "Thos Jefferson Esqr Monticello Virginia"; endorsed by TJ as received 31 Dec. 1818 and so recorded in SJL; additional notation by TJ beneath endorsement: "1817. Oct. 30. I inclosed to Delaplaine 12.D. for the first 3. N^{os} @ 4.D. a number: so this is p^d for." Enclosure: *Delaplaine's Repository*, vol. 2, pt. 1.

[1] Manuscript: "my."

From John Laval

SIR,   Philadelphia December 23ᵈ 1818

I have Sent, by this Morning's Mail, the Nautical Almanac for 1819 ($1–50/100) no English Edition Could be had in Philadelphia.

Mʳ Dufief is detained, in London, to attend the Sale of a fourth Edition of his F. & E. Nature Displayed. he has Sent, from England & France, a large assortment of Books in different Languages & Branches of Literature, & Amongst them, a Considerable Number of rare & Valuable Works, Some out of Print. Part of those are already Sold, but there remain, Still, many deserving the attention of the Erudite of the U.S. they Will be included in a Catalogue, Now publishing, a Copy of Which, When printed, I Will do myself the honor to forward for Your inspection & Selection—

I remain With the highest respect Sir, Your Very humble Servant

JOHN LAVAL

RC (DLC); dateline at foot of text; endorsed by TJ as received 31 Dec. 1818 from Laval writing for Nicolas G. Dufief and so recorded in SJL; additional notation by TJ beneath endorsement: "see Dufief." RC (DLC); address cover only; with PoC of TJ to Mathew Carey, 11 Mar. 1819, on verso; addressed: "Thos. Jefferson Esq. Monticello—Vᵃ"; franked; postmarked Philadelphia, 23 Dec.

The NAUTICAL ALMANAC sent by Laval was probably Edmund M. Blunt, *Blunt's Edition of the Nautical Almanac, and Astronomical Ephemeris for the year 1819* (New York, 1818; Poor, *Jefferson's Library*, 8 [no. 382]). F. & E.: "French and English."

From John Bent

SIR[1]   December the 24 1818

I Take this opportunity To Wright Theas few Loins To you to Let you Now that I want Some infermation from you how I Will get my Land I have Lost my Dis charge in alagany Near Pitts Burg Two miles on the alaganey about Mr Ben Jaman [. . .] I got it in april after Peace Whos made and I kin Prove By Mr John Smith I Saw him at Pitts Burg I have in the united states for Three years and god a onerable Dis Charge Wich Cant get my Land I Wish your as friend To inquire agint Jinner Buckner Wich Whos at Norfolk at that Time an Doctor Clark had Doctor a Ruptur in Service you Will Pleas To Wright To me and Direct To Stanards ville orange County viginia if you are a friend To a Soldier I have heard you are the Best friend To Soldiers No more from your Respect friend   JOHN BENT

RC (MHi); one word illegible; at foot of text: "Mr Thomas Jefferson President of the united states"; endorsed by TJ as received 14 Jan. 1819 and so recorded in SJL.

A missing and possibly related letter to TJ of 27 Dec. 1819 from a John "Bend"

is recorded in SJL as received 3 Jan. 1820 from Harrisonburg, with the additional bracketed notation that the author was "insane or drunk."

[1] Preceding this word Bent canceled "My friend."

From Joseph C. Cabell

DEAR SIR,   Richmond. 24th Decr 1818.

Conformably to your advice, I urged the friends of the University to hasten the proceedings of the House of Delegates upon that subject, and to get the Bill up to the Senate before Christmas. Unfortunately, however, the Bill is now lying on the table of the Lower House, after one reading & an order to print. As we met on 7th and 15 days are pretty fully employed in reading petitions, which this year are more numerous than usual, it would have been very difficult to avoid the delay which has taken place; especially as an artful opposition has been continually urging the necessity of[1] time to consider, and to bring forward their claims. From 30 to 40 members of the House of Delegates are now absent on a visit to their families, and it will be unsafe to take a vote on the bill till a week after christmas. Two strenuous efforts have at different times been made to get an adjournment of the Senate. On the first the vote was 10 to 5: on the second 9 to 5. But altho the attempt failed in both cases, yet 4 or 5 of the Senators have gone off without leave, and broken up the House. There are now about ten of us in town. Some of our best friends are in the country: & we shall suffer by their absence. The delay upon the University bill is truly to be lamented. The Hostile interests are daily acquiring new force by intrigue & management. The party opposed altogether to the University is growing so rapidly we have just grounds to fear a total failure of the measure. I this morning counted up 26 votes of this description on this side of the Ridge: and there are doubtless many others. Many of the Western members will take the same course, particularly if they lose the scite. If all the western votes could be united in opposition we shall certainly be defeated. Some of the west will certainly be with us on the Scite, and I hope a respectable portion will be for the bill on the passage. Yet if this portion should be small, it will be insufficient to save the bill from Eastern hostility. The friends of W^m & Mary demand[2] $5000, p^r annum, as the price of their concurrence: & in the event of refusal will carry off some votes. I have advised my friends not to enter into any compacts of the kind, and sooner will I lose the bill than I will give my assent to it. The party hostile to the University, come chiefly from the lower country, & are within convenient distance of W^m & Mary. The better educated part of them, whilst they, their sons, connexions or friends have been educated at W^m & Mary, quote Smith, the Edinburgh Review, & Dugald Stewart, to prove that education should be left to individual enterprize. The more ignorant part, pretend that the Literary fund has been diverted from its original object, the education of the poor: and accuse the friends of the university of an intention to apply all the fund to the benefit of the wealthy. Mr Archer of Amelia, very unintentionally, but very unfortunately, has given plausability to this charge. Two days ago, he offered a resolution to authorize the Committee of Schools & Colleges to consider of & report to the House on, the expediency of repealing that part of the Law relative to the poor. The resolution was laid on the table. The exhibition of such a resolution from a friend to the University, at this time, has produced great & perhaps irratreavable mischief. I have prevailed on him to consent not to call it up at all: or if another course should be preferred, to suffer it to be withdrawn. It will probably lie on the table.[3]—In regard to Charlottesville as a scite for the University, many liberal & enlightened persons feel difficulties from the smallness of the town. They think a town of some size necessary, to attract professors, to furnish polished society for students, to supply accomodations; to resist the physical force, & present the means of governing a large number of young men &^c. This last objection seems to make some[4] impression. Mr Johnson of Staunton arrived two days ago. He is very prudent and very remarkable on all occasions for reserving till the last moment, the disclosure of the opinion he means to advocate. On the day he arrived in the Senate Chamber, he went to the map of Virginia, and in a tone, half laughing & half earnest, observed to Genl Preston & myself that he always expected that those lines drawn across the state in the calculations published in the Enquirer, were not drawn in a proper manner: & proceeded to remark on the circumstance that the Eastern & western lines commencing at the middle of the mouth of the Chesapeake, were nearer to the Southern than northern side of the State. Should the bill get up to the Senate, it may be proper for me to be able to meet all possible objections on that subject. Perhaps Mr Johnson may take the course you expect of him; but if he does, I shall be greatly disappointed. I should therefore be much obliged if you will inform me, whether due[5] Eastern & Western, and due Northern & Southern lines, would materially change the position of the Center of population; or whether lines drawn in any other direction would materially vary the result; as also, whether, the mode of ascertaining the center, by the point of intersection of <u>only</u> two transverse lines, be liable to any well founded[6] objection. I have madison's map in my room, & shall make some calculations, but I ask you for information because yours would be more accurate than my own, particularly as to the relative portions of counties bisected by the lines. I will, if you desire it, make no other use of your letter than to enable myself to meet any objections to the present mode of drawing the lines. My motive for asking for information on the preceding subject, is not that I myself doubt, but that I may meet and dissipate the doubts of others.—You recollect no doubt the letter I wrote you last winter stating my impressions that certa[in cha]racters in the H. of Delegates were hostile to the location of the Univer[sity] [. . .] [Char]lottesville. I have ascertained that upon that subject I was entirely cor[rect.] I was also correct in my anticipation that they would go with the Board of Commissioners. They will now give us their support.—I lately wrote you that m[r] Hunter of Essex would unite with us. But in that, I was mistaken. my first apprehensions were well founded. He will be opposed to the measure altogether.

I am, D[r] Sir, most truly & faithfully yours,

JOSEPH C. CABELL

Poor old Col: Tatham is here, half deranged, in great poverty, avoided by every body, & trying to sell his collections to the Assembly, & to get his Lottery Law revived, in both which attempts I believe he will be disappointed.

RC (ViU: TJP-PC); mutilated at seal; addressed: "Thomas Jefferson Monticello"; endorsed by TJ as received 28 Dec. 1818 and so recorded in SJL; with possibly related calculation by TJ on verso. RC (DLC); additional address cover only; with PoC of TJ to Louis H. Girardin, 16 Mar. 1819, on verso; addressed: "M[r] Jefferson Monticello"; franked; postmarked Richmond, 24 Dec.

THE RIDGE: the Blue Ridge Mountains. When the annual report of the President and Directors of the Literary Fund was presented to the Virginia House of Delegates on 22 Dec. 1818, William S. ARCHER, of Amelia County, moved that it be referred to the House Committee of Schools and Colleges in order to investigate the possibility of repealing those sections of the 21 Feb. 1818 statute, "An Act appropriating part of the revenue of the Literary Fund, and for other purposes," not concerned with creating a state university (*JHD* [1818–19 sess.], 60; *Acts of Assembly* [1817–18 sess.], 11–5).

After unsuccessfully proposing amendments to TJ's Bill to Establish a University (printed above at 19 Nov. 1818), Chapman JOHNSON OF STAUNTON ultimately voted in favor of making Central College the University of Virginia (*JSV* [1818–19 sess.], 73 [25 Jan. 1819]). On 18 Dec. 1818 the surveyor William TATHAM petitioned the House of Delegates to name a new set of managers to oversee a lottery funding a geographical work of his, replacing those appointed by a 1791 statute. On 9 Feb. 1819 the General Assembly approved "An act concerning William Tatham" that appointed seven new lottery managers (*JHD* [1818–19 sess.], 49; *Acts of Assembly* [1818–19 sess.], 195).

[1] Cabell here canceled "delay."

[2] Sentence opening reworked from "W^m & Mary demands."

[3] A sentence here is heavily canceled and illegible.

[4] Word interlined in place of "most."

[5] Word interlined.

[6] Preceding two words interlined in place of "material."

From Robert Walsh

DEAR SIR   Philadelphia Decr 24th 1818

On my return, a few days ago, from a visit to Washington, I found here your obliging & very interesting letter of the 4th ins^t concerning Dr Franklin. I am the more grateful for the opinions and anecdotes you have Communicated, as I know how you are oppressed by the extent of your correspondence. What you have said as to Franklin's share in the Preliminaries, and to his relations with the Court of France, seems to me <u>decisive</u>, and will be of much importance in an historical point of view. Your personal testimony admits of no reply. The anecdotes are characteristic, and in themselves not a little piquant. The Biographical sketch which I undertook to write for Mr Delaplaine has been in print several weeks. He tells me that he has sent you a Copy of his third Volume, in which it is contained. I would venture to request you to cast your eye over my account of Franklin in some interval of leisure. My panegyric of the Philosopher is too lofty and unvaried, perhaps, but I think that most of my views of his character and services will have your approbation. I now send you the Analectic Magazine for this month, into which I have introduced a review of the last volume of Temple Franklin's Memoirs of his Grandsire. In the general Essay on the Life & Writings of this great man, which I propose to publish one day or other, I will avail myself of the valuable Communication which you have so kindly made. I have in my hands some other unpublished materials to which I attach much importance.

You will be pleased to accept my hearty acknowledgments for the volume of Count Destutt Tracy. The author is incalculably indebted to you for ushering him into the English world in a manner fitted to give him due weight & attract attention to him, in the outset. I have found time only to run through the book. I can perceive that it possesses unusial merit; and although it's doctrines are not precisely those which I have been accustomed to regard as the soundest, I shall be glad to co-operate in promoting it's currency.

Your Report concerning the University of Virginia was a rich feast to me, & cannot fail, I think, to be highly useful to the States at large. My fear is that the Legislating public of the country will not be à la hauteur of Your views, & suggestions. I trust that the Report is to be published in the pamphlet-form.—The Trustees of the University of Pensylv[al] have just created for me a Chair of General Literature. I mean to attempt a course of lectures; but the success of the experiment is doubtful in all respects.

I repeat my Sincere thanks for your Frankliniana, & for the flattering recollections of your family, and am,

Dear Sir, with profound respect, Your ob[t] serv[t]

ROBERT WALSH JR

RC (DLC); addressed: "Thomas Jefferson Esqr Monticello Virginia"; stamp canceled; franked; postmarked; endorsed by TJ as received 31 Dec. 1818 and so recorded in SJL. Enclosure: *Analectic Magazine*, vol. 12, no. 6 (Dec. 1818; Poor, *Jefferson's Library*, 14 [no. 925]).

À LA HAUTEUR: "up to the level."

[1] Preceding two words interlined.

From Joel Yancey

DR SIR   Poplar Forest 24th Dec, 18

Your two Boys Dick & Moses arrived here on Monday night last both on Horse-back without a pass, but Said they had your permission to visit their friends here this Xmass, yesterday two men came in pursuit of them for Stealing their Horse and Saddle, they found the horse here and Dick[1] acknowledged that he road it from albemarl, but that it was a stray, and that he was endeavouring to find the owner,[2] moses has made his escape, and Dick agrreed to take a whiping, which I thought was better than taking them before a justice of the Peace, which the men were determined to do unless they got some satisfaction, the owners of the horse William Hamner & Son both from your County, after getting their Horse was content to give him a very light whipping indeed not near Sufficient in my opinion to deter him from commiting a like offence, I have thought it probable they may be runaways and that both Horses is Stolen, the other[3] Horse, they Say is yours, which I have, and shall have taken care of until I here from you or the owner comes, should I not here from you before next Tuesday I Send them down with the Horse. In haste with great respect I am

y[r] mo ob[t]   JOEL YANCEY

P.S

The pork is ready, and as soon as your waggon comes[4] up I will send it off immediately, there is no beaves nor mottons this fall. I wrote you last Friday from Lynchburg   J. YANCEY

RC (MHi); at foot of text: "mr. Jefferson"; endorsed by TJ as received 28 Dec. 1818 and so recorded in SJL.

Yancey's letter of LAST FRIDAY, 18 Dec. 1818, not found, is recorded in SJL as received 28 Dec. 1818 from Lynchburg.

[1] Word interlined.
[2] Manuscript: "ower."
[3] Word interlined.
[4] Yancey here canceled "down."

To Abraham Lange

Monticello Dec. 25. 18.

On my return to this place in September I addressed a [let]ter to you, which having probably miscarried, I trouble you with a second repeating the request which I took the liberty of then making. it was to ask some of the beans which I saw and ate of at your house, a large bean eaten as a snap is with the hull on. you pointed out to me in your garden a red flowering bean which you said was the same, and you gave me about a dozen of them; but I wish as many as might plant a small patch in the spring, and would be glad to be informed at what time to plant them.   if quilte[d] [. . .] in linen bag, and wrapped in strong paper i[n] [for]m of a letter, and committed as a letter to mail, & directed to me at Monticello near Charlottesville they will come safe. a few of the beautiful white French bean or Haricot which you shewed me would be also accepted with thanks. I salute you with esteem & respect.   TH: JEFFERSON

PoC (DLC); on verso of reused address cover of Thomas Cooper to TJ, 18 Sept. 1818; edge trimmed and mutilated at seal; at foot of text: "Mons'r Lange"; endorsed by TJ.

Abraham Lange (d. ca. 1840), innkeeper, was a captain in the Augusta County militia during the War of 1812. His farm and mill in that county were situated on the road between Staunton and Warm Springs. TJ stopped at Lange's establishment en route to the springs in the summer of 1818 and approved of his accommodations. At the time of his death Lange owned personal property valued at

$2,696, including three slaves (DNA: RG 29, CS, Augusta Co., 1810–40; Butler, *Virginia Militia*, 49, 252, 279; TJ's Notes on Inns Between Staunton and Warm Springs and his Notes on Distances Between Warm Springs and Charlottesville, both printed above in a group of documents on Jefferson's Trip to Warm Springs, 6 Aug. 1818; Betts, *Garden Book*, 583; petition of citizens of Bath Co. and Augusta Co., [presented 28 Dec. 1829], Vi: RG 78, Legislative Petitions, Bath Co.; *Acts of Assembly* [1832–33 sess.], 96 [7 Mar. 1833]; "Peregrine Prolix" [Philip H. Nicklin], *Letters descriptive of the Virginia Springs; the roads leading thereto, and the doings thereat* [1835], 74–5; Augusta Co. Will Book, 23:290–1, 317–9).

The letter TJ ADDRESSED to Lange shortly after his 1 Sept. 1818 return to Monticello is not recorded in SJL and has not been found.

From Joseph Milligan

DEAR SIR   Georgetown December 25th 1818

The Box of Books which you mention in yours of the 9th has not yet reached me on the 11th the Potomack was closed with Ice which is now Six Inches thick this no doubt is the cause that prevents the box from coming: I have written to Mr Gray of Fredericksburg to have the box sent by the stages that now run from Fredericksburg to Alexandria

I have sent a Young man to Norfolk, Petersburg & Richmond to dispose of Political Economy he disposed[1] of twenty two copies in Norfolk he is now (judging by the last letter) in Richmond. I have desired him to present a copy to Mr Ritchie therfore I presume you will see it noticed in the Enquirer

I am now engaged in removing the Library of Congress from the General post office (Great Hotel) to the third story of the North wing of the Capitol that is taking it down from one third story to put in an other a labour that will employ me fifteen or twenty days In the present state of my business I would much rather have been without the job But as I have handled the books so much the Librarian and the Library Committee think they[2] have a claim in all cases where there is great labour and small profit

There has been an appropriation of $2000 this session to procure books If I can prevail with the committee[3] to get the agency to purchase them I would consider it worth one or two hundred dollars added to my business also they will want binding done if I can obtain that I shall not regret the labour that I am at present engaged in If I should want a reference as to capacity to execute those business would you object to the mention of your name by

yours respectfully   JOSEPH MILLIGAN

I sent a copy of Political Economy as a present to John Adams Esqr (Quincy near Boston)

RC (DLC); at foot of first page: "see next page"; endorsed by TJ as received 31 Dec. 1818 and so recorded in SJL. RC (ViW: TC-JP); address cover only; with PoC of TJ to James P. Preston, 11 Mar. 1819, on verso; addressed: "Thomas Jefferson Esqr Monticello Milton via [i.e., Virginia]"; franked; postmarked Washington, 25 Dec.

The YOUNG MAN was James Thomas. Without naming him, an article in the

Richmond ENQUIRER of 21 Dec. 1818 announced that Milligan's agent was in Richmond promoting Destutt de Tracy's work and ended with an extract from TJ to Milligan, [ca. 25 Oct. 1818]. For the establishment of the Library of Congress in the post office building that had formerly been Blodget's, the GREAT HOTEL, see George Watterston to TJ, 26 Apr. 1815, and note. "An Act to provide for the removal of the library of Congress to the north wing of the Capitol" included AN APPROPRIATION of $2,000 for the purchase of books (*U.S. Statutes at Large*, 3:477 [3 Dec. 1818]).

[1] Manuscript: "diposed."
[2] Manuscript: "the."
[3] Manuscript: "committe."

From Milton W. Rouse

SIR,   [ca. 25 Dec. 1818]

A stranger to you, I fear that I shall meet with a repulse, Young and inexperienced I know not how to proceed, but I hope that you will forgive my boldness, (perhaps impertinence) when I have acquainted you with the circumstances which have induced me to address you in this manner.—

I am so situated that I am deprived of every source of useful information. Not a book with which to nourish or instruct my mind I am compelled to live an ignorant spectator of ignorance. With truth I can say, "Happy are they who love to read, and are not, like myself, deprived of the means of gratification"[1]—While so many otherr young men are enjoying all the advantages of good books and men, I am doomed to live & dye in ignorance, & all this because I am not able to educate myself—

My ignorant, illiterate associates have no desire for reading or conversing upon any useful subject. With books they are entirely unacquainted. If I read I am despised—

If I attempt to converse upon any useful or interesting subject I am neglected even treated with contempt. But all this would be no obstacle, had I time to read, & good books, with which to nourish and sustain my fast declining mind, declining—for the want of nourishment In the summer I had no time for reading, but I fondly flattered myself[2] that I should have a few leisure moments this winter, especially evenings, that I could devot to that desirable object—but my hopes are blasted—It is for the interest of my employer that I should remain in ignorance, Had I time to read I should have no books. My employer has scarce a book in his house, and my wages will not enable me to buy one. even a dictionary I am unable to procure. The neares circulating library is 7 miles & that is good for naught—So great is my thirst for knowledge & so great is my inability to procure it, that I am driven almost to despair—Snatch me! O! snatch me! from my dreadful situation!, Perhaps you will think that I am imposing upon you; that I am[3] insane, but I can assure that I am in my right mind but I am so much confused at present that I scarce know what I write—I am a stranger to every good and wise man, I know not where to look for assistance. Having herd yourseff mentioned as a friend of learning—I have taken the liberty of addressing you, hoping that you will condescend to direct a few consoling lines to me as soon as possible after the receipt of this—Do contrive some way to rescue me from my dreadful situation, the labour of my hands shall repay you, I have been brought up to labour, but I cannot endure the thoughts of living & dying in ignorance

Sir this is nearly my first effort at composition I hope you will over-look its numerous defects

As this is unknown to any one, If you should conclude to let me re-main in my present awful situation, have the kindness to Destroy this, & let it remain unknown

If you will write to me immediately you shall know my exaxt situa-tion—   age business, &c.

Direct to Milton. W. Rouse Onondaga West Hill State New York[4]

Bury this in oblivion if you cannot assist me—& you will do me[5] a kindness[6]

RC (MHi); undated; addressed: "Mr Thomas Jefferson Monticello—Virginia"; franked; postmarked "Onon. Hol^w" (On-ondaga Hollow), 25 Dec.; endorsed by TJ as a letter from "Rouse W." received 10 Jan. 1819 and so recorded in SJL.

Milton W. Rouse (ca. 1800–24) fin-ished his schooling at the age of sixteen. He trained as a house carpenter, but ill health sometimes prevented him from working. In 1820 Rouse was unemployed in Oneida County, New York. A year later he was working as a carpenter in New York City, where he was also serv-ing in the 9th Artillery Regiment of the New York militia when he died (Rouse to TJ, 8 Nov. 1820; *Longworth's New York Directory* [1821]: 376; *New-York Evening Post*, 21, 23 Aug. 1824; *Minerva*, new ser., 1 [1824]: 334).

HAPPY ARE THEY . . . MEANS OF GRAT-IFICATION derives from book two of Fran-çois de Salignac de la Mothe Fénelon, *Les Aventures de Télémaque* (Paris, 1699; Sowerby, nos. 4305–7), the multiple American editions of which included *The Adventures of Telemachus, the Son of Ulysses* (Boston, 1797).

[1] Omitted closing quotation mark edi-torially supplied.
[2] Preceding two words interlined in place of "hoped."
[3] Rouse here canceled "a foo."
[4] Sentence added perpendicularly in margin of final page of letter.
[5] Rouse here canceled "one favour."
[6] Sentence on verso of address cover.

To Dabney Cosby

SIR   Monticello Dec. 26. 18.

I have nothing to do with the employment of the workmen for the Central college. that is the exclusive office of the Proctor. should the legislature adopt it for their University, the Proctor will immediately advertize for workmen of different kinds to send in their propositions and terms to him: on which occasion you will see what will be wanting and to whom your propositions must be addressed. Accept my best wishes & respects.   TH: JEFFERSON

PoC (MHi); on verso of reused address cover to TJ; at foot of text: "Mʳ Dabney Cosby"; endorsed by TJ.

To Louis H. Girardin

DEAR SIR   Monticello Dec. 26. 18.

Your letter of the 13ᵗʰ never came to hand till yesterday evening, and as mr Hall presses you in time I lose none in forwarding you the 1ˢᵗ vol. of Botta. if you should conclude to translate it, the other volumes shall be sent successively as they shall be wanting. Botta gives a list of the authorities he consulted: but in fact has chiefly followed Marshal & often merely translated him in his American facts, but even there transfuses into his narration his own holy enthusiasm for liberty of which his icy original had not one spark. his 2ᵈ great excellence over Marshal is in the foreign events of his history, in which he shines, while Marshal notes them either briefly or not at all. in making an extract therefore for publication as a specimen, you will of course be careful to collate the two, so that the extract selected may not be a translation from Marshal.

I thank you for the interest you are so kind as to express for my health. the trial of the Warmspring waters was very unlucky, and I was reduced very low. but I consider my health as perfectly reestablished. I salute you with great esteem and respect

                                        TH: JEFFERSON

RC (PPAmP: Thomas Jefferson Papers); addressed: "Mʳ L. H. Girardin Staunton"; franked; postmarked. PoC (MHi); on verso of reused address cover of Patrick Gibson to TJ, 14 Sept. 1818; hole in manuscript; endorsed by TJ. Recorded in SJL as sent "with 1ˢᵗ Botta."

Girardin's letter OF THE 13ᵀᴴ December 1818, not found, is recorded in SJL as received 25 Dec. 1818 from Staunton.

In his *Storia della Guerra dell' Indepenza degli Stati Uniti D'America*, 4 vols. (Paris, 1809; Sowerby, no. 509; Poor, *Jefferson's Library*, 4 [no. 134]), the first volume of which accompanied this letter, Carlo Botta cited John Marshall, *The Life of George Washington*, 5 vols. (Philadelphia, 1804–07; Sowerby, no. 496; Poor, *Jefferson's Library*, 4 [no. 133]), as one of the AUTHORITIES he consulted in preparing the work (1:ix).

From James Oldham

DEARE SIR   Staunton December 26. 1818.

I have returned heare from St Louis in the Missouri Territory much
disappointed in my engagement, the 1st of Janewary last I entered
into a contract with Benjamen James Harris of Richmond to perform
a grate deale of Building in & ajasent to the Town of St Louis, 10
hands, Sawyers & hewers ware sent from Richmond on the 8 of
Janewary last with all nesary tooles for Getting of lumber & arived
safe, a large quantity of Iron mongery was ordered from New York
and arived at Orleans in Aprail last, every thing nesary for a fare beginning was at hand, my part of the contract Mr Harris agreed was
performed, but Insisted on abolishing our contract on account of the
imbarest state of his afares in Richmond. If the Legislature accept
youre reporte on the university I Suppose theare will be a vast quantity of worke to be done the ensuing yeare and if you should have any
further management of the Buildings, I should be very thankful for
some of the worke to do, I am induced to beleave that I should be able
to give you every Satisfaction required.

With Grate Respect I Am Sir your Ob^t Servent.

J; OLDHAM

RC (MHi); at foot of text: "Thos Jefferson Esqr"; endorsed by TJ as received 31
Dec. 1818 and so recorded in SJL.

From John M. Perry

SIR   Central College dec^r 26. 1818
I inclose you the measurement of the Brick work made by Mr Minor
& Dinsmore—will you be pleased to Send the papers by tomorrow
mail—we are quite anxious to know what the price of the work is to be
Respectfully your obt & H. Set   JOHN M. PERRY

RC (CSmH: JF); addressed: "Thomas Jefferson Esquire Monticello"; endorsed by
TJ as received 26 Dec. 1818 and so recorded in SJL. Enclosure not found.

To Fernagus De Gelone

SIR   Monticello Dec. 27. 18.
I recieved yesterday the 2^d copy of De la lande's Logarithms and
your note of the 90.D. adding that the books would be forward[ed][1]
as soon as you should recieve a definitive answer to yours of the 15th.

I had considered mine of the 9th to mr Belair as an anticipation of that answer, inasmuch as it gave a specification of the books I had concluded to take, and covered the price of them. I will now however be more particular as to the others mentioned in your letter of the 15th & not in mine of the 9th

 Stephani Thesaurus Gr. I meant to decline taking because [I] found it cost more than it was worth my while to giv[e]
 Persoon fungarum et plantarum. declined for same reas[on]
 La Place Systeme—et Mecanique celeste, declined for t[he] same reason, and also because of 4to format, books of that size being too unhandy, & the 8vo format greatly preferred
 Tacite de la Malle. mr Belair had informed it was sold. if not sold I shall be glad to recieve it.
 Journal Bibliographique de la France. I shall be willing to recieve this instead of the Dictionnaire Bibliographique
 Sacrorum Bibliorum Concordantiae   ⎫ I had been informed that
 Dictionnaire de Medecine avec Lexicon ⎭ these also had been sold, and therefore neither the format nor price were stated to me. if you will be so good as to inform me of them, I will consider whether I take them or not. as I know nothing of them but from their titles, you would oblige me by stating their authors, their date & any other general information of them, & particularly whether the Lexicon is a Greek one, compiled specially for reading[2] the works of Hippocrates.

in the mean time send on the rest without detaining them for these two. a[ccep]t[3] the assurances of my respect.

PoC (MHi); on verso of reused address cover of Stephen Cathalan to TJ, 13 Aug. 1818; torn at seal; endorsed by TJ: "Fernagus de Gelone. Dec. 27. 18."

The NOTE from Fernagus De Gelone received 26 Dec. 1818 by TJ is not recorded in SJL and has not been found.

[1] Word faint.
[2] Word interlined.
[3] Word faint.

To John G. Jackson

DEAR SIR   Monticello Dec. 27. 18.
 I feel with great sensibility, the kind interest you are so good as to express on the subject of my health. my trial of the Warm springs was certainly ill-advised. for I went to them in perfect health, and ought to have reflected that remedies of their potency must have effect some way or other. if they find disease they remove it; if none, they

make it. altho' I was reduced very low, I may be said to have been rather on the road to danger, than in actual danger. I have now entirely recovered my strength, & consider my health as restored. But as to the value of my life, dear Sir, of which you speak so partially, it is now nothing. I may do for our University what others would do better were I away. my vicinity to the place alone giving me prominence in it's concerns. as to every thing else, I am done. enfeebled in body, probably in mind also, in memory very much, and all those faculties on the wane which are the avenues to life's happiness, I am equal to no pursuit useful to others, or interesting to myself, beyond such employment of my remaining time, as may protect me from the taedium vitae, not the least afflicting of the distresses of old age. I read with avidity, but have the sensations of the gallows when obliged to take up my pen. to yourself I sincerely wish a lengthened life of health and happiness. Th: JEFFERSON

RC (InU: Jackson Collection); addressed: "John G. Jackson esquire Clarksburg"; franked; postmarked Charlottesville, 29 Dec. PoC (DLC).

From John Martin Baker

SIR,   George Town DC. December 28th 1818.

It is with the most sensible Satisfaction that I learned from Mr Tucker, a few days since, of your happy re-establishing in Health.

I take the liberty to inclose, a Blank proposal, for a small Publication of facts, that some Notes, and memory enable me to communicate to paper, deduced from experience[1] during my residence in Spain in the Service of the United States, which I trust may be viewed, and found Commercially interesting: at the same time afford me some little means to Educate my three Younger children, two Daughters, and one Son. I Solicit Sir, your goodness in your Name to the Subscription, and ask the favor of your being so kind as to be pleased to transmit to me the same Signed.—

Mrs Baker, my Children and myself, unite in Prayer for your re-establishment in Health, and a series of Years with every Happiness this world can afford.—

I have the Honor to Subscribe myself, with the Highest Resp[ect] and Gratitude—Sir Your most Humbl[e] Obedient faithful Servant.—

JOHN MARTIN BAKER.

RC (MHi); edge chipped and trimmed; at foot of text: "To Thomas Jefferson. &c &c &c—Monti-cello"; endorsed by TJ as received 4 Jan. 1819 and so recorded in SJL. Enclosed prospectus not found, but see Baker to TJ, 4 Mar. 1819.

[1] Preceding two words interlined.

From José Corrêa da Serra

SIR   Washington. 28. December. 1818.

I have Lately received from you the report about the University of Virginia for which i give you my best thanks. Though you had been so kind to communicate it to me at Monticello, and the Leading ideas had remained in my mind, still a repeated and reflected perusal of it has still more impressed me with the soundness and fitness of the contents in all its parties.[1] May your Legislature adopt it, and may you enjoy the growth of this noble institution many years. It will be a most noble conclusion of the high services which you have rendered to America, because i consider an institution such as you have planned not only useful to yours and to the neighbouring states, but as a stimulant to the other though distant states.

I have not lost any occasion of knowing the state of your health, and am very glad to be informed to day by a Letter from Gilmer that it is perfectly recovered. Take now care of it for the sake of the work in which you are engaged; the Legislature may decree, but no body can execute it but the planner, i know your country.

Not to trouble you with microscopic observations, i inclose a bit of paper for Colonel Randolph, and remain always with the greatest respect and attachment

Your most obed[t] faithful serv[t]   JOSEPH CORRÈA DE SERRA

RC (DLC); endorsed by TJ as received 9 Jan. 1819 and so recorded in SJL. RC (MHi); address cover only; with PoC of TJ to Hugh Holmes, 4 Mar. 1819, on verso; addressed: "Thomas Jefferson Esqr Late President of the United States Charlottesville Albemarle C[ty] Virginia"; franked; postmarked Washington, 30 Dec. Enclosure not found.

[1] Omitted period at right margin editorially supplied.

To Louis A. Leschot

Dec. 28. 18.

Th: Jefferson sends to mr Leschot mrs Eppes's watch needing repairs, and the key needing a new pipe. her servant will be here till the middle of the week and it is hoped mr Leschot will do it in time for him to carry back, as she lives at a great distance, and opportunities of sending it are very rare. Th:J. will pay the cost of repairs, and will hope to recieve from mr Leschot at the same time the amount of the work done for him and the family at various times, which with[1] the cost of the gold watches first bought and which has been so long left in his hands, he proposes to pay him in a few days.

he wishes mr & mrs Leschot could come and dine here some day. he will send for them any day which will suit them, & he salutes them with friendship and respect.

RC (PPRF); written on a small scrap; dateline at foot of text. Not recorded in SJL.

On 8 Apr. 1819 TJ drew on James Leitch in Leschot's favor for "165.64 for watches" (*MB*, 2:1353).

[1] Manuscript: "with with."

From William Wirt

DEAR SIR   Washington Decem[r] 28th 1818.

Your letter of the 10th Ult[o] reached this place after I had set out for Baltimore on public business, which kept me from home a full month, tho' in the expectation, all the while, of returning on every succeeding day or two, at the farthest. I regret this delay, as I do most sensibly my misapprehension of your first letter relative to the proper court of probate of the will of General Kozciuzko: for I really understood you as apprizing me of the question, that I might be prepared to answer it, without delay, when called upon by the head of the Treasury department, and as expecting your answer through that department[1]—and under this impression, after waiting a reasonable time, I called on M[r] Crawford, and told him that I was ready to answer the enquiry whenever it should be presented to me officially; but he said there was no occasion for haste; and concurred with me in the opinion that proof of the will of General K. before any court of Virginia authorized by the laws of the State to receive such proof, would be sufficient for the object you have in view.—Proof, therefore, in the superior court of your county, which you seem to prefer, will avail fully to authorize the executor, or administrator with the will annexed, to with-draw the funds of the deceased from the hands of the United States.

You have recovered, I hope, from the indisposition with which you were so sorely afflicted this fall?—I pray Heaven to preserve you to your country and your friends, among whom you have no one more gratefully and ardently attached than   W[M] WIRT

RC (DLC); endorsed by TJ as received 5 Jan. 1819 and so recorded in SJL. RC (ViU: TJP-CC); address cover only; with PoC of TJ to Dabney Carr, 11 Mar. 1819, on verso; addressed: "Thomas Jefferson esquire Monticello (V[a])"; franked; postmarked. Tr (MdHi: Wirt Papers).

[1] Preceding eight words not in Tr.

From John Adams

DEAR SIR   Quincy Dec[r] 30th 1818 6 oClock[1]

Late last night I received Your Report and your translation of Tracy, for both of which, tho' I have read neither I thank you, but the full proof[2] of your returning health has given me more Pleasure than both. I envy your Eyes and hands and Horse. Mine are too dim, too tremulous

and my head is too dizzy for the Sovereign Doctor.[3]

All is now Still and tranquil. There is nothing to try Mens Souls nor to excite Men's Souls but Agriculture. And I Say God Speed the Plough and prosper Stone Wall.

Had I your Eyes and Fingers, and 100 years to live I could write an 100. Volumes in folio but neither myself nor the World would be the wiser or[4] the better for any thing that could be done by your assured Friend   JOHN ADAMS

RC (DLC); at foot of text: "President Jefferson"; endorsed by TJ as received 10 Jan. 1819 and so recorded in SJL. FC (Lb in MHi: Adams Papers).

Adams had also received a copy of Destutt de TRACY, Treatise on Political Economy, from Joseph Milligan (Adams to Milligan, 31 Dec. 1818 [Lb in MHi: Adams Papers]). For the transmission to Adams of TJ's letter to John Barnes of 11 Nov. 1818, in which TJ called his horse his SOVEREIGN DOCTOR, see note to Barnes to TJ, [30] Nov. 1818. The phrase TRY MENS SOULS comes from the opening sentence of Thomas Paine, The American Crisis (Norwich, Conn., [1776]).

[1] RC: "oCock." FC: "oclock."
[2] RC: "prof." FC: "proof."
[3] FC here adds "Horse."
[4] Preceding three words not in FC.

ENCLOSURE

Edward T. Channing to William S. Shaw

MY DEAR SIR   Dec. 10. [1818]

If you think it would not be asking too great a favour, I would thank you to request President Adams to forward this N° of the North American to President Jefferson. Our wish, as you know, is to have our book more generally known, & certainly then, we should place it in the hands of our distinguished men. I wish you in this to act as your own feelings direct, & you will excuse me if I have asked too much.

I am, dear Sir, yours sincerely,   EDW. T. CHANNING

RC (DLC: TJ Papers, 216:38638); partially dated at foot of text; addressed: "William S. Shaw Esq Boston."

Edward Tyrell Channing (1790–1856), educator, was born in Newport, Rhode Island. He entered Harvard University in 1804 but did not graduate due to his participation in a student rebellion in 1807. Channing thereafter studied law and was admitted to the bar in 1813. Harvard awarded him an honorary master's degree in 1819, the same year that it appointed him to the Boylston professorship of rhetoric and oratory. He held that position until his retirement in 1851. Channing was elected to the American Academy of Arts and Sciences in 1823. He died in Cambridge (*DAB*; *Harvard Catalogue*, 22, 50, 958; American Academy of Arts and Sciences, *Book of Members, 1780– Present* [2006], 72; Channing, *Lectures Read to the Seniors in Harvard College* [1856]; *Boston Daily Advertiser*, 11 Feb. 1856).

William Smith Shaw (1778–1826), attorney and librarian, was a nephew of Abigail Adams. He was born in Haverhill, Massachusetts, graduated from Harvard University in 1798, and afterwards served as John Adams's secretary, first in Quincy and then in Philadelphia and Washington, D.C., ultimately living with the Adams family for three years. In 1801 Shaw commenced the study of law in Boston. Admitted to the bar two years later,

he was clerk of the federal district court for Massachusetts for twelve years beginning in 1806. Shaw was a founder of the Anthology Society, and after that society became the Boston Athenaeum he served as its librarian, 1807–22, and secretary, 1807–23. He was elected to the American Academy of Arts and Sciences in 1810. Shaw died in Boston (*ANB*; *DAB*; American Academy of Arts and Sciences, *Book of Members*, 377; Joseph B. Felt, *Memorials of William Smith Shaw* [1852]; Lyman H. Butterfield, Richard Alan Ryerson, C. James Taylor, Sara Martin, and others, eds., *Adams Family Correspondence* [1963–]; *Harvard Catalogue*, 181; *Boston Commercial Gazette*, 1 May 1826).

Separately from this letter, TJ received the December 1818 issue (N° 22), part of vol. 8 of the *North American Review and Miscellaneous Journal*. Channing edited the journal from May 1818 until October 1819 (*DAB*).

From Kershaw & Lewis

SIR   Charleston 30ᵗʰ Decemʳ 1818

Agreeably to instructions from our much respected Friend Colº William Alston of George Town, we have put on board the Sloop Altezera, Capt J. B. Levy, for Richmond, a Barrel of Rice directed to you to the care of Captⁿ Bernard Peyton—we have inclosed a Bill of Lading to Capt Peyton and requested him to forward the Rice to your Residence at Monticello—the Freight is paid to Richmond.

with much respect We are Sir Your most Ob'd Servants

KERSHAW & LEWIS

P. S. The Box of Wine for Colº Alston arrived safe.

RC (MHi); endorsed by TJ as received 12 Jan. 1819 and so recorded in SJL. RC (MHi); address cover only; with PoC of TJ to Joel Yancey, 22 Feb. 1819, on recto and verso; addressed: "Thomas Jefferson Esqʳ Monticello Virginia"; stamped; postmarked Charleston, 30 Dec.

Kershaw & Lewis was a mercantile partnership formed by the factors Charles Kershaw (1760–1835) and John Lewis

(ca. 1777–1839) by 1813 in Charleston, South Carolina. Both men had emigrated from England, with Kershaw arriving in the city by 1788 and Lewis by 1801. The firm became Kershaw, Lewis, & Robertson by 1833, and Lewis continued to work as a factor in various partnerships after Kershaw's death (James H. Easterby, ed., *The South Carolina Rice Plantation as Revealed in the Papers of Robert F. W. Allston* [1945; repr. 2004], esp. 37–8,

377; Joseph G. B. Bulloch, *A History and Genealogy of the Families of Bellinger and De Veaux and Other Families* [1895], 37; Joshua W. Toomer, *An Oration, Delivered at the Celebration of the First Centennial Anniversary of the South-Carolina Society, in Charleston* [1837], 89; Jacob Milligan, *The Charleston Directory* [Charleston, 1794], 22; Alexander S. Salley, comp., *Marriage Notices in The South-Carolina Gazette and its successors* [1902], 101; John Dixon Nelson, *Nelson's Charleston Directory, and Strangers Guide* [Charleston, 1801], 91; [Charleston, 1816], 47; *Charleston Courier*, 21 Apr. 1813; gravestone inscriptions in Saint Philip's Episcopal Church, Charleston).

To William Radford and Joel Yancey

MESS^RS RADFORD & YANCEY   Monticello Dec. 31. 18.

I agreed the last winter with mr Matthew Brown of Lynchburg for the execution of certain brickwork at the Central College, for which he was to be paid the price at which similar work should be done in Lynchburg this present year 1818. that price is now to be settled, and as all the evidence on the subject must be found in Lynchburg or it's neighborhood, to which place I shall not be able to go until the spring, we have mutually agreed to refer it to you; and on behalf of the College I now sollicit your undertaking that office. in proof of the agreement I inclose you my advertisement and mr Brown's letter of agreement with the quantity and specification of the work done as estimated by referees. for the same reason of my inability to be in Lynchburg until the spring I must here make some observations which I should do verbally could I attend in person. mr Saml Harrison, to whose testimony I must refer you, informed me that he had an offer to do his work for 5.D. exclusive of the price of the bricks which would have been 8.D. more. on this information I have always expected that we should pay mr Brown 13.D. the thousand, for all except the oil brick. he says that the offer to mr Harrison was not for such work as ours. but I doubt the correctness of this suggestion. mr Harrison has his work done in the best manner, and such I presume was the understanding between him & the person offering. mr Brown alleges too that there is no sammel brick in our work, as there is in that in Lynchburg. if there be in Lynchburg, it is a cheat, for which a workman should pay instead of being paid. the law countenances no such infidelity.[1] the English statute allows 2. brick bats (half bricks) to be worked up in every 10. bricks. I am sure mr Brown will say candidly whether he has not used in our walls a greater than that proportion.   the advances of money to him have been ready and liberal, and his full paiment will not be delayed beyond April or May. could I have attended in person, I would have saved you the trouble of looking after evidence as to the prices at which work has been done this past season in Lynchburg. as it is I am obliged to request your consultation with employers as well as undertakers to satisfy yourselves on this head, and I will pray you to inclose to me by mail the papers now sent with your award of the rate of prices for each kind of work. with my apologies on behalf of the College for this trouble, I tender you the assurance of my great esteem and respect.

Th: Jefferson

RC (MH: Borgman Autograph Collection); addressed: "Messrs Joel Yancey & Wm Radford Poplar Forest." PoC (DLC); on reused address cover of DeWitt Clinton to TJ, 21 Sept. 1818; damaged at seal; endorsed by TJ. Enclosure: TJ's Advertisement for Brickwork, [by 7 Dec. 1817].

The LETTER OF AGREEMENT with Matthew Brown that was enclosed here may have been Brown to TJ, 26 Jan. 1818 (see note to TJ to Brown, 15 Jan.

1818). OIL BRICK was made using molds that were "sanded or oiled to alleviate the sticking" (Carl R. Lounsbury, *An Illustrated Glossary of Early Southern Architecture and Landscape* [1994], 49). SAMMEL (also samel, sammen, or salmon) bricks are soft due to underheating in the kiln (Lounsbury, *Illustrated Glossary*, 48; *OED*).

[1] Omitted period at right margin editorially supplied.

To George H. Richards

Sir   Monticello Dec. 31. 18.

Age and declining health having rendered me unequal to the labors of letter-writing, I can make but a short acknolegement of the obliging propositions of your letter of the 15th. in the various stations in which the public have thought proper to require my services, I have endeavored to discharge my duty with care and integrity. but I have seen thousands of my fellow citizens serving in their stations also with equal care and integrity. I have no claim therefore to merit for a faithful execution of trusts reposed, more than they have, nor any expectation, or even wish, that my biography should be noticed more than theirs. under this impression I have never noted in writing any particulars of my own life, and as to memory, that is too much impaired to furnish any thing worthy of confidence. you will, then, I flatter myself, have the goodness to excuse my declining the request of your letter, as I have uniformly done on other similar applications, and will be disposed to indulge the pressure of age unaggravated by the exactions of new toils and labours.

I feel a just sensibility for the sentiments you are so kind as to express towards myself and the course I have pursued. the approbation of my services by my fellow citizens is a great consolation and the richest reward I can recieve; and with my thankfulness to yourself particularly, I pray you to accept the tender of my great respect

TH: JEFFERSON

PoC (DLC); at foot of text: "Mr George H. Richards." Printed in *Richmond Enquirer*, 30 Mar. 1824, and elsewhere.

To James Riley

SIR   Monticello Dec. 31. 18.

The correspondence which mr Simpson mentions having commenced with me in Feb. 1793. while Secretary of state must have closed at the end of the same year, when I retired from that office. of it's particulars I have no recollection: but they are certainly to be found in the office of state. from 1801. to Mar. 1809. the conduct of mr Simpson, as Consul at Marocco, was of course under my observation. the opinion I formed of him was that he was attentive, zealous & faithful, and I considered him as one of the good servants of the US. I recollect his application for an enlargement of salary, and I have no doubt that the letter which he says 'he recieved by the Adams frigate, from the Secretary of State in 1802. mentioning the subject of his salary in such terms as had well nigh determined him to relinquish the office,' informed him of the sense of the Executive administration on that subject, and particularly of their incompetence to increase salaries fixed by law. he has now placed that question before the only authority competent to it, and what they ought to do is not for others to say.   I am very sensible of the kindness of the sentiments you are so good as to express towards my self. the approbation of my services by my fellow citizens is a great consolation, and the highest reward which I can recieve: and with my thankfulness to yourself particularly, I pray you to accept the assurance of my great esteem and respect   TH: JEFFERSON

PoC (ViW: TC-JP); on verso of re-used address cover to TJ; at foot of text: "Mr Riley"; endorsed by TJ.

TJ's correspondence as secretary of state with James Simpson, then the Russian consul at Gibraltar, COMMENCED with a letter from Simpson to TJ of 12 Feb. 1793 and ended with another from Simpson of 8 Oct. 1793 (*PTJ*, 25:182,

27:224). On 20 Apr. 1802 James Madison, TJ's secretary of state, informed Simpson in a letter dispatched via the ADAMS FRIGATE that, while the government would pay two bills as he had requested, the money would have to come out of his salary and that Madison had no authority to offer additional compensation (Madison, *Papers, Sec. of State Ser.*, 3:141, 431).

Estimate of Funds and Expenditures for Central College/University of Virginia

[1818–1819]

Funds, 1818

	D
1818. proceeds of Glebes	3,280.86
1st & 2d instalments of subscriptions	21,949
	25,229.86

Expenditures, 1818

	D
1818. 200. aˢ land purchased from Perry & Garth	1,540.
Proctor 200.D. Overseer 150.D	350.
laborers hire. 8. about	800
subsistence and miscellaneous[1] expences	500
Doric Pavilion [87,458 bricks] estimated @	3,411
South wing of Dormitories [184,325. br.]	
North wing of dᵒ [182,137. br.] estimated @ 13 D & ×ᵈ by 2. }	6,926
Corinthian Pavilion [123,717. br.][2] suppose @ $\frac{13).}{26)}$ × by 3. $\begin{matrix}3,843.\end{matrix}$	5,121
Balance remaining for 1819.	6,581.86
	25,229.86

Funds, 1819

	D
1819. Balance remaining of funds of 1818.	6,581.
3d instalment of subscriptions	12,615
annual endowment from Jan. 23. 1818.	15,000.
	34,196

Expenditures, 1819

	D
1819. Proctor 500. Overseer 100.	600.
laborers 14. about	1,400.
subsistence & Miscellaneous expences	1,000.
passage & wages of a stone cutter	625
Bursar @ [. . .]p.[c].? or salary	300
Doctor Cooper. salary	1,500
Perry's houses, and land. Mar. 1. Dec. 25 ½	4,000[3]
bringing water by pipes	300[4]
an Oxcart and team	220.
suppose	9,945[5]

	D
an Hotel	2700
a 3d Pavilion	4500
a 4th Pavilion	4500
26[6] Dormitories @ 350.D. each	9100[7]
	20,800
surplus to cover defects[8]	3,451
	34,196

MS (ViU: TJP); entirely in TJ's hand; undated; hole in manuscript; brackets in original.

TJ evidently composed this document in more than one sitting, beginning well after he completed a similar Estimate of Funds and Expenditures for Central College, printed above at 30 Dec. 1817, and ending about the time the Virginia General Assembly designated Central College as the University of Virginia on 25 Jan. 1819. Several of the figures estimated as expenses for 1819 are drawn from TJ's correspondence late in 1818. In his letter to TJ of 6 Oct. 1818, Thomas Cooper requested a salary of $1,500. The Agreement by John M. Perry to Sell Lands to Central College of 7 Nov. 1818 established payment dates of 1 Mar. and 25 Dec. 1819. TJ's salary estimate for a single stonecutter does not take into account the salaries for two stonecutters negotiated by Thomas Appleton and reported in his letter of 10 Nov. 1818, which TJ received 18 Feb. 1819. Three days after the passage on 25 Jan. 1819 of TJ's Bill for the Establishment of a University, printed above at 19 Nov. 1818, TJ wrote to Wilson Cary Nicholas laying out the possibility of beginning the third and fourth pavilions. Most likely at about that time he added the figures for these proposed structures in an ink different from the bulk of the document. As 1819 progressed more concrete figures replaced these speculative ones. At its first meeting, on 29 Mar. 1819, the newly appointed University of Virginia Board of Visitors selected Alexander Garrett as bursar and set his yearly salary at $250, not the $300 estimated here.

The DORIC and CORINTHIAN structures eventually became the University of Virginia's Pavilions VII and III, respectively.

[1] Reworked from "miscellanies."
[2] Omitted closing bracket editorially supplied.
[3] Reworked from what appears to be "2,000."
[4] Entry interlined.
[5] Reworked from what appears to be "7,645." Remainder of text added by TJ in a different ink, with further additions in pencil noted below.
[6] Number added by TJ in pencil.
[7] Number and table of sums to the right and below added by TJ in pencil.
[8] Preceding four words added by TJ in pencil.

To Joseph C. Cabell

DEAR SIR   Monticello Jan. 1. 19.

Altho' my revolt against letter writing has not permitted me to acknolege separately your several favors of Dec. 8. 14. 17. 24. as I recieved them, I am not the less thankful for their information. I take up my pen now on the subject of my estimate of the center of white population. you say it is objected that the commencement at the mouth of the Chesapeake is nearer the Southern than Northern limit on the coast. that is true; but the greatest part of what is North, is water. there is more land on the South than North. I do not think a fairer point of commencement can be taken & being a remarkable one I therefore took it. the point of commencement being determined, the direction of the line of equal division is not a matter of choice, it must from thence take whatever direction an equal division of the population commands. and the Census proves this to pass near Charlottesville, the Rockfish gap & Staunton. the blue ridge again, in the cross division is so natural a dividing line as to have been universally so considered, and a parallel course with that should therefore be taken for the line of equal division that way. they talk of a division by an E. and W. line; but our Northern boundary trending North of N. W.[1] while the Southern is E. & W. the fair direction is between the two as that is which I took. why should they divide by a parallel to our Southern more than to our Northern boundary? what reason can be given for laying off the Southern half in a parallellogram & the Northern in a triangle? not a single one but to bring the course of that line nearer to Lexington. the state itself being triangular, each half should be so.[2] an E. & W. line would take the line of equal division entirely from Staunton, but I do not believe it would from Charlottesville; and while a North & South line would take it entirely from Lexington, I believe it would be still as near to Charlottesville; and in my opinion run your lines in what direction you please, they will pass close to Charlottesville, and for the very good reason that it is truly central to the white population. however let those who wish to set up other lines in competition, make their own calculations. it is a very laborious business. mine took me 2. or 3. days, and I know there can be no inaccuracy in it, except from a single source. where a line divided a county into two parts, equal or unequal I could only estimate by my eye the proportion between the two parts. no doubt there is error in some of these, but probably as much one way as another, and that contrary errors balance one another. I am certain there will not be found much error in the whole result. but I am saying to you things which would occur to yourself, and yielding to the lex inertiae which, with respect to the use of the pen is now become, uncontroulably, the law of nature with me, I will place here the assurances of my affectionate esteem & respect

Th: Jefferson

RC (ViU: TJP); addressed: "Joseph C. Cabell esquire of the Senate of Virginia now in Richmond"; franked; postmarked Charlottesville, 2 Jan.; endorsed by Cabell. PoC (DLC); on reused address cover to TJ; damaged at seal; portions rewritten by TJ to correct a polygraph malfunction; endorsed by TJ.

[1] PoC: "the North West."
[2] TJ here canceled "if."

To Francis Eppes

DEAR FRANCIS   Monticello Jan. 1. 19.

Leschot has repaired mrs Eppes's watch and changed the pipe of the key, but the watch was so short a time in his hands that she could not be well regulated. she will therefore probably need further regulation to make[1] her keep good time.   I am sorry you are disappointed in your teacher. but it depends on yourself whether this is of any consequence. a master is necessary only to those who require compulsion to get their lessons. as to instruction a translation supplies the place of a teacher. get the lesson first by dictionary; and then, instead of saying it to a master go over it with the translation, and that will tell you whether you have got it truly.[2] Dacier's Horace is admirable for this. as to parsing you can do that by yourself both as to parts of speech and syntax. you can perfect yourself too in your Greek grammar as well alone as with a teacher. your Spanish too should be kept up. all depends on your own resolution to stick as closely to your book as if a master was looking over you. if Dr Cooper comes to us, he will open our grammar school the 1st of April. we shall be decided in a few days and I will let you know. you complain of my not writing to you, writing has become so irksome to me that I have withdrawn from all correspondence, and scarcely answer any body's letter. you are young and it is one of the best exercises for you. I shall hope therefore to hear from you often; but can write to you myself only when I have something to communicate or advise. present my respects to mrs Eppes and be assured of my constant affection.

TH: JEFFERSON

RC (DLC); addressed: "Mr Francis Eppes Millbrook." PoC (CSmH: JF); on verso of a reused address cover from James Monroe to TJ; endorsed by TJ.

Missing letters from Eppes to TJ of 22 Dec. 1818 and 12 Jan. 1819 are recorded in SJL as received from Mill Brook on 26 Dec. 1818 and 21 Jan. 1819, respectively.

[1] Reworked from "makes" in RC, with PoC unrevised.
[2] Word interlined.

From Alexander Murray

SIR   Frimley near Bagshot England January 1st 1819

I did myself the Honor of addressing, and inclosing to you, from the Bahamas some time ago two letters (one from my Deceased mother Lady Dunmore, & the other from my Sister Lady Virginia) calling on her Godfathers in your State to fulfil their promise, of making an ample provision for her—which promise, circumstances had before prevented her from bringing before them—but as both her Parents are now Dead; she has deemed it expedient to nominate, & give to me, & the Bearer John Stevens Esq[r], a Power of Attorney, to authorize us to use our endeavours to bring the Subject before the consideration of your State Legislature—in the accomplishment of which object—I feel it would be of the highest importance to her interest, to be able to profit by your friendly aid, & assistance in a case (in which if I am not mistaken you took at the time a very active and kind part) & which from your attention to my Brother Captain Murray, when on a visit to your Country, I am sanguine in the hope, that you will yet be induced to extend it to his Sister, as I feel conscious from your great influence among your fellow Citizens, that if the Subject should be brought forward under yours, & M[r] Monroe's Auspices (to whom I have already written on this head) that the most formidable obstacles to the measure will be removed, & that success would eventually attend this measure of her present application—so protected & recommended

I have the Honor to be &[a] Y[r] Humble Servant   A Murray

RC (DLC); at foot of first page: "Tho[s] Jefferson Esq[r] &[a] &[a] &[a] &[a]"; endorsed by TJ as received 10 Apr. 1820 and so recorded in SJL.

No letter to TJ from Charlotte Stewart Murray, Countess of DUNMORE, has been found, nor is one recorded in SJL.

On 10 Apr. 1820 JOHN STEVENS presented this letter to TJ in person, and in a letter dated Philadelphia, 5 May 1820, he reported to Murray that "I engaged M[r] Gilmer to do what might be necessary after I had seen M[r] Jefferson, at Monticello the seat of the latter 76 Miles Westwardly I arrived on the 10th. He told me he had some time ago received a Copy of the letter, he did not recollect that any such promise was ever made, altho Lady Dunmore was very much respected by all the Virginians, & expressed something of regret at not being encouraged to pay

his Respects to her Ladyship with his daughter at Paris some years afterwards, however he recommended my getting M[r] Gilmer whom he knew very well to search the Records, if any such was made he had no doubt it would now be made good agreeably to the fixed value of Land at that time about he thought 3£ Curr[y] per 100 Acres. I immediately wrote M[r] Gilmer to write me the result" (Tr in Vi: Personal Papers Collection, Murray Family Papers; at foot of first page: "The Hon[ble] A Murray"; at head of text: "Copy N[o] 2"; conjoined with Trs of other documents accompanying a memorial from Lady Virginia Murray to the Virginia General Assembly, Paris, 28 May 1824; memorial and enclosures printed in "Lady Virginia Murray and Her Alleged Claim Against the State of Virginia," *WMQ*, 1st ser., 24 [1915]: 85–101).

To James Oldham

Dear Sir   Monticello Jan. 1. 19.

I am really sorry for your disappointment[1] in your Western enter-
prise, altho' I did think at the time that a proficient in Architecture
was not likely to find as much emploiment in the new as old settled
part of the state. should the legislature adopt however the Central
college for their University there will be for years to come as much
work to be done as all the good workmen we can get can do; and we
mean to employ none but the best, as our houses altho small are to
be perfect models of chaste architecture and good taste. but[2] I have
nothing to do with the employment of the workmen. the Proctor of
the institution will advertize for undertakers[3] in every branch of building to give in the terms on which they will do their work, finding
themselves every thing, and how much they will undertake to compleat in the season. we expect to have about half a dozen houses, with
a long line of dormitories done the ensuing season. these houses are
generally about 35. feet front and from 25. to 40 in depth, finished
inside & out in the purest style of regular Architecture, and each
Undertaker may engage for 1. 2. 3 E^{t}c as he pleases. in the housejoin-
ery we shall make the Philadelphia printed book of prices the standard of reference, and each undertaker will have to say whether he
will work at those prices, or how much below or above them. we are
assured we shall have offers from Philadelphia to work considerably
below them. the advertisement in the public papers (the Enquirer)
from the Proctor will inform you when, how, and to whom to apply.
I shall be very glad to see you employed on it, & tender you my best
wishes and respects.   Th: Jefferson

RC (NjR: United States Letters Collection); addressed: "Capt James Oldham
Staunton"; franked; postmarked Charlottesville, 3 Jan. PoC (MHi); on verso of
reused address cover of Honoré Julien to
TJ, 14 Oct. 1818; endorsed by TJ.

[1] Manuscript: "diasppointment."
[2] Word interlined.
[3] Reworked from "undertakings."

From Charles Willson Peale

Dear Sir   Washington Jany 1st 1819.

soon after my arrival here I wrote to inform you of my object in
visiting this place, with the hope that my scribling might not be a
burden on your precious moments, and as I had said that I would
give you some account of my Portraits, Since I begin to think I shall

paint only one or two more at the present time, I will enumerate them. Viz^t The President, Mr Calhoun, Mr Adams, Mr Crawford, Mr Clay, Col^l Johnson, Mr Holmes, Mr Wirt, Mr Rufus King, Com^{re} Porter, and Com^{re} Rogers. Perhaps I may take the Portraits of Mr Tomkins, and the Sec^y of the Navy Mr Thompson, who are expected here daily. Should Genl Jackson arrive here shortly I may endeavor to obtain the favor of his setting.

Although there are many Gentlemen of Congress who wish the purchase of my Museum, yet I know by my conversation with several others who have not a conception of its Utility, therefore I shall not make an offer of it at this moment. But I am confident that the time will come, when they shall be sorry for having let it slip through their fingers. The education it is capable of diffusing through the mass of Citizens is all important. I have read a maxim of moral truth, "That the attainment of Happiness, Individual as well as Public, depends on the cultivation of the human mind."

Having laid aside all other persuits, except what may tend to the improvement of the Museum, I hope I may live long enough to place it on a permanant mount.

I conclude with my best wishes for your health and happiness in a length of days, most respectfully your friend   C W PEALE

Mr Epps will set to me in a few days.   C—P—

RC (MHi); lacking postscript; endorsed by TJ as received 10 Jan. 1819 and so recorded in SJL. RC (DLC); postscript and address cover only; with PoC of TJ to José Corrêa da Serra, 2 Mar. 1819, on recto and verso; addressed: "Thomas Jefferson Esqr Monticella Virginia"; with postscript beneath and oriented upside down to address; franked; postmarked. PoC (PPAmP: Peale Letterbook); lacking postscript.

THAT THE ATTAINMENT ... HUMAN MIND loosely quotes the British artist James Barry (Peale, *Papers*, 3:614; Barry, *An Account of a Series of Pictures, in the Great Room of the Society of Arts, Manufactures, and Commerce, at the Adelphi* [London, 1783], 40). In January 1819 TJ's son-in-law John Wayles Eppes (EPPS) sat simultaneously for a portrait by Peale and a miniature portrait by his niece Anna Claypoole Peale (Duncan), neither of which is known to survive (Peale, *Papers*, 3:684–6).

From Dominic W. Boudet

SIR,   Baltimore, January 2^d 1819.

A difficulty attached to the Subtilties of Etiquette and formality has often prevented many valuable discoveries of being known, those through whose ascendency alone Men of genius can possibly succeed being too often inaccessible; but, from a Knowledge of your liberality

of Sentiments, I feel a ready assurance that Scientifical characters
need no other introduction to you, Sir, than their merits and, consequently, that no further apology is necessary, in case of intrusion on
my Side.

In this confidence I have used the freedom of addressing you and
beg leave to have the honour of Communicating to you a Subjet of
National and Scientifical a nature on which your Sanction or Countenance would insure its highly important Success.

I have the honour to be, Very respectfully Sir, Your very humble
Servt   D. W. BOUDET

RC (MHi); endorsed by TJ as received 10 Jan. 1819 and so recorded in SJL. RC (DLC); address cover only; with PoC of TJ to James Breckinridge, 3 Mar. 1819, on verso; addressed: "Thomas Jefferson Esqr Mount-Cello Virginia"; franked; postmarked. Enclosure not found.

Dominic W. Boudet (d. 1845), artist, was a native of France who reportedly lived in Paris and studied under Jacques Louis David. By 1805 he was in Rich-mond with his father, Nicolas Vincent Boudet, with whom he operated acade-mies teaching art, dancing, and French. The pair were in Baltimore, 1806–08, Washington, D.C., 1810–12, and in Phila-delphia in 1814. The younger Boudet filed for bankruptcy in 1812. He unsuccessfully sought congressional support during the 1816–17 session for a national museum he wished to establish in Washington. In 1819 Boudet and his father worked on a massive painting of the 1814 Battle of Bal-timore, but he went bankrupt again when the city of Baltimore did not buy the com-pleted work. He continued to be peripa-tetic thereafter, painting and exhibiting his works in a variety of cities including Annapolis in 1819, Charleston, South Carolina, in 1820, New York City later in the 1820s and early in the 1830s, Bos-ton in 1831, New Orleans, 1833–34, and Charleston again by 1838. Boudet was exhibiting a painting in Baltimore when

he died (David Karel, *Dictionnaire des Artistes de Langue Française en Amérique du Nord* [1992], 108–9; George C. Groce and David H. Wallace, *The New-York Historical Society's Dictionary of Artists in America, 1564–1860* [1957], 67; Anna Wells Rutledge, *Artists in the Life of Charleston Through Colony and State From Restoration to Reconstruction* [1949]; Richmond *Enquirer*, 21 Mar. 1805; Balti-more *American and Commercial Daily Advertiser*, 17 Sept. 1806; *Baltimore Di-rectory and Citizens' Register* [1807]: 21; [1808]: 21; Washington *National Intel-ligencer*, 10 Oct. 1810, 16 June 1812; Bal-timore *American & Commercial Daily Advertiser*, 7 Aug. 1811, 29 Oct. 1845; *Alexandria Daily Gazette, Commercial & Political*, 26 May 1812; Benjamin Kite and Thomas Kite, *Kite's Philadelphia Directory for 1814* [Philadelphia, 1814]; *JHR*, 10:106 [26 Dec. 1816]; *JS*, 6:233 [13 Feb. 1817]; *Baltimore Patriot & Mer-cantile Advertiser*, 26, 28 Aug. 1818, 28 Sept., 13 Oct., 12 Nov. 1819, 24 Feb., 25 Mar. 1820; *City of Washington Gazette*, 25 Sept. 1819; Annapolis *Maryland Ga-zette and Political Intelligencer*, 9 Dec. 1819; DNA: RG 29, CS, Pa., Philadel-phia, 1820; *Longworth's New York Di-rectory* [1827]: 94; [1828]: 133; [1831]: 142; [1832]: 157; *Boston Masonic Mir-ror*, 17 Dec. 1831; Washington *Globe*, 12 Jan. 1833).

From Bernard Peyton

DEAR SIR   Rich^d 2^d Jany 1819

By Mr Johnson I send you a small Box which was deliverd to me a day or two since from Rocketts in <u>very</u> <u>bad</u> <u>order</u> & I have not since learnt where it is from, or any thing about it—I have had it recoopered and safely deliverd & hope it will reach you so

With great respect Dr Sir Your Mo: Obd: B PEYTON

RC (MHi); dateline at foot of text; addressed: "Thomas Jefferson Esqr Monticello"; endorsed by TJ as received 12 Jan. 1819 and so recorded in SJL.

From John Barnes

DEAR SIR   George Town Co^a 4^h Jany 1819.

Permit me to acknowledge your fav^r of the 21^t as it containd 2 Bank Notes for Seven dollars in paym^t for Gales & Seatons Acc^t—was 33^Cts over pay—

Moreover the pleasure Afforded me—in learning—your perfect State of health &^c—

with repeated Assurance of Esteem and respect. Your Obed^t servant   JOHN BARNES.

PS. I cannot but lament the unfortunate delay whereby, you are deprived receiving the growing Interest and dividends—of the late worthy & most respectable friend,—(of more than a $1000 per Ann^m)

RC (MHi); at foot of text: "Thomas Jefferson Esqr Monticello"; endorsed by TJ as received 17 Jan. 1819 and so recorded in SJL.   The late FRIEND was Tadeusz Kosciuszko.

From Thomas C. Flournoy

Columbus Ohio: 4th January 1819.

Permit me to renew my acquaintance, with one whom I esteem, very highly. Four or five years ago, I wrote you two letters, the last of which contained a fourth of July-speech. You were good enough to answer them both with promptness. Your first answer is dated 1st October 1812, your second 8th of August 1814. I have them yet, <u>in your own hand writing</u>, and will keep them till I die—indeed no money would buy them.

I see by the newspapers, that you have lately gone through a spell of sickness. I rejoice at your recovery. May you have good health and spirits for many years to come. No man can feel a more lively interest in your welfare, than I do: Indeed you are the only man I ever wrote to, without some acquaintance, except as a lawyer, upon business.

As a further introduction, suffer me to say a word or two more of myself. I am now twenty seven years of age;—unmarried. The two letters I formerly wrote you were dated at Georgetown, Kentucky, where I was born, and lived till I moved to this town, about two years ago. Since that I have practised law, with <u>tolerable</u> success. But I hate the law: it requires too much study. A military life is what pleases me best. During the last war, I performed two of the hardest campaigns, that went from Kentucky.—<u>as a volunteer</u>. This I mention as the proudest circumstance of my life.

At present, I have the honour to be Quartermaster General, for the state of Ohio, with the rank of Brigadier General. I was elected by the legislature some time last February.

I am well acquainted with two of your best friends in Kentucky— Colonel R. M. Johnson and M[rs] Porter, formerly Miss Latitia P. Breckinridge, daughter of the late Attorney general: The Colonel is a most excellent man: and M[rs] Porter, is certainly equal to any woman I ever saw.—but you know them both.

It would afford me great happiness, to receive a letter from you. Even your name "Th: Jefferson" written on a piece of paper, and directed to me, would be considered a very great compliment. Accept my best wishes for your happiness and welfare, and believe me yours sincerely.   THOMAS C. FLOURNOY.

RC (DLC); endorsed by TJ as received 17 Jan. 1819 and so recorded in SJL. RC (DLC); address cover only; with PoC of TJ to LeRoy, Bayard & Company, 21 Feb. 1819, on verso; addressed: "Thomas Jefferson Esq. Monticello Virginia" by "Mail"; stamp canceled; postmarked Columbus, 4 Jan.

From Alexander Macdonald

SIR.   104. Arch Street Philadelphia 4th January 1819.

It must be with diffidence, that an entier Stranger, can bring himself to address a character of your exalted reputation; and more particularly on Such an occasion, as I now have taken the liberty, to apply to you on. I am a person upwards of fifty years of age, who has experiencd Some disappointments in life; but possessing an unsullied reputation: Altho' under the necessity, of Seeking the means, for my future Support. I am Active and bless'd with good health. And beleive my happiness, is in your power: And Am Solicitous for the honor of being your Amanuensis, or humble Servant, in any Capacity, you may require.

prompted by the benign influence of that beneficent Spirit, that never forsook me, in Adversity! I make my desire known to you; And if I am so happy as to be admitted to the Situation, I Aspire to, I shall endeavor to render myself worthy of your friendship.

I have the honor Sir.

to Subscribe myself your very hb^{le} Serv.   A. MACDONALD

RC (ViU: TJP); at foot of text: "Thomas Jefferson Esqr &^{ca} &^{ca} &^{ca}"; endorsed by TJ as received 10 Jan. 1819 and so recorded in SJL.

Alexander Macdonald (b. ca. 1769) was a native of Scotland who became a naturalized citizen of the United States by 1824, the same year that he applied unsuccessfully to be the librarian at the University of Virginia. In 1825 he was working as an attorney in Philadelphia. An Alexander Allen McDonald had qualified at the Philadelphia bar on 23 Dec. 1824 (Macdonald to TJ, 6 Dec. 1824; *The Philadelphia Directory and Stranger's Guide, for 1825* [Philadelphia, 1825], 89; John Hill Martin, *Martin's Bench and Bar of Philadelphia* [1883], 290).

From Nathaniel Macon

SIR   Washington 4 Jany 1819

I have received and read with great pleasure the proceedings and report of the Commissioners for the University of Virginia; To improve the rising generation is a duty to God, the country & ourselves, those who do most toward it, deserve best of the nation; What man or what talents now in existence, can pretend to limit the progress of the human mind; Improvements in the united States have brought machines to do almost every thing but speak; and surely other branches of useful knowledge may be carried to the same perfection

Will you permit me, to take this opportunity to state to you, that I hav[e] for some time past, thought much of writing, to you, to ask you to inform me, for I know of no one else which could, how it happe[ns] that all the measures which turned the federalists out; have been & are now the fashion; I have not done so, because it mig[ht] be, that you were over done with letters, and did not wish to touch politics; I stop the pen & smother my inclination, to prevent an atte[mpt] which might be disagreeable

Accept my warm thanks for your kind remembrance, and my sincere wishes, that the remainder of your useful life, may be as easy and pleasant to yourself, as the past has been beneficial to our country, and believe me to be

Your friend   NATH[L] MACON

RC (DLC); edge chipped and trimmed; endorsed by TJ as received 10 Jan. 1819 and so recorded in SJL. RC (DLC); partial address cover only; with PoC of TJ to Simon Chaudron, 3 Mar. 1819, on verso; addressed (trimmed): "[. . .]s Jefferson Monticello Charlottesville Virginia"; franked.

To Joel Yancey

DEAR SIR   Monticello Jan. 4. 18. [1819]

Your letter of the 18th Dec. was not recieved till the 28th. that of the 24th came at the same time which proved that the first had lost a week at some of the intermediate post offices, and often they lose a fortnight. the bringing home some corn detained the waggon till now. it carries up some doors for the house which should be put in one of the rooms where they will be kept dry, and a box of wine to be put into the Cellar, as it requires a cool place. if the pork should weigh 7000 ℔ as you expect it is too much for two loads. you had better divide it into three, and our waggon shall go back with yours and bring the third. he carries a sowing of the forwardest peas I have ever met with, which I have directed[1] him to give to Nace. if he will sow them about the middle of February, I think I shall have them in my April visit. if you can send me the weights of the hogs killed, distinguishing how disposed of, I shall be glad of it, as I generally set these things down; as also a list of the stock. you do not say in your letter whether the flour is gone down, which it is necessary I should know, that I may know when I may draw. if not sent before the carriage of tob° comes into competition, I fear it will be difficult and dear getting it down. I wish you to hasten the tob° too as much as I can.[2] but I am sure you will do this and every thing else for the best. my entire confidence in you makes me quite easy under the accident of my long absence. I am with the best wishes for your health and welfare

Your friend & serv[t]   TH: JEFFERSON

P.S. a small box of books is sent to be put in one of the rooms

PoC (MHi); misdated; adjacent to signature: "M[r] Yancey"; endorsed by TJ as a letter of 4 Jan. 1819 and so recorded in SJL; on verso of an undated and unsigned note to TJ: "M[rs] Easton will thank M[r] Jefferson to Forward the enclosed shou'd M[rs] Trist have left Monticello" (enclosure not found).

For Yancey's letter OF THE 18TH DEC., see note to Yancey to TJ, 24 Dec. 1818.

[1] Manuscript: "dircted."
[2] Thus in manuscript.

From Thomas Cooper

DEAR SIR   Jan. 5. 1819 Philadelphia

I received a printed copy of your report, for which I thank you. It will serve to furnish more enlarged and more just ideas on the subject of education, than your countrymen have been accustomed to. I rejoice in the prospect of their being put in execution, whether I take any or no part in the Institution to be founded on them.

I have been enquiring for workmen as you desired, and I send you a man, whose honesty and industry I have entertained a good opinion of from near 20 Years observation. He asks so many questions that I have persuaded him to go to the place & look for himself, and make his own bargain. He is a Carpenter, & can command workmen: he can also induce bricklayers & brickmakers to come, if he determines to go himself: also a Tin man, & probably other trades: upon all this you will make your own enquiries in your own way. I have said nothing to him about prices.

I sent you about a month ago a discourse on the Connection between Medecine & Chemistry: by post.

I observe from your letter to Mr Short, that your health is likely to be established fully, the necessary defalcations of age excepted. I hope your active and most useful life, will yet be protracted to your own satisfaction,[1] and the public benefit, many years.

I beg my kind respects to Col. Randolph.   THOMAS COOPER

RC (ViU: TJP); endorsed by TJ as received 18 Jan. 1819 and so recorded (mistakenly dated 5 Jan. 1818) in SJL. RC (MHi); address cover only; with PoC of TJ to Patrick Gibson, 22 Feb. 1819, on verso; addressed: "Thomas Jefferson Esq Montecello By Mr Jared Richardson."

Jared Richardson, the man whose HONESTY AND INDUSTRY Cooper commended, was active as a carpenter in Philadelphia between 1809 and 1824 (*MB*, 2:1350; James Robinson, *The Philadelphia Direc-*tory for 1809 [Philadelphia, 1809]; DNA: RG 29, CS, Pa., Philadelphia, 1810, 1820; Robert Desilver, *The Philadelphia Directory for 1824* [Philadelphia, 1824]).

The DISCOURSE previously sent by Cooper was his work entitled *A Discourse on the Connexion between Chemistry and Medicine. delivered in the University of Pennsylvania, Nov. 5, 1818* (Philadelphia, 1818).

[1] Manuscript: "saitisfaction."

From Gabriel Crane

SIR   waynesville warren county Ohio Jan. 5–1819

It has fallen to my lot to make to You a very extraordinary and astonishing communication.[1] As the rest of the world I was untill a very short time since entirely unacquainted with the great mystery of the origin of our existance and of the existance of the astonishing objects and more Astonishing systematic operations with which we are surrounded and connected. At the period of time alluded to the great Creator and disposer of all revealed himself to me by intellectual communication being as he still remains perfectly invisible. The occasion of his revealing himself to me in this state of existance he inform'd me was to make a revelation of science to the world. Some of the principal causes that produce the effects and operations the developement of which is the object of scientific research being entirely beyond the reach of our experimental and speculative faculties must necessarily be revealed or we remain ignorant whilst in this state of the true philosophy concerning the things and operations that pertain to it. The revealing of this knowledge he farther informs me is an established regulation in his system of superintendance of our species in their state of Creation. From the general Ideas of the world concerning the Supreme and His establishment it would be natural to suppose that he would have employ,d some of his agencies to make a revelation of this kind—He informs me however that he has none but such as we are (angels &^{c} being fabulous) and we are constitutionally unable to execute such a mission in our permanent state of existance. This event which is So extraordinary and extremely astonishing to us in this world is one it appears that occurs to all in a very Short time after the Seperation of their Spirits and bodies by death—to use the Supremes observation concerning this circumstance He is generally in communion with our Spirits before our bodies are laid in their graves. The object of this communication is to obtain relief from circumstances that make it necessary for me to follow a daily evocation that is incompatible with a proper attention to the buisness of the Supreme— for this purpose I am instructed by Him to request You to Send me five thousand Dollars.[2] In corroboration of this relation he has directed and enabled me to send you a portion of the science alludded to—You will probably observe that it is written as tho' it was obtain'd by my own talents which circumstance is design'd as the revelation of it must not be even suspected by the world—It may like wise be proper to observe that notwithstanding some parts of the science is represented as uncertain Yet there is no uncertainty in it. but the want of sufficient circumstantial demonstration conformable to the scientific knowledge that is already possess'd by the world renders a very positive representation improper and impolitic. The exposition of the Element of light that I send You is as it will probably be eventually published—but that which is concerning the Comets is but a summary of the principal regulation and operations that relate to them.

The science will embrace a full explanation of all the great mysteries of nature—the properties and operations of the Elements the Electric matter and its operations and the regulations of the planetary system will all be correctly developed, and demonstrated as far as is practicable.

I am fully aware of the incredibility of this relation according to the Knowledge and ideas of the world—but I can only add in addition to the science (which I presume must itself be satisfactory) and I am instructed so to do as solemn an assurance of the truth of it as man can make. As the revealing of this event to You is calculated to impair Your[3] enjoyment unreasonably in this world by exciteing extraordinary anxiety concerning your future State I am directed by the Supreme to inform You that it will be Satisfactory.

You Saw perhaps and remember[4] a relation of a circumstance that was published in the public papers within two or three Years concerning a person in England who in the time of the late remarkable failure of the crops their was walking in company with others over a field of blasted grain and after surveying it raised his eyes towards the Heavens exclaiming—are You not ashamed God to blast the grain so. and instantly fell a corpse to the ground if you should not have been acquainted with this particular circumstance you will probably recollect others of the Same description—I advert to it in obedience to the direction of the Supreme to advise You of the certain consequence of an attempt to disclose the purport of this communication thro' incredulity—He also directs that You must not leave without first destroying it—   GABRIEL CRANE

PS As I was about to close the letter the Supreme directed me to add that if Your credence concerning this matter should be insufficient to induce you to comply with the request You must test the truth of it by endeavouring to communicate it to a friend—if You should be fearful of doing that and Yet persist in not complying with the requisition You will obviously be convicted of impropriety towards Him— And that if You are doubtful of the scienc[e] being reveal'd by Him You must admit me to be somewhat of a philosopher and You have no reason to expect according to Your knowledge[5] of Your species that one that was accustomed to contemplate and consider his works would commit so Heaven daring a crime as this would be if not true—

RC (MHi); edge trimmed; addressed: "To the Honourable Thomas Jefferson Virginia"; franked; postmarked Waynesville, 6 Jan.; endorsed by TJ as received 31 Jan. 1819 and so recorded in SJL; with additional notation by TJ: "mad," expanded to "madman" in SJL.

Gabriel Crane (b. ca. 1784), shoemaker and claimant to divine authority, was a native of New Jersey who settled about 1809 in Warren County, Ohio. Over several decades he wrote repeatedly to public figures and newspaper publishers detailing his revelations from God and requesting large sums of money or high political office. As of 1860 Crane still resided in Warren County and owned real estate valued at about $5,000 (*The History of Warren County, Ohio* [1882], 577, 872; Crane to TJ, 24 May 1819, 22 July 1825; Crane to James Madison, 25 July 1825, 9 Mar. 1828 [DLC: Madison Papers]; Bennington *Vermont Gazette*, 11 Oct. 1825; Chillicothe *Supporter, and Scioto Gazette*, 6 July 1826; Chillicothe *Scioto Gazette*, 2 Aug. 1827; *Philadelphia Album and Ladies' Literary Port Folio* 6 [1832]: 133; Boston *Zion's Herald*, 15 June 1836; Crane to William Henry Harrison, 1 Sept. 1840 [DLC: Harrison Papers]; DNA: RG 29, CS, Ohio, Warren Co., 1860).

[1] Omitted period at right margin editorially supplied.

[2] Omitted period at right margin editorially supplied.

[3] Manuscript: "You."

[4] Manuscript: "rememer."

[5] Manuscript: "knowledg."

ENCLOSURE

Gabriel Crane's Essay on Light as an Element

[ca. 5 Jan. 1819]

An exposition of the Element of Light

The principal properties of this Element are light and Heat—the former is probably constituted by a superior brightness similar to polished metal united with transparency and the peculiar color of the Element—where ever there is light this Element is with its particles in connection.[1] This position results from the long established fact that there is no other source of light or medium of sight and from the axiom that matter cannot operate beyond itself nor one Species or kind communicate its characteristic properties to another—That a connection of the particles is necessary to the display of this property it is reasonable to infer from the observation that the greatest accumulations of it in its diffused or disconnected State does not afford any light—There is obviously a much greater quantity of this Element in the atmosphere when the Sun is absent in the Summer Season than in the winter when it is preasent as is demonstrated by the heat Yet in the former there is comparitively extremely little light—which circumstance it is most reasonable to suppose[2] results from its disconnection—That the rays of the Sun in the winter Season are[3] sparse as to afford less heat than the quantity of that Element that is in a state of diffusion at the surface of the Earth in the summer Yet the matter that composes them is so much more dense and in a state of connection or cohesion (for the diffused matter it is presumed must be in contact) as to unite the particles in illumination—The single particles and the points of their unity when merely in contact being too small to operate upon our sight or to obviate in any degree the matters then excessive transparency—This Element passes through transparent substances in its state of cohesion the particles of those substances being globular have vacant space between them which with their fineness constitutes transparency. These positions result from the necessity of the Element of light,s being in that state to display its luminous property and the axiom that two particles of matter cannot occupy one point of space at the same time.[4] It is reflected by the turning of its rays without destroying its force or continuity and is connected with the intellectual seat of vision in man and the animals by the organs of sight,s being composed of transparent matter.

Heat is a pungent property of this Element and is correspondent to its quantity density and motion—the latter forces it into greater and closer contact with other substances against which it strikes and also increases the co-operation of its own particles by the pressure—Being immersed in this Element as in a flood if we rub two pieces of wood together it is forced into them by the motion and pressure untill the collection is sufficient and sufficiently dense to create a concentration when it assumes its state of illumination by a sudden addition of matter that is occasioned by the commencement of that operation—thus fire is produced by friction—Its production by the flint and steel is upon the same principle but is effected without the concentration— the violence of the operation and the peculiar adaption of the implements supply the comparative deficiency of matter (that is brot' into cooperation) by the extraordinary compression—the peculiar adaption of the flint consists in its hardness the fineness of its texture and the form of its particles which is calculated to leave but very little and irregular space between them this constitution prevents the particles of the Element of light from being easily forced into it and they are consequently more compressed[5] upon the surface where the fuel is simultaneously prepared by the seperation of small particles from the steel which is a combustible substance—

In the steel compactness hardness and combustibility are limited which constitutes its superior suitability for this operation.[6] Fire is continued and increased by the accession of matter that is in its state of diffusion and is brot' into contact with it[7] by the concentration—the correctnes of[8] this position is very obvious as instead of fire,s increasing when formed it would otherwise be immediately diffused by the emission. that it does emit and in proportion to the quantity that is in cooperation is demonstrated by the light and heat that is produced by it beyond the space that it occupies as we cannot be affected by Any matter without its comeing in contact with us. Flame is form'd and supported by the smoke which is composed of particles of the fuel that are carried off by the emission And the current of the concentration before they are perfectly calcined.

The cause of one substance being warmer than another is the difference of their textures by which the matter of heat passes less freely thro' some than others and it is therefore most dense where it meets with the greatest obstructions which constitutes the warmer substances—the Element of light is so much finer than the matter that composes the finest wool or fur as to pass between its particles. This Element is attached to combustible matter by a species of attraction, a combination of it sufficient to corrode is necessary to its cohereing and that which is in a state of diffusion then incorporates with it as they come in contact and as the fuel is prepared by the partial operation of that which is previously in connection with it—this necessary preparation is retarded by water in the fuel or prevented if the quantity be comparatively too great by the restraint of the operation and excess of evaporation—the operation is also diversified by the diversity in the textures and qualities of the different kinds of fuel.

The concentration is occasioned by the rarefaction of the atmosphere which destroys its equilibrium and the denser air moves to the rarified or weaker part untill the equilibrium is restored carrying with it the Element of light that is mixed among it—Rarefaction is a distention of the atmosphere by an accumulation of the Element of light between its particles which seperates them and thereby diminishes its gravity and the Element of light haveing none to these Elements does not supply the deficiency that is occasioned by its operation—the determination of the Element of light to pass off from the Earth by the difference of its gravity to its own centre from that of the adjoining Ether likewise aids in the operation and contributes to the uniformity of the course of the diffuseing[9] current. Gravitation is a property of matter by which the distinction of the Genera's and the Unity of the Species that compose them are preserved. it does not operate between distinct genera's—this is obvious from the Element of light,s passing off from the Earth which it could not do according to the law of gravitation if it operated between them— The Atmosphere Earth and Water are different species of matter[10] composeing one genera The Element of Light and Ether comprise another The varieties of matter that compose the different substances of the Earth are kinds of one Species. If the Sun does emit the matter of light and Heat it must necessarily receive a corresponding supply—the obvious diffusion of that which composes its rays its continuance when the Sun is absent—Its fluctuations and the very great quantity of it that is maintaind at the surface of the Earth as is demonstrated by the great number of the artificial collections that are daily form,d and may be increased almost without restriction together with the corroborateing operation of those collections render the apparent continual emission of a great quantity of the matter from the Sun unquestionable. As the emission is supplied by a return of the same matter there must be as great a quantity of it at the extremity of the atmosphere in opposition to the Sun on its return to that body as we receive from it which matter must have assumed another state by which its relative gravity is increass'd and rendered Superior to the obstacles that oppose its opperation—the change in the modification of it must likewise have rendered it incapable of passing between the particles of the atmospheric Element—and it cannot displace them by its gravity (which operates upon the atmospheric Element in that situation by the latters being in the direction of its Centre) it being the least of the two—This Element as before observed passes off from the Earth by its being of less gravity than the adjoining Ether—it probably resumes and continues its direction from the Sun untill it comes to the region of Ether that is of the same gravity as itself where it is most reasonable to suppose it is prepared for its return to that body in a manner similar to the preperation of vapour for its return to the Earth or perhaps in precisely the same that is by collecting in the rarified regions of Ether and condensing and forming into small globules by its own weight and liquid property. Its bias to the direction from the Sun when it leaves the Earth probably contributes in some degree to the difference of temperature between the day and night by its passing off more rapidly and in a greater ratio in the latter than the former—The emission of this Element is probably caused by the Element of Ether as the former does that of water this may be inferred from the cause,s operateing on the Earth as well as at the Sun and consequently cannot be local. The Element of Ether is considered as before observ'd a species of the Same genera as the Element of light—and is attached to the Sun as the atmosphere is to the Earth. it extends the emissions of the Element of light by the ordinary operation of the gravitateing principle on fluids (that is preserving an equilibrium by maintaining an[11] equality or regular gradation of the parts in density or gravity.) in conjunction with the velocity that is given to them by the operation of rarefying and seperateing them from the dense collections of the matter—this velocity is indicated by the emissions from the artificial collections of it upon the Earth extending in every direction from them to a very considerable distance almost instantaneously and in opposition to the current of the concentration—The Existance of the Element of Ether is intimated by the blue concave that is called the sky which must be composed of some kind of matter as void space would present no color—and the color that distinguishes it does not correspond to that of any other Element of which we have knowledge.

The temperature of the atmosphere is regulated very materially by its own constitution and construction—it thereby operates as the burning glass condensing the rays of the Element of light at the Surface of the Earth as at a focus that is formed by that implement—the Centre of a focus of the Element of light formed by the atmosphere or burning glass presents the greatest heat at the centre[12] which diminishes gradually towards the exterior; the rays being more compact and haveing greater velocity progressively as they approximate to the Centre this systematic variation is occasioned by the progression in the degrees of their variation from the course in which they came in contact with the concentrator—the forceing of them from their original direction counteracts the operation of the concentrator and diminishes their velocity in a corresponding proportion to the angle of alteration whereby they become more sparse and have less force in a regular gradation from the Centre to the exterior of the focus—This position is corroborated by the following observations the simularity of the form and constitutions of the atmosphere and burning glass and the operation of the latter which demonstrate the variation and gradation of the heat of the focus likewise by the progressive diminution of heat in ascending Mountains the atmosphere being a fluid consequently preserves an even surface whereby the Elevation of Mountains diminishes its depth and density upon them comparative with the common levil of the Earth which occasions a corresponding sparsity of the rays of light by the focus being greater in proportion to the surface of the concentrator. this It is presumed is the most if not the only rational explication of the coldness of mountains that can be deduced from our knowledge there being no other difference of local circumstances between them and the common levil of the Earth that is calculated to affect the temperature than the one adduced— that the difference in the density of the atmosphere in those situations does not occasion the diversity of their temperatures is demonstrated by the same diversity, occurring at the general surface of the Earth where there is no material or permanent dissimilarity in the density and is there occasioned by the movement of the focus of the Element of light[13] and the difference in the degrees of the heat of its parts.

The twillight and that which is generally[14] called Star light are produced by this operation of the atmosphere—The Sun being the larger body its rays consequently enter the atmosphere for more than half of its exterior extent and are sparsly conducted to the Earth the whole of the night—The Element of light as before observed does not afford the least degree of illumination in its diffused State which is frequently demonstrated by the collection of it in our Rooms And by the perfect darkness that ensues in the night when the

rays are all interupted And destroyd by the quantity and density of the inter-
poseing clouds—notwithstanding the diffused or disconnected matter does
not afford any light Yet it enables us to See condensed[15] collections of it much
farther than their emissions extend and likewise to perceive the interveneing
objects—It is by this latter circumstance that the light of night is apparently so
equeally diffused and connected nowithstanding the great Sparsity of the rays.

The rays of the Element of light are extremely fine streams that are form'd
by the Element of Ether which divides it as it extends and diffuses untill it
becomes indivisible[16] the cohesion of the particles that compose them is demonstrated and their astonishing flexibility by which they winde between the
particles of other matter for a vast distance without haveing their continuity
destroy'd strikeingly display'd in their reflection—The local variations of the
temperature of the atmosphere are occasioned by the difference in the operations of the Element of light on earth and water and by its transmission in its
state of diffusion by winds—In consequence of waters being transparent more
of the rays of light penetrate into it than into the Earth and consequently the
collection of that matter is greatest at the surface of the latter—difference of
soil also causes a variation of temperature—those which are termed dry which
admit water more speedily and to a greater depth into them than others present the greatest degree of heat on their surfaces which results from the
penetration of the matter of heat into the Earth in proportion to the quantity
of water that is mixed with it and from that matters receeding from dry soils
with less vapour in connection with it than from wet as vapour diminishes its
operation on other adjacent matter or bodies by obstructing the cooperation
of its particles—As water when mixed with Earth occupies the space that
would otherwise be vacant it might be inferr'd that such a mixture would
present more obstruction to the Element of light than dry earth.[17] It may
therefore be necessary to observe that transparent matter presents smoothe
surfaces that does not destroy the rays as those that are rough; they glance
from the former and pass on when not prevented by deficiency of space—but
the latter instantaneously destroys the greater part that comes in contact with
it—the rays being so fine that the least protuberance on the surface of other
matter is a direct and full obstruction and the forms of the particles of un-
transparent matter makes the incidental spaces between them irregular. the
apparent roughness of transparent substances when broken does not affect
this position it being occasioned by the unevenness of the general surface and
not the roughness of the particles—The partial condensation of the Element
of light in the atmosphere is occasioned by its connection with other substances by attraction as vapour and effluvia,s of most if not all the kinds of
matter that compose the Element of Earth—which obstructs its diffusion by
their gravity &c &c &c

The Comets are Spheres of the Element of light and are employ'd to contribute to the supply of the planets that are too far from the Sun to receive
a sufficiency of that essential Element from its rays—Their orbits are prescribed by the following operation of the gravitateing principle—If an inferior body be propell'd from that to which it gravitates in a line that diverges
from the centre of the latter it will return in a corresponding one so that a
perpendicular from the zenith of its Asscension to the centre of gravity will
divide its orbit into two equeal parts—Comets return towards the Sun by the
operation of gravitation and recede from it by the continuation of the force

that is acquired by that operation And by its own operation on the Element of Ether which is rarified by its rays and consequently as it moves in its orbit the denser Ether closes in behind it and constitutes a powerfull and Uniform impetus—the maximum of the Velocity of a Comet by gravitation takes place at the point of its orbit that is nearest to the sun which is in a line with the Centre of that body and the other extreme of its own orbit—its force by gravitation then precisely counterbalences its tendency to the centre of gravity and the other impetus constitutes a preponderance of power by which it resumes it course from the Sun—

The temperature of the planets being regulated by the Atmospheric Element as explaind in the exposition of the Element of light and in such a manner that an increase of it comparative to the size of the planet to which it is attached increases the temperature in a systematic proportion—and vice versa—Accordingly the atmospheres of the planets are adapted to their respective situations in the system and consequently those that are superintended by Comets have extremely large ones which receive from them a great quantity of the matter of heat and retain it in its State of diffusion—Those planets being such a great distance from the Sun that the gravitateing principle operates very feebly their on the Element of light and the Ether being very nearly of the same[18] degree of gravity it is retaind by the attraction of the Elements that compose the planets.[19] This attraction is the same that it is observd to have to our combustible and other matter at those planets it gives the Element of light a determination to their surfaces which occasions the wasteage in the abscence of the Comets to affect only the uper regions of the Atmosphere—Its concentrateing operation which eventuates in its greater[20] diffusion preserves the desired temperature at the surface of the Earth (as with us) by preventing it from too great an Accumulation—The wasteage results from occasional extraordinary concurrences of successive concentrations that diffuse upwards and carry a portion of the Element of light so far from the Earth that its tendency to the region of Ether that corresponds with it in gravity becomes superior to its attraction and it consequently is thereby entirely extricated from the elements and influence of the planet the diminution is partially supplied in the abscence of the Comets by the rays of the Sun which likewise affords a sufficiency of light—

MS (MHi); written entirely in Crane's hand on three numbered sheets, the first two folded to form four pages; undated.

[1] Omitted period at right margin editorially supplied.
[2] Preceding six words interlined in place of an illegible phrase.
[3] Word interlined in place of "tho' so."
[4] Omitted period at right margin editorially supplied.
[5] Manuscript: "compress."
[6] Omitted period at right margin editorially supplied.
[7] Word interlined in place of "the dense collection."
[8] Preceding three words interlined.
[9] Word interlined.
[10] Preceding two words interlined.
[11] Manuscript: "and."
[12] Preceding three words interlined.
[13] Preceding four words interlined in place of "heat."
[14] Manuscript: "generall."
[15] Word interlined.
[16] Preceding twelve words interlined in place of an illegible phrase.
[17] Omitted period at right margin editorially supplied.
[18] Manuscript: "sam."
[19] Omitted period at right margin editorially supplied.
[20] Word interlined.

From Solidor Milon

HONORABLE
MONSIEUR JEFFERSON, Baltimore Le 5. Janvier 1818. [1819]

Je vous demande pardon de la liberté que j'ose prendre en vous écrivant, Sans avoir l'honneur d'être connu de vous; mais ayant appris que vous etiés en recherche de maîtres capables d'instruire les Elèves du Collège que vous avez fait Elever, et me Sentant dans le cas de repondre à une partie de vos desirs, en enseignant le dessin, les belles Ecritures, la Science de la musique, le Chant, le forte-Piano, le violon, la Guittare, et la Danse; je m'offre à l'épreuve pour un mois, Sans aucun interêt Si vous n'êtes point Satisfait de ma personne, de ma manière d'enseigner, et des méthodes que je pratiquerai.

Je suis Italien, ayant fait mes Etudes et reçu mon Education en france, jeune homme, âgé de trente un an, je n'ai d'autres recommendations à vous offrir qu'une Conduite honorable et des mœurs intègres. J'ai été amené en Amerique par feu Mʳ George Crowninshield, lors de Son retour d'Europe Sur le Cleopras Barg de Salem. Mʳ Binjamin Crowninshield, Son frère, Ex Secretaire de la marine, que vous Connaissés Sans doute, pourra vous donner des renseignemens Sur ma personne et mes capacités, Si vous daignés lui en écrire.

En daignant prendre en Consideration la proposition que j'ai l'honneur de vous faire à mon égard, j'ose espérer que vous aurez lieu de vou[s] [a]pplaudir d'avoir employé un homme qui n'a d'autres ressources que dans Ses faibles talents, et d'autre recommendation que Sa vie privée, qui etant Connue de vous, pourra, peut'être, Elle Seule, Suffire pour lui meriter votre Consideration et votre Estime.

honorez-moi, je vous prie, d'une reponse, Et croyez-moi votre tres-Respectueux Serviteur. S. MILON

P. S. Dans quelques mois encore d'étude de la langue anglaise je pourrais enseigner les langues Italienne, et francaise, ainsi que l'arithemétique.

EDITORS' TRANSLATION

HONORABLE MR. JEFFERSON, Baltimore 5. January 1818. [1819]

Forgive me for taking the liberty of writing without having the honor of being known to you; but having learned that you were looking for teachers capable of instructing the students at the college you have built and feeling that I could satisfy some of your requirements by teaching drawing, penmanship, music theory, singing, the pianoforte, violin, guitar, and dancing, I offer myself on a one-month trial basis, with no obligation if you are not satisfied with me, my manner of teaching, and my methods.

I am Italian, educated in France, a young man of thirty-one, with no recommendations to offer you other than an honorable conduct and moral integrity. The late Mr. George Crowninshield brought me to America when he returned from Europe on the *Cleopatra's Barge* of Salem. Mr. Benjamin Crowninshield, his brother, the former secretary of the navy, whom you undoubtedly know, can inform you of me and my abilities, if you deign to write him on the subject.

By condescending to consider my proposition, I dare hope that you will congratulate yourself for employing a man with no resources other than his feeble talents and no recommendation other than his private life, which, once known by you, will perhaps, by itself, suffice to merit your consideration and esteem.

Pray honor me with a reply and believe me to be your very respectful servant.   S. MILON

P. S. After a few more months studying the English language I will be able to teach Italian and French, as well as arithmetic.

RC (MoSHi: TJC-BC); misdated; hole in manuscript; endorsed by TJ as a letter of 5 Jan. 1819 received five days later and so recorded in SJL. RC (DLC); address cover only; with PoC of third page of TJ to Joseph C. Cabell, 1 Mar. 1819, on verso; addressed: "To the honorable Mr Thomas Jefferson Esqr Monnt-Cello. Virginia"; franked; postmarked. Translation by Dr. Genevieve Moene. Enclosed in TJ to John Patterson, 31 Jan. 1819, and Patterson to TJ, 9 Feb. 1819.

Solidor Pierre (or Pierre Solidor) Milon (1787–1887), musician and educator, was born in Nice, then part of the kingdom of Sardinia, and may have studied music in Naples before serving in Napoleon's army. He met George Crowninshield when the latter toured Europe on his yacht, *Cleopatra's Barge*, and he returned with him to the United States, arriving in 1818 at Salem, Massachusetts. Soon thereafter Milon was granted a 160-acre tract in present-day Alabama at the French settlement known as the Vine and Olive Colony, but he sold this land in 1819 without ever having visited it. He was initially peripatetic, singing, performing on stringed instruments, and giving music lessons in Baltimore, Richmond, Norfolk, and Charleston, South Carolina. Except for some years in New York City, he spent

his later decades in Philadelphia, performing and teaching in both cities. In 1831 Milon published a pamphlet, *General Considerations on the Most Remarkable Natural or Artificial Defects to Which Singers are Liable*. Later in life he claimed that on his arrival in the United States he worked as a secret agent for Napoleon's brother Joseph Bonaparte and traveled on his behalf to Mexico and South America (Francis B. Crowninshield, ed., *The Story of George Crowninshield's Yacht Cleopatra's Barge* [1918], 223; Rafe Blaufarb, *Bonapartists in the Borderlands: French Exiles and Refugees on the Gulf Coast, 1815–1835* [2005], 178, 214; *Baltimore Patriot & Mercantile Advertiser*, 24 Sept., 27, 31 Oct. 1818, 25 Feb. 1819; Albert Stoutamire, *Music of the Old South: Colony to Confederacy* [1972], 101, 123, 268; *American Beacon and Norfolk & Portsmouth Daily Advertiser*, 24 Nov. 1819; Charleston *City Gazette and Commercial Daily Advertiser*, 28 Dec. 1819; DNA: RG 29, CS, Pa., Philadelphia, 1830, 1860–80, N.Y., New York, 1850; *New York Herald*, 11, 25 Mar. 1843, 8 Feb. 1844, 21 Mar. 1845; Thomas Louis Ogier, "A Reminiscence of Napoleon's Russian Campaign," *Potter's American Monthly* 11 [1878]: 52–4; *Philadelphia Inquirer*, 18, 19 Mar. 1887; Philadelphia *North American*, 21 Mar. 1887).

From William Alston

My dear Sir.   Clifton, near Geo. Town s° Ca 6th Jany 1819

I was very glad to see in the Intelligencer, sometime after the receipt of your very friendly letter, an extract of a letter from Monticello, mentioning that you were then quite recovered from the very painful complaints that had confined you for 3 months.—I have, at last, received the box of wine which you were So good as to send me. On its arrival at Charleston, it was Siezed by the Port Officer, because, he said, there was no certificate that the duties had been paid. Upon receiving this information, I addressed a letter to him, & enclosed a transcript of that part of your letter to me, respecting the Wine; and observed to him that, if he could suppose me capable of an intention to defraud the Revenue, he could not, after reading the extract from your letter, have any doubt on his mind that the duty had not been paid. The box was afterwards delivered to my Agent.— Messrs Kershaw & Lewis, my Factors in Charleston, have informed me that they have Shipped in the Sloop Altezera, J. B. Levy, Master, who sailed for Richmond on the 2^d inst^t, the barrel of rice I sent to them the 10th of December to be forwarded to you, which they have directed to the care of Capt. B. Peyton.—I think you will find the grains of this rice larger & much better polished than usual. There are a few rough grains intermixed, which must be picked out by the Cook before it is dressed for table. I will have the pleasure of sending you a further supply, sometime in February, & will endeavor to have it still higher polished, as the grains become firmer then, than at the time this was prepared. It will keep good much longer, as I observed to you in my former letter, the higher & more compleatly the grain is polished. My Daughter has written the enclosed directions, given to her by our Cook for dressing rice for the table; which I hope you may find useful.—I wish you, my very respected Sir, a happy new Year; and that you may live to enjoy multos et felices, is the very sincere Wish of one, who is, most truly, with [the] greatest respect & esteem,
        Yours   W. Alston

RC (DLC); dateline at foot of text; torn at seal; addressed: "The Honble Thomas Jefferson"; endorsed by TJ as received 17 Jan. 1819 and so recorded in SJL.

The EXTRACT seen by Alston was probably that from TJ to William Short, 10 Nov. 1818, which appeared in the Washington *Daily National Intelligencer*, 23 Nov. 1818.

A compilation of recipes by TJ's descendants includes DIRECTIONS for "South Carolina Rice pudding" from "Miss Alston" (MS in ViCMRL, on deposit ViU: Trist-Burke Family Papers, MSS 5385-f; in Cornelia J. Randolph's hand; undated).

MULTOS ET FELICES: "many and happy."

From John Patterson

Dear sir   Baltimore 6 Jany 1819—

I sent you yesterday, by the mail, a pamphlet, by Dr Potter of this City, on Contagion, which he gave to me for that purpose—Dr Potter is a man of genius, & his memoir has arrayed against him, a host of enemies among the advocates of the old system which he attempts to explode—

I have also, sir, to thank you for the pamphlet[1] containing the report of the Commissioners, respecting the University of Virginia, which you had the goodness to send me. There is no subject which interests me so much as the establishment of the University, & I hope soon to see it in operation—With my best wishes for the continuation of your health & happiness I am dear sir

Your Hble serv^t   JN^o PATTERSON

RC (CSmH: JF); endorsed by TJ as received 10 Jan. 1819 and so recorded in SJL. RC (DLC); address cover only; with PoC of first two pages of TJ to Joseph C. Cabell, 1 Mar. 1819, on recto and verso; addressed: "To Thomas Jefferson Esqr Milton V^a"; stamped; postmarked Baltimore, 6 Jan.

The PAMPHLET was Nathaniel Potter, *A Memoir on Contagion, more especially as it respects the Yellow Fever: read in convention of the Medical and Chirurgical Faculty of Maryland, On the 3d of June, 1817* (Baltimore, 1818; Poor, *Jefferson's Library,* 5 [no. 197]).

[1] Manuscript: "pamplet."

From Joseph C. Cabell

Dear Sir,   Richmond. 7th Jan: 1819

Your favor of 1st ins^t has been duly received, and I thank you for the information it contains. I also thank you for the copy of Tracy's work, which I received in a few days from the time it left you, but have heretofore omitted to mention.

In my last I gave you an account of our declining & gloomy prospects respecting the University. Just about Christmas, & from that period to the 1st ins^t, the success of the measure was despaired of. The Valley members first had united against us. Half the trans-Alleghaney members had followed them. The Residue were neutral and tending to the opposite party. Even my friend Thompson of Kenawha, who had theretofore kept up my spirits, acknowledged that he believed the greater part of the members from beyond the Alleghaney had determined to oppose us, and the remainder were not to be depended on. I was also assured by acquaintances from that quarter that the western Delegates were prepared to vote against the measure if a western site should not be preferred. In the lower parts of the State the opposition to the measure was great & growing, whilst a line of votes at the foot of the Blue Ridge, to the north & South of my district, and a scattering vote in other parts of the Eastern country were arrayed against us. In this state of affairs, with 6 or 8 very active & dexterous opponents, to contend with, and but few to aid me, I advised our friends to preserve a cheerful countenance & not to despair. Having lost, as I supposed, the western vote, I turned my views altogether to the East. The combination to the west, justified an appeal to Eastern feelings and interests. Our majority of votes on the East of the Ridge is 62. Putting down 22 of these for absentees, our majority would be reduced to 40; of these, if the opposition should obtain 21, of course, we should be defeated. I knew we should get some few votes to the west, but these I thought ought to be placed to the acc^t of absentees, inasmuch as 22 is but a small allowance. It was obvious therefore that it was necessary to reduce the opposition in the East to less than 20. For this purpose, it was essential to ascertain who were the opponents, and to contend for them, with the enemy beyond the mountain. In this enquiry I have encountered very great difficulty, from the absence of the Senators, & the want of experienced friends in the House of Delegates. But I have at length succeeded with respect to all the counties except a few low down on the south of James River. In the course of my search, I have had occasion to witness the vast & uncommon exertions of the opposite party. They had made great inroads into our ranks. whilst the greater part of our Eastern members seemed to be asleep. My mind has sought far & wide for the means of awakening the eastern people to a just view of their rights, and of exciting the friends of learning to an exertion of their powers. I have passed the night in watchful reflection, and the day in ceaseless activity. Our ranks are filled with clever young men, who will when the debate comes on, give us flowery speeches: but we want the practical[1] wisdom & efficient concert of the[2] year 1799. In this situation, I have sought to supply the defect, by conveying from person to person intelligence of our different views, & by endeavoring to reconcile differences of opinion, and to create harmony. I have written into the country for friends to come in, or to send letters to our aid. I have called on, & implored the aid of powerful friends out of the Legislature, such as Roane, the Nicholas's, Brokenbrough, Taylor, &^{c}. I have actually districted the country East of the Ridge, & obtained a promise from some gentleman of high standing & influence, to use his best efforts to remove the prejudices of members, & to counteract the movements of the opposite party. I have procured most of the Essays you have seen in the Enquirer, & furnished the topics of objection to some of our friends in the House of Delegates, with references to authorities for their refutation. Happily, sir, a counter current has been produced: and I am now confident of ultimate success. There are now 30 members on the East of the Ridge who have been prejudiced against the Bill. But the number will be reduced. And whilst many of these will vote with us on the site, I hope their votes on the passage will be at least in part counteracted. Some valuable friends have lately arrived. Capt: Slaughter of Culpepper: Chancellor Taylor: M[r] Pannel member of the board of public works: M[r] Hoomes of King & Queen: M[r] John Taleiferro of the Northern Neck: & Chancellor Green. The latter and myself were up untill 3 o'clock this morning, conversing on the means necessary to ensure success. I think he will be able to break down in some degree the influence of W[m] & Mary in the neck of Land from this to Hampton. Our friends are at last roused, and as ardent as you could desire. The course of things here will surprize and distress you. But, be assured, sir, I do not exaggerate, and we have been compelled to meet the opposition on their own ground. The liberal & enlightened views of great statesmen pass over our heads like the spheres above. When we assemble here, an eastern and western feeling supercedes all other considerations. Our policy now is to keep back the vote as long as possible. Thank Heaven! My health has sustained me and even improved in the anxious & trying situation in which I am placed. I hear you are still complaining. This intelligence comes thro' Col: Randolph, who I sought this morning, but could not find at M[rs] Randolph's. God Grant, Sir, that you may soon be entirely restored to perfect health, and that you may in a few weeks be cheered by the intelligence of the final success of the Bill for the University.

I am, D[r] Sir, most sincerely & faithfully y[r] friend

JOSEPH C. CABELL

RC (ViU: TJP-PC); torn at seal, with one word rewritten by Cabell; addressed: "Thomas Jefferson Monticello"; endorsed by TJ as received 10 Jan. 1819 and so recorded in SJL. RC (CSmH: JF-BA); additional address cover only; with PoC of TJ to Robert Taylor, 3 Mar. 1819, on verso; addressed: "Thomas Jefferson Monticello"; franked; postmarked Richmond, 7 Jan.

THE NICHOLAS'S: Philip Norborne Nicholas and Wilson Cary Nicholas. Cabell had sought Thomas Mann Randolph (COL: RANDOLPH) at the Richmond boardinghouse of his sister Mary Randolph.

[1] Cabell here canceled "experience."
[2] Cabell here canceled "days."

From Fernagus De Gelone

Sir.   New York January 7. 1819.
herein is the bill of lading of a box directed to you, care of Capt.
Bernard Peyton, Richmond, V^a, and Shipped on board the Schooner
Weymouth bound to that Place. the box contains:

1. Ducange, Glossarium mediæ & infimæ ætatis. 3. folio. bound in vellum				$.20.—
1. Dictionnaire Grec	français	de Planche 8vo	bound	6.25.
1. Suetone. Latin.	d^o	4. 8vo	d^o	7.50
1. Appien, Guerres Civiles.		3. d^o	d^o	7.—
1. Salluste, Dureau La Malle.		1. d^o	d^o	2.25.
1. henri IV, Perefixe. 12mo			Sewed	.87½
1. Affections catharrales, Cabanis. 8vo			d^o	.75.
1. Pline le Jeune, Lat. français. 3. 12° with panegyrique de Trajan.			d^o	2.87½
1. Denis d'halicarnasse. Antiquités Romains. Berenger. 6. 8vo Sewed				10.—

1. Epictetus. vellum. Bodoni. Greek Italian. 12° boards	5.37½
1. Journal, Bibliographie de la france. Years 1814. 15. 16. with tables and year 1817 without tables— (not furnished, because they are a little Spoiled with my own remarks)[1]—You will See the Subscription price is 18 francs a year	20.00.
	$.82.87½

You received from my Clerk Mr Belair	
1. Logarithmes Lalande. 18°	.87½
1. Diction. Grec, Planche, 8°	6.25.
1. Correspondance de fern. Cortez & Charles V	1.12½
	$.91.12½

I myself Sent you from York. 1. Logarithmes, Lalande	18°	.87½
Yesterday, I directed to you the 1^rst vol. of Tacite, Dureau La Malle. french Latin. the whole Shall go, 1. vol. at one time, and is		13.50.
I will direct you by the Same way (Mail)		
1. Geometrie de Le Gendre 1817		2.50
		$.108.00
I received from you		90.00
		$. 18.00

You will have a right to the continuation of Bibliographie de france,
if it is your wish. I have the N^os of 1818. to October.

With respect to antient books, I have a Single vol. of Cailleau's
Dictionnaire Bibliograph.—I had reserved it for myself. as I expect,

Sir, You will honour me with your custom and very high recommendation, it is at your disposal. it is complete in itself.

I have just opened Several boxes arrived from france. there is a Dictionnaire Pratique de Medecine et Chirurgie, Pougens. 1814. 2. 8vo $.4.50. it has no Greek Lexicon, but a Synonymy of old and new Chemistry.

There is also, h^{re} de l'Inquisition d'Espagne, par Llorente. 4. 8° 1818. an excellent book. $9.50.

I have resolved to open a book-Store in Georgetown (D.C.) within three weeks. Then I Shall be very happy to Serve you more at your wish. My establishment is well founded, but would perish if it was not encouraged. I however have the greatest hopes of a Success.

I am most respectfully. sir Your most humble and obedient Servant

FERNAGUS DE GELONE

RC (MHi); addressed: "Thomas Jefferson Esqr Monticelo. Milton. V^a"; franked; postmarked New York, 7 Jan.; endorsed by TJ as received 17 Jan. 1819 and so recorded in SJL; with notation by TJ at foot of text: "Jan. 22. 19. remitted 20.D."

François Bellanger (BERENGER) was the translator of Dionysius of Halicarnassus, *Les Antiquités Romaines*, 6 vols.

(Chaumont, 1800; Poor, *Jefferson's Library*, 3 [no. 25]; TJ's copy in ViHi). By February 1819 Fernagus de Gelone was operating a BOOK-STORE on Pennsylvania Avenue in Washington, D.C. (Washington *Daily National Intelligencer*, 25 Feb. 1819).

[1] Omitted closing parenthesis editorially supplied.

From Frederick A. Mayo

RESPECTED SIR   Richmond the 7. Janu: 1818 [1819]

Should have written before to your honour, but supposed it best to delay till all the books had been received, which has been done in good Order

As it respects[1] the direction given in your honours former letters, I shall be as particular as posseable, and do sincerely hope that Virginia will stand equal with other States, as it respects the execution of workmanship in the Line of my profession which will give pleasure

to Your Most Obedient & humble Servant

FREDERICK A MAYO

RC (MHi); misdated; at foot of text: "The Hon: Tho: Jefferson"; endorsed by TJ as a letter of 7 Jan. 1819 received three days later and so recorded in SJL.

[1] Manuscript: "respcts," here and below.

From Gulian C. Verplanck

SIR   New York Jan. 7th 1819

I take the liberty of sending you a copy of an anniversary discourse which I lately delivered before the Historical Society of this state. Whatever errors or faults it may have, I trust that the general purpose is such as you will approve. It is the inculcation of those great principles of freedom and toleration to the service of which your own talents have been so long, so gloriously and so efficiently devoted.

I am with great respect
Your obd^t servant   G. C. VERPLANCK

RC (MHi); endorsed by TJ as received 14 Jan. 1819 and so recorded in SJL. RC (MoSHi: TJC-BC); address cover only; with PoC of TJ to Fontaine Maury, 21 Feb. 1819, on verso; addressed: "Hon. Thomas Jefferson Monticello Virginia"; franked; postmarked New York, 7 Jan.

Gulian Crommelin Verplanck (1786–1870), public official and author, was a native of New York City who graduated from Columbia College (later Columbia University) in 1801. He read law and was admitted to the bar in 1807, although he never practiced. Beginning as a Federalist, over a long political career he was successively a Republican, a Jacksonian, and a Whig. Early on he ran afoul of DeWitt Clinton, who as New York City mayor presided over the trial of Verplanck and his fellow participants in the Columbia College commencement riot of 1811. Verplanck was a New York state assemblyman, 1820–23, and served in the United States House of Representatives for four terms beginning in 1825, chairing the Ways and Means Committee, 1831–33. He was a New York state senator, 1838–41. For four years beginning in 1821 Verplanck taught a course on evidences for the authenticity of Christianity at the General Theological Seminary of the Episcopal Church in New York. Throughout his career he published satirical verse and numerous essays, and after his retirement from politics he produced a three-volume edition of William Shakespeare's plays that included a biography of the playwright. Verplanck died in New York City (*ANB*; *DAB*; N: Verplanck Papers;

William Cullen Bryant, *A Discourse on the Life, Character and Writings of Gulian Crommelin Verplanck* [1870]; Robert W. July, *The Essential New Yorker: Gulian Crommelin Verplanck* [1951]; Milton Halsey Thomas, *Columbia University Officers and Alumni 1754–1857* [1936], 119; *New York Herald*, 19 Mar. 1870; gravestone inscription in Trinity Church Cemetery, Fishkill, N.Y.).

The GENERAL PURPOSE of the enclosed essay by Verplanck, *An Anniversary Discourse, delivered before The New-York Historical Society, December 7, 1818* (New York, 1818; Poor, *Jefferson's Library*, 5 [no. 165]; TJ's copy in ViCMRL, on deposit ViU), is "the commemoration of some of those virtuous and enlightened men of Europe, who, long ago, looking with a prophetic eye towards the destinies of this new world, and regarding it as the chosen refuge of freedom and truth, were moved by a holy ambition to become the ministers of the most High, in bestowing upon it the blessings of religion, morals, letters, and liberty" (pp. 7–8). The figures Verplanck profiled included Bartolomé de Las Casas; Roger Williams; George Calvert, 1st Baron Baltimore; William Penn; James Oglethorpe; Sir William Berkeley; Thomas Hollis; and Jean Luzac. His oration concludes with a defense of American contributions to the improvement of humanity, asserting that "the intellectual power of this people has exerted itself in conformity to the general system of our institutions and manners; and therefore, that for the proof of its existence and the measure of its force, we must look not so much to the works of

[563]

prominent individuals, as to great aggregate results; and if Europe has hitherto been wilfully blind to the value of our examples and the exploits of our sagacity, courage, invention and freedom, the blame must rest with her and not America" (p. 81).

Early in 1819 Verplanck also sent copies of his pamphlet to John Adams, James Madison, and John Marshall (Verplanck to Adams, 7 Jan. 1819 [MHi: Adams Papers]; Madison, *Papers, Retirement Ser.*, 1:403; Marshall, *Papers*, 8:254).

From John Wayles Eppes

DEAR SIR.   Washington Jan. 8. 1819.

Tracy's Political Economy & your Report on the University (which you were so good as to forward) have been received. As tokens of your continued friendly remembrance I look on them with great pleasure. The treatise of Tracy I had previously purchased & read & the Report on the subject of the University[1] had been forwarded by a friend from Richmond. This continued devotion of your time and Talents to promote the interest of your fellow citizens must afford great pleasure to your friends.

The value of your present would have been greatly increased by a few lines stating the present condition of your health. I know however your labours in this way and hope that my not writing will be attributed to the real motive "a fear of increasing them"—

With every wish for your health I am with affection & respect. yours.   JNO: W: EPPES

RC (ViU: TJP-ER); endorsed by TJ as received 14 Jan. 1819 and so recorded in SJL.

Late in 1818 Eppes wrote to his son that TJ had sent him Destutt de TRACY's *Treatise on Political Economy* and the *University of Virginia Commissioners' Report*, but he complained that with them TJ "did not however write a single line so that I know not how he is" (Eppes to Francis Eppes, Washington, 26 Dec. 1818 [NcD: Eppes Papers]).

[1] Manuscript: "Univesity."

From Joseph Jones

SIR   Coll^rs office. Petersburg 8^h January 1819.

I have received a letter p^r the Brig Planter of Petersburg Daniel Anderson master from marseilles dated 21^t October 1818 from Stephen Cathalan esq^r our consul, enclosing two Bills of loading one is for wines &c for you, and the other for Thomas Jefferson Randolph esq^r for wines. He writes me that he has sent all the things you wrote for except the <u>Smyrna raisins</u>, & the <u>Sans Pepins</u>, which he sayes he could not get in Town. He writes me he has been very sick from the 24.ʰ Septᵉʳ last until a few days past so that he has not been able to get the bills of cost of the several Articles, so as to make out the Invoice's, but that he will get them & send the Invoice's by way of Havre or Bordeaux as quick as possible, He sayes he had not time to write you now but will when he sends the Invoice's. He has consigned them to me as Collector at Petersburg and requested me to pay the Freight from marseilles¹ at 18 Dollars pʳ Ton. & 10 prcᵗ for Primage & average and to write you as soon as the Brig Arrives. the Brig has not got up to City point but is expected in a day or two. I will thank you for directions how to act. Here is the Contents of the bills of loading. Viz.

——

T.J.   one Cask in a double Cask containing 64 Gallons red wine.
Six boxes containᵍ each 50 bottles red wine in all 300 bottles.
one box containing 12 bottles Anchovies.
four Small boxes containᵍ each 12 bottles Sup fine olive oil in all 36 (he² says) but ought to be 48.
one basket containing nett ninety pounds American weight Macaroni.
one box containing Immortal Flowers.

——

R
T.J.   one Cask in a double Cask containing 32 Gallons red wine
two boxes containᵍ each 24 bottles red wine in all 48 bottles.

I am Sir with great respect Your obᵗ Serᵗ

JOSEPH JONES Collʳ

RC (DLC); idiosyncratic punctuation editorially omitted; endorsed by TJ as received 14 Jan. 1819 and so recorded in SJL. RC (DLC); address cover only; with PoC of TJ to James Madison, 19 Feb. 1819, on verso; addressed: "Thomas Jefferson esqʳ Late President of the United States. Monticello"; franked; postmarked.

Joseph Jones (1749–1824), public official, became a vestryman of Bristol Parish in 1773. He served as a captain in the Virginia militia during the Revolutionary War, eventually attaining the rank of major general of militia at the end of 1802. Jones also sat on the Dinwiddie County Committee of Correspondence during the Revolution. He later represented Dinwiddie in the Virginia House of Delegates, 1778–81 and 1784–88, and at the Virginia ratification convention in 1788, where he opposed the new federal consti-

tution. Jones served in the Senate of Virginia, 1788–89, was sheriff of Dinwiddie for about two years beginning late in the latter year, and became a presidential elector for TJ in 1800. He was appointed customs collector at Petersburg in 1811, and his duties were expanded to include those of surveyor of the revenue in 1821. Jones held both positions until his death (NcD: Jones Papers; Vi: Jones Family Papers; MB, 2:1364; WMQ, 1st ser., 19 [1911]: 289; 26 [1917]: 101; VMHB 9 [1902]: 414; 10 [1902]: 82; 17 [1909]: 250–1; Leonard, General Assembly; Merrill Jensen, John P. Kaminski, and others, eds., The Documentary History of the Ratification of the Constitution [1976–   ], 10:1538–41; CVSP; Richmond Virginia Argus, 22 Dec. 1802; JEP, 2:192, 3:227, 232, 235, 367 [25, 26 Nov. 1811, 14 Dec. 1820, 3, 15 Jan. 1821, 29 Mar. 1824]; Richmond Enquirer, 12 Feb. 1824;

Petersburg Hustings Court Will Book, 2:211, 216; gravestone inscription in Blandford Cemetery, Petersburg).

The letter of 21ᵀ OCTOBER 1818 from Stephen Cathalan to Jones is printed above as an enclosure to Cathalan to TJ, 30 Nov. 1818. PRIMAGE & AVERAGE were customary fees in a bill of lading generally charged as a standard percentage rather than broken down individually.

The former covered the loading and unloading of a shipment, while the latter paid for miscellaneous services, such as ship repairs and cleaning (*OED*; Joseph Kay, *The Law relating to Shipmasters and Seamen* [2d ed., 1894], 34).

¹ Manuscript: "marsiells."
² Omitted opening parenthesis editorially supplied.

From Joel Yancey

DR SIR   Poplar Forest 9ᵗʰ Janʸ 1819

Your letter by Jerry I received on Thursday night last, he delivered his load safe and I had the doors and books put in one of the rooms in the house and the wine in the cellar, the sowing of peas, shall be attended to, and I expect by the time Jerry returns, I Shall be able to Send you Some of those late peas, which you were pleased with last Summer, the letter to mʳ Radford & myself with the documents inclosed, I have Sent to mʳ Radford, and requested him to appoint an early day, for us to meet in Lynchburg to endeavour to settle that business, he informᵈ me he would attend to it one day next week as soon as any thing can be done, the documents and our award shall be Sent you by mail, In my letter of 18ᵗʰ December to you, I mentioned that 65 hogs would be Sent down, this was an error, the 12 that was to be Kept here for your use was included, after turning one out, that I did not wishᵈ to have Killᵈ, 4 for the overseers, and 20 for the negroes, 12 to be Kept here, there remained but 52 for Monticello, weighing 5309ᵗᵇ, the 12 would have made about the quantity I expected, as Jerry complains heavily of the roads, I shall divide what I send down into 3 loads, making about 2000 each, loading now¹ one waggon with pork, and the other, with lard, butter, soap and Some little things, making out the load with pork, the third will be all pork—there is Some bacon, a part of your last years Stock, which appears very good, except those pieces which are injured by the Rats, perhaps you would wish that sent down, if so, you will direct it, and it shall make part of the 3ʳᵈ load, the weights of all the hogs, and how desposed of and, a list of the Stock at both placees with Some other memoˢ youˡˡ find inclosed on a Seperate paper, the wheat was all delivered in Mitchels Mills before the first day of Decembʳ and I have been anxious to Send the flour off but carriage is so high, that I have thought and been advised, to wait till it comes down, which it must do, very Soon, it is now, from 8. to 9/– ℔ barrel. the To^{bo} is nearly all ready for prizing and shall be Sent off as Soon as practicable of which you Shall be advised, I certainly, think I am doing the best for you, I can here, but the turn out every year is So little, in proportion to the immense[2] capital that I am almost ready to acknowledge that I am incapable of managing it, there is Some improvement in the lands & plantations and a tolerable increase of Stock but the crops, is nothing in amont, to what they ought to be, last year the whole crop of wheat was 1250 bushels, of which 404, is sown 8 bushels Sold to the Overseer, and 848 deliver^d in the Mills, ½ crop To^{bo}. 12 or 15000[℔] say at both places, and not corn enough at Tomahawk to Serve the place, at B. creek not more than enough, and our prospect for the present year rather worse for corn than the last, as the Tomahawk field, and the upper field at B. creek comes in rotation, the chance for To^{bo} will be good, I shall therefore push for a full crop of To^{bo} the present year and not concern much with the [. . .] this year as we have as much meadow as we can Keep in good order, we want fresh land for corn and wheat, a great proportion of Several of the fields, is too much exhausted for coltivation, we have been unfortunate the last year also in the loss of Several Negroes, they had a bowel complaint prevailing among the children last Summer and fall which proved fatal to both of Edys, 2 of Amys, & 1 of Wills Sall, Nanny 1 born dead, Ceasar, and Joe all which deaths occured the last year, Joe died with a consumption, and Ambrose his Brother is going off rapidly with Same complaint, Dinah is pretty much the Same, does nothing, Maria has done nothing since she had a child, complains of a constant pain in her hip and back, I have had her blestered pretty Severely, and advice from the Doct^r but She will not acknowledge that she is any better, there are Several others, that are in the house, but I believe nothing seraous the matter, could you Send us a plough or two by Dick it would be of great Service to us, with very great respect and esteem

JOEL YANCEY

RC (MHi); one word illegible; endorsed by TJ as received 13 Jan. 1819 but recorded in SJL as received a day earlier. Enclosure not found.

For Yancey's letter OF 18TH DECEMBER, see note to Yancey to TJ, 24 Dec. 1818. B. CREEK: Bear Creek.

One of EDYS children who died around this time was Nancy. AMYS deceased children may have been Mahala and Madison. Milly, the daughter of Sally (WILLS SALL) and Gawen died about 1819. MARIA gave birth to her son James Hubbard on 16 July 1818 (Betts, *Farm Book*, pt. 1, 131, 168).

[1] Word interlined.
[2] Manuscript: "immese."

From Daniel Brent

DEAR SIR,   Washington, January 10. 1819.

I received your note of the 22ⁿᵈ of December, covering a Letter for General la Fayette, which I transmitted to the Collector of the Customs at New york immediately after it came to Hand, enclosed to mʳ Beasley, our Consul at Havre; and it is, I dare say, already forwarded by some vessel from the first mentioned place.

I have just received a Letter from mʳ Sheldon, Secretary of our Legation at Paris, dated the 5th of November, which contains the following paragraph—"The late election of the annual fifth of the Chamber of Deputies" (General la Fayette being one of the chosen) "has left the Ministry precisely as they were before; but the liberales have gained 14 or 15 members at the expence of the ultras; and this is a good deal out of 58, the whole number elected. The elections are now free and impartial, and may be taken as a fair expression of the popular sentiment." I have the Honour to remain, with sentiments of the Highest Respect and esteem, Dear Sir, your obedᵗ & very humble servant,   DANIEL BRENT.

RC (DLC); endorsed by TJ as received 14 Jan. 1819 and so recorded in SJL. RC (DLC); address cover only; with PoC of TJ to John H. Cocke, 19 Feb. 1819, on verso; addressed: "Mʳ Jefferson, Monticello"; franked; postmarked (faint) Washington, [1]1 Jan.

No NOTE OF THE 22ᴺᴰ OF DECEMBER from TJ to Brent has been found, nor is one recorded in SJL. The LETTER FOR GENERAL LA FAYETTE may have been TJ to Lafayette, 23 Nov. 1818, but it could also have been a separate communication transmitting copies of the *University of Virginia Commissioners' Report* and Destutt de Tracy, *Treatise on Political Economy*, which TJ dispatched to a number of his friends around that time. David Gelston was COLLECTOR OF THE CUSTOMS at New York City.

From "Common Sense & Co."

                                    Arendes (Hell) New London
INFERNAL WRETCH   Janʸ 12ᵗʰ 1819

What can be your thoughts on the distracted Country by your Philosophical arts & intrigues (**Embargoes** &c) for if the righteous is scarcely saved where will thee &c appear I wish you a warm reception—as also another whom would be duly gratified within the lower regions & as a Ferryman of Charons Ferry Boat built on the model of Gun Boat Nᵒ 1 I wish that you send me a Commodore worthy of notice & recommendations will be required endors'd on the back of Mazzies (Letter)—we your most truly petitioners[1] have reverence for

thy latter days & may the hour shortly come when Jefferson, Paine,
& Volney shall Furnish all the requistions of the lower Republic
We are your invisble [. . .]   COMMON SENSE & Co

RC (DLC); one word illegible; internal address on verso reading "**Th: Jefferson** **Late President of The U States Monticello Virginia**" embedded in ornamental swirl:

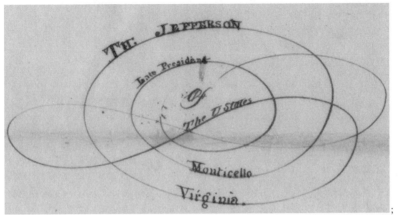

endorsed by TJ (trimmed) as an anonymous letter from a "blackguar[d]" received 22 Jan. 1819 and so recorded in SJL. RC (MHi); address cover only; with PoC of TJ to William Tudor, 31 Jan. 1819, on verso; addressed: "Honᵉ Thomas Jefferson Monticello Virginia"; stamped; postmarked Colchester, Conn., 12 Jan.

GUN BOAT Nᵒ 1 of the naval fleet that TJ ordered constructed during his presidency was commissioned in 1804. After

it was deemed unfit for ocean duty, it became part of the coastal defense force (Spencer C. Tucker, *The Jeffersonian Gunboat Navy* [1993], 38). MAZZIES (LETTER) was TJ to Philip Mazzei, 24 Apr. 1796, which sharply criticized the Federalist party and George Washington and was widely published in Europe and the United States beginning in 1797 (*PTJ*, 29:73–88).

[1] Manuscript: "petitoners."

From Jonas Horwitz

SIR!   Philadelphia Jan 12ᵗʰ 1818 [1819]

judge Thoˢ Cooper, informed me, that when in Virginia, he mentioned my name to you as professor, of Oriental literature, in the College of Charlotte-Ville under your auspices; & that you replied to him; if it could be joined with the German language, such a professorship might be instituted.

This induces me, to take the liberty of addressing you, the German is my Vernacular-tongue; & am not only master of it, but have actually now in my possession, a manuscript of a German Grammar, which

I composed some years ago {an[1] abridgement of Adelung the Johnson of Germany} for the use of Englishmen

Respecting the Hebrew &c. the enclosed proposals; & its recommendations which were written 7 years since may speak for themselves; but if required, I can obtain a letter of recommendation, signed by most of the Clergy, Advocates; & other literary Characters of this City; & I may say of almost half the Union {who had attended my lectures} in favour of both my talent for teaching, & proficiency in Oriental learning.

should it meet with your approbation, to have such a professorship in the Central College; & should you think me worthy of the station, you will oblige; & honour me much by answering this.

In hopes that this may find you in the best of health I have the honor to be   sir!   very respectfully—

Your Most Obt: J, HORWITZ

RC (ViU: TJP); misdated; at foot of text: "Thos Jefferson Esqr Monticello V[a]"; endorsed by TJ as a letter of 12 Jan. 1819 received five days later and so recorded in SJL. Enclosure: prospectus by Horwitz for a Hebrew Bible, [Philadelphia, before 1 Aug. 1813], decrying the scarcity of Hebrew-language bibles in the United States; commending the superior qualities of that of Everardus van der Hooght; proposing to publish an American edition of that work "without the points" (marks indicating vowels, repeated or varied consonants, punctuation, and pronunciation); announcing that it will be printed by William Fry on superfine paper using "a new pica Hebrew type" cast by Binny & Ronaldson and will cost $15 for a set of two octavo volumes; offering a discount on bulk purchases by educational institutions; including three testimonials for Horwitz and his project dated 5 Mar., 5 and 8 May 1812 by prominent clergy in Philadelphia and New York; requesting that subscriptions be returned by 1 Aug. 1813 to Thomas Dobson in Philadelphia; advertising other works by Dobson; and concluding with a sample page from the book of Genesis in Hebrew (printed text in ViU; undated).

Jonas Horwitz (1783–1852), physician and educator, was born in Berlin. He arrived in the United States in 1810, petitioned for citizenship in 1812, and in the following year advertised an evening school in Philadelphia at which he taught Hebrew, Chaldee, and Arabic. Horwitz received a medical degree from the University of Pennsylvania in 1815 and practiced medicine in Lexington, Kentucky, in 1816, and at a dispensary for the poor in Philadelphia in 1818. He continued to teach Hebrew in various locations, including the environs of Washington, D.C., 1819–20, and Raleigh, North Carolina, in 1822. Horwitz unsuccessfully petitioned to teach languages at Central College and in 1821 visited TJ at Monticello. By 1827 he had settled permanently in Baltimore, where he established a medical practice. Horwitz joined a unit of volunteer soldiers as a surgeon during the Mexican-American War. In 1850 he owned real estate valued at $10,000 (Jacob Rader Marcus, *United States Jewry 1776–1985* [1989], 1:360–2, 376; Horwitz's naturalization records, 8 May 1812 [DNA: RG 21, NPEDP]; Philadelphia *Democratic Press*, 25 Oct. 1813; *University of Pennsylvania Catalogue*, 575; Lexington, Ky., *Western Monitor*, 28 June 1816; *Rules and Regulations of the Northern Dispensary, for the Medical Relief of the Poor* [(Philadelphia, 1818)], 12; John Adems Paxton, *The Philadelphia Directory and Register, for 1819* [Philadelphia, 1819]; Samuel L. Mitchill to TJ, 4 May 1819; Washington *Daily National Intelligencer*, 15, 20 Nov. 1819; *Boston Daily Adver-*

tiser, 24 Nov. 1819; *Alexandria Gazette & Daily Advertiser*, 13, 17 Jan. 1820; TJ to Frederick W. Hatch, 9 Sept. 1821; Hatch to TJ, [received 10 Sept. 1821]; *Raleigh Register and North-Carolina Gazette*, 25 Oct. 1822; Eugene Fauntleroy Cordell, *The Medical Annals of Maryland, 1799–1899* [1903], 443–4; *Baltimore Patriot & Mercantile Advertiser*, 28 Apr. 1830, 28 Mar. 1831; DNA: RG 29, CS, Md., Baltimore, 1830–50; Horwitz, *A Defence of the Cosmogony of Moses* [(1838)]; *Matchett's Baltimore Director* [1831]: 187; [1851]: 133; Baltimore *Sun*, 1 July 1852).

Horwitz transferred the publishing rights to the project described in the enclosure to Dobson, who completed it (תורה נביאים וכתובים. *Biblia Hebraica*, 2 vols. [Philadelphia, 1814], with unpaginated note on publication history).

In a letter presumably given to TJ by Thomas COOPER during his autumn 1818 visit to Monticello, Horwitz asked Cooper to recommend him for a professorship of Oriental literature at Central College if the school "is intended to have the same standing {if not superior}" as Harvard, Yale, and the College of New Jersey (later Princeton University), all of which have such teaching positions and whose faculty, as well as "almost all the Clergy, besides many other literary Characters in the Eastern, Middle, & Western states have received the benefits of my instruction" (Horwitz to Cooper, Philadelphia, 11 Sept. 1818 [RC in ViU: TJP; addressed: "Thomas Cooper M.D. &C."; endorsed by TJ: "Horwitz J. to be Hebrew Professor"]).

[1] Inconsistent opening angle bracket editorially changed to a brace, here and below.

To Nathaniel Macon

DEAR SIR   Monticello Jan. 12. 19.

The problem[1] you had wished to propose to me was on[e] which I could not have solved; for I know nothing of the facts. I read no newspaper now but Ritchie's, and in that chiefly the advertisements, for they contain the only truths to be relied on in a newspaper. I feel a much greater interest in knowing what passed two or three thousand years ago, than in what is now passing. I read nothing therefore but of the heroes of Troy, of the wars of Lacedaemon & Athens, of Pompey and Caesar, and of Augustus too, the Bonaparte and parricide scoundrel of that day. I have had, and still have such entire confidence in the late and present Presidents, that I willingly put both soul & body into their pockets. while such men as yourself and your worthy colleagues of the legislature, and such characters as compose the Executive administration, are watching for us all, I slumber without fear, and review in my dreams the visions of antiquity. there is indeed one evil which awakens me at times, because it justles me at every turn. it is that we have now no measure of value. I am asked 18. Dollars for a yard of broadcloth, which, when we had Dollars, I used to get for 18/. from this I can only understand that a Dollar is now worth but 2. inches of broadcloth. but broadcloth is no standard of measure or value. I do not know therefore whereabouts I stand in the scale of property, nor what to ask, or what to give for it. I saw indeed the like machinery in action in the years 80. & 81. and without dissatisfaction; because, in wearing out, it was working out our salvation. but I see nothing in this renewal of the game of 'Robin's alive' but a general demoralization of the nation, a filching from industry it's honest earnings, wherewith to build up palaces, and raise gambling stock for swindlers and shavers, who are to close too their career of piracies by fraudulent bankruptcies. my dependance for a remedy however, is in the wisdom which grows with time and suffering. whether the succeeding generation is to be more virtuous than their predecessors I cannot say; but I am sure they will have more worldly wisdom, and enough, I hope, to know that honesty is the 1st chapter in the book of wisdom.   I have made a great exertion to write you thus much; my antipathy to taking up a pen being so intense that I have never given you a stronger proof, than in the effort of writing a letter, how much I value you, and of the superlative respect and friendship with which I salute you.

Th: Jefferson

PoC (DLC); edge trimmed; at foot of first page: "Nathaniel Macon esq."

¹ Word interlined in place of "question."

From Joseph Milligan

[before 12 Jan. 1819]

The page on the other side is a sample of Ricardo on political Economy & the principles of Taxation

I am urged by several members of Congress to print the book it will make such a Volume as Tracy

Ricardo is Reviewed in the 59th Nᵒ of the Edinburg Review

If I conclude to print it I will let you know

If I print it I will have it through the press before the 4th March

J: Milligan

RC (DLC: TJ Papers, 214:38207); undated, with date conjectured from TJ's reply. Possibly enclosed in Milligan to TJ, 25 Dec. 1818.

The enclosure on verso was a sample printed PAGE of Milligan's proposed edition of David Ricardo, *On the Principles of Political Economy, and Taxation* (London, 1817). The text of the sample page begins "If the necessaries of the workman could be constantly increased with the same facility" and ends "By producing, then, he necessarily becomes either the consumer of his own goods, or the purchaser and consumer of the goods of some other person." It is drawn from chapter 19 of the work and labeled at the top as p. 399. Milligan proceeded to publish the first American edition of this work in Georgetown in 1819, with the same title (Poor, *Jefferson's Library*, 11 [no. 701]). The text of the sample page enclosed here appears on pp. 299–300.

A review in the 59ᵀᴴ ɴº of the *Edinburgh Review* praised Ricardo for doing more for the science of political economy than any other writer, with the possible exception of Adam Smith (*Edinburgh Review* 30 [June 1818]: 59–87, esp. 60).

To Joseph Milligan

Monticello Jan. 12. 19.

Do, my good friend, let me have my books as soon as you can. of some of them I am in daily want. yet I mean not to hasten them to the prejudice of their being solidly done.

On the reciept of your letter proposing to republish Ricardo, I turned to the Edinburg review, and read that article. if you do republish, I wish, but doubt your seeing your own by it. it is a work in my opinion which will not stand the test of time & trial. if such men as Adam Smith, Malthus, Say, and Tracy, knew nothing of the nature of rent, or of the effect of capital on prices, it is not to be proved by such muddy reasoning as that of Ricardo, or of his Edinburg critic. their new discoveries of the errors of these great men will be like those of the errors of Newton, which almost every year produces from some half-sighted writer, who sees but a speck at a time of an expanded subject. yet, not having seen the whole work, I can only say, that neither the parts quoted, nor the supplementory reasonings of the Reviewer, are sufficient in my judgment to overthrow the theories of Smith, Malthus, Say and Tracy. the reputation of the work will, I think, fall as soon as it comes to be read. —make haste with my books and be assured of my esteem and best wishes.

Tʜ: Jᴇꜰꜰᴇʀꜱᴏɴ

PoC (DLC); on verso of reused address cover of Milligan to TJ, 17 Oct. 1818; at foot of text: "Mʳ Millegan"; endorsed by TJ.

From Mathew Carey & Son

ꜱɪʀ   Philad Jan 13. 1819

Enclosed we hand you statement of ⁹⁄꜀ for the past year, & remain respectfully Your obed servᵗˢ

√   M Cᴀʀᴇʏ & ꜱᴏɴ

RC (MHi); in the hand of a representative of Mathew Carey & Son; between dateline and salutation: "Hon Thoˢ Jefferson"; endorsed by TJ as a letter from Mathew Carey received 24 Jan. 1819 and so recorded in SJL. Enclosure not found.

From Simeon DeWitt

SIR   Albany Jany 13. 1819

I have had the temerity to advance a novel project for the consideration of our Legislature, now in session, and as it is of general concern I am induced to take the liberty of presenting you with the pamphlet which contains it. The pamphlet has only this moment come from the press and I have as Yet had no opportunity of learning opinions about it, except from a few friends of high standing in public life to whom I have shewn it in manuscript, who think well of the object and advised me to the publication. As every parent is partial to his child, so I think this offspring of mine, if adopted by the State, whose prosperity it is my duty to study, is calculated to do some good

You, Sir, are now considered as the chief of the surviving fathers of our beloved country, who as occasions offer do not cease to manifest Your paternal anxieties[1] for its welfare, and no where can there exist a greater deference for Your opinion on matters relating to the public good than in the State of New York.

An expression of your opinion therefore on the project now submitted would probably be decisive of its fate.

I would not have presumed to trouble You on this Occasion, if I did not think the subject of some importance and that You probably might feel some interest in it—

In reading the pamphlet you will of course bear in mind how different the condition and habits of our northern citizens are from those of the Citizens of the Southern States—

I am with the greatest regard Your most Obedient Humble servant

SIMEON DEWITT

RC (MHi); endorsed by TJ as received 22 Jan. 1819 and so recorded in SJL. RC (MHi); address cover only; with PoC of TJ to Charles K. Mallory, 27 Jan. 1819, on verso; addressed: "Thomas Jefferson Esquire Monticello Virginia"; franked; postmarked Albany, 13 Jan. Enclosure: DeWitt, *Considerations on the Necessity of Establishing an Agricultural College, and having more of the Children of Wealthy Citizens educated for the Profession of Farming* (Albany, 1819).

Simeon DeWitt (1756–1834), surveyor, was born in Wawarsing, Ulster County, New York, and studied in Schenectady before attending Queen's College (later Rutgers University), which awarded him a B.A. in 1776. At the outbreak of the American Revolution he enlisted as an adjutant in a local militia battalion and became a private when this unit was absorbed into another regiment. In 1778 DeWitt was appointed as assistant to the army's geographer-in-chief, and he took over leadership of that department two years later. From December 1780 he was attached to the main encampment of the Continental army making surveys and maps in aid of military operations, and after hostilities ceased he stayed on at George Washington's request, creating a cartographic history of the Revolutionary War based on field maps. DeWitt was named surveyor-general of the state of New York in 1784 and held the position for the remainder of his life, living for most of his career in Albany. He was active in various scholarly and educational organizations, including service to the University of the State of New York as regent from 1798, vice chancellor beginning in 1817, and chancellor from 1829 until his death. DeWitt was elected to the American Philosophical Society in 1787. He was a founder of the New York Society for the Promotion of Agriculture, Arts and Manufactures in 1793 and became its president in 1813. DeWitt also developed the settlement that eventually became Ithaca, New York, where he relocated permanently in 1831 (*ANB*; *DAB*; Theodoric Romeyn Beck, *Eulogium of the Life and Services of Simeon De Witt* [1835]; Worthington C. Ford and others, eds., *Journals of the Continental Congress, 1774–1789* [1904–37], 18:1118 [4 Dec. 1780]; Heitman, *Continental Army*, 196; Washington, *Papers, Confederation Ser.*, 1:34–6; APS, Minutes, 19 Jan. 1787 [MS in PPAmP]; DeWitt to TJ, 28 Aug. 1804 [MHi]; *New-York Spectator*, 11 Dec. 1834).

[1] Manuscript: "axieties."

From William Tudor

SIR,   Boston Jany 13^h 1819.

If the motive of this letter does not serve for my excuse with you, I have no other that I can offer for this intrusion—I have been for some months past endeavoring to collect materials for the life of James Otis who held so distinguished a place among the actors in the preparatory scenes of our immortal revolution. As my attention to his character was more particularly drawn by the letters of President Adams to my father, some of which have been published, I need hardly say that I did not undertake the task till I had been encouraged by his kind approbation. There are very few vestiges of him remaining except in printed documents; for in an unhappy period of mental alienation, he destroyed every paper in his possession; and his career was so prematurely arrested by this deplorable misfortune, that none of the cotemporaries of his intellectual powers now exist, except President Adams. It is therefore very difficult to find any letters of his writing. I wish very much to obtain copies of whole or extracts of letters that he may have written. It occurred to me that you might perhaps have received letters from him, or that you may have known some gentlemen from Virginia or the neighboring States who knew him and were in the habit of corresponding with him, and from whose families some documents of this kind might be obtained. Should this be the case, I hope I am not indiscreet in asking your good will to aid me in procuring them. I would leave nothing undone that depends upon me to do justice to this great patriot, and I know all your interests and sympathies must induce you to regard such undertakings with complacency. I beg you to accept my wishes for the prolongation of your health and happiness, and the assurance of my very high respect.   W. TUDOR J^R

RC (MHi); at foot of both first page and text: "President Jefferson Monticello"; endorsed by TJ as received 24 Jan. 1819 and so recorded in SJL.

William Tudor (1779–1830), author and public official, was born in Boston, studied at Phillips Academy in Andover, and graduated from Harvard University in 1796. He then embarked on a career in trade, sailing on business to Paris and Leghorn and subsequently to the West Indies on behalf of his brother Frederic Tudor. With his mother, Delia Jarvis Tudor, in August 1801 Tudor visited TJ at Monticello. He represented Boston for four one-year terms in the Massachusetts House of Representatives, 1810–11 and 1815–18, but his parents failed in attempts to place him in government positions at Marseille and London. Active in scholarly circles in Boston, Tudor was a founder of the Boston Athenæum in 1807, started the *North American Review* in 1815, joined the Massachusetts Historical Society in 1816, and published a biography of James Otis in 1823. President James Monroe appointed him United States consul at Lima in 1823. Four years later John Quincy Adams named him chargé d'affaires at Rio de Janeiro, where he died (*DAB; Harvard Catalogue*, 180; *PTJ*, 34:674,

35:94; DNA: RG 59, LAR, 1801–17; *Massachusetts Register and United States Calendar* [1811]: 18; [1816]: 17; [1817]: 17; [1818]: 17; Tudor, *Letters on the Eastern States* [New York, 1820], *Miscellanies* [Boston, 1821], and *The Life of James Otis, of Massachusetts* [Boston, 1823; Poor, *Jefferson's Library*, 5 (no. 148)]; *JEP*, 3:343–4, 579, 583 [8, 9 Dec. 1823, 24, 27 Dec. 1827]; Washington *Daily National Intelligencer*, 11 May, 10 July 1830).

Recently published LETTERS OF PRESIDENT John Adams to William Tudor (1750–1819) included one of 25 Feb. 1818 in which Adams stated that "I have been young and now I am old, and I solemnly say, I have never known a man whose love of his country was more ardent or sincere; never one, who suffered so much; never one whose services for any ten years of his life, were so important and essential to the cause of his country, as those of Mr. Otis from 1760 to 1770" (Baltimore *Niles' Weekly Register*, 11 July 1818; also quoted in Tudor, *Life of James Otis*, xviii). Adams expressed his APPROBATION of the younger Tudor's proposal to write a life of Otis in a letter to him dated 28 Aug. 1818 (Lb in MHi: Adams Papers).

To Joseph Jones

SIR   Monticello Jan. 15. 19.

I am very thankful to you for the trouble you have been so kind as to take with respect to my wines and other articles recieved from mr Cathalan of Marseilles. I import annually my wines from that place, and as there are not many vessels going thither from our ports, my correspondent is obliged to send them by any vessel which happens there to whatever port bound on her return, and consigns to the Collectors. I will ask the favor of you to have the articles sent to Richmond addressed to mr Patrick Gibson of that place, on whom I inclose you a draught for the amount of duties, freight and all other charges. if you are obliged to wait for the invoice for assessing the duties, you can use the draught for the immediate reimbursement of the freight & other charges which you have been so kind as to advance, and a second time for the duties. altho' I presume you could settle and draw for them also at once, the duties on wine being fixed, the cost of oil sufficiently known, and that of the Maccaroni having hitherto been charged to me at from 16. to 20. cents the pound, prime cost. I shall make it a point however to send you the invoice as soon as I recieve it. I am admonished to ask some attention and the usual forms of a receipt from the master of the vessel to whom committed, lest it get into the hands of the same who recieved for me at Petersburg the last year a cask of Scuppernon wine, of which I never heard more, nor could learn his name or abode. with my apologies for all the trouble I am giving you, accept the assurance of my great respect and esteem   TH: JEFFERSON

PoC (DLC); on verso of reused address cover of Lewis D. Belair to TJ, 9 Oct. 1818; at foot of text: "Mr Joseph Jones"; endorsed by TJ. Enclosure not found.

From Benjamin Waterhouse

DEAR SIR,   Cambridge 15th January 1819.
   Although answering of letters may have become an irksome task, the reading them may sometimes be an amusement. This idea has induced me to send you this. It has reference to future history, and has had its origin in the following occurrence: Mr Trumbull exhibited, a few weeks since, his national painting of "the Declaration of Independence' in the Town-hall of Boston. The picture has not given that general satisfaction the intimate friends of the painter probably anticipated. As a composition & painting, it is not thought to be a happy specimen of the State of the art in America, at this period; neither is it allowed to be altogether correct as it regards historical fact, as far as Massachusetts is concerned: Elbridge Gerry for example, has a very conspicious position, while Samuel Adams is scarcely discoverable in the croud of ordinary members. This drew forth a writer under the Signature of Historicus (Samuel Adams Wells, grandson of the eminent patriot) and this brought forth Tempus & Philo Tempus, and induced him to venture a sketch of the portraiture of that great man. They are here enclosed. Nothing passionate occurred in the short & liberal controversy. The painting is removed to Philadelphia, & all conversation relative to it ceased. Mr Trumbull was treated with great liberality in Boston, while all the remaining old whigs shooked their heads & sighed on seeing their Moses thrust almost out of sight. Some advised him to alter it; but the tories & their descendants said it was well enough, for that S. A. was so poor a man that he had every thing to gain, & nothing to lose by the revolution.

[577]

Tempus, by which the writer meant vox temporis, considers Samuel Adams as the great file leader of the Revolution; but as he was not greedy of fame, nor had he the Splendour of riches, nor the eclat of foreign embassies, nor his name spread abroad[1] by writing books, his character is not surrounded by that halo of glory which encircles even that of John Hancock. There was yet another cause: while Alexander Hamilton exerted all his influence & powers in favour of the return of the refugees & Tories, Samuel Adams exerted all his powers to prevent it. This drew on him the hatred of their descendents, the high toned federalists of Boston, & of the whole State.

A few months Since the rich men of Boston caused a fine bust of marble to be made by a French sculptor of John Adams, & placed it in the Town-hall, while the merits of Samuel Adams are passed over in Silence. This neglect induced Tempus to make the enclosed Sketch, to recall the half lost memory of Samuel Adams, and the few remaining old patriots of the revolution have shouted applause

Another reason for throwing this Sketch of S. A. before the public in the News papers, was to profit by the remarks & objections, should I ever venture to introduce the picture of that undeviating patriot into the history of our times. I cannot however conceal the strong desire I have to know your opinion of Samuel Adams. It is reported that Pres^t Jefferson has repeatedly said that Samuel Adams was the earliest, most active, & persevering man of the revolution. Should you give me your opinion, I would, if thought best, conceal it.

Should the history of our revolution, down to the conclusion of our late war appear, written in the manner of "Tempus," would the stile of it correspond with the subject?

If I am wrong in my opinion that Samuel Adams was the most meritorious man (his poverty, & all such things taken into consideration) in our revolution, I should deeply regret inserting it in permanent history.

I rejoice, in common with our countrymen, in the restoration of your health, and am with a high degree of respect

your ob^t serv^t BENJAMIN WATERHOUSE.

P.S. While you have ice & snow in the South, we in the North have our rivers & brooks free. The want of snow is lamented by our farmers, as a public calamity.

RC (DLC); addressed: "To Thomas Jefferson Late President of the United States Monticello Virginia"; franked; postmarked Cambridge, Mass., 18 Jan.; endorsed by TJ as received 27 Jan. 1819 and so recorded in SJL.

The newspaper dialogue HERE ENCLOSED between Samuel Adams Wells writing as "Historicus" and Waterhouse writing as "Tempus" and "Philo Tempus" consisted of six articles in the Boston Patriot and Daily Chronicle. Those authored by Wells appeared on 8, 15, and 19 Dec., while those by Waterhouse were published on 11, 16, and 29 Dec. 1818. Wells launched the discussion by describing his reaction to Trumbull's painting of *The Declaration of Independence*, emphasizing his doubts about the accuracy of the depiction and noting that the "lessons of history that we gain by painting are much more powerfully impressed upon the mind than those which are acquired by reading." Wells took particular issue with his grandfather Samuel Adams's "unfortunate position, pilloried in a manner between the shoulders of the two gentlemen beside him." Waterhouse responded that Adams "always preferred to stand in the back ground" and highlighted the longevity and fuller scope of literature as opposed to the ephemeral nature of paint and canvas. Continuing on 15 Dec., Wells encouraged biographical work on Adams and argued that Trumbull had a "*duty* to make known this in-

dividual to the public: and if he was indifferent to public rewards, it is equally the duty of his country to render to his memory that justice which he failed to demand for himself." A day later Waterhouse again insisted that historians, not artists, would render the durable portraits of historical leaders. Wells's last "Communication" in this series supplied a "schedule" of the members of Congress "at the time of the passing of the declaration," which could "perhaps give a more clear and distinct idea of the whole subject." In his own closing installment, "*A sketch or outline of the Picture of* SAMUEL ADAMS," Waterhouse provided a brief biography of Adams that "may be filled up by some future *Tacitus*."

VOX TEMPORIS: "voice of the times." For the FINE BUST OF MARBLE depicting John Adams, see Adams to TJ, 29 May 1818, and note.

[1] Manuscript: "aboard."

From John Forsyth

Washington Jany 16. 1819

J Forsyth presents his best acknowledgements to Mr Jefferson for the Copy of the proceedings and Report of the Commissioners for the University of Virginia & particularly for the flattering assurances inscribed upon it. For the work itself J Forsyth hopes the author will receive the highest of all human rewards an opportunity of witnessing the blessings it will confer upon his Country

RC (MHi); dateline at foot of text; endorsed by TJ as received 22 Jan. 1819 and so recorded in SJL. RC (DLC); address cover only; with PoC of TJ to John Patterson, 31 Jan. 1819, on verso; addressed: "Mr Jefferson Monticello Virginia"; franked; postmarked Washington, 18 Jan.

John Forsyth (1780–1841), attorney and public official, was born in Fredericksburg and raised in Augusta, Georgia, before matriculating at the College of New Jersey (later Princeton University). Following his graduation in 1799, he studied law in Augusta and was admitted to the bar in 1802. Forsyth enjoyed a long

political and diplomatic career, beginning with his selection as attorney general of Georgia in 1808. He served as a Republican in the United States House of Representatives, 1813–18, and was promoted to fill a vacancy in the Senate late in 1818. The following year Forsyth resigned his seat to accept appointment as minister plenipotentiary to Spain, serving in this capacity until 1823. He returned thereafter to the House of Representatives from 1823 until his election as governor of Georgia in 1827. After a single gubernatorial term Forsyth was elected to the Senate once more and occupied this position from 1829 until 1834. While serving as a senator he supported President Andrew

Jackson, who rewarded Forsyth for his opposition to Nullification and defense of the president's attack on the Second Bank of the United States with appointment as secretary of state in 1834. He held this office until the term of Jackson's successor, Martin Van Buren, ended in 1841. Forsyth died in Washington (*ANB*; *DAB*; Alvin Laroy Duckett, *John Forsyth, Political Tactician* [1962]; *JEP*, 3:174, 175 [11, 15 Feb. 1819]; Jackson, *Papers*; Washington *Daily National Intelligencer*, 23, 28 Oct. 1841; gravestone inscription in Congressional Cemetery, Washington, D.C.).

To John Bent

SIR   [M]onticello Jan. 17. 19.

I have just recieved your letter of Dec. 24. and am sorry it is not in my power to give you the information you request as to the steps you must pursue to get your bounty in land. but retired as I am from all public business and scarcely ever going from home, I have paid no attention to the subject on which you ask my advice, and am entirely ignorant of it. but the best thing you can do is to write your case to mr Barbour, your representative in Congress, who can advise you with certainty how to proceed. no man in the world is more capable of putting you on the right track, and none I am sure will be more ready to do it. wishing you may succeed in obtaining whatever may be your just rights, I tender you my respects   TH: JEFFERSON

PoC (MHi); on verso of reused address cover to TJ; dateline faint; at foot of text (faint): "[M^r] John Bent"; endorsed by TJ.

To Nathaniel Potter

Monticello Jan. 17. 19.

Th: Jefferson presents his compliments to Doct^r Potter and his thanks for his learned and ingenious treatise on contagion which he has been so kind as to send him. he has read it with great satisfaction, and the more as it maintains an opinion which has long been his own and which he once ventured to declare in a public document in the hope that it might induce foreign governments to relax their quarantine regulations which were so oppressive to our commerce. he salutes Dr Potter with esteem and respect.

PoC (MHi); on verso of reused address cover of John Adams to TJ, 20 Oct. 1818; dateline at foot of text; endorsed by TJ.

Nathaniel Potter (ca. 1770–1843), physician and educator, was born in Easton, Maryland, and received a medical degree from the University of Pennsylvania in 1796, having studied under Benjamin Rush. Potter began to practice medicine in Baltimore the following year. He worked at the Baltimore General Dispensary,

1802–05, and in 1808 became professor of the theory and practice of medicine at the College of Medicine of Maryland (later the University of Maryland's school of medicine), a position he held until his death. Potter published regularly, with his contributions to medicine including proof, through experimentation on himself, that yellow fever was not contagious. Active in numerous medical organizations, he served as president of the Baltimore Medical Society in 1812 and the Medical Society of Maryland in 1817, and he sat on the state board of medical examiners, 1803–19. Potter died in Baltimore (*ANB*; *DAB*; *University of Pennsylvania Catalogue*, 565; Lyman H. Butterfield, ed., *Letters of Benjamin Rush* [1951], 2:764;

George H. Callcott, *A History of the University of Maryland* [1966]; Potter, *A Memoir on Contagion, more especially as it respects the Yellow Fever: read in convention of the Medical and Chirurgical Faculty of Maryland, On the 3d of June, 1817* [Baltimore, 1818; Poor, *Jefferson's Library*, 5 (no. 197)]; DNA: RG 29, CS, Md., Baltimore City, 1830, 1840; Baltimore *Sun* and Washington *Daily National Intelligencer*, both 3 Jan. 1843; *Maryland Medical and Surgical Journal* 3 [1843]: 391–2).

The PUBLIC DOCUMENT in which TJ declared that yellow fever was not contagious was his annual message to Congress of 3 Dec. 1805 (*JHR*, 5:184).

To Joel Yancey

DEAR SIR   Monticello Jan. 17. 19. Sunday

The waggons arrived here on Wednesday a little after the middle of the day. we were under extreme sufferance for the want of a short job of hauling, and I thought it better to set both about it that they might go back together; and the rather as every day's stay enabled Johnny Hemings to add another plough frame. they will accordingly carry you three made on Thursday, Friday & Saturday, and will start tomorrow morning (Monday) I shall be very glad to recieve the latter peas I liked so much the last year and hope Nace has saved me a full sowing of them. I wrote you the last year that Dick had delivered all his articles safe and thought so at the time. but I learnt afterwards that he did not deliver a bag containing a bushel of dried peaches which [he] said had dropped thro a hole in the bottom of his waggon; altho' no hole was seen which could have let such a mass thr[o'.] this year his soap weighs 38. ℔ instead of 45 ℔. and the bar[rel] of apples is a little more than half full. these repeated accidents cannot but excite suspicions of him, sufficient to make us attentive in future. I will ask the favor of you to send by Jerry the Athenian poplars in the nursery of the garden. you will know them by the stems being ribbed, which distinguishes them from the Lombardy poplars & Aspens in the same place. their roots should be covered very thick with straw, tied firmly on, so that the cold may not reach the roots, which it very certainly kills. the old bacon may remain as I shall pass a great proportion of the ensuing year there.   The unproductiveness of our crops which you notice in your letter, is indeed a serious calamity, and the more so to me as 3. years of war, & 4. years of Goodman & Darnell had thrown me into arrears which will require 2. or 3. good crops to extricate me from. yet I do not ascribe it to any want of management in yourself, but to the impoverishment of our fields by constant culture without any aid of manure; and this cause will continue to increase. we must either attend to the recruiting our lands, or abandon them & run away to Alibama, as so many of our countrymen are doing, who find it easier to resolve on quitting their country, than, to change the practices in husbandry to which they have been brought up. straw will do something, good manure more, but nothing short of plaister and clover can recruit our extensive fields. the miracles this is working in this neighborhood can be believed only by those who see them. my fields here, which in my hands produced 4, 5. or 6. bushels to the acre, are now giving my grandson from 15. to 18. after one or two alternations only of plaister & clover. my neighbor Rogers, who while tenant [. . .] [Harv]ey's estate adjoining us, had reduced it to 5. bushels, now that [. . .] proprietor has made this last year from 25. to 30. bushels one[1] thro the whole of his fields, & all by plaister & clover. we must either go into the same course, or run away. if we cannot get the plaister carried up for 10.D. we must give 15. if not for 15. we must give 20. if you can make arrangements therefore for bringing up & grinding and will so inform me, I will write to Capt Peyton of Richmond to procure the plaister. then it may be necessary to buy the clover seed, but I hope never after the 1st year. the mortality among our negroes is still more serious as involving moral as well as interested considerations. they are well fed, and well clothed, & I have had no reason to believe that any overseer, since Griffin's time, has over worked them. accordingly the deaths among the grown ones seem ascribable to natural causes. but the loss of 5. little ones in a year induces me to fear that the overseers do not permit the women to devote as much time as is necessary to the care of their children: that they view their labor as the 1st object and the raising their child but as secondary. I consider the labor of a breeding woman as no object, and that a child raised every 2. years is of more profit than the crop of the best laboring man. in this, as in all other cases, providence has made our interests & our duties coincide perfectly. women too are destroyed by exposure to wet at certain periodical indispositions to which nature has subjected them. with respect therefore to our women & their children I must pray you to inculcate upon the overseers that it is not their labor, but their increase which is the first consideration with us. with respect to yourself my confidence is entire; and I am as

[582]

well satisfied [t]hat every thing under your eye is going on for the best as if I were there to see the fact. I know that the considerations under which you act are of a high & pure order, and it is a heart felt satisfaction to me to feel as well as to assure you of my sincere friendship & respect   TH: JEFFERSON

PoC (MHi); with first two pages on re-used address cover of Richard N. Thweatt to TJ, 29 Oct. 1818, and third page on verso of reused address cover of Bernard Peyton to TJ, 29 Oct. 1818; damaged at seal; at foot of first page: "Mr Yancey"; endorsed by TJ.

[1] Thus in manuscript, with a blank space preceding this word.

From Joseph C. Cabell

DEAR SIR,   Richmond. 4 p. m. 18th Jan: 1819

Grateful, truly grateful, is it to my heart, to be able to announce to you; the result of this day's proceedings in the House of Delegates. In Committee of the whole, the question was taken, after an elaborate discussion, on the motion[1] to strike the Central College from the Bill. The vote was as follows;—for striking out 69—against it 114—majority ag^t striking out 45. This is a decisive victory. Immediately after this decision, Mr Baldwin of Augusta, rose & made a most eloquent appeal to the Western Delegation, calling on them, to dismiss local feelings, & to unite with the majority, in the support of the measure. The Bill passed to a 3^d reading nem: con. Having left the House before the critical vote on the site, to avoid the shock of feeling, which I should have been compelled to sustain, I did not hear Mr Baldwin. But I am told the scene was truly affecting. A great part of the House was in tears: & on the rising of the House the eastern members hovered around Mr Baldwin: some shook him by the hand: others sollicited an introduction. Such magnanimity in a defeated adversary excited universal applause. The discussion must have produced a considerable effect. This morning Mr Hunter of Essex—an intelligent member, expressed great fears. The mode of drawing the lines was called in question—as favoring the Central College. I had prepared East & West & N & South lines, which threw the point of intersection somewhere near the S. end of Fluvanna. One of the Rockbridge Delegates suggested[2] another method of settling the pretensions of[3] rival sites, with a view to discredit the mode pursued by yourself. His idea was this—draw a line from one of the places to the other—bisect this line by another line runing across[4] the state. And the place which should be found on the side of the line, where the greatest mass of population should fall, would be nearest the center of population. This idea was suggested on saturday: & I did not hear of it till last night. I rose early this morning & with the assistance of Mr Hoomes of K. & Queen, my room mate, applied this rule: & found to the east of the Line 137,000 white inhabitants more than to the west. These tables were used in the debate. One of the Rockbridge delegates objected to the statement about the center of population lately published in the Enquirer: that the free negros & mulattos were included: the fact was admitted, & the coloured people deducted & the center still fell east of Charlottesville. I imagine you fell into the error of including the coloured population, by deducting the slaves from the Totals in the Census of 1810.—At a future day, I will give you further particulars, & inform you of the names of the gentlemen who have contributed to the happy results of this day.—I have just received Chancellor Carr's letter. The Hint was unnecessary: we shall take care of the bill in the Senate. I do not write to him,[5] because I suppose he has left you. I awoke two nights ago, about 3 o'clock with an alarming spitting of blood, which continued till 10' o'clock. It was probably brought on by exposure to bad weather & loss of sleep. I have been twice bled, & have taken medicine: & feel myself on the recovery.—I feel happy in the idea that this note will give you great pleasure.

  faithfully yours   JOSEPH C. CABELL

RC (ViU: TJP-PC); endorsed by TJ as received 22 Jan. 1819 and so recorded in SJL. RC (DLC); address cover only; with PoC of TJ to Joseph Miller, 30 Jan. 1819, on verso; addressed: "Mr Jefferson Monticello"; franked; postmarked Richmond, 18 Jan.

On 16 Jan. 1819 Rockbridge County delegate Andrew Alexander moved TO STRIKE THE CENTRAL COLLEGE FROM THE BILL naming it as the site of the University of Virginia. On the same day Briscoe G. Baldwin made a lengthy speech in the House of Delegates extolling the advantages of Staunton as a potential site for the university and calling on the eastern portion of the state to recognize both the importance of their western brethren and their efforts during the War of 1812 by locating the institution to the west. When it became clear on 18 Jan. that his advocacy of Staunton had failed, Baldwin nonetheless urged THE WESTERN DELE-GATION to support the creation of the University of Virginia in the interest of state unity (*Richmond Enquirer*, 19 Jan. 1819).

Nemine contradicente (NEM: CON.): "without opposition or dissent" (*Black's Law Dictionary*). John Bowyer, of Rockbridge County, objected to the MODE PURSUED by TJ for determining the center of the state's population, both for the arbitrary manner in which the lines were drawn and for the inclusion of free blacks in the population count (*Richmond Enquirer*, 19 Jan. 1819; see also TJ's Notes on the Geographic Center of Virginia's Population, printed above at 4 Aug. 1818).

[1] Word interlined in place of "question."
[2] Word interlined in place of "proposed."
[3] Cabell here canceled "<*the two*> Lexington & Charlottesville."
[4] Manuscript: "a cross."
[5] Preceding two words interlined.

From Mathew Carey & Son

Sir,   Philad[a] Jan. 18. 1819
We hope you will have the goodness to excuse the long delay of an answer to your favour on the subject of Baxter's Edition of Hume's England.

The arrangements of our business are incompatible with the undertaking such a work at present. Should any new plan take place, we shall give the subject that serious consideration, to which the high character you bestow on the work entitles it

Respectfully,

√ your ob[t] h[ble] serv[ts]   M Carey & son.

RC (MHi); in Mathew Carey's hand; dateline at foot of text; at head of text: "Hon Thomas Jefferson, Esq[r]"; endorsed by TJ as a letter from Mathew Carey received 24 Jan. 1819 and so recorded in SJL.

From Joseph Jones

Sir   Peters[bg]—Coll[rs] office 18[h] Jan[y] 1819
This morning I was informed by m[r] Patrick Durkin of the house of Durkin, Henderson & co. owners of the Brig Planter, Daniel Anderson master from marseilles that the Brig w[d] not come up to City point to unload but w[d] at Norfolk—I wrote you dated 8[h] Jan[y] 1819 by mail, that the Brig w[d] be up here in a few days, as they then told me.   our Consul at marseilles m[r] Stephen Cathalan has not yet sent me Invoice of your wines, olive oil, anchovies, macaronis, & immortal Flowers—I have nothing but a bill of lading for your things.— There are also one Cask of thirty-two Gallons red wine & two boxes of red wine for Thomas Jefferson Randolph esq[r] no Invoice, only a bill of lading.—as the Brig does not intend up here, until repaired I think you had better as soon as the Invoices come to hand, have the things for you & m[r] Randolph entered at Norfolk and I will endorse the Bills of Lading to any one you may direct me.

I am Sir with the greatest respect Your ob[t] Sert.

Joseph Jones Coll[r]

RC (DLC); idiosyncratic punctuation editorially omitted; endorsed by TJ as received 25 Jan. 1819 and so recorded in SJL. RC (MHi); address cover only; with PoC of TJ to James Eastburn & Company, 25 May 1819, on verso; addressed: "Thomas Jefferson esq[r] Late President of the United States. Monticello"; franked; postmarked Petersburg, 19 Jan.

From Joseph Milligan

Dear Sir Georgetown January 18th 1819

On the 15th instant I received the Box of Books to bind I exchanged two or three letters with Mr Gray of Fredericksburg befor I received them the delay has been between Fredericksburg and this place as during the frosty weather the steam boat has been laid up and the stages are not as yet regular but I trust the steam Boat will run again as the river is now entirely open and I trust as the weather yet remains mild that it will not again be closed this winter

Accept my best thanks for your kind caution in your Esteemed favour of the 12th respecting[1] Ricardo my intention is to take of a very small Edition say five or six hundred one half of which I will have engaged with the Members of Congress & officers of Government

Your Books are now in the Binders hands and shall be finished as speedily as is consistant with good work

Some years ago I published Malthus on Population I See that he has lately published a third Volume which when I can get I will put to press it is very highly spoken of When I get Ricardo through the press I will Send you a Copy

Yours respectfully JOSEPH MILLIGAN

RC (DLC); endorsed by TJ as received 22 Jan. 1819 and so recorded in SJL. RC (DLC); address cover only; with PoC of TJ to Wilson Cary Nicholas, 28 Jan. 1819, on verso; addressed: "Thomas Jefferson Esqr Monticello Milton virginia"; franked; postmarked (faint) Georgetown, [1]8 Jan.

Milligan's earlier edition of the work of Thomas R. MALTHUS was *An Essay on the Principle of Population; or, a View of its Past and Present Effects on Human Happiness*, 2 vols. (first American ed., Washington, 1809; for an earlier ed. see Sowerby, no. 2938). Malthus had LATELY PUBLISHED updates to the work as *Additions to the Fourth and Former Editions of An Essay on the Principle of Population* (London, 1817).

[1] Manuscript: "respeting."

To James Monroe

Monticello Jan. 18. 19.

You oblige me infinitely, dear Sir, by sending me the Congressional documents in pamphlet form. for as they come out by peice-meal in the newspapers I never read them. and indeed I read no newspapers now but Ritchie's, and in that chiefly the advertisements, as being the only truths we can rely on in a newspaper. but in a pamphlet, where we can go thro' the whole subject when once taken up, and seen in all it's parts, we avoid the risk of false judgment which a partial view endangers. on the subject of these communications I will venture a suggestion which, should it have occurred to yourself or to mr Adams as is probable, will only be a little labor lost. I propose then that you select mr Adams's 4. principal letters on the Spanish subject, to wit, that which establishes our right to the Rio-bravo which was laid before the Congress of 1817.18. his letters to Onis of July 23. & Nov. 30. and to Erving of Nov. 28. perhaps also that of Dec. 2. have them well translated into French, and send English & French copies to all our ministers at foreign courts, and to our Consuls. the paper on our right to the Riobravo, and the letter to Erving of Nov. 28. are the most important, and are among the ablest compositions I have ever seen, both as to logic and style. a selection of these few in pamphlet for[m]^1 will be read by every body; but, by nobody, if buried among Onis's long-winded and tergiversating diatribes, and all the documents; the volume of which alone will deter an European reader from ever^2 [opening] it: indeed it would be worth while to have the two most important of these published in the Leyden gazette, from which it would go into the other leading gazettes of Europe. it is of great consequence to us, & merits every possible endeavor, to maintain in Europe a correct opinion of our political morality. these papers will place us erect with the world in the important cases of our Western boundary, of our military entrance into Florida, & of the execution of Arbuthnot and Ambrister. on the two first subjects it is very natural for an European to go wrong, and to give in to^3 the charge of ambition, which the English papers (read every where) endeavor to fix on us. if the European mind is once set right on these points, they will go with us in all the subsequent proceedings, without further enquiry.   While on the subject of this correspondence, I will presume also to suggest to mr Adams the question whether he should not send back Onis's letters in which he has the impudence to qualify you by the term 'his Excellency'? an American gentleman in Europe can rank with the first nobility because we have no titles which stick him at any particular place in their line. so the President of the US. under that designation ranks with Emperors and kings, but add mr Onis's courtesy of 'his [e]x[ce]llency,' and he is then on a level with mr Onis himself, with the Governors of provinces, and even of every petty fort in Europe, or the colonies. I salute you with constant affection & respect.   TH: JEFFERSON

PoC (DLC); on portion of reused address cover to TJ; two words faint; at foot of first page: "President Monroe"; endorsed by TJ.

TJ probably read John Quincy Adams's 4. PRINCIPAL LETTERS ON THE SPANISH SUBJECT in *Message from the President of the United States, transmitting Copies of* the Remainder of the Documents referred to in his Message of the Seventeenth Ult (Washington, 1818; inconsistently paginated), which printed Adams to Luis de Onís of 23 July and 30 Nov. 1818 (also printed in *ASP, Foreign Relations,* 4:497–9, 545–6), and *Message from the President of the United States, transmitting, in pursuance of a resolution of the House of Representatives, such further information, in Relation to our Affairs with Spain, as, in his opinion, is not inconsistent with the public interest to divulge* (Washington, 1819; inconsistently paginated), which printed Adams's letters to George W. Erving of 28 Nov. and 2 Dec.

1818 (extract) (also printed in *ASP, Foreign Relations,* 4:539–45, 546–7).

Onís referred to Monroe as HIS EXCELLENCY in his letter to Adams of 6 Dec. 1817, printed in *Message from the President of the United States, transmitting the Correspondence between the Department of State, and the Spanish Minister, residing here, Showing the Present State of the Relations between the Two Governments* (Washington, 1818; possibly Poor, *Jefferson's Library,* 11 [no. 662]), 11–3.

[1] Edge trimmed.
[2] Word interlined.
[3] Manuscript: "into."

To Bernard Peyton

Jan. 18. 19. inclosed to Cap[t] Peyton the rec[t] for a box of books from Fernagus. also ment[d] the cask of rice which would be deliv[d] him from Charleston. all to be forwarded by Johnson's boats & exp. reimbursed by P.G.

also requested him to purchase & forward by Johnson 3. tons of Plaister to be paid for by P.G.

FC (MHi); summary in TJ's hand and endorsed by him. Enclosure not found.

P.G.: Patrick Gibson.

To John Adams

DEAR SIR   Monticello Jan. 19. 19.

About a week before I recieved your favor of Dec. 30. the 22[d] N[o] of the North American review had come to hand, without my knowing from what quarter. the letter of mr Channing to mr Shaw, which you have been so good as to inclose, founds a presumption that it was from mr Channing, and that he is the editor. I had never before seen the work; but have read this N[o] with attention and great satisfaction. it may stand boldly on the shelf by the side of the Edinburg Review; and, as I find that mr Channing has agents in George town and Richmond, where I can readily make the necessary payments, I shall write to one of them to enter me as a subscriber. I see with pride that as we are ahead of Europe in Political science, so on other subjects we are getting along side of them.

I hope you have read our University Report with approbation, as I am sure you will the work of Tracy, if you trouble yourself with such subjects. we are all atiptoe here in the hourly expectation of hearing what our legislature decides on the Report. being a good piece of a century behind the age they live in, we are not without fear as to their conclusions. we have to contend with so many biasses, personal, local, fanatical, financial E^{t}c. that we cannot foresee in what their combinations will result.

God bless you, and preserve you in good health & spirits.

TH: JEFFERSON

RC (MHi: Adams Papers); addressed: "President Adams Quincy. Mass."; franked; postmarked Charlottesville, 21 Jan.; endorsed by Adams as answered 29 Jan. PoC (DLC); on verso of reused address cover of Joseph Milligan to TJ, 30 Oct. 1818; endorsed by TJ.

Earlier in the month Jefferson family friend Hore Browse Trist reported from Monticello that "they expect every day to see in the papers that the University is fixed here but the Legislature being composed of ignorant drunken beasts they pay as little attention to that as they do to any thing else that is of consequence" (Trist to Nicholas P. Trist, 1 Jan. 1819 [DLC: NPT]).

From William C. Rives

DEAR SIR,   Richmond January 20th 1819.—

I have it in my power to congratulate you, at last, on an event, which constitutes a proud epoch in the history of Virginia. The Bill for the establishment of an University at the Central college was passed on yesterday in the House of Delegates by a majority of 141 to 28. Altho' the previous votes taken in the committee of the whole had left little doubt as to the final success of the measure, yet the result was much more decisively favorable than the most sanguine of us had allowed ourselves to hope for. The Bill, in every stage of it's progress, encountered a vehement, active & persevering opposition, on the floor of the house; and a system of intrigue & cabal was employed against it, out of doors, which, as being bottomed on feelings of local jealousy & conducted with great secresy, it was much more difficult to counteract. To triumph, under such circumstances, is a <u>double</u> <u>victory</u>, which must be peculiarly gratifying to every friend of science in Virginia.—Our success, however, was purchased at the price of an additional appropriation of twenty thousand dollars for the education of the poor. There still remain ten thousand dollars of the revenue of the Literary fund unappropriated, the greater part, if not all, of which

[589]

ought to go to the University. But whether it would be prudent, at this time, to make a farther experiment on the liberality of the Legislature, in relation to the university, is a question of great delicacy, which I am not prepared to decide. There would certainly be danger, in attempting to stretch the string too far, of breaking it.—Several of the existing establishments have already put in claims to the residuum of the fund—William & Mary, Hampden Sidney, & Washington Academy. I do not think that any of these applications will succeed; but if the university were to conflict with them by a contemporaneous motion, on it's own behalf, their defeat would be attributed to it's interference, & embody a host of enemies against it, that might be formidable hereafter. Whether, under these circumstances, it would not be politic to make a merit of our modesty, & to hold back until a future session of the Legislature, when the actual progress of the establishment will develope a demand for farther appropriations, & at the same time, afford the public a pledge for the ultimate fulfilment of their expectations, is the point now presented for consideration. I should be much pleased to know your views on the subject.—

I received, some time ago, the copy of Tracy's Political Economy which you were so kind as to send me. The numerous & embarrassing avocations, to which I am subject here as a member of the Legislature, have prevented me from reading it regularly; but so far as I have looked into it, I have found no difficulty in recognising the same vigorous & analytical mind that produced the Review of Montesquieu. It is among the many obligations which your countrymen are proud to acknowledge to you, that you have been the first to unlock to them these copious & profound sources of information in two of the most important studies connected with the happiness of human society.—

I have heard, with heart-felt satisfaction, of the entire restoration of your health, since I had the pleasure of seeing you; & sincerely hope that it will be given you to see the Institution, which has just risen into existence under your patronage, a monument, not unworthy of your fame, or of the love & veneration of your native State.—I beg you to accept assurances of my most profound respect & grateful affection.—

W C RIVES.—

RC (DLC); addressed: "Thomas Jefferson Esq. Monticello near Milton. in Albemarle County"; franked; postmarked Richmond, 21 Jan.; endorsed by TJ as received 24 Jan. 1819 and so recorded in SJL.

The Virginia House of Delegates approved the bill that would become "An act for the establishment of an University" on 19 Jan. 1819 by a MAJORITY of 143 to 28 (*JHD* [1818–19 sess.], 112). The ADDITIONAL APPROPRIATION from the Literary Fund of $20,000 for the education of the poor was included in the legislation as passed on 25 Jan. 1819 (*Acts of Assembly* [1818–19 sess.], 17).

On this date Rives applauded TJ in a letter informing John H. Cocke of the bill's success: "Among the many sources of congratulation that present themselves on this occasion, it is not the least with me that the man, to whom this country owes more than to any other that ever existed, with the exception of General Washington alone, lives to see the consummation of all his wishes in the establishment of an Institution, which will be a lasting monument to his fame. I sincerely hope that his years may be prolonged, in order that he may fix a character on an institution, which is itself to exert a decisive influence on the character of posterity" (RC in ViU: JHC).

From William Young

RESPECTED FRIEND,   Boston Jany. 20th 1819.—

The mention of your name in print, or conversation, always affords me a peculiar pleasure; and am always ready to defend your well merited fame, whenever I hear it called in question. But, my Honoured Friend, there is one thing, for which I am in want of data, when the subject is mentioned, and on which, I have heretofore ventured to presume:—It is, your opinion of the <u>sacred writings</u>, and the character of <u>Jesus Christ</u>, "The Saviour of Sinners"?

You have now arrived at a good old age,—have read "many books,"—have seen much of men in [var]ious situations of human nature,—and must now, from your accumulated experience, "be no longer in doubt, between two opinions."

The last words of D^r <u>Franklin</u>, to a young man, were in favour of the <u>truth</u> of Divine Revelation. <u>Washington</u>! <u>Newton</u>! and other great minds, were in favour of the truth of the claims of "The Holy Bible"!—Will you <u>favour</u> me; by sparing from your scientific labours, and literary pleasures; one hours writing in a letter on this subject? What are your views of the claims of <u>The Bible</u>, as being a Divine Revelation, from the <u>Supreme Being</u> by the inspiration of the prophets &c. And the character of <u>Jesus Christ</u>, as the Saviour of men, fro[m] the guilt and punishment, due for the transgressio[ns] of the law of God, according to the doctrins of the Apostles of the religion of Christ?—

The above favour will be very highly esteemed by yours &c very Respectfully.   WILLIAM YOUNG

RC (MHi); dateline beneath signature; mutilated at seal and edge trimmed; at foot of text: "Thomas Jefferson Esqr"; endorsed by TJ as received 31 Jan. 1819, with his additional bracketed notation: "fanatic," and so recorded in SJL.

A William Young was active as a gilder in Boston between 1820 and 1827 (*The Boston Directory* [1820]: 227; [1827]: 292).

When Yale College president Ezra Stiles queried him near the end of his life about his religious views, Benjamin FRANKLIN responded that he believed that God created the universe but that, although the moral and religious systems of Jesus were the best in the world, he had doubts as to his divinity (Franklin to Stiles, 9 Mar. 1790 [CtY: Stiles Papers]).

From Joseph C. Cabell

DEAR SIR,   Senate Chamber. 21st Jan: 1819.

On the 19th inst the University Bill passed the House of Delegates, only 28 members voting against it. Yesterday I moved its committment in the Senate. The Committee are Messrs Johnson, Alfred Powell, Taliaferro, Hoomes of K. & Queen, Mallory, Hay & myself. We met to-day at 10—Mr Mallory being absent. I had previously agreed with my friends to admit no amendments.[1] Mr Johnson proposed various amendments, begining with such as were unimportant, and proceeding to one of vital importance—viz to reduce the additional appropriation of 20,000$ for the education of the poor to $5000. We voted him down, after full discussion in the Committee. The committee has risen to meet again tomorrow so[2] as to give Mr Johnson an opportunity to offer other amendments. I now think he will make efforts to change the site in the House. But I think[3] you may be tranquil on this subject. The Bill will probably[4] be a law in three days from this time.

faithfully yours   J. C. CABELL.

P. S. My wife, hearing of my late attack of hemorage, has become very unhappy, and in conjunction with my Williamsburg friends, urges me to withdraw to that place. Happily I am getting over the attack, and my breast is much less sore than it was a few days past. I am strongly in hopes the rupture was confined to some of the Vessels of the throat. As soon as the University Bill passes I shall retire to Judge Coalter's and attend to my duties in the Senate, as my health will permit, from that place: and should it be necessary I will go to Williamsburg. But the connection of the Eastern & Western Waters, is a subject of great importance in itself and I have promised[5] to render every service in my power to Mr Thompson of Kenawha. Mrs C. will[6] come up on sunday with the Miss Coalters from Williamsburg.

RC (ViU: TJP-PC); endorsed by TJ as received 24 Jan. 1819 and so recorded in SJL. RC (MHi); address cover only; with PoC of TJ to John Steele, 25 May 1819, on verso; addressed: "Mr Jefferson Monticello"; franked; postmarked Richmond, 21 Jan.

[1] Manuscript: "admendments."
[2] Manuscript: "So so."
[3] Preceding two words interlined.
[4] Word interlined.
[5] Preceding nine words interlined in place of "on which I wish."
[6] Cabell here canceled "join me at Judge Coalter's."

From John C. Calhoun

DEAR SIR, Washington 21st Jany 1819

I have read with much interest the proceedings and report of the commissioners for the University of Virginia, with a copy of which you have honored me. The view presented by the report is concise and comprehensive; and the system of education, which it proposes, appears to me, to be excellent.

I most sincerely hope, that your effort in the cause of education may be crowned with complete success. Nothing is now wanting to produce this happy result, but the enlightened patronage of your state Legislature; and supported as the report of the Commissioners is, by the names of many of our most enlightened citizens, its favourable reception by the Legislature can scarcely be doubted.

The claim of M. Poirey has passed the House of Representatives;[1] and it will probably pass the Senate without difficulty.

That you may long continue to enjoy in the full possession of your health and faculties the gratitude of our country for your illustrious Services is my most ardent prayer. J. C. CALHOUN

RC (DLC); at foot of text: "Thomas Jefferson Es^r"; endorsed by TJ as received 27 Jan. 1819 and so recorded in SJL.

Joseph Léonard Poirey's CLAIM to compensation for service during the Revolutionary War passed in the United States House of Representatives on 15 Jan. 1819 and in the Senate on 17 Feb. 1819 (*JHR*, 12:189; *JS*, 8:273).

[1] Manuscript: "Representative."

From the Jefferson Benevolent Institution of Pennsylvania

RESPECTED SIR Philadelphia January 21^stl 1819

In Complyence With a Resolution of a Benevolent Institution Lately Estabblished In This City, Which have Highly Honoured Themselves In Assuming your Illustrious name? They Have further Unanimously Agreed That The Sec^y of The Said Institution Should Take The Liberty on Behalf of The Said Society to Address you, and Request your Approbation to be Considered a Honoured Member Thereoff—and further to Assertain The Birth of Our Pattern Which is a Day Calculated to be Celebrated In his Memory?

Signed On Behalf of The Jefferson Benevolent Institution of Pennsylvania LEWIS D BELAIR Sec^y

P S

Individuelly accept The Assurance of my most Profond Respect
for your Health[2] and Happiness,   L D BELAIR

RC (DLC); endorsed by TJ as a letter from Belair received 28 Jan. 1819 and so recorded (with additional bracketed notation: "Sec^y Benev soc.") in SJL. RC (DLC); address cover only; with PoC of TJ to William Wallace, 20 May 1819, on verso; addressed: "Thomas Jefferson Esqr Montecelo Near Charlotte Ville V^a p Mail"; stamped; franked; postmarked Philadelphia, 21 Jan.

The Jefferson Benevolent Institution of Pennsylvania was formed in Philadelphia on 16 Jan. 1819 and incorporated on 22 Mar. of that year. Members paid monthly dues and in turn received payments when ill and to defray funeral expenses. The preamble to the society's constitution indicated that the members, "taking the example of THOMAS JEFFERSON, Esq. late President of the United States, for our pattern, have assumed his illustrious name" (*Charter of the Jefferson Benevolent Institution of Pennsylvania* [Philadelphia, (1819)]; Robert Desilver, *The Philadelphia Index, or Directory, for 1823* [Philadelphia, 1823], lxxvi).

[1] Reworked from "20."
[2] Manuscript: "Helth."

From Bernard Peyton

DEAR SIR   Rich^d 21 Janu^y 1819

I was favor'd this morning with your esteem^d letter covering bill of Lading for a Box of Books from New York, which when received, as well as the Cask of Rice from Charleston, shall be forwarded by the first trip of Mr. Johnson's Boat—I will also take pleasure in purchasing and forwarding the Three tons Plaster mentioned, & present the bills to Mr. Gibson for payment when they shall reach a sum worth while—

I congratulate you with all my heart, as well as the state generally on the passage of the bill in the <u>lower</u> House for the establishment of a University at Charlottesville—not a doubt is entertained of its final passage in the Senate—   I have already a fine, promising Son growing up to be educated at that College, I hope to usefulness and respectability, if not to distinction—my greatest happiness would be to see him, even in a remote degree under your direction, as I sincerely hope he will—

With sentiments of real affection & respect Yours most Truely
BERNARD PEYTON

RC (MHi); endorsed by TJ as received 24 Jan. 1819 and so recorded in SJL. RC (MHi); address cover only; with PoC of TJ to Joel Yancey, 25 May 1819, on verso; addressed: "Thomas Jefferson Monticello Milton"; stamped; postmarked (faint) [Richmond?], 21 Jan.

To Thomas Cooper

TH: JEFFERSON TO DOCT^R COOPER　　　　Monticello Jan. 22. 19.

Mr Richardson had left us about an hour when I recieve[d][1] information from Richmond that the University bill had passed our house of Representatives by a majority of between 50. and 100 on different votes. altho' now certain of our establishment I will not[2] write to you finally till the bill is finally past. there are but 2. votes against it in the Senate. as soon as past we shall have a meeting of our Visitors, and form the new plan of operations.[3] in the mean time I will only say that we count upon you & in early spring, [as][4] I am sure I shall be authorised to write you a final letter to your mind. we have rented an excellent situation for you, opposite the College about 2. or 300 yards f[rom] it. I dare say you remarked & remember the house

Mr Richardson on his way here got badly bit in the leg by a [. . .] he left us this morning for Richmond from whence he expects to get a passage to Philadelphia by water.[5] but you will probably recieve this before you see him. Affectionate & friendly salutations.

PoC (ViU: TJP); on verso of reused address cover of Joseph Hutton to TJ, 2 Oct. 1818; dateline at foot of text; torn at seal; endorsed by TJ.

One day prior to this, TJ recorded loaning Jared Richardson $20. On 21 Jan. 1819 TJ also indicated that he had received $50 from James Leitch (*MB*, 2:1350). The latter sum was enclosed in an undated letter written and initialed by Leitch's clerk James Brown on his employer's behalf, which stated that "The enclosed $50 is in as small Notes as could be procured" (RC in DLC: TJ Papers, 214:38255; with PoC of TJ to Mathew Carey, 29 Jan. 1819, on verso; addressed: "Mr. Jefferson Monticello"; with additional notation of "$10" by Brown above address).

[1] Word faint.
[2] Word added in margin.
[3] Omitted period at right margin editorially supplied.
[4] Word faint.
[5] Preceding two words interlined.

To Fernagus De Gelone

SIR　　　　　　　　　　　　　Monticello Jan. 22. 19

Your favor of the 7th is recieved, and by that I percieve I am 18.D. in your debt, and therefore inclose you a 20.D. bill, the surplus of which may go into account.

I observe that l'Algebre d'Euler is not mentioned in your account. is this an omission of the account, or that the book has not been sent? you will find it mentioned in my letter of Nov. 16. in mr Belair's of Nov. 26. and finally in mine of Dec. 9. if you have not sent it, and still have a copy I shall be glad to reci[eve][1] it by mail, only observing now as always never to send a larger book than an 8vo by mail, nor more than one volume in a week, not to overburthen our village mail.

I had from you the last year a French translation of Euripides. in the report of the Institute to Napoleon (in Feb. 1808. I believe it was) M. Dacier mentions with approbation a translation of Aeschyle which I should be glad to get if you have it, and als[o] one of Sophocles if there be a good one in prose. in Kestleoot's notes on that discourse (chez Immerzeel. Hollande 1809) you will see the Aeschylus mentioned.   I salute you with esteem & respect

TH: JEFFERSON

PoC (MHi); on verso of reused address cover of John H. Cocke to TJ, 20 Oct. 1818; edge trimmed; at foot of text: "M. Fernagus de Gelone"; endorsed by TJ.

Recorded in SJL with additional bracketed notation "20.D."

[1] Word faint.

From Robert Patterson

SIR   Philadelphia Jany 23, '19.

Sometime in the beginning of winter, a young gentleman, Mr Trist, I believe, brought me a telescope which he said you had sent to be repaired. He also informed me that you had sent me a letter, but that he had left it, inadvertently, at Washington, with his portmantua & would forward it from N. york where he expected it would be sent. I have not yet, however, received it. The telescope was immediately put into the hands of Mr Davenport to be repaired, & after repeated calls & solicitations, he this day informed me that all the eye-glasses for celestial observations are missing, & cannot be supplied here.—He can however fit it up for land-observations, at a small expense—not exceeding $10—   You will please, Sir, to signify whether you will have it thus repaired—& in what manner to have it forwarded when completed—

I am, Sir, with the greatest esteem Your obed^t Servt—

R^T PATTERSON

RC (MHi); at foot of text: "Thomas Jefferson"; endorsed by TJ as received 31 Jan. 1819 and so recorded in SJL.

PORTMANTUA: an obsolete variant of "portmanteau" (OED).

To Simeon DeWitt

Sir   Monticello Jan. 24. 19.

Your favor of the 13th is duly recieved with the pamphlet it covered on an agricultural college, for which I pray you to accept my thanks. I have always thought that a professorship of Agriculture should make a part of the establishment in all our Universities, thro' which it's principles, and in some degree it's processes, might be taught, and our students retire to their homes from College, with a competent knolege of it's theory and an enlightened taste for it's practice. this is the more necessary in our country, where so great a proportion of the students are of the Agricultural character. whether it would be better to detach this branch from the other sciences, and to make of it a separate institution, I am not prepared to say. the proposition is new and would require consideration. but whatever opinion I might form on further consideration, I should be far from the presumption of[1] meaning that it should be offered to the public for their guidance. neither propriety nor inclination would permit me to obtrude myself as the director of public opinion. age, on the contrary, and the state of rest which it so much desires, urge a retirement from notice, and a resignation to the existing generation of the direction of their own concerns, which I do with more pleasure than I ever had in it's participation. you will then, Sir, I am assured, excuse my declining that portion of your request which would propose to add the slender effect of my opinion, if I had one, to the weighty considerations presented in your own pamphlet, and will be so good as to accept at the same time the assurance of my high respect and esteem.

Th: Jefferson

PoC (DLC); at foot of text: "Simeon   [1] TJ here canceled "having."
De Witt esq."

To Richard Duke

Sir   Monticello Jan. 24. 19.

The duties of a Proctor for the Central college are of two characters so distinct, that it is difficult to find them associated in the same person. the one part of these duties is to make contracts with workmen, superintend their execution, see that they are according to the plan, performed faithfully and in a workman like manner, settle their accounts, and pay them off. the other part is to hire common laborers, overlook them, provide subsistence, and do whatever else is necessary for the institution. for this latter part mr Barksdale is fully qualified: but the other part we have thought would be better done by a person more accustomed to that sort of business, and mr Garrett has given me a hope you would undertake this part. if you could devote two days in the week to it, it would be quite sufficient, but if this is incompatible with your other business, one day in the week would do. whatever agreement as to these particulars, or as to compensation, shall be arranged between mr Garrett and yourself, will be confirmed, and we should wish your entrance on your branch of the office as soon as we learn that the bill for the establishment of the University at the site of the Central College has passed both houses of legislature. I salute you with esteem & respect.

Th: Jefferson

RC (ViU: TJP); addressed: "Mʳ Duke near Lindsey's store"; franked; postmarked Charlottesville, 26 Jan. PoC (DLC); on verso of reused address cover of George Washington Jeffreys to TJ, 3 Nov. 1818; endorsed by TJ.

Richard Duke (1778–1849), artisan, came to Albemarle County in 1806 and in 1821 bought a milling complex known as the Rivanna Mills, which he ran with his brother James Duke. Both men also worked as carpenters. Duke subscribed $200 toward the establishment of Central College, but in 1819 he evidently declined TJ's offer to contract with and superintend the efforts of workmen at the University of Virginia and thus divide the duties of proctor with Nelson Barksdale. That same year he did become an Albemarle County magistrate. Duke was a director of the Rivanna Navigation Company in 1829 and served as county sheriff in 1847. He was in possession of twenty-eight slaves in 1820. Named a potential appraiser of TJ's estate in 1826, Duke did not serve. After his own death his personal property was valued at $228.77 (Duke family Bible records [ViU]; Woods, *Albemarle*, 181–2; Elizabeth F. Archer, "Paper Memories: Recalling the Dukes of Albemarle," *MACH* 59 [2001]: 87–9; DNA: RG 29, CS, Albemarle Co., 1810–40; James Duke and Richard Duke to John H. Cocke, 20 Apr. 1814 [ViU: JHC]; Master List of Subscribers to Central College, [after 7 May 1817], document 5 in a group of documents on The Founding of the University of Virginia: Central College, 1816–1819, printed above at 5 May 1817; K. Edward Lay, *The Architecture of Jefferson Country: Charlottesville and Albemarle County, Virginia* [2000], 213, 318; Admission of TJ's Will to Probate and Appointment of Appraisers, 7 Aug. 1826, Albemarle Co. Order Book [1826], 247; *Richmond Enquirer*, 24 Apr. 1829, 12 Jan. 1837, 9 Aug. 1839; Albemarle Co. Will Book, 21:133–4).

To Thomas C. Flournoy

Sir   Monticello Jan. 24. 19.

Altho' age, and the state of rest so grateful to it have obliged me to retire from the business of letter-writing, I feel myself bound by the kind expressions in your letter of the 4ᵗʰ inst. to acknolege it's reciept, and to return you my thanks for this proof of your good will.

the preference you express for a military vocation, over the labors of the law, may, by the circumstances of war, become valuable to our country. but every good citizen will deprecate the occurrence of these circumstances, and this employment of your services. I have lived to see my country labor thro' three wars, all of them finally succesful. yet I can pronounce from experience that one is enough for the life of one man.   I participate with particular pleasure in the praises you so justly bestow on our brave, honest, and patriotic Col° R. M. Johnson, whom no man living holds in higher estimation than my self. and the recollection your letter calls up of my late friend the Attorney Gen¹ Breckenridge, by the mention of his daughter, renews feelings of esteem & respect which I am happy to offer at the feet of mrs Porter, with the assurance of my continued attachment to his family.   the indisposition I lately experienced, in which you are so good as to [have]¹ felt an interest, has entirely ceased; but has not left me in the same confidence of continuing & firm health as heretofore.   but in sickness or health I tender you the assurance of my esteem and respect.   TH: JEFFERSON

RC (KyLoF: Thomas Jefferson, Miscellaneous Papers); addressed: "Thomas C. Flournoy esq. Columbus. Ohio"; franked; postmarked. PoC (DLC); on verso of re-used address cover of Joseph C. Cabell to TJ, 18 Nov. 1818; endorsed by TJ.

¹ Word, interlined in an unidentified hand in RC, is not in PoC.

To Abraham Lange

Monticello Jan. 24. 19.

Th: Jefferson presents his compliments to Mʳ Lange and his thanks for the two parcels of beans he has been so kind as to send him. they are safely recieved, and are quite sufficient in quantity to put him promptly into stock and with his acknolegements for the favor, he salutes M. Lange with esteem & respect.

PoC (DLC); on verso of a reused address cover from TJ to Francis Eppes; dateline at foot of text; endorsed by TJ.

A missing letter from Lange to TJ of 16 Jan. 1819 is recorded in SJL as received 20 Jan. 1819 from Calf Pasture.

To Gulian C. Verplanck

Monticello Jan. 24. 19.

Th: Jefferson presents his compliments to Mr Verplank, and his thanks for the Anniversary discourse before the Historical society of New York, which he has recieved and read with pleasure. it is a work of much erudition & research, with the high merit of bringing it into moderate compass, a merit so rare, and yet so valuable to the reader. with his acknolegements for this mark of attention, he prays mr Verplank to accept his respectful salutations.

RC (CSmH: JF); dateline beneath closing; erased phrase at foot of text in an unidentified hand: "My dear." PoC (MHi); on reused blank sheet with a wax seal; endorsed by TJ.

From Edmund Bacon

DEARE SIR.   25th Jany 1819.

It is some what possoble that I may[1] moove the comeing fall to the west. the certainty of my mooveing intirely depends upon an answer to a letter from me to my brothers which letter I have expected to recieve before now. should I moove I shall be Obliged to have a small waggon of some what the Kind of your old markit waggon and as I should be obliged to have it made and the time is not even at this time too soon to see whare I can have it done should it be wanting I have concluded that perhaps it might soot you to let your workmen make it or perhaps it may soot you to sell me the one you have I mean the old markit waggon

I am Yours &C   E: BACON

RC (ViU: TJP-ER); dateline adjacent to closing; idiosyncratic punctuation editorially omitted; addressed: "Mr Jefferson"; endorsed by TJ; additional notation by TJ beneath endorsement: "market waggon"; with apparently unrelated calculations in pencil on verso, possibly in TJ's hand.

[1] Bacon here canceled "still."

From Joseph C. Cabell

DEAR SIR,   Richmond 25th Jan: 1819.

The question on striking out the central College from the University Bill has just been taken in the Senate, and rejected by a vote of 16 to 7.

And I am happy to inform you that immediately thereafter, the question was taken on the passage of the Bill, and that it passed by a vote of 22 to 1.

I began to take some part in the discussion which has taken up all Saturday & to-day; but in my first effort, the blood vessel which had broken within me, opened again, & I was compelled to abandon the attempt, by the discovery that I was spitting blood. I am now under serious apprehensions on the score of my health. I have retired to Judge Coalter's, where Mrs Cabell met me on yesterday. Should I not get better, I must withdraw to Williamsburg.

Mr Watts voted for striking out the Central College. Mr Johnson made great exertions to get the Bill amended: but we voted him down very easily.

Yours faithfully   JOSEPH C. CABELL

RC (ViU: TJP-PC); endorsed by TJ as received 27 Jan. 1819 and so recorded in SJL; with additional notations by TJ beneath endorsement relating to his 28 Jan. 1819 reply: "send copy of bill. obtain derelict part of the 45,000. D of last year send him estimate." RC (DLC); address cover only; with PoC of TJ to John Vaughan, 28 May 1819, on verso; addressed: "Mr Jefferson Monticello"; franked; postmarked Richmond, 25 Jan.

Chapman Johnson made the motion ON STRIKING OUT the first section of the Bill to Establish a University (printed above at 19 Nov. 1818), which named Central College as the location of the new University of Virginia. After this amendment was defeated the bill passed in the Senate, with the only negative vote being cast by Joseph W. Ballard, the senator representing Isle of Wight, Prince George, and Surry counties (*JSV* [1818–19 sess.], 73; Leonard, *General Assembly*, 296).

To John H. Cocke

Monticello Jan. 25. 19.

Th: Jefferson with his compliments to Genl Cocke regrets much the having missed him both in going & coming from Charlottesville; he hopes he will do him the favor of coming here this evening, or tomorrow, as business of extreme urgency depends on it. he salutes him with friendship & respect

RC (ViU: TJP-Co); written on a small scrap; dateline at foot of text; addressed: "Genl Cocke." Not recorded in SJL.

From Wilson Cary Nicholas

My Dear Sir   Richmond Jan^ry 25. 1819

You have heard I know, that your College is made the University of Virginia. I call it yours, as you are its real founder, its commencement can only be ascribed to you, to your exertions & influence its being adopted can only be attributed. The object was always dear to me, it is doubly so, as it is now so compleatly identified with your fame. The sum given is too small but it will be increased I have no doubt from time to time. Perhaps it is as well to begin upon a small scale. It will be easier to get four competent professors than ten; & there may be a facility in governing a few that wou'd not be found if the number of young men shou'd be very large at first. The only difficulties I apprehend are in procuring good teachers & in governing the young men, both I fear will be very difficult in this country. It is indispensible that the masters shou'd be gent^n & command the respect of those they are to instruct & govern. Men of that description who are qualified are not to be had of our own growth, & are not often imported; but these are things you understand much better than I do. I hope your health & strength are perfectly restored. Be pleased to endorse the enclosed & return them to me by the first mail.

I am Dear Sir most respectfully   W. C. Nicholas

RC (DLC); endorsed by TJ as received 27 Jan. 1819 and so recorded in SJL. RC (MHi); address cover only; with PoC of TJ to de Bure Frères, 27 May 1819, on verso; addressed: "Thomas Jefferson Esqr Monti Cello Milton Va."; franked; postmarked Richmond, 25 Jan.

The ENCLOSED items sent for endorsement were probably promissory notes from Nicholas to TJ needed to renew Nicholas's bank loans, likely including a surviving one dated 6 Jan. 1819 and reading "Sixty days after date I promise to pay Thomas Jefferson Esqr or order ten thousand dollars without offset negotiable & payable at the office of the Bank of the U.S. at Richmond for value received" (MS in ViU: TJP; written in Nicholas's hand on a small scrap and signed by him; dateline added by Nicholas in a different ink; endorsed on verso by Nicholas and TJ, with additional notation in an unidentified hand: "W C nicholas 10000 March 7").

From Robert Walsh

Dear Sir   Philadelphia Jany 25th 1819

I send the Analectic Magazine for the present month. Circumstances have induced me to decline any further Co-operation in that journal, but Judge Cooper will still continue to supply it with an article from time to time. He has written for it a critique on De Tracy's Political Economy. I do not know what representation he has made of the book, or whether his studies have been of such a nature as to qualify him to pronounce judgment.

I have undertaken an Octavo of 500 or more pages—to be devoted to an exposition of the Historical & Moral Character, the Public Economy, and probable destinies, of these United States. An Outline is all that [can]¹ be given within the time & space to which I am obliged to restrict myself, but I hope to demonstrate that we are the most respectable and flourishing people on earth. The "Statistics" of Pitkin are too dry and technical; the "Statistical Annals"² of Seybert too ponderous & particular.

I need not say how grateful I should be for any hints from you with regard to the best plan for the attainment of what I venture to call my patriotic object.

Mʳ Benjamin Vaughan, and Dʳ Kirkland of the Harvard University are now in this City. On their way hither, they visited Mʳ Jay, & interrogated him concerning the Cooperation of Dʳ Franklin in the peace of 82. The testimony of Mʳ Jay corroborates the opinions which you were so kind as to communicate to me on the Subject. He attests that Franklin Seemed as tenacious of all points as his Colleagues, & had no intercourse with the French Cabinet other than that to which all the Commissioners were parties.

I am happy to find that the Legislature of Virginia have consulted the interests of the state and their own reputation, in the question of the University. What you have so skilfully and philanthropically projected, you will, I trust and expect, live to See either completely realized, or in a course of certain execution.

very faithfully & respectfully   ROBERT WALSH Jᴿ

RC (DLC); at foot of text: "T. Jefferson Esqʳᵉ"; endorsed by TJ as received 31 Jan. 1819 and so recorded in SJL. Enclosure: *Analectic Magazine*, vol. 13, no. 1 (Jan. 1819; Poor, *Jefferson's Library*, 14 [no. 925]).

The review by Thomas COOPER of Destutt de Tracy's *Treatise on Political Economy* appeared, signed with his initials, on pp. 177–91 of the March 1819 number of the *Analectic Magazine*. In it Cooper agreed with TJ's own displeasure with the style of the English translation, noting that "a more harsh and inelegant translation of any book we have seldom met with," and he questioned the "strange affectation of Destutt Tracy himself, in making the subject of political economy a part of the metaphysics of ideas. To us it appears, that a treatise on confectionary or on the art of dancing, is just as much connected with the nature of the will, and the physical formation of our wants and our means, as political economy" (p. 179). Nevertheless, Cooper recommended the work as "interesting to us, from the high standing and great respectability of the gentleman who edits it: for the importance of the subjects treated; and the ability with which they are discussed" (pp. 190–1).

Describing it as preliminary to a fuller discussion, Walsh eventually published his OCTAVO work, entitled *An Appeal from the Judgments of Great Britain respecting the United States of America. Part First, containing an Historical Outline of their*

[603]

Merits and Wrongs as Colonies; and Strictures Upon the Calumnies of the British Writers (Philadelphia, 1819; Poor, *Jefferson's Library*, 11 [no. 685]). The Treaty of Paris concluding the Revolutionary War was signed in 1783, not 82 (Hunter Miller, ed., *Treaties and other International Acts of the United States of America* [1931–48], 2:151–7).

[1] Omitted word editorially supplied.
[2] Omitted closing quotation mark editorially supplied.

From Patrick Gibson

SIR   Richmond 26th Jany 1819

Since writing to you on the 14th of last month, I have not had the pleasure of hearing from you nor has any of your Bedford flour yet been received

In next month I shall require some notes for renewal, you will therefore be pleased to send me blanks for that purpose

With much respect & regard

I am Your obt Servt   PATRICK GIBSON

RC (MHi); between dateline and salutation: "Thomas Jefferson Esqre"; endorsed by TJ as received 31 Jan. 1819 and so recorded in SJL.

From Joel Yancey

DR SIR   poplar Forest 18th Jany [before 26 Jan. 1819]

I received your letter by Dick & Jerry, this morning, they arrived here late, last Evening, I am very sorry that Dick, has faild to deliver his loads, he has many excuses, and seems now to be much mortified, I hope another case will not occur, I now send by Jerry the balance of the pork intended for monticello, in a box containing[1] 95 ps, also all the poplars that are in the gardens, we know them by the name of the balsam poplars. I send also a few of the latter peas, but have been desapointed in getting as many as I wish to have sent you at present, but still expect to be able to send you more in time for seeding, and plenty for your use here (reserved) mr Radford and myself have had one or two meetings in Lynchburg on the subject of assurtaining the price of Brick work during the last year in Lynchburg—it seems to me that mr Brown has considerable influence among the undertakers, and that most of the contracts have been made, with a View, to have a bearing on the contract at the C. College during the last year, they made lumping bargains (as they term it) and we as yet have not been able to satisfy ourselves, on the Subject, we again have appointed a day next week to make further[2] inquiry. but I fear that things have been so managed, that we shall not be able to make any award on the subject but more of this in a few days, when we shall send you our joint opinions—I am sorry to add another to the list of mortality, Ambrose who I mentioned in my last was Ill died last monday, Maria is better Dinah; much the Same, and several others complaining, but none in my opinion seriously[3] ill It would seem indeed, the mortality among the children—last year was occasioned from want of nursing and care of the mothers, but if it was, it was their mothers own fault, to my Knowledge they never was prohibited from going to their children when ever it was necessary, and particulurly, when they were sick, you will recollect that Wills Salls was sick, while you were here during the harvest, that you always found her with her child when you visited it, which was frequently[4] and as to Edy & Amy I think it will be a miracle if ever they raise a child, they appear to have no more care or concern at a Death of a child than a brute, Edy has had 5 and have lost them all and Amy 3 and lost 2. I have always enjoined it upon the overseers to suffer them to attend to their children, and Knowing it to be a particulur charge given me upon our first agreement I assure you paid particulurly attention to it myself also—expecting to write you again within few days I will conclude this hasty Scrawl, which I fear you will not be able to read, after expressing to you my graetfull acknowledgments for the confidence and friendship which you had the kindness to express for me and to assure you that my future conduct Shall be to endeavor to merit a continuance of it

JOEL YANCEY

RC (MHi); dateline at foot of text; partially and incorrectly dated, with evidence of misdating consisting of departure from Monticello of wagon carrying letter responded to here on morning of 18 Jan. 1819 (see TJ to Yancey, 17 Jan. 1819), and contradictory statement above that the wagon arrived at Poplar Forest the evening of 17 Jan. 1819; endorsed by TJ as a letter of 18 Jan. 1819 received eight days later and so recorded in SJL.

c. COLLEGE: Central College. In LUMPING BARGAINS building contractors or undertakers agree to complete projects for a single overall sum without specifying the tasks or wages of their workers or the costs of their materials.

[1] Yancey here canceled "pieces."
[2] Word interlined.
[3] Manuscript: "seriouly."
[4] Manuscript: "frequenty."

To Joseph Jones

SIR   Monticello Jan. 27. 19.

I wrote on the 15th inst. in answer to your obliging favor of the 8th since which that of the 18th has come to hand. in consequence thereof I have this day written to mr Mallory Collector of Norfolk, to pray him (if the rules of office permit) to enter and pay the charges & duties on my articles at Norfolk and to forward them direct to Richmond. I have taken the liberty of saying you would [i]mmediately forward to him the bills of lading, which I n[ow re]quest you to have the goodness to do and to accept my tha[nks for] the kind trouble you have taken with the assurance [of] my great esteem & respect.

                                                              TH: JEFFERSON

PoC (DLC); on a reused blank sheet with a seal tear; at foot of text: "Joseph Jones esq."; endorsed by TJ.

To Charles K. Mallory

SIR   Monticello Jan. 27. 19.

I have just learnt that the brig Planter Capt Anderson bound from Marseilles to Petersbg has put in to Norfolk for repairs. she has on board for myself and my grandson Thos J. Randolph the articles noted below, which were consigned by mr Cathalan of Marseilles to the Collector of Petersburg, bills of lading only sent to him, & an invoice promised immediately, mr Cathal[a]n[1] being sick at the moment of the vessel's departure. mr Jones collector of Petersbg writes me that [by?] information from the house of Durkin, Hendersons & co. the brig [. . .] unload at Norfolk. but whether she does or not it is so much more expeditious & safe for them to be forwarded to Richmond direct, that, if the rules of office will permit it, I will request the favor of you to consider the consignment to yourself, enter the articles at your office, and forward them immediately to Richmond addressed to mr Gibson who will pay your draught for all expences and duties. I write this day to mr Jones to forward you the bills of lading, and the moment an invoice is recieved I will transmit it to you. in the mean time I think it probable you can settle the duties and draw for them without awaiting the invoice, the duties on the wines being fixed, and you can estimate the oil, anchovies & Maccaroni. this last article has cost me generally at Marseilles from 16. to 20. cents the pound. with my apologies & thanks for this trouble accept the assurance of my great esteem & respect   TH: JEFFERSON

TJ. 1. cask, in a double cask containing 64. gall[s] red wine.

6. boxes contain[g] each 50. bottles red wi[n]e, in all 300. bottles

1. box containing 12. bottles anchovies.

4. small boxes containing each 12. bottles superf. olive oil, in all 36. bottles. there are probably however only 3. boxes, as 5. gallons was the quantity written for.

1. box containing nett 90. ℔ Maccaroni. and 1. box of flowers (a present)

R. 1. cask in a double cask containing 32. gall[s] red wine [of
TJ Roussilon. same as the 64.][2]

2. boxes containing each 24. bottles red wine, in all 48. bottles

P.S. you will oblige me by a line of information what is, or can be done in this case

PoC (MHi); on verso of reused address cover of Simeon DeWitt to TJ, 13 Jan. 1819; torn at seal and hole in manuscript; final postscript in left margin perpendicular to text; at foot of text: "Charles K. Mallory"; mistakenly endorsed by TJ as a letter of 7 Jan. 1819 but correctly recorded in SJL.

[1] Word faint.
[2] Brackets in original.

To Joseph C. Cabell

Dear Sir   Monticello Jan. 28. 19.

I join with you in joy on the passage of the University bill, and it is necessary you should send me a copy of it without delay, that the visitors may have a meeting to see and to do what it permits them to do for the furtherance of the work, as the season for engagements is rapidly passing off. but we shall fall miserably short in the execution of the large plan displayed to the world, with the short funds proposed for it's execution. on a careful review of our existing means, we shall be able this present year to add but two pavilions and their dormitories to the two already in a course of execution, so as to provide but for 4. professorships; and hereafter we can add but one a year; without any chance of getting a chemical apparatus, an astronomical apparatus with it's observatory, a building for a library with it's library E[t]c.[1] in fact it is vain to give us the name of an University without the means of making it so. could not the legislature be induced to give to the University the derelict portions offered to the pauper schools & not accepted by them; I mean so-much for example of last year's 45,000 D. as has not been called for, and so much of this year's 60,000 D. as shall not be called for. these unclaimed dividends might enable us to compleat our buildings & procure our apparatuses, library E[t]c which once done, a moderate annual sum may maintain the institution in action. I shall be happy to hear of the improvement of your health, and salute you with affectionate respect

TH: JEFFERSON

RC (ViU: TJP); addressed: "Joseph C. Cabell of the Senate of Virginia now in Richmond"; franked; postmarked Charlottesville, 30 Jan.; endorsed by Cabell as answered 4 Feb. PoC (DLC); on verso of a reused address cover from Wilson Cary Nicholas to TJ; endorsed by TJ.

On 21 Feb. 1818 the Virginia General Assembly passed "An Act appropriating part of the revenue of the Literary Fund, and for other purposes," which devoted an annual payment from the Literary Fund of 45,000 D. to educating the poor (*Acts of Assembly* [1817–18 sess.], 13–4). An additional allocation of $20,000 for this purpose is described above at William C. Rives to TJ, 20 Jan. 1819.

[1] Omitted period at right margin editorially supplied.

From Fernagus De Gelone

SIR   New York January–28. 1819.

I had no copy of Euler's Algebra, when I Sent you the last box in the beginning of this month. I found one per chance this morning in private hands . . . 2 8[vo] in boards. $.4.50.

I received yesterday the honour of your letter with a note of $20. which was too much by 2 dollars.   2.00.
                                                                      .2.50

I Send you per mail this day the 1[rst] vol. of Euler's Algebra, and next week the 2nd Shall be Sent. I Still owe you the 3rd, 4th, 5th and 6th vol. of Tacitus.

As to any good translation of Eschylus and Sophocles, I have none and Know none in town. I will try to procure them here or from Europe.

I am most respectfully Sir Your most humble obedient Servant

FERNAGUS DE GELONE.

RC (MHi); ellipsis in original; endorsed by TJ as received 7 Feb. 1819 and so recorded in SJL. RC (DLC); address cover only; with PoC of TJ to James H. McCulloch, 7 Feb. 1820, on verso; addressed: "Thomas Jefferson Esq[r] Monticelo. Milton V[a]"; franked; postmarked New York, 28 Jan.

From "Franklin"

CITIZEEN JEFFERSON SIR   Kentucky 28 Jan^{ry} 1819

As I am as old a man as your self, And as I see our Ministers, and the Diff^t state goverments going headlong to destruction I have above forward^d you a scroul for your perusal on John Q Adams conduct in his Negociation with Don Onis, in their entercourse, and exchange of notes; on the Subject of the Flarda^s Cession, and on fixing the West line of the Lousiana purchase, as youl see the great sacrifice he offers in making the Sabine, and the Red river, the line of a Devision, Cant you Arrest this offer, by useing your enfluence before its carry^d into effect. As I mean to publish that note, I forward you, in all our western papers unless I hear from washington its laid Aside.

The state Bank Mania, with the state Bank paper doll^s will undoubtly ruin the finance of the nation, and Jeopardize a Dissolution of the Union, if not spedily check^d and arrested—This State bank system if it runs its race, untill it dies a natural death, will sink One hundred times, as much property as the old continental money did, And all this evil has taken place under the Adminstration of two of your own pupills, which its said you have rais^d for the express purpose, and by your influence they[1] were plac^d in the chair of State, which they have fill^d in rotation—As Madison and his party pul^d down the fabrick, the Unit^d State bank, that Hambleton had fix^d our currencey on, and so open^d the flood gates of State banks and ruin^d our Currencey, And in Silunce altho he must have seen the evil, quit[2] the Chair, without ever bearing his Testimoney Against it, to the publick,—And Monroe is equally faulty by his Silence every Session in his Speech^s Crying peace, peace, and prosperity, when there is Neither in our land, As their is a great^r evil Stalking through^t o[ur] [Lan]d. than if their was One thousand African Lions, let loose uninter[...] our Slack of Horses, Cattle, hogs & Sheep,—as long as[3] this swingling false, Spurious, unstable state paper dollars exists,[4] a curse equal to a pestilance, Destroying, all faith, entigrity or confidence, between Man and Man, ruiening endustry, encouraging the swingling class of the Comenity, ruening the Ignorant and unwary Class—those two mens Administation, if twelve or Sixteen years, will sink more property, than One hundred years Administer^d as well as your eight was.

I have been Surpris^d at your Silence on the Subject, of this great National evil surly its not out of sight to you, And I am afraid Monroes Silence is caus^d by the next four years race, he has to run. that has shut up his eyes, and Mouth, as he sees the State bank Mania, rages so generally throughout the Union. Dewitt Clinton, apears to have the most independant Soul, of all the state Govenors, you see he Scouts the State Banks System, and has gave the Alarm in his two last yearly Speeches to the Legislater, I could wish you would think with me, and fix him in your old Chair of State, as I am sure that Neither his eyes or mouth would be shut, but would proclaim this worst of evils, and try to halt and correct it, as the last Legislater of Kentucky by their Late Litter of forty Six independant banks May convince one and all, States cant act with sound Discretion in money Matters, of course ought not to have the pow^r—I hear some Legall Men say the Unit^d State constitution, Deprives the Diff^t States, to Issue paper money or Issue bills of credit, And say its Ileagal for them to grant or charter a Company, to exercise a power, they[5] dont possess themselves.

This queston ought to be laid before the high federal Court and if so declare their State charters voy^d. Now if you can be instrimental and can find a cure for this great national evil youl render more es-ential sarvice than you ever did Since you drew our Declaration of Independance.   FRANKLIN—

RC (DLC); subjoined to enclosure; dateline at foot of text; mutilated at seal; addressed: "Thomas Jefferson Esqr Mon-ticella Virginia"; stamp canceled; franked; postmarked Lexington, 1 Feb.; endorsed by TJ as an anonymous "Political" letter received 14 Feb. 1819 and so recorded in SJL.

"Franklin" also wrote TJ as "Zed" on 3 Feb. 1819.

[1] Manuscript: "the," here and later in sentence.
[2] Manuscript: "quite."
[3] Preceding three words interlined.
[4] Word interlined.
[5] Manuscript: "the."

ENCLOSURE

Address by "Franklin" to Western Citizens

To ALL THE WESTERN CITIZEENS   [ca. 28 Jan. 1819]

you all remember when Jefferson purchas Lousiana, the Hue in Cry the yankey federalist rais^d against it, for giving such a enormous Sum as fifteen Million Doll^s for it, Scouting the Idea, it being so large a wild a Teritory en-larging our bounds, so as to endanger a Dissolution of the Union, And that they[1] were Copying after Mother Britton, runing the Nation in debt so as to Create a Enormous National debt, And when the purchase was known, F can Testify the heart felt Joy, that apear^d in every Mans countenance, who had made choice of the western world for his Residence and planted his money in the soil,—And what think you now of Eastern, influence or Ignorance, which you please to call it, when that interst are going to give at least one half of the soil of your purchase away without receving one cent for it, which cost you Seven Million five Hundred thousand Dollars—you all have seen Don Onis and John Q Adams interchange of Notes on the Subject of the Cession of East and West Florada to us, And Adams for our claims for Spoilations on him, And on fixing the boundary line on the west side of Lousiana of the purchase, And you have seen what Onis asks of the Executive, more than two thirds of the purchase that was made by making Missora river the line, the center river, and largest river of the whole purchase. And you see Adams, informs Onis, that in his former Note to him on the subject it was so clear and explicite, that it could not bear any other explanation or refutation, than it contain^d, As it was a fact we purchas^d the great Missisippi river, with all its branches and all their tributary streams runing into them, and youl all agree that is sound plain doctrine,—And you all know there is four, large branches or Rivers, emptys in, Ohio, Missora, Arkensaw, and Red river, and the Ohio, the Smaulest of the four, by one half, red river being More than Double its length, and double its water, Now think and figure to yourselves, setled as you are on each side of the Ohio to its scourse, and Ohio fix^d in the chanel of red river is in, and the title of the fee simple indisputable, what your feeling would be, and how you would act, If John Q by his Mandate would lay off^2 all you on the west or northside of the Ohio to Don Onis and Spain, with all its population, then such is the present offer made of the west side of red river, with all its tributary streams runing in, the Division begining at the end of the 32 degree of No Latitude thirty or forty miles above Nachitochus to its scourse, And at present their is 500 families setled 300 miles above on both sides of the river, by this youl see what a dreadful sacrifice, he is making of National property, as the soil at congress price, will bring Ninty to One hundred and fifty Million doll^s, and worth fifty florada^s, as if they^3 were sunk twenty fathoms under water, it would be a great acquission gain^d to us, as it will be a bill of cost to us and a grave to destroy our population, and the soil not worth a cent, there cant be the least necessity to hurry the Cession, as we have it in possession, and sure I am Spain will never take the expence on them again, to maintain the posts. Neither does^4 Don Onis make any demand on us, as a renumeration for those Florada^s. his only object apears to have fix^d of the Lousiana sale at the time the Session is made; and that line at as Great a Distance from the Mexican^5 Mine as practicable, and can bully John Q into his measures so as to prevent the American population setling near their Vicinety, from the best information I ever could gain, or ever publish^d,^{6} we purchas^d from france all the soil they^7 ever held on the Mexican Gulph, and their is the best information, they were in possession of the mouth of riodenorte river, as Original possessers, long before they took possession of New Orleans, and doth not com^n Sence and true policy say, why settle the west Lousiana line at this day, when a few years hence, time will give it us, As spain has Ten thousand times as much soil, as she can protect, defend, or occupy, by setlers, and europe and all the world can see, the power of Spain, has pass^d the Rubican and is faling into a state of Non existance—Good Authority asserts John Qs offer^d lines from the mouth of the Sabine river, to the Mouth of Riodenorte river will give up more Sugar soil, than ever can be rais^d in the Island of^8 Jamaica, in the highest State of cultivation—Soil much want^d for the consuption of the Union, which we have a clear title to—Now after reading thus far, can any of you see the Necessity and haste for making this great National sacrifice,—As the west side of red river, can raise Truble the produce, than all the New England States.

And more than Double the size of either the North or the south side of the Ohio to is scource, Queirey.

Has not John Q a prompter or adviser in making this unpresident[d] offer and Sacrifice, and who is the Man or Men, who Advis[d] it—perhaps the old Scotch womans, Observation, may elucidate it.—being in Cincinnatas shortly after the Session of Congress rose the first after Monroes tour to the Eastward—a young buck observed we may soon be keeping looking out for Monroe, to eat some of our Western Beaf, and potatoes.

The old woman reply[d], it will be a lang, lang, look then, why so says he,— dinna yee Zee, hee[s] fond of carbs, ousters fish and sichna things suits iss pallatt bettar,—dinna yee Zee hees tain John Q an aw the fish eaters Parnar-ship, wee him, in they Goverment, an yeel Zee heel sweam or sink wee theme, Aund gin yee dinna find me spaying, trueas yee maw sete my Gugement doon, nott wourh a Groate.   FRANKLIN

MS (DLC: TJ Papers, 214:38253); entirely in the hand of "Franklin"; with covering letter subjoined; undated.

MOTHER BRITTON: Great Britain. F: "Franklin."

Luis de Onís transmitted Spain's expectations concerning border negotiations with the United States in his letter to Secretary of State John Quincy Adams of 24 Oct. 1818. Adams's response of 31 Oct. was CLEAR AND EXPLICITE regarding the Mississippi: "The right of the United States to the river Mississippi, and all the waters flowing into it, and to all the territories watered by them, remains as entire and unshaken by any thing now adduced by you as by any thing which had ever preceded it in the discussions between the two Governments. It is es-tablished beyond the power of further controversy; nor could it answer any use-ful purpose to reproduce proofs which have already more than once been shown, and which, remaining unimpaired, must henceforth be considered by the United States as not susceptible of refutation" (*ASP, Foreign Relations*, 4:526–31, quote on p. 530).

[1] Manuscript: "the."
[2] Manuscript: "of."
[3] Manuscript: "the."
[4] Manuscript: "does Does."
[5] Manuscript: "Mexincan."
[6] Manuscript: "pulish[d]."
[7] Manuscript: "the," here and twice more in this sentence.
[8] Preceding three words interlined.

From Alexander Garrett

D[R] SIR   Thursday morning 26th [28] Jan[y] 19.

I now send you Latrobes price book: Mr. Dinsmore yesterday mentioned to me that he had heard with regret, that you were dissatisfied with the contract made with him, and beg'd me to assure you, that he would take no advantage of any mistake you may have made in that contract; that he will be entirely satisfied to work by the printed prices of the book now sent you. not even insisting on the correction of those by Latrobe.

You have no doubt learnt that the University bill passed the Senate on saturday last by a vote of 22 to 1.

I present you with a rock fish, of which I beg your acceptance
Respect^y Your Ob^t S^t   ALEX: GARRETT

RC (ViU: TJP); misdated; addressed: "Mr: Jefferson Monticello"; endorsed by TJ: "Dinsmore James." Enclosure: *The Book of Prices adopted by the House Carpenters of the Borough of Pittsburgh, February 15, 1813* (Pittsburgh, 1813; Poor, *Jefferson's Library*, 6 [no. 243]).

TJ's Bill to Establish a University (printed above at 19 Nov. 1818) PASSED THE SENATE and became law on Monday, 25 Jan. 1819, not SATURDAY (*JSV* [1818–19 sess.], 73).

To Wilson Cary Nicholas

DEAR SIR   Monticello Jan. 28. 19.

Yours of the 25th came to hand last night and I sincerely join with you in joy on the passage of the University bill. but it will be in a great measure on paper only with our present funds. the funds we transferred to the public, with what may be saved of the 1st year's endowment may enable us to build this year a 3^d and a 4th pavilion so as to accomodate 4. professors; but after this year we cannot add a pavilion a year with it's dormitories, and what will be an University without a chemical apparatus, an astronomical apparatus with it's Observatory, a Library building and it's library E^tc. I wish the legislature could be induced to give for these purposes the derelict portions of the appropriations for the pauper[1] schools, I mean the portions of the 45,000 D. not accepted by the different counties. a great deal of the pauper appropn will either be unclaimed or embezzled by jobs. we have few paupers in this country, and the labor of these cannot be spared by their parents because they are paupers. they are so sparse also that they could not be brought together. the want of elementary education in the lower class is not from want of means in the parents, but of masters; none but cripples or invalids being willing to devote themselves to inactivity. ever & affectionately yours

                                             TH: JEFFERSON

PoC (DLC); on verso of reused address cover of Joseph Milligan to TJ, 18 Jan. 1819; at foot of text: "W. C. Nicholas esq."; endorsed by TJ.

[1] Word interlined in place of "primary."

From James Riley

HONOURABLE SIR   Washington Jan.ʸ 28, 1819

On my arrival in this City a few days since I had the honour of receiving your favour acknowledging the receipt of mine & mr Simpsons Petition which has since been laid before the Senate

For your goodness I beg you to accept my most unfeigned thanks, I shall send a copy of your letter to mr Simpson & have great hopes that it will cause congress to view his situation in a more favourable light,

I have now the pleasure to send you a Copy of my Narrative which you will do me the honour to accept

And with the truest sentiments of Veneration & esteem, I am Sir your most humble & most devoted admirer & servant

JAMES RILEY

RC (ViW: TC-JP); at foot of text: "Honˡᵉ Thomas Jefferson"; mistakenly endorsed by TJ as a letter of 28 Jan. 1818 received 31 Jan. Recorded in SJL as a letter of 28 Jan. 1819 received three days later. Enclosure: Riley, *An Authentic Narrative of the loss of the American Brig Commerce* (3d ed., New York, 1818; Poor, *Jefferson's Library*, 7 [no. 334]; TJ's copy in CSmH, inscribed on flyleaf to "Honˡᵉ Thomas Jefferson Late President of the United States From his most devoted grateful & Obedient Servant James Riley Washington. Jan.ʸ 1819," with William K. Bixby's bookplate).

To William C. Rives

DEAR SIR   Monticello Jan. 28. 19.

I sincerely join in the general joy on the passage of the University bill, and by such majorities as bespeak a friendly patronage hereafter. in a letter of this date to mr Cabell I have requested him to send me a copy of the bill that the visitors may meet and do at once what the law permits them to do, as the season for engagements is rapidly passing off. but we shall fall miserably short in the execution of the large plan displayed to the public. on a careful review of our funds we shall be able this present year to add but two pavilions & their dormitories to the two now in hand, so as to provide but for 4. professorships of the ten proposed, and hereafter we can add but one annually; without any chance of procuring a chemical apparatus, an astronomical apparatus with it's observatory, a building for a library with it's library Eᵗc. could not the legislature be induced to give to the University the derelict portions offered to the pauper schools & not accepted by them? I mean, for example, so much of the last year's 45,000.D. as has not been called for, and so much of this year's 65,000.D. as shall not be called for. these unclaimed dividends might enable us to compleat our buildings, & procure our apparatuses, library E^{t}c which once done, the institution might be maintained in action by a moderate annual sum. could it have any ill effect to try this proposal with the legislature? you who are on the spot can best judge. ever & affectionately Yours   TH: JEFFERSON

RC (DLC: Rives Papers); addressed: "William C. Rives esq. of the H. of Delegates of Virginia now in Richmond"; franked; postmarked Charlottesville, 30 Jan.; endorsed by Rives. PoC (DLC); on verso of reused address cover of Robert Walsh to TJ, 8 Nov. 1818; endorsed by TJ.

From John Adams

DEAR SIR   Quincy January 29th 1819

If I am not humble I ought to be, when I find myself under the necessity of borrowing a juvenile hand to acknowledge your kind favour of the 19th I have read your university report throughout with great pleasure, and hearty approbation; Of Tracy's report I have read as much as I could, the Translation appears to me an original written with all the purity, accuracy, and elegance, of its author in his maturest age if it can destroy the Parasite Institutions of our country it will merit immortal honor.

The Medici rose to the despotism of Europe, ecclesiastical, & political, by the machinery of banks, hundreds of mushrooms or Jonah's gourds have sprung up in one night in America by the strength of the same rotten manure, how has it happened that the bank of Amsterdam has for so many years conducted all most all the commerce of Europe without making any profit to the proprietors and how has it happened that religious liberty, fiscal science, coin, & commerce, & every branch of political economy should[1] have been better understood and more honestly practised in that Frog land, than any other country in the World?

Your letter shall be communicated without loss of time to Mr Shaw and consequently to Mr Channing by your friend

JOHN ADAMS

RC (DLC); in an unidentified hand, signed by Adams; endorsed by TJ as received 7 Feb. 1819 and so recorded in SJL. RC (DLC); address cover only; with PoC of TJ to James Madison, 16 Feb. 1820, on verso; addressed in an unidentified hand: "President Jefferson Monticello Virginia"; franked; post-

marked Quincy, 29 Jan. FC (Lb in MHi: Adams Papers).

In the Bible, God causes GOURDS to grow overnight (Jonah 4.6–10). FROG LAND: The Netherlands (*OED*).

[1] Preceding seven words not in FC.

To Mathew Carey

SIR   Monticello Jan. 29. 19.

Your favors of the 13th and 18th reached me both on the 24th and I now inclose you 15.D. in bills of the US. bank to cover the balance of 14.75 D stated in your account.

I observe that Baines's History is merely what it's title announces, that of the <u>Wars</u> of the French revolution. he consequently passes over in 20. or 30. pages the preliminary troubles of France which produced those wars, and which occupy 2. of the 7. vol^s of the inestimable history of Toulongeon, & by far the most interesting and instructive part of the history of the French revolution. I had begun to read Baines, but the unwieldiness of a 4to vol. in my old & feeble hands rendered it too fatiguing, and I have laid it by, supposing that before this they have published an 8vo edition in England[1] and that if you should get an 8vo copy you will have the goodness to exchange it with me for the 4to which will be a great obligation. has your religious Olive branch been published yet? I shall be glad of a copy when it is. I salute you with friendship and respect.

                                                TH: JEFFERSON

RC (DLC: TJ Papers, ser. 9); at foot of text: "Mr Matthew Carey"; with calculation at foot of text in an unidentified hand. PoC (DLC); on verso of James Brown (for James Leitch) to TJ, [ca. 21 Jan. 1819] (see note to TJ to Thomas Cooper, 22 Jan. 1819); hole in manuscript, with damaged word rewritten by TJ; endorsed by TJ. Recorded in SJL with additional bracketed notation "15.D."

Carey's RELIGIOUS OLIVE BRANCH, eventually published as *A Roland for an Oliver. Letters on Religious Persecution* (Philadelphia, 1826), was issued anonymously as the work of "A Catholic Layman."

[1] Preceding two words interlined.

To Joseph Miller

DEAR CAPTAIN   Monticello Jan. 30. 19.

I shall want a supply of good corks to bottle our beer and cyder, as soon as they can be got. it is so provoking to lose good liquor by bad corks, and so uncertain to get them good from Richmond that I had rather trespass on your friendship to get them for me in Norfolk, where I expect better ones can be got, and selected by your better judgment. I therefore inclose you a 5. Dollar bill, and I will pray you to send me the amount of it in good corks. I imagine the steam boats give a quick opportunity of sending them to Richmond where it will be better I believe to address them to Capt Peyton, who has more to do with the Milton boats than mr Gibson, and can probably forward them quicker. I salute you [with] [fri]endship & respect.

Th: Jefferson

PoC (DLC); on verso of reused address cover of Joseph C. Cabell to TJ, 18 Jan. 1819; torn at seal; at foot of text: "Cap.ᵗ Joseph Miller"; endorsed by TJ. Recorded in SJL with additional bracketed notation "5.D."

To Lewis D. Belair

Sir   Monticello Jan. 31. 19.

I recieve with due sensibility the mark of attention which the benevolent institution, in whose name your letter of the 21ˢᵗ is written, has been pleased to manifest, by proposing me as an honorary member of their institution. aged, & distant as I am little benefit to the society can result from my services: but such as they may be will be at their command. of this Sir, be pleased to assure them, and of my thankfulness for the honor of having my name associated with theirs.

Accept yourself at the same time the tender of my great respect and esteem.   Th: Jefferson

PoC (DLC); at foot of text: "M. Lewis D. Belair"; endorsed by TJ. Printed in *Charter of the Jefferson Benevolent Institution of Pennsylvania* (Philadelphia, [1819]), which notes at head of text that it was *"received the 5th of February, and recorded in the minutes of the 9th of February, 1819."*

To John Patterson

Dear Sir   Monticello Jan. 31. 19.

Your favor of the 6ᵗʰ was rec.ᵈ in due time, with D.ʳ Potter's pamphlet, for which I thank you, and have read it with satisfaction. I join with you in joy on the passage of our University bill, and the majorities of 143. to 28. in one house, and of 22. to 1. in the other, give hopes of a liberal patronage hereafter, of which there will be need, and the funds in hand. not doubting the interest you take in this institution, of which your subscription was so honorable proof, I inclose you a letter with a request to enquire for us into the character and qualifications of the writer. from it's style and contents I should conjecture him respectable; but an ounce of fact is worth a pound of conjecture. his drawing,¹ dancing, music, would suit us. his Italian and French may be useful for a while: but I propose to write to Professor Pictet of Geneva for a professor of modern languages, where French, Italian

& German are almost natively spoken. as I shall not answer mr Milon's letter until I hear from you, I pray you to make the enquiry as promptly, but as thoroughly also as your convenience will permit, and with your information to return me his letter.—Your friends in our neighborhood are well. Jane & Jefferson lately presented us their 3ᵈ daughter. we are preparing a house for them to remove to at the place called Tufton, about a mile from us, and with which we shall be glad to be made your joint head quarters in future visits to those who jointly & severally regret their loss by your removal. of one of these accept the affectionate & respectful salutations.

TH: JEFFERSON

P.S. now dayly & hourly expecting our Italian Stonecutters to arrive at Baltimore I hope mr Hollins will be on the watch not to let them stay there a day, and I join you in commission with him. a water passage to Richmᵈ addressed to Capt Peyton would be a good conveyance.

RC (NjP: Andre deCoppet Collection). PoC (DLC); on verso of reused address cover of John Forsyth to TJ, 16 Jan. 1819; mutilated at seal; at foot of text: "John Patterson esq."; endorsed by TJ. Enclosure: Solidor Milon to TJ, 5 Jan. [1819].

Mary Buchanan Randolph, the 3ᴰ DAUGHTER of Jane H. Nicholas Randolph and TJ's grandson Thomas Jefferson Randolph, was born on 23 Nov. 1818 (Shackelford, *Descendants*, 1:214).

[1] Omitted comma at right margin editorially supplied.

To William Tudor

SIR   Monticello Jan. 31. 19.

Your favor of the 13ᵗʰ was recieved on the 24ᵗʰ and I extremely regret that it is not in my power to give you any information on the subject of mr James Otis. my acquaintance with the Eastern characters began with the first Congress. mr Otis not being a member, I had never any personal acquaintance or correspondence with him. Colᵒ Richard Henry Lee of Westmoreland county had, I know, an active correspondence, from the early dawn of our revolution, with gentlemen of that quarter, and with none more probably than mr Otis, who was then so conspicuous in the principles of the day. it is probable he preserved mr Otis's letters, and that his family now possesses them. of them I have no knolege, as their residence is in a part of the state very remote from mine. but a certain & easy channel for your communication with them would be thro' any member of Congress from your state, and the member from the Westmoreland district of ours.

who he is, I cannot tell you, so entirely am I withdrawn from all attention to public affairs, and so thoroughly satisfied to leave them to the generation in place, in whose hands, from the advancing state of knolege, they will be at least as wisely conducted as they have been by their predecessors. with this scanty information all however which I possess, I pray you to accept the assurance of my high respect and esteem.   TH: JEFFERSON

RC (Christie's, New York City, 2000); addressed: "W. Tudor esquire Boston"; franked; postmarked; endorsed by Tudor. PoC (MHi); on verso of reused external address cover of "Common Sense & Co." to TJ, 12 Jan. 1819; endorsed by TJ.

To Benjamin Waterhouse

DEAR SIR   Monticello Jan. 31. 19.
    Your favor of the 15th was recieved on the 27th and I am glad to find the name and character of Samuel Adams coming forward, and in so good hands as I suppose them to be. but I have to regret that I can add no facts to the stores possessed. I was the youngest man but one in the old Congress, and he the oldest but one, as I believe. his only senior, I suppose, was Stephen Hopkins, of and by whom the honorable mention made in your letter was richly merited. altho' my high reverence for Samuel Adams was returned by habitual notices from him which highly flattered me, yet the disparity of age prevented intimate and confidential communications. I always considered him as more than any other member the fountain of our important measures; and altho' he was neither an eloquent nor easy speaker, whatever he said was sound and commanded the profound attention of the House. in the discussions on the floor of Congress he reposed himself on our main pillar in debate, mr John Adams. these two gentlemen were verily a host in our councils. comparisons with their associates, Northern or Southern, would answer no profitable purpose, but they would suffer by comparison with none. I salute you with perfect esteem & respect.   TH: JEFFERSON

RC (MBCo: Waterhouse Papers); at foot of text: "Dr Waterhouse." PoC (DLC).

Edward Rutledge (1749–1800) was the YOUNGEST member of the Second Continental Congress in 1776. The oldest were Benjamin Franklin (1706–90) and STEPHEN HOPKINS (1707–85), and several others were older than Samuel Adams

(1722–1803) (*ANB*). In two of the newspaper articles enclosed to TJ in his letter of 15 Jan. 1819, Waterhouse referenced Hopkins, stating first that "The character of STEPHEN HOPKINS, who was many years governor of the Colony of Rhode Island and Providence Plantation, is but little known, beyond a circle of old men in that State. His '*rights of the Colonies*,' and his correspondence with SAMUEL

ADAMS, will constitute his portrait in history—It is a reflection on his native town that it has never appeared before." Later, when describing a "paralytic shaking of the head and arms" that afflicted Adams, Waterhouse noted that "*Stephen Hopkins*, the Samuel Adams of Rhode-Island, experienced the same affection full 30 years before his powers of mind failed" (*Boston Patriot and Daily Chronicle*, 16, 29 Dec. 1818).

Appendix

Supplemental List of Documents Not Found

JEFFERSON's epistolary record and other sources describe a number of documents for which no text is known to survive. The Editors generally account for such material at documents that mention them or at other relevant places. Exceptions are accounted for below.

From R. F. Patrick, 11 May 1818. Recorded in SJL as received 18 May 1818 from Nelson County.

From R. N. Harrison, 24 June 1818. Recorded in SJL as received 18 July 1818 from New York.

From Mr. Driscoll, 6 Aug. 1818. Recorded in SJL as received 1 Sept. 1818 from Charleston, South Carolina.

To Mrs. Wandell, 6 Sept. 1818. Recorded in SJL, with additional notation: "on the subject of my watch."

From Joseph Antrim, 30 Nov. 1818. Recorded in SJL as received 8 Dec. 1818 from Lynchburg.

From Charles Bizet, 30 Nov. 1818. Recorded in SJL as received 9 Dec. 1818 from Washington.

From John Donne, 3 Dec. 1818. Recorded in SJL as received 31 Jan. 1819 from Louisville.

INDEX

Aberdeen, University of. *See* King's College (later part of the University of Aberdeen)

Abregé des Dix Livres d'Architecture de Vitruve (Vitruvius; ed. C. Perrault), 314n, 342, 343n, 391

Abstracts of Calculations, to ascertain the Longitude of the Capitol, in the City of Washington (W. Lambert), 314

Academy of Natural Sciences of Philadelphia: identified, 12:505n; journal of, 53, 250n; TJ elected to, 52–3

An Account of Expeditions to the Sources of the Mississippi (Z. M. Pike), 100, 101, 107, 227, 228n

acoustics: collegiate education in, 195, 208, 214, 215n

An Act appropriating part of the revenue of the Literary Fund, and for other purposes (*1818*), li, 160, 163n, 179–80, 182, 189, 209–10, 223n, 339–40, 405n, 484, 511, 516n, 608n

An act concerning William Tatham (*1819*), 516–7n

An Act for laying a Duty on Goods, Wares, and Merchandises imported into the United States (*1789*), 378, 380n

An act for the establishment of an University (*1819*), 402, 473n, 591n

An Act for the relief of Oliver Evans (*1808*), 128–9, 131

An Act to provide for the removal of the library of Congress to the north wing of the Capitol (*1818*), 520, 521n

An Act to regulate the duties on certain wines (*1819*), 439n

Adams, Abigail Smith (John Adams's wife): death of, 49n, 392, 469, 479; friendship with F. A. Van der Kemp, 479, 482n; health of, 324; identified, 6:298n; relationship with J. Adams, 70; TJ sends greetings to, 49, 309

Adams, John: on banks, 615; busts of, 49, 69, 70n, 578; on Christianity, 69; correspondence of published, 575, 576n; on death and dying, 70, 324, 471–2; and death of A. S. Adams, 392; and *The Declaration of Independence* (J. Trumbull), 472; and Destutt de Tracy's writings, 529, 589; diplomatic service of, 466–7; family

of, 324; friendship with TJ, 309, 469; friendship with F. A. Van der Kemp, 41n, 479; on God, 471–2; health of, 48, 472, 480, 529; identified, 4:390–1n; introduces H. Holley, 48, 69; letters from, 69–71, 138–9, 324–5, 471–2, 529, 615; letters to, 48–9, 309, 392, 588–9; as member of Continental Congress, 619; as minister to Great Britain, 331; and J. Monroe, 239, 240n; on Napoleon, 69; on the Netherlands, 615; opinion of sought, 575, 576n; and origin of American Revolution, 48, 69; portraits of, 331; praised, 482; proposed biography of, 496n; reading habits of, 69; reflects on his life, 138; *A Selection of the Patriotic Addresses, to the President of the United States. together with The President's Answers* (ed. W. Austin), 33, 47; sends works to TJ, 138, 529, 588; on state of politics, 529; TJ on, 27, 28; TJ sends works to, 529; and TJ's health, 442, 529; works sent to, 72n, 520, 564n, 589; on writing, 69

Adams, John (of Richmond): as character reference, 419

Adams, John Quincy: and appointments, 125; identified, 12:91–2n; portraits of, 540; relationship with J. Adams, 69; as secretary of state, liii, 119, 155, 236n, 246, 280, 282n, 445, 504, 587–8, 609–12; and subscriptions, 22n; works sent to, 31n

Adams, Samuel: as member of Continental Congress, 578–9n, 619, 620n; and origin of American Revolution, 69, 577–8; signer of Declaration of Independence, 332

Adams, USS (frigate), 533

Additions to the Fourth and Former Editions of An Essay on the Principle of Population (T. R. Malthus), 586n

An Address, delivered at the meeting at the Agricultural Society of Jefferson County, December 29, 1817 (J. Le Ray de Chaumont), 71, 72n, 172n

Adelung, Friedrich: works of, 569–70

Adlum, John: correspondence with TJ published, 351n; identified, 1:587n

The Adventures of Telemachus, the Son of Ulysses (Fénelon), 521, 522n

Aeneid (Virgil), 206–7n

Bryant, Lemuel: and J. Adams, 138
Buck Island (Albemarle Co.): slate from, 92
Buffalo (steamboat), 254
building materials: bricks, 64, 112, 203n, 524, 531–2, 534; cement, 343–4, 362; cement, Roman, 410; ironmongery, 95–6, 524; lead, 381; lumber, 524; nails, 381, 399; pine, 399; poplar, 387; shingles, 399; slate, 92, 97–8, 99, 117; tarras, 343–4, 362; timber, 96; tin, 380–1; zinc, 381
Bukaty, Franciszek: Polish envoy in London, 54, 55n, 282n
Bunker Hill, Battle of (*1775*): J. Trumbull's painting of, 331, 332
Burdett, Francis, 77
Burgoyne, John: as general, 114
burgundy (wine), 121
Burr, Aaron (*1756–1836*): alleged conspiracy of, 3; family of, 243
Burton, Hutchins Gordon: identified, 11:51n; and wine for TJ, 126, 173, 283, 287, 350
Burwell (TJ's slave; b. *1783*). *See* Colbert, Burwell (TJ's slave; b. *1783*)
Burwell, William Armistead: identified, 2:105–6n; letter from, 438–9; in U.S. House of Representatives, 438–9; visits Monticello, 415, 439n
Busti, Elizabeth May: and portrait of C. Wistar, 40
Bute, John Stuart, 3d Earl of: anecdote of, 462
Butler, Pierce: wine preferences of, 243
Butler, Samuel (ca. *1765–1826*): and Baltimore *Niles' Weekly Register*, 497; identified, 10:385n; letter from, 497
butter: sent to TJ, 566

Cabanis, Pierre Jean Georges: *Observations sur les Affections Catarrhales*, 342, 358, 394, 474, 494, 561
Cabell, Joseph Carrington: and Central College subscription, 161, 170; and Destutt de Tracy's writings, 558; and establishment of Central College, 170; and establishment of University of Virginia, 170, 398–9, 401–2, 407, 472–3, 490–1, 497–8, 498, 514–6, 535–6, 558–60, 583–4, 592, 600–1, 607–8; health of, 325, 334, 398, 407, 473, 498, 560, 584, 592, 601, 608; identified, 2:489–90n; invites TJ to

visit, 334; letters from, 170, 334–5, 398–9, 472–3, 490–1, 497–8, 498, 514–7, 558–60, 583–4, 592, 600–1; letters to, 407, 535–6, 607–8; and P. Poinsot's land grant, 427; possible congressional candidate, 398; proposed visit to Williamsburg, 473, 498, 592, 601; and recruitment of University of Virginia faculty, 398, 399n, 407; as Va. state senator, 398, 592; visits Monticello, 334. *See also* Central College Board of Visitors
Cabell, Landon: and Central College subscription, 161
Cabell, Mary Walker Carter (Joseph C. Cabell's wife): travels of, 407, 592, 601
Cabell, William (*1759–1822*): and Central College subscription, 161; delivers letter, 170
Cabell, William H.: advises J. C. Cabell, 497; as University of Virginia commissioner, 182, 183, 223
Caesar (TJ's slave; *1774–1818*): death of, 567
Caesar, Julius: mentioned, 571
Cailleau, André Charles: as publisher, 343n, 561–2
Calhoun, John Caldwell: identified, 12:300n; letter from, 593; letters to, 140–1, 435–6; C. W. Peale paints, 540; and J. L. Poirey's military service claims, 140, 414, 415n, 435, 593; as secretary of war, 140; and subscriptions, 22n
Callaway, George: and Central College subscription, 161; identified, 4:165n
Calvin, John: as religious leader, 481; TJ on, 160
Cambden, Benjamin: land of, 221
Campbell, George Washington: identified, 7:354–5n; as minister plenipotentiary to Russia, 78, 94, 118, 119n, 125
canals: books on, 477n; James River Company, 488; in N.Y., 245, 312–3; in Va., 592
Capitol, U.S.: heating system of, 409n; B. H. Latrobe works on, 58; Library of Congress moved to, 520; longitude measurement at, 314; J. Trumbull's paintings for, liii, 328, 328–9, 330, 331–3, 390, 400 (*illus.*)
Carey, Henry Charles. *See* Mathew Carey & Son (Philadelphia firm)

INDEX

342, 343n, 358, 394, 474, 476, 494, 561

Dictionnaire Grec-François, dédié a son altesse sérénissime Le Prince Camba-cérès, archichancelier de l'empire (J. Quenon), 32

Dictionnaire portatif et de prononciation, Espagnol-Français et Français-Espagnol (J. L. B. Cormon), 369

Didot, Firmin: publishes work, 358

Didymus Chalcenterus: edits Homer's *Iliad* and *Odyssey*, 293

A Digest of the laws of England (J. Comyns), 53

Digges, Thomas Attwood: on C. Bagot, 76–7; family of, 77; health of, 77, 93; identified, 1:517n; letter from, 76–9; letter to, 93–4; proposed visit of, 76; recommends F. C. Fenwick, 78, 94; sends seeds to TJ, 77–8, 94; Washington residence of, 77

Dinah (TJ's slave; b. *1766*): health of, 605; on Poplar Forest slave list, 387

Dinsmore, James: as builder for Central College, 64, 380–1, 399, 524, 612; and Central College subscription, 162; delivers papers, 370; identified, 1:136n; letter from, 399; Report on Tin to Central College Board of Visitors, 380–1

Dionysius of Halicarnassus: *Les Antiquités Romaines* (trans. F. Bellanger), 342, 391, 394, 413, 474, 494, 561, 562n

Discours de L'Empereur Julien, contre les Chrétiens (Julian; trans. J. B. de Boyer), 295

A Discourse concerning Unlimited Submission and Non-Resistance to the Higher Powers (J. Mayhew), 138

Discourse, delivered at the Consecration of the Synagogue of קְ"ק שארית ישראל *in the City of New-York, on Friday, the 10th of Nisan, 5578, corresponding with the 17th of April 1818* (M. M. Noah), 30, 65–6

A Discourse on the Connexion between Chemistry and Medicine (T. Cooper), 546

Discours sur les Progrès des Sciences, Lettres et Arts (ed. J. L. Kesteloot), 147, 394–5, 428, 596

Divers, George: identified, 1:157–8n; letter to, 117; reports on TJ's health, 395; TJ visits, 109, 111–2, 117

Dobson, Thomas: as publisher, 570n, 571n

Dodge, Joshua: as consular candidate, 9; identified, 11:488–9n

Donald, Andrew: property of, 385

Donne, John: letter from accounted for, 621

Dorsey, John Syng: as university professor, 45, 429

Dort, Synod of (*1618–19*): and colonial N.Y., 481

Dougherty, Joseph: appointed superintendent of federal buildings, 289, 307; identified, 1:3–4n; letter from, 289; letter to, 307; and porter business, 289; seeks Senate doorkeeper appointment, 289

drawing: instructors for University of Virginia, 419, 555, 617; study of, 198, 218

Drayton, John: federal judge, 318, 319n

Driscoll, Mr.: letter from accounted for, 621

drunkenness. *See* alcohol: abuse of

Duane, James: as member of Continental Congress, 333n

Duane, William: H. Dearborn on, 3; and Destutt de Tracy's works, 421, 422n; as editor of Philadelphia *Aurora*, 50, 475; identified, 1:49n; letter to, 475; and Republican supporters, 149

Du Cange, Charles Du Fresne: *Glossarium ad Scriptores Mediæ & Infimæ Latinitatis*, 342, 358, 394, 474, 494, 561

Ducatel, Julius Timoleon: identified, 176n; letter from, 175–6; and TJ's correspondence, 147, 175–6

Duclos, R.: edits *Dictionnaire Bibliographique, Historique et Critique des Livres Rares*, 343n, 394, 413, 474, 494, 525, 561–2

Dufief, Nicolas Gouin: identified, 3:98n; *Nature Displayed*, 513; travels to Europe, 513

Dugnani, Antonio: identified, 8:328n; TJ introduces G. Ticknor to, 236–7, 338

Duke, Richard: identified, 598n; letter to, 597–8; as potential proctor for University of Virginia, 597–8

Dumfries (ship), 291, 440, 492

Dunbar, John, 344

Epicurus (Greek philosopher), 258, 267n

Ἐπικτήτου Ἐγχειρίδιον. Manuale di Epitteto (Epictetus; trans. "E. Pilenejo" [G. M. Pagnini]), 394, 413, 428, 474, 494, 561

Episcopalians: beliefs of, 481, 482n; and education, 452; TJ subscribes for minister, 476n; in Va., 341

Eppes, Francis Wayles (TJ's grandson): and Central College, 175, 278, 321, 428–9, 483; clothing for, 321; education of, in Lynchburg, 17; education of, at Monticello, 18; education of, at New London Academy, 175, 292, 321, 458, 483; education of, TJ on, 278, 537; education of, with Baker family, 321, 428–9, 483; health of, 428; identified, 4:115n; letters from, 175, 428–9; letters from accounted for, 537n; letters to, 278, 537; mentioned, 279; relationship with father, 17

Eppes, John Wayles (TJ's son-in-law): and Central College, 17–8; and Central College subscription, 17–8, 321–2; identified, 1:337–8n; invites C. A. Rodney to visit, 311n; letter from accounted for, 18n; letters from, 321–2, 564; letter to, 17–8; library of, 429; portraits of, 540; relationship with son, 17, 321; and TJ's health, 564; as U.S. senator, 429; visits Monticello, 488; and wine for TJ, 126, 127n, 173

Eppes, Martha Burke Jones (John Wayles Eppes's second wife): identified, 2:127n; TJ sends greetings to, 537; watch of, 527, 537

Ernesti, Johann August: edits Graecum Lexicon Manuale (B. Hederich), 429

Erving, George William: identified, 2:32n; as minister plenipotentiary to Spain, 237, 587, 588n; TJ introduces G. Ticknor to, 236, 237

Esquisse et Vues Préliminaires d'un Ouvrage sur l'Éducation Comparée . . . et Séries de Questions sur l'Éducation (M. A. Jullien), 153

Essai de Géologie (Faujas de Saint-Fond), 147, 476

Essai Général d'Éducation physique, morale, et intellectuelle (M. A. Jullien), 153

Essai sur la Turquoise et sur la Calaite (G. Fischer), 118, 119n, 145

An Essay on the principle of population (T. R. Malthus), 586

Estienne, Henri (Stepani; Stephani): edits Θησαυρὸς τῆς Ἑλληνικῆς Γλώσσης. Thesaurus Graecae Linguae, 342, 343n, 358, 494, 525

The Ethereal Physician: or Medical Electricity Revived (T. Brown), 346–7, 378

ethics: collegiate education in, 195, 214, 403; TJ on study of, 198, 217–8

Ἠθικὴ Ποίησις: Sive Gnomici Poetæ Græci (ed. R. F. P. Brunck), 295

Euclid: The Elements of Euclid (R. Simson), 476; writings of, 17, 441

Euler, Leonhard: Élémens d'Algèbre (trans. J. G. Garnier), 394, 413, 428, 474, 595–6, 608; as mathematician, 382–3

Eulogium Sacred to the Memory of the Illustrious George Washington (B. O. Tyler), 21n

Euripides: Les Tragédies d'Euripide (trans. P. Prévost), 596

Europe: public opinion in, 586–7; relations with U.S., 586–7; TJ on titles of nobility in, 587

Evans, Oliver: asserts patent rights, 128–9, 131; identified, 7:109n

Evening Amusements; or, the Beauty of the Heavens Displayed (W. Frend), 59

Everett, Jesse: and medical use of electricity, 347n

The Evidence and Authority of the Christian Revelation (T. Chalmers), 19

Ewell, James: The Medical Companion, 73n; The Planter's and Mariner's Medical Companion, 73n

exercise, physical: at college, 198, 218

Exposition du Système du Monde (P. S. Laplace), 342, 359, 494, 525

Fables of Æsop and others (trans. S. Croxall), 477

Fabroni, Angelo: Historiae Academiae Pisanae, 377

Fagg, John: and Central College subscription, 162; identified, 12:71n

Fairfax, Ferdinando: identified, 4:425n; letter to, 34; sends work to TJ, 34

Fair Trader (ship), 10, 16, 171, 240, 443

Fanny (TJ's slave; b. 1788; daughter of Abby): on Poplar Forest slave list, 387

Holland, Henry Richard Vassall Fox,
3d Baron: introduction to requested,
239, 339
Holley, Horace: identified, 12:405n;
introduced to TJ, 48, 69
Hollins, John: identified, 2:197–8n; and
stonecutters for Central College, 618
Holmes, David: C. W. Peale paints, 540
Holmes, Hugh: identified, 6:114–5n;
introduces G. Blackburn to TJ, 234;
letters from, 234–5, 468; letter to,
507; as University of Virginia com-
missioner, 182, 183, 223, 234; visits
Monticello, 468, 507; and wine from
S. Cathalan, 468, 506, 507
Homer: *Iliad*, 293; *Odyssey*, 293; study
of, 429
Hooe, John: and establishment of
University of Virginia, 473n
Hoomes, Thomas Claiborne: and
establishment of University of
Virginia, 560, 584, 592
Hopkins, Stephen: as member of
Continental Congress, 619–20
Horace: *Oeuvres d'Horace* (ed. A. Da-
cier), 537; quoted by J. Adams, 69,
70n; study of, 175
Horne, John. *See* Tooke, John Horne
horses: falls from, 302; owned by TJ,
228; theft of, 518; TJ rides, 28, 29n,
94, 111, 117, 233, 286, 388, 529
Horwitz, Jonas: and Hebrew-language
Bible, 570, 571n; identified, 570–1n;
letter from, 569–71; seeks position at
University of Virginia, 569–71
Hosack, David: identified, 8:467–8n;
and N.Y. board of agriculture, 249
hospitals: and university education, 197,
217
Hot Springs (Bath Co.): TJ on, 243; TJ
visits, 228, 242, 243; visitors to, 242
Houdetot, Elisabeth Françoise Sophie de
La Live de Bellegarde, comtesse d':
family of, 397
household articles: alum, 147; bed-
clothes, 17; beds, 17, 68, 112, 169,
226, 386, 387; blankets, 386, 387;
bottles, 15, 243; corks, 15, 616–7;
mattresses, 17, 169; razor case, 76; sal
ammoniac, 73; soap, 566, 581. *See also*
building materials; clothing; tools
House of Representatives, U.S.:
chaplains to, 425; and taxes, 378–80;
Ways and Means Committee, 438,
439n. *See also* Congress, U.S.

Howell, Samuel: transports flour, 13
Hubbard, Cate (TJ's slave; b. *1747*): on
Poplar Forest slave list, 387
Hubbard, James (TJ's slave; b. *1818*):
birth of, 387, 567
Hudson, John: and Central College
subscription, 162
Hudson, John (editor): edits *Flavii
Iosephi Hebraei Opera Omnia Graece
et Latine* (Josephus), 476
Hudson River, 114
Huger, Daniel Elliott: as congressional
candidate, 318, 319n
Hume, David: *The History of England,
from the Invasion of Julius Caesar to
the Revolution in 1688*, 24, 410–2,
585; quoted, 487, 489n
Humphreys, Charles: signer of
Declaration of Independence, 329,
330
Humphreys, David: anecdote of, 464
Hunter, James: and establishment of
University of Virginia, 473, 516, 583
Hunter, Robert: Campbell Co. inn-
keeper, 126; identified, 9:20n
Huntington, William: identified, 157n;
letter to, 157; as merchant, 349; TJ
invites to Monticello, 157
Hunts, Mr.: and estate of Major Walsh,
431–2
Hutchinson, James, 148
Hutton, Charles: *A Course of Mathematics*, 382
Hutton, James: as geologist, 102, 480,
482n
Hutton, Joseph: identified, 297n; letter
from, 297; sends prospectus to TJ,
297
Hyde de Neuville, Jean Guillaume:
identified, 4:374–5n; letter from,
459–61; letter to, 489–90; reports on
French affairs, 459–60, 489; and
tariffs, 460; visits Monticello, 490
hydraulics: collegiate education in, 208,
215n
hydrodynamics: collegiate education in,
208, 215n
hydrostatics: collegiate education in,
208, 214n

ideology: collegiate education in, 195,
209, 214, 215n, 403
Iliad (Homer): TJ orders, 293
Independence Day. *See* Fourth of July

JEFFERSON, THOMAS (*cont.*)
subscriptions, 469, 470, 471, 475, 477, 479, 486, 487n, 497, 506, 542, 571; orders books, 33, 42, 53, 100–1, 107, 126, 291, 305, 342, 346, 358–9, 368, 391–2, 394, 413, 428, 439, 449–50, 469, 474, 524–5, 561–2, 588, 595–6, 608; packing and shipping of, 93, 293, 474, 594; preferred physical characteristics, 455, 476, 616; purchases from de Bure Frères (Paris firm), 291, 293, 296, 335, 424, 440, 492; reading habits of, 48; receives works, 33, 34, 53, 55, 57, 59, 64, 65–6, 67, 71, 96–7, 100, 107, 142, 143–4, 145, 153, 160, 304, 312, 312–3, 378, 382, 440, 441, 470, 597, 600, 617; sends books, 421, 422n, 476, 523, 529, 558; shelving arrangement, 476; subscriptions, 43, 60, 72, 143–4, 310, 327, 526, 588; works sent to, 19, 30, 32, 36, 41, 42n, 47, 75, 87, 98, 100, 106, 118, 119n, 124, 126, 127, 132, 137, 138, 147, 148–50, 157–8, 174, 175, 236, 245, 247, 288, 297, 314, 317, 322, 345, 346–7, 350, 366, 408, 425, 436, 458, 511, 512, 513, 517, 529, 530n, 540–1, 546, 558, 563–4, 574, 614 (*See also* Library of Congress; Poplar Forest [TJ's Bedford Co. estate]: library at)

Business & Financial Affairs
account with E. Bacon, 169; account with S. Cathalan, 10, 240, 291, 443–4, 445n, 446, 449; account with de Bure Frères, 296; account with Fitzwhylsonn & Potter, 165; account with S. Girard, 252; account with J. Leitch, 142n, 165, 166–7, 169, 595n; account with Mathew Carey & Son, 47, 100, 106, 107, 573, 616; Account with *National Intelligencer*, 470, 486, 487n, 506, 542; account with R. Perry, 112; account with C. Peyton, 430, 437; account with J. Vaughan, 252; account with W. Watson, 59n; bonds with van Staphorst & Hubbard, 88; buys and sells slaves, 430, 437; debt to P. Mazzei, 252, 471, 486, 508–9; debt to N. & J. & R. van Staphorst, 42–3, 43–4, 88, 141; debt to J. Neilson, 370;

endorses notes for W. C. Nicholas, 14, 123–4, 126, 283–4, 391, 602; investments for W. Short, 488, 489n; Invoice from Stephen Cathalan, 14–5, 16–7, 447–8; and T. Kosciuszko's American investments, 320–1, 542; and T. Kosciuszko's estate, 154, 155–6, 319, 351–2, 384, 528; and lease of Lego, 355; and lease of Shadwell mills, 355–6; and lease of Tufton, 355; lines of credit in Europe, 31, 45, 68, 79, 113n, 252, 291; loan from Bank of Virginia, 18, 79, 91, 95, 131, 141, 165, 277, 283, 323, 326, 459, 475, 492, 604; loan from Second Bank of the United States, 18, 42, 79, 91, 95, 101, 131, 141, 159, 165, 165–6, 168, 171, 173, 277, 283, 285, 289, 323, 326, 459, 475, 492, 604; loans money, 595n; and P. Mazzei's property, 373; Notes on Mutual Assurance Society Policy, 34–5; orders wine from S. Cathalan, 14–5, 16, 316–7, 506, 564–5, 606, 607; pays taxes, 356, 393; Promissory Note to Edmund Bacon, 324; Promissory Note to Thomas Jefferson Randolph, 251, 285, 289, 326; rent due TJ, 322; sale of Albemarle Co. land proposed, 276; and W. Short's property, 37–8, 73–4 (*See also* Barnes, John; Gibson, Patrick; Gibson & Jefferson [Richmond firm]; Henderson case; Mutual Assurance Society; Peyton, Bernard)

Correspondence
anonymous letters to, 318–9, 499–500, 501–3, 503, 568–9, 609–10; extortion letter, 546–8; fatiguing to, 57, 424, 526, 537, 572; filing system for, 74; gifts of, 474n; letter of condolence, 392; letter of introduction from, 337; letters of application and recommendation from, 244, 301–2, 511–2; letters of application and recommendation to, 78, 122–3, 125, 128, 292, 399–400, 418–21, 429–30, 431–4, 450–5, 485–6, 493–4, 500–1, 513–4, 521–2, 543–4, 555–6, 569–71; letters of introduction to, 99, 152, 271–2, 290, 325, 508, 546; and P. Mazzei

cal Society of New-York, 288n;
mentioned, 378
Mœurs et coutumes des Romains
(J. P. Bridault), 295
Molly (TJ's slave; b. *1814*): proposed
sale of, 437
Le Moniteur Universel (Paris newspaper). *See* Gazette nationale, ou, Le
Moniteur universel (Paris newspaper)
Monroe, James: and appointments, 118,
125, 145, 146, 280, 282n, 301–2, 308,
317; and S. Cathalan, 8–9; W. J.
Coffee's terra-cotta bust of, 49;
forwards correspondence to TJ, 285,
286; friendship with Baron Holland,
239; health of, 225; identified,
1:349n; introduces W. King, 508;
introduces J. R. Poinsett, 271; letters
from, 150–1, 225–6, 271–2, 276,
285–6, 299–300, 415–6, 508; letters
to, 286, 301–2, 308, 586–8; mentioned, 499; and V. Murray's claim,
538; names Highland estate, 276;
C. W. Peale paints, 426, 540; plans
to visit Loudoun Co., 151; presidency
of, 3, 77, 78, 150n, 150–1, 249, 253,
280, 282n, 445, 588n, 609–10; as
presidential candidate, 149; presidential messages of, 414, 415n, 415, 416n,
422–4, 424, 587–8; presidential
tour, 612; and South American affairs,
299, 300n, 415, 586–7; TJ on, 571;
and TJ's land, 276; and J. Trumbull's
historical paintings, 328, 333; visits
Loudon Co., 150; visits Montpellier
(J. Madison's Orange Co. estate), 313;
works sent to, 81–3, 367n. *See also*
Central College Board of Visitors;
Highland (J. Monroe's Albemarle Co.
estate)
Monteagle (C. Peyton's Albemarle Co.
estate): dispute over, 284
Montepulciano (wine): TJ orders, 11,
166; TJ recommends, 243, 302
Montesquieu, Charles Louis de Secon-
dat. *See* Destutt de Tracy, Antoine
Louis Claude: *Commentary and
Review of Montesquieu's Spirit of
Laws*
Montgomery, Richard: *The Death of
General Montgomery in the Attack on
Quebec* (J. Trumbull), 332; as general,
330
*The Monthly Register, and Review of the
United States*: bound for TJ, 368

MONTICELLO (TJ's Albemarle Co.
estate): brewery at, 616–7; cisterns at,
343–4, 362; corn crop at, 134; cotton
used at, 109; described, 23, 24, 25,
27; dining at, 28; Entrance Hall, 28;
fish for, 99; flour from, 141, 277, 283,
285, 289, 322, 326, 393; insurance
on, 34–5, 35, 44, 44; routes to, 287;
rye crop at, 167; schooling at, 18;
wheat crop at, 173

Visitors to
Beaven, Baker, 99; Burwell, William
A., 415, 439n; Cabell, Joseph C.,
334; Carr, Dabney (*1773–1837*),
584; Cocke, John H., 601; Coffee,
William J., 49, 362, 364; Coles,
Isaac A., 334; Cooper, Thomas,
308, 395, 571n; Corrêa da Serra,
José, 395; Eppes, John Wayles,
488; Hale, Salma, 22, 23, 24, 25,
26–9; Harris, Levett, 118, 119;
Harrison, Mr., 271; Holley, Horace,
48; Holmes, Hugh, 468, 507;
Huntington, William, 157; Hyde de
Neuville, Jean Guillaume, 490;
Kean, Andrew, 461; King, William
(of Maine), 508; Lowndes,
William, 315n; Madison, Dolley
and James, 109, 180; Maury,
Matthew, 290; Murray, John, 538;
Poinsett, Joel R., 271; Preston,
Francis, 485; Preston, James P.,
325; Randolph, David Meade
(*1798–1825*), 493n; Roane, Spencer,
180; Short, William, 488, 489n;
Stevens, John, 538n; Trist, Hore
Browse, 589n; Tudor, Delia J.,
576n; Tudor, William (*1779–1830*),
576n; Weems, Mason Locke, 410

Montpellier (Montpelier; J. Madison's
Orange Co. estate): visitors to, 76,
79n, 93, 94n, 313, 315n
Montreal: construction techniques in, 381
Moore, Richard Channing: as character
reference, 420n; identified, 10:151n
Moore, Thomas (*1760–1822*): engineer
to Va. Board of Public Works, 59n
Moore's Ford (Albemarle Co.), 276n
moral philosophy: works on, 295
More, Hannah: works of, 441
Morellet, André: *Mélanges de Littérature
et de Philosophie*, 396–7
Mormons: and Christian primitivism,
267n

INDEX

Nature Displayed (N. G. Dufief), 513

The Nautical Almanac and Astronomical Ephemeris (E. M. Blunt): sent to TJ, 513

The Naval Gazetteer; or, Seaman's Complete Guide (J. Malham), 36

navigation: bound pamphlets on, 455, 457n; elementary education in, 196, 215; study of, 368, 369, 449. *See also* Rivanna River

Navy Department, U.S.: building superintendent for, 289, 307; gunboats of, 568, 569n; ordnance for, 7n; proposed work on, 22n

Neilson, John: identified, 5:299–300n; letter to, 369–70; TJ forwards letters to, 369; TJ's debt to, 370; and work at Bremo (J. H. Cocke's Fluvanna Co. estate), 129–30

Nelson, Hugh: identified, 1:500n; visits Washington, D.C., 77

Nelson, Thomas: signer of Declaration of Independence, 329

Nestor (mythological character): TJ compared to, 384n

The Netherlands: J. Adams on, 615; Bonaparte, Louis (king), 147

Nevil, Zachariah: and Central College subscription, 161

A New Abridgment of the Law (M. Bacon), 53

The New American Practical Navigator (N. Bowditch), 36, 53, 368, 369, 449

A New and Impartial History of England (J. Baxter), 410, 412, 413n, 585

New Hampshire: agriculture in, 149; judicial reform in, 87n; legislature of, 87, 101; militia of, 87n; politics in, 25; praise for, 23, 25; prison reform in, 87n; and War of *1812*, 87n

New Israelites: and Christian primitivism, 267n

New Jersey, College of (later Princeton University): students transfer to, 450–1, 454n; and taverns, 396

New London, Va.: academy at, 17, 18, 175, 292, 321, 457, 483

New Orleans: descriptions of, 255; and France, 611; port of, 95–6, 524; steamboats at, 254. *See also* Batture Sainte Marie, controversy over

newspapers: Baltimore *Niles' Weekly Register*, 456, 477, 497; *Boston Daily Advertiser*, 578–9n; bound for TJ, 456; Charleston *City Gazette and Commercial Daily Advertiser*, 130n; *Daily Compiler and Richmond Commercial Register*, 471; French, 42, 459–61; New York *National Advocate*, 328–30, 331–4, 502n; *New-York Public Sale Report*, 479; Philadelphia *Aurora*, 475; Philadelphia *Democratic Press*, 383–4n; Philadelphia *National Gazette and Literary Register*, 465n, 467n; politics of, 436, 475; TJ on, 94, 106, 311, 586, 587. *See also National Intelligencer* (Washington newspaper); *Richmond Enquirer* (newspaper)

The New Testament, in an Improved Version, upon the basis of Archbishop Newcome's New Translation: with A Corrected Text, and Notes Critical and Explanatory, 305, 439, 469

Newton, E. I.: business partnership of, 375–7

Newton, Sir Isaac: gravitational theory of, 257, 267n; mentioned, 102, 573; religious beliefs of, 591

Newton, Thomas (*1742–1807*): and W. Short's Green Sea lands, 37–8, 73–4

New York (city): Academy of Fine Arts, 328n; cement in, 343–4; *National Advocate*, 502n; New York Institution for the Deaf and Dumb, 328n; *New-York Public Sale Report*, 479; J. Trumbull's *Declaration of Independence* exhibited in, 328. *See also* Gelston, David: collector at New York

New York (state): agriculture in, 71, 72n, 172; board of agriculture, 249; and canals, 245, 312–3; Dutch inhabitants of, 39–40; *A Memoir on the Antiquities of the Western Parts of the State of New-York. Read before the Literary and Philosophical Society of New-York* (D. Clinton), 288, 312; public records of translated, 39–40, 480–1

New-York Historical Society: addresses to, 563–4, 600; identified, 7:120n

New-York Public Sale Report (newspaper), 479

Nice: U.S. consul at, 9, 245–6, 308, 316–7, 444; wine from, 9, 240, 241, 246, 316, 445n, 447, 468, 507

Nicholas (TJ's slave; b. *1818*): traded to T. J. Randolph, 437n

Nicholas, George: and proposed dictator for Va., 274

Sacchetti, Franco: *Delle Novelle di Franco Sacchetti Citadino Fiorentino* (ed. G. Poggiali), 39, 41n
saddles, 518
sainfoin, 75
Saint John's College (Annapolis), 451, 454n
Saint Louis: construction in, 95, 524
Saint Mary's College (Baltimore), 451, 452, 455n
Saint Petersburg: U.S. consul at, 118–9, 145
Saint Thomas (Danish West Indies): U.S. consulship at, 122–3
sal ammoniac (ammonium chloride): medicinal use of, 73
Sallust: *Oeuvres de Sallust* (trans. J. B. Dureau de la Malle), 342, 358, 394, 474, 494, 561
Sally (Sal) (TJ's slave; b. *1777*): and child rearing, 605; family of, 567
salt: manufacturing, 6, 35; shipment of, 10
Sampson, Richard: and proposed Albemarle Co. road, 275
San Concordio, Bartolomeo da: *Ammaestramenti degli Antichi*, 39, 41n
Sanderson, Joseph McClellan: *Biography of the Signers to the Declaration of Independence*, 477–8; identified, 478n; letter from, 477–8
Sanderson & Ward (Baltimore firm): as print sellers, 478n
Sandy (TJ's slave; b. *1807*): proposed sale of, 437
San Lorenzo, Treaty of (*1795*), 150–1
Sapieha, Anna, 115
Saratoga, N.Y.: British surrender at, 115
Sardinia: Victor Emmanuel I, 316
Sasserno, Joseph Victor Adolphus: consulship for, 9, 240–1, 245–6, 301–2, 308, 316–7, 444; identified, 11:655n; letters from, 245–6, 316–7; and wine, 240, 241, 246, 308, 316
Sasserno, Victor: death of, 301; family of, 301–2
Say, Jean Baptiste: economic theories of, 573; identified, 7:420n
Say, Thomas: as scientist, 249–50, 253, 280
Scheffer, Charles Arnold: works of, 55
schools and colleges: Asbury College (Baltimore), 452, 455n; Baltimore College, 451–5; classical, 457; College of New Jersey (later Princeton

University), 396, 450–1, 454n; Cumberland College (Nashville, Tenn.), 451; C. de Montcarel's Richmond school, 418–21; Frederick Academy (Md.), 450–1, 454n; Hampden-Sydney College, 590; Harvard University, 138, 238; King's College (later part of the University of Aberdeen), 138, 139n; New London Academy, 17, 18, 175, 292, 321, 457, 483; Saint John's College (Annapolis), 451, 454n; Saint Mary's College (Baltimore), 451, 452, 455n; TJ sends works to, 476; University of Glasgow, 453; University of Pennsylvania, 45, 102, 105n, 174, 226, 233, 249, 255, 269, 270, 429, 430n, 518; Washington Academy (later Washington and Lee University), 590; Washington College (Chestertown, Md.), 454n; Washington College (later Washington and Lee University), 180–1. *See also* Central College; Virginia, University of; William and Mary, College of
Schuring, Jan: as publisher, 40
Schuyler, Philip: as general, 114; as member of Continental Congress, 333n
Schweighaeuser, Johannes: edits Ἀππιανοῦ Ἀλεξανδρέως Ῥωμαϊκῶν Ἱστοριῶν τὰ Σωζόμενα *Appiani Alexandrini Romanarum Historiarum quæ supersunt* (Appian), 295; edits *Herodoti Musae sive Historiarum Libri IX* (Herodotus), 295
science: and divine revelation, 546–8. *See also* specific disciplines
scientific instruments: barometers, 348; mirrors, 5–6; quadrants, 348; sextants, 385; telescopes, 323, 596; theodolites, 385. *See also* surveying
Scotchtown (Bath Co.): tavern at, 230, 231, 232
sculpture: W. J. Coffee's terra-cotta busts, 49, 344. *See also* Jefferson, Thomas: Portraits
scuppernong (wine), 126–7, 173, 277, 283, 287, 577
Seaton, William Winston: editor of Washington *National Intelligencer*, 469; identified, 6:506n
Secretary's Ford (Albemarle Co.): road at, 275
seeds: bean, 519, 599; chicory (succory), 303, 361, 438; kale, sea, 325; kale,

INDEX

seeds (*cont.*)
sprout, 111; lentil, 278; oat, 75; pea, 278, 545, 566, 581, 604; rutabaga, 75, 111; rye, 75; sainfoin, 75; sent by TJ, 111, 303; sent to TJ, 77–8, 85, 94, 131, 140, 141, 165, 278, 307, 315; tobacco, 438; wheat, 75, 77–8, 94

A Selection of the Patriotic Addresses, to the President of the United States. together with The President's Answers (ed. W. Austin), 33, 47

Seminole Indians, 286n

Senate, U.S.: and appointments, 289. *See also* Congress, U.S.

Senegal: and wine, 16, 443

Septuaginta Interpretum (ed. J. E. Grabe), 293, 295

Serrier, Michel Raymond: as physician, 443

Sète. *See* Cette (Sète), France

Seventy-Six Association (Charleston, S.C.): forwards orations, 157; identified, 4:107n; letter from, 157–9; toasts of sent to TJ, 130n

sextant: TJ uses, 385

Seybert, Adam: identified, 1:172n; *Statistical Annals*, 603

Shackleford, Zachariah: and Central College subscription, 162

shad: TJ purchases, 99

Shadwell mills: builders at, 476n; flour from, 13–4, 18, 120, 141, 355–6; flour mill at, 116, 277; improvements to, 116, 120; and T. E. Randolph, 13–4, 116; rent for, 322; road at, 276n; TJ's insurance for, 34

Shakespeare, William: *Hamlet* referenced, 499, 500n

Shaw, William Smith: conveys letters to and from TJ, 529, 530n, 615; identified, 530n; letter to, from E. T. Channing, 529–30; mentioned, 588

Shaw's Tavern (Bath Co.), 230, 231, 232

sheep: and chicory (succory) cultivation, 438; at Poplar Forest, 386. *See also* merino sheep

Sheldon, Daniel: as secretary of U.S. legation in Paris, 445, 568

Shepherd (TJ's slave; b. *1809*): on Poplar Forest slave list, 387

Sherman, Roger: signer of Declaration of Independence, 331, 390

Short, William: on books, 396–7, 488; on France, 397; identified, 1:39n;

investments of, 488, 489n; lands of near Norfolk (Green Sea lands), 37–9, 73–4; letters from, 37–9, 395–7, 487–9; letters to, 73–4, 383–4, 510–1; publication of correspondence with TJ, 383–4n, 487, 546, 557; and TJ's health, 383–4n, 395–6, 487, 488, 510–1; and University of Virginia, 396, 487–8, 511; visits Monticello, 488, 489n

Silliman, Benjamin: and *American Journal of Science*, 82, 83n, 310, 327; identified, 12:626–7n

Silsbee, Nathaniel: as character reference, 4

Simms, Charles: as collector at Alexandria, 14, 16n, 171, 253, 254n, 345, 443, 445n; and goods for TJ, 345; identified, 4:221n; letters to, 171, 345

Simms, William Douglass: as deputy collector at Alexandria, 253, 277; forwards wine to TJ, 253; identified, 10:194n; letter from, 253–4

Simons, Edward Peter: identified, 158–9n; letter from, 157–9; and Seventy-Six Association, 157

Simpson, James: petition of, 504–6, 533, 614; as U.S. consul at Gibraltar and Tangier, 504–5, 533

Simson, Robert: *The Elements of Euclid*, 476

Siro (brig), 241, 443

Sketches of the Life and Character of Patrick Henry (W. Wirt): criticism of, 274–5; opinions on, lii; and origin of American Revolution, 48; preface to, 24

Sketches of the Principles of Government (N. Chipman), 33, 47

Sketch of the Internal Improvements already made by Pennsylvania (S. Breck), 174

Skipwith, Fulwar: as consul general at Paris, 431–2

slate, 92, 97–8, 99, 117

Slaughter, John: identified, 12:49n; and proposed Albemarle Co. road, 275

Slaughter, Philip: and establishment of University of Virginia, 560; as University of Virginia commissioner, 182, 183, 223

slavery: in North Africa, 504–5, 506n, 614

slaves: accused of theft, 518, 581; J. Barbour's, 25; beaten, 518; blankets

[674]

THE PAPERS OF THOMAS JEFFERSON are composed in Monticello, a font based on the "Pica No. 1" created in the early 1800s by Binny & Ronaldson, the first successful typefounding company in America. The face is considered historically appropriate for The Papers of Thomas Jefferson because it was used extensively in American printing during the last quarter-century of Jefferson's life, and because Jefferson himself expressed cordial approval of Binny & Ronaldson types. It was revived and rechristened Monticello in the late 1940s by the Mergenthaler Linotype Company, under the direction of C. H. Griffith and in close consultation with P. J. Conkwright, specifically for the publication of the Jefferson Papers. The font suffered some losses in its first translation to digital format in the 1980s to accommodate computerized typesetting. Matthew Carter's reinterpretation in 2002 restores the spirit and style of Binny & Ronaldson's original design of two centuries earlier.

✧